Chinese American Voices

The publisher gratefully acknowledges the generous
contribution to this book provided by Sue Tsao

Chinese
American Voices

OcLc record

From the Gold Rush to the Present

EDITED WITH INTRODUCTIONS BY

Judy Yung, Gordon H. Chang, and Him Mark Lai

UNIVERSITY OF CALIFORNIA

Berkeley   Los Angeles   London

University of California Press, one of the most distinguished
university presses in the United States, enriches lives around the
world by advancing scholarship in the humanities, social sciences,
and natural sciences. Its activities are supported by the UC Press
Foundation and by philanthropic contributions from individuals
and institutions. For more information, visit www.ucpress.edu.

University of California Press
Berkeley and Los Angeles, California

University of California Press, Ltd.
London, England

Library of Congress Cataloging-in-Publication Data

Chinese American voices : from the gold rush to the present /
    edited with introductions by Judy Yung, Gordon H. Chang, and
    Him Mark Lai.
        p.   cm.
    Includes bibliographical references and index.
    ISBN 0-520-24309-9(cloth : alk. paper)—ISBN 0-520-24310-2
    (pbk. : alk. paper)
        1. Chinese Americans—History—Sources.   I. Yung, Judy.
    II. Chang, Gordon H.   III. Lai, H. Mark.
E184.C5C479   2006
973'.04951—dc22   2005021227

Manufactured in the United States of America
15   14   13   12   11   10   09   08   07   06
10   9   8   7   6   5   4   3   2   1

The paper used in this publication meets the minimum requirements of ANSI/NISO Z39.48–1992 (R 1997) (*Permanence of Paper*).

For Eddie (J. Y.)

Vicki, Chloe, and Maya (G. H. C.)

and Laura (H. M. L.)

CONTENTS

ILLUSTRATIONS

xi

PREFACE

The story of the Chinese in America has been curiously told. In most accounts, they have been mute. Although they have been integral to this country's history, their voices have rarely been included by either their historical contemporaries or subsequent writers. Although one historian of their experience even described them as "silent sojourners,"[1] in fact, they were ignored. They were laborers who helped build much of the American West in the nineteenth century, but they were not asked what they felt about their toil; they were the victims of murderous violence, social ostracism, and discriminatory legislation, but they were not asked for their reaction; their lives were described variously as quaint and exotic, as depraved and threatening, and more recently as successful and exemplary, but they were not asked to describe their own lives in their own terms. Missionaries, journalists, and historians may have written about what the Chinese in America did or what was done to them, but they often neglected to consult the Chinese themselves.

The first scholarly book devoted entirely to the Chinese in America appeared as early as 1909. *Chinese Immigration,* by Mary Roberts Coolidge, a sociologist who espoused many causes, was as much an attack on unscrupulous labor leaders and opportunist politicians behind the anti-Chinese movement as a defense of the Chinese, whom she saw as indispensable labor in the building of the American West.[2] Openly sympathetic to the Chinese, Coolidge tried to discuss their social life, community organizations, and customs, but she fell short because her source materials (government

---

1. Gunther Barth, *Bitter Strength: A History of the Chinese in the United States, 1850–1870* (Cambridge, Mass.: Harvard University Press, 1964), p. 7.
2. Mary Roberts Coolidge, *Chinese Immigration* (New York: Henry Holt, 1909).

reports, missionary observations, and political tracts) were virtually all written in English by non-Chinese.

Perhaps the most influential writer about the Chinese after Coolidge was historian Gunther Barth. His *Bitter Strength,* published fifty-five years after Coolidge's pioneering work, did include some Chinese primary sources. But whereas Coolidge argued that the Chinese were just as assimilable as European immigrants, Barth argued that they were not immigrants but sojourners whose foreign ways and indentured status had brought on their troubles. A number of historians, most notably Elmer C. Sandmeyer, Stuart Miller, and Alexander Saxton, also probed into the causes behind the anti-Chinese movement, but they came up with different conclusions.[3] Nevertheless, by choosing to focus on the excluders rather than the excluded, and in failing to use primary sources generated by the Chinese themselves, their works did little to improve America's understanding of Chinese Americans.

A breakthrough came when sociologists Stanford Lyman, Rose Hum Lee, S. W. Kung, and Betty Lee Sung began researching and writing about the development of social organizations and family life among Chinese Americans as well as the impact of racial discrimination on their efforts to assimilate into mainstream society.[4] Although they used few Chinese primary sources, their roots, connections, and investigations in the Chinese community enabled them to provide considerable texture and depth to understanding Chinese American life. They were followed in the 1970s by a new generation of scholars who were inspired by the new social history to study "history from the bottom up." In their efforts to document how the Chinese actually experienced and understood their own lives in America, they conducted oral histories and searched for writings by the Chinese themselves, be they on the walls of the Angel Island immigration station, in old Chinese-language newspapers, or in personal papers stored in dusty boxes in the basements of family homes.[5]

Their historical approach and findings allowed new issues to be addressed: How did the Chinese organize their lives and communities in America? How

3. Elmer Sandmeyer, *The Anti-Chinese Movement in California* (Urbana: University of Illinois Press, 1973); Stuart Miller, *The Unwelcome Immigrant: The Immigrant Image of the Chinese, 1785–1882* (Berkeley: University of California Press, 1969); and Alexander Saxton, *The Indispensable Enemy: Labor and the Anti-Chinese Movement in California* (Berkeley: University of California Press, 1971).

4. Rose Hum Lee, *The Chinese in the United States of America* (Hong Kong: Hong Kong University Press, 1960); S. W. Kung, *Chinese in American Life: Some Aspects of Their History, Status, Problems, and Contributions* (Seattle: University of Washington Press, 1962); and Betty Lee Sung, *Mountain of Gold* (New York: Macmillan, 1967).

5. See, for example, Victor and Brett De Bary Nee, *Longtime Californ': A Documentary Study of an American Chinatown* (New York: Pantheon Books, 1972); Tin-yuke Char, *The Sandalwood Mountains: Readings and Stories of the Early Chinese Immigrants in Hawaii* (Honolulu: University of Hawaii Press, 1975); Him Mark Lai, Genny Lim, and Judy Yung, *Island: Poetry and History of Chinese Immigrants on Angel Island, 1910–1940* (San Francisco: HOC-DOI, 1980); and Diane Mark and Ginger Chih, *A Place Called Chinese America* (Dubuque, Iowa: Kendall/Hunt, 1982).

did they regard their work, social, and family lives here? What were their perceptions of America, including its culture, politics, values, and attitudes? How did the Chinese relate to other ethnic groups and respond to racial discrimination and exclusion? How and why did they maintain transnational kin, political, and cultural relations with their homeland? And how did the experiences of the early immigrants compare with those of subsequent generations of American-born Chinese and the large influx of Chinese immigrants after 1965? Addressing these questions contributed to opening new vistas on American social history generally and new understandings of its cultural and political histories.[6] In recent years, there have been several efforts to synthesize the written accounts of the Chinese in America, combining the early studies that explored the political and social dimensions of the "Chinese question" with the new social history to interpret the experiences of Chinese Americans along with those of other Asian Americans.[7] Moreover, in-depth scholarship on a range of Chinese American subjects continues to be produced by young scholars, including third- or fourth-generation Americans and foreign students from China with valuable biliterate skills.[8]

While progress has been made in writing more nuanced, sophisticated, and meaningful history about Chinese Americans, much remains to be done in

6. See, for example, James W. Loewen, *The Mississippi Chinese: Between Black and White* (Cambridge, Mass.: Harvard University Press, 1971); Lucy M. Cohen, *Chinese in the Post–Civil War South: A People without a History* (Baton Rouge: Louisiana State University Press, 1984); Sandy Lydon, *Chinese Gold: The Chinese in the Monterey Bay Region* (Capitola, Calif.: Capitola Book Company, 1985); Sucheng Chan, *This Bitter-sweet Soil: The Chinese in California Agriculture, 1860–1910* (Berkeley: University of California Press, 1986); L. Eve Armentrout Ma, *Revolutionaries, Monarchists, and Chinatowns: Chinese Politics in the Americas and the 1911 Revolution* (Honolulu: University of Hawaii Press, 1990); Renqiu Yu, *To Save China, to Save Ourselves: The Chinese Hand Laundry Alliance of New York* (Philadelphia: Temple University Press, 1992); and Charles J. McClain, *In Search of Equality: The Chinese Struggle against Discrimination in Nineteenth-Century America* (Berkeley: University of California Press, 1994).

7. See Roger Daniels, *Asian America: Chinese and Japanese in the United States since 1850* (Seattle: University of Washington Press, 1988); Ronald Takaki, *Strangers from a Different Shore: A History of Asian Americans* (Boston: Little, Brown, 1989); and Sucheng Chan, *Asian Americans: An Interpretive History* (Boston: Twayne, 1991).

8. See, for example, Madeline Hsu, *Dreaming of Gold, Dreaming of Home: Transnationalism and Migration between the United States and South China, 1882–1943* (Stanford: Stanford University Press, 2000); Erika Lee, *At America's Gate: Chinese Immigration during the Exclusion Era, 1882–1943* (Chapel Hill: University of North Carolina Press, 2002); Mae Ngai, *Impossible Subjects: Illegal Aliens and the Making of Modern America* (Princeton: Princeton University Press, 2004); John Kuo-Wei Tchen, *New York before Chinatown: Orientalism and the Shaping of American Culture, 1776–1882* (Baltimore: Johns Hopkins University Press, 1999); Xiaolan Bao, *Holding Up More Than Half the Sky: Chinese Women Garment Workers in New York City, 1948–92* (Urbana: University of Illinois Press, 2001); Shehong Chen, *Being Chinese, Becoming Chinese American* (Urbana: University of Illinois Press, 2003); Yong Chen, *Chinese San Francisco, 1850–1943: A Trans-Pacific Community* (Stanford: Stanford University Press, 2000); Huping Ling, *Surviving on the Gold Mountain: A History of Chinese American Women and Their Lives* (Albany: State University of New York Press, 1998);

uncovering important primary material. Contrary to popular and scholarly opinion, the Chinese have generated extensive documentation about their experiences here. In English as well as in Chinese, this material spans a wide spectrum: immigration case files, the records of business and community organizations, legal and government documents, personal manuscript collections, speeches, testimonies, and correspondence; and of published materials, there are oral history interviews, magazines and newspapers, pamphlets and newsletters, autobiographies, poems, and folk songs. These materials record the history of the Chinese since their early days in America.

Some of this primary material has been reproduced in the past,[9] but most of it has remained obscure and inaccessible to the general reader. *Chinese American Voices* aims to correct this historical amnesia and to encourage an appreciation of the texture and depth of Chinese American history from the perspectives of the Chinese themselves. It is the first effort dedicated to presenting primary documents generated exclusively by Chinese Americans, writing in English or Chinese, from their arrival during the California gold rush to the present day. We attempt to cover a broad spectrum of experiences that reveal the diversity of socioeconomic status, gender, generation, geographic affiliation, political perspective, and cultural lifestyle among Chinese Americans. We purposely excluded primary documents that have been widely published elsewhere; thus, much of the material in this volume appears in print for the first time or is reprinted from hard-to-find publications.

Chinese American Voices is very much a collaboration of three historians who have devoted most of their lives to researching, writing, and teaching Chinese American history. Having each developed extensive research collections through the years, we began the project by combing our own libraries for materials written by Chinese Americans themselves. This included going through our voluminous collections of journal articles, news clippings, and unpublished papers as well as secondary sources for citations of Chinese voices that speak to different aspects of their lives in America. Working together, we collected over three hundred documents, from which we selected some sixty for inclusion in this anthology. In some instances, we conducted additional oral history interviews, looked through Chinese newspapers on microfilm, surfed the Internet for new voices, and combed

---

and Xiaojian Zhao, *Remaking Chinese America: Immigration, Family, and Community, 1940–1965* (New Brunswick, N.J.: Rutgers University Press, 2002).

9. See Paul Jacobs and Saul Landau with Eve Pell, *To Serve the Devil:* vol. 2: *Colonials and Sojourners* (New York: Vintage Books, 1971); Cheng-tsu Wu, *"Chink!": A Documentary History of Anti-Chinese Prejudice in America* (New York: World Publishers, 1973); R. David Arkush and Leo O. Lee, eds., *Land without Ghosts: Chinese Impressions of America from the Mid–Nineteenth Century to the Present* (Berkeley: University of California Press, 1989); and Franklin Odo, ed., *The Columbia Documentary History of the Asian American Experience* (New York: Columbia University Press, 2002).

through local libraries and archives for additional materials to fill in certain gaps.

What were we looking for? Of utmost importance were documents and stories that touched upon and revealed certain important moments or turning points in Chinese American history: the Chinese Exclusion Act of 1882; the Sino-Japanese War and World War II (1937–1945); the Cold War and the Confession Program (1950s); the civil rights movement and the Immigration Act of 1965; U.S. normalization of relations with China in the 1970s; and the rise in hate crimes beginning with the Vincent Chin case in 1982. Thus, we included such entries as the Angel Island poem "Detention in the Wooden Building"; an interview with World War II veteran Eddie Fung; testimonies by victims of McCarthyism; and community reactions to the Vincent Chin and Wen Ho Lee cases.

Second, we wanted to challenge the stereotypes of Chinese Americans as silent sojourners, passive victims, and the model minority by providing actual examples of social agency and political activism throughout Chinese American history. This was not difficult, as it is usually outspoken community leaders and activists who leave the best records behind. Examples of such documents include Norman Asing's letter to Governor Bigler protesting his racist remarks about the Chinese in 1852; the testimony of the Chinese-American Citizens' Alliance before a congressional committee to reform the Immigration Act of 1924; the activity reports of the Chinese Women's Association in New York during the war years; and Shui Mak Ka's speech before twenty thousand garment workers on strike in New York City in 1982.

Probably the most difficult documents and voices to find were those that truly represented a diverse population in terms of gender, socioeconomic background, generation, and geographic affiliation. Because of our own backgrounds and research interests, our initial selections tended to focus too much on California, immigrants from Guangdong Province, the working class, women, and leftist politics. We tried to correct these biases in our final selections by including an equal number of male voices; stories of immigrants from Taiwan, Fujian, and Vietnam since 1965; interviews with Chinese Americans who live in the Midwest and South; poems and essays by the younger generation about what it means to be Chinese American, mixed race, or gay/lesbian; and success stories like those of David Ho, an AIDS researcher, and Gary Locke, governor of the state of Washington.

Finally, we included some entries that we found irresistible because of their unique point of view and poignant sentiments. Such a find was a newspaper column by Liu Liangmo in the *China Daily News* telling of his friendship with singer and actor Paul Robeson and how he got Robeson to introduce a popular Chinese war song, "March of the Volunteers," to American audiences. Another unique find was "I Want to Marry an American Girl" by Eddie Gong, who we later discovered served in the Florida state legislature from 1963 to

1972. Probably the most poignant pieces in the anthology are the folk songs sung by "living widows" left behind in China and an 1876 report on the difficulties involved in finding the remains of Chinese laborers who had died in America.

We chose to divide *Chinese American Voices* into three parts, corresponding to three distinct periods in the development of Chinese American history and life experiences. Part I (1852–1904) covers early Chinese immigration and the anti-Chinese movement, which culminated in the passage of the Chinese exclusion acts, ending large-scale immigration of Chinese into the United States; Part II (1904–1943) covers the modernization of Chinese America during the exclusion period, and the impact of the Sino-Japanese War and World War II on the Chinese community; and Part III (1943–2003) covers the Cold War era, the liberalization of immigration policies, and efforts on the part of the Chinese to become an integral part of America. To lend meaning and context to the documents and personal stories, we provide an overview history of major developments in each period at the beginning of each section. We also introduce each document with background information on the author and comments on its historical significance, and end each document with a list of references for further reading and investigation.

An important and unique feature of this anthology is the inclusion of Chinese primary documents that have been translated into English. The writing style of the originals varied considerably. Some, for example, were composed in the formal, classical style, which made translation difficult. For others, especially documents and creative expressions generated in the mid–twentieth century, we attempted to convey not only the literal meaning but the tone and expressive flavor as well. Following standard practice, we used the Hanyu Pinyin system for Chinese proper nouns, except in cases where the names have been commonly spelled in a different romanization system or spoken in Cantonese or another dialect. Although an attempt was made to be consistent in the Chinese transliteration within each document, no attempt was made to be consistent throughout this book. A Chinese glossary is provided in the appendix for clarification.

We make no claim for comprehensiveness. We recognize that we have been highly selective in our choices, and that these choices reflect our own interpretations of Chinese American history, perhaps our personal biases and values as well. Our aim, however, is for a wide range of Chinese American voices to be heard and for this anthology to complement the many accounts of Chinese American life and experiences that already exist and those that will be produced in the future. We hope our collective efforts here will lead readers—whether scholars, writers, students, or the general public—to engage in further reading and investigation, and that they will come to see Chinese Americans not as silent sojourners or perpetual foreigners, but as an integral part of American history and life.

ACKNOWLEDGMENTS

It has taken the three of us over ten years to complete *Chinese American Voices: From the Gold Rush to the Present.* Such a monumental project could not have been possible without the assistance of many friends, colleagues, librarians and archivists, and community contacts. We are fortunate to have had four excellent translators, Ernest Chin, Marlon Hom, Ellen Yeung, and Shiree Teng, who helped us render the Chinese-language documents into English.

We are indebted to the following individuals for their help in suggesting, locating, and in some instances interpreting the primary documents included in this anthology: Xiaolan Bao, Ko-lin Chin, Michaelyn Chou, Philip Choy, Colleen Fong, Marlon Hom, Peter Kiang, Bob Lee, Sandy Lee, Nellie Leong, Gordon Lew, Raymond Lew, Charles McClain, Ruthanne Lum McCunn, Franklin Ng, Mae Ngai, Vu Pham, Wei Chi Poon, Bill Strobridge, John Kuo-wei Tchen, Mi Ling Tsui, Wanda Wang, Wang Xing Chu, Brad Wong, Eddie Wong, Elaine May Woo, Renqiu Yu, Xiaojian Zhao, and Helen Zia.

We wish to also thank Eddie Fung, David Ho, Daphne Kwok, Bonnie C. Lew, Ah Quon McElrath, Sheila Chin Morris, and Johnny Wong for allowing us to include their interviews in this anthology; Roger Daniels, Ruthanne Lum McCunn, Franklin Odo, and Vicki Ruiz for their critical readings of the manuscript; the Senate Committee on Research at the University of California, Santa Cruz, and the Center for East Asian Studies at Stanford University for granting us research funds to complete this book; Monica Mc-Cormick, Mary Severance, Niels Hooper, and Anne Canright of the University of California Press for their editorial guidance; and last but not least, Eddie Fung, Vicki Chang, and Laura Lai, for their unflagging support and sustenance throughout.

PART ONE

Early Chinese Immigrants, 1852–1904

The first Chinese to immigrate to the United States in the mid–nineteenth century came principally from the Pearl River Delta of Guangdong Province in southeastern China. Attracted by stories of the California gold rush, they came not only as miner-prospectors, but also as artisans, merchants, and students. Many more arrived as laborers to work in Hawaii's plantations and the mines, railroad lines, farmlands, fisheries, and factories of the American West. From 1852 until 1882, when the Chinese Exclusion Act was passed, over 300,000 Chinese entered the United States. They were part of an international migration of labor from Asia linked to the global expansion of European capitalism, in which workers, capital, and technology moved across national borders to profit entrepreneurs.

After China was defeated in the Opium War by Britain and forced to open to outside trade and political domination, life for the Chinese people in Guangdong Province deteriorated. Aside from suffering increased taxes, forfeiture of land, competition from imported manufactured goods, and unemployment, they also had to contend with problems of overpopulation, natural calamities, bandits, and the devastation caused by peasant rebellions and the ongoing Punti-Hakka interethnic feud. Because of their coastal location and their early contact with foreign traders, many were drawn to America by news of the gold rush and by labor contractors in search of young, able-bodied men to work in the New World. Moreover, a strong entrepreneurial tradition had emerged among some of the Chinese in this region, causing them to seek new opportunities abroad. By the latter part of the nineteenth century, emigration patterns were firmly established, and many villages in the Pearl River Delta came to depend on the remittances of men who had gone overseas for work.

Like other immigrants in America at this time, many of these Guangdong men intended to strike it rich and return home. More than half of them were married, but most did not bring their wives and families. Because of cultural mores against women traveling abroad, limited economic resources, and the harsh living conditions in the frontier West, it was cheaper and safer to maintain a split household and support the family in China from across the ocean. But later, when Chinese men wanted to bring their families to join them in America, they were prevented from doing so by anti-Chinese immigration laws. The absence of women set the patterns of nineteenth-century Chinese immigration and community development apart from those of most other immigrant groups, resulting in a bachelor society marked by social vices and a decades-long delay in the emergence of a sizable native-born generation.

The reception the Chinese received in the United States was hostile almost from the start. Arriving at a time when European Americans, imbued with a strong sense of manifest destiny and white supremacy, were expanding into the American West, laying claim to its lands and riches, Chinese immigrants fell victim to racial discrimination and class exploitation. Although some welcomed the Chinese as new members of the American family, many in the country saw them as cultural threats, labor competition, and racial inferiors. Even before their arrival, many white Americans held pejorative ideas about the Chinese based on false images and assumptions about their land of ancestry. China, in their view, was a backward, heathen, and degenerate country, and its people, especially its poor, part of the dregs of humanity. They were not seen as the stuff from which "real" Americans were made. Moreover, the racial difference of the Chinese set them apart, with white Americans considering them as a separate people, akin to other subordinates such as Africans, Mexicans, and American Indians.

As a result, the Chinese faced racist laws and actions almost from the moment of their arrival. As early as 1852 the California state legislature enacted a Foreign Miners' Tax, which was aimed particularly at the Chinese miners. Until it was repealed in 1870, the tax accounted for $5 million, a sum representing between 25 and 50 percent of all state revenue. As hostile miners resorted to physical violence to expel the Chinese from the mines and a number of mining counties passed resolutions and special taxes to exclude them, Chinese miners fanned out into gold fields throughout the West, reworking leftover claims abandoned by white prospectors or hiring themselves out to work borax deposits and mine coal and quicksilver. Not only did their hard labor reap immense profits for mining corporations, but the Chinese also contributed to the economy by supplying goods and services to miners—hence the development of Chinese camps throughout the mining areas.

In addition to mining, Chinese workers were also closely associated with the expanding railroad industry that boomed in the mid and late nineteenth century. Inspired by dreams of tapping the riches and markets of Asia and the resources of the western part of the country, American entrepreneurs pushed for the building of a transcontinental railroad that would link up the country and expedite trade between the two coasts. In this effort the federal government provided railroad barons with incentives of $16,000 to $48,000 and one square mile of land for each mile of track laid—land that had been taken from the American Indians. Even so, in the 1860s the Central Pacific Railroad, facing the rugged terrain of California's Sierra Nevada and the scarcity of reliable labor, made little progress on the western end of the railroad line, until they hired Chinese workers. These workers proved so capable and effective that some 12,000 to 14,000 Chinese, four of every five men hired by the Central Pacific, were soon put to work in all phases of construction—leveling roadbeds, boring tunnels, blasting mountainsides, and laying tracks. The work was hard as well as dangerous. To carve a roadbed out of the granite promontory of Cape Horn, towering 1,400 feet above the American River, Chinese laborers lowered themselves from the top of the cliff in wicker baskets to drill holes and light explosives, pulling themselves up before, hopefully, the gunpowder exploded beneath them. Working through two severe winters in the High Sierras, the Chinese lived in caverns carved out below the snow level and were often victims of snow slides and avalanches. While no record was kept of the number of lives lost in this endeavor, one newspaper reported that there must have been at least 1,200 deaths, based on the 20,000 pounds of bones that were shipped back to China before the completion of the railroad in 1869. Chinese labor was also instrumental in laying tracks and telegraph lines throughout the western states.

From the 1860s to the 1910s, Chinese farmers helped to make California into the nation's premier agricultural state. Chinese labor was used to reclaim swamplands in the Sacramento–San Joaquin River Delta, increasing the land value from $1–$3 an acre to $20–$100 an acre. They helped to lay the foundation of the wine industry in Napa and Sonoma by constructing roads, stone bridges, rock walls, wine cellars, and irrigation ditches. They cleared land; planted, pruned, and harvested grapes; and made wine. The farming skills that they brought with them from China were put to good use in the growing of citrus fruits, beans, peas, sugar beets, and hops—commercial crops that became the mainstay of the state's agricultural economy. As tenant farmers and truck gardeners, the Chinese specialized in potatoes, garden vegetables, fruits, peanuts, and celery. Chinese vegetable peddlers became a common sight in many towns as housewives came to depend on their fresh produce. In other parts of the country as well as in Hawaii, Chinese helped to develop new varieties of flowers, fruits, and vegetables, including jasmine, the Bing cherry, Gim orange, Chinese cabbage, and taro.

Chinese also entered the fishing industry along the West Coast and proved adept at fishing, curing, and canning. In the 1860s and 1870s Chinese fishing villages dotted the California coastline and ringed San Francisco Bay. Chinese fishermen caught a variety of fish, shrimp, and abalone, which they dried and sold locally or shipped to China, Japan, and the Hawaiian Islands. In fact, it was the Chinese who introduced abalone meat and the decorative shells to white Americans. By the mid-1870s, Chinese workers also made up the bulk of the labor force in salmon canneries in the Pacific Northwest. In the young cities of the West, they could be found as domestics and laundrymen, but also as workers in the developing factories, such as in San Francisco's woolen, cigar, shoe, and garment industries. Once the Chinese learned the trade, they would pool their capital to start their own small factories, specializing in inexpensive lines such as ready-made clothing, undergarments, slippers, and boys' shoes to avoid competing with white manufacturers. They proved to be such hard workers that after the Civil War, labor recruiters tried to bring them to the Deep South to replace former slaves and to factory towns in the Middle Atlantic and New England states as strikebreakers.

Thus, when an economic depression hit the West in the 1870s, anti-Chinese sentiment and violence broke out among white workers, farmers, and fishermen who saw the Chinese as unfair competition and the cause of all their economic woes. Denis Kearney and the Workingman's Party, based in San Francisco, became the most vocal forces in making the Chinese racial scapegoats. Throughout the West in the 1870s and 1880s, murderous mobs regularly stormed Chinese settlements, looting, lynching, burning, and expelling the Chinese. Their goal to drive the Chinese out of all areas of profitable employment and ultimately out of the country was finally realized with the help of opportunistic politicians who pressured Congress to pass the Chinese Exclusion Act of 1882. The act prohibited the entry of Chinese laborers for ten years and barred Chinese from becoming naturalized U.S. citizens. Only diplomats, students, teachers, merchants, and visitors were exempted. The ban on Chinese labor, which was applied to Hawaii after it became a territory of the United States in 1898, was made indefinite in 1904 and not repealed until 1943.

The message behind the anti-Chinese movement was evident: the Chinese were tolerated as long as there was use for their labor to help develop the economic infrastructure of the American West. Racist attitudes, policies, and practices sought to prevent them from settling down, owning land, becoming naturalized citizens, intermarrying, or integrating into mainstream society. But the Chinese refused to be driven out of the country. Many moved to eastern and midwestern cities and to the South, where they could find work and where their presence was better tolerated. By the turn of the century, Chinese could be found in every state of the union. They worked where they could, usually in agriculture, domestic service, restaurants, or laundries, and they clustered in Chinatown communities that sprang up in many towns to serve their social, economic, and political needs. There, they could shop for Chinese foods and supplies, look for work, socialize with kinsmen, frequent brothels, attend Chinese operas, worship at temples, observe traditional holidays and customs, and find protection from racial persecution. In the larger Chinatowns, family and district associations, fraternal organizations, and labor guilds were formed for social control, mutual help, and labor arbitration. Tongs or secret societies involved with prostitution, gambling, and drugs also thrived, and the stiff competition for control of these illegal activities often led to assassinations and fights, known as tong wars.

In response to racial discrimination, the Chinese found ways to pool together resources to start businesses, sustain strikes and boycotts, and use the judicial system and diplomatic channels to defend their civil rights. By so doing, they contributed significantly to the molding of American constitutional jurisprudence and expanding notions of fairness under the law. For example, in the 1862 case of *Lin Sing v. Washburn,* the California Supreme Court nullified a law imposing an onerous tax on Chinese immigrants only. In the landmark cases of *Wong Kim Ark v. United States* (1898) and *Yick Wo v. Hopkins* (1886), the U.S. Supreme Court confirmed the citizenship of any native-born person and equal protection of the law for all residents irrespective of race or nationality. The Chinese consulate was also instrumental in pressuring the U.S. government to honor its treaties with China and in seeking retribution on behalf of Chinese victims of discriminatory laws and racial violence.

The situation was different for Chinese in the Hawaiian Islands, where racial discrimination was not as virulent as on the mainland. Recruited in large numbers to work in the sugar plantations beginning in 1852, Chinese laborers soon moved on to raise livestock, grow rice, taro, coffee, garden vegetables, and fruits, and eventually become shopkeepers and skilled craftsmen in Honolulu and other towns. Because they had been encouraged to bring their wives to work in the cane fields and were allowed to marry native Hawaiian women, the Chinese in Hawaii were able to develop family life and integrate into the larger society at an earlier date than on the mainland. Nevertheless, learning from the experiences of their counterparts on the mainland, the Chinese in Hawaii early on formed organizations to provide fellowship, social control, protection, and arbitration. They also maintained close ties to their homeland and culture, establishing their own newspapers, schools, and temples even as they planted roots in Hawaii.

Chinese immigrants left few records and documents about their experiences in America during this early period. Although some were literate, many were not. Furthermore, the constant struggle for survival and the attitude that they were only in the country temporarily meant they had little time, energy, or inclination to record their experiences. Very few letters, diaries, or other written records survived in either China or the United States. The destruction of wars, revolutions, and great social upheavals took its toll as well. What have survived are a few letters, editorials, speeches, petitions, reports, and ephemeral material produced by the Chinese that were published or retained by the Chinese government and religious or social organizations

in America. There are also some memoirs from these early years, and poems or folk songs handed down through the generations. The following selections draw from these types of rare material.

We begin this section with three folk songs sung by women in the Pearl
River Delta lamenting the long family separations caused by their husbands'
sojourns in Gold Mountain. Although we failed to find any personal accounts
of Chinese miners, farmers, fishermen, factory or domestic workers, we were
able to include the reminiscences of five immigrants who came to America
in the nineteenth century: Wong Hau-hon, a railroad worker; Huie Kin, a
community leader and the first Chinese minister in New York; Wen Bing
Chung, who came with the Chinese Education Mission in 1871; Sing Kum,
an abused slave girl who found refuge in a San Francisco mission home; and
a Mrs. Teng, who came to Hawaii as a bond servant in 1891. The remaining
voices in this section attest to the individual and collective efforts of Chinese
immigrants to establish communities, protest racial discrimination, maintain
ties with China and Chinese traditions, and make America their home. Especially poignant and disturbing are two reports, one documenting the atrocities committed against Chinese miners at Rock Springs, Wyoming, in 1885,
and the other describing the difficulties involved in locating and returning
the remains of the deceased to China. We end the section with a selection
of letters from emigrant family members, complaining about problems at
home and beseeching their men to return soon. Together, these voices provide us with a glimpse of who some of the early immigrants were and how
they tried to establish meaningful lives in the inhospitable environment of
nineteenth-century America.

Songs of Gold Mountain Wives

The large majority of Chinese who came to the United States in the nineteenth century were men, and a good number of them—although young—were married with families left behind in their home villages. Cultural mores dictated that their wives remain in China to tend the fields and care for the in-laws and children. Many husbands, after going abroad to Hawaii, the United States, and elsewhere for work, sent remittances home to support the family, and some eventually returned to the Pearl River Delta with their newly acquired wealth. Many others, however, never returned home, and restrictive immigration laws made family reunification in the United States difficult. This often meant a life of widowhood for the wives of Gold Mountain men. The lyrics of the following folk songs reflect the sadness of separation and the women's longing for eventual reunion.

As a record of the grieving voices of Gold Mountain wives, the following three folk songs have a special poignancy. The first was sung by women in the Siyi region of the Pearl River Delta. It is a rarity in that it expresses the sojourner's sentiment rather than that of the women who were left at home. The second song, "Yik Jook, Yee Jook" ("First Admonition, Second Admonition"), comes from the Hakka villages in the outlying areas of Hong Kong. (In the nineteenth century, Siyi men tended to go to the U.S. mainland, while Hakka men went to Hawaii.) The third song is a popular ditty that questions the pros and cons of marrying any Gold Mountain man.

In the second reign year of Haamfung,[1] a trip to Gold Mountain
    was made.
With a pillow on my shoulder, I began my perilous journey.
Sailing a boat with bamboo poles across the seas,
Leaving behind wife and sisters in search of money,

---

1. The second reign year of Haamfung (Xianfeng) of the Qing dynasty was 1852.

7

No longer lingering with the woman in the bedroom,
No longer paying respect to parents at home.

SOURCE: Marlon K. Hom, *Songs of Gold Mountain: Cantonese Rhymes from San Francisco Chinatown* (Berkeley: University of California Press, 1987), p. 39.

.   .   .

YIK JOOK, YEE JOOK

I beg of you, after you depart, to come back soon,
Our separation will be only a flash of time;
I only wish that you would have good fortune.
In three years you would be home again.

Also, I beg of you that your heart won't change,
That you keep your heart and mind on taking care of your family;
Each month or half a month send a letter home.
In two or three years my wish is to welcome you home.

SOURCE: Tin-Yuke Char, *The Sandalwood Mountains: Readings and Stories of the Early Chinese in Hawaii* (Honolulu: University Press of Hawaii, 1975), p. 67.

.   .   .

O, just marry all the daughters to men from Gold Mountain:
All those trunks from Gold Mountain—you can demand as many
    as you want!
O, don't ever marry your daughter to a man from Gold
    Mountain:
Lonely and sad—a cooking pot is her only companion!

SOURCE: Marlon K. Hom, *Songs of Gold Mountain: Cantonese Rhymes from San Francisco Chinatown* (Berkeley: University of California Press, 1987), p. 46.

OTHER REFERENCES

Marlon K. Hom, "Gold Mountain Wives: Rhapsodies in Blue," *Chinese America: History and Perspectives*, 2002, pp. 32–35.

Madeline Hsu, *Dreaming of Gold, Dreaming of Home: Transnationalism and Migration between the United States and South China, 1882–1943* (Stanford: Stanford University Press, 2000), pp. 90–123.

Judy Yung, *Unbound Voices: A Documentary History of Chinese Women in San Francisco* (Berkeley: University of California Press, 1999), pp. 113–23.

To His Excellency Governor Bigler
(1852)

Norman Asing

Sentiment toward Chinese arriving in California took a decidedly negative turn in 1852, the year that twenty thousand Chinese arrived for the gold rush. That spring, a committee of the California assembly issued a report that condemned Chinese and other foreign miners as the greatest threat to the well-being of the state's mining districts. The report called for national and state measures to deal with the problem.

One week after the report's release, Governor John Bigler, in a special message to the state legislature, called for immediate, specific measures to "check the tide of Asiatic immigration" into California. He acknowledged that his call broke with the "long cherished and benevolent policy" of the United States to welcome immigrants from all lands, but it was necessary because the Chinese as "coolie labor" were undesirable additions to the state. He argued that because of cultural, racial, and other differences, they would never be able to assimilate and were incapable of becoming good citizens. As evidence, he maintained that not a single "Asiatic" had applied for citizenship, a claim Norman Asing addresses in his rejoinder, along with other charges made by Bigler. The Daily Alta California, *one of California's leading newspapers at the time, published Asing's remarks on April 25, 1852.*

Also known as Sang Yuen, Norman Asing was from the Huangliang Du region of the Pearl River Delta. He traveled to Europe and America around 1820 on a ship from Macao. When the ship berthed in New York City, he decided to stay. According to his rejoinder, he later became a merchant in Charleston, South Carolina, and also a Christian and a naturalized U.S. citizen. Not much else is known about Asing except that he was listed in the 1850 San Francisco city directory as the proprietor of a Chinese restaurant at Kearny and Commercial Streets, and in the 1854 directory as a foreign consul. He was also one of the founders of the Yeong District Association and an eloquent spokesman for the Chinese community.

Sir:

I am a Chinaman, a republican, and a lover of free institutions; am much attached to the principles of the government of the United States, and therefore take the liberty of addressing you as the chief of the government of this State. Your official position gives you a great opportunity of good or evil. Your opinions through a message to a legislative body have weight, and perhaps none more so with the people, for the effects of your late message have been thus far to prejudice the public mind against my people, to enable those who wait the opportunity to hunt them down, and rob them of the rewards of their toil. You may not have meant that this should be the case, but you can see what will be the result of your propositions.

I am not much acquainted with your logic, that by excluding population from this State you enhance its wealth. I have always considered that population was wealth; particularly a population of producers, of men who by the labor of their hands or intellect, enrich the warehouses or the granaries of the country with the products of nature and art. You are deeply convinced, you say, "that to enhance the prosperity and preserve the tranquility of this State, Asiatic immigration must be checked." This, your Excellency, is but one step towards a retrograde movement of the government, which, on reflection, you will discover; and which the citizens of this country ought never to tolerate. It was one of the principal causes of quarrel between you (when colonies) and England; when the latter pressed laws against emigration, you looked for immigration; it came, and immigration made *you what you are*— your nation what it is. It transferred you at once from childhood to manhood and made you great and respectable throughout the nations of the earth. I am sure your Excellency cannot, if you would, prevent your being called the descendant of an immigrant, for I am sure you do not boast of being a descendant of the red man. But your further logic is more reprehensible. You argue that this is a republic of a particular race—that the Constitution of the United States admits of no asylum to any other than the pale face. This proposition is false in the extreme, and you know it. The declaration of your independence, and all the acts of your government, your people, and your history are all against you.

It is true, you have degraded the Negro because of your holding him in involuntary servitude, and because for the sake of union in some of your States such was tolerated, and amongst this class you would endeavor to place us; and no doubt it would be pleasing to some would-be freemen to mark the brand of servitude upon us. But we would beg to remind you that when your nation was a wilderness, and the nation from which you sprung *barbarous,* we exercised most of the arts and virtues of civilized life; that we are possessed of a language and a literature, and that men skilled in science and the arts are numerous among us; that the productions of our manufactories, our sail and workshops, form no small share of the commerce of the world; and that for centuries, colleges, schools, charitable institutions, asylums, and hospitals, have been as common as in your own land. That our people cannot be reproved for their idleness, and that your historians have given them due credit for the variety and richness of their works of art, and for their simplicity of manners, and particularly their industry. And we beg to remark, that so far as the history of our race in California goes, it stamps with the test of truth the fact that we are not the degraded race you would make us. We came amongst you as mechanics or traders, and following every honorable business of life. You do not find us pursuing occupations of degrading character, except you consider labor degrading, which I am sure you do not; and if our countrymen save the proceeds of their industry from the tavern and the gambling house to spend it in the purchase of farms or town lots or on their families, surely you will admit that even these are virtues. You say you "desire to see no change in the generous policy of this government as far as regards Europeans." It is out of your power to say, however, in what way or to whom the doctrines of the Constitution shall apply. You have no more right to propose a measure for checking immigration, than you have the right of sending a message to the Legislature on the subject. As far as regards the color and complexion of our race, we are perfectly aware that our population have been a little more tanned than yours.

Your Excellency will discover, however, that we are as much allied to the *African* race and the red man as you are yourself, and that as far as the aristocracy of *skin is* concerned, ours might compare with many of the European races; nor do we consider that your Excellency, as a Democrat, will make us believe that the framers of your declaration of rights ever suggested the propriety of establishing an aristocracy of *skin*. I am a naturalized citizen,[1] your Excellency, of Charleston, South Carolina, and a Christian, too; and so hope you will stand corrected in your assertion "that none of the Asiatic class," as you are pleased to term them, have applied for benefits under our naturalization act. I could point out to you numbers of citizens, all over the whole continent, who have taken advantage of your hospitality and citizenship, and I defy you to say that our race have ever abused that hospitality or forfeited their claim on this or any of the governments of South America, by an infringement on the laws of the countries into which they pass. You find us peculiarly peaceable and orderly. It does not cost your State much for our criminal prosecution. We apply less to your courts for redress, and so far as I know, there are none who are a charge upon the State, as paupers.

You say that "gold, with its talismanic power, has overcome those natural

1. Norman Asing may indeed have been a naturalized citizen because although the 1790 Naturalization Law limited naturalization to "free white persons," some eastern courts were willing to naturalize Chinese.

habits of non-intercourse we have exhibited." I ask you, has not gold had the same effect upon your people, and the people of other countries, who have migrated hither? Why, it was gold that filled your country (formerly a desert) with people, filled your harbors with ships and opened our much-coveted trade to the enterprise of your merchants.

You cannot, in the face of facts that stare you in the face, assert that the cupidity of which you speak is ours alone; so that your Excellency will perceive that in this age a change of cupidity would not tell. Thousands of your own citizens come here to dig gold, with the idea of returning as speedily as they can.

We think you are in error, however, in this respect, as many of us, and many more, will acquire a domicile amongst you.

But, for the present, I shall take leave of your Excellency, and shall resume this question upon another occasion, which I hope you will take into consideration in a spirit of candor. Your predecessor pursued a different line of conduct towards us, as will appear by reference to his message.[2]

I have the honor to be your Excellency's very obedient servant.

Norman Asing

SOURCE: *Daily Alta California,* May 5, 1852, p. 2.

OTHER REFERENCES

Gunther Barth, *Bitter Strength: A History of the Chinese in the United States, 1850–1870* (Cambridge, Mass.: Harvard University Press, 1964).

Roger Daniels, *Asian America: Chinese and Japanese in the United States since 1850* (Seattle: University of Washington Press, 1988).

Charles McClain, *In Search of Equality: The Chinese Struggle against Discrimination in Nineteenth-Century America* (Berkeley: University of California Press, 1994).

---

2. In 1851 Governor John McDougal had called for the further immigration and settlement of Chinese in California.

The Founding of *Golden Hills' News* (1854)

As a result of the California gold rush, San Francisco grew from a sleepy Mexican vil-lage to become the largest city in the state in the 1850s. As different ethnic groups set-tled in the area, newspapers sprang up to fill their needs. In 1853 there were twelve newspapers in the city, including three in French and one in German. On April 22, 1854, the first Chinese-language newspaper was launched by William Howard[1] to serve the growing population of Chinese immigrants. According to the following edi-torial, the newspaper was aimed at Chinese merchants who had come to California to provide goods and services to the gold miners. Handwritten with a Chinese brush, it was printed on four tabloid-size pages and initially came out twice a week. Because of low readership, it was reduced to a weekly publication, and ceased publication after a year. Nevertheless, it marked the birth of Chinese American journalism and the begin-nings of a stable community.

My goal in establishing the newspaper is to serve the business community, to broaden knowledge, to give expression to opinions and sentiments, and to inform readers about government affairs. Currently the state of Califor-nia has become a gathering place for the world. Every immigrant group has its own newspaper except for the Chinese. As a result, although the Chinese merchants are many in number, they have no influence. Because they are uninformed, they have no way to exercise their freedom of choice. Even though they participate in American society, they lack real understanding and are easily manipulated and deceived by unscrupulous elements. When it comes to government affairs, their ignorance causes them to suffer abuse and mistreatment at the hands of corrupt officials. Though they have ranged

---

1. Probably William D. M. Howard, who arrived in San Francisco in 1839 and was active in the Presbyterian Church and in public life.

far and wide, yet they labor under restrictions and cannot develop themselves. How can one not sigh with regret? Since I feel strongly about this situation, I have founded a newspaper called *Golden Hills' News* to record in Chinese the commercial news and government affairs happening every day. It will be published every Wednesday and Saturday for your reading pleasure. If you respected gentlemen should have business announcements, I would be pleased to publish them on your behalf. In this way, the merchants and businessmen will profit, knowledge will increase, opinions and sentiments will be shared, government affairs will be understood, and the Chinese community will, in no small means, also benefit.

SOURCE: *Golden Hills' News,* July 29, 1854. Reprinted in Him Mark Lai, "19 shiji Meiguo Huawen baoye xiaoshi [Short history of Chinese journalism in America during the 19th century]," in *Huaqiao Huarenshi yanjiuji* [Collection of studies on the history of Chinese overseas], vol. 2, ed. Liang Chuhong and Zheng Min (Beijing: Haiyang Chubanshe, 1988), pp. 381–92. Translator: Ellen Yeung.

OTHER REFERENCES

H. M. Lai, "The Chinese-American Press," in *The Ethnic Press in the United States: A Historical Analysis and Handbook,* ed. Sally M. Miller (New York: Greenwood Press, 1987), pp. 27–43.

Karl Lo and Him Mark Lai, *Chinese Newspapers Published in North America, 1854–1975* (Washington, D.C.: Center for Chinese Research Materials, Association of Research Libraries, 1977).

Letter by a Chinese Girl (1876)

Sing Kum

Among the small number of Chinese women who immigrated to America in the nineteenth century, some came as the wives of merchants, but the majority were young women who had been kidnapped, tricked, or purchased from poor peasant families in southern China to be prostitutes. According to the federal census, some 70 percent of the Chinese women in San Francisco were prostitutes in 1870. As indentured slave girls, they were usually confined in brothels and, according to the terms of their contracts, worked without wages in order to repay debts incurred in their sale and passage to America. They endured brutal, degrading conditions, and many died from disease and mistreatment after just a few years.

The lucky ones escaped bondage by buying out their contracts, running away, or seeking protection from the police or mission homes in Chinatown. In the following account, Sing Kum writes about how she ran away from an abusive mistress to seek refuge at the Methodist Mission Home founded by Rev. Otis Gibson in 1870. According to Gibson's book, The Chinese in America, *when he opened the mission door at midnight that fateful Sunday, "a Chinese girl in dirty, ragged clothes rushed in hurriedly and immediately ran upstairs. When asked what she wanted, she replied in Chinese, 'I want to go to the school for Chinese girls—my mother whips me all the time, and I have run away from her,—let me go to the school before they catch me.'" Sing Kum was allowed to stay at the Mission Home, where she learned to read and write in English and Chinese, and eventually worked as an assistant teacher.*

Miss B,—

You ask me to write about my life. I can not write very well, but will do the best I can.

I was born in Sin Lam, China, seventeen years ago. My father was a weaver and my mother had small feet. I had a sister and brother younger than myself. My father was an industrious man, but we were very poor. My feet were never bound; I am thankful they were not. My father sold me when I was about seven years old; my mother cried. I was afraid, and ran under the bed to hide. My father came to see me once and brought me some fruit; but my mistress told me to say that he was not my father. I did so, but afterward I felt very sorry. He seemed very sad, and when he went away he gave me a few cash, and wished me prosperity. That was the last time I saw him. I was sold four times. I came to California about five years ago. My last mistress was very cruel to me; she used to whip me, pull my hair, and pinch the inside of my cheeks. A friend of mine told me of this place, and at night I ran away. My friend pointed out the house. I was very much afraid while I was coming up the street; the dogs barked, and I was afraid my mistress was coming after me. I rang the bell twice, and when the door was opened I ran in quickly. I thank God that he led me to this place. I have now been here nearly three years. I am very happy, for I do not have those troubles which I had before. I have kind friends, but most of all, I am thankful that Jesus died to save me. God has given me the Bible to read, which teaches me that "Straight is the gate and narrow is the way that leadeth unto life." I was very bad before I came here. I used to gamble, lie, and steal. Now I love Jesus, and by God's help I will try to be obedient, and do those things which will please him.

Yours truly,
Sing Kum
San Francisco, January 4, 1876

SOURCE: Rev. O. Gibson, *The Chinese in America* (Cincinnati: Hitchcock & Walden, 1877), pp. 220–21.

OTHER REFERENCES

Lucie Cheng Hirata, "Free, Indentured, Enslaved: Chinese Prostitutes in Nineteenth-Century America," *Signs: Journal of Women in Culture and Society*, 5, no. 1 (autumn 1979): 3–29.

Peggy Pascoe, *Relations of Rescue: The Search for Female Moral Authority in the American West, 1874–1939* (New York: Oxford University Press, 1990).

Anthony Peffer, *If They Don't Bring Their Women Here: Chinese Female Immigration before Exclusion* (Urbana: University of Illinois Press, 1999).

Benson Tong, *Unsubmissive Women: Chinese Prostitutes in Nineteenth-Century San Francisco* (Norman: University of Oklahoma Press, 1994).

Judy Yung, *Unbound Feet: A Social History of Chinese Women in San Francisco* (Berkeley: University of California Press, 1995).

Documents of the
Chinese Six Companies
Pertaining to Immigration

*Violence against Chinese miners, which started soon after their arrival in the early
1850s, continued to escalate and spread to Chinese of all walks of life in the next two
decades. While assaults against individual Chinese became commonplace throughout
the West, one of the worst cases of mob violence was the 1871 attack on the Chinese community in Los Angeles that took the lives of some twenty or more Chinese, with over a
dozen lynched in the streets while their homes were looted. As the industrial depression
hit California and state and local legislative efforts to stop Chinese immigration proved
fruitless, the anti-Chinese movement went national.*

*The presidential election year of 1876 marked a turning point in that movement,
as both the Republican and Democratic parties adopted planks in their platforms that
called for restrictions on Chinese immigration along with other anti-Chinese measures.
The Democrats were especially vicious in their attack, claiming that Chinese workers
were being used as tools of monopolies and that they constituted unfair competition to
white workers. In March the Democratic mayor of San Francisco, Andrew Jackson
Bryant, publicly condemned Chinese immigration and called on the city's Board of
Supervisors to draw up a list of grievances that would be sent to Washington, D.C.,
and circulated throughout the country. He also called for a public rally to dramatize
the issue.*

*On April 5, some twenty thousand people gathered in the largest meeting ever held
on the West Coast up to that time to listen to a score of prominent speakers denounce
the presence of Chinese in California and their further immigration. In response, leading officials of the important district associations in San Francisco Chinatown, collectively known as the Chinese Six Companies, along with the Chinese YMCA, publicly issued "A Memorial to President Grant." Attached to this was a twenty-page tract
written by Professor August Layres, entitled "The Other Side of the Chinese Question."
Layres was known as an outspoken defender of the Chinese, and in his essay he re-
butted charges that the Chinese were economically detrimental to the state.*

The accusations made against the Chinese were economic and social in nature. The Chinese were said to be draining the state of its wealth and not contributing to its general welfare. Moreover, they were accused of bringing immorality into the state through prostitution, gambling, and drugs and, more generally, of being culturally incompatible with American life. Exclusionists also blamed the Chinese Six Companies for flooding the country with "coolie labor," which it allegedly exploited for its own commercial benefit. In fact, the officers of the Six Companies were often among the most respected members of the Chinese community. Not only had they tried to eliminate prostitution and encouraged Chinese immigrants to lead moral lives, but they had also looked for ways to reduce the number of arrivals from China, even though 80 percent of immigration at this time was coming from Europe. The three documents that follow (the second and third explicitly) attest to such efforts.

President Grant was the first president to draw public attention to the Chinese immigration issue. He did so in brief comments made in his annual addresses in 1874 and 1875, in which he expressed a willingness to consider some limits on Chinese immigration. According to several contemporaneous accounts, the first document presented here, "A Memorial from Representative Chinamen in America, 1876," proved an effective response to the accusations made against the Chinese, though it failed to stop the anti-Chinese tide. A few years later, Congress passed the Chinese Exclusion Act of 1882, which prohibited the further entry of Chinese laborers into the United States and denied the Chinese naturalization rights.

A MEMORIAL FROM REPRESENTATIVE CHINAMEN IN AMERICA (1876)

To His Excellency U. S. Grant, President of the United States of America:

Sir:

In the absence of any Consular representative, we, the undersigned, in the name and in behalf of the Chinese people now in America, would most respectfully present for your consideration the following statements regarding the subject of Chinese immigration to this country:

  I. We understand that it has always been the settled policy of your Honorable Government to welcome immigration to your shores from all countries, without let or hindrance.

    The Chinese are not the only people who have crossed the ocean to seek a residence in this land.

  II. The Treaty of Amity and Peace between the United States and China makes special mention of the rights and privileges of Americans in China, and also of the rights and privileges of Chinese in America.[1]

---

1. The Burlingame Treaty of 1868 called for free migration between countries and equal treatment of travelers and residents within both countries, but forbade the right to naturalization.

The directors of San Francisco's Chinese Consolidated Benevolent Association, popularly known as the Chinese Six Companies. (Courtesy of the Bancroft Library, University of California, Berkeley)

III. American steamers, subsidized by your Honorable Government, have visited the ports of China, and invited our people to come to this country to find employment and improve their condition. Our people have been coming to this country for the last twenty-five years, but up to the present time there are only 150,000 Chinese in all these United States, 60,000 of whom are in California, and 30,000 in the city of San Francisco.[2]

IV. Our people in this country, for the most part, have been peaceable, law-abiding and industrious. They performed the largest part of the un-skilled labor in the construction of the Central Pacific Railroad, and also of all other railroads on this Coast. They have found useful and re-munerative employment in all the manufacturing establishments of this Coast, in agricultural pursuits, and in family service. While benefiting themselves with the honest reward of their daily toil, they have given

2. According to the U.S. Census, there were 63,199 Chinese in the United States in 1870 and 105,465 in 1880.

satisfaction to their employers, and have left all the results of their industry to enrich the State. They have not displaced white laborers from these positions, but have simply multiplied the industrial enterprises of the country.

V. The Chinese have neither attempted nor desired to interfere with the established order of things in this country, either of politics or religion. They have opened no whisky saloons, for the purpose of dealing out poison and degrading their fellow men. They have promptly paid their duties, their taxes, their rents and their debts.

VI. It has often occurred, about the time of the State and general elections, that political agitators have stirred up the minds of the people in hostility to the Chinese, but formerly the hostility has usually subsided after the elections were over.

VII. At the present time an intense excitement and bitter hostility against the Chinese in this land, and against further Chinese immigration, has been created in the minds of the people, led on by His Honor the Mayor of San Francisco and his associates in office, and approved by His Excellency the Governor, and other great men of the State.

These great men gathered some 20,000 of the people of this city together on the evening of April the fifth, and adopted an address and resolutions against Chinese immigration. They have since appointed three men (one of whom we understand to be the author of the address and resolutions) to carry that address and those resolutions to your Excellency, and to present further objections, if possible, against the immigration of the Chinese to this country.

VIII. In that address numerous charges are made against our people, some of which are highly colored and sensational, and others, having no foundation whatever in fact, are only calculated to mislead honest minds and create an unjust prejudice against us.

We wish most respectfully to call your attention, and, through you, the attention of Congress, to some of the statements of that remarkable paper, and ask a careful comparison of the statements there made with the facts of the case; and

(a) It is charged against us that not one virtuous Chinawoman has been brought to this country, and that here we have no wives nor children.

The fact is that already a few hundred Chinese families have been brought here. These are all chaste, pure, keepers-at-home, not known on the public street. There are also among us a few hundred, perhaps a thousand, Chinese children, born in America.

The reason why so few of our families are brought to this country is, because it is contrary to the custom and against the inclination of virtuous Chinese women to go so far from home, and because the frequent outbursts of popular indignation against our people have not encouraged us to bring our families with us against their will.

Quite a number of Chinese prostitutes have been brought to this country by unprincipled Chinamen, but these, at first, were brought from China at the instigation and for the gratification of white men. And, even at the present time, it is commonly reported that a part of the proceeds of this villainous traffic goes to enrich a certain class of men belonging to this Honorable nation—a class of men, too, who are under solemn obligation to suppress the whole vile business, and who certainly have it in their power to suppress it, if they so desired.

A few years ago our Chinese merchants tried to send these prostitutes back to China, and succeeded in getting a large number on board the out-going steamer; but a certain lawyer of your Honorable nation (said to be the author and bearer of these resolutions against our people), in the employ of unprincipled Chinamen, procured a writ of "habeas corpus," and brought all those women on shore again, and the Courts decided that they had a right to stay in this country if they so desired. Those women are still here, and the only remedy for this evil and also for the evil of Chinese gambling lies, so far as we can see, in an honest and impartial administration of Municipal Government in all its details, even including the police department. If officers would refuse bribes, then unprincipled Chinamen could no longer purchase immunity from the punishment of their crimes.

(b) It is charged against us that we have purchased no real estate. The general tone of public sentiment has not been such as to encourage us to invest in real estate, and yet our people have purchased and now own over $800,000 worth of real estate in San Francisco alone.

(c) It is charged against us that we eat rice, fish and vegetables. It is true that our diet is slightly different from the people of this Honorable country; our tastes in these matters are not exactly alike and cannot be forced. But is that a sin on our part, of sufficient gravity to be brought before the President and Congress of the United States?

(d) It is charged that the Chinese are no benefit to this country. Are the railroads built by Chinese labor no benefit to the country? Are the manufacturing establishments, largely worked by Chinese labor, no benefit to this country? Do not the results of the daily toil of a hundred thousand men increase the riches of this country? Is it no benefit to this country that the Chinese annually pay over $2,000,000 duties at the Custom House of San Francisco? Is not the $200,000 annual poll tax paid by the Chinese any benefit? And are not the hundreds of thousands of dollars' taxes on personal property, and the Foreign Miner's tax, annually paid to the revenues of this country, any benefit?

(e) It is charged against us that the "Six Chinese Companies" have secretly established judicial tribunals, jails and prisons, and secretly exercise judicial authority over the people. This charge has no foundation in fact. These Six Companies were originally organized for the purpose of mutual protection and care of our people coming to and going from this country. The Six Companies do not claim, nor do they exercise any judicial authority whatever, but are the same as any tradesmen or protective and benevolent societies. If it were true that the Six Companies exercise judicial authority over the Chinese people, then why do all the Chinese people still go to American Tribunals to adjust their differences, or to secure the punishment of their criminals?

Neither do these Companies import either men or women into this country.

(f) It is charged that all Chinese laboring men are slaves. This is not true in a single instance. Chinamen labor for bread. They pursue all kinds of industries for a livelihood.

Is it so then that every man laboring for his livelihood is a slave? If these men are slaves, then all men laboring for wages are slaves.

(g) It is charged that the Chinese commerce brings no benefit to American Bankers and Importers. But the fact is that an immense trade is carried on between China and the United States by American merchants, and all the carrying business of both countries, whether by steamers, sailing vessels or railroad, is done by Americans. No China ships are engaged in the carrying traffic between the two countries.

Is it a sin to be charged against us that the Chinese merchants are able to conduct their mercantile business on their own capital? And is not the exchange of millions of dollars annually by the Chinese with the banks of this city any benefit to the banks?

(h) We respectfully ask a careful consideration of all the foregoing statements. The Chinese are not the only people, nor do they bring the only evils that now afflict this country. And since the Chinese people are now here under solemn treaty rights, we hope to be protected according to the terms of this treaty.

But, if the Chinese are considered detrimental to the best interests of this country, and if our presence here is offensive to the American people, let there be a modification of existing treaty relations between China and the United States, either prohibiting or limiting further Chinese immigration, and, if desirable, requiring also the gradual retirement of the Chinese people, now here, from this country. Such an arrangement, though not without embarrassments to both parties, we believe, would not be altogether unacceptable to the Chinese Government, and, doubtless, it would be very acceptable to a certain class of people in this Honorable country.

With sentiments of profound respect,

Lee Ming How, President Sam Yup Company.

Lee Chee Kwan, President Yung Wo Company.

Law Yee Chung, President Kong Chow Company.

Chan Leung Kok, President Ning Yung Company.

Lee Cheong Chip, President Hop Wo Company.

Chan Kong Chew, President Yan Wo Company.

Lee Tong Hay, President Chinese Young Men's Christian Association.

SOURCE: Rev. O. Gibson, *The Chinese in America* (Cincinnati: Hitchcock & Walden, 1877), pp. 315–23.

OTHER REFERENCES

Najia Aarim-Heriot, *Chinese Americans, African Americans, and Racial Anxiety in the United States, 1848–1882* (Urbana: University of Illinois Press, 2003).

Andrew Gyory, *Closing the Gate: Race, Politics, and the Chinese Exclusion Act* (Chapel Hill: University of North Carolina Press, 1998).

Him Mark Lai, "Historical Development of the Chinese Consolidated Benevolent Association/*Huiguan* System," *Chinese America: History and Perspectives*, 1987, pp. 3–51.

Stuart Miller, *The Unwelcome Immigrant: The American Image of the Chinese, 1785–1882* (Berkeley: University of California Press, 1969).

Alexander Saxton, *The Indispensable Enemy: Labor and the Anti-Chinese Movement in California* (Berkeley: University of California Press, 1971).

A MEMORIAL TO THE STATE OF CALIFORNIA TO BAR PROSTITUTES (1868)

Subject of petition: The sale of women into prostitution is a violation of the law and the import of prostitutes should be prohibited.

When the United States first began to develop California, there were newspaper advertisements seeking to attract people from all nations. Consequently the Chinese came to mine gold and engage in trade. All countries were regarded as one nation and the people from the four seas as one family. Moral standards were high and the laws strict and clear. The sale of people into slavery was strictly forbidden. From this, one can see the moral integrity of this great nation.

If the trafficking of slaves is prohibited by law, how then can the abduction of women and forcing them into prostitution be permitted? Since Chinese prostitutes began arriving in 1852, the number has been increasing steadily, and will soon reach 10,000. In truth, most of these women originated from decent families, but have been purchased by racketeers and forced to be prostitutes. Lured by them, commercial travelers from other countries and young men as well indulge in pleasures of the flesh to the point that they are reluctant to return home, squandering their money and neglecting their businesses. The industrious become idlers; the rich become poor. Poverty leads to shamelessness; shamelessness breeds lawlessness. Thus crime is on the rise as thievery and robbery occur more and more, causing strife and disorder. This [prostitution] has become a disease for the country. Moreover, there are those who have been infected with vene-real disease resistant to medical treatment. As a result, quite a few lives have been ruined through the years. The repercussions from this are too many to enumerate.

The Chinese prostitutes here do not bear offspring, nor do they add to the tax coffers. They do not make a single contribution to society but in-stead cause a lot of harm. They really should not be allowed to stay, not even for a day. That is why in 1863 the city government of San Francisco allowed the Chinese Six Companies to send back to Hong Kong women who could be proven to be intended for prostitution. A record of this is still on file. As a result, morals improved in the few years following the ban. The racketeers, however, unwilling to give up their lucrative business, have resorted to lies and brazenly claim that the women are really concubines. As a result, the situation has become worse than before. Now when a prostitute becomes in-fected with disease, she is denied medical treatment and hidden away in a dark corner of some basement. And when she dies, no one comes forward to identify her. Fortunately, thanks to the compassion and kindness of your government, she is given a coffin and decent burial. Alas, such cruelty is re-ally beyond description.

We believe the case of selling women into prostitution is the same as that of selling people into slavery and should also be outlawed by your country. We have traveled far across the ocean to be sojourners in California. When we enter your country we usually acquaint ourselves with your laws and do all we can to abide by them. We work peacefully in our trade and are grate-ful for your government's favors. Now, seeing the terrible harm done to so-ciety by prostitution, we respectfully petition Your Excellency, who is in charge of this land and whose magnanimous kindness extends to all corners of the earth like the brilliant midday sun. We humbly and earnestly beseech Your Excellency to instruct your official in charge of shipping in the State to or-der the general managers of the big ships and the owners of steamboats and sailboats to carefully check for the stamp of the Chinese Six Companies to verify that the holder is really a maidservant or concubine before she is al-lowed to disembark. If our official stamp is missing, the woman must have been abducted and will be forced to prostitute herself to make money for racketeers, and, regardless of her age, must not be permitted to disembark. Only then can the continuous influx of prostitutes be checked. From now on, they can only leave but not enter. In this way we will rid society of this evil, thereby benefiting not only the country, but also California, where com-mercial travelers will be left in peace.

We humbly beg Your Excellency to execute this order, for which, we, the sojourners, will be exceedingly grateful.

12th day of the 2nd fourth month of the 7th year of Tongzhi [June 2, 1868][3]

SOURCE: California State Archives, Sacramento. Translator: Ellen Yeung.

A LETTER WRITING CAMPAIGN TO DISCOURAGE IMMIGRATION (1876)

The Chinese Six Companies is asking our fellow clansmen not to make the long sea voyage to the United States so as to avoid bringing trouble on the community. The reason we have been subjected to all kinds of harassment by the white people is that many of our Chinese newcomers are taking jobs away from them. And yet, if we take a look at the wages of the Chinese workers in the various trades, we can see that they are shrinking day by day. This is also due to the large number of our fellow clansmen coming here. If up to 10,000 people come here, even if they do not take away 10,000 white men's jobs, they will still drive down the wages of 10,000 workers in various trades. It's inevitable. If this trend is not stopped, not only will the white men's harassment continue, causing a great deal of trouble for our community, but even skilled Chinese workers will have difficulty finding jobs and will lose their livelihood. If it is hard for the Chinese who are already here, imagine how much worse it will be for the newcomers.

Therefore, in an effort to prevent disaster before it strikes, the members of the Six Companies believe that the best course of action is to have each person in California write a letter home exhorting his clansmen not to come to America. And who would doubt such advice when it originates from a kinsman? This is much better than our posting thousands and thousands of notices. If the trend should cease and fewer clansmen come here, first, further trouble from the white people would be avoided; second, wages will stop shrinking; third, there will be no worry about newcomers being detained. Everyone will benefit. Just a single word from you will do a world of good. For this reason we are urging every one to write home.

The Chinese Six Companies
15th day of the 3rd month, Guangxu[4] 2nd year [April 9, 1876]

SOURCE: Reverend Otis Gibson Papers, Ethnic Studies Library, University of California, Berkeley. Translator: Ellen Yeung.

3. The year 1868 is a leap year in the Chinese calendar and there were two fourth months. Tongzhi is the reigning title of the eighth emperor of the Qing dynasty.

4. Reigning title of the ninth emperor of the Qing dynasty who ruled from 1875 to 1908.

The Second Exhumation and Return of the Remains of Our Departed Friends to the Homeland (1876)

Traditional Chinese belief held that the souls of the dead could not rest until they were interred in the soil of their native village. Village burial and ancestral worship were also important for the surviving relatives of the deceased in order for them to pay proper respects to the departed. These customs played an important part in the social life of the Chinese. Death away from the home village, therefore, posed a difficult problem for Chinese immigrants in the nineteenth century.

One of the first things that a new arrival to Gold Mountain would do was arrange for his body to be shipped to China for burial should he meet with an unfortunate accident. This he usually did through his district association, many of which established a separate organization, known as a shantang *(charity hall), for this purpose. Funds came from exit fees that members were required to pay before leaving for China or from special fundraising efforts on the part of the district association. As described in the following poignant account by "bone collectors" from Panyu District, a great deal of expense and trouble went into the task of collecting and preparing the remains of the deceased for reburial in China.*

One of the reasons many Chinese in America tenaciously retained their connections to China and Chinese traditions had to do with their deep estrangement from American life and society. Unaccepted here, many Chinese immigrants persisted in their view that "fallen leaves return to their roots." The remains of thousands of Chinese were returned to China in the nineteenth century for burial. Even for those buried in American cemeteries, the racist practice was to keep them segregated from others, and if unattended, their graves were often vandalized. Thus, until the founding of the People's Republic of China in 1949 damaged relations between China and the United States, and the situation for Chinese Americans improved, the common practice was to exhume the bones and return them to China.

San Francisco is more than 20,000 miles from China. When the Americans opened up the frontier lands, they purposely used homesteading and gold

Chinese cleaning the bones of the dead, 1879. (Courtesy of Philip P. Choy)

mining to attract immigrants. That was why the Chinese flocked to California like ducks to water. Yet who knows how many of them died with their ambitions unattained, their dreams unfulfilled. Instead, their spirits could not return to their homeland since their bones were buried in foreign soil. They could only gaze longingly toward home, and their anguish deepened with each passing of Ching Ming.[1]

One cannot but feel regret at such stories. Therefore, in 1858, Xianfeng[2] eighth year, those of us formerly from Panyu assembled our fellow expatriates and proposed the establishment of the Cheung Hau Association.[3] We drew up a special rule: successful returnees to China would each donate ten American dollars; those who were well off could donate more if they wished. In this way we collected funds and hired workers to locate and exhume the remains of our fellow countrymen to be sent back to their native village so that, properly interred, they could forever enjoy the offerings due to the dead. Even as early as 1862, Tongzhi[4] first year, after we finished the exhumation and shipment, we were already worried that our funds would not last and

1. The "Bright and Clear Day" Festival occurs on April 4, 5, or 6 each year, during which time the Chinese visit and clean the gravesites of their ancestors.
2. Reigning title of the seventh emperor of the Qing dynasty.
3. District association for the expatriates of Panyu.
4. Reigning title of the eighth emperor of the Qing dynasty.

began making contingency plans. At that time, it so happened that the Jui Ying Building and attached business were up for sale. The asking price was a little over $26,000. So we took out a bank loan of $8,000 and bought the property at its full price. We then made additions to the building and were soon making loan payments to the bank with income from the property. Any surplus was saved for future use and strict accounting was kept.

In 1874, during the Ching Ming Festival, when young and old gathered to pay their respects to the dead, we saw rows and rows of neglected and overgrown graves. The tomb markers had all been stripped away by the white people. Fearing that everything would disappear without a trace, we assembled others on our return and discussed the situation. We all agreed on exhumation. Unfortunately, there was only a little over $8,000 left in the account. Worried that this meager sum would not be enough to cover such a big undertaking, we therefore decided to lower the association dues to $5. Messrs. Wong Kai and So Mo were elected to travel to other foothill towns to collect the money and canvass for more donations.

It was the height of summer. Along the way Wong Kai and So Mo became sick with influenza in the sweltering heat and had a really difficult time. Fortunately, thanks to the generosity of our friends, Wong and So collected several thousand dollars, not quite enough to finance the whole project, but a good addition to the start-up fund. After we notified everyone, we elected Gong Yan to do the exhumation and Fung Biu to be the supervisor. We had hoped the two men would work closely together, but unexpectedly, the two had a falling out. . . . Subsequently, we elected Chan Dak Gwong as exhumer and Mok Fai Bak and Jau Dung Sing as supervisors. Unfortunately, Mok and Jau passed away halfway through the project. We then chose Yuet Chung Paak to fill the post, and the exhumation finally proceeded as planned.

From east to west, north to south, their trail took them not only to various parts of the United States, but also to Victoria, British Columbia. The team left no graves unchecked. They investigated every single report regarding remains of our compatriots from Panyu. Any body, which had not decomposed, would be put in a box made from lead, and then sealed inside a wooden box. As for those who had perished in a watery grave, those who had been victims of foul play and whose bodies had been hidden in some secluded place, those whose bodies had been stolen by the white people to make fish bait, or those whose graves were missing markers and therefore unidentifiable, their names were inscribed on a silver plate, which was placed in a "spirit" box and shipped back to the homeland.

From the beginning of the project in 1874 to its completion in 1876, a total of 858 coffins and 24 "spirit" boxes were used. Ten dollars were paid for each individual, and sacrifices with young animals were performed. The remains were shipped home on a steamer with Leung Naam assigned as escort. More than $40,000 was expended. Such was the situation as of November 1876.

The task this time was much more difficult than the previous one had been. The dead were many, and their graves were scattered, some far away, some nearby, requiring many different trips. The most difficult task was trying to get to Salmon River, Idaho, where Mr. Wong Sei was buried. His grave was located in an isolated area, thousands of miles from the nearest town, not on the route of any boat or vehicle. The exhumation team had to hire horses and mules to take them there. They traveled by day and rested by night, sleeping outdoors in the wild, risking attacks by wild beasts. The whole trip took them more than fifty days. The next most difficult search was for the remains of Messrs. Jau Taan and Lok Gau, who were buried in Memphis, Tennessee. Although close to the U.S. capital and accessible by train, it was still over 10,000 miles away, not a short journey that could be completed in a day. The other difficult sites to get to included Ma-che-haang-mei, where Mr. Chui Waan was buried, Ha-si-jin-ji, where Mr. Sin Siu was buried, Ma-sun-dong, where Mr. Chan Woon Sui was buried, and Bok-fat-lik, where Mr. Jau Hing was buried.[5] Some of these places were on high mountains, and some were in deep valleys. Neither horse nor vehicle could travel on those narrow winding trails. Still, the team managed to carry out their mission. With such effort and dedication on the part of the living, surely the dead can rest in peace. What was most tragic was the case of Mr. Choi Gei Gwong, who died on his way back to Guangdong Province. Since the ship he was on passed by Honolulu, he was buried there. Although the five people who handled the matter are still living, his tombstone has long since vanished, so nothing could be done. There are probably some remains that have not been recovered, but after all, it is not humanly possible to find all of them. Since we have completed the task that we set out to do, I am recording the events as they occurred from beginning to end.

·SOURCE: Yuk Ow, Him Mark Lai, and Philip Choy, eds., *A History of the Sam Yup Benevolent Association in the United States, 1850–1974* (San Francisco: Sam Yup Benevolent Association, 1975), pp. 253–54. Translator: Ellen Yeung.

OTHER REFERENCES

Linda Sun Crowder, "Mortuary Practices in San Francisco Chinatown," *Chinese America: History and Perspectives*, 1999, pp. 33–46.

Marlon K. Hom, "Fallen Leaves' Homecoming: Notes on the 1893 Gold Mountain Charity Cemetery in Xinhui," *Chinese America: History and Perspectives*, 2002, pp. 36–50.

5. The American names of these four places cannot be deciphered from the given Chinese names. See Chinese Glossary for the Chinese names.

Reminiscences of a Pioneer Student (1923)

Wen Bing Chung

As a result of the early evangelical efforts of American missionaries in China, beginning in 1818 small groups of Chinese youths were brought to this country for an education. Although their numbers were small, they played an important and colorful role in history. Many of the students were associated with Yung Wing, who came to the United States in 1847 under American missionary sponsorship. He completed his middle school education at the Monson Academy in Massachusetts and became the first Chinese to graduate from an American college (Yale) in 1854. Upon his return to China, he successfully persuaded Chinese officials to sponsor the Chinese Educational Mission and send 120 young men to the United States for a Western education. The intention was that they would bring back technological skills to help China develop into a strong and prosperous nation. Among the students was Wen Bing Chung, who came with the second delegation in 1873.

The effort ended abruptly in 1881 because of fears that the students were becoming too Americanized and because of deteriorating relations between the two countries. About one hundred of the Educational Mission students returned to China; many assumed important positions in education, business, government, and the military. Wen Bing Chung became one of China's foremost engineers and superintendent of customs in Suzhou. The following excerpts are taken from a speech that he gave to a group of students at the Customs College in Beijing on December 23, 1923, in which he recalled the purpose and impact of the Chinese Educational Mission on China as well as his student days in the United States.

I am going to relate to you this evening: how the Chinese Government was persuaded to despatch the first government students to the United States of America to be educated. I will give you a succinct account only, because it will occupy too much of your valuable time, and is too long and tedious a narrative, covering as it does a period of more than fifty years.

Wen Bing Chung.
(La Fargue Collection,
Washington State
University Libraries)

It was in 1870 that some unfortunate missionaries were killed by the rough elements in Tientsin.[1] The Chinese officials had great difficulty in engaging the service of [an] efficient interpreter and translator to help them in the case, and were often obliged to fall upon the assistance of foreigners, thus experiencing great inconvenience during negotiations with the consular representatives.

About this time the officials were informed of the arrival at Shanghai of a young Cantonese student who had but recently returned from the United States after graduating with honors in the Yale University. The young man was Yung Wing, a village urchin in the district of Hsiang Shan, Kwangtung

1. In response to rumors of kidnapping and other abuses circulating against the missions in Tientsin, a riot broke out that resulted in the deaths of twenty-one Westerners and thirty Chinese Christians, and the destruction of buildings belonging to the French consul and the missionaries.

Province. He attracted the attention of a missionary by his bright and smart appearance, and was afterwards taken by the latter to America. With slender resources but with a determined mind, he worked his way first through the primary schools and then finished brilliantly at Yale. As he made his debut into the world, his first thought was to realize a dream that he had nourished during his college days. The dream was to induce the Chinese Government to despatch students to the United States for education so that in due time China would have [a] sufficient number of Western educated men to administer the affairs of the state so as to elevate the status of the country to an equal footing with foreign nations.

Having received an invitation from the great Viceroy Li Hung Chang to proceed north immediately, Yung Wing came to Tientsin in time to help in the negotiation and settlement of the case of the murdered missionaries, to the satisfaction of all parties concerned.

Viceroy Li was highly pleased with Yung Wing's services. He asked Yung Wing what he could do for him. Yung Wing saw his opportunity; there and then he disclosed his cherished dream; he pointed out to the Viceroy the importance of sending government students to America, and with growing intercourse with the Western people, the great advantages that China would reap in diplomacy, commerce and industry through the knowledge and experience acquired by the students abroad.

The Viceroy was impressed by Yung Wing's earnestness and enthusiasm and he promised to give him his support. There was, however, a slight drawback. Although Li Hung Chang was then the senior Viceroy in the Empire, he was loath and even timid to be the first and only advocate of an educational commission to the United States. The idea was too advanced for conservative China. Therefore, he sought to interest Viceroy Tseng Kuo-fan of the Liang Kiang Provinces and Ting Yi-chang of the Min-Cheh Provinces in Yung Wing's scheme, and succeeded to influence them to present a joint memorial to the Throne emphasising the benefit of sending government students abroad to be educated. In due course the memorial was sanctioned by the Throne.

Yung Wing was at once appointed Commissioner of Education and Chen Lan Ping Co-Associate Commissioner; these two were to have full charge and control of the students during their education in the United States.

Yung Wing's plan was to despatch thirty students each year for four consecutive years, making a total number of one hundred and twenty boys. A school was established at Shanghai in 1870, in order that prospective students should undergo a course of Chinese studies and a preliminary one in English. Examinations were held semi-annually for the selection of bright and competent students.

It is unnecessary to dwell at any length over the school days of these students. Suffice it to say that as boys will always be boys, the students of those days did not differ from those of today. They did not, however, have any tennis, football, basketball and other games, nor any holiday except during the Chinese New Year, Fifth Moon and Eighth Moon festivals. Much study and little play was the order of the school.

The inspector of the school was an autocrat. He believed in the use of the bamboo for the maintenance of discipline, and applied it with vigour on those who lagged in their studies. Still he was remembered by the students in after years with some affection, for although he put the fear of the Big Stick into them, he also made them learn the characters, the knowledge of which proved most useful on their return to China. . . .

The first batch of thirty students after passing the examination were despatched to the United States in 1871; the second batch in 1872; and the third and fourth in 1873 and 1874, respectively. Prior to their departure, the students were provided with a "pukai"[2] and a small trunk containing a few long gowns, "maqua"[3] and other sundries. They were instructed how to behave before the officials and trained in the rules of etiquette. . . .

The voyage across the Pacific was made in twenty-eight days, a long and tiresome voyage. Luckily for the students, the sea was calm and the days were bright and cheerful. They had got over their *mal de mer* and spent their time on deck, gazing at the blue expanse or watching a school of flying fishes disporting themselves. Occasionally, a whale spouting a column of water skyward would cause a flutter of excitement on board. Games were organized on board for the boys, and the days soon flew by before the students realized the steamer was sailing through the Golden Gate and the voyage had come to an end.

The sights that greeted the students in the harbour of San Francisco remained vividly in their memories for years afterwards. The steam launches and ships moving or anchored at their berths—the neat looking cottages on the lower levels and the stately mansions peering through the foliage of well kept lawns,—the business houses clustering like bees in the centre of the city—all seemed very grand to the students.

Soon the steamer was along the wharf. The students were driven to the Palace Hotel, a nine-story building, which was then the largest building in San Francisco. They tarried three days in this beautiful city, spending their time in sight-seeing; and enjoying themselves hugely.

It was not without a tinge of regret when the students had to leave San Francisco and board the train which was to transport them across the American Continent, a distance of more than 3,000 miles, in six days and six nights. A special car was reserved for the students. The train stopped three times a day to allow the passengers to get down to eat, as there was no dining car at-

2. Bedding.
3. A Mandarin jacket worn over a man's traditional long gown.

tached to the train. There were restaurants near or at the station. Standing at the restaurant door were two men, one ringing a bell and another beating a gong in order to attract the patrons. Fifteen minutes were allotted for eating, and hence when the train stopped for meal time, the passengers would race for the nearest restaurant and the same undignified scramble for the train would take place on the first sound of the bell for the train to start. In this way, the meals during the six days on the train were gobbled down with much discomfort.

During the first part of the journey, the train passed many tunnels in getting through the Rocky Mountains, and after that for four days it ran over the vast prairie land, and at the stations along the route the students saw genuine red Indians, natives of the American Continent, dressed in their original costumes, with eagle feathers projecting from their black hair, their faces painted in different colours, similar to the painted actors on the Chinese stage, and armed with bows and arrows. . . .

When the students arrived at New York, they remained one night in a hotel and [the] following day took a train for Springfield in the State of Massachusetts. On their arrival they stayed in a hotel where they were presented to Dr. Yung Wing,[4] who had left China several months before the students, in order to make the necessary preparations for their education. The next day Dr. Yung Wing assigned the students to their respective teachers who had come to take the students away to their own homes in the various parts of the States and who were to have the guardianship over them during their term in America. The students were distributed in twos and fours and placed under the care of their guardians. Those students who were advanced enough in English were sent to schools while the others were given private lessons at home.

At first the students wore the Chinese dress. Their long gown and "maqua," with their plaited queues, made them look like girls to the Americans. It was, to say the least, very embarrassing that each time the students ventured out of doors, they would draw a crowd that would follow and call them "Chinese girls." For the sake of convenience and less publicity, the students after they had been in America for some months prevailed upon the Chinese commissioners to allow them to adopt the costume of the country.

The students being all under fifteen years old were quick to receive impressions of the new life and to assimilate American ideas and ideals, retaining them permanently even to this day. They entered into the spirit of the schools, played baseball and football, and fought their way with the fists in true American style. After a few years the boys had become thoroughly Americanized breathing the air of freedom and independence, but they had

---

4. Although Wen Bing Chung addresses Yung Wing as Dr. Yung Wing throughout his speech, he did not have a doctorate degree.

their hard times, too. They were allowed one dollar a month for pocket money, a paltry pittance as they grew older and their amusements and pleasures increased in proportion.

The progress made by the students in their studies was steady and satisfactory, but one of the two Chinese Commissioners, a Hanlin,[5] was alarmed at the rapid rate [at which] the students were becoming imbued with the spirit of their environments—they were developing into more like go-ahead Americans in their ways than the humble and sedate subjects of the Emperor. This official sent a memorial to the Throne, stating that the students would soon fast turn into foreign devils unless they were sent home at once. Unfortunately for the students, the memorial was sanctioned, and a decree was issued for their recall.

It was a sad day when the students received the news that they were to be sent home. The majority of them were one or two years from their graduation; it was heartbreaking to have their scholastic career brought to an untimely termination. The students called a mass meeting and delegated a party to interview Dr. Yung Wing with the hope of getting the latter to intercede with the Government on their behalf. Dr. Yung Wing calmed the students by telling them they were only going to China for a vacation and would soon be back to America to finish their studies. It was on this assurance that the students consented to return to China, but alas! Not half a dozen ever went back.

The students had formed strong ties of friendship with the people they stayed with, and with the American boys in schools and colleges. So when the date of their departure was set, it was with saddened hearts that they bade good-bye to their friends and scenes of boyhood. It should be mentioned that the students carried with them most grateful memories of the kind and almost parental treatment they received from their American guardians and teachers.

On the homeward journey in 1881 the students stopped over at San Francisco, and while they were waiting for their steamer they received a challenge from the Oakland baseball team, which they were glad to accept by way of diversion. Now the Chinese nine had a twirler that played for Yale, and could do some wonderful curves with the ball, although in those days it was underhand pitching. Before the game began, the Oakland men imagined that they were going to have a walk-over with the Chinese. Who had seen Celestials playing baseball forty years ago? But the Oakland nine got the shock of their life as soon as they attempted to connect with the deliveries of the Chinese pitcher; the fans were equally surprised at the strange phenomenon— Chinese playing their national ball game and showing the Yankees some of the thrills in the game. Unimaginable! All the same, the Chinese walloped

5. In reference to Woo Tze-teng, who was a Hanlin or a member of the Imperial Academy.

them, to the great rejoicing of their comrades and fellow countrymen. This was the last baseball game the Chinese team played, for they never got together again afterwards.

These students that went to study in America from the year 1871 to 1881 were pioneers, paving the way for future students and dispelling the superstitious fear that held the better classes of our people from sending their sons to America and Europe. But on their return home, they were not greeted with open arms by the Government. On the contrary, when they landed at Shanghai, they were at once taken to the native city and locked up in a large building. They were not allowed out; and this restriction on their liberty was very much resented by these boys, fresh from the land of the Free. One day being unable to resist the temptation of seeing the sights, outside the wall, one of the students who happened to be the baseball pitcher and also a good boxer gave the guards a severe jolting for trying to bar his passage out. The matter was reported to the director in charge of the students, who saw the unreasonableness of detaining the students as prisoners and therefore permitted them on parole to go out and come back before dark.

Not long after their return, the students were despatched by the Government to different parts of the country. Then commenced their life battles in earnest. The students were poorly paid, most of them receiving four taels[6] a month; they suffered great hardships in the struggle for existence. They encountered prejudice and strong opposition from the literary and official classes, who declared that the students had become "foreign devils" and were of "no use to the country." By dint of patience and perseverance and plodding along for years, these students gradually convinced the Government of their integrity, loyalty and patriotism. Finally the Government showed its appreciation of the students by appointing them to high offices of trust and responsibility.

It may interest you if I mention a few of these pioneer students whose achievements will always be remembered by their old school mates. During the college days, one of the students Mr. Chung Mun-yao was the coxswain that steered the Yale University boat to victory against Harvard University for two consecutive years. The famous pitcher of the Chinese team, after struggling for twenty years, rose on his own ability and merits to many high and important government positions, such as the Haikuan Taotai[7] at Hankow, Tientsin, Foreign Minister in the Ching Dynasty, and Minister of Communications in the Republic. This baseball pitcher, Mr. Liang Tung-yen, is the uncle of the Peding Champion tennis player of the Customs College, of which he was one of the founders. The first premier of the Republic of China was Mr. Tong Shao-yi, one of [the] pioneer students, who was also the founder

6. Four taels of silver was little better than the wages of Chinese laborers at the time.
7. Chief of Customs.

and the first Associate Director-General of the Shui Wu Chu[8] in 1906. In the military and naval service, many have been promoted to the ranks of admirals and generals. Among them is Admiral Tsai Ting-kang, the present Associate Director-General of the Shui Wu Chu. In the naval battle of Yalu, 1894, a pioneer student, Admiral Woo Ying-foo, won the much coveted Manchu title of Bahtuhlu[9] for conspicuous bravery. The Kin-Chang Railroad was built by the late Chief Engineer Jim Tien Yu, a pioneer student. Many others have gained fame and honour in different fields of activities.

Such then were the pioneer students who had the courage in those days to face the perils of a long and uncertain voyage across the Pacific and an overland journey of more than 3,000 miles; who lived in an alien land, in order to learn its language, science and literature; who on their return demonstrated to their countrymen the wisdom as well as the benefit of commercial and friendly intercourse with occidental nations, thereby strengthening and enriching their own country and bringing about in time the brotherhood of nations. The pioneer students have served their days and generation; they have given the best of their life energy to the building up of a new China.

Of the 120 pioneer students, more than half have gone over to the Great Beyond. But those remaining, although they have passed three score years, show no sign of diminished activity; and many are still in the saddle, for few could afford to retire on their humble savings. This latter fact speaks for the honesty of the pioneer students as a whole. But the field of their usefulness is ever lessening as the years advance.

You, young gentlemen, after your graduation from this College, must carry on the noble and loving task to make this great Republic of ours strong and prosperous among the leading nations of the world. Now, as students of the Customs College, you have a special part to perform. Since China's commerce is gradually expanding and more ports will be thrown open to foreign trade, the establishment of customs houses will be on the increase, and more qualified assistants for the Service will be required. This Customs College will be able to supply the Service with competent men. Therefore, the future before you is full of bright prospects and your career will be of the most promising character. The hard work that you put into your studies will not be in vain, for in due season you will be amply rewarded.

SOURCE: Chinese Educational Mission, Thomas Edward La Fargue Papers, Manuscripts, Archives and Special Collections, Washington State University Libraries, Pullman, Washington.

8. Imperial Telegraph Administration.
9. A title conferred during the Qing dynasty for active service in the field that carries with it the right to wear the peacock feather.

OTHER REFERENCES

Doris C. J. Chu, *Chinese in Massachusetts: Their Experiences and Contributions* (Boston: Chinese Culture Institute, 1987).

Thomas La Fargue, *China's First Hundred* (Pullman: State College of Washington, 1942).

Ruthanne Lum McCunn, "Yung Wing and the Chinese Educational Mission," in *Chinese American Portraits: Personal Histories, 1828–1988* (San Francisco: Chronicle Books, 1988), pp. 17–25.

Yung Wing, *My Life in China and America* (New York: Henry Holt, 1909).

Reminiscences of an Old
Chinese Railroad Worker (1926)

Wong Hau-hon

Although many of the early Chinese who came to North America in the nineteenth cen-
tury were engaged in mining and railroad construction in the far West, very few records
of their experiences remain. This recollection by Wong Hau-hon, who worked on the
Canadian Pacific Railway (CPR), may well be the only existing account. Although it
tells of his experiences as a railroad worker in the mountainous terrain of British Co-
lumbia in western Canada, the harsh working conditions were similar to those faced
by Chinese workers on the Central Pacific line in the United States.

Chinese first began to enter Canada in the mid–nineteenth century as miners, and
between the years 1881 and 1885 over ten thousand Chinese were recruited from San
Francisco and China to work on the British Columbia section of the transcontinental
railroad. The CPR labor contractor in charge of overseeing the Chinese testified before
the Canadian government that approximately six hundred Chinese were killed dur-
ing the railway's construction, mainly due to frequent accidents, poor food, and weather
conditions. This averaged four Chinese lives for every mile of track laid. The actual
number of deaths is most likely higher, although Wong Hau-hon's estimate of three thou-
sand is probably too high. The numbers, however, reflect the railroad's fearsome repu-
tation among the Canadian Chinese.

Wong hailed from Xinhui District in Guangdong Province and offered these recol-
lections in 1926, soon after Canada tightened its laws against Chinese immigration.

I first came to Canada in 1882 (the 8th year of Guangxu)[1] on a sailing vessel. There were ninety or so fellow Chinese on the same ship. We debarked
at Westminister in mid-March of that year.

After a few days ashore, I set out on foot with a group of about four hundred Chinese to join the railroad construction crews at Yale [British Columbia].

---

1. Reigning title of the ninth emperor of the Qing dynasty who ruled from 1875 to 1906.

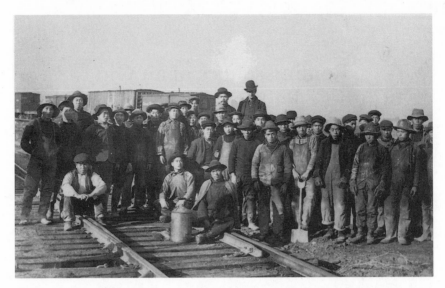

Chinese work crew on the Canadian Pacific Railway, 1884. (British Columbia Archives #D-07548)

In the daytime we walked and at night we slept in cloth tents beneath the trees. Those who did not have tents hung up their blankets to act as makeshift shelters.

After our arrival at Yale, we had worked only two days when the white foreman ordered the gang to which I was assigned to move to North Bend. We started on our way at seven in the morning; there were many Chinese in our traveling group. The weather was bad, for it rained all day, and we were all wet and cold. Among our traveling companions there were some arrivals who were unaccustomed to the exposure of the Canadian climate and sickened. Some died as they rested beneath the trees or lay on the ground. When I saw this I felt miserable and sad. Fortunately I was in more robust health and continued my journey until I reached the destination.

When we arrived at North Bend, we pitched our tents by the river. But the river level rose because of the recent rains and within a week we had to move our camp three times. The floods also severed the road from Vancouver to North Bend in several places so that pack trains could not come through. Our food supply was cut off and our store of provisions dwindled.

Our foreman then ordered us to pack up and return to Yale. So, although already suffering pangs of hunger, we had to start on our way immediately. When we were passing China Bar on the way, many of the Chinese died from an epidemic. As there were no coffins to bury the dead, the bodies were stuffed into rock crevices or beneath the trees to await their arrival. Those whose burials could not wait were buried on the spot in boxes made of crude thin planks hastily fastened together. There were even some who were buried in the ground wrapped only in blankets or grass mats. New graves dotted the landscape and the sight sent chills up and down my spine.

When we returned to Yale, we worked there for a while. Then the foremen ordered us to move to Hope. At that time I belonged to gang No. 161. Each gang consisted of about thirty workers and I heard that there were more than 380 gangs.

The work at Hope was very dangerous. On one occasion, there was a huge rock on the slope of the mountain that stood in the railroad's path and must be removed by blasting before the tracks could go through. However, the sides of the rock were nearly perpendicular all around and there was no easy way to reach the top. The workers had to scramble to the top by use of timber scaffolding and by ropes fastened to the rock. After they reached the top they drilled holes in the rock to hold the dynamite charges.

I was one of the workers who were assigned the task of drilling. Each morning I climbed the rock, and after I had finished the day's work I was lowered again by rope. I remembered that in blasting this rock more than three hundred barrels of explosives were used.

When blasting, all of the workers usually hid away in a safe place. But in spite of this there was one, Leung, who was killed. Actually Leung had already gone behind another hill, where he thought he would be safe. He then sat on the hillside and lit his pipe while he waited for the blasting to proceed. Unexpectedly, a huge boulder thrown up by the blast landed on the hillside where Leung was sitting and rolled down the slope, hitting him in the back. We heard a piercing shriek, and by the time we reached him Leung was already dead.

Another incident occurred about ten to fifteen miles west of Yale. Dynamite was used to blast a rock cave. Twenty charges were placed and ignited, but only eighteen blasts went off. However, the white foreman, thinking that all of the dynamite had gone off, ordered the Chinese workers to enter the cave to resume work. Just at that moment the remaining two charges suddenly exploded. Chinese bodies flew from the cave as if shot from a cannon. Blood and flesh were mixed in a horrible mess. On this occasion about ten or twenty workers were killed.

In 1883 I moved from Hope to Thompson River and worked there a month. Fortunately I suffered no accidents. Later I moved again to work in a barren wilderness for more than a year. There, more than one thousand Chinese laborers perished from epidemics. In all, more than three thousand Chinese died during the building of the railroad from diseases and accidents.

I am now sixty-two and I have experienced many hardships and difficulties in my life. I am proud of the fact that we Chinese contributed much to the development of transportation in Canada. Yet now the government is enforcing forty-three discriminatory immigration regulations against us. The Canadian people surely must have short memories!

SOURCE: *East/West,* May 5, 1971, p. 6. Translator: Him Mark Lai.

OTHER REFERENCES

Ping Chiu, *Chinese Labor in California, 1850–1880: An Economic Study* (Madison: State Historical Society of Wisconsin, 1967).

James Morton, *In the Sea of Sterile Mountains: The Chinese in British Columbia* (Vancouver: J.J. Douglas, 1974).

Alexander Saxton, "The Army of Canton in the High Sierra," *Pacific Historical Review* 35, no. 2 (May 1966): 141–52.

Edgar Wickberg, ed., *From China to Canada: A History of the Chinese Communities in Canada* (Toronto: McClelland & Stewart, 1982).

Memorandum No. 29
to Envoy Zheng (1882)

Huang Zunxian

Following their conquest of China in 1644, the Manchus (Qing dynasty) for decades had forbidden Chinese emigration to prevent loyalists to the dethroned Ming emperor from going abroad. This policy changed after the ratification of the Burlingame Treaty of 1868, which allowed for free migration between China and the United States and the right of China to appoint consuls at U.S. ports. After repeated requests by the Chinese Six Companies for the Qing regime to send officials to protect the interests of Chinese in America, two Chinese ministers, Chen Lanbin and Yung Wing, were finally appointed to Washington, D.C., in 1875. The two men had previously been assigned to supervise the Chinese Educational Mission in New England in 1872. Once made aware of the many problems facing the Chinese in California, they requested and were granted the authority to appoint a consul general in San Francisco. In 1881, Zheng Zaoru, known for being a skilled diplomat, replaced the two ministers in Washington and served as envoy until 1885. He appointed Huang Zunxian, a scholar from Guangdong, to be the consul general of San Francisco.

As the following report from Consul Huang to Envoy Zheng shows, both were in constant communication with one another over matters of grave concern to Chinese immigrants. Their job was to defend the Chinese against racial discrimination and mistreatment according to the stipulations of the Burlingame Treaty. This included making appeals to the U.S. government, filing lawsuits, and seeking reparations on behalf of wronged individuals. During Zheng's four-year term of office, he did what he could to protest treaty violations in the Chinese Exclusion Act, to fight discrimination against Chinese laundrymen, to stop the trafficking of Chinese women, and to negotiate indemnities for victims of the Rock Springs massacre in 1885. Although he was successful in many of these cases, his frustrations in dealing with lawlessness and violence against the Chinese soon led him to request a transfer. Consul Huang, known for his mediation skills in San Francisco Chinatown, left office at the same time.

Your Excellency's letter No. 27 arrived on the ninth day of this month, followed by letters No. 28 and No. 29 on the twenty-fifth and twenty-seventh, respectively. I have studied each of them carefully and understood their contents. The following is my report, in which I have attempted to provide information and responses, per your instructions.

Regarding the matter of Chinese laborers borrowing passage [through the United States], a subject which your Excellency has repeatedly discussed with the State Department, I have just learned that the U.S. Attorney General has written to the State Department advising that, in view of the new Exclusion Act and treaty regulations, Chinese laborers in transit through the United States are considered to be different from those contracted to work here and this therefore does not infringe on the new Exclusion Act restricting entry of Chinese laborers. If this is the case, the right of passage is permitted and all Chinese laborers residing in South America and the West Indies will be grateful for this act of kindness and glad for the convenience they will enjoy in their travels. I wonder if your office has received any dispatch about this from the State Department. Please advise if there are additional stipulations.[1]

As for new ordinances against laundry facilities, they were first challenged and refuted by our attorney. Then, in the middle of October, the regulatory board drafted a new ordinance with seven articles. The Chinese who have come to the U.S. to work are generally engaged in mining, road construction, and restaurant work. The only area where they can offer any kind of competition to Americans is the laundry business. Laundries can be found in numbers in cities everywhere. For example, just in the city of San Francisco, there are five to six thousand people engaged in laundry work. In the laundries, clothes are allowed to pile up, creating fire hazards. Water consumption is high and filthy conditions exist. Sometimes laundry workers carouse through the night, disturbing the neighbors, causing ill feelings, and attracting hostility. That is why laundries are often sued. A new ordinance was passed last year stipulating that only brick buildings are allowed to house laundries. This year another ordinance passed that requires recommendations from twelve property owners in the vicinity before a laundry can commence operation. Both the above-mentioned laws were repealed. This time, there is a new ordinance with seven articles. Article Five bans operation between ten o'clock in the evening and six in the morning. Article Six prohibits the sheltering of people with communicable diseases. In truth, both articles should be observed. The same also applies to the third and fourth

1. It was due to Zheng's diplomatic skills that President Chester Arthur first vetoed the Chinese Exclusion Act, reduced the period of immigration suspension from twenty years to ten years, and allowed Chinese laborers passing through the country to be exempted from the Exclusion Act.

articles about fire prevention and sewage construction, which are not unreasonable. Yet I am genuinely concerned by the Board's requirement of a license. I'm afraid that the process is just an excuse to cavil and find faults so as to drive laundries out. I have no choice but to challenge them in court. At the present time I have instructed the laundries to continue operation under prior regulations and have also retained attorneys to represent us, since the new law is about to take effect and legal action should begin before long. In my opinion, even if we are fortunate enough in getting the new law repealed, we should still instruct the laundries to establish formal guidelines to regulate themselves so as not to cause trouble in the future.[2]

The Ma Din case was tried in a local court at the end of the tenth month of the lunar calendar. One man pushed a Chinese off a building. Another man assembled a crowd by beating a gong and encouraged them to use thick ropes to pull down the building. The Americans who witnessed what happened, who lent the gong and who supplied the ropes, all came forward to testify. Yet, despite the many reliable depositions, the presiding judge handed down the decision to acquit. (McAllister was assigned to handle this case, but he refused.)[3] The attorney, [Thomas] Riordan, said he heard that the two men spent a huge sum of money to hire attorneys and to bribe all the investigating officers. That was why they were acquitted. "Those characters paid a heavy price in this case, so that should serve as a warning against similar crimes," added Riordan. "But if one wants to get them convicted, it is close to impossible. It happened in a small community where honest men are few and the so-called officials are no better than the criminals." Earlier, the foreman, Seeto, presented a list of damages totaling a little over a thousand dollars (not really a heavy loss in my estimation); nevertheless the official in charge rejected it for lack of proof. Riordan also said, "If we want compensation, we need to have the case moved and tried at some other court. However, I'm afraid it will cost too much and the loss will outweigh the gain." At present, the three other men arrested with the two culprits have not been tried yet; presumably they will also be acquitted. I have not decided whether further action should be taken to deal with Seeto's loss. After the whole case is settled, I will have the attorney make a copy of the entire trial proceedings and forward it to Your Excellency.

2. The Chinese laundrymen would eventually take their fight all the way to the U.S. Supreme Court, resulting in the famous 1886 *Yick Wo v. Hopkins* decision, which determined that the San Francisco ordinances discriminated against the Chinese and violated the "equal protection" clause of the Fourteenth Amendment to the Constitution.

3. Hall McAllister, of the established law firm McAllister and Bergin, was the lead counsel in the *Yick Wo v. Hopkins* case and had been retained by the Chinese community a number of other times.

It was recently reported in the newspapers that the Treasury Department[4] dispatched an agent, Yu Sun, to Port Townsend, Washington, to investigate the case of a group of Chinese laborers and immoral Chinese women attempting to enter the United States in violation of the new law. Port Townsend borders Victoria, British Columbia. Recent reports revealed that a dozen or so Chinese women were shipped from Hong Kong to Victoria. Local Chinese businessmen brought charges before the British authorities that these women are prostitutes. An official investigation followed but no evidence was found. Nevertheless, the media reported that those prostitutes were in fact destined for the United States, so a Treasury agent was sent to look into the matter. The new Exclusion Act restricts entry of Chinese laborers and is never meant to bar women. In a recent case in Portland, not only was a Chinese woman allowed entry, it was also ruled that a woman can enjoy the same rights as her husband; if a Chinese laborer is here, his wife and daughters are permitted to be here as well.[5] The only problem is that among the female population in San Francisco, there are more prostitutes than decent women. Every time a [Chinese] prostitute arrives, fighting would erupt among the Triad members[6] who battle each other for a share of the profits, even resorting to kidnapping. Because of the money that can be made, impoverished Tanka[7] people and unscrupulous merchants plot and scheme to get women to the United States. (A woman brought to San Francisco, for example, can fetch over a thousand dollars. Leung Tai Kee, a trading company in Hong Kong, is actually a trafficker in prostitutes, and responsible for shipping those prostitutes who came here in the second lunar month this year. It is said that the owner of that company came from a well-off family but suffered a financial setback this year due to a shipwreck, and now he will stop at nothing to make money.)

The issue is constantly on my mind. On one hand, I really don't want the new Act to ban Chinese women as well; on the other hand, in light of what is happening in San Francisco, neither do I want prostitutes to come here under false pretenses to create trouble. In a previous report, I submitted a proposal to refute the new Exclusion Act. I suggested that before the Chi-

4. The first Bureau of Immigration was established within the Treasury Department in 1891. Before then, the collection of customs and inspection of ships were within the purview of the Treasury Department. It was not until 1940 that immigration came under the supervision of the Department of Justice.

5. Two years later, in the cases of *Ah Quan* and *Ah Moy*, the federal court would rule that wives of Chinese laborers assumed their husbands' status as laborers and were therefore barred from entry.

6. Triads were secret societies that engaged in criminal activities such as gambling and prostitution.

7. A loose term for people who live and make their living on boats in the South China coastal region.

nese authorities issue a passport, any woman who wants to come to the United States must first show proof of sponsorship from a business owner in San Francisco, subject to verification by the Consul General who will then issue a certificate. Only with this certificate in hand is the person eligible for a passport. In this way we can stop fraud and abduction and eliminate trouble. I await your decision on the feasibility of my proposal.

SOURCE: Huang Zunxian, "Shang Zheng Yuxuan qinshi bingwen [Reports to Envoy Zheng]," in *Jindai ziliao* [Contemporary historical documents] (Beijing: Zhongguo Shehui Kexue Chubanshe, 1984), pp. 54–55. Translator: Ellen Yeung.

OTHER REFERENCES

R. David Arkush and Leo O. Lee, eds., *Land without Ghosts: Chinese Impressions of America from the Mid–Nineteenth Century to the Present* (Berkeley: University of California Press, 1989).

Charles J. McClain, *In Search of Equality: The Chinese Struggle against Discrimination in Nineteenth-Century America* (Berkeley: University of California Press, 1994).

Shih-shan Henry Tsai, *China and the Overseas Chinese in the United States, 1868–1911* (Fayetteville: University of Arkansas Press, 1983).

Memorial of Chinese Laborers at Rock Springs, Wyoming (1885)

One of the worst outbreaks of anti-Chinese violence occurred at Rock Springs, Wyoming, in 1885. As recounted below by Chinese residents and survivors of the attack, the riot was triggered by the refusal of Chinese miners to join white miners in a strike for increased wages. However, it should be pointed out that racial hostilities had been festering since 1875, when Chinese laborers were first hired by the Union Pacific Company as strikebreakers to replace white miners. In the 1885 incident, the Knights of Labor, seeking to eliminate Chinese competition for jobs, instigated the violence, in which a mob of armed white men opened fire on defenseless Chinese miners, killing twenty-eight and wounding fifteen, and burning all seventy-nine shacks belonging to the Chinese.

Chinese minister Zheng Zaoru immediately sent three officials to investigate the situation, including Huang Sih Chuen, consul at New York. They were able to substantiate the damages and cause of the massacre as set forth in the following memorial. However, despite their thorough report and the eyewitness accounts that were submitted to Congress, none of the rioters were punished. Zheng then resorted to arguing for indemnities on the basis of U.S. constitutional and treaty obligations to good effect, so that President Grover Cleveland was moved to convince Congress to appropriate $150,000 to cover property losses detailed in Zheng's report.

The gruesome details and outpouring of emotions in the aftermath of the massacre speak to the vulnerability of the Chinese caught in the cross fire of labor conflict and racial hatred as well as to their courage, dignity, and dogged determination in seeking justice in America. Appended to the memorial, but not reproduced here, were detailed lists of those killed and wounded in the riot as well as of property losses sustained by Chinese residents in the respective camps.

Massacre of the Chinese at Rock Springs, Wyoming, 1885. (Courtesy of
the Bancroft Library, University of California, Berkeley)

Rock Springs, Wyo., September 18, 1885
Hon. Huang Sih Chuen, Chinese Consul

Your Honor:

We, the undersigned, have been in Rock Springs, Wyoming Territory, for
periods ranging from one to fifteen years, for the purpose of working on the
railroads and in the coal mines.

Up to the time of the recent troubles we had worked along with the white
men, and had not had the least ill feeling against them. The officers of the
companies employing us treated us and the white man kindly, placing both
races on the same footing and paying the same wages.

Several times we had been approached by the white men and requested
to join them in asking the companies for an increase in the wages of all, both
Chinese and white men. We inquired of them what we should do if the companies refused to grant an increase. They answered that if the companies
would not increase our wages we should all strike, then the companies would
be obliged to increase our wages.[1] To this we dissented, wherefore we excited their animosity against us.

---

1. Their employer, Union Pacific Coal Department, had cut their wages the year before in
response to the economic depression.

During the past two years there has been in existence in "Whitemen's Town," Rock Springs, an organization composed of white miners, whose object was to bring about the expulsion of all Chinese from the Territory.[2] To them or to their object we have paid no attention. About the month of August of this year notices were posted up, all the way from Evanston to Rock Springs, demanding the expulsion of the Chinese. On the evening of September 1, 1885, the bell of the building in which said organization meets rang for a meeting. It was rumored on that night that threats had been made against the Chinese.

On the morning of September 2, a little past 7 o'clock, more than ten white men, some in ordinary dress and others in mining suits, ran into Coalpit No. 6, loudly declaring that the Chinese should not be permitted to work there. The Chinese present reasoned with them in a few words, but were attacked with murderous weapons, and three of their number wounded. The white foreman of the coal-pit, hearing of the disturbance, ordered all to stop work for the time being.

After the work had stopped, all the white men in and near Coal-pit No. 6 began to assemble by the dozen. They carried firearms, and marched to Rock Springs by way of the railroad from Coal-pit No. 6, and crossing the railroad bridge, went directly to "Whitemen's Town." All this took place before 10 o'clock A.M. We now heard the bell ringing for a meeting at the white men's organization building. Not long after, all the white men came out of that building, most of them assembling in the bar rooms, the crowds meanwhile growing larger and larger.

About 2 o'clock in the afternoon a mob, divided into two gangs, came toward "Chinatown," one gang coming by way of the plank bridge, and the other by way of the railroad bridge. The gang coming by way of the railroad bridge was the larger, and was subdivided into many squads, some of which did not cross the bridge, but remained standing on the side opposite to "Chinatown"; others that had already crossed the bridge stood on the right and left at the end of it. Several squads marched up the hill behind Coal-pit No. 3. One squad remained at Coal-shed No. 3, and another at the pump-house. The squad that remained at the pump-house fired the first shot, and the squad that stood at Coal-shed No. 3 immediately followed their example and fired. The Chinese by name of Lor Sun Kit was the first person shot, and fell to the ground. At that time the Chinese began to realize that the mob were bent on killing. The Chinese, though greatly alarmed, did not yet begin to flee.

Soon after, the mob on the hill behind Coal-pit No. 3 came down from the hill, and joining the different squads of the mob, fired their weapons and pressed on to Chinatown.

2. The Knights of Labor, which entered the Wyoming scene in 1883, had demanded the discharge of all Chinese employed by the Union Pacific.

The gang that were at the plank bridge also divided into several squads, pressing near and surrounding "Chinatown." One squad of them guarded the plank bridge in order to cut off the retreat of the Chinese.

Not long after, it was everywhere reported that a Chinese named Leo Dye Bah, who lived in the western part of "Chinatown," was killed by a bullet, and that another named Yip Ah Marn, resident in the eastern end of the town, was likewise killed. The Chinese now, to save their lives, fled in confusion in every direction, some going up the hill behind Coal-pit No. 3, others along the foot of the hill where Coal-pit No. 4 is; some from the eastern end of the town fled across Bitter Creek to the opposite hill, and others from the western end by the foot of the hill on the right of Coal-pit No. 5. The mob were now coming in the three directions, namely, the east and west sides of the town and from the wagon road.

Whenever the mob met a Chinese they stopped him, and pointing a weapon at him, asked him if he had any revolver, and then approaching him they searched his person, robbing him of his watch or any gold or silver that he might have about him, before letting him go. Some of the rioters would let a Chinese go after depriving him of all his gold and silver, while another Chinese would be beaten with the butt ends of the weapons before being let go. Some of the rioters, when they could not stop a Chinese, would shoot him dead on the spot, and then search and rob him. Some would overtake a Chinese, throw him down and search and rob him before they would let him go. Some of the rioters would not fire their weapons, but would only use the butt ends to beat the Chinese with. Some would not beat a Chinese, but rob him of whatever he had and let him go, yelling to him to go quickly. Some, who took no part either in beating or robbing the Chinese, stood by, shouting loudly and laughing and clapping their hands.

There was a gang of women that stood at the "Chinatown" end of the plank bridge and cheered; among the women, two of them each fired successive shots at the Chinese. This was done about a little past 3 o'clock P.M.

Most of the Chinese fled towards the eastern part of "Chinatown." Some of them ran across Bitter Creek, went up directly to the opposite hill, crossing the grassy plain. Some of them went along the foot of the hill where Coal-pit No. 4 stood, to cross the creek, and by a devious route reached the opposite hill. Some of them ran up to the hill of Coal-pit No. 3, and thence winding around the hills went to the opposite hill. A few of them fled to the foot of the hill where Coal-pit No. 5 stood, and ran across the creek, and thence by a winding course to the western end of the "Whitemen's Town." But very few did this.

The Chinese who were the first to flee mostly dispersed themselves at the back hills, on the opposite bank of the creek, and among the opposite hills. They were scattered far and near, high and low, in about one hundred places. Some were standing, or sitting, or lying hid on the grass, or stooping down on the low grounds. Every one of them was praying to Heaven or groaning with pain. They had been eyewitnesses to the shooting in "Chinatown," and had seen the whites, male and female, old and young, searching houses for money, household effects, or goods, which were carried across to "Whitemen's Town."

Some of the rioters went off toward the railroad of Coal-pit No. 6, others set fire to the Chinese houses. Between 4 o'clock P.M. and a little past 9 o'-clock P.M. all the camp houses belonging to the coal company and the Chinese huts had been burned down completely, only one of the company's camp houses remaining. Several of the camp houses near Coal-pit No. 6 were also burned, and the three Chinese huts there were also burned. All the Chinese houses burned numbered seventy-nine.

Some of the Chinese were killed at the bank of Bitter Creek, some near the railroad bridge, and some in "Chinatown." After having been killed, the dead bodies of some were carried to the burning buildings and thrown into the flames. Some of the Chinese who had hid themselves in the houses were killed and their bodies burned; some, who on account of sickness could not run, were burned alive in the houses. One Chinese was killed in "Whitemen's Town" in a laundry house, and his house demolished. The whole number of Chinese killed was twenty-eight and those wounded fifteen.

The money that the Chinese lost was that which in their hurry they were unable to take with them, and consequently were obliged to leave in their houses, or that which was taken from their persons. The goods, clothing, or household effects remaining in their houses were either plundered or burned.

When the Chinese fled to the different hills they intended to come back to "Chinatown" when the riot was over, to dispose of the dead bodies and to take care of the wounded. But to their disappointment, all the houses were burned to ashes, and there was then no place of shelter for them; they were obliged to run blindly from hill to hill. Taking the railroad as their guide, they walked toward the town of Green River, some of them reaching that place in the morning, others at noon, and others not until dark. There were some who did not reach it until the 4th of September. We felt very thankful to the railroad company for having telegraphed to the conductors of all its trains to pick up such of the Chinese as were to be met with along the line of the railroad and carry them to Evanston.

On the 5th of September all the Chinese that had fled assembled at Evanston; the native citizens there threatened day and night to burn and kill the Chinese. Fortunately, United States troops had been ordered to come and protect them, and quiet was restored. On the 9th of September the United States government instructed the troops to escort the Chinese back to Rock Springs. When they arrived there they saw only a burnt tract of ground to mark the sites of their former habitations. Some of the dead bodies had been buried by the company, while others, mangled and decomposed, were strewn on the ground and were being eaten by dogs and hogs. Some of the bodies were not found until they were dug out of the ruins of the buildings. Some had been burned beyond recognition. It was a sad and painful sight to see the son crying for the father, the brother for the brother, the uncle for the nephew, and friend for friend.

By this time most of the Chinese have abandoned the desire of resuming their mining work, but inasmuch as the riot has left them each with only the one or two torn articles of clothing they have on their persons, and as they have not a single cent in their pockets, it is a difficult matter for them to make any change in their location. Fortunately, the company promised to lend them clothing and provisions, and a number of wagons to sleep in. Although protected by Government troops, their sleep is disturbed by frightful dreams, and they cannot obtain peaceful rest.

Some of the rioters who killed the Chinese and who set fire to the homes could be identified by the Chinese, and some not. Among them the two women heretofore mentioned, and who killed some Chinese, were specially recognized by many Chinese. Among the rioters who robbed and plundered were men, women, and children. Even the white woman who formerly taught English to the Chinese searched for and took handkerchiefs and other articles.

The Chinese know that the white men who worked in Coal-pit No. 1 did not join the mob, and most of them did not stop work, either. We heard that the coal company's officers had taken a list of the names of the rioters who were particularly brutal and murderous, which list numbered forty or fifty.

From a survey of all the circumstances, several causes may be assigned for the killing and wounding of so many Chinese and the destruction of so much property:

(1) The Chinese had been for a long time employed at the same work as the white men. While they knew that the white men entertained ill feelings toward them, the Chinese did not take precautions to guard against this sudden outbreak, inasmuch as at no time in the past had there been any quarrel or fighting between the races.

(2) On the 2nd day of September, 1885, in Coal-pit No. 6, the white men attacked the Chinese. That place being quite a distance from Rock Springs, very few Chinese were there. As we did not think that the trouble would extend to Rock Springs, we did not warn each other to prepare for flight.

(3) Most of the Chinese living in Rock Springs worked during the daytime in the different coal mines, and consequently did not hear of the fight at Coal-pit No. 6, nor did they know of the armed mob that had assembled in "Whitemen's Town." When 12 o'clock came, everybody returned home from his place of work to lunch. As yet the mob had not come to attack the Chinese; a great number of the latter were returning to work without any apprehension of danger.

(4) About 2 o'clock the mob suddenly made their appearance for the attack. The Chinese thought that they had only assembled to threaten, and that

some of the company's officers would come to disperse them. Most of the Chinese, acting upon this view of the matter, did not gather up their money or clothing, and when the mob fired at them they fled precipitately. Those Chinese who were in the workshops, hearing of the riot, stopped work and fled in their working clothes, and did not have time enough to go home to change their clothes or to gather up their money. What they had left at home was either plundered or burned.

(5) None of the Chinese had firearms or any defensive weapons, nor was there any place that afforded an opportunity for the erection of a barricade that might impede the rioters in their attack. The Chinese were all like a herd of frightened deer that let the huntsmen surround and kill them.

(6) All the Chinese had, on the 1st of September, bought from the company a month's supply of provision and the implements necessary for the mining of coal. This loss of property was therefore larger than it would be later in the month.

We never thought that the subjects of a nation entitled by treaty to the rights and privileges of the most favored nation[3] could, in a country so highly civilized like this, so unexpectedly suffer the cruelty and wrong of being unjustly put to death, or of being wounded and left without the means of cure, or of being abandoned to poverty, hunger, and cold, and without the means to betake themselves elsewhere.

To the great President of the United States, who, hearing of the riot, sent troops to protect our lives, we are most sincerely thankful.

In behalf of those killed or wounded, or of those deprived of their property, we pray that the examining commission will ask our minister to sympathize, and to endeavor to secure the punishment of the murderers, the relief of the wounded, and compensation for those despoiled of their property, so that the living and the relatives of the dead will be grateful, and never forget his kindness for generations.

Hereinabove we have made a brief recital of the facts of this riot, and pray your honor will take them into your kind consideration.

SOURCE: *U.S. House Report* (1885–1886), 49th Congress, 1st Session, no. 2044, pp. 28–32.

OTHER REFERENCES

Arif Dirlik, ed., *Chinese in the American Frontier* (Lanham, Md.: Rowman & Littlefield, 2001).

Craig Storti, *Incident at Bitter Creek: The Story of the Rock Springs Chinese Massacre* (Ames: Iowa State University Press, 1991).

Shih-shan Henry Tsai, *China and the Overseas Chinese in the United States, 1868–1911* (Fayetteville: University of Arkansas Press, 1983).

3. Legal status accorded to countries with which the United States wished to trade.

A Chinese View of the
Statue of Liberty (1885)

Saum Song Bo

The following letter by a Chinese immigrant in response to the building of the Statue of Liberty pedestal in 1885 was first published in the New York Sun *newspaper and later reprinted in the monthly periodical* American Missionary. *Just three years before, Congress had passed the Chinese Exclusion Act, barring further immigration of Chinese laborers to this country and denying Chinese immigrants the right to become naturalized U.S. citizens. Excluded from political participation and denied civil rights as symbolized by the Statue of Liberty, Chinese immigrants such as Saum Song Bo considered it an insult that they were being asked to contribute funds toward the building of the statue. To add salt to the wound, the statue was a gift from France, which that same year had defeated Chinese troops in Indochina and begun to colonize the area that is now Vietnam.*

Sir:

A paper was presented to me yesterday for inspection, and I found it to be specially drawn up for subscription among my countrymen toward the Pedestal Fund of the Bartholdi Statue of Liberty.[1] Seeing that the heading is an appeal to American citizens, to their love of country and liberty, I feel that my countrymen and myself are honored in being thus appealed to as citizens in the cause of liberty. But the word liberty makes me think of the fact that this country is the land of liberty for men of all nations except the Chinese. I consider it as an insult to us Chinese to call on us to contribute toward building in this land a pedestal for a statue of Liberty. That statue represents Liberty holding a torch which lights the passage of those of all

---

1. The Statue of Liberty was designed by Augustus Bartholdi and given to the United States by the French in memory of the two countries' alliance during the American Revolution. An additional $270,000 had to be raised among the American people to build the statue's pedestal.

nations who come into this country. But are the Chinese allowed to come? As for the Chinese who are here, are they allowed to enjoy liberty as men of all other nationalities enjoy it? Are they allowed to go about everywhere free from the insults, abuse, assaults, wrongs and injuries from which men of other nationalities are free?

If there be a Chinaman who came to this country when a lad, who has passed through an American institution of learning of the highest grade, who has so fallen in love with American manners and ideas that he desires to make his home in this land, and who, seeing that his countrymen demand one of their own number to be their legal adviser, representative, advocate and protector, desires to study law, can he be a lawyer? By the law of this nation, he, being a Chinaman, cannot become a citizen, and consequently cannot be a lawyer.

And this statue of Liberty is a gift to a people from another people who do not love or value liberty for the Chinese. Are not the Annamese and Tonquinese [Tonkinese] Chinese, to whom liberty is as dear as to the French? What right have the French to deprive them of their liberty?

Whether this statute against the Chinese or the statue to Liberty will be the more lasting monument to tell future ages of the liberty and greatness of this country, will be known only to future generations.

Liberty, we Chinese do love and adore thee; but let not those who deny thee to us, make of thee a graven image and invite us to bow down to it.

SOURCE: *American Missionary*, October 1885, p. 290.

OTHER REFERENCES

Sucheng Chan, ed., *Entry Denied: Exclusion and the Chinese Community in America, 1882–1943* (Philadelphia: Temple University Press, 1991).
Philip P. Choy, Lorraine Dong, and Marlon K. Hom, *The Coming Man: 19th-Century American Perceptions of the Chinese* (Hong Kong: Joint Publishing Co., 1994).
Charles J. McClain, *In Search of Equality: The Chinese Struggle against Discrimination in Nineteenth-Century America* (Berkeley: University of California Press, 1994).

Reminiscences of an
Early Chinese Minister (1932)

Huie Kin

Even before Chinese immigration to the United States became significant in the mid–nineteenth century, American missionaries were in China spreading the Gospel. In addition to their evangelical work, they helped establish a web of social ties between the two countries. On returning to the United States, they worked among Chinese immigrants. Although the missionaries were only modestly successful in winning converts, many of the early Chinese American Christians played leading roles in their communities as educational, social, and religious leaders. Huie Kin was one of these.

Born Huie Kin-kwong ("Light of Scholarship") in 1854 in a poor village in Sunning (now Taishan) District, Guangdong Province, he emigrated to the United States in 1868 at the age of fourteen. He and other youngsters in his village had caught "gold fever" after hearing stories from villagers who had returned from California. Huie initially settled in Oakland, where he worked as a houseboy for several different families. One of his employers taught him to read and write English, and introduced him to Christianity. After he was baptized in 1874, he became a leader in the local Chinese Sunday school. Several years later, at the age of twenty-six, Huie entered the Lane Theological Seminary in Cincinnati, Ohio, at the urging of his "spiritual father," Dr. Nathaniel Eells, pastor of the Oakland Presbyterian Church.

In 1885 he became the first Chinese Christian minister in New York and one of the prominent leaders of the local Chinese community. He actively propagated the Gospel among the local Chinese, attended to the needs of the poor, and tried to bridge the divide between the Chinese and white American communities. He married Louise Van Arnam, a volunteer mission worker and daughter of a New York police officer. The two had six daughters, all of whom married Chinese professional men and went to China to live with them, and three sons, who married white American women and stayed in the United States. Late in life, Huie Kin returned to China and in 1932, two years before his death, published his memoirs, from which the following excerpts are taken. His recollections include many vivid memories of his youth in China, his

57

Huie Kin family portrait, ca. 1911. *Front row:* Louise, Ruth, Huie Kin, Arthur, Louise Van Arnam, Albert, Dorothy, and Alice. *Back row:* Caroline, Irving, and Helen. (Courtesy of the Huie Kin descendants)

adolescence in Oakland, his religious education, many travels, encounters with promi-
nent Chinese political and educational leaders, and the building of the First Chinese
Presbyterian Church in New York City.

AN IMMIGRANT BOY

On a clear, crisp, September morning in 1868, or the seventh year of our Emperor Tongzhi, the mists lifted, and we sighted land for the first time since we left the shores of Kwangtung over sixty days before. To be actually at the "Golden Gate" of the land of our dreams! The feeling that welled up in us was indescribable. I wonder whether the ecstasy before the Pearly Gates of the Celestial City above could surpass what we felt at the moment we realized that we had reached our destination. We rolled up our bedding, packed our baskets, straightened our clothes, and waited.

In those days there were no immigration laws or tedious examinations; people came and went freely. Somebody had brought to the pier large wagons for us. Out of the general babble, someone called out in our local dialect, and, like sheep recognizing the voice only, we blindly followed, and soon were piling into one of the waiting wagons. Everything was so strange and so exciting that my memory of the landing is just a big blur. The wagon made its way heavily over the cobblestones, turned some corners, ascended a steep climb, and stopped at a kind of clubhouse, where we spent the night. Later, I learned that people from various districts had their own benevolent societies, with headquarters in San Francisco's Chinatown. As there were six of them, they were known as the "Six Companies." Newcomers were taken care of until relatives came to claim them and pay the bill. The next day our relatives from Oakland took us across the bay to the little Chinese settlement there, and kept us until we found work.

In the sixties, San Francisco's Chinatown was made up of stores catering to the Chinese only. There was only one store, situated at the corner of Sacramento and Dupont streets, which kept Chinese and Japanese curios for the American trade. Our people were all in their native costume, with queues down their backs, and kept their stores just as they would do in China, with the entire street front open and groceries and vegetables overflowing on the sidewalks. Forty thousand Chinese were then resident in the bay region, and so these stores did a flourishing business. The Oakland Chinatown was a smaller affair, more like a mining camp, with rough board houses on a vacant lot near Broadway and Sixteenth Street. Under the roof of the houses was a shelf built in the rear and reached by a ladder. Here we slept at night, rolled in our blankets much in the manner of Indians. . . .

My first job was in a family as general help, earning $1.50 a week with board. There lingers still in my memory the vision of the ubiquitous apple sauce on the table, which I soon got so sick and tired of that I would have given anything for a Chinese meal. Our culinary tastes play an important part in the psychology of homesickness. We were told on Scriptural authority that the one thing that marred the otherwise joyous exit of the Israelites from the land of their serfdom and their triumphal journey to their new home in Canaan was the longing for the meats and drinks they were accustomed to in Egypt, and when the good Lord heard their pleading and sent them a flock of wild geese, or something of that sort, the people ate so heartily that many died of acute indigestion. One of the homely remedies we have in China for homesickness is to take along a bit of native earth, mix it with water, and drink it when one is in a strange land. I do not know what its therapeutic effect is on our internal workings, but at least it soothes one's feelings. . . .

MISSIONARY WORK IN NEW YORK

Chinatown then [1886] lay on both sides of Mott Street and was filled with gambling houses, which, in open daylight, carried on their nefarious trade, stripping poor workingmen of their earnings. It was a little Monte Carlo, but without its glamour, and its uncrowned prince was Tom Lee, head of the On Leong Association and known among Americans as the "Mayor of Chinatown." We were then young, full of ardor to right the wrongs of the world, and decided to wipe out the evil business, even though we knew that the most powerful organizations were behind it, and the city police, for some reason, were maintaining a tolerant attitude towards it. We secured the backing of Mr. Anthony Comstock, secretary of the Society for the Prevention of Crime. We went into the gambling houses dressed as ordinary workmen, mingled with the habitués and got to know the proprietors or operators by sight. With the incriminating information in hand, we had warrants issued, and even took part in the raids, quite unaware of the personal risk we were running. Very soon [missionary workers] Guy Maine [a.k.a. Yee Kai Man], Joseph Singleton [a.k.a. Chew Mon Sing], and I were spotted men.[1] The gamblers threatened us with physical violence if we did not leave them alone; and when they found us unmoved, approached us with attractive offers to share their profits. One evening some armed men tried to waylay me along a certain street which I usually took to return to the mission, but somehow I took into my head to return by a different way and thus avoided the encounter. On another occasion, when we were leaving the Tombs, after having successfully prosecuted some gamblers, a man came up from behind and aimed something at my head; fortunately, Mr. Allen Williams knocked the assailant down before he could do any harm. Mr. Allen Williams was the agent to an insurance company from which I had just taken out a policy. It was a coincidence that he should be there, but the rumor spread in Chinatown that the insurance company maintained a bodyguard for Huie Kin. Taking out life insurance policies was then quite a novel thing with our people.

Another incident of a similar kind happened a few years later. It was Sunday and, as usual, church service was to commence at 2 P.M., and men would drift in and find a welcome, whether they were members or strangers. As I was leaving my study to go up to the pulpit, I noticed three men entering the church whom I suspected to belong to the group that had attempted to kill me. I told Mrs. Huie of my suspicion, leaving her to deal with them as best as she could without disturbing the audience. Mrs. Huie met them in the vestibule, greeted them cordially, as was her custom, and ushered them to seats in the very front row in the church. The men sat down sheepishly, stayed about five minutes, and slipped out. I do not believe any permanent good was done by our activities, but we did stir things up so that the police had to close all the gambling houses. They remained closed for a year or so.

Once a meeting held at the Second Avenue Presbyterian Church was addressed by a lady missionary from China. A number of our people, as well

1. Both Guy Maine and Joseph Singleton were Christian converts who had arrived in New York City in the 1880s. Maine established the Sunday school of St. Bartholomew's Episcopal Church, and Singleton was director of the Chinese Mission of the United Congregational Church, interpreter for U.S. Customs, and a member of the Chinese Reform Party.

as I myself, attended. The lady spoke fervently for the cause of evangelizing China's millions, and drew a vivid and impressive picture of the social and spiritual transformation that Christianity was making in the land of Old Cathay. The address was well received by the audience until the speaker, in her desire to bring out the contrast between Christian and heathen civilization, overdid herself in painting a black picture of Chinese homes without a ray of redeeming love, little children crushed under inhuman cruelty, women denied an education and treated as the plaything of the predatory male, etc. The storm broke when she generalized that all Chinese men beat their wives without cause. One Chu vehemently remonstrated in his broken English against this obvious exaggeration: "Fourteen year in China, no Christian, no beat wife one time." I also stood up to say that in my own village I had never seen a man beating his wife. The lady asked me how many wives my father had. I replied that he had only one wife, my mother; and as a return thrust, I added that it seemed that even preachers in Christian America sometimes could not avoid difficulties with their wives. This roused ripples of laughter in the audience, for just at that time the newspapers were featuring the domestic troubles of a prominent minister in the city. . . .

MY MARRIAGE

Our people have a belief that marriages are made in heaven, hence the importance of consulting fortune tellers beforehand to make sure that the birth cycles of the prospective bride and groom harmonize with each other, thus insuring matrimonial happiness. In the West people make matches first, and then consult the fortune mender (psychiatrist, psychotherapist, and what not) afterwards. Whether marriages are made in heaven or on earth, there is such a thing as love at first sight, an inner urge and conviction beyond the reach of conscious reasoning that one has found his lifemate. That was how I felt when I first met Miss Van Arnam. Even the fact that she was of another race made no difference to me, and neither could the social prejudice against international marriages stand in my way. Our common interest in mission work brought us together frequently, and, like any young man bent on winning a fair maiden, I made use of every opportunity to cultivate her good opinion and strengthen the bonds that held us together. I frequented the prayer meetings at the Dewitt Memorial Chapel, Twenty-Ninth Street and Seventh Avenue, where Miss Van Arnam had her practical training. No doubt at first she merely regarded me as an interesting Chinaman engaged in Christian work, and attributed my presence at these prayer meetings to religious zeal. I invited her to help us at the mission and consulted her about our work. More and more her interest in the Chinese people grew, acquaintance deepened into friendship, and friendship ripened into life comradeship.

I confided the matter to Dr. George Alexander, my pastor and chairman of our Mission Committee. With his usual acumen, the good doctor asked to see the young lady. So I took Miss Van Arnam to see him. Salutations over, Dr. Alexander, with infinite tact, asked whether she had thought of the fact that centuries of a different culture lay behind the life of the young man whom she had decided to accept as her husband. Miss Van Arnam replied that she realized the difference in our racial and cultural backgrounds, but she believed that back of us both was the Lord God, who created all races of one blood and meant them to live together in mutual service. We left with our pastor's blessing.

We next called on her parents at Troy to obtain their consent to the marriage. Mr. Van Arnam said that he liked me personally well enough, but how could he entertain the thought of his daughter living under the stigma of having married a Chinaman? Her pastor, a kindly old gentleman of the conservative school, was genuinely perturbed. "You marry a Chinaman?" he said to her; "Why, you could marry any man in the Troy Conference. . . . And have you considered where would your children stand?" Miss Van Arnam's reply was at once dignified and to the point. She said that if God should bless our home with children, she would bring them up in the fear of the Lord and educate them for a useful life in the world, trusting that they would be able to take their place, the equal of any other young men and women. She saw her mother alone, who told her that she was old enough to know what she was doing and that she would not stand in the way of her happiness.

We were quietly married by Dr. Alexander on April 4, 1889, the ceremony being witnessed by a small group of intimate friends, including Mr. K. P. Lee, of the Chinese Legation, and Mr. Chang Foyin, of Columbia Law School.[2] After the church service, a reception for the Chinese community was held at our Mission. For our honeymoon, we visited Washington, D.C., where, through the introduction of the Legation, we called on President Harrison, who very graciously presented to Mrs. Huie a bouquet of flowers from the White House Conservatory. . . .

ASSISTING DR. SUN YAT-SEN

In the summer of 1903 we spent our vacation in visiting the World's Fair at St. Louis, Mo., and seeing old friends on the Pacific Coast. In San Francisco we met Dr. Sun Yat-sen, then a political refugee from China with a big prize on his head. As he was proceeding to New York, we urged him to stop at our Mission. This he did, but he got there before we returned. Our Bertha who

2. Most likely Kwai-pan Lee and Chang Hon-yen, both former students of the Chinese Educational Mission. Chang became the first Chinese lawyer in the United States when he received his law degree from Columbia University in 1886.

received him explained that no accommodation was available except a small room at the head of the stairs on the fourth floor with only a sky-light. Without saying who he was, Dr. Sun took the little room and moved in with his suit-cases. Later he was transferred into a bigger and better lighted room. Here he spent the summer months and with him were the brothers Wang Chung-hui and Wang Chung-yao, sons of my old friend Rev. Wang Yu Cho of Hongkong, at that time studying at Yale and at Columbia respectively. What they were working on nobody in the house had any inkling of, but we were later told that the first draft of the Constitution of the Chinese Republic was made there. . . .

Dr. Sun was advocating a more drastic policy, namely, to overturn the Manchu Regime and make China a Republic. Kang [Youwei, the reformer] and Sun could not see eye to eye in this matter. The business interests were opposed to a revolution. Dr. Sun's following was mostly among the laboring and student classes. When he was staying at our place, a threatening letter came demanding that we oust him or else our Mission would be boycotted by the Chinese people. In reply, I made a public announcement that the Mission was not interested in politics and was open to all comers whatever their political views. In time Dr. Sun's persistent and self-sacrificial efforts bore fruit. Especially the younger elements, students and workers alike, rallied around him and joined his secret revolutionary organization, the Tung Meng Hui, precursor of the Kuomintang. A fascinating and fluent speaker, well informed about world affairs and backed by his unselfish devotion to the national cause, undaunted courage and a romantic career, Dr. Sun could hold his audiences spellbound for hours at a time, whether they numbered by the hundreds and thousands or only a handful. He was at his best when in the quiet of the night, with a small group of followers gathered around the lamp-light, as often happened in the back-rooms of the little laundries in New York City, he spoke to them about the military reverses and diplomatic failures of China and expounded his programme for the liberation and self-rule of the Chinese people. He often appeared weary and worn in body, but always enthusiastic for his cause and never down-hearted.

His next visit to New York was in July 1910 when he returned from England shortly before the Revolution actually broke out at Wuchang in central China. Dr. Sun spent the evening with us, talking about his plans until three in the morning. He said that everything was ready for the revolution to start but they needed more funds and suggested that on his return from San Francisco and Portland in the fall, he be introduced to some American sympathizers who were financially able to help the movement. I did speak to Mr. Thomas Denney of Wall Street, a classmate of Mr. Yung Wing at Yale. But Dr. Sun did not come back. He was in England when the Wuchang uprising in November 1911 precipitated the revolution and he hurried back to the old country to head up the new Republican Government in Nanking. . . .

"ALL THINGS TO ALL MEN"

From the very beginning a great deal of my time was taken up with helping individuals in trouble, such as illness, lawsuits, misunderstanding with their American landlords, financial difficulties, home problems, etc. Like other immigrants, the Chinese people find life difficult in America on account of differences in language and ignorance of the customs, which in turn cause misunderstanding with the people of other races. Such difficulties can become very serious, but they are also easily adjusted, if properly handled by those who happen to know the language and usages of the land, and have friends on both sides of the line. Hence people came to me for such friendly advice and help that I could give without difficulty, though involving much time and energy. When a foreigner is in good health and able to earn his own livelihood, he can well take care of himself, but when he gets sick, is laid up, and without employment, he is pitifully helpless. He cannot afford private medical attention and yet does not know where the hospitals are or how to get in. So every year, I brought a good number of sick Chinese to the hospitals. . . .

Charlie Hin kept a basement laundry and came to our Sunday School at 14 University Place. One winter Sunday, he was not at the Mission. We found him sick with pneumonia in his basement laundry, almost dying. He refused to go to the hospital, for he had heard of doctors taking out the patients' eyes while they were under ether. I assured him I would personally go with him and visit him every day. He got well, and thenceforth he could not say enough about the clean linen and fine treatment they gave him at the hospital; he thought that the doctors and nurses were like angels. While he was convalescing in the hospital, I told him that I had an invitation from our Chinese minister at Washington, D.C., and had to be away for several days. Charlie got excited and wanted me to take him out of the hospital that very day. This was impossible; his importunity won and I had to cancel my trip. . . .

The Mission door bell rang vigorously at 4 o'clock, one March morning. On opening the door, I found a Chinese brother who had walked up from Chinatown in the rain. He rushed into the church, saying, "I come worship, I come worship," knelt before the pulpit and "kowtowed" as he would in a temple. I stayed with him, gave him some hot drink, and quieted him. He kept complaining, "I lost my soul; man died in Chinatown taken my soul away; can't you see I have only a head, soul gone?" I told him that he had come to the right place and that we would do all we could to have his soul restored to him. We arranged for him to be taken care of in a hospital for mental disorders. The man got well, recovered his reason and was never troubled again with the malady.

In one year, I introduced as many as eighty-one sick persons to the hospitals. That was in 1923, two years before my retirement. I became a familiar figure to the gate-keepers, and the patients were known as "Huie's patients." I knew the doctors and nurses and social workers at the Presbyterian Hospital best of all, and for their care of the Chinese patients, these strangers without a home and often without friends or relatives, I can never adequately express my indebtedness. I recall in particular Dr. Charles Young, Superintendent of the Hospital, and Dr. Fisher preceding him. I would take up a sick man and Dr. Young would put his arm in mine and together we would go to a ward. He would speak to the head nurse: "This is Huie's patient." This was sufficient: however crowded the ward, a bed was found for "Huie's patient." They were all wonderful to the Chinese. Often a patient had nothing with which to pay his hospital bill; I would appeal to the Superintendent and he would remit the fee. In return, every year I went around among the Chinese restaurants and laundries to take up a collection for the hospital.

All sorts of people sought my help, both known and unknown to me. Whenever a case seemed hopeless, it would be referred to me. One night, I received word that a white woman in Chinatown wanted to see me. She was dying and wanted to speak to a clergyman. I went down with Mrs. Huie. The front door of the building, opening on the Bowery, was found locked. We went through the Chinese theatre, down a rope ladder, through a sub-basement, up a flight of stairs and got to her room. We talked with her, prayed with her and comforted her as best as we knew how, a young woman of another nationality, an actress by profession, who had drifted into the Bowery and was dying of the dreaded T.B. She passed away the next day.

Tom, 15, was a difficult boy to manage. His uncle thrashed him, and he in turn hit the uncle. He was charged with attempted murder and committed to the Jefferson Market Court detention-house. Our Mission was then at 26 West 9th Street, not far from the Market. I went to see the boy and sent him some Chinese food every evening. At the trial, I was present. He put his arms around my neck, clung to me and promised that he would be good, if I would take him home. I pleaded with the judge and the judge agreed to leave him in Mrs. Huie's custody. We had him in the old house with our own children for several weeks until he found work. Tom's uncle, of course, did not like my interference in his family affairs and for a long time avoided me and our Mission. Years afterwards I met him, explained that my interference was for the boy's own good, and we were reconciled. . . .

Some years ago it was a common practice for Chinese to be smuggled into the United States from Canada. At Plattsburg, N.Y., they would try to get in and be arrested. Certain lawyers who were in the business on a commission basis, namely, a fixed sum for a successful entry, would get as witnesses Chinese residents with registration papers, to testify that they had known the individuals in question in San Francisco, were present at the shaving of the baby's hair (which was equivalent to a baptism certificate), etc. In this way they would get into the country, with good registration papers issued to them as native-born. My contention was that so long as a Chinese was in the country, with or without registration paper, he should not be molested. It was up to the Government to keep them out, but once within the country, they should be left alone.

An amusing incident occurred in Buffalo. A Chinese had bought a ticket for China and was on his way. At Buffalo, he was arrested and detained, because he could not produce his registration paper. I was asked to go and straighten up the case. I called on the Commissioner of Immigration and explained that the man was really on his way to China; he had no registration paper, but there was his ticket for the journey. The Commissioner would not believe us and said that the United States Government would deport the person. So I got the man to give me his ticket and collected the refund for him, while the United States provided him with a free trip back to the old country.

Ling Fong was an inmate of a bad house. Word came through to the Mission that she wanted our help to secure her freedom. We got Mr. William Beecher interested in the case. Mr. William Beecher was a well known lawyer of New York, once a district attorney and son of Dr. Henry Ward Beecher, the famous preacher. We arranged for her to escape from the house. She stayed for a week in the Beecher home and then came to our house. At that time, we were living at Sackman Street, Brooklyn. The keepers of the house discovered her escape and traced her movements to our place. So a group of them came and demanded her return. It so happened that, only a few minutes before, the girl had left with Mrs. Harriet Carter, a Baptist mission worker, to attend a court session in New York. There was a street car station at the back of our block and it seemed that the men had come around to the front of the house one way and the women had gone the other way and so they did not meet. Mrs. Huie alone was in with our son Irving. The men fiercely demanded the Chinese girl.

Mrs. Huie: "There is no Chinese girl here."

The men: "You have her."

Mrs. Huie: "Then look through the place, and if I have her, take her away and my house too."

The men searched the place, looked into closets, crawled up the attic, and of course, left in a threatening mood but empty-handed. At the trial, Mr. Beecher prosecuted the girl's keeper; she was given her freedom and brought back to our house. Two weeks later she was transferred to a Home for Girls at 23 East 11th Street, where she made herself very useful. The Superintendent became much interested in her and spoke to her about her spiritual welfare. One morning before daybreak, Ling Fong excitedly rapped at the Superintendent's door and called, "Get up, get up; I talk to God, He talk to me."

She was baptized by Dr. Alexander. Afterwards she married a Chinese restaurant proprietor, maintained a beautiful home and adopted a number of orphaned children, whom she cared for and sent through school. . . .

The forty years of my ministry were filled with cases of the kind I have here given, helping my countrymen in time of distress. It is true some of the younger people went through the Mission to positions of high standing in business and in political life, but they are a very small minority. The majority were composed of humble workingmen and tradesmen—strangers in a strange land, unknown beyond the narrow circle of their own nationality, whose existence in the community was without significance and left not a record because they were without vote or citizenship. But I was glad that my lot was cast among them and that in living among them and working for them, I seemed to get a clearer insight into the mind and spirit of that Great Galilean, who lived so close to his people, that their joys became his joys, and their sorrows, his sorrows. Without trumpeting and heralding, the work of our Mission Church was carried on from year to year, hidden away in a humble corner of the gigantic metropolis, ministering to a neglected but self-respecting nationality group of five thousand souls.

SOURCE: Huie Kin, *Reminiscences* (Peiping: San Yu Press, 1932). Reprinted by permission of George L. Trigg.

OTHER REFERENCES

Arthur Bonner, *ALAS! What Brought Thee Hither? The Chinese in New York, 1800–1950* (London: Associated University Presses, 1997).

Leong Gor Yun, *Chinatown Inside Out* (New York: Barrows Mussey, 1936).

Timothy Tseng, "Chinese Protestant Nationalism in the United States, 1880–1927," in *New Spiritual Homes: Religion and Asian Americans,* ed. David K. Yoo (Honolulu: University of Hawaii Press, 1998), pp. 19–51.

Wesley Woo, "Chinese Protestants in the San Francisco Bay Area," in *Entry Denied: Exclusion and the Chinese Community in America, 1882–1943,* ed. Sucheng Chan (Philadelphia: Temple University Press, 1991), pp. 213–45.

Bow On Guk (Protective Bureau)
(1887)

Learning from the experiences of their counterparts on the U.S. mainland, Chinese community leaders in Hawaii were quick to act at the first signs of anti-Chinese agitation. In the early 1880s, when Hawaii was still an independent kingdom, organizations such as the Workingmen's Party and the Anti-Asiatic Union began protesting Chinese competition and pressing the government to pass legislation that would restrict Chinese immigration and economic activities. The fear was that the anti-Chinese movement would lead to physical attacks on Chinese residents or their places of business, as happened on the mainland. In 1887 representatives of the Chinese community met under the auspices of the United Chinese Society[1] to form the Bow On Guk (Protective Bureau) to defend Chinatown in Honolulu from any violent attacks. Handbills such as the following were distributed to solicit financial support for the new organization. Chinese immigrants were told to put aside their intra-ethnic and political differences and take collective action to protect their lives and property. Members voluntarily paid a one-dollar fee, and merchants, twenty-five cents for each hundred dollars of business handled that year. In this way, several thousand dollars were collected to acquire a two-story building for the headquarters of the Bow On Guk. Funds were also used to purchase rifles and hire watchmen to patrol the Chinatown area at night. Fortunately, no physical attack occurred. Nevertheless, the establishment of the Bow On Guk reflected a strong sense of group consciousness and collective action in the face of growing anti-Chinese sentiment in Hawaii.

We Chinese in Hawaii left our home villages to make our fortunes. At first we lived peacefully and happily, but later on conflicts arose among ourselves

---

1. The United Chinese Society, the Hawaiian counterpart of the Chinese Six Companies on the mainland, was established in 1884 to provide mutual aid, social control, and protection among the Chinese in Hawaii.

as we cut each other's skins.[2] And because of this weakness we were frequently subject to foreign exploitation. Fellow countrymen, don't say that a spark of fire cannot burn a large plain nor that a tiny cloud cannot cause a rainfall, for drops of water will form a river and a little work each day will move a mountain. If we are not harmonious among ourselves and promote friendship among our countrymen, how can we protect our property and life? This is why the establishment of a Protective Bureau in Hawaii is the most pressing need. Remember the massacre of Chinese in Peru,[3] also the driving out of Chinese in the United States and the burning of stores there. Beware that we don't fall into the same trouble. Although we see that the interests of the Chinese should be protected here, we cannot go on without financial support. Let all our fellow countrymen come together to defend themselves. Since we need money urgently, we are sending people to canvass for funds. We sincerely hope that all countrymen, no matter how rich or poor, open their purses that this worthy work might be accomplished. The fur patched together becomes a coat; the pollen gathered by the bees becomes honey. May we all be in accord with one another, cooperate, and eliminate all suspicion. If we can accomplish this, we can protect ourselves and live happily. This is the purpose of our organization. Please sign your name.

SOURCE: Clarence Glick, *Sojourners and Settlers: Chinese Migrants in Hawaii* (Honolulu: Hawaii Chinese History Center and the University Press of Hawaii, 1980), p. 216.

OTHER REFERENCES

Tin-Yuke Char, *The Sandalwood Mountains: Readings and Stories of the Early Chinese in Hawaii* (Honolulu: University Press of Hawaii, 1975).

Adam McKeown, *Chinese Migrant Networks and Cultural Change: Peru, Chicago, Hawaii, 1900–1936* (Chicago: University of Chicago Press, 2001).

2. This is in reference to the ongoing feud between two Chinese ethnic groups in Hawaii—the Hakka and the Punti.

3. This is in reference to the cruel treatment of Chinese coolies in the sugar plantations and guano mines of Peru.

Why Am I a Heathen? (1887)

Wong Chin Foo

One of the most prolific writers in the English-language press among the Chinese in America was a man named Wong Chin Foo. He first came to the United States in 1868 as a seventeen-year-old student sponsored by Christian missionaries. After completing his studies, he returned to China, but because of his political activism, he was forced into exile, first to Japan and then back to the United States in 1873. For the next twenty years, until he slipped into obscurity, Wong spent most of his time in the East and Midwest, writing and speaking publicly about Chinese culture and the plight of the Chinese in America. He is credited with starting a weekly newspaper in New York titled Chinese America *in 1883, the first Chinese American voters association in the United States in 1884, and the Chinese Equal Rights League to campaign for the repeal of the exclusion laws in 1892. Wong's essays appeared in prominent periodicals such as the* North American Review, Chautauquan, Cosmopolitan, Atlantic Monthly, *and* Harper's Weekly.

The following essay, "Why Am I a Heathen?" appeared in the North American Review *in August 1887 and tells why, even though he had a Christian education, Wong chose to remain true to Confucian ideals of morality and goodness. In his provocative and sarcastic style of speaking, Wong exposed the hypocrisy he saw in the prejudiced actions of American Christians against Chinese Americans. The essay provoked a response from Yan Phou Lee, whose rejoinder, "Why I Am Not a Heathen," follows this selection.*

Born and raised a heathen, I learned and practiced its moral and religious code; and acting thereunder I was useful to myself and many others. My conscience was clear, and my hopes as to future life were untrimmed by distracting doubt. But, when about seventeen, I was transferred to the midst of our showy Christian civilization, and at this impressionable period of life Christianity presented itself to me at first under its most alluring aspects; kind Christian

Wong Chin Foo.
(Courtesy of Wong
Chin Foo Collection,
New York)

friends became particularly solicitous for my material and religious welfare, and I was only too willing to know the truth.

I had to take a good deal for granted as to the inspiration of the Bible—as is necessary to do—to Christianize a non-Christian mind; and I even advanced so far under the spell of my would-be soul-savers that I seriously contemplated becoming the bearer of heavenly tidings to my "benighted" heathen people.

But before qualifying for this high mission, the Christian doctrine I would teach had to be learned, and here on the threshold I was bewildered by the multiplicity of Christian sects, each one claiming a monopoly of the only and narrow road to heaven.

I looked into Presbyterianism only to retreat shudderingly from a belief in a merciless God who had long foreordained most of the helpless human race to an eternal hell. To preach such a doctrine to intelligent heathen would only raise in their minds doubts of my sanity, if they did not believe I was lying.

Then I dipped into Baptist doctrines, but found so many sects therein, of different "shells," warring over the merits of cold-water initiation and the method and time of using it, that I became disgusted with such trivialities; and the question of close communion or not, only impressed me that some were very stingy with their bit of bread and wine, and others a little less so.

Methodism struck me as a thunder-and-lightning religion—all profession and noise. You struck it, or it struck you, like a spasm,—and so you "experienced" religion.

The Congregationalists deterred me with their starchiness and self-conscious true-goodness, and their desire only for high-toned affiliates.

Unitarianism seemed all doubt, doubting even itself.

A number of other Protestant sects based on some novelty or eccentricity—like Quakerism—I found not worth a serious study by the non-Christian. But on one point this mass of Protestant dissension cordially agreed, and that was in a united hatred of Catholicism, the older form of Christianity. And Catholicism returned with interest this animosity. It haughtily declared itself the only true Church, outside of which there was no salvation—for Protestants especially; that its chief prelate was the personal representative of God on earth, and that he was infallible. Here was religious unity, power, and authority with a vengeance. But, in chorus, my solicitous Protestant friends beseeched me not to touch Catholicism, declaring it was worse than my heathenism—in which I agreed; but the same line of argument also convinced me that Protestantism stood in the same category.

In fact, the more I studied Christianity in its various phases, and listened to the animadversions of one sect upon another, the more it seemed to me "sounding brass and tinkling cymbals."

Disgusted with sectarianism, I turned to a simple study of the inspired "Bible" for enlightenment.

The creation fable did not disturb me, nor the Eden incident; but some vague doubts did arise with the deluge and Noah's ark; it seemed a reflection on a just and merciful Divinity. And I was not at all satisfied of the honesty and goodness of Jacob, or his family, or their descendants, or that there was any particular merit or reason for their being the "chosen" of God, to the detriment of the rest of mankind; for they so appreciated God's special patronage that on every occasion they ran after other gods, and had a special idolatry for the "Golden Calf," to which some Christians allege they are still devoted. That God, failing to make something out of this stiff-necked race, concluded to send his Son to redeem a few of them, and a few of the long-neglected Gentiles, is not strikingly impressive to the heathen.

It may be flattering to the Christian to know it required the crucifixion of God to save him, and that nothing less would do; but it opens up a series of inferences that makes the idea more and more incomprehensible, and more and more inconsistent with a Will, Purpose, Wisdom, and Justice thoroughly Divine.

But when I got to the New Dispensation, with its sin-forgiving business, I figuratively "went to pieces" on Christianity. The idea that, however wicked the sinner, he had the same chance of salvation, "through the Blood of the Lamb," as the most God-fearing—in fact, that the eleventh-hour man was entitled to the same heavenly compensation as the one who had labored in the Lord's vineyard from the first hour—all this was absolutely preposterous. It was not just, and God is Justice.

Applying this dogma, I began to think of my own prospects on the other side of Jordan. Suppose Dennis [Denis] Kearney, the California sand-lotter, should slip in and meet me there, would he not be likely to forget his heavenly songs, and howl once more: "The Chinese must go!" and organize a heavenly crusade to have me and others immediately cast out into the other place?[1]

And then the murderers, cut-throats, and thieves whose very souls had become thoroughly impregnated with their lifelong crimes—these were they to become "pure new-born babes"—all within a few short hours of a death-preparation—while I, the good heathen (supposing the case), who had done naught but good to my fellow heathen, who had spent most of my hard earnings regularly in feeding the hungry, and clothing the naked, and succoring the distressed, and had died of yellow fever, contracted from a deserted fellow being stricken with the disease, whom no Christian would nurse, I was unmercifully consigned to hell's everlasting fire, simply because I had not heard of the glorious saving power of the Lord Jesus, or because the construction of my mind would not permit me to believe in the peculiar redeeming powers of Christ!

But, then, it was gently insinuated: "Oh, no! You heathen who had not heard of Christ will not be punished quite so severely when you die as those who heard the gospel and believed it not."

The more I read the Bible the more afraid I was to become a Christian. The idea of coming into daily or hourly contact with cold-blooded murderers, cut-throats, and other human scourges, who had but a few moments of repentance before roaming around heaven, was abhorrent. And suppose, to this horde of shrewd, "civilized" criminals should be added the fanatic thugs of India, the pirates of China, the slavers, the cannibals, et al. Well, this is enough to shock and dismay any mild, decent soul not schooled in eccentric Christianity.

It is not only because I want to be honest, and to be sure of heavenly home, that I chose to sign myself "Your heathen," but because I want to be as happy

1. Denis Kearney was an anti-Chinese agitator who rose to political fame as leader of the Workingmen's Party of California in the late 1870s. He was known for his demagogic speeches and the refrain "The Chinese must go," which he delivered at outdoor rallies to stir anti-Chinese sentiment among the white working class.

as I can, in order to live longer; and I believe I can live longer here by being sincere and practical in my faith.

In the first place, my faith does not teach me predestination, nor that my life is what the gods hath long foreordained, but is what I make of it myself; and naturally much of this depends on the way I live.

Unlike Christianity, "our" Church is not eager for converts; but, like Free Masonry, we think our religious doctrine strong enough to attract the seekers after light and truth to offer themselves without urging, or proselytizing efforts. It pre-eminently teaches me to mind my own business, to be contented with what I have, to possess a mind that is tranquil, and a body at ease at all times,—in a word it says: "Whatsoever ye would not that others should do unto you do ye not even so unto them." We believe that if we are not able to do anybody any good, we should do nothing at all to harm them. This is better than the restless Christian doctrine of ceaseless action. Idleness is no wrong when actions fail to bring forth fruits of merit. It is these fruitless trials of one thing and another that produce so much misery in Christian society.

If my shoe factory employs 500 men, and gives me an annual profit of $10,000, why should I substitute therein machinery by the use of which I need only 100 men, thus not only throwing 400 contented, industrious men into misery, but making myself more miserable by heavier responsibilities, with possibly less profit?

We heathen believe in the happiness of a common humanity, while the Christian's only practical belief appears to be money-making (golden-calf worshiping); and there is more money to be made by being "in the swim" as a Christian than by being a heathen. Even a Christian preacher makes more money in one year than a heathen banker in two. I do not blame them for their money-making, but for their way of making it.

How many eminent Christian preachers sincerely believe in all the Christian mysteries they preach? And yet it is policy to be apparently in earnest; in fact, some are in real earnest rather from the force of habit than otherwise; like a Bowery auctioneer who, to make trade, provides customers too—to keep up the appearance of rushing business. The more converts made, the more profit to the church, and the more wealth in the pocket of the dominie. . . .

If we do anything charitable we do not advertise it like the Christian, nor do we suppress knowledge of the meritorious acts of others, to humor our vanity or gratify our spleen. An instance of this was conspicuous during the Memphis yellow-fever epidemic a few years ago,[2] and when the Chinese were virulently persecuted all over the United States. Chinese merchants in China donated $40,000 at that time to the relief of plague-stricken Memphis, but

2. In 1878 a yellow-fever epidemic devastated the city of Memphis, killing more than five thousand residents and causing the city to go bankrupt.

the Christians quietly swallowed the sweet morsel without even a "thank you." But they did advertise it, heavily and strongly, all over the world, when they paid $137,000 to the Chinese Government as petty compensation for the massacre of 23 Chinamen by civilized American Christians, and for robbing these and other poor heathen of their earthly possessions.[3]

In matters of charity Christians invariably let their right hand know what the left is doing, and cry it out from the house-tops. The heathen is too dignified for such childish vainness.

Of course, we decline to admit all the advantages of your boosted civilization; or that the white race is the only civilized one. Its civilization is borrowed, adapted, and shaped from our older form.

China has a national history of at least 4,000 years, and had a printed history 3,500 years before a European discovered the art of type-printing. In the course of our national existence our race has passed, like others, through mythology, superstition, witchcraft, established religion, to philosophical religion. We have been "blest" with at least half a dozen religions more than any other nation. None of them were rational enough to become the abiding faith of an intelligent people; but when we began to reason we succeeded in making society better and its government more protective and our great Reasoner, Confucius, reduced our various social and religious ideas into book form and so perpetuated them.

China, with its teeming population of 400,000,000, is demonstration enough of the satisfactory results of this religious evolution. Where else can it be paralleled?

Call us heathen, if you will, the Chinese are still superior in social administration and social order. Among 400,000,000 of Chinese there are fewer murders and robberies in a year than there are in New York State.

True, China supports a luxurious monarch, whose every whim must be gratified; yet, withal, its people are the most lightly taxed in the world, having nothing to pay but from tilled-soil, rice, and salt; and yet she has not a single dollar of national debt.

Such implicit confidence have we Chinese in our heathen politicians that we leave the matter of jurisprudence entirely in their hands; and they are able to devise the best possible laws for the preservation of life, property, and happiness, without Christian demagogism, or by the cruel persecution of one class to promote the selfish interests of another; and we are so far heathenish as to no longer persecute men simply on account of race, color, or previous condition of servitude, but treat them all according to individual worth.

3. In reference to the Rock Springs massacre in 1885, when twenty-eight Chinese men were killed and fifteen wounded. In response to Chinese diplomatic pressure, Congress appropriated $150,000 to cover indemnities.

Though we may differ from the Christian in appearance, manners, and general ideas of civilization, we do not organize into cowardly mobs under the guise of social or political reform, to plunder and murder with impunity; and we are so far advanced in our heathenism as to no longer tolerate popular feeling or religious prejudice to defeat justice or cause injustice. . . .

We do not embrace our wives before our neighbor's eyes, and abuse them in the privacy of home. If we wish to fool our neighbors at all about our domestic affairs we would rather reverse the exhibition—let them think we disliked our wife, while love at home would be the warmer.

I would rather marry in the heathen fashion than in the Christian mode, because in the former instance I would take a wife for life, while in the second instance it is entirely a game of chance.

We bring up our children to be our second selves in every sense of the word. The Christian's children, like himself, are all on the lookout for No. 1, and it is a common result that the old people are badly "left" in their old age. . . .

Christians are continually fussing about religion; they build great churches and make long prayers; and yet there is more wickedness in the neighborhood of a single church district of one thousand people in New York than among one million heathen, churchless and unsermonized.

Christian talk is long and loud about how to be good and to act charitably. It is all charity, and no fraternity—"there, dog, take your crust and be thankful!" And is it, therefore, any wonder there is more heart-breaking and suicides in the single state of New York in a year than in all of China?

The difference between the heathen and the Christian is that the heathen does good for the sake of doing good. With the Christian, what little good he does he does it for immediate honor and for future reward; he lends to the Lord and wants compound interest. In fact, the Christian is the worthy heir of his religious ancestors.

The heathen does much and says little about it; the Christian does little good, but when he does he wants it in the papers and on his tombstone.

Love men for the good they do you is a practical Christian idea, not for the good you should do them as a matter of human duty. So Christians love the heathen; yes, the heathen's possessions; and in proportion to these the Christian's love grows in intensity. When the English wanted the Chinamen's gold and trade, they said they wanted "to open China for their missionaries." And opium was the chief, in fact, only missionary they looked after, when they forced the ports open. And this infamous Christian introduction among Chinamen has done more injury, social and moral, in China than all the humanitarian agencies of Christianity could remedy in 200 years. And on you, Christians, and on your greed of gold we lay the burden of the crime resulting; of tens of millions of honest, useful men and women sent thereby to a premature death after a short miserable life, besides the physical and moral prostration it entails even where it does not prematurely kill! And this great national curse was thrust on us at the points of Christian bayonets. And you wonder why we are heathen? . . .

In public affairs, it is either niggardliness that puts a premium on dishonesty, or loose extravagance for show, that encourages political debauchery and jobbery. In general, businessmen are lauded as great financiers who actually conspire to buy laws, place judges, control senates, corner and regulate at will the price of natural products; and, in fact, act as if the whole political and social machinery should be a lever to them to operate against the interests of the nation and people. In a heathen country, such conspirators against social order and the general welfare would have short shrift.

Here in New York, the richest and the poorest city in the world, misery pines while wealth arrogantly stalks. The poor have the votes, and yet elect those who betray them for lucre to corporate and capitalistic interests; and the administration of justice—in fact, the whole system of jurisprudence—is to stimulate crime rather than prevent it. As to preventing poverty, or rendering it less intolerable, that is the most remote thought of religious and political local administration.

It is no wonder, under such circumstances and conditions, that New York is a most heavily taxed city, and the worst governed for the interests of New York. "Public office a public trust?" Rather, it is a form to be worked, Christian-like, for all it is worth. Public spiritedness and moral worth have no value or utility in "practical" Christian politics. Such civic virtues "don't pay."

Do as we do. Give public office to the competent. Pay them well. If they are inefficient or indifferent, remove them at once. If dishonest, morally or financially, kill them as traitors.

"It is better that a child knows only what is right and what is wrong than to have a rote knowledge of all the books of the sages, and yet not know what is right and what is wrong." Collegiate education does not necessarily make a youth fit for the duties of life. And men like [Abraham] Lincoln, [Horace] Greeley, and other such Americans prove it. "The most successful youth in life is not the most learned, but the most unblemished in conduct." So say the heathen. But here, it is called smart when a boy is merely impudent to the old, and it is "smartness," and is excused by the phrase that "boys will be boys," when a boy throws a stone with malice to break someone's window, or do some injury. And parents of such a boy, while they chide, will secretly chuckle, "He's got the makings of a man in him."

It is our motto, "If we cannot bring up our children to think and do for us when we are old as we did for them when they were young, it is better not to rear them at all." But the Christian style is for children to expect their parents to do all for them, and then for the children to abandon the parents as soon as possible.

On the whole, the Christian way strikes us as decidedly an unnatural one; it is everyone for himself—parents and children even. Imagine my feelings, if my own son, whom I loved better than my own life, for whom I had sacrificed all my comforts and luxury, should, through some selfish motive, go to law with me to get his share prematurely of my property, and even have me declared a lunatic, or have me arrested and imprisoned, to subserve his interest or intrigue! Is this a rare Christian case? Can it be charged against heathenism?

We heathen are a God-fearing race. Aye, we believe the whole Universe-creation—whatever exists and has existed—is of God and in God; that, figuratively, the thunder is His voice and the lightning His mighty hands; that everything we do and contemplate doing is seen and known by Him; that He created this and other worlds to effectuate beneficent, not merciless, designs, and that all that He has done is for the steady, progressive benefit of the creatures whom He endowed with life and sensibility, and to whom as a consequence He owes and gives paternal care, and will give paternal compensation and justice; yet His voice will threaten and His mighty hand chastise those who deliberately disobey His sacred laws and their duty to their fellow man.

"Do unto others as you wish they would do unto you," or "Love your neighbor as yourself," is the great Divine law which Christians and heathen alike hold, but which the Christians ignore.

This is what keeps me the heathen I am! And I earnestly invite the Christians of America to come to Confucius.

SOURCE: *North American Review* 143, no. 2 (August 1887): 169–79.

OTHER REFERENCES

Arthur Bonner, *ALAS! What Brought Thee Hither? The Chinese in New York, 1900–1950* (London: Associated University Press, 1997).

John Kuo Wei Tchen, *New York before Chinatown: Orientalism and the Shaping of American Culture, 1776–1882* (Baltimore: Johns Hopkins University Press, 1999).

Qingsong Zhang, "The Origins of the Chinese Americanization Movement: Wong Chin Foo and the Chinese Equal Rights League," in *Claiming America: Constructing Chinese American Identities during the Exclusion Era,* ed. K. Scott Wong and Sucheng Chan (Philadelphia: Temple University Press, 1998), pp. 41–63.

Why I Am Not a Heathen:
A Rejoinder to Wong Chin Foo
(1887)

Yan Phou Lee

A month after Wong Chin Foo's essay "Why Am I a Heathen?" appeared in the North American Review, *Yan Phou Lee wrote the following rebuttal in defense of Christianity while boldly condemning bigots for their un-Christian ways. Born in 1861 in Xiangshan District, Guangdong Province, Lee had come to the United States in 1873, at the age of twelve, as a member of Yung Wing's Chinese Educational Mission and had completed his first year at Yale College when the group was recalled to China in 1881. He managed to return to the United States with the help of U.S. missionaries and had just graduated from Yale when he wrote this rejoinder. He later went on to work at various jobs—farming, business, court interpreting, and journalism—before returning to China in 1931 to become editor of the* Canton Gazette, *a bilingual newspaper.*

Yan Phou Lee's autobiography, When I Was a Boy in China, *was published in 1887. Like Wong Chin Foo, he lectured widely on Chinese manners and customs, and often defended the Chinese in the press. His other well-known work, "The Chinese Must Stay," in response to Chinese exclusion, appeared in the* North American Review *in April 1889.*

I draw a sharp distinction between Religion and Ethics. Religion pertains to the heart. Ethics deals more with outward conduct. Religion inculcates principles. Ethics lays down rules. Religion without Ethics is like a disembodied spirit; Ethics without Religion is a body from which the soul has fled. The most intelligent form of Heathenism, namely, Confucianism, never taught the "'relations and acts of individuals toward God," the Ruler of the Universe. Confucius inculcated a lofty morality, but left Religion to shift for itself.

"Born and raised a heathen, I learned and practiced its moral and religious code," by worshiping the prescribed number of idols, and I was useful to others, though not to myself, because I helped to fatten the lessees of the

Yan Phou Lee.
(Frontispiece in
*When I Was a Boy
in China*, 1887)

temples, incense-venders and idle priests. "My conscience was clear," because I knew not what I was doing, "and my hopes as to the future life were undimmed by distracting doubt," simply because they were never very bright. In fact, I was not precocious enough to think much on the subject.

I came under Christian influences at the age of thirteen, and I am ashamed to confess that I did not take to Christianity kindly at first, and for three years to come, for it takes a long time to weed out error, and my Chinese friends and teachers had taken special pains to prejudice my mind against Christianity. But in 1876 that grand man of God, Mr. Moody, came to proclaim the Gospel in Springfield, Mass. I attended the meetings and listened to his presentation of the truth with wonder, and, at length, with conviction of my lost estate, of my need of redemption. I had a personal interview with Mr. Moody, and was strengthened in my resolution to be a Christian. That was one of the happiest periods of my life. I did not join the church then, as friends advised me to wait; for it was feared that the Chinese Commissioner of the Educational Mission, to which I belonged, might send me home before I got well started on the right road. I identified myself with Christians, and took part in all religious exercises; and certainly friends there are who can testify that I became more gentle and more thoughtful of others. I got along well with my studies, because my mind was free and I had learned concentration. When the Chinese students were recalled in 1881, I went home with the rest. The mandarins made some attempt to draw us back to heathenism, with varying success. Not confident of my strength to stem the current that was setting in toward heathenism, I left the naval school as soon as I could get leave of absence, went to Canton, and joined the Presbyterian Church in charge of Rev. Dr. A. P. Happer. I had to give up the government service and heathenism at the same time; but do you suppose I regretted it?

I did not bother myself with the peculiarities and shortcomings of different denominations. It mattered little to me which sect I identified myself with. For the frailties of human nature are no part of Christianity. They are the very things it teaches us to overcome. There are as many conceptions of Christianity as there are men who give any thought to the subject. But Christianity is one; it is like its head, the same yesterday, today, and forever. It appears to be distorted on account of the human medium through which it must pass. But the very fact that so many people misunderstand it, misapply its principles, and abuse its privileges, is proof positive of its Divine origin. Whatever is human can be understood of man; whatever is from God can only be apprehended imperfectly by man.

Thus, I not only discriminate between Christianity in the abstract and Christianity in the concrete, but also between its correct application and its perversion. There was at one time a dyspeptic who preached a crusade against eating. He argued that, because a great many men abused it, and injured themselves by eating too much, and ruined their health by defying its rules and violating its principles, therefore the whole doctrine and practice of eating was a humbug. He said, moreover, that eating, instead of giving health and maintaining life, was every day making people sick, and in some cases people had actually died from eating. In consequence of such representations, he converted a great many to his views, and was hailed as a great deliverer of mankind. The more zealous of his followers eschewed eating, and, as they persisted to the last, of course they died. Then people began to open their eyes, and said: "Since without eating we die any way, while *with* eating we may live to a green old age, we will stand by eating and let those cranks do as they please." The doctrine and practice of Christianity is very much like the doctrine and practice of eating.

I did not have much difficulty in believing the Bible to be an inspired book. If the wickedness and imperfections of men obscured the mercifulness and goodness of God, it was a great pity; but that is no argument against Christianity. Clouds may get between me and the sun, but I believe it is there, and that it shines all the same.

I did not profess to comprehend the Divine Will, Purpose, Wisdom, and Justice, in the plan of Salvation. What a conceited fool you would have called me if I did! I accepted the truth as it is told in the Bible, and confessed that there were things that I could not comprehend, and was not expected to comprehend.

If others believe that a man can enter heaven by repenting at the eleventh hour, what is that to me? How should that destroy my faith in the saving grace of Christianity? Such, indeed, is its power to change the heart of man, that even if Dennis [Denis] Kearney should slip into the Heavenly Jerusalem, he would be lamb-like and would be heard to say: *"The Chinese must stay!* Heaven is incomplete without them."

It is very easy to misinterpret the Bible. Some minds are so crooked that everything which goes through invariably comes out crooked. Some men understand the Bible literally. Others take each verse out of its context and tack it to some other place, and the result is something like this: "And Judas went out and hanged himself," "Go and do thou likewise!"

The reason why I am enabled to sign myself a "Christian" is because I am endowed with the faculty of reason, which I have supplemented with formal logic and *a desire to tell the truth.*

Heathenism teaches nothing if it does not teach fatalism and the control of Destiny. If it does not go so far as predestination, it is because its notions of a future life are a confused heap of nonsense.

Now, my faith teaches me to cultivate my mind, rectify my heart, and to make my conscience delicate and sensitive. It bids me to be tolerant, charitable, and just to my fellow-men. It tells me to faithfully discharge my duties, public and private. It gives me the requisite strength to act the good citizen and the true husband. It commands me to accord to others their rights, and to take nothing that is not my due. Finally, it teaches me how to discharge my duties towards God, Father and Preserver of us all.

I not only discriminate between Christianity and its professors, but I also discriminate between true Christians and hypocrites. Confucius says: "It is impossible to carve on rotten timber." Christianity is not responsible for the acts of morally rotten men, and yet, where there is any soundness at all, it has demonstrated its power to heal and to save. I think that ministers should be paid according to the work they do. The laborer is worthy of his hire. But I am not "down" on all ministers because some betray their trust. I do not believe that all Christians are worldly because I have met some conspicuous cases of worldliness among them.

Organized charities may seem to lack sympathy, and, perhaps, have too much of red tape to be vigorous; but private charity is too apt to be indiscriminate, and too liable to be imposed upon, so that, instead of relieving the distress of the really deserving, it may encourage shiftlessness and idleness. Neither method of relief is perfect. But that is owing to the sinfulness of man, which Christianity alone can cure. When the Chinese were persecuted some years ago—when they were ruthlessly smoked out and murdered— I was intelligent enough to know that Christians had no hand in those outrages; for the only ones who exposed their lives to protect them were Christians. The California legislature that passed various measures against the Chinese was not Christian, the Sandlotters[1] were not Christians, nor were the foreign miners. They might *call* themselves Christians, but I don't call a man a great genius simply because he *claims* to be one. Let him *do* something worthy of the name first. You shall know a man by his works. If there is any sentiment in this country in favor of the Chinese today, it is only to be found in the Christian church. I don't forget that that Congress (which was most liberal and most jealous of the national honor) that finally voted the magnificent indemnity,[2] was influenced and urged on by Christian opinion as expressed in petitions and the press. If there was no Christianity in this land, things would be too hot, not only for the Chinese, but for all who form the base of the social pyramid.

I flatter myself that I am broad, and entertain cosmopolitan views. For while I glory in China's ancient civilization, her extensive literature, and lofty philosophy, I am aware that other nations are superior to her in science and the arts. While I am proud of China's philosophers, statesmen, and heroes, I can admit that other countries have also produced great men.

Murders and robberies may be pretty frequent in New York State, but who knows how many are committed in China in a year? If foreigners have such paradises in their native countries, why do they persist in staying *here?* For my part, I am content to stay and cast my lot with the good people of this country, who, you will find, are mostly Christians.

I do not confound Christian congregations with cowardly mobs organized for arson and murder, and I deny that Christianity encourages the young to abuse the aged. Granting that there is more wickedness in the neighborhood of a single church district of one thousand people in New York than among one million heathen in China, that only proves that one thousand heathen in New York have a greater capacity for wickedness than one million heathen in China.

By no torturing of Aristotelian logic can I connect heartbreaking and suicides in New York with Christian charity, and wherever I have met with any "fraternity" I invariably found it in the Christian church. Having been a heathen myself, and an associate of the heathen, I am competent to say that they never do any good without expecting a return, or gaining some merit. The true Christian does good for the love he has toward all God's creatures. When I was in need of friends, Christians befriended me. Christians helped me to return to this country, and they said nothing about it either. When I was in

1. In reference to Denis Kearney and other agitators who made speeches at outdoor rallies to instigate riots against the Chinese.

2. In reference to the indemnity of $150,000 appropriated by Congress to cover losses suffered by Chinese victims of the Rock Springs massacre in 1885.

doubt about the advisability of returning to college, Christian friends gave me encouragement and promised help. When I undertook to work my way through college, Christian people assisted me in pursuing that course. They got me to lecture, and aided me in the disposal of my literary wares. When I stood on the commencement platform to denounce the anti-Chinese policy of this government, it was the Christians who strengthened me with their enthusiasm and their applause. It is the Christian who looks on me as his equal, and who thinks that the Chinese are as well endowed, mentally, as he. The true Christian is the friend of the poor, the down-trodden, and the oppressed of all countries. When the famine was at its height in China, some twelve years ago, Christian missionaries went into the doomed districts to heal the sick and relieve the distressed.

If England were a truly Christian country, as she *claims* to be, the Opium War would have never taken place. Christianity is nowhere so explicit as where it warns people against the sin of covetousness. If Mephistopheles persuaded John Bull Faustus to sell his soul for gold, I don't see what Christianity has to do with it. Were half the Christians running mad after the Golden Calf, Christianity would still be the only saving religion in the world.

The ways of the American heathen and the Chinese heathen are wonderfully alike. Only the American may become a Christian whenever he chooses with greater facility than the Chinese. That is not saying, however, that the American heathen may not be worse than the Chinese.

I fervently believe that if we could infuse more Christianity into politics and the judiciary, into the municipal governments, the legislature and the executive, corruption and abuses would grow beautifully less. The Christian men are the last hope of the Republic. The final appeal is to be made to the Christian sentiment of the nation.

I have the misfortune to be a college-bred man; but a collegiate education does not necessarily disqualify one for the duties of life. A classical education would not have injured men like Lincoln and Greeley, but they had something better than that,—they had a Christian education. No greater praise can we give them than this: They were *Christian* gentlemen.

The duties of parents and children are reciprocal. The Americans lay more stress on the duty of parents towards their children, while the Chinese insist too much on the duty of children towards their parents. Both have departed from the golden mean. Christianity alone can restore harmony in the domestic relations. Neither foolish parents nor undutiful children are the products of the Christian religion. They are such either from imperfect training or natural depravity. Water, and air, and sunlight are beneficent things, but when applied to some seeds, fine fruit-trees spring up from the soil; when applied to others, poisonous weeds overrun the land. In the last case, water, air, and sunlight are misused. So the perversion of Christian teachings has produced many poisonous weeds.

It is hard to tell what a heathen fears or what he believes. It is some consolation to know that he does believe in something. He is slightly better off than the atheist. There are good men among the heathen. Such men you will find to be just, reasonable, honest, and truthful. Christianity would make such men perfect almost. But a bad heathen is quite the reverse.

I have some confidence left yet that Christianity will survive this last and most terrible of attacks. Indeed, I am silly enough to believe that that religion, which flourished in spite of the Pharisee and the Sadducee, which survived the persecutions of the Caesars, and finally supplanted them, which passed through the Dark Ages of ignorance and barbarism undimmed in lustre, which rose serenely after the terrible French Revolution, will continue to reign supreme so long as eternity itself shall endure.

Christianity has demonstrated its fitness to supply my spiritual needs. Its authenticity as a history no reasonable man can deny. I believe, I accept, its truths, as I hope to be happy in this life and to enjoy a blessed immortality in the life to come.

Do you wonder that I am a Christian? I cordially invite all heathen, whether American, or English, or Chinese, to come to the Saviour.

SOURCE: *North American Review* 145, no. 3 (September 1887): 306–12.

OTHER REFERENCES

Thomas La Fargue, *China's First Hundred* (Pullman: State College of Washington Press, 1942).

Yan Phou Lee, *When I Was a Boy in China* (Boston: D. Lothrop Co., 1887).

Amy Ling, "Yan Phou Lee or the Asian American Frontier," in *Re/collecting Early Asian America: Essays in Cultural History,* ed. Josephine Lee, Imogene L. Lim, and Yuko Matsukawa (Philadelphia: Temple University Press, 2002), pp. 273–87.

The Geary Act:
From the Standpoint
of a Christian Chinese (1892)

Jee Gam

The Geary Act of May 5, 1892, extended the provisions of the Chinese Exclusion Act for another ten years and also required all Chinese in the United States to obtain certificates of residence within one year or face deportation. Among the community leaders who spoke out against the Geary Act was Jee Gam. One of the earliest Chinese to be baptized and admitted into the First Congregational Church of Oakland in 1870, he was a missionary worker and court interpreter at the time he wrote this essay. His main arguments were that the Geary Act was unjust, un-Christian, and an outright violation of the Burlingame Treaty of 1868.

The Chinese consul and the Chinese Six Companies went so far as to advise the community against registering while their attorneys fought the law in the courts. In Fong Yue Ting v. United States, *the U.S. Supreme Court ruled the Geary Act constitutional on the basis of public interest and necessity. To avoid wholesale deportation, Congress passed the McCreary Amendment of 1893, extending registration for another six months. Despite the eloquent and reasoned appeals of Jee Gam and other defenders of the Chinese, the Chinese Exclusion Act was made indefinite in 1904 and not repealed until 1943.*

During the last six months this act has been more talked about than any other question in America. You can hardly take up a daily paper, a magazine, or any religious paper, without finding something about the Geary Law. The Chambers of Commerce, the Board of Trade, the mass meetings, the religious conventions, preachers in their pulpits, in fact all clubs and societies have discussed this question. Every individual from the lowest to the highest has spoken on it. Some are for it; others are against it. Even the judges of the highest tribunal in America differ in opinion concerning it.

I have been requested to write on it, and have with great reluctance consented, because it is a hard question to handle. Yet I feel it my duty to try.

I am a Chinaman and a Christian. I am not any less Chinese for being a follower of Christ. My love to Jesus has intensified rather than belittled my love for my native country. I am proud of China, for it is a great country. I admire her, for she has a wonderful future. What a glorious nation she will be when she embraces Christianity! I praise her authentic history, for it goes back 4,800 years.

I honor all things that are honorable in my country. I blush for whatever has marred her record. I pray for her daily, that she may speedily become a Christian nation.

I am in some sense also an American, for I have lived in America almost twice as long as in China. I love this country. I teach my children who are native-born Americans to sing the National hymns. And just as I rejoice in whatever is honorable to America, and commend her example to my countrymen, so I am pained when unjust and oppressive laws are permitted to be placed upon her statute books. Such a law as the Geary Act seems to me to be one which dishonors America, as well as injures my countrymen and native land.

It dishonors America as a breaking of solemn pledges—for the Chinese were invited here by the Americans. Mr. Burlingame was one of the most prominent representatives of the U.S. who gave us this invitation.[1] He assured China that a million Chinese laborers could find welcome and employment on the Pacific Coast alone. These invitations were endorsed by express treaties. China took these invitations and treaties in good faith. Her people came, but not in such a number as need call forth the alarm of the Americans, for in the period of 40 years there were less than two hundred thousand Chinese that ever put their feet on America's soil. But the laborers from Europe and especially from Ireland, who have no more right to be in America than the Chinese have, and perhaps much less, began to kick, and demand that "the *Chinese must go.*" Sandlot agitators and other demagogues saw in this an opportunity to get famous, and also to gratify their greed by echoing the cry in Congress; and the anti-Chinese Scott Act, in 1882, was the outcome of that agitation.[2] This act, though prohibiting the coming of Chinese laborers, said that those already here were at liberty to go and return as they pleased; and when they should go the Government was to give them return certificates. Accordingly there were over 20,000 Chinese la-

1. Anson Burlingame, who was the American minister to China in 1860, negotiated the Burlingame Treaty of 1868 on behalf of China. The treaty recognized the right of free migration and guaranteed the reciprocal privileges of residence and travel on the basis of most favored nation treatment, with the exception of naturalization.

2. The Scott Act was actually passed in 1888, a presidential year. Its passage came on the heels of an aborted U.S.-China treaty and was motivated by electoral politics in California and the Western states.

borers that went to China with such certificates. Not one of these certificates was ever honored. Thus another solemn pledge was broken. It is said that no Chinese shall be allowed to become citizens of the United States. One of the charges against the Chinese is that they do not become naturalized, but this act said they shall not be. So not only is there no consistency in blaming the Chinese for not becoming citizens, but this act is a direct violation of the Burlingame treaty, which guaranteed the Chinese the same rights as those of the most favored nation.

Now the Geary Act is even worse, for it not only prohibits the Chinese laborers from entering into the United States, but compels the deportation of those that are lawfully here, which is virtually an act of war.

So this Geary Act is an oppression of the weak. China is a great and powerful nation, but not just now in condition to fight a power like America. At any rate, America thinks so, and it looks to us cowardly for her to take undue advantage of a weaker nation. We all despise a man who stabs another in the back; how much more despicable when the person so attacked is weaker than he!

See how this law injures China.

1. It discriminates against her subjects. It says all Chinese laborers must register or be deported, but says this of no others. If America is fair in her dealing, she ought never for a moment to allow discrimination to exist within her borders. Her laws ought to be applicable to all people, regardless of nationality. To single out the despised Chinese, the only people who hold no votes, shows cowardliness. Would America venture to enact a similar law against any of the European powers?

And now, what harm is in the registration law? Why do the Chinese object? Every American has to register. These have been the questions and assertions of many friends. My answer to these is as follows: An American if he fails to register forfeits only the right of voting at that particular election. For that no harm can come to him. But there is a vast difference in the Geary registration, for it means that the Chinese must register, or be forcibly removed from this country. So one registration is voluntary, while the other is compelled. In other words, the former law makes a person a free man, the other law makes one a slave, a criminal, or even a dog. For the only class that are required to give photographs are the criminals, and the only animal that must wear a tag is a dog. The Chinese decline to be counted in with either of these classes, so they refuse to register, and I do not blame them;

2. A registration paper will add trouble to its owner instead of protection.[3] A laborer will have to carry the paper with him wherever he goes. Suppose

3. According to proponents of the Geary Act, it was supposedly passed to protect legal Chinese residents.

he is in a strange town, and some hoodlums should play the part of officers, and should demand the showing of his paper, and, when he complies, suppose they should immediately tear it to pieces. Now, how can this man prove his loss? He has no witness but himself, and the Court will not believe him unless he has some white witness to corroborate his testimony. Consequently, his request for a renewal will be denied. Not only so, but they must charge him with having sold his papers. If he gets clear once, when he goes into the next town he is liable to be arrested again, and he will have no rest until he is deported.

3. This Act withdraws some sacred rights such as in the Declaration of Independence are declared to be inalienable. The right to a free, untrammelled pursuit of happiness, the right of habeas corpus, the right to be adjudged innocent until proven guilty. The Geary Act says, when a Chinese is arrested under the provision of this Act, he shall be adjudged to be unlawfully within the United States, *unless* he shall establish by *affirmative proof,* to the satisfaction of such Justice, Judge or Commissioner, his lawful right to remain here. Now if that law which says every person arrested and charged with a crime is presumed to be innocent until he is proven guilty will hold good for a white man, *why not for a Chinaman also?* In other words, the people must make out a case against the accused before he can be convicted of the crime charged. If he choose to be silent, the law says that is his privilege, and judgment must not be entered against him for doing so. This also should apply to the Chinese as well as other people, but the Geary Act says No, and therefore it is un-American, barbarous and inhuman. It is unchristian, for it is contrary to the teaching of Christ.

All this is so plain to us that we did not for a moment suppose that it could be declared constitutional, and therefore did not register. Furthermore, if we registered we would be traitors in the eyes of our countrymen. The course of our Christian work would be greatly hampered; for ever since they have heard that the American Christians, and especially the ministers, are against this Geary Act, and have repeatedly petitioned the Government to repeal the same, not only do they feel *very grateful,* but we feel greatly encouraged. They naturally expected the Chinese Christians to cooperate with them in their efforts to have the law tested, and so we did. Therefore our brethren have said that they would rather take the chance of being deported than to be charged with disloyalty; rather sustain the cause of Christ than disgrace it.

If the United States should enforce this disgraceful Geary law, China will most assuredly retaliate. The lives of missionaries and the properties of missions will be in danger. The leading commercial interest, which is now held by America in China, will be given to the nations of Europe. If America can afford to lose that, I am sure China can also. But is that the best policy? Not conflict, but peace and harmony. Let not this infamous act mar the progress of Christianity in China, as the English opium has done: for while the gospel sent to China by the people of England is saving one soul, her opium, that she so wrongfully and selfishly forced into China, is destroying a thousand.

I never can forget the remark made by the Chinese mandarin to a British minister: "Sir, I wish you would take back with you the opium your country sent us." What a blush went over the face of the British representative! What a great stumbling block to Christianity! Let America regain her good name by repealing the Geary law.

Our sincere thanks are due to all our Christian friends. Their sympathy and prayers have greatly comforted us; and may God overrule all injustice and wrong to His glory, and the final triumph of the right!

SOURCE: *Our Bethany* 3, no. 4 (February 1892): 5.

OTHER REFERENCES

Bill Ong Hing, *Making and Remaking Asian America through Immigration Policy, 1850–1990* (Stanford: Stanford University Press, 1993).

Charles J. McClain, *In Search of Equality: The Struggle against Discrimination in Nineteenth-Century America* (Berkeley: University of California Press, 1994).

Wesley Woo, "Chinese Protestants in the San Francisco Bay Area," in *Entry Denied: Exclusion and the Chinese Community in America, 1882–1943,* ed. Sucheng Chan (Philadelphia: Temple University Press, 1991), pp. 66–75.

Leaves from the Life History
of a Chinese Immigrant (1936)

Elizabeth Wong

The Chinese were first recruited to Hawaii as contract laborers to work on the sugar-cane plantations in 1852. Because of the low pay and harsh working conditions, many left upon completion of their contracts and turned to farming, growing rice, or shop-keeping. By the 1880s, Chinese owned a third of the businesses in Honolulu and had become an important part of the growing mercantile class. Unlike most Chinese la-borers in Hawaii, they enjoyed the comforts of having wives, families, and servants.

Chinese bond servants, or mui tsai *as they were called, either came with the fam-ily from China or could be imported from China. Under the* mui tsai *system, poor par-ents who sold their daughter into indentured service usually stipulated in the deed of sale that the girl be freed through marriage when she turned eighteen. If the girl was lucky, her master would treat her well and marry her off to a good husband. If un-lucky, the girl could be treated like a slave, suffer sexual and physical abuse, or be sold into prostitution. This is the story of one lucky* mui tsai *who came to Hawaii in 1891.*

LIFE IN A CHINESE VILLAGE

"Lucky come Hawaii? Sure, lucky, come Hawaii," said Mrs. Teng,[1] pushing back her black hair with her hands, which showed signs of hard labor. "Be-fore I come to Hawaii I suffer much. Only two kinds of people in China, the too poor and the too rich. I never can forget my days in China," she said, her mouth falling into a smile revealing a pretty good set of teeth. She is pro-portionally built for her five feet four.

"In a small crowded village, a few miles from Hongkong, fifty-four years

---

1. Author's note: I am using a fictitious name for the lady who has given me her life ac-count. She has used broken English and Chinese. I shall translate her Chinese accordingly and shall try not to alter her style.

ago I was born. There were four in our family, my mother, my father, my sister,[2] and me. We lived in a two-room house. One was our sleeping room and the other served as parlor, kitchen, and dining room. We were not rich enough to keep pigs or fowl, otherwise our small house would have been more than overcrowded.

"How can we live on six baskets of rice which were paid twice a year for my father's duty as a night watchman? Sometimes the peasants have a poor crop, then we go hungry. During the day my father would do other small jobs for the peasants or carpenters. My mother worked hard too for she went every day to the forest to gather wood for our stove. . . .

"Sometimes we went hungry for days. My mother and me would go over the harvested rice fields of the peasants to pick the grains they dropped. Once in a while my mother would go near a big pile of grain and take a handful. She would then sit on them until the working men went home. As soon as they go we ran home. She clean and cook the rice for us two. We had only salt and water to eat with the rice. Today when I hear my children grumble about the food I wish they could experience what I went through and what the children in China are doing to relieve their hunger.

"Father was suffering from dysentery so my mother went out to look for herbs. My father told me to take the baby out to play and not to come back until late. Being always afraid of him I gladly took the baby out. We were three houses away watching a man kill a chicken. Pretty soon a man came to call me to go home for my father is dead. I ran with my brother on my back and stopped at the door of our house. I took one look at my father dangling from the ceiling and started to run to where I don't know. . . .

"Poor people are buried in mats, but mother bought a coffin for my father. She had asked the carpenter to give her a few weeks to pay for the coffin and the man agreed. My mother called me to her and put me on her lap.

"'Do you want me to remarry or will you be a good girl and go to stay with a certain lady,' she said. I told her that I do not want her to remarry but I will go with the lady so that she will have money to pay for my father's coffin. If she did marry again I would have a hard time looking for her when I came big. I leaned my head against her breast and if I knew that was the last time I would be so near to her I would have let my brother cry alone.

"I heard my mother tell this go-between lady that she wants me put in the hands of a lady or man who would come to Hawaii because she has heard Hawaii is a land of good fortune. All the other people who went to Hawaii sent money home every time. (My mother has never told me that I was being sold as a slave until I came to Hawaii my mistress called me names.)

"My mother took off my mourning robes, dressed me in a colored dress

2. She means brother, as that is all she refers to in the remaining interview.

with a red string on my hair. I went with this lady to the big house of Mr. Chin, two miles from our village. He was to look me over and I seem to be his choice for he took out ninety dollars to give to my mother. Every year in my age was worth ten dollars. I wished I were older than nine so that my mother could get more money.

"Before the actual parting I was happy and glad to go because I knew I was helping mother. When my mother and me went out of the house I took one look behind and did not want to go. I cried and begged and asked to stay at home. For once I had the sympathy of the neighbors. They cried and told me that I must be a good girl and go so that my mother can get the money to pay the coffin. I quickly wiped my eyes and went with my mother. When we got to this place we went to give our offerings to the temple god. It was eleven o'clock when we came to the gate of Mr. Chin's house. We stayed outside until it was twelve. It is said that it is bad luck to enter a master's house when the time is odd, it must be even time. Again the parting was hard. I ran after my mother but my master held me. He gave me a silver spoon, a jade bowl, sweets, and cakes—all that I always longed for. I was glad to stay forever. Next time when my mother came I did not care to go with her. I was so poor for a long time that those sweet and pretty things took a great hold on me.

"A lady in that house told me that Hawaii had big, fat, very sweet sugar cane—it was better than honey. I crazy for cane that I just waited for the day to come to Hawaii. She also told me that there was hardly anything to do but after I came I found out that this was not true.

LEAVING THE ANCESTRAL VILLAGE

"In 1891 my master and me sailed on the 'Billy Jack' to go to my new mistress in Hawaii. We slept on canvas cots and had cheap meat and cabbage for every meal. We could not land in Honolulu because there was a small pox on board ship. We went directly to San Francisco and stayed there for two months. I never saw the shape of the land for I was below the ship. When we came back to Hawaii I was locked in the immigration office for three weeks. How happy I was when my boss came to me. I went to meet my mistress who was never pleasant to me.

"The first thing I asked my master was a piece of sugar cane. He said that there is none around the place where we live. How sad I was for I expected cane to be all around.

"Mr. Chin was the owner of a large carpenter shop on Nuuanu street. He had many workers. They cooked our meals and they ate in the shop. I always took the meals home for the family. We lived behind the shop. I had to wash clothes, clean the house and the basin. I also waited on the table and when the family was served then I took my bowl to my master for food. I always ate separately from the family table. Whenever I go back for a second helping my mistress would glare at me. Being afraid I used to press the rice in my bowl so that I had my fill and avoided her glance. Although she called me a 'slave girl,' a good for nothing girl, and beat me unmercifully, I was happy to be in Hawaii. At least I had food in my stomach and ate with a silver spoon.

ON THE ROUGH ROAD TO WESTERNIZATION

"Being a 'China Jack' I was tempted by the good taste of the first cookie my mistress gave me. I saw her hang the can on the kitchen wall. As soon as she left the house I helped myself to a cookie and a cup of tea. In my little party she caught me. She took the ruler and beat my fingers to and fro, to and fro. They were all black and blue and she kept on until the ruler broke.

"One day after I had swept the house, washed the clothes, I went out to play with the neighborhood children who wanted to have some fun with the 'China Jack.' I was having a good time when my mistress yelled 'slave girl' at me. I went into the house expecting and prepared for the outcome. Afraid that the children outside would hear she stuffed my mouth with a dirty rag and beat me with a bamboo rod. I struggled but of no use. After her anger or jealousy was satisfied she made me clean the house again.

"Before I was real dumb. I was afraid to go to school on account of my mistress not giving me money to buy tablets and pencils. I didn't know how to explain to the teacher that my mistress would not give me money for books. I used to hide from the teacher. My mistress said that a 'China Jack' like me need not go to school. I sorry I no go before.

"I used to go to a shoe maker's and take needles from him, for my mistress refused to let me use her needles. Behind her back I learned how to sew. When I was sixteen she went to China for four months. I made sure I learned how to sew dresses for myself. Every ten cents that I earned for sewing button holes for the neighboring tailor I saved to buy materials. When my mistress returned from China she wanted me to sew for her. I wasn't very eager because she, herself, wanted to stop me from learning.

"The following year the plague invaded Honolulu. Chinatown was burned down.[3] All I can remember is that we went to live at Kalihi, then to Vineyard. We had little to do.

MARRIAGE—A RELEASE FROM RESTRAINTS

"I believe the turning point of my life came when I was eighteen. One morning I overheard my master scold my mistress for wanting to marry me off to

3. On December 12, 1899, a death in Chinatown was diagnosed as caused by the bubonic plague. The Board of Health ordered a sanitary fire, which got out of control; as a result, Chinatown was burnt down in the Great Chinatown Fire of January 20, 1900.

a man not of my same group. He said that long ago my mother made him promise that I be married to someone of my own group—Pun Dee [Punti].[4] He said that it is only fair to present the recent case [suitor] to me. I hurried away from the door and waited to be called any minute. I went before them. My master who was always nice to me said that my mother would be happy to know that I am married and on my own. He said that a merchant, a Mr. Teng, from Wailuku, Maui, is looking for a bride. He is well-to-do but is forty years old. You are only eighteen. I leave the matter up to you. If he told me that the man was sixty I would have gladly said 'yes.' Here was my chance to escape from the harsh words of my mistress. Better than suffer some more I accepted. How he looks like I did not know but with that thought of freedom in mind I slept peacefully for the first time.

"As a fee for my master's successful matchmaking my future husband sent him one hundred fifty dollars, a roast pig, five hundred cakes, a half dozen bottles of wine, and a half dozen chickens. All day I was buying things to take up to my new home. A lady took me down to the boat and when I landed at Kahului I was met by my brother-in-law who took me home to my husband. I became Mrs. Teng. My husband was almost bald but he was very nice to me.

CONTACTS WITH THE HOME VILLAGE

"Right after my marriage I asked my husband to write back to my village in search of my mother. Lucky he asked my former boss for help. I told him of my hard times and how I came to Hawaii. He sent my mother fifty dollars along with that first letter. I was very happy that I cried when I received my mother's letter telling me that my brother is eleven and is watching cows. I wrote home and sent her money to send my brother to school. I only longed to see my mother again. I think I would fall in her arms and cry for days but I never had that chance. She died a year after my husband's death in 1921.

BETWEEN TWO CULTURES BUT ADJUSTED PHILOSOPHICALLY

"The young people of today are very much changed. I cannot understand my daughter-in-law who never trusts me with her son. I am his grandmother. She is so afraid that I might put germs on him. When I have a slight cold I cannot go near him. How can I put germs on him? If he is healthy he gets no germs. The small children in China don't have enough to eat and no

4. The Punti were the original inhabitants of Guangdong Province, as opposed to the Hakka, who came from northern and central China and settled in the Guangdong area three hundred years later. The two groups differed in speech, customs, and economic interests and had a running feud dating back to the Taiping Rebellion (1850–64).

clothing and yet they don't die. The children in Hawaii have all the good food and clothing so why should they get sick?"

With a wistful smile she went on commenting about her mistress. She said that no matter how rich you are or how much better you are than the other person never look down upon him because some day you may be in that person's position. "Today, my mistress lives in a one-room house on Vineyard Street. Her husband, three sons, and two daughters are dead leaving a son-in-law who told her to get out of his home. Now she know what poor means. She gladly calls me her 'daughter' and even if she was mean to me I let that be forgotten. When I see her in town I give her a dollar or two. If she was nice to me maybe I would have been a little more glad to help her.

"My children call me a 'jew' because I do not spend for clothes or other unnecessary luxuries. It is not that; I shudder at the thought of being poor. I was poor for a long while, that much suffering is enough for me. I can not spend here and there because someday I want to buy new refrigerator, pay for doctor's bills, and pay for any emergency. I must save so that I may have money on hand.

"I am proud of my children. They are very good children and have helped me lots. I am looking forward to the day when I will have my sons, daughters, and in-laws, and grandchildren with me. At present they are scattered on Maui, Kauai, and Oahu. I lucky come Hawaii."

SOURCE: *Social Process in Hawaii* 2 (1936): 39–42.

OTHER REFERENCES

Tin-Yuke Char, *The Sandalwood Mountains: Readings and Stories of the Early Chinese in Hawaii* (Honolulu: University Press of Hawaii, 1975).

Clarence E. Glick, *Sojourners and Settlers: Chinese Migrants in Hawaii* (Honolulu: Hawaii Chinese History Center and the University Press of Hawaii, 1980).

Arlene Lum, ed., *Sailing for the Sun: The Chinese in Hawaii, 1789–1989* (Honolulu: University of Hawaii Center for Chinese Studies, 1988).

Kam Wah Chung Letters
(1898–1903)

The following Chinese letters were found in the Kam Wah Chung Company Building in John Day, Oregon. During its heyday in the 1870s and 1880s, John Day had a population of five to six hundred Chinese inhabitants who had come for the gold rush and stayed to work in the mines, ranches, farms, and logging camps. The Kam Wah Chung store, first established by local Chinese in 1871, was sold in 1886 to Ing Hay, better known as Doc Hay for his Chinese medicinal skills, and Lung On, an educated and shrewd businessman. Together, they turned the store into a successful business enterprise, selling general groceries and supplies as well as Chinese foods and goods. The store also served as an employment agency, social center for Chinese bachelors, and post office for the writing, receiving, and sending of mail.

After the deaths of Lung On and Doc Hay, the store was turned over to the city, and in 1967 it was restored to the way it had been in 1940. During the restoration, letters from China and other parts of the Western states were found. Some were addressed to Doc Hay or Lung Ong; others were letters that were either never sent or picked up. Outgoing mail to China generally reported on one's well-being with a sum of money enclosed. Incoming mail from China generally talked about problems at home and asked for money or the sojourner's early return. As the following letters indicate, Doc Hay and Lung On were married men who had left families behind in China. Despite repeated pleas from their families, they wrote infrequently, rarely sent money home, and never returned to China. In contrast, the first letter from an unknown husband to his wife in China is laden with bitterness at his unfruitful sojourn in America and their painful separation. Like the folk songs sung by Gold Mountain wives in China, these letters remind us of the hardships suffered by family members on both sides of the ocean because of Chinese exclusion and financial considerations.

Dr. Ing Hay,
John Day, Oregon.
(Oregon Historical
Society #OrHi 26468)

An unfinished letter to a wife in China.

From an unknown husband, via the Kam Wah Chung Co., John Day, Grant County, Oregon.

Undated.

My Beloved Wife:

It has been several autumns now since your dull husband left you for a far remote alien land. Thanks to my hearty body I am all right. Therefore stop embroidering worries about me.

Yesterday I received another of your letters. I could not keep the tears from running down my cheeks when thinking about the miserable and needy circumstances of our home, and thinking back to the time of our separation.

Because of our destitution I went out, trying to make a living. Who could know that fate is always opposite to man's design? Because I can get no gold, I am detained in this secluded corner of a strange land. Furthermore, my beauty, you are implicated in an endless misfortune. I wish this paper would console you a little. This is all that I can do for now . . .

.   .   .

Lung On,
Chinese merchant,
John Day, Oregon.
(Oregon Historical
Society #OrHi 53840)

From a mother in China.

To a son at John Day, Grant County, Oregon.
February 2, 1898.

Chin-hsin[1] My Son, Take Notice:

We are all very well at home, so don't worry about us. But your mother worries about you all the time. I cannot sleep and eat well because I am always thinking of you. You have been away from home for years. During that time, your second elder brother died, then your father died, and then your eldest brother died, too. Although I know that fate was the cause of their death, I still cannot but grieve deeply. I am old and weak now and I may die at any moment.

---

1. The names in these letters were transliterated in Mandarin rather than Cantonese, most likely because the translator, Chia-lin Chen, is Mandarin-speaking.

I hope you will be home and get married while I am alive, so that I might die with my eyes closed without grievance. I also hope that you will take care of Ah Fung, your nephew. Help him get a wife and establish their home, so that both your father and eldest brother might feel relieved under the ground.

You should save some money and should come back at least next year. I know my days are numbered. You won't see me any more; I may already be gone by the time you come back. Would you feel sorry then?

The twenty dollars which you sent me last June was received. So I guess you are all right and that relieves me a little. However, so long as you are not home, I am in suspense. Come back, don't forget your mother, please.

Your Mother.

.   .   .

From Lung On's father in China.

To Lung On, John Day, Oregon.
July, 1899.

Lung On, My Son:

Your business has proved profitless for a long time now. You should get rid of it or sell to some one else. Come home as soon as you can. Don't say "no" to me any more. There are too many gossips in our village; that makes me uneasy. You are my only son. You have no brothers, and your age is near forty but still without a male offspring.[2] You should think carefully. If you neither make a fortune abroad nor have a son at home, your loss is double. So why not come home before it is too late? Uncle Shang-sui owns many businesses in Canton, you can choose a suitable position for yourself. Under his wing you can settle down and start your own business. A man who does not have any long-range plans should have an immediate goal. Since you cannot make money in one place you should try somewhere else. Be flexible in accordance with circumstances. You have been away from home for seventeen years, you know nothing about our domestic situation. Anyway you should return even only for a visit. Sell the business to someone else, this is the wisest. We need you, and you must come back. I cannot tell you

2. Lung On came from a well-to-do family in Xinhui District, Guangdong Province, and was well educated in the Chinese classics and self-taught in English. Leaving a wife and daughter behind, he emigrated to the United States in 1882 and became a successful businessman in John Day, Oregon. It is not clear why his father thinks he is "profitless," but the rumors about his gambling, womanizing, and Western ways were probably true. Lung On passed away and was buried in John Day in 1940. He left half of his fortune to his daughter in China, but because of the severed diplomatic relations between China and the United States, she was never able to claim it.

all that I have in my mind in this short letter. Come back, let our family get united and enjoy the rest of our lives.

Your Father, Chu-chia.

. . .

From Lung On's wife, China.

To Lung On, John Day, Oregon.
Undated.

My Husband-lord:

I have received the two gold rings and ten dollars which you sent me via Mr. Wang. According to Mr. Wang, you are indulging in sex, and have no desire to return home. On hearing this I am shocked and pained. I have been expecting your return day after day. Your mother is completely blind. The housework is oppressing, and I have no one to give me a hand. If you have any conscience, please come back immediately. If you return, all the hardships I have suffered would be nothing as compared to the rejoicing of seeing you on your return. But alas, I don't know what kind of substance your heart is made of . . . Your daughter is now at the age of betrothal and it is your responsibility to arrange her marriage . . .

Your Wife.

. . .

From Doc Hay's father, Taishan District, Guangdong, China.

To Doc Hay, John Day, Oregon.
May 28, 1903.

Take Notice, My Son:

You have been away for more than a decade. Men go abroad in order to earn money to support their families, but you have not sent us money or letters since then. Everyone at home is anxious and worried, even in their dreams. I am disturbed and confused. Are you intending to let us starve to death? If you had sent no money back because of your bad business then I would not blame you. But I have been told that your business is booming, and you have made much money. Why don't you send some back? Even if you don't think of your mother and me, you should think of your wife and son. But you think only of yourself and enjoy your life alone without considering us. This is not suitable for a man of high character.[3]

I remember what you had said when we were both in Gold Mountain. You

---

3. Ing Hay came from a poor family in Taishan District, Guangdong Province. He emigrated with his father to the state of Washington in 1883, leaving behind a wife, son, and daughter. Trained

said, "Let the old go back home and rest. Let the young seek fortune abroad." You were exactly right when you made that remark. I have been back and you have sent no money.[4] Prices are sky-rocketing here, everything is expensive. I don't have any income, since I am unemployed. The small amount of money which I had brought back from Gold Mountain is gone. I am planning to borrow but there is no door to knock on. We are in a desperate situation. We cannot get along any more. My grandson—your son—is growing up and needs schooling. The tuition fee is much more than living expenses. Your mother is approaching the age of sixty. Her birthday is in August. Of course you know the date. Are you going to express what a son should for his mother on that day?

Send some money immediately to meet the urgent need at home. Come back whenever you can get a little fortune so that would bring about your family's reunion.

Your Father, Ing Du-hsieh.

SOURCE: Chia-lin Chen, "A Gold Dream in the Blue Mountains: A Study of the Chinese Immigrants in the John Day Area, Oregon, 1870–1910," Master's thesis, Portland State University, 1972, pp. 141–68.

OTHER REFERENCES

Jeffrey Barlow and Christine Richardson, *China Doctor of John Day* (Portland, Ore.: Binford & Mort, 1979).

Ruthanne Lum McCunn, "Ing Hay, Healer, and Lung On, Entrepreneur," in *Chinese American Portraits: Personal Histories, 1828–1988* (San Francisco: Chronicle Books, 1988), pp. 57–61.

---

in traditional Chinese medicine, he became a well-known herbal doctor in John Day, where he settled, died, and was buried in 1952. It is unclear why he chose to neglect his family in China.

4. Doc Hay's father returned to China in 1887.

PART TWO

Life Under Exclusion, 1904–1943

The exclusion years were marked by racial and class strife in the larger society as well as social and political upheavals within the Chinese community. Conditions for the Chinese did not improve until World War II, when China and the United States became allies and Chinese Americans were encouraged to participate in an all-American effort to defend democracy and defeat fascism. Until then, the exclusion acts remained in force, and Chinese in the United States had to endure not only the legal limitations set by discriminatory legislation but also racial prejudice as a daily fact of life. As Chinese immigrants found loopholes in the exclusionary laws by which they could enter the country, efforts were made to enforce the exclusion laws more stringently at the ports of entry and to pass further restrictive immigration laws that barred Chinese wives from joining their husbands in America. Chinese immigration reached its lowest point when only ten persons were admitted in 1887. As one Chinese immigrant remarked in 1904, when Congress extended the Chinese Exclusion Act indefinitely, "They call it exclusion, but it is not exclusion, it is extermination."[1]

The Chinese, however, refused to be driven away or become passive victims of racial discrimination. As political and economic conditions in China remained unstable throughout the first half of the twentieth century, some Chinese circumvented the restrictive immigration policies by smuggling themselves across the borders or coming posed as wives or children of U.S. citizens and merchants, who were legally allowed to enter the country. As a result, families began to develop and a small native-born population slowly took root. On the eve of World War II, the Chinese population climbed mod-

---

1. Chan Kiu Sing, cited in Mary Roberts Coolidge, *Chinese Immigration* (New York: Henry Holt, 1909), p. 302.

estly to 77,504, while the male-female ratio decreased from a high of 27:1 in 1890 to 2.9:1 in 1940. A so-called second generation of Chinese Americans finally emerged, and when combined with the growing numbers of those claiming derivative citizenship, their total population outnumbered the foreign-born population in 1940.

In the mainland and in Hawaii as well, the Chinese principally lived in urban areas where they concentrated in noncompetitive fields, working in ethnic enterprises in Chinatown, domestic service, or operating small laundries, restaurants, and grocery stores. Some men found seasonal employment in agriculture or in canneries, while many women worked in garment factories and food-processing plants. Others moved to the Midwest or the South, where they established small businesses in out-of-the-way places, often serving as the "middleman minority" between the white and black communities. Chinese restaurants that offered such Chinese American dishes as chop suey, chow mein, and fortune cookies could be found in almost every state. A few Chinese entrepreneurs tried their hands at manufacturing, food processing, shipping, and banking, but most of these ventures failed due to insufficient capital, managerial inexperience, and racial discrimination. Although many Chinese in Hawaii became skilled workers, office and retail employees, and professionals before World War II, these same opportunities would not open up for Chinese on the mainland until after the war. In essence, formal segregation and informal discrimination kept the Chinese in marginal areas of the American economy and society.

Those with families here had an economic advantage, since the family could live on the business premises and family members worked without wages, so that overhead remained low. Family and work life was thus closely integrated and marked by strict discipline, long hours of toil, constant frugality, and collective effort. However, compared to the nineteenth century, marital relationships were more interdependent as wives not only bore the responsibilities of running the household, raising the children, and maintaining Chinese cultural practices but also worked alongside their husbands to provide for their families.

Out of a strong sense of familial obligation and Chinese nationalism, many Chinese immigrants continued to keep close economic and political ties to their homeland. They were aware that the racial oppression and humiliation they suffered in America were due in part to China's weak international status and inability to protect its citizens abroad; thus, they focused their political attention and energies on helping China become a stronger and more modern country, even as they worked to change their unfavorable image and treatment in America. Sizable amounts of money were sent to China to support family and relatives, business enterprises, and educational institutions. On the question of how to liberate China from foreign domination, the overseas Chinese were divided in their support of the Zhigongtang, which favored restoring the Ming emperor; Kang Youwei's Baohuanghui, which advocated a constitutional monarchy; and Sun Yat-sen's Tongmenghui, which finally succeeded in overthrowing the Qing dynasty and establishing a democratic republic in 1911. They were united, however, in their support of China's War of Resistance against Japan from 1931 to 1945, contributing more than $25 million toward Chinese war bonds and refugee relief.

In retrospect, the exclusion years constituted a period of isolation, economic and political strife, and social transformation in the Chinese community. Discrimination remained virulent on the Pacific Coast, and the Chinese were kept out of the professions and trades, segregated in schools and theaters, refused service in public places, and prohibited from buying land, living in white neighborhoods, and sending for their wives from China. Within the community, merchant associations, trade guilds, and tongs fought over control of the distribution and commercial use of limited space and economic resources, while political factions disagreed over the political future of China. In an effort to establish social order, nurture business, and protect family life, merchants and social reformers established new institutions, including Chinese schools, churches, hospitals, and newspapers, as well as Western-style organizations like the Chinese Chamber of Commerce, Chinese-American Citizens' Alliance (CACA), and the Chinese YMCA and YWCA. They also worked closely with Protestant missionary workers and law enforcers to eradicate prostitution and opium dens, stop the bloody tong wars, educate women and children, and improve the public image of their community.

Although unwelcomed and targeted by the American labor movement earlier, Chinese workers were encouraged to participate in boycotts and strikes in the 1920s and 1930s, earning the right to become members of major unions, such as the National Maritime Union and International Ladies' Garment Workers' Union. In New York City laundry workers organized the Chinese Hand Laundry Alliance and were successful in opposing a local ordinance that discriminated against Chinese laundries. Chinese garment workers in San Francisco stayed on strike for 105 days until they won a better union contract from Joe Shoong's National Dollar Stores. In the political arena, CACA, representing the interests of the second generation, spoke up at congressional hearings and succeeded in protecting the right of Chinese merchants and U.S. citizens to bring their wives into the country, as well as the right of American-born Chinese women to marry Chinese aliens without losing their U.S. citizenship.

Coming of age in the 1920s and 1930s, many second-generation Chinese Americans experienced cultural conflicts in attempting to follow both Chinese and American values and customs. Despite their ability to speak English, their high educational attainment, and their Western outlook, they found themselves confined to living in segregated quarters, working at low-paying jobs, and excluded from participation in mainstream society. Most Chinese

Americans accommodated discrimination by creating their own bicultural identity and lifestyle. At home they continued to speak Chinese and observe Chinese customs, but in their social life outside, they were no different from other Americans in going to the movies, attending parties and picnics, and participating in sports and club activities, albeit in a segregated setting. To circumvent job discrimination, they resorted to working in Chinese-owned businesses or setting up professional practices in Chinatown communities. Encouraged by their parents and by political developments in China, some opted to go to China for better job opportunities and to put their talents to better use in the service of their ancestral homeland. With the advent of war in China, however, most were forced to return to the United States.

World War II proved to be a major turning point for Chinese Americans, providing them with unprecedented opportunities to improve their socio-economic and political status and become full participants in an all-American war effort. Because of China's allied relationship with the United States, American attitudes toward the Chinese turned favorable. Touted as loyal sons and daughters of Uncle Sam by the mass media, over 12,000 Chinese Americans served in the armed forces, thousands more worked in the shipyards and defense industries, and Chinese women throughout the country did their part on the home front—fundraising, pushing war bonds, and volunteering for Red Cross, USO, and civil defense duties. With the labor shortage, Chinese Americans were able to find jobs for the first time in private companies, civil service, and professional fields outside Chinatowns. In contrast, after Japan attacked Pearl Harbor, Japanese Americans were regarded as "enemy aliens," stripped of their civil rights, and herded into concentration camps, where many remained for the duration of the war. Then, in December 1943, as a goodwill gesture to China and to counter Japanese propaganda in Asia, Congress repealed the Chinese Exclusion Act and assigned the Chinese an annual quota of 105. With repeal came the right for Chinese to become naturalized U.S. citizens. The exclusion era had finally come to an end.

As the Chinese population in the United States became more established, immigrants and the second generation began speaking up for themselves and their community. Many of the documents in this section address issues of racial discrimination and exclusion: Ng Poon Chew and an anonymous Angel Island poet speaking out against the mistreatment of Chinese immigrants; CACA appearing before Congress to argue against a clause in the Immigration Act of 1924 that kept Chinese couples and families apart; the Chinese Hand Laundry Alliance in New York Chinatown declaring war on a local ordinance that unfairly discriminated against Chinese laundries; and political activist Happy Lim extolling revolutionary struggle on behalf of the working class. Joining them are the political voices of Chinese seeking to help develop or defend their homeland: Chin Gee Hee asking for donations to help build a railroad in Taishan; the Chinese Women's Association in New York drumming up support for the war effort in China; and Lim P. Lee reporting on a community picket at the San Francisco waterfront to protest the shipping of scrap metals to Japan in 1938. Especially heartwarming is Liu Liangmo's story of how he got singer and actor Paul Robeson to introduce the Chinese war song "March of the Volunteers" to the American public.

Unlike Part I on the nineteenth century, here there is no scarcity of voices to describe the work, family, and social lives of Chinese Americans during the exclusion period. Included in this section are the firsthand accounts of two Chinese immigrants who came to the United States in the 1920s: Gong Yuen Tim, who became a successful produce grower in central California, and Helen Hong Wong, who worked alongside her husband in his restaurant and laundry businesses in the Midwest. In addition to their stories, we have an interview with Anna May Wong at the height of her career as an actress; the observations of social worker Pardee Lowe on the aspirations and lifestyles of the second generation; and the unusual experiences of PFC Eddie Fung, the only Chinese American to be captured by the Japanese in World War II. We end this section with journalist Gilbert Woo's sarcastic commentary about the repeal of the Chinese Exclusion Act, which many considered a major turning point in Chinese American history.

The Treatment of the Exempt Classes of Chinese in the U.S. (1908)

Ng Poon Chew

In 1904 the Chinese Exclusion Act was extended indefinitely; but white labor, business groups, and political demagogues were still not satisfied. As they clamored for more stringent enforcement at the ports of entry, certain classes that had been exempt from exclusion by treaty, namely, officials, teachers, students, merchants, and travelers, fell victim to harsh treatment at the hands of zealous immigration officials. Chinese reaction to this abuse led to the 1905 boycott of American goods in China. A noted Chinese leader and eloquent speaker, Ng Poon Chew, was sent by the Chinese Six Companies on a speaking tour to explain the situation to Americans. Part of his efforts was the publication of the following pamphlet on the unfair treatment of the exempt classes.

A native of Taishan District in Guangdong Province, Ng Poon Chew immigrated to Gold Mountain in 1881 with high hopes of making his fortune. Instead, he converted to Christianity while studying English at a Presbyterian mission in San Jose, California, going on to graduate from the San Francisco Theological Seminary and become an ordained minister in 1892. In 1900, he started the Chung Sai Yat Po *daily newspaper.*

A popular lecturer on the Chautauqua and Lyceum circuits, Ng Poon Chew was one of the few educated Chinese Americans who could speak out effectively against anti-Chinese legislation and discriminatory practices. Well versed in law and politics, he quoted liberally from leading politicians, including President Theodore Roosevelt, on the discriminatory nature of the Exclusion Act, and argued that its enforcement broke treaty provisions, damaged relations between the United States and China, and caused undue hardships on the exempt classes. Although Ng did not go as far as to demand repeal of the exclusion laws, he did argue persuasively for upholding treaty obligations and putting a stop to the harassment of Chinese immigrants at U.S. borders.

Ng Poon Chew,
1911. (Courtesy of
Philip P. Choy)

After a quarter of a century of Chinese Exclusion, many people take it for granted that Exclusion has become a fixed policy of the Government of the United States, and that the vexed Chinese question is finally and permanently settled, as far as this country is concerned. The exclusion of Chinese laborers may have become a fixed policy with the United States, but the treatment of the exempt classes is not settled and will not be until it is settled aright with justice to all.

The Chinese Exclusion Law, as now enacted and enforced, is in violation of the letter and spirit of the treaty between this country and China, and also in opposition to the original intention of Congress on the subject. As long as this law remains on the statute books in its present shape, and is carried out by methods such as are now in vogue, the Chinese question will continue to be a vexatious one in the United States, as well as a fruitful source of irritation between America and China; and it will continue to hinder the upbuilding of commercial interests between the two great countries.

During twenty-five years the Chinese exclusion policy has steadily increased in stringency; as Senator [George] Hoar said on the floor of Congress, the United States enforced the exclusion laws first with water, then with vinegar, and then with red pepper, and at last with vitriol. The Exclusion Law has been carried out with such vigor that it has almost become an extermination law. The Chinese population in the United States has been reduced from 150,000 in 1880 to 65,000 at the present time.[1] During these twenty-five years much injustice and wrong have been heaped upon the Chinese people by the United States in the execution of its exclusion policy, and now it is time that this great nation should calmly review the whole question thoroughly and revise the law, so that it may come within the spirit of the treaty, and at the same time fulfill the original intention of Congress, namely: the exclusion of Chinese laborers, and the admission of all other classes. . . .

In the year 1880 China and the United States signed a treaty[2] by which China agreed to the suspension or limitation for a reasonable period of the emigration to this country of Chinese laborers, both skilled and unskilled; and the United States agreed that all other classes of Chinese should come and go as freely as the subjects of the most favored nation. Article I of the treaty reads as follows:

> Whenever in the opinion of the Government of the United States the coming of Chinese laborers to the United States, or their residence therein, affects or threatens to affect the interests of that country, or to endanger the good order of the said country or of any locality within the territory thereof, the Government of China agrees that the Government of the United States may regulate, limit or suspend such coming or residence, but may not absolutely prohibit it. The limitation or suspension shall be reasonable, and shall apply only to Chinese who may go to the United States as laborers, other classes not being included in the limitation. Legislation taken in regard to Chinese laborers will be of such a character only as is necessary to enforce the regulation, limitation or suspension of immigration, and immigrants shall not be subject to personal maltreatment or abuse.

And Article II reads as follows:

> Chinese subjects, whether proceeding to the United States as teachers, students, merchants or from curiosity, together with their body and household servants, and Chinese laborers who are now in the United States, shall be allowed to go and come of their own free will and accord, and shall be accorded all the rights and privileges, immunities and exemptions which are accorded to the citizens and subjects of the most favored nation.

1. According to the U.S. census, there were 105,465 Chinese in 1880, 107,488 in 1890, 89,863 in 1900, and 71,531 in 1910.

2. This is in reference to [James] Angell's Treaty of 1880, which marked the end of free migration guaranteed by the Burlingame Treaty of 1868 by giving the United States the exclusive right to regulate Chinese immigration. Soon after, Congress passed the Chinese Exclusion Act of 1882.

This treaty is still in force, and yet only a very limited number of Chinese other than laborers are now admitted, and by no means as freely as even the laborers of other nationalities.

The unwarranted limitation of the exempt classes of the Chinese—who have a right to come under both treaties and laws—to a few persons of a very few occupations, has come about chiefly through political agitation to secure the votes of workingmen, and by the strong anti-Chinese prejudice of immigration officers, who were themselves often representatives of labor organizations. All Chinese, except laborers, had a right to come and go freely under the treaty and even under the first restriction law of 1882, and this was acknowledged by both nations for eighteen years, although immigration officials, in some instances, enlarged the definition of laborers as so to include persons not technically of that class.

But in 1898 the Attorney General of the United States decided that the true theory of the law was not that all Chinese who were not laborers could come in, but that only those could come who were expressly named in the law. If this were correct, the law itself was a violation of the treaty; but, in fact, this ruling violated the clear and originally accepted meaning of the treaty and of the laws passed in execution of it. The American immigration officials, however, made it a pretext for excluding all the Chinese they could, even of the five classes named in the treaty. It appeared to be their ambition to deny all Chinese admission, and any one admitted was regarded as a lost case. The phrase "officials, teachers, students, merchants and travelers for curiosity or pleasure," was used in the treaty merely by way of illustration and before 1898 had been generally so interpreted, but the Attorney General's decision gave opportunity for limiting even these classes still further.

From this time on the exempt classes of Chinese were limited by enlarging the definition of laborers to include many who were not laborers, and by narrowing the definitions of teacher, student and merchant so as to exclude many who were certainly of these classes. For instance, it was declared that a teacher was one who teaches the higher branches in a recognized institution of learning; a student was one who pursues the higher branches in a recognized institution of learning, facilities for which are wanting in his own country or in the country from which he came; a merchant was one who carried on business in a fixed place, in buying and selling, in his own name. If a merchant, who does a million dollars worth of business a year, invests one dollar in a hotel or restaurant business or in a manufacturing concern, in a mining venture or railroad enterprise, his status as a merchant is at once vitiated, and he is denied admission, or deported if already admitted. As a result Chinese traders, salesmen, clerks, buyers, bookkeepers, bankers, accountants, managers, storekeepers, agents, cashiers, interpreters, physicians, proprietors of restaurants and laundries, employers, actors, newspaper editors, and even preachers and missionaries of Christianity, are excluded from the shores of the United States. A Chinese by the name of Wah Sang was admitted to this country as a student in theology, and as long as he was a student he was allowed to remain in the country; but when he completed his course in theological training, and entered into active service in preaching the Gospel to his countrymen under the auspices of the Methodist Church, he was arrested in Texas as a laborer, was tried and ordered deported in February, 1905, the court sustaining the contention of the immigration officials that a preacher is a laborer, and therefore subject to the operation of the Exclusion Law.

This exclusion by regulation, not justified by treaties or laws, has been carried much further so as to harass and inconvenience Chinese merchants, students and others in many ways. The United States demands a certificate of admission, with many personal details, signed by officials of the Chinese Government and of the United States; but when the certificate has been secured in proper form and every requirement has been met, the holder is not sure of being able to enter the United States; for the immigration officials re-examine him and often detain and sometimes deport him on petty technicalities. For the practice with the immigration officials is to regard every Chinese applicant for admission as a cheat, a liar, a rogue and a criminal, and they proceed to examine him with the aim in mind of seeing how he may be excluded, rather than of finding out whether he is legally entitled to land. For many years the certificate has been no guarantee that its holder could be admitted, though he might be a great merchant or a student coming to study at an American university.

In 1904 there arrived at the port of San Francisco a Chinese gentleman from the Straits Settlement,[3] with the intention of taking up a post-graduate course at Columbia University, he being a graduate of one of the great American universities in the Eastern States, and having taught English in colleges in Shanghai and Singapore for several years; yet, on account of trifling technical defects in his papers, he was detained for a long time at the detention shed on the Mail docks in San Francisco,[4] and finally deported.

Among the passengers on board the steamer *Ivernia,* which arrived at Boston on June 1st, 1905, from Liverpool, were four Chinese students, the three King brothers and their sister, Miss T. King, who had completed a three years' course in the University of London. These four students were of high official family in Shanghai, and they were on their way home, intending simply to land at Boston and cross to Canada to take the Canadian train for Vancouver. They were armed with passports signed by the American Ambassador,

3. The colonial name for Malacca, Penang, and Singapore under British rule.
4. Until the Angel Island Immigration Station opened in 1910, Chinese immigrants arriving at San Francisco were detained in a two-story shed at the Pacific Mail Steamship Company wharf to await inspection and clearance to land.

the Honorable Mr. Choate, who was their personal friend, certifying as to their status and intention, yet they were held on board while the very lowest and ignorant classes from southern Europe, that came in the steerage, were freely permitted to land. They would have been shipped back to England had not some local American merchants interested themselves in the case. After they were photographed and bond of five hundred dollars each given, they were permitted to land and cross to Canada. All these inconveniences and humiliation were accorded them, simply because the immigration officials at that port contended that they found some technical defect in their papers.

Furthermore, Chinese residents of the exempt classes are limited and harassed by official regulations in going to and from China, in bringing in their wives and children, and in many ways are treated as the subjects of other nations are never treated by the United States. Ladies of highly respectable families have been asked all sorts of questions in the examinations by the immigration officials which they would not dare to mention in the hearing of American ladies.[5] A boy of ten years of age, whose father was a prominent merchant, arrived in San Francisco with his parents. After a long investigation the parents were admitted and the boy ordered deported on the ground that he had *trachoma*,[6] although the American officers at the port of departure had given them a health certificate and although Americans on board the vessel testified that the ship's doctor had examined the eyes of all the second cabin passengers without disinfecting his hands. The Secretary of Commerce and Labor refused to reverse the decision of deportation. There have been a number of instances where Chinese merchants returning from a trip to China with their wives and families have been allowed to land but have had their wives and children deported.

For years the *Bertillon System,* used for the identification of criminals in the United States, has also been used to identify departing Chinese of all classes who wished to return.[7] The system has only been abandoned during the last few months because the Department at Washington failed to supply the different Bureaus with sufficient men to operate it.

Although the Geary Law of 1893 [1892], which required resident Chinese laborers to obtain a certificate of residence and to be photographed, did not require the exempt classes nor their wives and children to obtain a

5. Because Chinese prostitution was still rampant in San Francisco at the time, immigration officials commonly treated each Chinese woman seeking admission as a potential prostitute.

6. Beginning in 1903, trachoma or conjunctivitis in the eye was considered dangerously contagious and grounds for denying admission.

7. Originally invented by French scientist Alphonse Bertillon in the 1880s, the Bertillon System relied on detailed measurements of different parts of the body to determine the age of a person. It was mainly applied to Chinese returning from a visit abroad.

certificate, the regulations of the immigration bureau require officials to arrest every Chinese found without a certificate. Consequently any Chinese merchant, student or physician who was in this country at the time of registration and did not get a certificate is now liable to arrest and imprisonment.[8]

Under these regulations many of the exempt classes have been held up in various ways, at many places and times, by the immigration officials in their zeal to enforce the Chinese Exclusion Laws. The exempt classes, thus arrested, are put to great expense and inconvenience before they are released by United States Commissioners. Once an attache of the Chinese Legation at Washington was held up while traveling through Arizona on official business, and put to much inconvenience and indignity before he was released by order of the Department at Washington. In order to find some who might be without certificates, the whole Chinese quarter in Denver and in Boston was surrounded, and all Chinese found without certificates, whether merchants or not, were arrested and herded in close confinement, until their status was decided by the court.[9]

In 1904 the United States sent a special minister to China to invite the Provinces to make exhibits at the Louisiana Purchase Exposition, and promised their representatives a most cordial welcome. The Viceroys of the Provinces issued proclamations and many exhibits were prepared, but when the merchants and their employees arrived they were treated by the immigration officials as if they were laborers attempting to enter the country unlawfully. Some of them were so much offended that they returned at once to China; others decided not to set out from China; and those who reached St. Louis were treated throughout the Exposition like suspected criminals.

In that year there arrived at the port of San Francisco four Chinese gentlemen from Shanghai, three of whom were exhibitors at the St. Louis Fair, and the other a delegate from the Synod of China to attend the Presbyterian General Assembly at Buffalo, N.Y. Their papers were submitted to the American Consul in Shanghai, who passed upon them as being properly made out, and the gentlemen were assured that they would meet with no difficulties when they arrived in San Francisco. But they were denied landing by the immigration officials on the ground that their papers did not state the length of time the applicants had held their respective professions before they started for America. They were held at the detention shed, while strenuous efforts were made by their friends, both white and Chinese, who

8. The Geary Act of 1892 extended the Chinese Exclusion Act for ten years and required all Chinese laborers to carry a certificate of residence or be subjected to deportation.

9. During the early 1900s, police and immigration officials routinely raided Chinatowns in various cities and jailed offenders without warrant. One of the best-known raids occurred in Boston in 1903. Of the 234 Chinese arrested, 45 were deported.

appealed to the Department at Washington and to the Chinese Legation; orders were finally received by the immigration officials in San Francisco to land these men on bonds. After incurring an expense of more than one hundred and fifty dollars in perfecting their bonds, they were permitted to leave the shed and go on their way "rejoicing" and breathing the "sweet air of liberty." This was the treatment they received when they accepted America's invitation to participate in the World's Fair. . . .

It is well known that the discourteous treatment of merchants and students by immigration officials was the principal cause of the boycott of American products in China in 1905. Although this boycott was shortly suppressed by the Chinese Government, it was an expression of the bad feeling which had arisen between the two countries because of violation of the treaty and accumulated sense of injustice.[10] Thirty years ago there were nearly 200 Chinese students in the United States pursuing their education; when they returned to China they became leaders of the people and reported that the Americans were a friendly and honorable nation. But since the passage of the Geary law especially, students of all grades except post-graduate have been excluded. They go to other countries, and when they return to China do not speak favorably of the United States; and those who have received indignities in America have also returned home full of resentment, and urge their countrymen to resist the violation of the treaty. . . .

Chinese laborers of all classes have been excluded from the United States by mutual agreement, and the Chinese themselves are not now asking for any change in this arrangement; but they do ask for as fair treatment as other nationalities receive in relation to the exempt classes. Since the first restriction law was passed the United States has received as immigrants more than two million Austro-Hungarians, two million Italians and a million and a half Russians and Finns. Each of these totals is from five to seven times the whole amount of Chinese immigration of all classes during thirty years of free immigration, seventy times the amount of immigration of the Chinese who were not laborers. Even if the number of the exempts under a just interpretation of the treaty should rise to 10,000 in one year, it would still be less than one one-hundredth of the total immigration to the United States in one year. During the fiscal year 1907 there came to the United States from Europe 1,280,000 immigrants; whereas, during the thirty years of free Chinese im-

---

10. In the summer of 1905, at the urging of overseas Chinese, tens of thousands of people in more than twenty cities and towns in China launched a boycott against American goods to protest the abusive enforcement of the Chinese Exclusion Act. Ng Poon Chew took a strong stand in support of the boycott and did his part to help fundraise among the Chinese in America. Although the boycott was suppressed by the Qing government in 1906, it did succeed in decreasing the volume of American exports to China and influencing President Theodore Roosevelt to issue an executive order to put a stop to the Chinese immigration abuses.

migration, the largest number of Chinese found at any one time in the United States was one hundred and fifty thousand.

The question is not now of the admission of laborers, but whether other Chinese who are entitled to come under both law and treaty shall receive the same courtesies as people of other nations, and shall be relieved from many harassing regulations. They must no longer be detained, photographed and examined as if they were suspected of crime. Americans desire to build up a large trade with the Orient, but they can scarcely expect to succeed if the United States Government continues to sanction the illegal and unfriendly treatment of Chinese subjects. President Roosevelt has said that if the United States expects justice it must do justice to the Chinese, and certainly the Americans cannot expect to obtain the trade of the Orient by treating the Chinese with discourtesy. . . .

SOURCE: Ng Poon Chew, "The Treatment of the Exempt Classes of Chinese in the United States: A Statement from the Chinese in America," pamphlet, San Francisco, *Chung Sai Yat Po,* 1908.

OTHER REFERENCES

Corinne K. Hoexter, *From Canton to California: The Epic of Chinese Immigration* (New York: Four Winds Press, 1976).

Erika Lee, *At America's Gate: Chinese Immigration during the Exclusion Era, 1882–1943* (Chapel Hill: University of North Carolina Press, 2002).

Delbert L. McKee, *Chinese Exclusion versus the Open Door Policy, 1900–1906* (Detroit: Wayne University Press, 1977).

Lucy E. Salyer, *Laws Harsh as Tigers: Chinese Immigrants and the Shaping of Modern Immigration Law* (Chapel Hill: University of North Carolina Press, 1995).

Detention in the
Wooden Building (1910)

In 1910 a new immigration station was built at Angel Island in San Francisco Bay expressly to accommodate Chinese and other Asians immigrating to the United States. For the next thirty years, until a fire destroyed the station in 1940, approximately 175,000 Chinese immigrants passed through Angel Island, where they were singled out for long detentions and intense cross-examinations to prove their right to enter the country according to the Chinese Exclusion Act. A number of the Chinese detainees left poems that they wrote or carved into the barrack walls, recording their journey to America, their longing for families back home, and their outrage and humiliation at their mistreatment in the muk-uk *(wooden building).*

The following poem was not written on the barrack walls but sent by a Chinese detainee to the Chinese World *newspaper,[1] where it was published on March 16, 1910. It is the earliest and longest extant poem expressing the Chinese response to their detainment at Angel Island. Similar to other poems that have been found at Angel Island, it was written in the classical style and rich with references to heroic figures who had overcome adversity. Reflecting the strong feelings of Chinese nationalism at the time, the newspaper exhorted its readers to help restore China's wealth and glory and thereby wipe out the humiliation suffered by the Chinese at Angel Island. Interestingly, fifteen lines that advocated the overthrow of the Qing dynasty and restoration of Han Chinese rule were deleted from the poem, most likely because the newspaper supported reform, rather than obliteration, of Qing rule.[2] A year later, the same poem in its entirety*

1. The *Chinese World* newspaper was founded as the weekly *Mon Hing Bo* in 1891. It was given its English name, *Chinese World*, when the Baohuanghui, or Chinese Reform Party, gained control of the newspaper in 1899. It began publishing daily in 1901, and its Chinese name was changed to *Sai Gai Yat Po* in 1908.

2. The Manchus conquered China in 1644 and ruled as the Qing dynasty until they were overthrown by Sun Yat-sen's Revolutionary Party in 1911.

One of many Chinese poems still visible at Angel Island today. (Photo by
Chris Huie)

appeared in the Xinning Magazine, *which was intended for the emigrant community in Taishan District. According to the editor's note at the end of this version, the
poem was published to arouse the sympathy and appreciation of the sons of overseas
Chinese so that they would not squander their fathers' hard-earned money. There were
also minor textual differences between the two versions. We have chosen to translate
and reprint the* Xinning *version here.*

My mind often recalls Su Wu who, in maintaining his unyielding
    loyalty to the Han Dynasty, would rather endure the biting
    snow in the freezing frontier,[3]
And the King of Yue who, in reminding himself to seek revenge
    against the State of Wu, would sleep on firewood and lick the
    bitter gall bladder.[4]

3. During the Western Han dynasty, Su Wu (140–60 B.C.) was sent by the Chinese government as envoy to the Xiongnu, a nomadic people north of the Chinese empire. Detained there
for nineteen years, he refused to renounce his loyalty to the Han emperor.

4. Goujian was king of the state of Yue (in the present province of Zhejiang). In 494 B.C.
he was ignominiously defeated by King Fucha's armies from the state of Wu. Two decades later,
Yue recovered and returned to defeat Wu. During Yue's recovery period, it was alleged that
King Goujian slept on firewood and tasted gall bladder in order not to forget the bitterness
and humiliation of his defeat.

Our ancestors have met adversities;
They have overcome hardships;
Their trials and tribulations are duly recognized in the history
     books.

Showing their might before the barbarians,
     Calming the anxiety within themselves—
That would resolve my life-long yet unfilled ambitions.
And yet,
My generation is indeed unlucky;
Our lives have been most unfortunate.
We drift like tumbleweed in a foreign country;
And suffer the fate of detention as in Youli.[5]

When we bade farewell to our village home,
We were in tears because of survival's desperation.
When we arrived in the American territory,
We stared in vain at the vast ocean.
Our ship docked
And we were transferred to a solitary island.
Ten *li*[6] from the city,
My feet stand on this lonely hill.
The *muk-uk* is three stories high,
Built as firmly as the Great Wall.
Room after room are but jails,
And the North Gate firmly locked.

Here—
Several hundreds of my countrymen are like fish caught in a net;
Half a thousand Yellow Race are like birds trapped in a mesh.
As we lift our heads and look afar,
The barbarian reed pipes all the more add to our anguish and
     grief.
As we cock our ear and try to listen,
The horses' neighing further worsens our solitude and sorrow.

During the day, we endure a meal of crackers and cheese,
     Just like Yan Hui eating rice and water;[7]

---

5. King Wen (ca. 12th century B.C.), founder of the Zhou state, was held captive at Youli because the last Shang king regarded him as a potential threat to his rule. His son, King Wu, later defeated the Shang and established the Zhou dynasty.

6. One *li* is approximately one-third of a mile.

7. Yan Hui (521–490 B.C.), the poorest of Confucius's disciples, ate very simply and yet was content.

At night, we wrap ourselves in a single blanket,
    Just like Min Qian wearing clothes made of rush.[8]
We wash in the morning in salty tidal water;
We drink murky water to quench our thirst.[9]
In this newly open facility
Neither land nor water is in harmony with us.
Drinking the water makes many cough;
Eating the meal causes many to have sore throats.
A hundred ailments come about;
Our pain and sufferings are beyond words!

At times the barbarians would become angry with us,
They kick and punch us severely.
By chance, in their sudden cruel moment,
They would point their guns at us.
They scrutinize us like Prince Qin inspecting his soldiers;[10]
They trap us with schemes like Han Xin's multiple levels of
    encirclement.[11]
Brothers cannot share words, separated by faraway mountains;
Relatives cannot comfort each other, divided by the distant
    horizon.[12]
Inside this room—
    Neither Heaven nor Earth answers my cries.
Outside this prison
    A hundred birds chirp in grief in the mournful woods.
    A thousand animals run in fright among gloomy clouds
        and mist.
This is indeed living with nature, amidst trees, rocks, deer, and
    wild boars!

Alas! Heaven!
So desolate is this sight

8. Min Ziqian (536–487 B.C.), or Min Sun, a disciple of Confucius, was treated cruelly by his stepmother when he was young. She used to clothe him in rushes, which failed to keep out the winter cold.

9. At the time, the immigration station did not have any freshwater tanks. Drinking water came from a spring, which at one point contained traces of fecal contamination (letter from Acting Commissioner L. C. Steward to the Commissioner General of Immigration, December 19, 1910).

10. Li Shimin was a general before he became the second emperor of the Tang dynasty (A.D. 627–649).

11. Han Xin (d. 196 B.C.) was an important general who served the first emperor of the Han dynasty.

12. Chinese detainees were not allowed visitors for fear of collusion before the immigration interrogation.

It is disheartening indeed.
Sorrow and hardship have led me to this place;
What more can I say about life?
Worse yet,
A healthy person would become ill after repeated medical
    examinations;
A private inspection would render a clothed person naked.
Let me ask you, the barbarians:
    Why are you treating us in such extreme?
I grieve for my fellow countrymen;
    There is really nothing we can do!

All the tall bamboo from Zhongnan Mountain cannot inscribe
    our words of frustration.[13]
All the water in the Eastern Sea will not cleanse our sense of
    humiliation.
Perhaps, we can be—
Like Emperor Min of Jin who didn't reject the shame of wearing
    a blue garb and serving wine,[14]
Like Li Ling who pounded his chest in agony for his Han army
    surrendering to the Huns.[15]
Our ancestors have encountered such misfortune—
Why does our present generation endure the same?
In a moment of desperation,
    What more can one say?
In waiting with concealed weapons for the right moment to
    arrive—
    It is nothing but pure fantasy.

Alas,
Such tyranny of the White Race!
Such tragedy of the Yellow Souls!
Like a homeless dog forced into a confining cage,
Like a trapped pig held in a bamboo cage,
Our spirits are lost in this wintry prison;
    We are worse than horses and cattle.

13. This idea is taken from a proverb, which alludes to crimes so numerous they will not
fit on slips made from all the bamboo in the Zhongnan Mountains. The ancient Chinese often
wrote on bamboo slips.
14. In A.D. 316 Emperor Min of the Jin dynasty was captured by the Xiongnu and forced
to perform such humiliating acts as serving wine to the victors.
15. Li Ling (d. 74 B.C.), a Han general, led an army of foot soldiers against the Xiongnu.
After fighting against great odds, he was forced to surrender.

Our tears shed on an icy day,
   We are less than the birds and fowls.

In my exile to the ocean's end,
I have found enjoyment in reading newspapers.
It is said that
My old country, my native soil—
   Split apart like pea pods
   Cut up like melons.
I mourn that
My motherland, my native culture—
   Swallowed by wolves,
   Digested by the tigers.

It is my wish:
Someone like Chen She will drop the ploughs on the field,[16]
Someone like Tian Heng will raise the righteous banner,[17]
And pick up the weapons—
Leveling the State of Qin,
Wiping out the State of Wu.

Just take a look at China today:
We the Han people must take over.
Otherwise—
We will be butchered;
We will be enslaved;
We will be subjugated.
There is a difference between the true ruler and the imposter.[18]

How can we bear witness:
Four hundred million Chinese people, again, enslaved by other
    nations?

---

16. Chen She (d. 208 B.C.) led the first large-scale peasant rebellion recorded in Chinese history, against the Qin imperial government in 209 B.C. His forces soon expanded from nine hundred to several tens of thousands as he proclaimed himself a royal sovereign. However, he was defeated by a Qin army and subsequently assassinated by his chariot driver, who chose to surrender to the foe.

17. Tian Heng (d. 202 B.C.) was a descendant of the nobility in the state of Qi that was absorbed into the Qin empire. Toward the end of the Qin dynasty, he and his cousin led many former soldiers of Qi in a revolt to reestablish the state of Qi. However, he was defeated by the Han and fled with five hundred followers to an island. Soon afterward, the Han emperor summoned him to Luoyang, where he killed himself. When his followers on the island heard the news, they all committed suicide.

18. This is a critique of the inept rule of the Qing government in power at the time.

Five thousand years of civilization, like in India, obliterated?[19]
We feel grievious,
How can we suppress our cries?

SOURCE: *Xinning Zazhi* 28 (1911): 76–78. Translator: Marlon K. Hom.

OTHER REFERENCES

Him Mark Lai, Genny Lim, and Judy Yung, *Island: Poetry and History of Chinese Immigrants on Angel Island, 1910–1940* (San Francisco: HOC-DOI, 1980).

19. During this period when China was threatened by foreign powers, Chinese patriots often used India, which was then ruled by the British, as an example to alert their countrymen to the threat of foreign aggression against China's sovereignty.

Letter Asking for Support to Build the Sunning Railroad (1911)

Chin Gee Hee

In 1911, when the following letter was written to the Chinese Six Companies for help, Chin Gee Hee was halfway to completing a railroad line in Sunning, now Taishan District, that was to bring industrial and commercial prosperity to the region. It was a dream born and nurtured in Seattle, Washington, where Chin had become a successful businessman and labor contractor. A native of Taishan, home province of most Chinese who had immigrated to America, he had hoped that the Sunning railroad would facilitate transportation and trade within Taishan and eventually connect the region to the rest of China, Southeast Asia, and Europe.

Chin Gee Hee was born in Langmei Village in 1844. Although he came from a poor family, he found a way to emigrate to the United States as a young man. Settling in Port Gamble, Washington, he worked as a laborer, launderer, and cook at a lumber mill before moving in 1873 to Seattle, where he started the Quong Tuck Company, a general store that recruited laborers for the railroads. As a labor contractor and general agent for all the Pacific steamship companies, Chin took an active part in helping to develop the transportation system in Washington. Thus, he came to understand the importance of modern transportation to the development of China.

In 1904 Chin Gee Hee founded the Sunning Railroad Company with fellow Taishanese Yu Cheuk. The two men were successful in raising $1.4 million by selling shares at $2.50 each to overseas Chinese in North America, Australia, Singapore, and Hong Kong. He returned to Taishan to oversee construction of the railroad in 1906. Within three years, he managed to lay thirty-one miles of tracks, linking Doushan to Taishan City and Gongyi, at a cost of $2.7 million. Needing another $1.3 million to complete the second section from Gongyi to Jiangmen, he sent the following letter of appeal to the Chinese Six Companies in San Francisco.

Dear Sirs:

Our company is undertaking the construction of the Jiangmen extension of the Sunning Railroad. Survey work began during the eleventh lunar month

125

Chin Gee Hee at work in Seattle, Washington. (University of Washington Libraries, Special Collections, A. Curtis 1281)

of last year. To date foundation has been laid up to Fenshuijiang, and, in another seven miles or so, we will reach the city of Xinhui. Tracks are currently laid up to Dawang City. The stretch from Gongyi to the Niuwan coast is already open to construction vehicles. The Xinhui City segment will probably be finished before the year is over or by next spring. As for the segment from Xinhui City to Jiangmen and Baishi, the plan is to begin survey and testing at the beginning of the seventh lunar month. The entire line will be completed around the Duanwu Festival [5th day of the 5th lunar month][1] next year and open for trains.

However, the whole extension measures eighty to ninety miles, and up to

1. Also known as the Dragon Boat Festival, the day is rooted in fertility rites to ensure abundant rainfall in South China and is celebrated with dragon boat races and offerings of *joong* (rice wrapped in bamboo leaves) in honor of China's renowned poet and patriot Qu Yuan.

$1.2 or $1.3 million is needed. The stock offering this time, which began in the eighth lunar month last year, only netted slightly more than $300,000, and that included out-of-town sales. The shortfall is quite large and our need for money is desperate. Previously when we sold shares to raise capital for the Sunning Railroad, we amassed over $2 million in a few months. What is the reason for the earlier enthusiasm and the current apathy? I wonder if it is because the overseas Chinese are unfamiliar with China's way of conducting business and might have been deceived by false rumors, or been led astray by mischief makers, and, as a consequence, a lot of misgivings are keeping potential shareholders away.[2] That would indeed be most unfortunate. Yours truly, who is in charge of the project, has taken on a heavy responsibility, and, without the necessary capital, is like the proverbial good wife who cannot produce a meal for the lack of rice. Earlier this month I traveled to Hong Kong for a fundraising meeting. Fortunately, the various [Taishanese] business leaders stationed in or visiting Hong Kong, who understood what was at stake and who were interested in the public good, each offered a loan of $5,000. In a few days we had pledges of over $100,000. Once again construction materials could be purchased. This was a favorable development for the railroad project, for which I am eternally grateful. However, the money is really a loan, with an agreed-upon interest rate of 8 percent per month, to be repaid at the end of one year. Those who would like to convert their loans into shares can do so if they wish. Other ways of securing loans and soliciting contributions would invariably involve all kinds of complications. That is why this enthusiastic response by our Taishan compatriots is rare, like a piece of perfect jade. However, this is a stopgap measure and by no means perfect. We still need to intensify our efforts in getting enough shareholders to meet our goal of $1.2 or $1.3 million. Only then can we rest assured.

I am hereby forwarding to you the agreement reached in Hong Kong to be made available for public perusal, and to be sent to other associations. And I am including a serious plea to all you gentlemen to publicize in the newspapers the fundraising efforts for this present project to extend the Sunning Railroad to Jiangmen, in the hope that our overseas clansmen will be moved to come forward and help. Everyone knows the benefits the railroad will bring, and if we can clarify the misunderstandings so that everyone will work together, it will not be difficult to build a mountain from earth, and form a river from streams. Our problem lies in our lack of leadership to dis-

---

2. Rumors had been spreading among the local Taishanese that the railroad would harm the natural environment and the people's livelihood. In addition, Chin Gee Hee had been criticized for poor management and not keeping his word to rely only on Chinese capital to build the railroad. However, he had not anticipated the hefty bribes he had had to pay government officials for permission to build and run the railroad; as a result, he had been forced to borrow from foreign banks.

pel the existing misconceptions. My company has proposed that as soon as we raise $4 million, the old shares from the Sunning Railroad included, we will stop issuing any more stocks. We hope that you gentlemen will do your best to help advance this project and persuade your clansmen to buy shares now so as to avoid disappointment when they are no longer available.

We wish you gentlemen at the Chinese Six Companies good health and success.

Your humble servant,
Chin Gee Hee
Tenth day of the sixth lunar month [1911]

After receiving Chin Gee Hee's letter, the Chinese Six Companies responded by encouraging overseas Chinese to invest in the Sunning Railroad. The railroad, totaling eighty-two miles and costing $4.8 million, was completed in 1920. Although it did shorten traveling time and lowered shipping costs, it failed to bring prosperity to Taishan. Throughout the 1920s, the operation was plagued by bandits, unpredictable foreign markets, political wars, and extortion. In the end, Chin was unable to raise the necessary funds or political support to connect the Sunning Railroad to China's other railroad lines, and thereby realize his dream of transforming Taishan into a commercial center. Moreover, in 1926 the Nationalist regime in Guangzhou, using labor-management disputes in the company as a pretext, ousted Chin from the management and took over control of the railroad. The ousted Chin suffered a partial mental breakdown and died in his birthplace, Langmei Village, in 1929. A decade later, with the onset of war, the Chinese government ordered all local railroads, including the Sunning Railroad, be dismantled to stop the advancement of Japanese troops. It was never rebuilt, but in 1984, a statue of Chin Gee Hee was restored in the town square of Taishan City to commemorate a native son's loyalty and contribution to his homeland.

SOURCE: Liu Pei Chi, *Meiguo Huaqiao shi, xu bian* [A history of the Chinese in the United States of America, vol. 2] (Taipei: Liming Wenhua Shiye Gufen Youxian Gongsi, 1981), pp. 266–67. Translator: Ellen Yeung.

OTHER REFERENCES

Lucie Cheng, Yuzun Liu, and Dehua Zheng, "Chinese Emigration: The Sunning Railroad and the Development of Toisan," *Amerasia Journal* 9, no. 1 (1982): 59–74.

Madeline Hsu, *Dreaming of Gold, Dreaming of Home: Transnationalism and Migration between the United States and South China, 1882–1943* (Stanford: Stanford University Press, 2000).

Willard Jue, "Chin Gee Hee, Chinese Pioneer Entrepreneur in Seattle and Toishan," *The Annals of the Chinese Historical Society of the Pacific Northwest*, 1983, pp. 31–38.

Ruthanne Lum McCunn, "Chin Gee-hee, Railroad Baron," in *Chinese American Portraits: Personal Histories, 1828–1988* (San Francisco: Chronicle Books, 1988), pp. 47–55.

Admission of Wives of American Citizens of Oriental Ancestry (1926)

Chinese-American Citizens' Alliance

In response to growing nativism and anti-Japanese agitation, Congress passed the Immigration Act of 1924. Also known as the National Origins Act, it was aimed at excluding "undesirable" immigrants, namely Southern and Eastern Europeans and all aliens ineligible for citizenship—a category that applied only to those of Asian descent. Thus Chinese alien wives of both U.S. citizens and merchants who had previously been admitted into the United States were deemed "undesirables." Not only were Chinese men having a hard time finding wives in America because of the skewed sex ratio and prohibitions against interracial marriages between Chinese and whites, but now those who already had wives in China would not be able to send for them.

Upset by this turn of events, the Chinese community challenged the new restrictions in court. On May 25, 1925, the Supreme Court ruled that Chinese alien wives and minor children of noncitizen Chinese merchants would be allowed into the country, whereas alien wives of American citizens would be excluded. This decision was particularly disturbing to the Chinese-American Citizens' Alliance (CACA), a fraternal organization that was established in 1895 to improve the sociopolitical status of the American-born Chinese. As CACA argued in the following pamphlet, all men, Chinese included, have the natural and legal right to the companionship of wives. Moreover, why should alien Chinese merchants have more rights than U.S. citizens of Chinese descent? Finally, CACA attempted to put to rest the question of assimilability of Chinese Americans by pointing to evidences of Americanization among their second-generation peers. As a result of CACA's efforts, Congress amended the law in June 1930 to permit the entry of Chinese alien wives of U.S. citizens, but only those who were married prior to May 6, 1924. It was not until after World War II, with the passage of the War Brides Act, that immigration of Chinese women increased; and not until the Immigration Act of 1965 put every nation on an equal par that sex parity among Chinese Americans was finally reached.

(This pamphlet, prepared for submission to the Committee on Immigration and Naturalization of the House of Representatives, Sixty-ninth Congress, first session, is issued by the United Parlor, Native Sons of the Golden State, Chinese-American Citizens' Alliance, an organization composed of American citizens of the Chinese race, having for its object and purpose the fostering of patriotism and good citizenship, the head offices of the organization are at 1044 Stockton Street, San Francisco, Calif. Its subordinate lodges are scattered throughout the United States.)[1]

This is a plea for relief from a hardship imposed upon a certain class of citizens of the United States by the immigration act of 1924.

The Supreme Court of the United States has recently decided that section 13 of the act excludes from admission to the United States the alien Chinese wives of American citizens.[2] There are in the United States many American citizens of the Chinese race who are married to alien Chinese women, resident in China. Under the decision of the Supreme Court these American citizens are permanently separated from their wives, unless they abandon the country of their citizenship and take up their residence abroad in a country which will permit their wives to reside with them. The hardship of this situation is so apparent that it is felt that a mere statement of the case is all that is required to show the necessity for an amendment to the act which will permit the admission of these women.

Until the passage of the act alien Chinese wives of American citizens of the Chinese race were eligible to admission to the United States. The courts had repeatedly held that they were admissible and the immigration department admitted them upon proof of their status.

It is a well-known fact that the Chinese male population of this country far outnumbers the Chinese female population and that the Chinese male resident here, desiring to marry, must in most cases go to China to seek a wife of his own race, the number of Chinese females resident here being too restricted to supply the demand. Such being the conditions obtaining, under the law as it now stands, most of our Chinese-American citizens must of necessity remain unmarried or if elected to go to China, there to marry, must either give up their residence and virtually give up their citizenship here or live separate and apart from their wives, who are debarred from admission to the United States under section 13 of the immigration act of 1924.

1. CACA was initially named the United Parlor of the Native Sons of the Golden State, but the desire to became a national organization led to the name change in 1915. Throughout Chinese American history, CACA has been instrumental in challenging discriminatory laws and policies, protecting the legal rights of Chinese Americans, and encouraging Chinese American participation in electoral politics.

2. This is in reference to *Chang Chan et al. v. Nagle,* in which the Court ruled that alien wives of American citizens were not admissible whereas alien wives of Chinese merchants were.

The only solution of the problem, the immigration act remaining un-amended, would be the marriage of the Chinese-American citizen resident here to a woman not of his own race, and this is not only undesirable and inadvisable from the viewpoint of both white and Chinese, but contrary to the laws of many of the States of the Union, the intermarriage of white persons with persons of the Mongolian race being prohibited in the States of Arizona, California, Idaho, Missouri, Utah, Wyoming, Mississippi, Oregon, Nebraska, Texas, and Virginia.

Marriage is an institution sanctioned, encouraged and fostered by civilized society and by the state. Civilized society has always recognized the right of a man to marry, and when married, his right to the society and companionship of his wife. Civilized society recognizes the fact that "it is not good for man to be alone," and that marriage and the association of a man with his wife constitute the greatest safeguard of public morals.

In all probability, when the immigration act of 1924 was being considered by Congress, the fact that section 13 of the act would prohibit the admission of the alien Chinese wives of American citizens was not called to its attention, and it is felt that, had it been, there would have been added to section 13 a proviso allowing their admission.

It is not presumed that the unnatural condition in the respect herein pointed out in which the American citizen of the Chinese race finds himself as a result of section 13 will be allowed to stand. The Supreme Court could only interpret the law as it was written by Congress. It could not disregard the literal and plain language of the law in an effort, by strained construction, to avoid its hardships upon a worthy class of American citizens which has done its duty to its country both in time of peace and in time of war.

Therefore it is from Congress that the relief must come, and it is to Congress that the American citizen of the Chinese race confidently looks for an amendment to section 13 which will give him that legal right to the companionship of his wife which is in consonance both with natural law and with the customs and usages of civilized society.

It is not deemed necessary to argue the matter further, for as was intimated at the outset of these observations, a mere statement of the case is all that is believed necessary in the presentation of this matter.

ALIEN CHINESE WIVES OF CHINESE MERCHANTS ADMISSIBLE

It might not be out of the way, however, to call attention to the fact that while the immigration act of 1924 prohibits the admission of the alien Chinese wife of an American citizen, the Supreme Court of the United States has recently held that the act permits the admission of the alien Chinese wife of an alien Chinese merchant, who is resident in the United States. In other words, the act gives greater rights to the alien Chinese resident here than it accords to our own citizens of the Chinese race. It is submitted that an American citizen in his own country should certainly be accorded rights at least equal to those given to an alien resident here.

THE AMENDMENT SUGGESTED

Subdivision (c) of section 13 of the immigration act of 1924 reads as follows:

> (c) No alien ineligible to citizenship shall be admitted to the United States unless such an alien (1) is admissible as a nonquota immigrant under the provisions of subdivision (b), (d) or (e) of section 4 or (2) is the wife, or the unmarried child under 18 years of age, of an immigrant admissible under such subdivision (d), and is accompanying or following to join him, or (3) is not an immigrant as defined in section 3.

It is requested that there be added by amendment a fourth clause to subdivision (c), to read substantially as follows: "or (4) is the wife of a citizen of the United States."

Such an amendment would give to the American citizen of the Chinese race the same right to the admission to this country of his wife which he always enjoyed and to which he was entitled prior to the passage of the immigration act of 1924, which right was taken away from him by that act.

SUPPLEMENT

There are now pending in Congress two bills—one, S. 2358, and the other, H.R. 6544, identical in language, amendatory in the immigration act of 1924, designed to relieve the situation of hardship referred to in the foregoing "Plea for Relief." Under this proposed amendatory legislation, the alien wives ineligible to citizenship of citizens of the United States would have restored to them the right of admission to the United States. This right of admission existed until July 1, 1924, and was recognized under the so-called Chinese exclusion laws.

The humane aspect of this proposed amendment to the immigration law can not, we assume, be questioned, for the unnatural hardship of the permanent separation of an American citizen from his wife is so apparent as not to require discussion. The home is the basis of the life of the nation, and without a wife and mother a home can hardly exist. A law permanently separating a husband from his wife is an unnatural law, contrary to common humanity and the institutions of civilized society, and indefensible from the standpoint of morality, and it is submitted that such a law has no place upon the statute books of any civilized country. . . .

This brings us to the consideration, whether any valid reason exists why the relief afforded in the proposed amendment should not be granted in view of the admitted principle that—

"Our Government owes its first duty to our own people and that no alien, inhabitant of another country, has any legal rights whatever under our Constitution and laws."

The Government's first duty is to our own citizens, but it is to our own citizens that the relief accruing under these bills is to be afforded. Those of our citizens who have wives of the class referred to are as much citizens of our country as those whose wives are of the Caucasian race, and shall we deny to them the companionship of their wives and the comforts of a home, and to their children, who by law are American citizens, the fostering care of a mother's love?

ASSIMILABILITY

It has been suggested that in allowing these alien wives, ineligible to citizenship, a home with their husbands in this country, we are permitting a multiplication in this country of Orientals not assimilable with Americans, as are other races. Is this true? This brings us to the question of assimilability. Does the child of the Chinese race, born and reared in this country, assimilate American thoughts and customs and ideas? In other words, does he become and is he a real American, speaking our language, following our customs, living as we live, and thinking as we think, and true to his duty as an American citizen?

The mere answering of these questions abstractly in the affirmative—and the facts of the case not only admit of, but require such an answer—can hardly convey to those who have not come in contact with the American born child of Chinese parentage as true and clear an impression of the situation as a few concrete typical illustrations would afford. Therefore, there are submitted in the pages which follow, a few cuts, showing typical groups of Chinese American families, that is, families whose alien Chinese parents emigrated to this country from China, and have here given birth to and here reared their families. These illustrations could be multiplied indefinitely, but a few typical illustrations it is believed will suffice. These children, born and reared here, speak the English language, were educated or are being educated in our public schools and colleges, wear the American dress, follow American customs, live in homes as typically American as do Caucasian children, and being surrounded by the same environment as Caucasian children, grow up with the same ideas and follow the same pursuits as Caucasians and are in every respect true Americans, loyal to their country and an asset to the State.

A HISTORICAL VIEW

In the days of anti-Chinese agitation on the Pacific coast, preceding and for a time following the enactment of Chinese exclusion legislation, the Chinese residents here were in effect an outcast people, suffering humiliation, persecution and social ostracism, and naturally their children born here were reared under such circumstances as to make assimilation by them of American customs and thoughts and ideas, and perhaps even speech, practically impossible and not to be expected. But as time has gone on, the people of the Pacific coast, satisfied with the existing exclusion legislation and its economic results, have unconsciously tempered and humanized their views with respect to their Chinese population, and the Chinese children born here, reared under more pleasant surroundings, and not subjected to that humiliation and persecution and ostracism which in the earlier days obtained, have had opened to them the opportunities for Americanization, which they have most readily accepted and imbibed. No longer denied the advantages of our public schools, colleges, and universities, with the opportunities for religious, recreational, and proper social life opened to them, treated humanly by the Caucasians with whom they come in contact, they have developed into true Americans. They look upon this country of their birth as their country, having no dual allegiance, and speak, dress, think, work and act as Americans.

Having in view the American born Chinese child of the present day, the old idea of nonassimilability must fall, when the conditions which now exist are presented and considered.

But adherents to the old view, in support of their theory of nonassimilation, bring up the subject of intermarriage. Intermarriage between persons of the Caucasian and Chinese races is considered inadvisable and unwise by Caucasians and Chinese alike, but intermarriage has nothing to do with assimilation by persons of the Chinese race of American customs and ideas, or with the question whether a Chinese child born and reared here becomes in every respect a true American. We have in this country a large Jewish population, which has come to this country from Europe and which includes many of our most eminent Americans and some of our best citizens. Intermarriage between the Jew and the Gentile is very rare, and yet no one would contend that because the Jews rarely marry outside their own race they lack one element of assimilability.

Religion and intermarriage have nothing to do with the issue of assimilability.

CASE OF FAMILY OF SING KEE, SAN JOSE, CALIF.

Father and mother born in China. Oldest son, also called Sing Kee, born Saratoga, Calif.; served in United States Army in France, being awarded

Distinguished-Service Cross; Army citation accompanying same reading as follows:

"For extraordinary heroism in action at Monte Notre Dame, west Fismes, France, August 14–15, 1918. Although seriously gassed during shelling by high explosive and gas shells, he refused to be evacuated and continued, practically single-handed, by his own initiative, to operate the regimental message center relay station at Monte Notre Dame. Throughout this critical period he showed extraordinary heroism, high courage, and persistent devotion to duty, and totally disregarded all personal danger. By his determination he materially aided his regimental commander in communicating with the front line."

Fortunately he and his wife arrived in the United States June 16, 1924, and she was admitted. If his wife had arrived after July 1, 1924, she would not have been admissible. He is now an interpreter in the United States Immigration Service in New York.

CASE OF PAUL YEE OF OAKLAND, CALIF.

Birth place, San Francisco; occupation, drayman. Educated in Berkeley and Oakland. Father and mother born in China; came to United States about 40 years ago. Father died in California, mother living with Paul Yee. Paul Yee owns his own home and other real property in Oakland. Paul Yee went to China in 1924 and there married Jee Shee, arriving in the United States with her July 23, 1924, less than one month after the immigration act of 1924 went into effect. Jee Shee was consequently denied admission by the immigration authorities and is now at liberty temporarily on bond and living with her husband in Oakland, where she had a son born to her on February 3, 1926. A number of other women, wives of Chinese-American citizens, who arrived in the United States after July 1, 1924, are also temporarily at liberty on bond. Are these women to be torn from their husbands?

AS TO HOW MANY PERSONS WOULD BE AFFECTED BY THE PROPOSED AMENDMENT

It is impossible to state exactly how many persons would be affected by the proposed amendment, but the United States census of 1920 affords some basis of calculation. The "ineligible to citizenship" races in the United States consist largely of Chinese and Japanese, and of these races only such as are citizens of the United States are affected by the proposed amendment.

The number of Chinese in the United States, according to the 1920 census, is 61,639, of which 53,891 are males and 7,748 are females. Of the total Chinese population of 61,639, 43,107 are foreign born and 18,532 native born. Of the 18,532 native-born Chinese, 13,318 are males and 5,214 females. Of the total female Chinese population of 7,748, the 1920 census shows 3,047 married and 4,302 single, 371 widowed, 15 divorced, and 13 whose marital condition is not reported. Of the 4,302 Chinese females classed as single, 3,340 were under 15 years of age at the time of the census and 962 were 15 years or over.

Adding to the 4,302 single females, the widowed (371), the divorced (15), and those whose marital conditions is not reported (13), we have a total of 4,701 Chinese females without husbands. Of this number a large proportion are children not of marriageable age and some are women practically beyond marriageable age, so that the number of Chinese women available for marriage in this country is very small and out of all proportion to the single Chinese male population, which according to the 1920 census is 27,167. The number of widowed Chinese males is given as 1,355, of divorced 66, and those unreported as to marital condition is 510. The great disparity between the male and female Chinese population is due to the fact in the early days of Chinese immigration very few Chinese females came here.

When the above figures are considered, it is apparent why the Chinese-American citizen must, in most cases, seek his wife in China. As time goes on, the situation will naturally gradually change, and the ratio between the sexes gradually equalize itself, due to the birth here of Chinese children, but until it has so equalized itself, most of our male Chinese-American citizens must either seek a wife in China or remain unmarried. This statement is made having in mind the accepted principle that it is inadvisable for a Chinese to marry outside of his own race.

The proposed amendment would, of course, also apply to American citizens of the Japanese race, but practically its field of operation among the Japanese would be very small, almost negligible, for most of the Japanese unmarried males in the United States are alien Japanese, whose wives when such Japanese marry would not be admissible under the proposed amendment. The total Japanese population of the country is given in the 1920 census as 111,010 made up of 72,707 males and 38,303 females. Of the total Japanese population, 20,672 are classed as native born, 15,404 being males and 14,178 being females, and only 658 native-born Japanese were 21 years or over at the time of the census. It will be seen, therefore, that the native-born Japanese in the country—and the proposed amendment could apply to no others—are largely children, and the sexes being almost equally divided, this class will practically take care of itself in the matter of marriage.

SOURCE: *Hearings before the Committee on Immigration and Naturalization,* House of Representatives, 69th Congress, 1st Session, February 16, 1926 (Washington, D.C.: Government Printing Office, 1926), pp. 38–42.

OTHER REFERENCES

Sucheng Chan, "The Exclusion of Chinese Women, 1870–1943," in *Entry Denied: Exclusion and the Chinese Community in America, 1882–1943*, ed. Sucheng Chan (Philadelphia: Temple University Press, 1991), pp. 94–146.

Sue Fawn Chung, "The Chinese American Citizens Alliance: An Effort in Assimilation, 1895–1965," *Chinese America: History and Perspectives*, 1988, pp. 30–57.

Mae Ngai, *Impossible Subjects: Illegal Aliens and the Making of Modern America* (Princeton: Princeton University Press, 2004).

Xiaojian Zhao, *Remaking Chinese America: Immigration, Family, and Community, 1940–1965* (New Brunswick, N.J.: Rutgers University Press, 2002).

"Just plain old luck and good timing"

Reminiscences of a Gold Mountain Man (1988)

Gong Yuen Tim

The following memoir was written in Chinese by Gong Yuen Tim for his children in 1988 on the sixth anniversary of his wife's passing. It was discovered by historian Him Mark Lai when he interviewed Gong in 1990. Lai promptly had it translated and published in Chinese America: History and Perspectives, *the annual journal of the Chinese Historical Society of America. With minor editing, we have included it in this anthology as a rare firsthand account of one Chinese immigrant's struggles to succeed in America.*

In 1920 Gong Yuen Tim left his young bride, Low Hop Yee, in Huaxian, Guangdong Province, and emigrated to the United States. In 1931, after working as a laundryman for eleven years and after Congress amended the Immigration Act of 1924 to admit Chinese wives of U.S. citizens, he was finally able to bring her to America. Like many other Huaxian immigrants, they entered the produce business and later operated a supermarket in California's Central Valley. They also raised a family of seven children.

Throughout his detailed and at times touching memoir, Gong attributes his success to hard work, luck, and Bodhisattva's blessings. But as his story reveals, he also had the benefit of a supportive family and kin network, reminding us of the importance of ethnic solidarity for the early Chinese immigrants and the advantages of having a devoted wife by one's side in Gold Mountain. Aside from being hardworking and resourceful throughout his life, Gong was known to be a loving husband and father as well as a respected member of the Chinese community. When he passed away in 2001 at the age of ninety-eight, a funeral cortege of eighty cars and three marching bands gave him a grand send-off to the Chinese cemetery in Colma, California.

COMING TO GOLD MOUNTAIN

I came from a family of poor peasant background for three generations. Like his grandfather and father before him, my father, Man Dak, farmed on ten

Gong Yuen Tim in the driver's seat, 1930. (Courtesy of Mary Gong)

mou of leased land[1] near the ancestral Lok Cheung Village in Huaxian [District]. He had seven sons and five daughters but no money. It was really a hard-luck life for everyone.

When I was eight years old, our paternal uncle Chaap Kuen sponsored Older Brother Yik Hau to come to Gold Mountain. After that, we received remittances from America and I was able to attend school for eight years. When I was fifteen years old, Yik Hau had me come to Gold Mountain as a paper son.[2] The perilous journey aboard the *Shunyo Maru* lasted for thirty-one days. I reached First City [San Francisco] in February 1921 and was detained at the [Angel Island] Immigration Station for two days.

The economy was bad when I landed; I couldn't find any work. It was not until April that year that I finally found work ironing clothes at Hop Lee Laundry. There was a rule at the laundry: a newcomer must apprentice for twenty weeks. When you were an apprentice, the laundry fed you, but you didn't get paid. After that you would become a regular worker. I endured those 140 days before I began to earn ten dollars a week.

In 1923 the Hop Lee partners, all ten of them, saw that I had been a hard

1. One *mou* equals 733½ square yards; 6.6 *mou* equal one acre.
2. During the exclusion period, many Chinese immigrated by assuming bogus identities as sons of merchants or U.S. citizens.

worker. Besides that, I was the only person at Hop Lee with a driver's license. Hence they made me a partner; I was in charge of pick-up and delivery. We kept our books on the laundry this way: Each Saturday evening we tabulated the income and expenses. We would divide whatever amount we made into eleven shares. Our earnings varied weekly—sometimes each of us cleared twenty or thirty dollars; sometimes only a few dimes! At any rate, I calculated my total 1923 earnings to be less than $500.

SENDING FOR MY WIFE

By 1928 I was twenty-three years old and had been in America for eight years. I wanted to return home to China for a visit. I taught a partner to drive in order to take care of the pick-up and delivery. Then I prepared for my home-bound journey. I had saved, including the coins in my pants pockets, only $450. I spent $85 on a boat ticket and, through a lawyer, over $10 for an exit permit. In addition, I made out a money order for $1,000 in Hong Kong dollars so that I would have money for my return fare from Hong Kong. At that time, the exchange rate was U.S. $1 to $5.70 in Hong Kong currency. So I spent U.S. $175 for that money order. I also bought a Western suit for $30, and a pair of leather shoes for $3. After all these expenditures, I only had a little over $100 left in my pocket. Yet I went home "triumphantly" with that much cash on hand!

I reached home on the fifteenth day of the eighth lunar month in 1928. Two weeks later I had a benediction banquet and invited all my friends and relatives for a feast. While everyone was having a wonderful time, I was counting how much money I had left—less than $100! I racked my brain trying to figure out what to do from then on. I figured that if I avoided all socializing by returning to school for perhaps a year with Mr. Yim Geng of the Lik Bui Village, I could save whatever I had left. I kept this game plan to myself and didn't share it with anyone.

I returned to Gold Mountain in February 1930 and had to work like a mule all over again. I had planned to return to the States with my wife.[3] However, the laws barred wives of [Chinese] American citizens from immigrating. In 1931, the Chinese-American Citizens' Alliance spent $5,000 on an attorney to file a lawsuit against United States Immigration. They won, and the law against the immigration of wives was lifted. I immediately applied for a visa to visit China again. However, I was flat broke. So I borrowed $400 from Uncle Wah Fong and commissioned a lawyer to file a petition for me to return to China to bring my wife over. I quickly prepared a "coaching

---

3. Lau Hop Yee was married to Gong Yuen Tim at the tender age of thirteen. Three weeks after their marriage, Gong took off for America.

book," and sent it to my wife, telling her to memorize the contents well.[4] As soon as I got back to China again, I went to the American consulate in Hong Kong and filed all the necessary papers. It took many rounds of running back and forth. Finally, everything was completed and I took my wife to Hong Kong. A week later we set sail for the United States.

Upon our arrival in First City, my wife was detained at the Angel Island Immigration Station for processing. She made several mistakes and was denied entry by the immigration office. She was about to be deported, but fortunately she was into the sixth month of her pregnancy. The deportation was delayed. Immediately I talked to my lawyer and spent $300 on bribes. (Naturally I borrowed from Uncle Wah Fong again. So now I owed him a total of $700.) Finally, my wife was released after spending a total of thirty-nine days at the Immigration Station. I took her to our home, which I had rented earlier. It was a one-bedroom apartment located a few buildings across from Hop Lee Laundry [at 538 Jackson Street]. The rent was nine dollars a month, including water, electricity, and garbage. We settled down at last.

SELLING RICE WINE ON THE SIDE

My son Leung was born on March 16, 1932. His birth cost me twenty-five dollars. I had saved up, so I knew I could handle it. However, Mrs. Yeung, our landlady, was so delighted by the birth of my son that she suggested I should have a "ginger and red egg" party for Leung's one-month-old celebration. At that time a banquet table cost twenty dollars; I couldn't afford that kind of luxury. Knowing that I was poor, Mrs. Yeung told me to buy two dozen eggs, which cost fifteen cents per dozen, a bottle of ginger pickled in vinegar, and a bottle of red dye. She helped me cook the eggs and colored them red. Afterward, I took them over to my co-workers at Hop Lee, announcing the birth of my son. My ten partners each gave a quarter in a *leisi!*[5] As I look back at those days, I shiver and wonder how I ever got through.

Mrs. Yeung also suggested to my wife that since times were tough, she would show her how to make rice wine in order to earn some money. Our son Leung was one year old and she couldn't find any work. Well, she tried to sew at Ou Lei Sewing Shop one block from our apartment. She took Leung to the shop with her. For two weeks, she made five dollars and twenty cents. As for myself, I only made a little over a dollar a day. Making wine was a better option. Mrs. Yeung had done it herself some few years earlier. Now that her husband was making a good living working in the lottery business, she had stopped making rice wine. However, she still had all the equipment.

4. Coaching books provided information about one's family background that immigration officials were likely to ask in the United States.

5. A red envelope for lucky money.

Mrs. Yeung told me to get a one-hundred-pound sack of ground sweet rice, which cost $1.90, and a pack of yeast cakes. She then taught my wife how to cook the rice in the kitchen, pour it into four large earthen containers, and then let it ferment for a month at the back of the apartment. Afterward the containers were heated, one by one, for about two hours; each would yield one gallon of rice wine. In one night's work we made four gallons. Our cost was about five cents per gallon.

I drove down to the Chinese shrimp camps in the southern part of the city [Hunter's Point] and sold the wine at the price of one dollar per gallon. The workers at the shrimp camps were dirt poor. They even asked for credit for a one-dollar sale.

One day I went to the Ferry Terminal [Pier No. 5] to pick up laundry. A group of Filipinos there asked if I had any Chinese rice wine for sale. I immediately recognized the jackpot for our business. I said yes and that it cost four dollars a gallon.

When I got home that evening, I took out the rice wine in gallon jugs and poured out half of the wine into another jug. I boiled some hot water, sweetened it with rock sugar, and mixed the water with the rice wine in the jug. The wine was sweet and yellowish, and the Filipinos loved it! They said, "Wow! Chinese wine tastes great! Bring us as much as you can!" With this, I cleared eight dollars per gallon! Some time later, when I was picking up laundry at the shrimp camps, the Chinese there asked me, "Ah Tim, why don't you bring us any rice wine anymore?"

I replied, "Hell, I'm now selling my wine at the price of eight dollars per gallon, cash! You choosy guys want 90 percent proof and pay only one dollar a gallon and on credit. Forget it!"

By the end of the year my wife and I had saved over $100. I told my wife, "This is your hard-earned money. Chinese New Year will be here in a few days. What would you like to get yourself for the New Year?" She said that she would like a gold coin bracelet and a jade brooch. Right away I took her to Tin Fook Jewelry Shop on Jackson Street and let her pick what she wanted. Together the bracelet and brooch cost less than $100.

A FARMHAND IN THE VALLEY

By January 1934 I was still making about a dollar a day at Hop Lee Laundry. I saw no bright future working like that. Furthermore, I still owed Uncle Wah Fong $700 and I had to think of a way to pay him back. My wife and I talked about what to do. We concluded that I should find something else. Well, talk about timing. One morning Village Brother Hoi Ping came to my place and delivered a letter from my paternal cousin Yim Hei, who had a 160-acre vegetable farm in Madera. My cousin asked me in the letter to work for him. He would pay me sixty dollars a month. In addition, he said in the letter that

my wife could also earn a dollar or so every day sorting and bundling vegetables in the barn. He would also hire my brothers Seung and Tai, who had
just arrived from China a few months earlier.

I borrowed a truck from Uncle Wah Fong and moved to Hoi Ping's farm.
We started working the next day. Seung got up, washed his face, put on his
new overalls, and asked Clan Brother Dai Gai, "Older Brother Dai Gai, what
do you want me to do today?"

Dai Gai suggested, "Why don't you drive the tractor and plow the field?
This tractor's easy to operate. Just turn on the ignition and shift into gear
with the stick shift."

Seung confidently drove off to the field. It was five o'clock in the morning and there was a cool breeze. He said, "Easy work." By ten in the morning the sun was hot; the exhaust from the tractor was hotter. It was close to
120 degrees driving the tractor. By twelve noon, he drove back for lunch and
said to me, "This is like working in hell! I might make some money, but I'd
rather skip it altogether." He refused to work the next day.

Younger Brother Tai, however, was exactly the opposite of Seung. On the
first day he asked Dai Gai to assign him some work. I said to him, "Brother
Tai, you're only fifteen years old. Relax, you'll have lots of time to earn money.
But right now I want you to go to school for at least one year before you start
working. Besides, you will get out of school by 3:30 P.M. every day. You can
work in the barn after school, bundle the vegetables, or whatever. You'll still
earn a quarter or more a day. You know, you'll learn English at school and
that will help you in the future."

Well, he attended the same school Hoi Ping's daughter Giu attended.
Every day after school he went to the barn and bundled the vegetables. Hoi
Ping then said to him, "Well, you don't go to school on Saturdays and Sundays, so why don't you work during these two days? I'll pay you a dollar a
day!" Tai was overjoyed because he was able to make an additional eight dollars a month working during the weekends, while earning a quarter or so a
day during weekdays.

So I began my hardworking days at Hoi Ping's vegetable farm. On September 14 my daughter Lai Heung was born. I delivered her. No doctor or
midwife. My wife could not work after childbirth. At night she changed di-
apers and fed the baby. I would start working at five in the morning and drive
the tractor out to the farm. My day's work ended at eleven or twelve o'clock
at night.

My second daughter, Lai Gyuen, was born on December 26, 1935. Again
I played doctor at her birth. The small house in which we lived was a forty-
dollar ready-built trailer. It was freezing cold in the winter. So I went into
town and bought a small iron stove before Lai Gyuen was born. I collected
discarded pieces of wood for firewood and burned them to keep the room
warm. Lai Gyuen was born at three in the morning. I was out in the field on

the tractor working by five o'clock! Well, I was only thirty then. I could take anything and everything.

WORKING FOR UNCLE WAH FONG

In February 1936, Uncle Wah Fong came to talk to me. "I'm making a trip back to China. After I leave, no one will drive my truck to San Francisco for delivery." He wanted to ask me to work for him while he was gone. So I moved to work for Uncle Wah Fong, whose farm was huge—400 acres in size. Beyond my wildest imagination, Uncle Wah Fong paid me ninety dollars a month and put up a forty-dollar trailer on the farm for my family. After he made all the arrangements, he took off for China. I felt grateful for his generosity and worked hard on his farm. Well, I had to; otherwise, how could I take such a high wage?

Uncle Wah Fong had nearly a hundred Filipino farmhands; he paid them around nine or ten dollars a week. They worked from dawn till dusk. He also hired about twenty Chinese farmers, paying them accordingly, with the highest at sixty dollars a month and the lowest at thirty dollars, and fed them three meals a day. So, I felt good and grateful that I was paid so much. I worked extra hard to earn my keep. For at least three nights a week, I drove the delivery truck to First City. During the days when there was no delivery, I would drive the tractor and plow the field and supervise the Filipino farmhands.

The delivery trip to First City was not an easy drive. It was a distance of 160 miles from Madera to First City. It took eight hours, nonstop, to drive the truck, which weighed more than ten tons with a full load. After I unloaded the truck, which took over an hour, it would be three or four o'clock in the morning. I would then rent a $6.50 room at the Mandarin Hotel on Jackson Street and sleep for a few hours. At seven I would get up and check on the prices of vegetables and their sale. Then I would drive the empty truck back, and by three or four o'clock in the afternoon I would be back in Madera. Right away I would drive the tractor out to the field and work until dark. After supper, I would work in the barn rinsing the vegetables. I usually stopped at around eleven o'clock. By then I would have worked more than eighteen hours a day! Well, I didn't mind the hard work. I was paid to do that.

It was also my good fortune that my wife worked just as hard alongside me. She earned over a dollar a day working in the barn. She started working before sunrise for over ten hours a day. At night she took care of the children's needs—sewing clothes, knitting sweaters, whatever. I remember in 1936, when it was close to Chinese New Year, I took the family with me to First City to buy some Chinese provisions for the New Year. The night before New Year's Eve, we reached First City at three o'clock in the morning. As usual I rented a $6.50 room at the Mandarin and we slept until dawn. We finished running around at noon and took the children to lunch. Afterward we walked down to the Produce Market, where I had parked the truck (it was too large to drive inside Chinatown). On our way there my wife held onto our four-year-old Leung with her left hand and two-year-old Lai Heung with her right hand. On her back was one-year-old Lai Gyuen. And she was seven months pregnant with Lai Yuen. As for me, I was carrying all the Chinese foodstuffs with both hands. As we walked down Jackson Street to the Produce Market, the white folks stared at us. What a sight!

At year's end in 1936 Uncle Wah Fong returned from China. He was extremely pleased to see that I had managed his farm superbly. Anyway, I told him, "The delivery truck is getting too old, and besides, it's too small. Why don't you get a five-ton, ten-wheeled Westmoreland instead? But that will cost $2,700." Immediately he agreed, without a second thought. And he went with me to buy one, paid full in cash.

The next day I drove the truck on a delivery trip to First City with a load of over ten tons of vegetables and melons. The truck had a huge engine that burned gasoline like mad. I filled up with eighty gallons when I started. By the time I reached First City, the tank gauge showed that it was almost empty. Well, gasoline cost about ten cents a gallon then. Still, it was not at all economical. So I asked the dealer why it consumed so much gasoline. He said, "That's because the truck has a large gasoline motor. If you switch it to a diesel engine, it'll be seven times more powerful and the diesel fuel would cost only five cents a gallon. However, it will cost $2,700 to make that change." Immediately Uncle Wah Fong put out another $2,700 in cash to change the motor. Altogether that truck cost him $5,400. By today's value, it would be close to $100,000! My co-workers on the farm began to slander me, saying that I had conned Uncle Wah Fong!

However, lucky for me, in January 1937 Uncle Wah Fong planted forty acres of spinach. Ordinarily a case of spinach sold for about one dollar. But the Teamsters went on strike at that time, and all vegetables were in short supply at the Farmers Market in San Francisco. The price of spinach reached three to four dollars a case. During the strike I drove out to First City every night for two weeks straight, with a full load of over three hundred cases of vegetables per trip. We cleared over $10,000 just for that! Uncle Wah Fong and the farmers thought I was some kind of a wonder man to foresee such a move. Well, without that big truck, we wouldn't have been able to ship over three hundred cases of vegetables per trip. Hell, I was no fortune-teller. It was just plain old luck and good timing. Nevertheless, everybody shut up after that.

TO BE MY OWN BOSS

On January 23, 1937, my daughter Lai Yuen was born. Of course I played doctor again during delivery. My wife went back to work at the barn three days after the birth.

I learned in July that Uncle Kai Yee had passed away in Chinese Hospital [in San Francisco] and that there was no one to take over his produce business in Visalia. When he was alive, he had worked with his wife. His wife did not speak English; she became totally helpless after he died.

At that time I had just paid back Uncle Wah Fong the $700 plus $60 interest. My wife and I discussed whether or not we could buy Uncle Kai Yee's business. By doing that, we could at least become our own bosses and expand the business in the future. It would be a lot better than working for someone else for the rest of our lives. Besides, I remembered when Uncle Kai Yee was alive, he came to see me on a few Sundays and suggested to me, "Dear Nephew, what you are doing is hard work. Why don't you do what I do—get a truck and sell produce? At least you'll have Sundays all to yourself."

Well, I told Uncle Wah Fong that I was leaving. Of course he was not pleased. He said, "Tim, if you're leaving because I'm paying you too low, I'm ready to pay you $120."

"It isn't that," I said. "You pay me more than what I deserve. It's just that I have so many kids and I have to plan for our future. I thought it would be better if I could start my own business. It is not that I am quitting on you. I just want to let you know, so you can find a replacement."

Seeing that I was determined, he said, "Well, how in the world can you come up with $500 to pay Kai Yee's wife for the business?" I did come up with that money. How? Well, my wife saved up all her earnings from working in the barn. In addition, she put aside all the money that our friends and relatives gave to our children during Chinese New Year. She kept the money, a total of $550, in a savings account at a bank that is now called Bank of America.

So I moved my family to Visalia. My wife and I had only twenty-seven dollars in our possession. We couldn't afford to stay in a hotel, nor could we find a house to rent ahead of time. We were going to take our chances when we arrived in Visalia. We left Uncle Wah Fong's farm at eight o'clock in the morning. Approximately four miles down the road, my wife told me to stop the car beside a big tree by the roadside. Well, she had brought along some incense, candles, and what-have-you. She got out of the car and walked over to the tree. She lit these sacrificial items and started praying under it. "Almighty Bodhisattva! Almighty Heaven! Give us your blessing that we'll find a place to stay! Give my Tim your blessing that he'll earn $5,000!" I thought she was crazy. Anyway, we continued on our way afterward.

Well, that was a Sunday. When we got to Visalia, we learned that a village brother, Chan Hung, and his wife had just rented a large, six-bedroom house a few months before. It cost him thirty dollars a month. I proposed to him, "How about letting me lease half of the house for the time being? You live in the front, and we'll live in the back. When I find a place to stay, we'll move out." Well, just like that and we found a place to stay right away!

I had to come up with some cash by nightfall for Village Brother Siu Jong to buy the produce in Fresno. Fortunately, I was able to borrow $100 from Uncle Si Jing. Early next morning I had to get up and go to the Produce Market to pick up the produce. By eight in the morning I hit the road with Uncle Kai Yee's widow to sell the produce. The first day we had fewer than twenty customers, taking in only $6.80. On the second day we went to the mountains and had over twenty customers, taking in $19.20.

It was frustration beyond description for two weeks. Most of the customers were twenty or thirty miles away from Visalia. There were huge orange groves. Uncle Kai Yee's widow did not know the addresses, she only knew how to get there: turn left, turn right, over this street corner, whatever. . . . Worse yet, she was grieving and mourning over her husband's death. Something might remind her of him along the way and she would start crying. It bothered the hell out of me. But what could I do? Not much but to bear with her during those two weeks. Finally, after a couple of months of hustling, I picked up more customers, close to forty orders a day. By month's end I subtracted all the expenses and still had $150 in profit. Not bad at all.

Well, every day I drove the truck around trying to make new sales. I remember well the day before Thanksgiving that year, when I worked late into the evening. By the time I finished with the last customer, it was ten o'clock at night. I didn't get home until eleven. The kids were all asleep, but my wife was still up, knitting jackets and sweaters. She had cooked supper for me. After the meal she went with me to the garage and took care of all the odds and ends and prepared for tomorrow's business. We didn't go to bed until one or two o'clock. By seven in the morning I had to be up and go to the Produce Market to pick up my vegetables. A long day's work!

A PERMANENT HOME OF OUR OWN

Of course, as business picked up, I became all the more ambitious. I was fanatic; I didn't feel tired at all working long hours everyday. However, I was concerned with the fact that we didn't have a permanent home. Chan Hong and his wife had no children; they were quiet and neat people. However, we had noisy children. Sometimes they cried at night and asked for food, disturbing everybody's sleep. Chan and his wife might not say anything, but I felt bad about it. My wife and I talked it over and decided to find another place to live. Every Saturday and Sunday afternoon we would take the children and drive all over town, looking for a place to move into. But it was not at all easy. There were rental units, but when the landlords saw the children, they would always say, "Sorry, I've rented the place out this morning." It was like this for several months, until January 1, 1938.

My son Leung and Uncle Chau Dou's son Syu were in the same first grade. Uncle Chau Dou's house was about two blocks away. Syu would always come over to play with Leung after school. On New Year's Day it was no work for me. Syu came over and the first thing he said was, "Uncle Tim, there's a 'For Rent' sign out there." My wife and I walked over to take a look. Well, it was a "For Sale" sign. For the last couple of months, when we went house-hunting during the weekends, we usually would pass by this house, and we had always said to each other, "I wish this house were for rent." The house was located on the outskirts of town. It had a large open area in the back and two big trees in front at the corner. It was perfect—we could raise chickens and grow Chinese vegetables. Well, all this time we just drooled over the prospect, but the place was not for rent. Unexpectedly, with this new development, it was better than a dream come true! My wife and I immediately went knocking at the door. The landlord was a young man, about nineteen years old. He said he had found a job in Fresno and was putting the house up for sale, asking for $1,300. He would take $500 for the initial payment and the rest of the $800 could be paid by a three-year installment of $27 per month.

Boy, what luck! However, we had saved up only $300. I asked Uncle Chau Dou to lend me $300. He agreed in no time. So I arranged to go with the white man to City Hall on January 17 at ten o'clock in the morning to complete the ownership transfer. At nine o'clock that morning I went to see Uncle Chau Dou at Gong's Market to get the loan. Well, Gong's Market was only two blocks away from City Hall. I thought I would have the money right away. I didn't realize that the Market was a partnership among three brothers. Uncle Chau's younger brother, Uncle Chong, was in charge of all the money. The three brothers had to co-sign all the checks. Well, the three of them went into a room and talked it over. I was standing outside waiting nervously. The wall was partitioned by a thin fiberboard, and I could hear Uncle Chau Dou screaming, "Hell! Tim is not using this money to gamble! What's there not to trust?" Finally they co-signed the $300 check and gave it to me. My feeling at that moment was beyond words. After all the paperwork was done, I consulted the lunar calendar for an auspicious day and we moved in two weeks later.

LEAVING POVERTY BEHIND

After a while my produce business turned the corner. I made over $200 a month, after subtracting all the expenses. My wife and I were so happy. In fact, it was all the more wonderful because our son Seung was born on February 14, 1938! I didn't go out to sell produce that day. So I went to the garage and checked out the truck, oiling it and making minor repairs on the engine. Well, the garage was across the street from Kerby, a big restaurant. Kerby used one hundred pounds of potatoes and one case of lettuce every day. Its boss asked me if I would be interested in making that kind of delivery every morning. Of course I said yes, and just like that, I signed up a big customer. This big order increased my business volume by 50 percent! By the end of the month I took in over $400 after deducting all expenses. (At that time a worker earned $70 or $80 at the most if he worked for someone else.)

Well, we were not poor anymore! Kerby's boss was impressed, and he told the chef that from now on, I would be responsible for providing the restaurant with the vegetable items on the menu. Well, that gave me a great idea. I recalled that over ten produce trucks would be parked at the produce market every night. The owners would sort out the leftover vegetables and throw the unsellables into dumpsters. I took that discarded produce home and asked my wife to clean it out and store it in a large refrigerator. We took the good ones and cut them up nicely, and I would then deliver them to the chef at Kerby. The chef liked what I did because my cleaning and cutting saved him a lot of work. Well, I didn't spend any money on those vegetables! By the end of the month I made over $600 in profit.

Now I could hire a contractor to fix up my house and build a big double garage with a large refrigerator inside. Everything turned new and splendid at home. I was not a struggling poor soul anymore! In June 1939 I paid $900 in cash for a brand new, four-door Hudson sedan. Well, no one bought new cars in those days!

Just that week Uncle Hing's eldest son, Hok Jik, died. My wife and I drove our brand new car up to Madera for the funeral. Everybody stared at us and gossiped among themselves: "Tim couldn't afford a car like that. It must be a rental." Well, Clan Brother Victor walked over to my car and checked the registration. He told everybody, "It is Tim's car!"

When we first moved down to Visalia, my wife would always remind me, "Tim, everybody looks down on you. Show them that they are wrong about you." So I worked extra hard and I worked until midnight. Now everybody saw that I had become rather rich since I left two years ago. We showed them at last!

In 1942 the United States government inducted many men into the armed forces because of the war in Europe. I was too old for the draft because when I first came to the United States, I was two years older on paper than I really was. Besides, I had a large family to support. As my workers packed and left for the army, I made up my mind to take care of everything myself. I would get up earlier to go to Fresno to buy wholesale produce; then I would be home by early dawn. My wife and I worked together to clean and sort the produce for sale. To my surprise, even though I lost all my workers, my business volume increased several times! I cleared over $1,000 a month. My wife and I were delighted by the turn of the business. Ever since then, on every second day of the Lunar New Year, we always cook *faat choi* [a hairy seaweed whose name sounds like the word "prosperity"]. I always pick up a chopstickful of *faat choi* and pray: "Let me have it."

A TRIUMPHANT RETURN TO CHINA

I was ambitious all those years! In June 1947, however, I received a letter from my father saying that my mother was extremely ill and wanted to see her grandchildren before she died. I had known for a long time that my mother was in poor health. Besides, she was already seventy-five years old. I would be an unfilial son to deny her last wish. I discussed the matter with my wife, and we decided that since I was only forty-three years old, I still had time. Besides, I had saved up over $50,000! I planned to return home to buy some land and build a four-story house. Furthermore, my children were growing. I wanted them to study some Chinese. And mostly, I wanted to make my mother happy.

After [selling my business to my Clan Brother Lou Hou], I left with my family for First City to make preparations for the trip to China. We purchased first-class tickets and packed everything into nine trunks, each weighing over three hundred pounds—kids' toys, skates, BB guns, whatever. On November 8 we went on board the SS *President Gordon* for Hong Kong. Ming Leung was fifteen years old; Lai Heung, thirteen; Lai Gyuen, twelve; Lai Yuen, ten; Ming Seung, nine; and Lai Ngan, five.

On November 24 we arrived in Hong Kong. I was going to take a ferry to Canton City immediately, but I learned that the Chinese government was in chaos. A journey by boat in southern China was dangerous because pirates were all over. I was told that it would be better if I went by land. However, I would have to pay a hefty sum of duty for all the goods I was bringing home. It was suggested to me that I should get someone to help me through the back door with customs. It took five days and altogether close to $2,000 to make all the arrangements.

As I entered the village, I saw Father, who, with a worried look, shook his head and said, "What took you so long?" (Well, I did write from the States that I would be home by November 25th. I didn't figure on the delay in Hong Kong.) Father continued, "Your mother doesn't look well at all."

I took my wife and six children into my mother's room. She was lying in bed, eyes closed. She was thinner than a vine and pale as a ghost, hardly breathing. I felt her hand, which was as cold as a popsicle. All my children came to the bedside and said, "Hello, Grandma." Each of them presented her with two United States gold coins. (Well, back in the States I'd told them that Grandma loved gold coins from America, so they got that as presents for her.) My kids kept calling her, "Grandma, Grandma!" After a while she finally half-opened her eyes and squeezed out a faint smile. If we'd come home an hour or two later, I believe that would have been it. My wife and I were so relieved that she was alive. Bodhisattva was on our side again!

The family had a big feast that evening. The maid, Ah Jum, fed my mother. Everyone was surprised that she ate some food. Well, after that my

Gong Yuen Tim with his family in China, 1948. (Courtesy of Mary Gong)

wife and the children and I would keep her company every day. She was so happy that after two weeks she was able to get out of bed. With Ah Jum helping her, she would walk to the front door. We made sure that Ah Jum had all kinds of food for her. Now that she was happy, my wife and I were also very happy.

Since returning home, I did notice, however, that the Chinese currency had dropped in value rather rapidly; it was worth less daily. My bank checks were in American currency, so I was not affected by the devaluation too much. Anyway I hired a builder to build me a four-storied mansion and an agent to buy some farmland. Every day my wife and I went shopping at the marketplace; we spent quite a lot—rolls and rolls of Chinese money. My father was a frugal man; he was startled by our spending spree. He reminded me, "Your house is only half built! Besides, you need to have some money for your trip back to America!"

I said, "Don't worry. I have paid in full for the house. I still have a lot of money in American bank checks. If you want to buy eight or ten *mou* of farmland, I'll buy them for you!" Father was so happy to hear me say that.

Well, the house was finally completed. I spent $15,000 on it. On the fourth day of the fourth lunar month in 1948, my first son was married and we all moved into the new house. What a day of celebration! We had a fifteen-course banquet—abalone, shark fins, and all kinds of exquisite delicacies. All the friends and relatives were invited—altogether 128 tables! I specially ordered a forty-foot string of firecrackers from Canton City for the occasion!

It was bright and clear that day. Relatives and friends presented us with fifteen roasted pigs, sixty baskets of ham on shank, and several baskets of firecrackers. When the firecrackers were lit, the entire alley was clouded with smoke, and we couldn't see anyone. Mother, supported by the maid Ah Jum, went up to the top floor of the house to view the excitement—people bustling all over and a line of people carrying my daughter-in-law's dowry coming into our house. She was brimming with joy.

Well, everything was done—house built and land bought. The next thing was for me to hire a teacher to teach my children the books. After that I had done all that we must do. For the next few months we spent most of our time in the marketplace. We would buy goodies for my parents to eat. On the seventh day of the seventh month, my mother died in her sleep. As for my wife and me, I truly believe we had been very filial to her.

COMING BACK TO AMERICA

One day in February 1949 I went to Canton City. There I saw a lion dance and dragon parade celebrating a decisive victory in Chui Jau against the Communist insurgents. When I went to the bank for some Chinese currency, the exchange rate had doubled. I felt something was wrong, because the Chinese money shouldn't drop so badly if it was a decisive victory for the government. The more I thought about it, the more I became nervous about the prospect of staying in China. After returning home, I talked to my wife and children about going to the United States Consulate in Hong Kong to prepare ourselves to return to the United States. Soon after that my wife and I took our children on board the SS *President Wilson* for America. Our son Ming Leung returned later because his bride's visa was being processed.

Well, my obligation of filial piety was the main reason for calling it quits in America two years before. I thought I would make my parents happy and proud with my triumphant and successful return. I had sold my business and house in the States; what would become of us now? I was worried during those fifteen days crossing the Pacific. My wife noticed my sour face and said, "No need for that. Bodhisattva will protect us."

We arrived in First City at six in the morning. I took my wife and children by taxi to Chinatown. We stayed in the basement of the Yat Ging Lau [Restaurant] for the time being. After lunch I tried to see if I could get someone to drive us back to Visalia. Well, talk about luck! I met this man Louie who had just bought a new truck. He said he planned to be a mover in Chinatown. I said, "Well, would you be interested in moving our stuff to Visalia today?" He said he had not driven out of town before. I said, "I have been driving trucks all my life. I'll drive it to Visalia, and you just drive it back. It's a distance of 220 miles." My wife and I moved all our belongings to the truck. We also made a canvas canopy to cover the truck bed so that our five children could have some cover along the way.

At twelve midnight we started down Highway 99. I was concerned about what to do when we reached Visalia—where to take my children, where to settle down again. . . . I kept thinking about all this as I drove along. It was almost dawn by the time we reached Fresno. I passed Hobbs-Parson Produce Market and saw Lou Hou's truck parked there. I stopped and went over to talk to him, "This is Wednesday, why are you here so early?"

Lou said, "I was invited to a baby party and stayed overnight at my in-laws' place here." Before he finished, he added, "Brother Tim, I'd like to return the truck and the produce business to you." Well, I thought he was joking and I didn't pay attention to him. I got back to Louie's truck and continued on to Visalia.

I stopped at Third Uncle Bing's place, unloading my luggage with him for the time being. Well, Aunt Leung Ju was visiting Third Aunt. Third Aunt said, "Why don't you leave your kids here for tonight?" And Aunt Ju also suggested, "Yes, you and your wife could stay with us in my daughter Siu's room. She's in college in Los Angeles." Well, that solved the sleeping arrangements for the night. Right away I went to Third Uncle Bing's market to find out how I could get a car. Living in the valley without a car was like being a cripple. Both Third Uncle and hare-lipped Hoi gave me a car key, saying, "Use the car for the time being." I drove over to a Buick dealer and bought myself a used, full-sized Buick.

When I went back to the market, Uncle Chan Yum was there too. He said to me, "Tim, I rented a house two months ago for thirty dollars a month. I painted the place over. I also bought a new refrigerator and a new stove; I plan to move in there in a few days. But if you need a place to stay, why don't you move in first? When you find your own place, I'll move in after you move out."

Well, just like that my housing problem was solved. It was something I wouldn't dare dream would happen. It must have been some supernatural help!

Next morning I got my children back to school. Afterward my wife and I were alone in the house. We looked at each other. What next? I was already forty-four years old. It wouldn't be easy for me to find a job. Even if I could find one, it would, at the most, pay $250; it wouldn't be enough for household expenses. I came to regret my trip back to China, for which I sold off my business and house. Well, I couldn't take back what I had done.

For two weeks we couldn't come up with anything to resolve our worries. Then suddenly one day my wife said, "On our way past Fresno, didn't Lou

Hou say he wanted to sell the business back to you? Why don't you go and ask him if it's for real?"

I said, "He's only joking. I don't think it's for real." But her suggestion made sense. That day was Wednesday. I knew Lou would return from Fresno at three o'clock in the afternoon. I took my wife in our Buick and went to see Lou.

As we drove near Kingsburg, we saw Lou returning with his truck. I stopped him and asked if what he said that morning in Fresno was serious. He said, "Of course I'm serious. I want to go into the supermarket business now." I asked him for how much he would sell the business back. He said, "Two years ago you sold it to me for $7,200. I'll take back that amount." My wife and I were so relieved and happy. We went home and immediately killed a chicken and offered thanks to Heaven. I made over $1,000 the first month after I took the business back.

GETTING INTO THE SUPERMARKET BUSINESS

On Chinese New Year in 1950, another daughter, Lai Sim, was born. By then I had saved over $10,000 in the bank. In 1952 I felt that my truck was getting old; besides, it was getting too small for the business. I traded it in for a brand new 1952 big truck. My business picked up further.

A year later, Cousin Lau Som came to visit us. He noticed that all my children were growing and that they did not work after school. He said to me, "Cousin Tim, with all your growing kids, you should find a supermarket. They could pitch in and I am sure you'd make more money."

My wife and I agreed. Every Saturday afternoon and every Sunday, we would drive around to find a nice lot to build a modern supermarket. Well, I knew I couldn't compete in First City. We aimed to open our store in a small city. We drove around thirty small towns and couldn't find anything that we liked.

On September 1, I attended a wedding party in First City. I drove home to Visalia along Highway 33. I went through Patterson and saw a lot that I really liked. However, it was not for sale. A few days later I went back to Patterson to show my wife what I saw. Anyway, her eyes were sharp. She noticed a "For Sale" sign by a tree on that lot. There was only a telephone number on that sign. I immediately called. Well, a doctor in Modesto owned that lot and he was selling it for $15,000. I put down a deposit immediately.

Afterward I drew up my own design for the structure, hired a contractor, and ordered all necessary materials. I rushed about and got everything done by December 20. Well, our market had its grand opening on June 15, 1954. My elder son Leung had just been discharged from the military after serving in the Korean War. He had worked as a helper in the butcher shop owned by Third Uncle Bing ever since he was nine years old. He was a pro in the butcher shop. So I put him in charge of the meat department. As for my produce business and house in Visalia, I sold them all for only $3,600 to Chan

Yum. It was dirt cheap, but I was grateful for his generosity to my family when we first returned to Visalia.

I only had a little over $30,000 in savings to start the market. Everything was bought on credit—the mortgage, the machines, the grinder, the band saw, the truck, the cashier's machines. I had to pay monthly installments for three years for six major items. Fortunately, business was good. Still, I couldn't hire any help. Instead my wife and my children pitched in. Everyone worked until eleven or twelve o'clock. Even my twelve-year-old daughter, Lai Ngan, would come after school and work behind the third checkout cash register. Well, it was like this for three years until we paid off everything and didn't owe anybody anything anymore.

TIME TO TAKE IT EASY

On July 1, 1957, I took off my apron. I bought a new car and moved back to First City with my wife. I would go to the market for a few days each week and spend the rest of the week in First City. Well, I had enough savings by then. I might not be considered very rich, but I was not that poor. Both my wife and I had worked very hard in the old days; now it was time to relax for a change. So I spent most of the time driving around in our Cadillac and had a nice time with my wife.

We had retired and we were taking it easy, no more rushing about. In the summer we would take a pot of nicely brewed Pu-erh tea and a box of dim sum, and drive my air-conditioned Cadillac to either Golden Gate Park or Seal Rock. We would sit under the shade of a tree and enjoy ourselves. Life was without worry for us now. Sometimes we would prepare a pot of steamed rice with dried scallops and preserved pork belly and drive to a mountain campsite. Under tall trees we would put out our cots and relax, eat our food, and enjoy nature's beauty.

During those twenty years of retirement, my wife and I were always together, enjoying everything and sharing happiness and laughter. On August 10, 1980, when she was cutting her toenails, she accidentally cut her toe. She thought it was something minor, but it became a serious infection. She was hospitalized at St. Francis Hospital for an operation. She was there for 101 days and came home on January 22, 1981. During her stay our five daughters took turns keeping her company twenty-four hours a day. After she came out of the hospital, I would also drive her all over for fresh air. If she said she wanted to eat a certain something, I would get it for her. For instance, once she said she remembered eating some fried fish in a restaurant in Modesto. I immediately called up all my daughters and made arrangements to eat a fish dinner in that restaurant at Coffee Street in Modesto. I wanted to keep her happy all the time.

Well, on February 19, 1982, my wife was hospitalized again at St. Francis

Hospital because of a stroke. On March 8, at three o'clock in the afternoon, she passed away peacefully, holding onto my hands. She was seventy-seven.

I had many sleepless nights after she passed away. In our fifty years together, it was my wife who constantly encouraged me to move up. Sometimes because of financial problems, I would become so frustrated that for no reason I would yell at her just to vent my frustration. She would take all that abuse with a smile. I remember one Saturday when I came home earlier than usual. When I entered the house, I saw her holding a duster, about to punish one of the children. When she saw me walk in, she stopped, turned to me with a smile, and fetched me my slippers instead. I felt so bad that she had to keep up with disciplining the children and with making me happy at home. But I have thought it over. Had I died before her, she would have had a more miserable time than I am having now. With that thought, I feel a bit more relieved and can close my eyes to sleep.

During the spring and autumn festivals, I get some flowers and go to the cemetery; I wipe her tombstone clean with a white handkerchief and talk to her: "Wait for me, I am coming. We will be together again in our next life."

SOURCE: Gong Yuen Tim, "A Gold Mountain Man's Memoir," *Chinese America: History and Perspectives*, 1992, pp. 211–37. Translator: Marlon K. Hom.

OTHER REFERENCE

Him Mark Lai, "Chinese Regional Solidarity: The Hua Xian (Fa Yuen) Community," in *Becoming Chinese American: A History of Communities and Institutions* (Walnut Creek, Calif.: Alta Mira Press, 2004), pp. 143–76.

"I was the only Chinese woman in town"

Reminiscences of a Gold Mountain Woman (1982)

Helen Hong Wong

The voices of Gold Mountain women are finally entering the public record. Judy Yung met and interviewed Helen Hong Wong in 1982 while researching the history of Chinese women in America. A petite and spry woman of seventy-four years, Wong immigrated to the United States as a merchant's wife in 1928. During the interview she spoke quite openly about her detention experience at Angel Island, her hardworking life in the Midwest, where she was often the only Chinese woman in town, and her struggles raising a family of four children during the depression years. Although she never realized her Gold Mountain dream of a life of wealth and leisure, she nevertheless found fulfillment in her work, family, and community. Wong made her home in Chicago, where she passed away in 2001 at the age of ninety-one. Her story is one of the few first-person accounts we have of life in the Midwest, where Chinese immigrants such as her husband went to start small businesses in the 1920s.

A HARD LIFE IN CHINA

I was born in Hom Gong Village in Sunwui District [in 1909]. My *goong* [grandfather] and father owned a hemp business in the nearby town of Nam How. The Chans and the Lums were feuding and we were caught in the middle. As a result, our house was burnt down in a fire and we had to run to *jo poh*'s [grandmother's] home in Ngui Hoi. We didn't have much money. Just put some bedding and clothes in some large baskets—the kind with handles that you pull rope through to carry things—and had some hired hands help us carry them to *jo poh*'s. I was only eight months old and my brother was four.

After four years of hiding there, we went to Gong Moon [a seaport] to live. Then when I was seven we moved to Hong Kong. We had a hard life then. There was no work for women or children. My father worked at a fur-

Helen Hong Wong in
Hong Kong, 1928.
(Courtesy of Helen
Hong Wong)

niture store. He only made a few dollars a day, so we could only afford to rent one room for the four of us—my father, mother, brother, and me. Then came my baby sister, so I had to help my mother wash clothes, cook meals, and carry the baby. My brother got to go to school and he eventually became a carpenter at sixteen. They were just starting to educate girls, but my mother wouldn't let me go to school. There was no time and no money. If there was any money, we would have bought some *mui nui* [slavegirls] to help us out. After dinner, we would make rattan chairs. Since my mother had bound feet and couldn't go out, I had to do all the shopping as well. So there was no time to play, hardly any time to sleep.

I lived in Hong Kong from seven years old until I got married and left for America. It wasn't an arranged marriage or a modem marriage. A friend of my old man [husband] introduced us. My father knew this friend. He was a *gamsaanhaak* [Gold Mountain man] and had a restaurant business in Fort Wayne, Indiana. He sold it to a cousin for $20,000 and returned to China. But he spent a lot of money coming back. Bought a house in Hong Kong for a few thousand Hong Kong dollars. Got sick and had to pay medical bills. Spent all his money. Then they needed him to go back to help with the failing restaurant business, so we left soon after we were married.[1]

DETAINED AT ANGEL ISLAND

Where we lived in Hong Kong we could see the harbor where many of the big ships docked. Every time we heard the tooting of the ship, we would watch all the *gamsaanpoh* [Gold Mountain women] get off the ship, wearing all their jewelry and followed by their *mui nui*. We would dream about going to Gold Mountain. So when I had the chance to make the trip, I was overjoyed.

We [she and her husband] came together on the ship. It took twenty-one days. I wasn't seasick at all. Ate six meals a day—breakfast in our room at six, a second breakfast in the dining room at eight, lunch at twelve, tea at three, dinner at six, and evening snack at nine. It was a Japanese ship. We had second-class tickets, so we were allowed to go on deck. There were many Chinese but most were in steerage.

When we got to San Francisco, they were originally going to interrogate us on the ship. But it was a Saturday, so we had to go to Angel Island.[2] He [husband] stayed in the men's barracks with his friend's son while I stayed in the women's barracks. Both he and the boy answered wrong. They were very strict then and we had not prepared for the interrogation.[3] They asked all kinds of questions, about the type of stove we used in the village, how many tiles on the floor, even how many steps in the stairs. I had lived in Hong Kong all those years and didn't remember anything about the village. They asked where you lived, where is the kitchen, and your lineage going back generations. How could anyone remember all that?

I answered wrong and they would not let me land. So we had to appeal the case. I was stuck there from the beginning of October to the beginning of January the next year. I still remember the Jesus woman[4] bringing us each

1. According to her daughter, Nellie Leong, there was a big age difference. Helen Hong Wong was eighteen, while her husband was in his fifties.
2. Between 1910 and 1940 newly arrived Chinese immigrants were processed at the Angel Island Immigration Station in San Francisco Bay, where they were locked up for weeks and sometimes months and subjected to intense cross-examinations to prove their right to enter the country.
3. In anticipation of the interrogation, most Chinese immigrants memorized coaching books that had been sent to them by relatives in America. The books provided questions and answers about one's family background that immigration inspectors might ask.
4. Deaconess Katharine Maurer (1881–1962) was appointed by the Methodist Episcopal Church in 1912 to administer to the needs of immigrants at Angel Island.

a parcel at Christmas: cloth, toothbrush, towel, and other toiletries. There was a woman from Heungshan [District] who had to stay here for three years with her son and daughter. Her husband made the mistake of mentioning his first wife's name. When she saw the Christmas tree again, she said she had seen it three times. Three times, can you imagine that?[5]

The women's barracks was one big room with three tiers of beds. We only used the bottom two tiers. Young children generally stayed with the mothers and slept in the bottom bed. Everyone got along. There were people from Sunwui, Heungshan, Sunning [Districts]. There were very few women then, but there was always someone coming or going.[6] Every ship always had a few that failed the interrogation. We weren't allowed visitors. Couldn't talk to anyone or receive any mail or packages directly. They were afraid of coaching notes being sneaked in. Every time we went to the big dining hall to eat, a foreign woman would stand by the door to watch, afraid that the [Chinese] kitchen staff might sneak you coaching notes. The kitchen staff was known to hide coaching notes under the plates of food. If you weren't caught, you would take the note upstairs and read it in the bathroom. Then you would light a match, burn it, and flush it away. I never received any coaching notes, but I saw others.

[About the food,] there was a long table with two dishes of food, one at each end of the table. Do you know what it was? Pork steamed with *gum jum* [a vegetable] in a basin. Or bok choy and pork in soup. People could add their own dishes. Fried ham and eggs cost twenty-five cents. Or your friends might send some canned fish or food down [from San Francisco].

We could stay in the breezeway [sitting area adjacent to the sleeping area]. The younger ones could play ball outside. We really couldn't go anywhere. Besides, we had to be available in case they phoned to call us to go downstairs for the interrogation. The Jesus woman was willing to go shopping for us. I had her buy me some material so I could do some sewing by hand. Time passed quickly. We had our meals every day. Then we would watch the people play outside. We just had to wait to hear when we would be landed.

[About the poems on the walls,] not many. But people said the person who wrote one of the poems in the bathroom committed suicide.[7] What did we know? At that time, only one out of ten knew how to read. There were always people arriving and leaving. Those who answered right could go to

5. The average stay for Chinese immigrants at Angel Island was two to three weeks. Those who failed the interrogation and chose to appeal their cases through administrative channels in Washington, D.C., usually had to stay locked up at Angel Island for another three or four months. For those whose cases went through the court system, their stays could be prolonged up to two years.

6. There were anywhere between 200 and 300 Chinese men and 30 to 50 Chinese women at Angel Island at any one time.

7. To vent their frustrations and express their feelings of loneliness, anger, and humiliation, Chinese immigrants wrote poetry on the barrack walls. Unfortunately, the administration

the city; those who answered wrong couldn't. Some stayed years, like the woman who said she had seen the Christmas tree three times. During the time we were there, there was a woman who got deported. That was considered very sad because so much money had already been spent.

After Helen Hong Wong was allowed to land, she stayed with her husband in San Francisco for one week at a cousin's home. Then they took a train to Chicago, stayed there for one week, and went to live in Fort Wayne, Indiana.

LIFE DURING THE GREAT DEPRESSION

When you heard people talk in China, you wanted to come. But when you actually arrived, you usually wouldn't like it. There were very few Chinese women in Fort Wayne then. Just a few dozen Chinese in town, two restaurants and two laundries run by bachelors. I was the only Chinese woman. Even in [Chicago] Chinatown, when we lived at this hotel above the Universal Restaurant for a week, I would look out and never see a Chinese woman walk by. No one for me to socialize with, I felt lonely.

We lived upstairs above the restaurant and I would come down to help. Peeled potatoes, cut vegetables, washed the rice, helped with the dishes, everything. I was young then and didn't feel it was hard work. When I had free time I took my daughter [Lilly], who was a little over a year old, with me and went browsing in the dime store. No one bothered me. Fort Wayne had an open marketplace on Tuesdays, Thursdays, and Saturdays. So at night, I would go there and walk around. When I had the second daughter, Nellie, I didn't go out as much.

When we first arrived, the restaurant business wasn't bad. We made $200 during lunch time. But come 1930 it was difficult. People had no jobs and no income. Then we made only $2 during lunch time. The department store business was slow too. In 1932 we closed the restaurant because we couldn't pay the rent.

We moved to Chicago for a year. We had nothing to eat. The government was giving out corned beef, cabbage, potatoes, and bread to needy families, but my old man was afraid to go stand in line. Instead, he borrowed money from gamblers in Chinatown. Rice only cost 80 cents for one hundred pounds.

We rented a flat with six rooms for $19. But there was no electricity, even when my son [William] was born, because we couldn't pay for it. During the winter the windows were all frosty and we closed all the doors and stayed in

---

building where the women were housed was destroyed in a fire in 1940, so no records remain of women's poetry. There are also very few documented cases of suicide, but many of the detainees remember hearing stories of suicide.

Helen Hong Wong
after her arrival in Fort
Wayne, Indiana, 1930.
(Courtesy of Helen
Hong Wong)

one room. Wrapped the two girls with blankets. We could only afford one
bushel of coal for the week, which cost 90 cents. It got to be 40 degrees in
the house.

No one in Chinatown had any money, just a quarter or a half dollar in
their pockets, no dollar bills. A year later, a friend opened a laundry and we
moved to Anderson, Indiana, to work for him. That's how we got into the
laundry business.

THE LAUNDRY BUSINESS

We lived above the laundry in two rooms. [Their fourth child, Betsy, was born
in Anderson.] I helped out with the wash, pressing, and ironing. It was hard
work, long hours. We did everything ourselves. We hardly slept. There was
no time for anything else. We worked Monday through Saturday, even Sun-

day if we didn't finish on time. Or I would clean house on Sunday. We did this for four years. Then the nephew came from Hong Kong and caused trouble. So we left and went to Kokomo, Indiana, to open our own laundry.

Kokomo was a small town about one and a half hours away. We lived on the premises again. Business was so-so. We started making $20 a week and that grew to a $100 a week. It was still hard work from morning to night, washing and ironing four hundred shirts a week. If we got behind, no Sunday off, nor time to sleep. I helped at the front when someone came to pick up laundry. Even though I couldn't read, I knew how to find the package by number. There was no time for anything else, only time to go get my hair cut. Again, we did this for four years. It was always four or five years and we would move again. Then their father died. It was wartime and there was no one available to hire. I couldn't do it alone, so I moved to Chicago, where I had friends.

WORKING AT A COOKIE FACTORY

I found a job working for relatives at the Dong Kee Bakery. Only made $20 a month working over ten hours a day. After work, I had to do all the cooking and housework, but the kids helped out. Stayed there about three years, from 1944 to 1947. It wasn't a better or a worse job, just a matter of having enough to eat and a place to live. There wasn't anything to put in the bank. I wanted to send money to my brothers in Hong Kong, but I couldn't.

I left the bakery to go work for Nabisco cookies, folding boxes, packing cookies. My Italian landlady's daughter found the job for me. I was the second Chinese to be hired. Everyone was good to me, called me Mama, Mama. They asked me why I never complained to the union. There really was no reason to. I took the bus to the west side at 5:10 A.M. in the winter; 5:30 A.M. in the summer. I had to take three buses. Worked until 3:15 P.M. The hours were better. It was only 75 cents an hour when I started, but the foreigners [white employers] always have better working conditions—raises, insurance, vacation benefits. But by the time I got home and had dinner, I was tired and went straight to bed. Besides, there really wasn't much going on then. Not like now. I retired in 1977.

REFLECTIONS ON LIFE IN AMERICA

There are advantages to being a woman in America. There were hardly any jobs for women in China and it was considered a loss of face if girls went to work. Now, [Chicago] Chinatown has more people, businesses, and activities. The churches have English classes and job training. Women who come from China today can find a job within a month or two even if they don't speak English. The sewing factory, shoe factory, bobby pin factory will hire them, although they pay Chinese less than the other workers.

Women have more rights in America. They can run the household, not like in China where the mother-in-law dictates. Even when the husband sent money home, the mother-in-law kept it. But I must admit that my Gold Mountain dream was not fulfilled. Instead of becoming a rich *gamsaanpoh,* I ended up working like a slave. When I came in 1928, things were cheap. String beans were 2 cents a pound; pork chops were 25 cents for three pounds. But no one had any money to spend and there was no food in the house. We didn't know any better at the time, only that we saw these *gamsaanpoh* with all this jewelry, fine clothes, and *mui nui.* So we assumed life was easy in Gold Mountain. But there was no gold to be picked up. Instead, we all had to work hard.

SOURCE: Helen Hong Wong, interview with Judy Yung in Chinese, Chinese Women of America Research Project, June 17, 1982, San Mateo, California.

OTHER REFERENCES

Him Mark Lai, Genny Lim, and Judy Yung, *Island: Poetry and History of Chinese Immigrants on Angel Island, 1910–1940* (San Francisco: HOC-DOI, 1980).

Huping Ling, *Surviving on the Gold Mountain: A History of Chinese American Women and their Lives* (Albany: State University of New York Press, 1998).

Judy Yung, *Chinese Women of America: A Pictorial History* (Seattle: University of Washington Press, 1986).

Second-Generation Dilemmas
(1930s)

Pardee Lowe

George Cooper Pardee Lowe, born in 1904 in San Francisco, was named after the governor of California at the time. He has the distinction of being the first Chinese American to write a full-length book, Father and Glorious Descendant *(Little, Brown, 1937). The autobiography introduced readers to Chinese American life by telling the story of the author's relationship with his father, whom he loved and respected. Good-humored in tone, the book nevertheless firmly criticized racial prejudice in America and recalled critical moments of anti-Chinese discrimination in this country.* Father and Glorious Descendant *was a commercial success and went through several editions. Lowe's work was also published in major publications, including* Asia, *the* Atlantic Monthly, Survey Graphic, *and* Yale Review.

Pardee Lowe had prepared well for his writing efforts. He graduated from Stanford in 1930, where he studied Chinese, English, history, and public speaking. He was a star member of the university debating club and completed a thesis on the history of anti-Chinese prejudice in the United States. After graduation, he went to Harvard, where he received an MBA in 1932. He also had many friends among college-educated Chinese Americans and was personally familiar with the Chinese communities because of the family business and his own church activities.

After finding that his MBA opened no doors, Lowe returned to San Francisco and began to conduct extensive sociological research on the Chinese community, completing a major study of its demographic, economic, social, historical, and cultural features. His efforts included extended personal interviews and firsthand reports of living conditions. He completed much of this work for the State Emergency Relief Administration, but his efforts were never published. He apparently hoped to include his work in a later collaboration with a Stanford sociologist, but it too never materialized.

The following "case histories," as he called them, are a few of the fascinating human-interest accounts Lowe completed as part of his research efforts. They offer poignant insight into depression-era Chinese American lives. Lowe's own candid personal com-

Portrait of Pardee
Lowe in 1946.
(Courtesy of
Anita Lowe)

mentaries also unintentionally reveal his own frustrations and inner conflicts about being a well-educated and ambitious Chinese in a racially restrictive society.

Lowe pursued many interests in his long life: business, the military, academia, and government. He even earned a doctoral degree in Russian studies from the University of California, Berkeley, in the 1950s. He joined the U.S. State Department and was stationed in Taiwan for many years in the 1960s, after which he served as an educator in the Middle East and Africa, working for the State Department and UNESCO. Pardee Lowe died in 1996 at the age of ninety-two.

ELEVATOR BOY

This is a brief case history of an American-born Chinese young man who has had several years of college but has never graduated (1937):

1909	Born in San Francisco of parents who emigrated from China.
1915–1923	Educated in public grammar schools of Chinatown; also attended Chinese language schools.

1923–1927	Enters American high school, gives up Chinese school, and takes to athletics.
1928	Matriculates at University of California but fails to pass examinations. Spent time in Chinatown playing athletics, in attending dances and other social activities. Stated that "he couldn't find time to study; too many distractions in Chinatown."
1931	After a few more failures in examinations, he quits college to work in a Chinatown store. He drives a truck for a Chinese butcher store. Discharged, he claims, because he was not polite enough. Failed to greet the numerous bosses each morning according to traditional forms of Chinese etiquette. Was making $50 per month, including found [room and board].
1932	Becomes a potato sorter, working with a group of Chinese "gangs" on the waterfront. Makes about $30 per month. "Just enough for spending money," he explains, "And I must rely upon my folks for board and room." When the C.W.A. [Civil Works Administration] was formed in the winter of 1932, he was one of the many Chinese who joined up. "Found the pay swell," "best he ever earned," "they treated him like a white-man."
1933	When C.W.A. is closed up, he attempts to get on the rolls of the State Emergency Relief Administration work relief projects. Fails because investigation discloses that his family has just enough income to take care of him.
1934–1935	He has taken to doing odd jobs; anything to provide him with spending money. He has driven for the gambling houses, worked as busboy in Chinese restaurants, served as a waiter, houseboy. The last I heard of him he was working in a Jewish hospital as an elevator boy. At that time he was threatened with the loss of this job, since all Chinese employees of the hospital were being discharged in compliance with the demands of the other (non-Chinese) workers that their jobs be given to "white" people.

OWN COMMENTS: This is a fairly typical case of a Chinatown youth who has failed to make either an educational adjustment or vocational adjustment to the hyphenated world in which he lives. Chinatown has "unfitted" him for work in its own community and he lacks something, aside from racial factors, which makes it difficult for him to hold a job in the American community.

When I have talked to him at the Y.M.C.A., where he is a member, he has been quite frank with his ideas. He would like to get married but sees no prospect of supporting a wife. He feels that his wife no doubt could find and manage to hold on to her job; but he does not see any permanent vocational employment for himself. As he put it, "I have no money of my own. I have a high standard of living, but I see no chance of ever realizing it. There are no steady jobs for the likes of me. What future is there for me?"

The young man drifts. He consoles himself with the social life that Chinatown has to offer. Every cent he makes he spends on clothes, "good times," while, as he expresses it, "my family gets angrier and angrier." His family would want him to find a job that would be permanent, so that he can marry, settle down, and forget all his foolishness.

"In fact," he adds, "they would be willing to loan me the money on which to marry if I would only agree. But what for?" he questions. "I would only be tying myself down, forever in debt. Forced to do whatever the old folks say. As long as I don't marry, I'll still be able to keep my independence, to do as I please."

Actually, however, the young man hasn't the independence he imagines. His freedom of action is definitely limited. He can find no job among Americans. He has thus far failed to hold one among his own people. His economic opportunities are limited and precarious, apt to be cut off at any time. If it were not for the generosity of his parents who keep him with room and board, he would never be able to maintain the high personal standard of living which he desires.

China holds no place for such an individual and the young man realizes this.[1] His only chance for a living, good or bad, is in Chinatown. But whether the young man has yet awakened to this fact or not remains to be discovered. Some of his more serious comrades have warned him of the danger of drifting. But he seems, or gives the impression, of being wholly enamored of American ways. He is ashamed of the old culture; and makes every effort to be as American as possible. This is manifested in every conceivable manner possible—in dress, speech, slang, ideas, sports, entertainment, and reading matters.

PULLMAN STEWARDESS

This is the brief case history of a second-generation American-born Chinese girl (1936).

---

1. Second-generation Chinese Americans who went to China during the 1930s for employment opportunities and/or nationalist reasons were generally well educated or trained in aviation.

She is born in San Francisco's Chinatown. Is about 28 years of age, with a high school education. Appears to have only a little formal Chinese education, although she speaks it well. Has no family and lives at the Chinese Y.W.C.A., considered to be the finest living accommodations in Chinatown.

She works on the Overland Limited railroad train of the Southern Pacific as a girl stewardess. She must wear Chinese clothes, namely jacket and trousers, but detests the idea. She makes $80 a month, plus tips. Explains that her monthly total income varies between $125 and $150 per month. Finds her work not too distasteful. The cultured and professional American classes she finds very interesting and tolerant. Can't stand salesmen and their families. Their ignorance of Chinese-American ways antagonizes her. Says: "They always are so surprised to see me reading American books and magazines and exclaim, 'Oh! Do you read English too?' They also are amazed at my fluent English. As if we could not speak, read or write. It gets my goat!" Explains that she has very little to do on the trains except to manicure fingernails and give high-class maid service to the wealthy travelers who desire it. Is extremely well thought of by the train-crew who treat her with respect. Has little to do with the Pullman porters or dining-room waiters. While somewhat sorry for their racial plight, she expresses the typical American woman's aversion toward Negroes. Compares the situation of the Chinese in this country with them, realizes that there isn't much future for a native-born Chinese. Concludes, "My job is not bad at all. There aren't many girls who can make as much as I do and the work is not difficult. I am satisfied to hang on to it until I get married."

She is engaged to a native-born Chinese college student, who is majoring in physical sciences. Just as soon as he receives his degree they plan to go back to Canton and live. Feels that China is the only place for American-born college graduates to live. Admits that the adjustments will be terrific, but is willing to make the attempt. Since there are so many who have returned and made the grade, she feels that she and her fiancé should be able to do likewise. States: "In China, we can be somebody. We can even walk the streets, without being stared at. I understand that there is a feeling of 'belonging' that is absent in America."

Although she has never explained the reason, she does feel racial discrimination very keenly. Speaks very strongly on the point of intermarriages. "I hate the idea of Chinese boys marrying white girls." When pressed for the reason, explains that such unions, so she has read and believes, end "unhappily." Her attitude in regard to interracial relations, however, is not consistent, for in the next breath she speaks with pride of her American and Japanese friendships, mainly with boys of her own age. Does not hesitate to go out with them if they invite her. This was before her engagement. Since she has promised _____ to accept him, she has discontinued her old interracial friendships. Concludes, "I might still go out with some of my old boy friends (regardless of race) if it were not for the fact that Chinatown gossips. The 'talk' is so bad that one gets a bad reputation immediately. It would never do for me to court disaster since my boyfriend is studying in the East and I would have no opportunity to explain to him in person why I accepted So-and-So's invitation. Therefore, I have considered it wisest not to go out with anybody except girls. I protect myself that way."

Despite an income of approximately $150 per month, she finds herself almost broke every month. Explains, "Easy come, easy go!" "When I stop off at Chicago," she continues, "I go to all the best shops and buy presents for myself and my friends." Insists upon $14 shoes . . . evidently because this compensates for her racial disadvantages. Maintains charge accounts at a number of the more exclusive shops in San Francisco and Chicago.

OWN COMMENTS: Typical native-born girl. Not exceptionally good-looking but has a very attractive, vivacious manner. Well turned out. Is extremely attractive in Chinese garments, which she detests. Her American clothes, however, err on the side of being a little too stylish. In other words, she, due to her opportunities of observing the wealthy society women on the Pullman trains, buys what they do, anticipating the style trend.

While stressing her Chinese background, herself, she is or gives the appearance, except for racial physical characteristics, of being just another American girl. In other words, her actions belie her claims. From the tone of her conversations, I gather that she would gladly remain in America and become an American if it were possible. Because of the advantage of money and travel, she unconsciously adopts a patronizing air toward the young people of her own race.

Have met her a number of times. Best opportunity for observation was when I made my last trip eastward. Observed that she kept very much alone, nothing much to do. Gather the impression that the Southern Pacific Company and the Pullman Company wish to exploit the Chinese atmosphere as much as possible. Even the bar stewards on many of these crack trains are Chinese, usually older men who are American-born. She had nothing to do with the bar-steward, explaining, "It's a better idea not to get too friendly with anybody—train crew or passengers—on a Pullman train. You never can tell what will happen."

Adds: "My best times on duty have been with well-to-do people of our own race, who are glad to have somebody to talk to. Also with cultured Americans, such as college professors, who seem to have a sympathetic understanding of our problems."

CONSUL GENERAL'S BANQUET

This long report begins with a careful description of a dinner hosted by the consulate general of China in San Francisco for prominent "second-generation" Chinese Amer-

icans in an effort to improve relations between the consulate and the Chinese community. Lowe included the following comments in his report about the second-generation guests.

The general characteristics of this group may be drawn as follows: Approximately one-quarter of the group were born and raised outside of Chinatown. In fact, the most interesting individuals, the ones who had become famous in the community either from a professional or social service viewpoint, were non-Chinatownians, driven back into S.F. Chinatown in order to find a place to exercise their talents and training. Practically all, men and women, are of the middle-class bourgeoisie. With hardly an exception, they are children of comparatively poor families who have early come into contact with Christian missionaries, their schools and training. As a result of this contact, their parents have been able to get ahead in business because of their knowledge of English or of American customs and the children have received the education and much of the training of Americans. Most of them have had to work their way through college since the family due to the large number of children cannot support them. This also accounts for the large number of the group who have attended the state university rather than some private college.

Practically all of the living of this group is gotten through Chinatown or the Chinese. Only one doctor (a woman) and one architect depend upon Americans for their source of livelihood. They live on a hyphenated Chinese American standard of living and where their income is sufficient, they are expected to support their parents and their brothers. (This includes purchase of homes, sending the brothers and sisters to college, aiding them to get started in business or helping them to get married.) In the period of prosperity, namely before 1930, when professional competition in the community was not so keen and everybody had money, this group was comparatively very well off. It owned its own homes, or lived in luxuriously furnished apartments, owned high priced automobiles, dabbled in the stock market, took extensive vacations, and gave constant and expensive parties both to their American and Chinese friends. Despite the depression, this group still manages to hold its own economically. Even though it may constantly run into debt, the old standards of living are still maintained.

With one or two exceptions, all of the men have married girls who have not had the same educational training as themselves. This can be explained by the fact that the old style families did not believe in giving their daughters more than high school training. Those girls who did succeed in acquiring a college education were of unusual character and ability and usually seldom married. Marriage was difficult for them, for few of the uneducated Chinese dared ask them for their hand and the group of college-educated Chinese was highly limited.

It is interesting to note that out of this small group of 100 or so young people there were four who had contracted interracial marriages, all of them outside of the state of California. A Chinese male artist had married an American college girl (non-Californian); a Chinese lawyer (from Hawaii) had married an American woman teacher in Honolulu; a Chinese woman insurance broker had married an American architect (non-Californian); and a Chinese male research assistant had married an American musician (non-Californian). All four inter-married couples were present at the banquet. No discrimination was shown.

Although most of the group has been married for some time, only about 15 couples (out of a total of 50) had children. Two couples had three children each, two couples had two, and the rest, 11 couples, had one each. (Since then, 1933, some four years have passed, and of the same total group, there have been only 5 babies added.) From general conversation with couples in this group and from general hearsay, there is definite indication that birth control is being practiced. The mothers of this group invariably go to the hospitals for confinement and are accustomed to both pre- and postnatal medical attention; also to the well-baby clinical services. Child rearing for them is less arduous than for their parents, who usually raised six or more children at the same time, but more expensive since they will not accept anything but the best for their infants.

The foods eaten by this group are mainly American; breakfast and lunch is always American; much of it being ordered from the Chinatown restaurants. The main meal of the day, dinner, is usually Chinese. Quite often the main dishes are also ordered from Chinatown's Chinese restaurants. The ease with which this can be done and the economical prices charged for dishes induce housewives to constantly fall back on this practice. If desired, no meals need to be prepared at home. Should one be hungry at any time during the 24 hours, day or night, a simple phone call will bring piping hot Chinese or American meals to one's home within 15 minutes.

Clothing is always as expensive as the couple can afford. For the women, at least, much of their time is spent in shopping for American clothes, which are the external symbols of prosperity. To be in style is very important for one's local personal prestige. One woman's organization boasts that none of the members ever attend their numerous social functions in the same costume twice. While there is not the same competitive stress on clothing among the men-folk, there is no apparent slovenliness. This desire for neatness in appearance and for fashionable men's clothes stems from a desire to appear no different than other non-Chinese Americans in the eyes of the general public. In other words, there is an intense desire for conformity, which finds its expression (or one of them) in wearing the same style of men's clothing. Man for man, the Chinese-American white-collared individual far outshines the American in neatness of dress and in style. As one young Chinese-American put it, "It's bad enough to be a Chinese in America without drawing added attention by being shabbily or improperly dressed. Besides, no one wants to be classified as a 'greenhorn' newly arrived from the old country."

Housework is not a very important item with the women of this group, especially for those who live in the modern apartments. Vacuum sweepers, carpet cleaners and modern cleaning equipment make household cleaning comparatively easy. Where many of the meals are ordered from the Chinatown restaurants, dish washing is unnecessary, as the restaurant dishes are invariably returned unclean. In case of heavy housecleaning such as washing windows and cleaning kitchen walls, Negroes and Filipinos are hired at the rate of $2 per day to do the work. Very little of the laundry is done at home, except for the women's personal linen. Chinatown's laundries are good, speedy and cheap.

There is much leisure for the wives of the professional group, if they are disposed to enjoy it. Where their children are old enough to go to both Chinese and American schools, little of their time is required to train them. For those whose husbands' incomes are insufficient to meet the ever-expansible wants of a typical middle-class Chinese-American family, the wives usually engage in some occupation such as working the garment-sewing factories (a social as well as an economic activity), serve as clerks in stores, or do odd jobs. Where the husband's income is sufficient, however, outside work for the wife is no longer a necessity. For such a fortunate wife, there are innumerable outlets for her social activities. First and foremost, there are the countless games of ma jong and bridge which are played every afternoon and evening in the homes of many of the wealthier groups of Chinatown. Ma jong, particularly, does not draw the line between generations of Chinese women. At the same table may be found women who are grandmothers, young matrons, and even girls not yet out of high school. The latter group [is] fairly rare and are only invited to play where there are insufficient players. According to the older women, it is not right for young children not yet economically self-sufficient to gamble. The point to be emphasized, however, is that by means of ma jong and other games of amusement the older and younger generations of women in Chinatown are brought very close together. The ma jong table becomes the training-school, as it were, where the older generation of women pass on the traditional lore by word of mouth to the younger Americanized women. Bridge is mainly a younger generation game and is mainly indulged in when the women's modern social groups get together for their periodic teas and celebrations. Poker and blackjack are Western card games in which the older women sometimes join the younger ones.

For the women who do not care for games, there are other outlets. She may join any one of a score of clubs sponsored by Chinese, religious or educational organizations. The chief of these, of course, is the FIDELIS CO-TERIE. This organization is like the Junior League in conception and in its activities. Stress is laid on giving monthly luncheons at the very best American hotels, periodic parties at home, entertainments for "sweet charity's sake." As observed, the organization is made up of the non–college educated wives of the more successful professional men of Chinatown (including San Francisco and the East Bay). The organization tends towards snobbery and aims to be exclusive. Presumably divorcees and the poor are ineligible for membership. Whether because the younger college graduates do not wish to be associated with a group with ultra-Babbitt virtues, or whether it is because they do not have the income with which to meet the excessive expenses attached to such a membership, it is nevertheless true that few of them join this group. The age of most members is in the forty-year group. This also constitutes a barrier. So often has the boast been heard from members of this organization that its motto should read, "Money can do anything!"

Most of these women are able to drive automobiles. In the wealthier families the wife always has her own car. Weekend trips and long automobile excursions during vacation periods are very common.

For the men, fishing, the cultivation of indoor fish pools, trap shooting, hunting, golf, motoring, as well as the common forms of gambling—usually poker and ma jong—are the chief recreations. To this should be added "good food."

Religion does not play too prominent a part in the lives of this group. Although all are members of early Christian families and have a "sound" Protestant training, few are actually active church members. They do, however, send their children to Sunday School in order, as they express it, "to learn how to do good," "to learn morality," and to "keep them out of mischief." They subscribe to their churches during financial campaigns but not generously. They observe baptisms and deaths and weddings in the Christian manner, but aside from these family crises they do not participate actively in religious rites. Easter and Christmas see them usually attending church. Their attendance is conditioned partly by their own childhood training, partly by their desire to conform to the ideals of their non-Chinese fellow citizens, and where they have children, by the desire to see their children perform in the services.

This group does not believe in the old Chinese religious superstitions. It is not above tolerating them, however, and will, if compelled, observe them at funerals, weddings, christenings, etc. Its dominant religious beliefs are colored by Protestant Christianity—as are its morals.

As a group the second-generation professionals and their wives believe in performing their American citizenship duties. They do this not only in order to justify their citizenship but also to impress the outsiders (namely Americans) that they are worthy of this privilege. It might be mentioned also that they vote in order to protect their own interests as much as possible. For the last two presidential elections, this group has been evenly divided between the Republicans and Democrats. As with the Americans, the same motives impelled each group of Chinese professionals to vote as they did. The wealthier Chinese believed that Republicanism would preserve their status better, while those not so well to do wanted the Democrats to win so that they could get better jobs. It was a case of the "Haves" versus the "Have Nots." A secondary factor was the belief that the Republicans were primarily pro–Open Door and friendly to China and that the Democrats were more inclined to let such a dangerous policy lapse. It was also believed that the Republicans would give the Chinese a better deal since they have been traditionally pro-Chinese as regards the Chinese domiciled in this country. The Democrats were still considered to be anti-Chinese through and through. Neither of these last two factors, however, had much to do in swaying the Chinatown electorate.

While voting at every opportunity, these professionals and their families are none too hopeful that every right, implicit as well as explicit, will be granted them by the American government. Such a goal will eventually be attained, they believe, if Chinese immigration restriction continues and the Chinese become entirely Americanized and the Americans a little more understanding and tolerant of the Chinese-American background. In order to achieve this end, this group always eagerly joins any Chinatown organization whose purpose is to improve the conditions of Chinatown and its inhabitants. "The Oppose Anti-Exclusion" activities of the Six Companies; the Americanization efforts of the native-sons organization; and the civic improvement efforts of the Chinatown Progressive Association meet with its approval.

This group believes in keeping healthy. It relies mainly upon Western medicine and medical methods. However, it is willing to also experiment with Chinese herbalists and herbs where Western medicine fails to give relief. Healthy recreation, mainly out-of-doors, and the pursuit of hobbies represent health-contributing activities.

This group also believes in the Community Chest communal type of care for the "down and out" of Chinatown. However, in regard to its own personal family, it still retains the old sense of familial responsibility. It does not particularly favor the old methods of caring for the unable, which relied upon the district organizations and sub-organizations.

Little of the news either of Chinatown or of the outside world is obtained by this group from Chinatown's five [Chinese-language] newspapers. Reliance is mainly based upon the reading of the American daily newspapers for outside news; the *Chinese Digest* for news about the Chinese second generation; and gossip and the "grapevine telegraph" for news about the old folks in Chinatown.

In conclusion it might be well to speak a little about what the dinner party that the Consul General gave was for. When the Consul General, a native-born Chinese of Singapore, educated partly in China and then in the higher institutions of the United States, became the Consul General of San Francisco, he wished to bring about a closer sense of cooperation between the consulate and the older and younger generations of Chinatown. In order to meet the most representative group of the younger people, he had his consulate staff prepare an invitational list. A series of American banquets in a Chinatown dine and dance palace followed. The first and chief banquet was the one which I attended. It was an extremely representative group of second-generation young people. The program of the evening included dancing and speeches. The speeches included one for the introduction to the newly arrived Consul General and the other was made by the Consul General himself. The gist of the latter's remarks was that the separation of the viewpoint of the younger and older generation of Chinatown was both great and tragic; and that unless such a gap were bridged, he could see little hope for the future of the community; and that it would be his duty to see that such a gap should be bridged.

For the two years that this Consul General served here, he did all that he possibly could to bridge this gap. While he did not succeed in any great measure, he did contrive to win the affections of the younger generation. In the minds of the younger generation, he represents the best Consul General yet sent by the Chinese Government. Because of his efforts, they believe that the Chinese Government is actually a little bit interested in the welfare of the Overseas Chinese.

SOURCE: Pardee Lowe Collection, Hoover Institution on War, Revolution and Peace, Stanford University.

OTHER REFERENCES

Pardee Lowe, *Father and Glorious Descendant* (Boston: Little, Brown, 1943).

K. Scott Wong and Sucheng Chan, eds., *Claiming America: Constructing Chinese American Identities during the Exclusion Era* (Philadelphia: Temple University Press, 1998).

Judy Yung, *Unbound Feet: A Social History of Chinese Women in San Francisco* (Berkeley: University of California Press, 1995).

I Am Growing More Chinese— Each Passing Year! (1934)

Anna May Wong

In this interview with Los Angeles columnist Harry Carr, twenty-nine-year-old Anna May Wong reflects on her Chinese American identity at the pinnacle of her successful career as a film actress. The second child in a family of seven children, Wong was born in Los Angeles in 1905. She made over sixty films in an acting career that spanned two world wars and that, more often than not, was limited by stereotypical and demeaning roles of the Mongol slave or spurned Chinese mistress. As she tells Carr in this interview, Anna May Wong had always wanted to be an actress, even if it meant going against the wishes of her parents, who operated a laundry outside Chinatown. Opportunities opened up to her because she was in the right place at the right time, but also because she was persistent, hardworking, and talented. However, racial discrimination in the guise of American orientalism and "yellowface" typecasting prevented her from ever realizing her full potential in Hollywood.

At the time of this interview, she had just returned from a successful tour in Europe, where she played leading screen and stage roles and was widely acclaimed by German and British critics. In the afterglow of her European achievements, Anna May Wong spoke with self-confidence and assurance about her future as a Chinese American actress. No longer the "defensive little Hollywood flapper," she said, she now found "solace and philosophy in the tradition of my own people."

With every passing year I feel myself more Chinese; it is as though I were taking up the heritage of my race. Yet I have never seen China.

My father came from a little town near Canton.[1] He is Chinese to the bottom of his soul, charitable, tolerant, wise.

I was born in Los Angeles. My real name is Wong Luie Song[2]—which

1. In other accounts, Anna May Wong said that her father, Wong Sam Sing, was born in Michigan Bluffs, California, and her mother, Lee Gon Toy, was born in Oakland, California.

2. Anna May Wong usually spelled her Chinese name Liu Tsong.

Anna May Wong in
the 1930s. (Courtesy
of Elaine Mae Woo)

means "Yellow Frosted Willow." I did not learn to speak English until I went
to school.

My first school was in the old building on California Street. I was very miserable. The American boys used to chase me around at recess, called me a
Chink and pulled my little pigtail.

I don't think I resented it bitterly or ever hated them. To me it was a vague
impersonal danger and misery. Later I went to another public school where
I was treated kindly.[3] When I was old enough, my father sent me in the evenings
to a native Chinese school where I learned to read and write Chinese.

NO SHINING STUDENT

I am afraid I did not shine as a student, either by day in the American schools
or in Chinese in the evenings. The whole thing seemed like a vague dream.

3. The racial harassment got so bad that her parents ended up sending the children to the
Chinese Mission School in Chinatown. Later, Anna May Wong attended Los Angeles High
School, where she said she faced no discrimination.

However, I must have tried hard because Chinese writing is terribly complicated and difficult and I learned to read and write.

At a very early age, I went movie-crazy. I used to play hookey from schools to go to the 5-cent movies. With Chinese logic, my father used to protest that if I had to be a bad girl and play hookey, why didn't I play hookey from the American school, which cost him nothing, instead of the Chinese school where he had to pay tuition.

We always celebrate Christmas at our little house. My sister Ying begged for a big doll with flaxen curls who would squeak Mama and Papa when her tummy was squeezed. I asked for a whole lot of little dolls. I had a purpose:

MY BED A STAGE

Using my bed for a stage, I arranged the tiny dolls for actors and made up all sorts of dramas of my own. When my brother Jimmy got old enough, I pressed him into service and we two acted plays that I made up. Jimmy, being all boy, finally struck and refused to play-act any more.

One day I happened to see a movie in which was a Chinese actor. I ran around to an old Chinese who helped out the movies by getting Chinese actors for them. He looked me over critically. "Well," he said, "you are a big girl and you have big eyes; you will do." I felt flattered until I learned that he had just had an order for 600 Chinese actors in a hurry and hadn't been able to find but fifty.[4]

SO I RAN HOME

I ran home and announced to my parents that I had decided to be a motion-picture star. To say they were displeased is not to express the idea. They simply hit the ceiling. The Chinese had old-fashioned notions about play-acting.

I defended myself, saying that I didn't see anything wrong with a business in which so many of their old friends were engaging. They were staggered. Just then a squadron of buses stopped at our house to pick me up. There were about 150 Chinese on the way to the studios to play extra parts and my father and mother knew most of them. They stayed so long gossiping in front of the house that the picture was kept waiting; but meanwhile I had slipped without further objection into the van.

That first day I simply walked around with a mob of Chinese. Later the director told me to come back for another picture in which I could play a part as one of three girls who could carry lanterns. I felt the responsibility for the whole movie industry on my shoulders.

4. James Wang, an actor and casting agent, was looking for Chinese extras for the film *The Red Lantern* (1919).

I had noticed that actresses were "made up" on the sets, so I produced a grand scenic version of myself. I borrowed my mother's rice powder rag and fairly kalsomined my face. With the most painstaking effort, I managed to curl my straight Chinese hair. As a finishing touch, I took one of our Chinese red papers, wet it and rubbed off the color onto my lips and cheeks.

The director looked at me with astonishment and gasped: "Good God!"

Two costume women, under his orders, seized me, rubbed off my fine red cheeks and washed down my head until they got the curl out of my hair.

When the picture came out, I went without lunch for more than a week to save money enough to take five girl friends up to the top gallery of the old California Theater on Main Street to witness my triumph.

All we saw were three dim Chinese girls walking by with lanterns. "Which is you?" my girl friends asked. "I . . . I don't know," I faltered. "I think I must be the outside one."

I had a long wait, but finally Mickie Neilan gave me a real part. I was the Chinese mistress of Noah Beery in a drama.[5]

Finally I was lucky enough to be cast in an early picture of Norma Talmadge's—made in color.[6] I had a tragic part in which I had to cry. I cried so that I could not stop crying. Finally the cynical assistant director called out: "Someone throw Anna May Wong a raft."

I had in the meantime become Anna May. We chose the first name because all of the children of our family had American names with four letters. I added the name "May" because Anna Wong didn't sound well and I liked the suggestion of springtime in "May."

My big chance came through Douglas Fairbanks when he gave me a part in "Thief of Bagdad."[7]

Just as I was finishing that picture, I had an offer to go to Germany.

I felt it was a crisis in my life. In a way I was running away from something that was beginning to develop into at least a good chance of a career in Hollywood—yet the door opened and I walked through.

There have been three events that were psychological mileposts in my life.

The first was when the worm turned, so to speak, and I ceased to be on the defensive. When I was about 17, a truck came booming down the street and the driver yelled for me to get out of the way. He called me "Chink." To my own surprise I blazed back a remark equally insulting at him and he wilted. That was the turning of a corner for me.

5. Marshall Neilan took a liking to Anna May Wong and wrote the part of Toy Sing for her in *Bits of Life* (1921).

6. In *The Toll of the Sea* (1922), Anna May Wong played the leading role of Lotus Flower, who dutifully commits suicide after her white lover abandons her for someone of his own race.

7. Anna May Wong's supporting role as the "Mongol slave" in *The Thief of Bagdad* (1924) stole the show, and from then on she was known as Hollywood's "Oriental siren."

NEXT MILEPOST: BERLIN

My next milestone was in Berlin. The first picture in which I appeared made a hit.[8] Crowds waited in the lobby for me to come out. Weaving my way through that pack of admiring fans, I seemed suddenly to be standing at one side watching myself with complete detachment. It was my Chinese soul coming back to claim me. Up to that time I had been more of an American flapper than Chinese. That was also the turning of a corner.

Other film offers came up in Germany, but the producer of my first picture advised me to go to France and to England first, then come back to Germany.[9]

That early stay in England was a wonderful experience for me. The English are a cool, detached, broad-minded people. I made warm friendships that helped me. I studied German, French and music.

Strange to say, the more deeply I studied, the more did my Chinese blood call to me. I found solace and philosophy in the tradition of my own people.

My friends say that my appearance and manner have changed since my early Hollywood flapper days. I know that I feel differently in my consciousness.

I don't believe that anything would ever worry me again. Those pigtail pulling days of my terror and unhappiness could never come back.

TIMELESSNESS, A SAVIOR

I suppose what I feel is the racial philosophy of the Chinese, and that philosophy could be expressed as timelessness.

This is such a short life that nothing can matter very much either one way or another. I have learned not to struggle but to flow along with the tide. If I am to be rich and famous, that will be fine. If not, what do riches and fame count in the long run?

Above all else, Chinese blood beckons to a great tolerance. Sometimes one hears that even the Chinese coolies have a feeling of superiority. That is not strictly true. What he feels for other and more hectic struggling races is a vast pity. He feels sorry for them as one feels sorry for a squirrel madly running around a wheel in a cage. Nowhere to go and taxing his strength to get there.

Chinese are imbued with the consciousness that each of us is only a link in a long life chain. The important thing is the family. What does it matter that one link shines more brightly than another? Chinese are good business men, but a Chinese merchant never hurries and never struggles. He keeps his same little shop and saves his money.

8. Anna May Wong received rave reviews for her performance in *Song* (1928), in which she portrayed a German-Malayan woman in a doomed love affair with a white man.

9. Richard Eichberg, an independent German producer, was Anna May Wong's mentor and adviser during her European tour.

CHINA IS ROOTED SOUNDLY

Time adjusts all things. China knows that it is rooted in sound philosophy and inward strength. It has gone its slow serene way and seen empires rise and fall; nations rise to grandeur and power; then to perish.

It is the Chinese way to sit still, enjoy each day and each period of life— serene in the knowledge that an all-wise Providence is working out a plan of which each of us is a part.

We can't hurry the slowly grinding mills of the gods; and we do not wish to.

China will be a great nation one day. We know that. What does it matter if it is in this decade or next century or the century after that.

· I—that flustered, worried, defensive little Hollywood flapper—found happiness when I ceased to worry about time.

No one can give me what belongs to some one else; and no one can take away that which is mine.

In 1935 Anna May Wong was turned down for the leading role of O-lan in The Good Earth, *and the part was given instead to the white actress Luise Rainer. Devastated, she traveled to China for ten months to study Chinese theater and to visit her father, who had retired to his home village in Taishan. There, to her dismay, she was chastised for portraying roles that demeaned the Chinese. On her return to the United States, she found roles in films that were more sympathetic to the Chinese, as in* Daughter of Shanghai (1937), *thanks to the allied relationship between China and the United States during the war years. She also did her part for the war effort by fundraising for China and by entertaining American troops in Alaska and Canada. Then she faded into obscurity, working only intermittently in film and television, until she died of a heart attack in 1961 at the age of fifty-six.*

SOURCE: *Los Angeles Times Sunday Magazine,* September 9, 1934, p. 3. Reprinted by permission of the *Los Angeles Times.*

OTHER REFERENCES

Anthony B. Chan, *Perpetually Cool: The Many Lives of Anna May Wong* (Lanham, Md.: Scarecrow Press, 2003).

Judy Chu, "Anna May Wong," in *Counterpoint: Perspectives on Asian America,* ed. Emma Gee (Los Angeles: Asian American Studies Center, UCLA, 1976), pp. 284–89.

Graham Russell Gao Hodges, *Anna May Wong: From Laundryman's Daughter to Hollywood Legend* (New York: Palgrave Macmillan, 2004).

Karen Leong, *The China Mystique: Pearl S. Buck, Anna May Wong, Mayling Soong, and the Transformation of American Orientalism* (Berkeley: University of California Press, 2005).

Anna May Wong, "The True Life Story of a Chinese Girl," *Pictures,* August 1926, pp. 28–29, 106–8; September 1926, pp. 34–35, 72, 74–75.

Declaration of the Chinese Hand Laundry Alliance (1933)

The anti-Chinese movement that culminated in the passage of the Chinese Exclusion Act of 1882 succeeded in reducing the overall Chinese population as well as driving Chinese workers out of the more desirable occupations. By the turn of the century, one out of every four Chinese men was eking out a living as a laundryman. Although laundry work required ten to sixteen hours a day of tedious and menial labor, Chinese gravitated to it because it did not require English fluency or much capital. The largest concentration was in New York City, where there were estimated to be 3,550 Chinese laundries when the Great Depression hit.

In 1933, the non-Chinese laundries in New York City convinced the Board of Aldermen to pass a city ordinance requiring all laundrymen to pay an annual licensing fee of $25 and a security bond of $1,000. It also required U.S. citizenship of all laundry operators. The new law was obviously intended to drive the Chinese competition out of business. When the Chinese Consolidated Benevolent Association (CCBA) proved ineffectual in dealing with the crisis, the Chinese laundry workers took matters into their own hands and created the Chinese Hand Laundry Alliance (CHLA).

The following declaration, supported by 254 laundrymen, came out of CHLA's founding meeting. The Alliance went on to successfully challenge the new law. The licensing fee was reduced to $10 and the security bond to $100, and, most important, Chinese were exempted from the citizenship requirement. Reflecting the rise of radical politics in the country at the time, it was the first time that a leftist group had openly challenged the power structure of New York Chinatown.

Soon after, CHLA's membership grew to more than 3,000 and the organization became actively involved in supporting China's War of Resistance against Japan while criticizing Chiang Kai-shek's Nationalist regime. In the 1960s and 1970s, the CHLA supported the civil rights movement and called for the normalization of U.S.-China relations. By then, however, its membership had dropped to about 100 as a result of

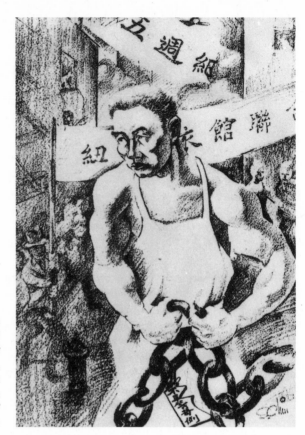

Artwork from
the cover of a 1938
Chinese Hand Laundry
Alliance pamphlet,
showing a laundryman
breaking the chain
of "unequal laws."
(Courtesy of Renqiu Yu)

FBI harassment during the McCarthy period and the overall decline of the hand laundry business.

Ever since China's fence of insulation was broken by European and American capitalist-imperialism, the Chinese socioeconomic basis was fundamentally shaken.[1] The rural economy was bankrupt, and urban industries shut one after another. Unable to make a living [in China], we were forced from our families, to leave our hometowns, and to go overseas to seek petty profits. But we do not have large amounts of capital to invest in commerce, therefore most of us in this country are engaging in the hand laundry business. So, this trade became the lifeline of the Chinese community, and our wives and children back home depend on it too.

---

1. In reference to foreign incursions into China in the second half of the nineteenth century.

Recently the New York City Council of Aldermen proposed a discriminatory ordinance against hand laundries. If the ordinance is unfortunately passed and becomes effective on July 1, tens of thousands of Chinese laundrymen would be stranded in this country and our wives and children back home would be starved to death. . . . That's why we have to fight against it with every effort.

However, we Chinese laundrymen in New York City never had a formal organization of our own. The organization that existed in the past exploited us in disguised names.[2] It failed to protect our interests and, worse, it damaged our business. This has been proven by our experiences in the past. Therefore we have to organize a formal organization that truly represents our own interests in this campaign to fight the discriminatory ordinance. Without such an organization, there is no hope to abolish the discriminatory ordinance. The CCBA and the organizations under its control cannot represent our case to the City government. They are but taking this chance selfishly to serve their interests.

Based on these reasons, we set up the preparatory committee of the New York CHLA, expecting to establish as early as possible an organization that truly represents the interests of the Chinese hand laundries. [With such an organization] we can not only unite ourselves to fight the City government collectively so as to abolish the discriminatory ordinance, but also prevent such discrimination from occurring again in the future. Moreover, our own organization will be able to solve the problem of the rapid decline of service charges as a result of competition among hand laundries. Collective efforts will make the service charges rise again. In short, to establish a collective organization is indeed an urgent task for us.

—Two Hundred Fifty-four Hand Laundrymen

SOURCE: *Chinese Nationalist Daily*, April 24, 1933, p. 1, and as translated in Renqiu Yu, *To Save China, to Save Ourselves: The Chinese Hand Laundry Alliance of New York* (Philadelphia: Temple University Press, 1992), p. 35. Reprinted by permission of Renqiu Yu.

OTHER REFERENCES

Peter Kwong, *Chinatown, N.Y.: Labor and Politics, 1930–1950* (New York: Monthly Review Press, 1979).

Him Mark Lai, "To Bring Forth a New China, to Build a Better America: The Chinese Marxist Left in America to the 1960s," *Chinese America: History and Perspectives*, 1992, pp. 3–82.

Leong Gor Yun, *Chinatown Inside Out* (New York: Barrows Mussey, 1936).

Paul Siu, *The Chinese Laundryman: A Study of Social Isolation* (New York: New York University Press, 1987).

2. According to sympathizers in the CHLA, previous laundrymen's guilds had been more interested in extracting fees and dues from their members than in representing their interests.

Chinese Women's Association Condensed Report for the Years 1932–1936

The Japanese attack on China drew women from all walks of life into the public arena to do their part for the war effort. Soon after Japan occupied Manchuria in 1931, women's organizations formed across the country—in New York, San Francisco, Chicago, Seattle, and Portland—to do fundraising, propaganda, and Red Cross work. One of the earliest and most effective groups was the Chinese Women's Association (CWA) in New York. As early as October 14, 1931, it fired off letters to newspaper editors who had been advocating that the United States stay out of the war in China. Calling this stance "immoral" and "cowardly" in view of Japanese war atrocities in China, the women argued that the United States should uphold its earlier pledge to help settle all international disputes by peaceful means. The organization was successful in mobilizing Chinese women in New York to raise over $30,000 for the relief of war refugees within a year's time.

As this rare report of Chinese women's activities indicates, CWA also played a major role in helping immigrant women and their daughters adapt to life in America, promoting better relations between Chinese Americans and the larger society, and providing social services to the Chinese community in New York City. The modern, middle-class aspirations of the group reflected the background of its leaders. Theodora Chan Wang, the chairwoman who wrote this report, held a master's degree from Columbia University and had served as the general secretary of the Chinatown YWCA for ten years prior to founding CWA. Moreover, the stated purposes and activities of the organization speak to the changing gender role and increased political activism among Chinese women in America that were inspired by the war and the times.

The record of this Association's steady increase in membership to over 350 together with its great activities during the last five years speaks for itself. For the sake of clarity, I wish to divide this report into three parts: (I) The purpose, (II) The activities and (III) The future plans of this Association.

PART I—THE PURPOSE

New York Chinatown, with a population of almost 10,000, is the second largest Chinese community center in the U.S.A. With a Chinese population of about 16,000, San Francisco already can claim to have two organizations for Chinese women. But here in New York, at the time when this Association was formed, there was not even a single club room being provided for Chinese women. When the Gen. Sec'y of Chinese Y.W.C.A. in San Francisco sent me a beautifully engraved invitation card announcing the grand opening of its new 6-story "Y" building with its spacious auditorium, dormitories, gymnasium and swimming pool,[1] I immediately sent her the following telegram, "HEARTY CONGRATULATIONS AND BEST WISHES ON THE GRAND OPENING OF YOUR NEW BUILDING." It was such a beautiful women's club building located at 965 Clay St., San Francisco, Calif., that it was no wonder they felt very proud of their new headquarters.

According to the law of supply and demand, surely there must be some good reason for a beautiful building like that to come into existence. In order to prove my point, I will take New York Chinatown as a concrete example. We have here, as I mentioned above, a total Chinese population of almost 10,000. But, due to the U.S. Immigration restrictions, out of this total, we have here only about 250 Chinese families—with an average of about four children in each family. You will thus notice that the male and female ratios amongst the Chinese are all out of proportion. Then again, due to a peculiar trait of the Chinese race as a whole, they do not mingle with people of other nationalities as readily as they should. Furthermore, as we all know, the figure on illiteracy among the overseas Chinese is rather high. According to a statement issued recently by the Chinese National Association of the Mass Education Movement, the percentage of illiterates was over 85 percent. For these and various other reasons, the Chinese are somewhat forced to live closely by one another, and to try to be self-sufficient unto themselves. With most of our elder residents in Chinatown, although they are living right in the heart of this great metropolis, yet they know so very little about American home life and its higher standard of living that they might as well be still living in a village back in China.

Although we have here quite a few men's clubs, societies, etc., nevertheless, there is in the whole of Chinatown not one social organization for Chinese women and their children. The elder people, being used to suffer solitude, may be content to remain at home most of the time. But with the young people of the second generation, they positively refuse to tolerate such con-

---

1. The new Chinese YWCA building in San Francisco, designed by Julia Morgan and built with funds from the local YWCA and Chinese community, did not have a swimming pool, but the girls were allowed to use the swimming pool at the Chinese YMCA.

ditions any longer. Yet, due to a lack of social and club facilities in China-town, the boys can only amuse themselves with an occasional picture show or else they will patronize undesirable pool rooms. As for the girls, the only diversion they can have outside of dish washing, house cleaning and other family drudgeries, is for them to follow the boys to movies. As a consequence, they oftentimes fall into bad company. To safeguard these youngsters' moral as well as their physical well-being, and at the same time, to improve their mothers' standard of living, is what this Association has been laboring so hard to accomplish. In the club room of this Association, the Chinese mothers and these young persons of the second generation are provided with a place where they may exercise, amuse or try to improve themselves socially, men-tally, spiritually and physically—and under wholesome conditions.

In brief, the particular purposes for which this Association is formed are as follows:

(a) TO PROMOTE, CREATE AND MAINTAIN SOCIAL FELLOWSHIP AND COM-PANIONSHIP AMONGST THE OVERSEAS CHINESE WOMEN AND THEIR FRIENDS;
(b) TO PROMOTE, STIMULATE, CREATE AND MAINTAIN BETTER UNDER-STANDING OF THE CHINESE AND THEIR CUSTOMS, HISTORY AND PROBLEMS, AND TO THAT END TO PROVIDE A PLACE OF MEETING AND ENTERTAINMENT;
(c) TO ARRANGE AND CONTRACT FOR OUTINGS, PICNICS AND EXCURSIONS FOR THE MEMBERS, THEIR FAMILIES AND FRIENDS;
(d) TO PROMOTE CLOSE COOPERATION AND UNDERSTANDING AMONGST ITS MEMBERS AND THOSE OF SIMILAR ORGANIZATIONS;
(e) TO RENDER PRACTICAL SERVICES TOWARDS THE WELFARE OF CHINA AND THAT OF THE OVERSEAS CHINESE IN THE UNITED STATES OF AMERICA.

PART II—THE NATURE AND SCOPE OF ACTIVITIES

A. SOCIAL ACTIVITIES:

1. On Sept. 1st, 1934, at Port Arthur Restaurant, 7 Mott St., New York City, an elaborate testimonial dinner was given by members of this As-sociation in honor of our greatest modern hero, General Tsai Ting-kai. Gen. Tsai, as is well known, was the commander of that famous 19th Route Army, who so successfully repulsed the Japanese from Shanghai in 1932.

There were present at our welcome banquet more than 200 of our members and friends, who seemed to represent the whole female Chi-nese community here in the East. Gen. Tsai was ushered in by Mrs. Chun Doshim, Chairman of the Reception Committee. He made such a rousing speech, which was full of meaning and inspiration, that all those present seemed to be deeply touched. In consideration of the huge crowd waiting patiently outside, his address had to be broadcast by loud-speakers installed on Pell and Mott Streets. He was accompanied on this occasion by his secretary, C. S. Mark, Esq., and General Tom Kai Shau, who so bravely defended the Woo Sung ports during the combined Japanese Army and Navy attack. . . .

Upon his arrival in the city from Europe aboard S.S. "Olympic," Gen. Tsai was met down the bay by a delegation from this Association in the company of that of the seven largest local Chinese organizations. Three planes flown by members of the Chinese Aviation Association also went along to circle around his ship at quarantine in his honor.

At the West 14th St. Pier, there were thousands of residents from local Chinese communities together with more than two hundred automobiles bearing reception committees waiting there to greet our "Saviour of Shanghai." With a motorcycle police escort, we finally managed to reach Mott Street, where a crowd estimated at between 7,000 to 8,000 people gave him another rousing reception. The streets were so crowded that all automobile traffic, with the exception of cars carrying the reception committees, was kept off Chinatown.

2. Another Reception Committee was sent only recently to welcome Dr. C. T. Wang, former Minister of Foreign Affairs, upon his arrival in this city on June 13th, 1936. Due to the fact that this Association is the only Chinese women's organization in existence here in New York, we have often been called upon to participate in all receptions of importance. Ever since we succeeded in raising that record sum of $30,000 during the year 1932 for the relief of Chinese war and flood refugees, the importance of this Association has grown considerably, and its name is known far and wide.

3. In order to make the mothers and their children feel more at home, many kinds of indoor games have been introduced in our clubrooms. They all seem to enjoy the games very much. At times, we also have on hand high school girls reading to them aloud the current events of China.

4. Your Association has been acting as hostess to club members of many other nationalities, such as Italian, Greek, Russian, etc. Large delegations from out of town have also come to visit us from time to time.

5. Arrangements have often been made for our members to visit, as guests and in small groups, some of those refined American and Chinese homes. In this way, many of our members get their first glimpse of a real American home life. As a result of these visits, classes have been formed for them to study table manners, interior decoration, etc.

6. The Chinese Mothers' Club celebrated its 16th Anniversary last year

on April 11th. Among those present were many American friends and other celebrities.

7. During the last few years, our Girls Boxing Teams were frequently being called upon by American clubs to give sword and shadow boxing exhibitions. From the many letters of thanks which we have since received, we are pleased to learn that our friends always seem to enjoy seeing this, our national art of defense.

8. Our last Double-Tenth Anniversary Party was quite a picturesque affair. There were present more than 100 mothers together with their children. Members from our "Girls Dramatic Club" presented a charming play in costume.

B. INTELLECTUAL ACTIVITIES:

1. Being a member of the Chinese National Association of Mass Education, this Association was fortunate in securing the service of several volunteer leaders to teach some of our elders simplified Chinese characters. It is hoped that some day there will be less illiterate mothers left in our community.

2. During the last few years, frequent sightseeing trips were made by club members to visit different museums, art centers, expositions, telephone exchanges, great industrial factories, etc. These trips have always proved to be very popular and educational.

3. Reading Clubs have been formed by several groups. Members often bring their own books, magazines, etc. to serve as reading and discussion material.

4. Several religious and semi-religious institutions have invited members of our different clubs to hear lectures and to review their educational and artistic exhibits held in their auditoriums. We shall always welcome such invitations from other institutions.

5. Public relationship departments of two industrial concerns were kind enough to have several short and informative motion pictures shown, free of charge, to our members. We shall always appreciate such courtesies.

C. SPIRITUAL ACTIVITIES:

Introducing those who wish to join churches, Sunday schools, etc. without discrimination as to denomination. Being free from all rivalry and partiality in our recommendation, this Association is in an admirable position to act as a "Central Religious Clearing House."

D. PHYSICAL ACTIVITIES:

1. One fine day last summer, a group of our younger members drove out to Port Washington for deep sea fishing. Although their catch was not

very big, still they all managed to have a wonderful time. Through the kindness and generosity of friends of this Association, both the motor boat and the automobile were placed at our members' disposal free. Hiking, picnicing and camping in different parts of the country also have been indulged in by our members from time to time.

2. Due to lack of space and facilities, we have not much opportunity for outdoor sports. Our younger members have been wanting for some time to form a C.W.A. Basket-Ball Team and a Tennis Team so that one day they may be in a position to compete with other teams. If the service of competent instructors can be secured, we feel confident that strong teams can result from the materials we have on hand. The young ladies are also very fond of swimming, dancing, etc.

E. CHARITABLE ACTIVITIES:

During this prolonged depression, there has been much destitution in New York Chinatown. This Association has been trying to do its duty in cooperating with other charitable organizations in the distribution of food tickets. At the present writing, we still give out entirely free about one hundred food tickets every week. From time to time, our members also sell flowers and give boxing exhibitions towards the relief of suffering from hunger and cold. Other similar works are: visiting Chinese patients in hospitals, interpreting for members unacquainted with the language of their country, helping to solve unemployment problems and to adjust immigration, housing and renting troubles, etc.

F. PATRIOTIC ACTIVITIES:

Whatever may be the world's pronouncement on Japan's aggression against peace-loving China, humanity cannot regard its wanton bombing and killing of Chinese civilians—men, women and children—without feeling a sense of horror and repugnance.

Doubtlessly, you have often read in your newspapers and magazines of such atrocities and massacres committed by the Japanese militarists in China. Generally, a squadron of Japanese bombing planes suddenly appears in the air, skimming over a village, town or city, and without the least bit of warning, showers bombs on its inhabitants. At first, the American press reported such cases in some detail; as these cases of shameful wasting of human lives occurred regularly, they have since ceased to be interesting topics for news columns. But we Chinese, who read in almost every mail from our people in China of these outrages, naturally resent such barbarous actions in our innermost hearts.

During the last few months, the zone of this "unofficial" war has widened considerably—farther southwest and westward. Consequently, more and more war refugees have fled from their homes located both

Chinese women participating in a parade in New York City to raise money (thrown into the Chinese flag) for war relief in China. (Courtesy of Museum of Chinese in the Americas)

within and without these bombarded zones. To a great extent, all such refugees have been taken care of by charitable and philanthropic organizations in China. However, the combined resources of these institutions did not prove adequate to cope with this dreadful situation. That they have not been adequate may be testified to by the many urgent cable appeals addressed to this Association as well as to many other Chinese organizations throughout the world.

To raise funds to meet these urgent appeals, members of this Association held on Feb. 28th, 1932, a dragon parade and street dances in which our symbolic lion was made to appear several times. Due to the spontaneous and generous response on the part of our compatriots as well as of American sympathizers, we succeeded in raising the record sum of $7,694.46 in one day. With this sum in hand, we immediately transferred by telegraph $31,000 in Shanghai local currency to the Shanghai Consolidated Benevolent Association and Shanghai Emergency Hospital for the relief of the wounded and maimed war refugees.

Because of further urgent appeals from China and entreaty from the seven most influential local Chinese organizations, this Association decided to hold a GRAND CHARITY BAZAAR for the relief of China's war refugees. Thanks to the generosity of our Elders, we were allowed free use and access of the entire 3-story Chinese Public School Building for this occasion from Mar. 27th to April 3rd, 1932, inclusive. The main features of the Bazaar included exhibitions of articles of Chinese arts, paintings and crafts. For its stage program, there were Chinese Opera given by our "Girls Dramatic Club" members, fencing and shadow boxing, dramas and plays as well as numerous other entertainments. There were, of course, the usual dragon parades and street dances with our mythological lion always at the head of each parade. . . . During this Bazaar, thanks to the wholehearted cooperation from all conceivable Chinese Associations, Tongs, Clubs, Leagues, Societies and many American organizations, we succeeded in raising a grand total of U.S. $19,189.33. As soon as the receipts were audited, in the solemn presence of both our governmental and local representatives, several cable transfers of a total of $75,486 in Shanghai currency were rushed to those trustworthy representatives in China above mentioned for relief works.

Encouraged by previous success in our money-raising abilities and for such a worthy cause as flood relief, we once again inaugurated a Financial Campaign from April 15th to 23rd, 1933, inclusive, for funds towards the relief of China flood refugees. We raised during that week a total of $3,804.76, equivalent to $10,000 in Shanghai currency.

A recapitulation of funds raised by this Association on the three occasions mentioned above follows:

DATE	OCCASION	U.S. DOLLARS AND/ OR SHANGHAI DOLLARS	
2/28/32	Dragon Parade	$ 7,694.46	$ 31,000.00
3/27–4/3/32	Grand Charity Bazaar	19,189.33	75,486.00
4/15–4/23/33	Financial Campaign	3,804.76	16,000.00

Grand total . . . . $30,688.55 and/or $122,486.00

PART III—OUR FUTURE PLANS AND ASPIRATIONS

A. FOR THE IMMEDIATE FUTURE:

From the above, it will be noted that in order for this Association to properly carry on the activities enumerated, it will need the wholehearted support and cooperation of every one of our members as well as of our friends. Unless these are assured, a great many worthy causes, no matter how urgent their appeal may be, would inevitably have to be neglected or sacrificed due to lack of assistance, means and facilities. Furthermore, we are constantly in need of all kinds of club leaders, and volunteer instructors in arts and crafts. We sincerely hope that we may continue to merit your support.

B. FOR THE NEAR FUTURE:

I hope I have succeeded in a small measure to prove to your satisfaction that there really is need for such an organization as the Chinese Women's Association working on behalf of the Chinese Community in New York City. Since it was organized five years ago, through the generosity of our Elders, we have been allowed to make our headquarters in the Annex Building of the Chinese Public School. In order for us to expand in the not too distant future, we will want to have an association building of our own somewhat similar to the ones which San Francisco Chinatown already possess. In regard to this tentative plan, which I have had in mind for a long time, I had since had several occasions to discuss the same with a few of our influential and patriotic Elders. They all agreed with me that we should have a 5-story Association Building of our own containing:

(a) One dormitory large enough to accommodate from 20 to 25 people;
(b) An auditorium with seating capacity for about 500 people;
(c) A modern gymnasium;
(d) An entire floor for offices, play rooms, reading rooms, club rooms, library, etc.

To erect such a building on a plot of 60 × 120 feet will cost something in the neighborhood of $30,000. To this will have to be added another $20,000, as endowment fund—the income derived from such an investment ought to be sufficient to meet both running and overhead expenses. With regard to this sum of $50,000, we have already received from several influential and public-spirited Chinese organizations as well as our Elders' assurances to the effect that they will help to raise the first half of $50,000, i.e. $25,000, on the condition that we, the Executive Committee and members, will agree to raise the second half of $50,000, from some American philanthropists. The Chinese Y.M. and Y.W.C.A. in San Francisco were fortunate in securing quite a substantial contribution from such philanthropical American friends as Captain Robert Dollar of the Dollar Steamship Lines, Mrs. Marshall Hale, etc., which encourages me to hope that we too here in New York may one day be blessed with some such financial help towards the building of our own larger headquarters from such well known philanthropists as perhaps the Rockefellers, Mrs.

Andrew Carnegie, Gen. James G. Harbor, William M. Chadbourne, Esq., etc. Offhand, this may sound like a large order, but with faith, love, hope and hard work, which members of this Association do possess in great abundance, let us hope that this expansion program of ours may soon get started, if possible, before these depression prices for building materials and labor costs go up. Incidentally, such building activity like ours will contribute in no small measure towards the relieving of the present unemployment situation.

Respectfully submitted,
CHINESE WOMEN'S ASSOCIATION, INC.
[Signature]
Theodora Chan Wang
Chairman, Executive Committee

SOURCE: *The Chinese Women's Association Fifth Anniversary Special Issue* (New York: Chinese Women's Association, 1937), microfilm, New York Public Library, pp. 59–62.

OTHER REFERENCES

Peter Kwong, *Chinatown, N.Y.: Labor and Politics, 1930–1950* (New York: Monthly Review Press, 1979).

Hua Liang, "Fighting for a New Life: Social and Patriotic Activism of Chinese American Women in New York City, 1900 to 1945," *Journal of American Ethnic History* 17, no. 2 (winter 1998): 22–38.

Judy Yung, *Unbound Feet: A Social History of Chinese Women in San Francisco* (Berkeley: University of California Press, 1995).

Song of Chinese Workers (1938)

Happy Lim

Happy Lim was one of the best-known "working-class intellectuals" among the Chinese in America. He was also one of the most enigmatic members of the community. The FBI knew him as Hom Ah Wing, Lin Chien Fu, and a dozen other aliases. As one FBI intelligence report conceded, the agency had "encountered considerable difficulty in ascertaining the identity of LIM insofar as birth or naturalization, previous employment, and residence in the United States." Lim had confused not only the FBI, but also virtually everyone else who thought they knew him.

    According to information Lim submitted to the federal government, he was born in Kaiping District, Guangdong Province, in 1907 and entered the United States in 1922 as a U.S. citizen. Lim claimed that his father had been born in the United States and was therefore himself a citizen. Federal agencies accepted this claim, until the early 1960s when Lim became a target of government investigation and deportation efforts. He was accused of being in the country under false pretenses and of being a member of the Communist Party. Lim successfully frustrated the deportation attempt, but only after years of dogged effort. In truth, he had lived most of his adult life as a prominent member of the left wing. In the 1930s as a writer and painter, he had joined several leftist cultural clubs in the Chinese community. He had also been an officer in the Chinese Workers' Mutual Aid Association (CWMAA), an important Chinese workers' group in San Francisco during the depression. And indeed, he admitted he had been a member of the Communist Party, USA, from 1942 to 1945.

    Happy Lim had little formal education, but studied poetry and the arts on his own, even as he labored in poor-paying jobs throughout his life. He lived a lonely existence in "bachelor hotels" around the San Francisco Bay Area, working as a busboy and cook in restaurants and in shipyards during the war years. His writings extolled revolutionary struggle, exposed the ills of capitalist society such as lynching and poverty, and encouraged multiracial unity and political struggle. Lim also wrote about love and romance and about experiences, real and imagined, he had had while traveling

*around America. His writing style was simple and direct. He wrote almost exclusively
in Chinese and was most influenced by Walt Whitman and the proletarian literature
of revolutionary China.*

*In the last decade of his life, Happy Lim associated with the new activism that had
emerged in Asian American communities. He continued to write, but he suffered increasingly from serious health problems, including blood disorders. He endured am-
putations of all his toes. On New Year's Day, 1986, he died alone of pneumonia in
his dingy one-room residence in San Francisco Chinatown.*

The following poem, "Song of Chinese Workers," was first published in Hezuo
*(meaning "working together"), the official publication of CWMAA, under the pseu-
donym Jian Fu ("tough man").*

Years ago, long before 1938,
Our ancestors, sailing by boat, crossing the vast ocean,
Leaving behind the family,
Arrived on this land, America.

At that time, America was but a barren land
Of mountain ranges with no sight of humanity.
Through our ancestors' tireless work, reclaiming,
Turning it into high-rising metropolises today.

Take a look: That piece of earth—the forest, the mines,
Don't you see our ancestors' blood and sweat?
Take a look: That railroad, the ranches and factories,
Don't you know that they are our ancestors' handiwork?

Once the air-horn blasted, it's time to work.
They picked up their spades and chisels,
Working from sunrise to sunset,
Busily reclaiming the arid deserts and barren hills.

Not knowing the year or the month, just daylong labor;
But they don't harbor a bit of resentment.
At times, there might be frustrating moments—they just
     swallowed hard.
Just like that—they lost their youth and later their lives.

Don't they ever know:
Their blood and sweat have become shackles of their own
     oppression?
Don't they ever realize:
Their labor contributes to the fattening of someone else's belly?

Looking back, that was a century ago.
Now, we are again crossing the perilous seas, and have arrived.

Happy Lim in the
1930s. (*East Wind*,
winter/spring 1985)

But we are not fools like our ancestors;
We have our own lifestyle different from theirs.

That long dark endless path—
We walk it no more.
Let us make it clear: You're a blood-sucking devil;
Don't ever think of using us to forge your selfish power again!

We are an awakened collective; we are organized.
We have learned how to survive, to fight, and to forge our
    solidarity.

From now on, we are no longer submissive slaves;
We will unite with the White workers for an indivisible alliance.

There may be, at times, traitors in our ranks:
Slandering our darker looks and colored hair.
They are the yellow-belly lackeys;
They will not last long in our camp.

We have seen through the traps set by our enemy;
We will not blindly crawl into them like in the old days.
We should be able to enjoy what we have produced.
As long as we are resolute in the struggle, we will overcome.

With our blood we will rinse clean the shame of our predecessors;
With our life we will challenge the tyrannical enemies.
We have firmly built a formidable castle.
Our power and strength shall reach the sky.

Let's not be discouraged by a little setback;
Let's not be overjoyed by a small victory.
If we fall, we shall stand up again;
Our enemy will bow to us despite its arrogance.

The bandits in Asia have now gone berserk in our ancestral
     homeland;[1]
We have reached the critical stage of agony and pain.
We have made self-sacrifices to defend our motherland
And for the dawning of a new social order.

SOURCE: *Hezuo,* no. 2 (April 1938): 8–10. Translator: Marlon K. Hom.

OTHER REFERENCES

Him Mark Lai, "To Bring Forth a New China, to Build a Better America: The Chinese Marxist Left in America to the 1960s," *Chinese America: History and Perspectives,* 1992, pp. 3–82.
Happy Lim Collection, Hoover Institution on War, Revolution and Peace, Stanford University.

1. In reference to the Japanese attack and occupation of China.

Chinatown Goes Picketing (1938)

Lim P. Lee

Although China did not formally declare war against Japan until 1937, the War of Resistance informally began in 1931 after Japan attacked Mukden and occupied northeastern China. Almost immediately, Chinese Americans across the country put aside their differences and did what they could to help save China. During the next fourteen years of war in China, they donated their hard-earned savings, boycotted Japanese products, participated in protest parades and rallies, and supported the training of Chinese American pilots for the Chinese air force.

Written by social worker Lim P. Lee for the Chinese Digest,[1] the following detailed account of a successful picket protesting the shipping of scrap iron to Japan provides insight into the Chinese community's patriotic fervor and united stance on behalf of the war effort in China. Everyone—young and old, men and women, the political right and left, Christian and secular groups—participated. Highly organized and determined to make their point, the pickets succeeded in gaining the support of the longshoremen and calling national attention to the need for an embargo of war materials to Japan.

San Francisco's waterfront has been the scene of many labor wars but it was only last month that the Sino-Japanese war was carried to its Embarcadero. The "zero hour" was 11 A.M., Dec. 16, and the "stragetic withdrawal" was 2 P.M., Dec. 20, 1938, and what *did* happen has attracted nation-wide attention and is a story worth re-telling.

By the "grapevine method"—the most effective [form of] communication

---

1. A social worker, journalist, and later postmaster of San Francisco, Lim P. Lee (1910–2002) wrote about social issues in the Chinese American community through his "Sociological Data" page in the *Chinese Digest*, a newspaper intended for second-generation Chinese Americans that was published from 1935 to 1940.

Chinese pickets at the San Francisco waterfront, 1938. (Courtesy of Labor
Archives and Research Center, San Francisco)

in Chinatown—Chinatownians heard that "something will happen" at the
waterfront on Dec. 16, and all interested in picket duty for the good of China
were to meet at 10:30 A.M. at the corner of Stockton and Clay streets. By
11:00 more than 200 volunteers answered the call to the colors. Singing,
yelling, and cheering, they were carted down by trucks to Pier 45. There they
were met by [European] Americans, Greeks, Jews, and other volunteers of
many nationalities, 300 in number, 100 more than the Chinese forces. Lying on Pier 45 was a Greek tramp freighter, the *S. S. Spyros,* loading implements of death—scrap iron for the bombs of Japan! I. Bib Tolins, the director
of the United Committee for the Boycott of Japanese Goods, held a short
strategy meeting, and the demonstration was on!

Lieutenant Governor–elect Ellis Patterson of California, a true liberal and
a statesman—if there ever was one—fired the opening gun, saying: "Speeches
have been made, the press has denounced the shipment of war materials to
Japan, all progressives have expressed themselves for democracy against the
aggressor, but you are doing something about it! Congress is about to
meet. . . . *Pressure your Congressmen,* that they must ask Congress to put through
an embargo on aggressor nations and declare Japan to be an aggressor."

When the American longshoremen started for lunch, the pickets very
courteously but firmly pleaded, "Longshoremen, be with us! Longshoremen, be with us." Smilingly and good-naturedly the pickets continued until
1:00 P.M., then asked among themselves: "Will the longshoremen return to

work?" A few did, but the majority of them honored the Chinese picket lines, and the few that worked were so ashamed that they dropped their hooks shortly and joined their comrades. "Victory! Victory!" the call was shouted through Chinatown and the pickets began to arrive in trucks, in street-cars, in automobiles. The radio and the press flashed the news to the nation:— Chinese pickets tied up scrap iron to Japan and American longshoremen refused to load implements of destruction! This lasted until 5 P.M.

By the time the news was flashed back to Chinatown, pigs were being roasted for the nourishment of the Chinese pickets and American sympathizers. Soda pop, coffee, hot tea, sandwiches, oranges, Chinese buns were streaming toward the waterfront to feed the pickets and the longshoremen. Chinese came in from Stockton and valley towns; they marched in from Palo Alto and Peninsula cities; and thousands poured in from the Bay Area till the climax of the picketing numbered 5,000 strong and more!

Then an ultimatum was issued to the pickets on Dec. 19, at 12:00 noon. The committee of the United Chinese Societies met with the representatives of the Waterfront Employers' Association, and the labor relations committee of the International Longshoremen and Warehousemen's Union, Local 1–10, met with the same representatives of the shipowners, and through their president, Mr. Almon E. Roth, the ultimatum was issued: the Chinese must remove the picket lines, the longshoremen must go back to work, or the shipping of San Francisco and the West Coast would be tied up as a consequence of the failure to accept the dictate of the Waterfront Employers' Association. However, Mr. Roth expressed "personal sympathies" for China, but as a business principle, commerce in San Francisco cannot be interrupted. (Even such commerce that goes to Japan to become bombs to be rained on innocent Chinese civilians, women, and children must go on as a matter of "business principle.")

The longshoremen met the same evening, and Mr. B. S. Fong, president of the China War Relief Association of America and chairman of the committee representing the United Chinese Societies, pleaded with the longshoremen to respect the picket lines. Dr. Le Shan Peng, secretary of the National Committee of China's YMCA and director of Hankow's six refugee camps, gave an impassioned plea for the longshoremen to stand by China. After the Chinese representatives left, the longshoremen voted not to cross the picket lines even if there were one Chinese picket on duty. However, they instructed their officials to negotiate with the Chinese for an amicable solution but specifically told their officials "not to let the Chinese down."

The emergency council of the United Chinese Societies was summoned for a night session, and a committee of eleven was empowered to negotiate with the longshoremen for an "amicable solution." The committee met with the officials of the International Longshoremen and Warehousemen's Union at 12 noon on Dec. 20. Mr. Henry Schmidt, spokesman for the longshoremen, told the Chinese representatives that the C.I.O. Council had passed a resolution to instruct the secretary to call all labor, fraternal, civilian and religious organizations for a coastwide conference to study and promote the embargo on all materials to Japan. Thus the demonstration the Chinese staged has served the purpose of calling the attention of the American public to the seriousness of the embargo question, and that the conference should be called immediately. The picketing of the S. S. *Spyros* was borne solely by the longshoremen, and they had voted to stand by the Chinese as long as they continued picketing in spite of the threat of the closing of the San Francisco port and the tie-up of West Coast shipping. But the more important issue was to get the American people to act together, and that the longshoremen pledged to do.

Mr. B. S. Fong spoke for the Chinese committee, expressing the heartfelt thanks of the Chinese people to the longshoremen in honoring the picket lines. The wages that the longshoremen lost far exceeded in value the cargo that could be lost by the shipowners, but the Chinese people had found out who their true friends were. The Chinese pickets were withdrawn at 2 P.M. Dec. 20, and marched en masse to the Waterfront Employers' Association and protested their mercenary action. Then they circled to the longshoremen's headquarters to express the appreciation of the Chinese people. Thus ended the Sino-Japanese war on San Francisco's waterfront. Then 5,000 marched in a mile-long parade through downtown San Francisco and back to Chinatown, where a mass meeting was held and a national campaign for an embargo on war materials for Japan was launched!

SOURCE: *Chinese Digest,* January 1939, pp. 10–11.

OTHER REFERENCES

Him Mark Lai, "Roles Played by the Chinese in America during China's Resistance to Japanese Aggression and during World War II," *Chinese America: History and Perspectives,* 1997, pp. 75–128.

Judy Yung, *Unbound Feet: A Social History of Chinese Women in San Francisco* (Berkeley: University of California Press, 1995).

Paul Robeson:
The People's Singer (1950)

Liu Liangmo

Little has been written about the history of Chinese–African American relations in the United States. One source of insight is the China Daily News *(CDN), a left-leaning newspaper that was founded in New York in 1940 and almost destroyed by Mc-Carthyism in the 1950s. Closely aligned with the Chinese Hand Laundry Alliance,* CDN *reported on the organization's efforts to build better relations with the African American community and gain its support for China's War of Resistance against Japan. The newspaper also wrote editorials and published letters from readers that expressed the need for Chinese Americans to improve their attitudes toward African Americans and to recognize that both groups shared a common history of racial oppression.*

In July 1950, CDN *began publishing a column, "The America I Know," written by Liu Liangmo, who was connected with the YMCA in China. Known for pioneering the use of choral music to arouse support for the war effort, he had come to the United States in 1940 to escape Kuomintang (Chinese Nationalist Party) harassment. Liu was instrumental in organizing a choral group among members of the Chinese Youth Club in New York. He also wrote a regular column on the war in China for the African American newspaper* Pittsburgh Courier. *Liu returned to China in 1949, soon after the founding of the People's Republic of China.*

His column in CDN *ran for one month and primarily railed against racial discrimination, U.S. imperialism, and the anti-Communist hysteria building up in America. The following excerpt from "The America I Know" focuses on his friendship with the famous African American singer, actor, and civil rights activist Paul Robeson, and on how he got Robeson to introduce "Chee Lai" ("March of the Volunteers"), which would later become the national anthem of the People's Republic of China, to the American audience.*

The individual most representative of the black people's struggle and their fighting spirit is none other than their own famous singer, Mr. Paul Robeson, whom I first met over nine years ago (1940). I had just come to this country, bringing with me many Chinese songs of resistance, which I hoped to introduce all over the U.S. However, being a new arrival with hardly any contacts or connections, I could do little on my own and was at a loss as to how to achieve my goal. It was then that I thought of Robeson, whose fame had reached me even when I was in China, and whose sonorous voice I had already heard on the silver screen and on gramophone records. I thought if only I could get Robeson to sing the songs of resistance, there could be nothing better. But then it was merely a dream on my part.

After I got to New York, I happened to mention Robeson at a friend's house and my desire to meet him. "I know Robeson quite well," said this friend. "Let me give him a call and see if he's at home." When he finished his phone call, he turned to me and said in delight, "He'll be right over." Within half an hour, Robeson was actually there. When I looked up, I almost jumped with fright. At six feet four or five inches tall,[1] with an imposing physique, he seemed to have come from the land of giants. Compared to him, I was a dwarf. But then he smiled that warm, friendly smile of his, and with his big, strong hands grasping mine, he greeted me affably. "You just came from China? Wonderful! Wonderful!" From that moment, we were like old friends.

Robeson was very interested in the War of Resistance by the Chinese people because both the blacks in America and the Chinese in China were suffering from oppression. The fact that the Chinese rose up in firm resolve to fight against Japanese imperialism made the blacks sympathetic to our cause and proud of our struggle.[2] Besides filling him in on the war effort in China, I also told him about the Patriotic Song Movement among the common people.[3] He became very excited and asked me to sing for him some of the songs of resistance and some of our Chinese folk ballads. Emboldened by his request, I opened my mouth and let myself go. He listened intently and silently. Some of the songs he asked me to repeat, "March of the Volunteers" being one of them. After my singing, he thanked me profusely and left.

Several weeks later, my friend asked me to join him for a Robeson recital at the famous Lewisohn Stadium in New York. I accepted his invitation with pleasure. That night, under a canopy of stars, six to seven thousand people listened to Robeson's magnificent voice give expression to songs of struggle

---

1. Robeson was actually six feet two inches tall.

2. As early as 1937, Robeson was speaking out against Japanese aggression in China.

3. The People's Choral Society that Liu Liangmo started in Shanghai in 1935 grew from ninety people to more than a thousand, with branches in Guangzhou, Hong Kong, and other cities. It was one of the most influential groups in the Resist Japan and Save the Nation Choral Movement. For example, the People's Choral Society drew an audience of five thousand at its third concert, held at Ximen Athletic Field on June 7, 1936. Two months later, the Nationalist government forced the group to disband. Liu left for the United States in 1940.

from many nationalities. His baritone was rich and powerful, and his Russian, French, German, Yiddish, and Spanish pronunciation extremely accurate.[4] The conclusion of each song was met with frenzied applause and cheers. To me, the most special thing about that recital was the fact that the performer on stage and the audience off stage had bonded as one. In America, I have yet to encounter a musician who is more loved by his audience than Robeson because he is indeed a great singer of the people.

The high point of the Robeson recital actually came after the official program was over, when it was request time for the audience. Robeson stood smiling in the middle of the stage while the crowd shouted out their favorites, all of which Robeson graciously sang for them. When the audience called out their requests, the clamor was reminiscent of that at a stock exchange. Yet, as soon as Robeson started to sing, a hush would fall over the stadium as the crowd listened to him in complete silence. That evening, Robeson sang the Negro spiritual "Let My People Go," which tells how Moses led the Jews before the Egyptian Pharaoh to protest the oppression to which they had been subjected. He also sang from the famous movie *Show Boat* its theme song, "Ol' Man River," which talks about how blacks in the southern part of the United States were persecuted. Then there was also the well-known American labor song, "Joe Hill," narrating the story of the miner leader who was hounded to death by capitalists.

At the end of those songs, Robeson suddenly held his hand up for silence. "Tonight, I want to sing a song for the heroic Chinese people in battle," he announced. "The title of the song is 'Chee Lai!'" And in perfect Mandarin Chinese, he sang our "March of the Volunteers." I listened with excitement and pride. Then the audience clamored for an encore. From then on, "Chee Lai" began to circulate among the progressive people in the United States. After that event, I organized a youth chorus among the overseas Chinese laundry workers. Through this choral group, the songs of resistance also spread throughout the overseas Chinese communities in the U.S.

In the spring of 1941, several friends suggested that Robeson and our Chinese youth chorus make a gramophone record together, using the proceeds from its sales to help the war effort in China. Robeson readily agreed and offered his services for free.[5] As we were collaborating on the recording, I had a chance to witness his drive and commitment. He worked on perfecting his diction for every word and phrase, at the same time striving to grasp the nuances of the text. He practiced repeatedly, singing again and again,

4. Robeson was a serious scholar of singing, and a master of several languages.

5. Robeson had already given his support on several occasions for Chinese war relief. One of the biggest benefit concerts was held on April 25, 1941, when Robeson sang to an audience of six thousand at the Uline Arena in Washington, D.C. The event was cosponsored by the Washington Committee for Aid to China and the National Negro Congress.

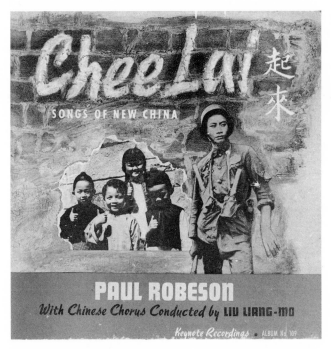

Album cover of Paul Robeson's recording of "Chee Lai."
(Courtesy of Him Mark Lai)

until everyone, including himself, was totally satisfied before he would record. The album was titled "Chee Lai" and featured Robeson singing "March of the Volunteers" and "Flower Drum Song," and the youth chorus singing "The Hoeing Song," "Soldiers and People Working Together," and "To the Enemies' Rear." After the record came out, thanks to the wonderful voice of Robeson, "Arise, ye who refuse to be slaves" could be heard all over America.[6] Eventually, even public school children could sing the song.

I discovered that not only did he master the Chinese lyrics, he also became very interested in Chinese literature. He carried constantly in his bag the *Sanzi Jing*,[7] and whenever he had a free moment he would take it out

6. *Chee lai,* meaning "arise," is found in the first line of the lyrics to "March of the Volunteers," the Chinese version of "La Marseillaise." The words were written by Tian Han and the music was set by Nie Er in 1935.

7. The classic literacy primer formerly used by Chinese children to learn their first characters, the entire text is organized in groups of three characters, hence the title *Sanzi Jing,* or *Trimeter Reader.*

and discuss with us the form, meaning, and sound of Chinese characters. One really cannot help but admire him for his thirst for learning.

In school, Robeson had proven himself a dedicated student. He was admitted into one of the oldest American universities, Rutgers, and later earned his law degree with highest honors [from Columbia University]. A star athlete as well, he was ranked among the top sixteen American football players.[8] After graduation, he could have practiced law; however, the chance discovery that he could sing made him realize that he could use his voice to awaken his people and thus serve them in another way.[9]

The greatness of Robeson is due not only to his talent in singing, but also to the way that he uses his voice to fight for black people and all oppressed people in the world, and to challenge American imperialism. Today, Robeson has become the most courageous and progressive warrior in the United States. Neither the threats issued by the Committee on Un-American Activities nor the disturbances created by reactionary veterans could silence his heroic voice.[10] Robeson is not only a singer respected by all Americans, but also a singer esteemed by people all over the world.

SOURCE: *China Daily News,* July 13, 14, 15, and 17, 1950. Translator: Ellen Yeung.

OTHER REFERENCES

Martin Duberman, *Paul Robeson* (New York: Alfred A. Knopf, 1988).

Him Mark Lai, "To Bring Forth a New China, to Build a Better America: The Chinese Marxist Left in America to the 1960s," *Chinese America: History and Perspectives,* 1992, pp. 3–82.

Jeffrey Stewart, ed., *Paul Robeson: Artist and Citizen* (New Brunswick, N.J.: Rutgers University Press, 1998).

Renqiu Yu, *To Save China, to Save Ourselves: The Chinese Hand Laundry Alliance of New York* (Philadelphia: Temple University Press, 1992).

8. Robeson was named first on the roster of the All-American college team at Rutgers and played professional football for the Akron Pros and the Milwaukee Badgers to support himself through law school.

9. Robeson also quit law because the white secretaries in the law firm refused to take dictation from him, a black man.

10. During the McCarthy period, Robeson was hounded by the Committee on Un-American Activities because of his outspoken views on racism and his high regard for the Soviet Union and the new China. He was harassed, stopped from traveling and speaking abroad, and so discredited that African American organizations and white American fans turned against him. On August 27, 1949, a demonstration by veterans' organizations before a scheduled concert in Peeksill, New York, culminated in a riot that left 140 persons seriously injured.

The Founding of McGehee Chinese School (1944)

Jew Baak Ming

As the Chinese population dispersed throughout the United States in the early part of the twentieth century, communities developed with attendant business, political, social, and educational institutions along the Pacific Coast, in the Midwest, along the Eastern seaboard, and throughout the South. Between World Wars I and II, a significant number of Chinese settled in rural Mississippi and Arkansas, primarily operating grocery stores that served black customers. As family life took root, parents became concerned about the Chinese education of their children.

In 1939 the Chinese community in Arkansas, consisting of approximately four hundred residents, established a Chinese language school in McGehee in the southeast corner of the state. The following history of this Chinese school is taken from the annual report of the Arkansas Chinese Association, which was founded in 1943 to promote the welfare of the local Chinese and to help with the war effort in China. Although short lived—McGehee Chinese School closed within two years because of World War II—its existence demonstrates the strong commitment that Chinese immigrants have always had to instill Chinese culture in the next generation.

A decade ago, many of the married Memphis Chinese, concerned with their children's education and well-being, began moving to Arkansas. Those who believed strongly in education noticed that just in the southeast corner of Arkansas there were already forty to fifty school-aged Chinese children. As there were no Chinese schools, however, any attempt to instill Chinese culture was difficult. Within the family, parents were busy working and had no time to attend to the task, and the children were in danger of becoming corrupted by the immoral customs of American society.

In the spring of 1939, Messrs. Jew Ji Faan, Jau Fung Gui, Ho Man Gwong, Go Hap Yuen, Yu Gau San, Jew Cheuk Faan, and Lam Yam Yin proposed unanimously to establish a Chinese school. A school board was formed for that purpose, with Mr. Ho Man Gwong as the board president, Messrs. Jew Ji Faan and Jau Fung Gui as directors to assist with all the planning. The town of McGehee was chosen for the school site because it was centrally located and easily reached by transportation from anywhere—be it north, south, east, or west—within a radius of sixty miles. The operating expenses came from the Chinese community. The first fundraising campaign netted around U.S. $1,000. Normally the Chinese students would attend American school, so [Chinese] classes were held only once a week on Sunday. That was because the Arkansas Chinese were not concentrated in one area and it was difficult to hold classes at night. The regular teachers were zealous volunteers from the community who had a certain level of Chinese education. During summer vacation, however, professional teachers were hired to teach full time, and their salaries were solicited from the students.

The school was named the McGehee Chinese School. The school building—a spacious store located at the edge of town—was rented, renovated, and the interior painted white. The desks and chairs were donated by Mr. Yu Gau San, games and classroom supplies by Mr. Jew Ji Faan, and maps and other classroom reference books by Mr. Jau Fung Gui. Mr. Ho Man Gwong undertook to do all the installations and setting up in the school. As a result, the school was well equipped and the building neat and clean.

In the summer of 1940, Mrs. Ng Yiu Ming, who formerly taught at Greenville Chinese School, was formally hired. A teacher for many years in China and fluent in both the Cantonese and Mandarin dialects, Mrs. Ng was a very effective teacher, and extremely patient with her many students. Every day the students came to school, those living far away traveling a round trip of about one hundred miles. Lunch took place at Mr. Ho Man Gwong's, at a nominal price. Despite the hot summer weather, the students never flagged in their enthusiasm for learning. Often there were various kinds of sports meets and artistic and cultural competitions. The Student Council was very efficient, and all the events ran smoothly and orderly. Every year there was a picnic. It was a social event to which the entire community was invited.

This writer was a volunteer teacher at one time, and also assisted in the planning of the McGehee school. I felt that interest in the school among the Chinese community was very high. In 1941, there were plans to introduce improvements, to do away with tuition and textbook fees, and to construct a school building and dormitory. Unfortunately, after Pearl Harbor, the people in charge either enlisted for service or moved away. Moreover, there was a strict government ration on gas and rubber tires. The operation of the school therefore came to a halt. All the school supplies, equipment, textbooks, and $160 in funds were entrusted to the custody of Mr. Jau Fung Gui. As for the future organization and management of the school, I hope the Chinese community and the various board members and association members [of the Arkansas Chinese Association] will work together to draw up a comprehensive plan.

Evidently, another Chinese school was not started in Arkansas until 1995, at which time the Chinese population had grown to over two thousand with the influx of immigrants from China, Taiwan, and Hong Kong. That same year, there was reportedly a total of 634 Chinese schools in the United States.

SOURCE: *Annual Report of the Arkansas Chinese Association,* 1944, pp. 24–25. Translator: Ellen Yeung.

OTHER REFERENCES

Him Mark Lai, "Chinese Schools in America," in *Becoming Chinese American: A History of Communities and Institutions* (Walnut Creek, Calif.: Alta Mira Press, 2004), pp. 271–362.

Shih-Shan Henry Tsai, "The Chinese in Arkansas," *Amerasia Journal* 8, no. 1 (1981): 1–18.

"There but for the grace of God go I"

The Story of a POW
Survivor in World War II (2002)

Eddie Fung

Approximately twelve thousand Chinese Americans served in the U.S. armed forces during World War II. We know of only one who was captured by the Japanese in the Pacific campaign and put to work on the Burma-Siam Death Railway, made famous by the film Bridge on the River Kwai. *Eddie Fung was among the 61,000 Allied prisoners of war and 250,000 Asian civilian laborers used to build the railway that stretched 262 miles through the tropical jungles of Burma and Thailand. Working under brutal slave labor conditions, the men completed the railroad in a record 14 months at the cost of 16,000 POW and 70,000 Asian lives. Fung was one of the lucky survivors.*

Born in 1922 in San Francisco Chinatown, Fung was the seventh child in a family of eight children. His father was a watchmaker and jeweler; his mother was a housewife and seamstress. Early on, Eddie resented the restrictions of Chinatown life and developed an interest in horses. At the age of sixteen, he ran away to Midland, Texas, to become a cowboy. It was while he was working as a cattle ranch hand that he decided to volunteer for the Texas National Guard, which later became known as the Lost Battalion after it was captured by the Japanese in Java on March 8, 1942.

In the following interview with Judy Yung, Eddie Fung, a small but solidly built man, recalls with sharp clarity and a poignant sense of humor what it was like working on the Burma-Siam railroad and how he was able to survive forty-two months of humiliation and brutality as a POW of the Japanese. This is a story about service to one's country, loyalty to one's comrades, the basic instincts of survival, and the recovery of one's ethnic identity.

"I'M GOING TO BE A SOLDIER!"

When the army came to the ranch in the early forties to buy horses, we had the horses all groomed. After they picked the horses, they started telling

Eddie Fung with
his sister Grace after
the war. (Courtesy
of Eddie Fung)

me about the army. Of course, they were talking from the officer's point of
view. Said all they did was play polo. They asked me if I wanted to be a houseboy. I said, "No, I don't think so." But then I decided, "Holy smoke, that's
another place where I can be around horses. I can join the cavalry." So I
went up to the army recruiting station and asked them if I could join up.
He said, "You have to take the physical and the I.Q. test." So I went through
all that. And he said, "You have to get your parents' permission." (Back in
those days, the required age was twenty-one; I was only seventeen.) So I gave
my mother as a reference. The recruiting sergeant came back and said,
"Your mom said definitely, she does not want her son to be a soldier." When
I found out I couldn't be a soldier, naturally, I'm going to be a soldier. So
when the sergeant said, "Really, you don't want to be in the army, do you?"
I said, "Yes, I do." And he said, "I'll tell you what. There's a National Guard
Armory in town. All you have to do is go there and they'll sign you up regardless of your age. By November you'll be in the army because the Na-
tional Guard will be federalized."

*After basic training at Lubbock and Camp Bowie in Texas, Fung found himself part
of the 2nd Battalion, 131st Field Artillery, 36th Division, aboard the USS* Repub-

lic, *heading toward Pearl Harbor for a destination with the code name "PLUM" on November 21, 1941.*

"CAPTURED BY THE JAPANESE"

The Pensacola convoy of eight thousand men was supposed to be reinforcement and supplies for the Philippines. But after Pearl Harbor was bombed, we were instructed to head south to avoid the Japanese. Then the news came that Cavite Naval Yard [in the Philippines] had been bombed out, so there was no point in the convoy going there because you couldn't unload. They decided to divert the whole convoy to Brisbane, Australia. So we landed in Brisbane on the 22nd of December, just before Christmas in '41. Then on January 1, our battalion of artillery was sent to Java, or Indonesia as they call it. We landed in Soerabaja on January 11, '42. For a while, we were taking care of the 19th Bombardment Group aircraft, doing anything to help—gas up the airplane, take care of the armament, load 50-caliber belts and bombs.

Then the Japanese led a three-prong attack to take Java from both ends of the island. It was the largest amphibious operation at this point of the war and the Allied forces on the island were no match. Our entire Asiatic fleet had been destroyed in the Battle of the Java Seas and we had had no air control to begin with. For seven days we basically provided fire support for the Australian troops. The navy was put under Dutch command, and that was one of the reasons why they had so much trouble, because communications was lousy and they had never worked together. We were fighting up in the area west of Batavia (near Jakarta) for two days and were chased back. Then March 8, orders were sent out by the Dutch commander that all troops were to surrender. Of the 906 American soldiers and sailors who were captured by the Japanese, 668 were sent to Burma to help build the railway.

Have you ever heard the term "hellships"? The Japanese can squeeze more men into a confined space than anyone in the world. I swear to God, our group of 191 Americans was squeezed into a hold no larger than this room [approximately 30 × 30 feet]. You couldn't even breathe! The first night on the way to Singapore wasn't bad, but from Singapore to Rangoon . . . To this day, people see me running around in a T-shirt and they ask me, "Aren't you ever cold?" "No," I said, because all I have to do is think back to October of '42. We spent three days in the harbor of Singapore below the water line, in the hold of the ship, which had hauled rice as the last cargo. And the cargo before that was horses. So we had horse manure and rice fermenting, and we were sweating until we were dry and dehydrated. Water was in short supply and I broke out in a heat rash. I swore to God, if I ever got out of there, I would never, never complain about heat again. [It was so crowded that the men had to take turns sitting, squatting, standing or laying down while suffering from seasickness, dysentery, and malaria.]

"WORSE THAN BUILDING THE TRANSCONTINENTAL RAILROAD"

We worked ten days then got a day off, for 10 cents a day. We got one holiday, the Emperor's Birthday on April 29. We got up at four in the morning,
had *jook* [rice gruel] with a little ginger and sugar for breakfast, got our tools,
marched out to the job site, worked until lunch time, when we got rice and
vegetables, and kept working until the work was done. The average was fourteen hours a day. You were lucky if you got six hours of rest. We had the easy
stretch of the railroad at the north end because the south end was horrible.
Because we were such a small group, roughly two hundred people, we were
put in with the Australians, which was a good thing because Australians and
Texans got along famously. [The other Allied POWs were British and Dutch.]

We were used as a mobile force, meaning that we went wherever the trouble spot was and we would try to straighten it out. So at the beginning, the
civilians were used to cut out the right-of-way—three meters, roughly ten
feet. They would clear the jungles, and of course, it grows back almost as
fast. Then you have to cut and fill, which is the basic of almost any railroad
work. In other words, you want as level a road as possible. You lay down the
cross ties and rails on each side. Then you start drilling holes for the spikes.
Next, you pound in the spikes. Then there will be a Japanese engineer to
measure it's a one-meter track and to make sure the alignment and spacing
are correct. Then you would make little rocks from big ones for ballast. That's
what holds the cross ties in place. Aside from cut and fill and building bridges,
we were used mostly for loading and unloading supplies, like the rails and
cross ties. The first time they put a hundred kilos on the backs of some of
my Texan friends who were used to hard work as ranchers, they almost died
(a kilo is 2.2 pounds). That's when I realized the body can do amazing things.
All you have to do is to take care of it.

I don't think anyone who worked on the railroad got off without injuries,
because we were down to the G-string [a loin cloth] and our bare feet. In
the beginning, we all had clothes, but because of mildew, everything falls
apart. We were given no prisoner clothes, no shoes. The centipedes were this
long *(motions about one foot long)*, and tarantulas were the size of a dinner plate!
We also had to look out for snakes and scorpions. It was hot year round.
Where we were, we could get 400 to 600 inches of rain during the monsoon
season. It was like being under Niagara Falls. The humidity will kill you, if
the tropical diseases didn't get you first, because the Japanese refused to provide us with any medicine.

The Japanese never got used to the Americans. The first time we had to
unload a bunch of rails—they're about thirty feet long, run seventy pounds
to a foot—the Japanese were screaming at us to hurry: until they realized
we were trying to be efficient. The engineers would not bother to learn English, because once they got the work layout, they're not around anymore.

The Korean guards would make sure we weren't loafing on the job. Slapping, beatings, and torture were common. We found out after the first two months that they were dead serious about getting this railroad build, so we just went ahead and did it. You learned to work at a rate that does not incur the wrath of the guards. There's no official tea break, but if you need a drink, you go ahead and do it. Just don't linger. It was worse than the Chinese building the transcontinental railroad!

Speedo started in May of '43. That was when they found out they couldn't finish the railroad in one year. So they figured, "Okay, let's speed everything up." No more days off, and they just kept increasing the workload, from 1.5 cubic meters per man per day to 2.2, then to 2.8, and 3.2 meters [1 meter = 39¼ inches]. It didn't matter if it was mud, soft dirt, sand, or rock. The job had to be done before you left for the day. Of course, May is the beginning of the rainy season. So combined with the additional workload and the rainy season, it's more difficult. That was the most intense period of construction. Everybody was under pressure. During the speedo period, they even got sick people up to work, anyone who could walk. I was down to 60 pounds [from 103 pounds at the beginning of the war] and sick with malaria and dysentery, still I had to do hard work every day. You can do almost anything when you're forced to. Sabotage didn't do any good because you knew the job had to be done, but we sabotaged when we could. There was no point in trying to escape. The Japanese had a very cute system that worked in Java. Any Allied soldier was worth $10 dead and $1 alive. So there was no fear of natives bringing you in alive. You were worth more dead. The first three Australians who tried to escape were caught and executed.

"THERE BUT FOR THE GRACE OF GOD GO I"

We had native civilians helping—Malaysians, Indonesians, Thais, Burmese—but they died like flies. You would think they would fare better because they live in that country, but there's one thing they didn't have: organization. We were still a military unit, and we looked after each other. We had basic sanitation, no matter how crummy it was. When we got to a camp, you located your kitchen, you located your latrines, you took care of the simple things that would contribute to your hygiene. The natives never did because they worked as individuals. Another example: our basic ration was one pound of rice per *working* man per day. So if only half of the camp is working, immediately you're on half ration. But everyone shares. It was a perfect socialistic state. When the officers got paid their $20 per month, they would put $10 into what we called the Red Cross fund to take care of the people who couldn't work. Without being told, we formed tribes of two, three, or four people to look after one another. If one guy is sick, the other two guys remember to boil drinking water for him and to pick up his rations. Let's say

STORY OF A POW SURVIVOR IN WORLD WAR II   217

the worst happens and the three guys are sick; another group will look after their group. And no one keeps score. You do it willingly because "there but for the grace of God go I." Regardless of how we kidded each other about being with the navy, marines, or army, we were an American unit and we knew we had to pull together. You knew that you were not going to be alone.

But then we were lucky; we had Dr. [Henri] Hekking as our camp doctor. He was the one who kept our losses down. In our group of 191 people, we lost only 13 people in the year and a half that we were in the jungles. The other larger group of 470-odd Americans lost 120 men. Dr. Hekking was born and raised in Java, but went to medical school in the Netherlands. The British didn't consider him a qualified medical officer, so here he was, just surplus. Captain Fitzsimmons contributed his wristwatch, and Lieutenant Lattimore a pocket watch, and they used the watches as a bribe to the Japanese to get us Dr. Hekking. It turned out that he was magic because he had learned herbal medicine from his grandmother. He would tell us what kind of herbs and eatable greenery to look out for in the jungles.

There's nothing I won't do for Dr. Hekking, like scrounging at nighttime, or what we called "moonlight reconnaissance." One time I stole a hundred pounds of sugar. A friend of mine, Slug Wright, worked in the Japanese kitchen, and he told me, "Watch out, Eddie, they mined the kitchen because they've been losing so much stuff." I decided, no, it doesn't matter, because they got to have a safe way in and out. So all we have to figure out is where they walk. Then I decided, no, there's an easier way. So what I did was untie enough of the vines that held the bamboo walls together so that I could remove the wall and sneak in. Well, one of the things I saw was this hundred-pound sack of sugar. The trick about scrounging is that you have to get in and get out. You don't fool around. So I dragged the hundred pounds out and put the wall back together again. Okay, now, the trick is when you steal something, you can't keep it, because there's no refrigeration, and the Japanese conduct snap searches. So what you do is distribute it. First thing I thought about is Dr. Hekking, because he takes care of the sick people. And sugar is like a treat. So I divided it between Dr. Hekking and the kitchen. Everybody got a taste of it.

I guess the best haul I ever made was a case of quinine. We were working in Kanchanaburi, Japanese headquarters, for about a week. There is a medical officer who had his supplies there. So Dr. Hekking said to me one day, "When you're out on the working party, see if you can scrounge some quinine; I'm almost out." He knew that I was allergic to quinine. He said, "Do what you can, but don't get in trouble." The first day I found where the medical supplies were, and there were four cases of quinine. I didn't know very much about trading with the natives. What I should have done was to steal the quinine, sell it to a native, take the money, and give it to the doc to buy the quinine, so I wouldn't be caught. Instead of that, I got the case of quinine. I took it out bottle by bottle, twenty-four bottles in a wood crate with straw. Then I got the case back in order, put the top back on, minus the quinine, and put the case on the bottom. I figured it will take some time before the Japanese medic gets to the bottom case.

I was in charge of the food baskets that day. And as a rule, the guards don't search each and every group going back to camp. It's almost an instinct or intuition, "They're not going to search me." The question was, "Do you bring back four, five bottles at a time, or try to take the whole thing in?" My instinct said, "Do it once. If you're caught, you're caught." If you take it back six bottles at a time, you take four times the chance. So I took all of it in. There was an Australian who was helping me carry the pole. He said, "Eddie, you'll get us killed." I said, "No, they're not going to search us." So I put some bananas on top. And I said, "I'll give you half for helping me carry it in." He said, "What are you going to do with it?" I said, "Give it to the doc for the hospital." "Now," he said, "if you're going to do that, I'll help you carry it in." We got it in. So I told the Australian, "You can take half to your doctor if you want." He said, "Let's see what your doctor wants first." He said, "If he's a good bloke, he'll share it with us." And that's what doc did. He shared it with all the other doctors. I wasn't scared, but you know what the Japanese are going to do. Well, besides beating you up, they'll turn you over to the *kempeitai*, which is the Japanese equivalent of the S.S. They're mean! But as far as I was concerned, Doc saved my life twice, so I'm beholden to him. He knows I'll take chances whenever he needs something. In fact, I asked him before I did that, "You want a microscope, they got a microscope in there, and a nice wooden case." He said, "Eddie, I would love that microscope *(sounding exasperated)*, but where am I going to hide it?"

"WHAT IT IS TO BE CHINESE"

My worst moment came in May '45. The reason I can remember the month is because May is the beginning of the rainy season, and '45 was, of course, our last year, even though we didn't know it at the time. It wasn't a vision but a feeling that I would never see my mother again, who was still alive when I left, that I would not be able to go home and tell her face to face, "Okay Mom, I understand what you and Pop were trying to tell me, what it is to be Chinese, and how to be a Chinese." I just had the feeling that I wasn't going to get the chance to do that. There was never a time when I was more down, even when I had the dysentery and malaria at the same time. So I lived with the fact that I'm an unfilial son, because as it turned out, my mom died in May. There's two ways that I put it. If there's a heaven and a hell—an afterlife— and wherever they are, my parents will know that I'm trying to live the life they taught me to live. If there isn't an afterlife, I will know that I'm trying to live the way they taught me to live. So either way it will work out.

I came to feel strongly about my ethnic identity when we first got to the jungle, and Captain Fitzsimmons called me in one day and said, "Eddie, I can change your service record so it reads that you're half Chinese." And I said, "Why would we do that, Captain?" He said, "They may not be as rough on a half Chinese." My father had died in 1940, so I told Captain Fitzsimmons, "My father would turn over in his grave if I did that. Let's just take our chances and leave it the way it is." That was when I realized that I am Chinese. There's nothing I can do to change that. Culturally, I'm Chinese. Philosophically, I'm Chinese. But earlier, I had denied it because that was the thing that made Chinatown a ghetto to me. I suddenly realized that regardless of whether you're a prisoner in Chinatown or in a war camp, that doesn't make you any less or any more of a man than what you are. It doesn't matter what the rest of the world thinks, you're still that person. Being a prisoner made me realize that. I had this pathological fear of being a Chinese in the clutches of Japanese hands because I had been brought up to believe that Chinese and Japanese are traditional enemies. It was at that moment I knew that I could not deny who I am. I wasn't extra proud of it. I wasn't ashamed of it. I just knew that's the reality of it. I am Chinese, period.

"GENTLEMEN, THE WAR IS OVER"

Each of us had a different liberation date. Mine is the 19th of August. We knew something strange was going on because we went out three days in a row to work, and each time we were told to go back to camp. The fourth time they called us to the parade grounds at ten o'clock in the morning. The British bugler sounded assembly. That had never happened before. And we just had that feeling, "God, maybe this is it." We were all assembled in the parade ground, and British Warrant Officer Stimson, who was in charge of the camp, announced, "Gentlemen, the war is over and we are free." That was it. Later, we found out about the annihilation orders, that the Japanese were to kill any prisoners who might get in the way of the last-ditch fight.

I haven't had a hard day since that day, because to me, being taken prisoner has been the focal point of my life. I was a snotty-nose kid, just out for adventure, thinking that was all there was to life, not realizing that there's more that you're intended to do. Otherwise, you're just taking up breathing space. I've never regretted the war or the experiences because it taught me something, gave me the self-confidence that I could resolve any problem and take care of any situation that comes up.

After the war Eddie Fung served six months in the air force, worked as a butcher in Bakersfield, California, while attending junior college, and went on to study at Stanford University, majoring in chemistry. He worked as a metallurgical technologist at the Livermore National Laboratory until he retired in 1977. Every year around Au-

gust 15, Fung faithfully attends the reunion of the Lost Battalion Association in Texas as the sole Chinese American member of the most decorated Texan unit of any war.

SOURCE: Eddie Fung, interview with Judy Yung, August 17, 2002, San Francisco, California.

OTHER REFERENCES

Gavan Daws, *Prisoners of the Japanese: POWs of World War II in the Pacific* (New York: William Morrow, 1994).

"History of the Lost Battalion," Lost Battalion Association, 2nd Battalion, 131st Field Artillery, USS *Houston* Survivors, 2002 Roster, pp. iv–vii.

Marjorie Lee, ed., *Duty and Honor: A Tribute to Chinese American World War II Veterans of Southern California* (Los Angeles: Chinese Historical Society of Southern California, 1998).

K. Scott Wong, *Americans First: Chinese Americans and the Second World War* (Cambridge, Mass.: Harvard University Press, 2005).

One Hundred
and Seven Chinese (1943)

Gilbert Woo

At the time that Gilbert Woo[1] wrote the following satire on repeal of the Chinese Ex-clusion Acts, Congress was in the midst of debating the issue. The Citizens' Commit-tee to Repeal Chinese Exclusion, which consisted of China scholars, writers, and church leaders, lobbied heavily for the Magnuson bill. If passed, the bill would repeal the fifteen Chinese exclusion acts passed between 1882 and 1913, establish an annual quota for Chinese immigration, and grant naturalization rights to Chinese in the United States. On the surface, the legislation appeared to be dealing racial discrimination a blow, but Gilbert Woo, a liberal journalist at the Chinese Times *newspaper,[2] saw it for what it was—a token gesture and an insult to Chinese Americans.*

In the following article, which appeared in his newspaper column "Qizhi" or "I Wish to Inform You,"[3] Woo pokes fun at the debate over the small quota as well as at the arguments that labor unions and veterans' organizations were raising over po-tential job competition and the threat of interracial marriages should Congress pass the bill. But given the international situation—with China as a wartime ally to the United States—Congress decided to vote for repeal, and President Franklin Delano Roosevelt signed the bill into law on December 17, 1943, technically ending 62 years of Chinese exclusion.

1. Gilbert Woo (1911–1979) was one of the most widely read columnists in the Chinese Amer-ican press. He was born in Taishan District, Guangdong Province, and immigrated to the United States in 1932. In his forty-year career as a journalist, he consistently advocated for equal rights in American society, social reforms in the Chinese American community, and prosperity in China.

2. Founded by the Chinese-American Citizens' Alliance in 1924, the *Chinese Times* is a daily Chinese-language newspaper that claims to speak for American citizens of Chinese descent.

3. Gilbert Woo began writing the column on March 9, 1943. The title, "Qizhi," comes from the formal phrase commonly used at the beginning of a Chinese letter, "I wish to inform you." The column ran in the *Chinese Times* for over a year, covering a wide range of topics such as housing issues, the internment of Japanese Americans, and developments in China.

Gilbert Woo reading
the *Chinese Pacific
Weekly.* (Courtesy
of Lucy Huang)

Should the Chinese Exclusion Act be repealed, then 107 Chinese[4] will enter
the United States every year. As a result, the attention of all those who oppose the repeal seems to be focused on these 107 individuals.

These 107 individuals—ah, you can truly be proud of yourselves. In number there are not enough of you to make up a full set of mahjong tiles; yet
in power you can scoop up the moon's reflection in the water.[5]

Do you know that an American boxer claims he can take on 100 men? So
actually, they can summon a boxer and he alone can beat you black and blue
in the face. And yet, believe it or not, just hearing about you strikes terror
into the hearts of millions of Americans.

There used to be a Sergeant York in the United States, who, single-hand-
edly, captured over 100 German soldiers.[6] So actually, an army sergeant alone
is enough to tie all of you up. And yet, believe it or not, just mentioning you
causes millions of Americans to lose sleep and appetite.

4. The annual allotment for Chinese immigration was later fixed at 105.
5. Meaning, "to achieve the impossible."
6. Sergeant Alvin Cullum York served in Europe during World War I.

An American robber with one single machine gun can hold off 5,000 policemen. So actually, the head of a gang of robbers alone can mow you down like so much wheat. And yet, believe it or not, just speaking about you sets millions of Americans trembling.

Actually, one single streetcar is enough to take you to Seal Rocks.[7] One single apartment building is enough to hold all of you and you will not even have to fight over the bathroom. Five pounds of coffee is enough to give you insomnia all night. Five *jin*[8] of *wujiapi*[9] is enough to make you so drunk you cannot tell left from right. One porky pig is enough to give you the runs. You are not supermen, nor are you celestial beings. And yet they fear you more than the government troops feared the 108 bandit-heroes of Liang-shanpo.[10] Come to think of it, we might as well petition Congress and request special permission to increase the number by one to make it 108 individuals. But, on second thought, since Wu Song killed his sister-in-law, he would not fit in here.[11] We had best leave him in China.

They say that once the 107 of you manly fellows arrive, you will compete with the tens of millions of Americans for bread and thus drive down the living standards of the United States and cheapen the labor force. Do you really have such power? Or can this be some trick concocted by your Mr. Zhiduoxing?[12]

They say that once the 107 of you manly fellows arrive, you will introduce the problem of yellow and white marriages to this country. Now I am really confused. Are not your ranks filled with people like Lu Zhishen?[13]

Ah, you 107 manly fellows! I cannot help but prostrate myself in admiration. And when you finally arrive, we will be at the dockside to welcome you, loudly exclaiming, "Long live Liangshanpo!"

As historians and political analysts have correctly pointed out, the Chinese exclusion laws were repealed in 1943 as a goodwill gesture to China and to counter Japanese propaganda in Asia. The repeal did little to rectify the exclusion of Chinese immigrants, as the token annual quota of 105 was applied to Chinese people from any part of the world. As for Gilbert Woo, outspoken articles like this one would eventually cost him

7. A cluster of rocks off the coast of San Francisco where sea lions like to gather.

8. A Chinese measurement, one *jin* is equivalent to half a kilogram.

9. Potent Chinese liquor.

10. The headquarters of a group of 108 outlaws who battled corrupt officials, as immortalized in the eighteenth-century Chinese adventure novel *Shuihu Zhuan (The Water Margin)*, first translated as *All Men Are Brothers* by Pearl S. Buck.

11. Wu Song, one of the bandit-heroes, killed his adulterous sister-in-law to avenge the murder of his brother.

12. Zhiduoxing is the nickname for the resourceful Wu Yong, the mastermind strategist among the bandit-heroes.

13. Another member of the bandit-heroes of Liangshanpo, Lu Zhishen was a monk and therefore a man who must remain celibate.

his job at the Chinese Times. *He went on to write for the* Kuo Min Yat Po (Chinese Nationalist Daily) *before establishing his own newspaper, the* Chinese Pacific Weekly, *in 1946. He remained Chinatown's liberal voice and conscience until he died in 1979 at the age of sixty-eight.*

SOURCE: *Chinese Times,* September 7, 1943; reprinted in *Hu Jingnan wenji* [Selected works of Gilbert Woo] (Hong Kong: Xiangjiang Chuban Youxian Gongsi, 1991), pp. 37–38. Translator: Ellen Yeung.

OTHER REFERENCES

Him Mark Lai, "A Voice of Reason: Life and Times of Gilbert Woo, Chinese American Journalist," *Chinese America: History and Perspectives,* 1992, pp. 83–123.

Fred Riggs, *Pressure on Congress: A Study of the Repeal of Chinese Exclusion* (New York: Columbia University Press, 1950).

L. Ling-chi Wang, "Politics of the Repeal of the Chinese Exclusion Laws," in *The Repeal and Its Legacy: Proceedings of the Conference on the 50th Anniversary of the Repeal of the Exclusion Acts* (San Francisco: Chinese Historical Society of America and Asian American Studies, San Francisco State University, 1994), pp. 66–80.

Becoming an Integral
Part of America, 1943–2003

Sweeping changes in immigration, domestic, and foreign policies irrevocably changed the composition and lives of the Chinese American population during the second half of the twentieth century. In the afterglow of World War II, Congress passed the War Brides Act of 1945 and Alien Wives Act of 1946, which allowed over seven thousand Chinese women to enter as nonquota immigrants and join their husbands in America. This, in turn, generated a baby boom and noticeable infusion of family life in urban Chinatowns such as those in San Francisco, Los Angeles, New York, and Boston. But after China turned Communist in 1949 and the Chinese fought against Americans in the Korean conflict a year later, U.S.-China relations deteriorated. The anti-Communist hysteria that followed in the 1950s forced overseas Chinese to sever ties with their homeland. At the same time, changes in domestic policies encouraged them to set down roots and become an integral part of America. Anti-Chinese laws, which for decades had denied the Chinese fundamental civil rights and legal protection, were revoked one by one, enabling them to intermarry with whites, own land, and find better jobs and housing outside Chinatown boundaries. These new developments opened up opportunities for the Chinese to move out from the shadows of exclusion and become fuller participants in American life.

As the country entered the Cold War era, a series of refugee acts were passed which admitted approximately thirty thousand professionals, entrepreneurs, intellectuals, and ex–government officials escaping unstable political conditions in China. The Chinese population in the United States swelled from 117,629 in 1950 to 237,292 in 1960. Unlike earlier Cantonese immigrants, many of these newcomers were well educated, cosmopolitan, spoke the Mandarin dialect, and came from central and northern China. Arriving at a time when conditions were turning favorable for Chinese Americans and when their scientific and technical skills were in demand by America's military-industrial complex, they had little trouble finding work in their fields, housing in the suburbs, and social acceptance in middle-class circles.

However, at the same time that America welcomed political refugees from Communist countries, it sought to persecute Communist sympathizers at home. In 1955 Everett Drumwright, U.S. consul in Hong Kong, raised the issue of fraudulent entry on the part of Chinese immigrants and with it the implicit accusation of Communist infiltration. To avoid tying up the courts with deportation cases, immigration authorities in cooperation with alarmed leaders in Chinatown instigated the Confession Program, by which paper sons could confess and assume their true identities with a guarantee against deportation. Only fourteen thousand volunteered to do so. Although the program presented the Chinese with an opportunity to clear their immigration status, it also exerted undue pressure on those who did not want to implicate relatives by their confessions. Federal agents, taking advantage of the program, were known to make periodic sweeps through Chinatowns in search of Communist sympathizers. Politically left groups, such as the Chinese American Youth Club and the Chinese Hand Laundry Alliance, all fell victims to the "red scare," while the Kuomintang (Chiang Kai-shek's Nationalist regime in Taiwan) took advantage of the political situation to strengthen its control and influence over Chinatown politics and institutions.

The paranoia and mental anguish suffered by Chinese in America during this period served to dampen their interest in China politics as well as any involvement in left-wing political activities. Many went out of their way to prove they were all-American, and at the same time to take advantage of improved opportunities after the war for socioeconomic and political advancement. Chinese American baby boomers, growing up in the era of the atom bomb, suburban living, drive-in movies, television, and rock 'n' roll, were encouraged by the mass media to give up their ethnic identity and conform to white middle-class standards. But in so doing, they encountered cultural conflicts at home and found that race and gender still mattered in the working world, especially if one had been brought up to be obedient, reserved, and collective-minded rather than independent, assertive, and outgoing.

Although 1960 U.S. census data show that a larger proportion of Chinese Americans, as compared to their white counterparts, graduated from college, and that they had moved up the occupational ladder from manual labor, domestic service, and clerical work to technical, sales, and professional fields, statistics also show that Chinese Americans did not have the same earning power as white men and women with comparable backgrounds. In other words, their earning power was not commensurate with their level of education. Owing to racial discrimination, cultural barriers, media stereotypes, and the lack of role models and career counseling, Chinese Americans were segregated into the lower-paying, nonmanagerial sectors of the primary labor market. More Chinese Americans were accountants, health technicians, and secretaries than were lawyers, physicians, and business executives. Nevertheless, some were able to distinguish themselves in new fields of endeavor, such as the arts, higher education, and politics.

Meanwhile, the Chinese in Hawaii were still assimilating faster than their counterparts on the mainland. In 1960, 74 percent of the Chinese working population was concentrated in white-collar jobs, and the Chinese had the highest median income of all ethnic groups in the islands. By 1970 the average family annual income among Chinese in the Honolulu metropolitan area was 40 percent higher than the comparable average for Chinese on the mainland, and the Chinese outmarriage rate in Hawaii was 30 percent as compared to 13 percent on the mainland. Chinese business tycoons were making a fortune, while stimulating commerce and travel between the mainland and the islands. After Hawaii attained statehood, Hiram Fong became the first and only Chinese American to be elected to the U.S. Senate, where he served from 1959 to 1977.

Then came the civil rights movement and the passage of the Civil Rights Act of 1964 and the Immigration Act of 1965. The first piece of legislation prohibited discrimination in education, employment, and public facilities on the basis of race or sex. It paved the way for the establishment of affirmative action programs in education and employment to make up for past discrimination. This in turn leveled the playing field and opened up opportunities for Chinese Americans to get ahead. The second major piece of legislation ended the discriminatory quota system of selecting immigrants by national origin and placed China on an equal footing with other countries at twenty thousand immigrants annually. Intended to promote family reunification and attract highly educated and skilled workers to the United States, the Immigration Act made a major impact on the Chinese American population in terms of numbers and diversity. By the end of the century, the Chinese population had increased dramatically, from 430,000 in 1970 to 2.8 million, and 71 percent of the population was foreign born. Initially, most of the immigrants came from Taiwan and Hong Kong, but political turmoil in Cuba, Peru, Burma, Indonesia, the Philippines, and Vietnam soon brought thousands more from these areas as well. Direct emigration from China was not possible until diplomatic ties between China and the United States were restored in 1979.

Because immediate family members of U.S. citizens were counted as nonquota immigrants, actual Chinese immigration went well beyond its annual quota of twenty thousand. Many of the new immigrants, joining their spouses and families after many years of separation, came from the rural areas of Guangdong Province. Primarily non-English-speaking and lacking marketable job skills, they settled in urban Chinatowns, where they eked out a living in the ethnic economy, mainly in food stores, restaurants, and garment sweatshops. Their arrival injected new life into the Chinatown communities, creating new demands for Chinese food, goods, services, and entertainment. However, the large influx also compounded already existing ghetto conditions of overcrowded and substandard housing, unemployment and underemployment, and inadequate health care, recreational space, and childcare services. Furthermore, the absence of both parents away at work and the pressures of adjusting to American life led to intergenerational conflicts within the home and increased juvenile delinquency in the community.

Fortunately for the new immigrants, they were arriving at a propitious moment, for just then President Lyndon B. Johnson's War on Poverty program was getting into full gear. In response to the demands of the civil rights movement, federal funds had been allocated to provide social services to minority communities suffering poverty conditions. A new generation of Chinese American liberals, going against the "better judgment" of the Kuomintang-controlled Chinatown establishment, marched in demonstrations and filed class action lawsuits to ensure that the Chinese community received its share of public funding, social services, and protection against racial discrimination. New community-based organizations were formed to help Chinese immigrants learn English, acquire job skills, and cope with their new lives in America. While the civil rights movement inspired the founding of national organizations like Chinese for Affirmative Action and the Organization of Chinese Americans to fight for civil rights, bilingual education, and affirmative action, the black power movement spurred a new generation of Chinese American radicals to engage in revolutionary politics as a way to address social issues in the community. Moreover, after the United States normalized relations with China in 1979, the Chinese American community, which had been sorely divided on the two-China issue for thirty years, was finally able to break away from Kuomintang control and redirect their energies and financial resources toward American politics and the welfare of the community.

As U.S. involvement in the Vietnam War escalated after the Tet offensive in 1968, Chinese Americans were not spared from the negative impact of that conflict. Some lost their lives at the battlefront; some returned to their communities traumatized. Others became politicized by the antiwar movement at home and chose to unite with other Asian Americans to protest what they perceived to be a racist and immoral war. When the war ended in 1975, over one million Vietnamese, Laotian, and Cambodian refugees were admitted into the United States. Approximately 35 percent of those from Vietnam were ethnic Chinese "boat people" who had escaped in overloaded vessels after being forced out by the new Communist regime because of their prominent role in the country's former capitalist economy as well as the heightened tensions between Vietnam and China. Many of the refugees spoke Cantonese, but there were also those who spoke the Chaozhou, Hakka, Minnan, or Hainan dialects. Sharing a common Chinese cultural background, they gravitated toward Chinatowns for employment, grocery shopping, and social services. But arriving at a time of economic recession and anti-Asian backlash, they were not always welcomed by the Chinese community or the larger American society. Once they got back on their feet, however, many went on to establish small businesses adjacent to Chinatowns or in Vietnamese enclaves in California—Westminster, Long Beach, San Diego, and San Jose.

Then beginning in the mid-1980s, they were followed by thousands of Chinese from Fujian Province, across the strait from Taiwan, all seeking a better livelihood in America. Unable to qualify for admission under the current immigration laws, they resorted to paying "snakeheads" enormous fees to smuggle them into the country. Their voyages to America were often fraught with danger and hardships. The majority settled in New York Chinatown, where they were indentured into low-paying jobs in the underground economy and forced to live in squalor in order to pay off their debts. Those caught in transit—as in the case of 286 Chinese passengers packed into the hold of the *Golden Venture* freighter in 1993—were either deported or imprisoned for as long as three years while awaiting hearings on their applications for political asylum.

Not all immigrants arriving after 1965, however, have had to start at the bottom. A significant number coming from Taiwan, Hong Kong, and different parts of China as part of the "brain drain" have been able to find well-paying jobs in America's expanding technological economy. Many who initially came as foreign students were able to acquire status as permanent residents on graduation by finding jobs in certain professional fields or by marrying U.S. citizens. Because of the Tiananmen Square incident in 1989, when a mass protest of college students advocating political reform in China was quashed by armed troops, another sixty thousand students and scholars from China were allowed to become permanent residents after President George H.W. Bush issued an executive order to that effect. Others who came with capital and entrepreneurial skills in response to the Immigration Act of 1990 have been able to invest profitably in restaurants, supermarkets, shopping centers, hotels and motels, banks, real estate, and computer technology. Their returns have allowed them to realize the American dream of economic success, and their contributions to the prosperity of this country have been immense, judging by the wealth they have generated in Pacific Rim trade, Silicon Valley, and new Chinese suburbs in San Gabriel Valley and Monterey Park, California; Flushing and Brooklyn, New York; Houston, Bellaire, and Richardson, Texas; and even Chamblee, Georgia. However, these wealthy immigrants have not always been welcomed with open arms by their white American neighbors. For example, in Monterey Park, also known as Little Taipei, the arrival of Taiwanese immigrants with capital has been viewed by local residents as an economic and cultural invasion of their community. A bumper sticker says it all: "Will the last American out of Monterey Park please take the American flag with them?"

In general, however, the large influx of Chinese immigrants, combined with improved U.S.-China relations and a renewed commitment to multi-culturalism in this country, has led to a proliferation of Chinese institutions and a broader acceptance of Chinese cultural practices in America. Chinese cuisine, fashion, music, martial arts, temples, schools, newspapers, literature, and films have developed at a fast pace to meet the new demands of a grow-ing Chinese immigrant population. New regional, professional, and social organizations have been established by recent immigrant groups, while at the same time, older family and district organizations in Chinatowns have had to revamp their purposes and services to remain relevant to the needs of a changing population. Chinese restaurants are more popular than ever, and such foods as potstickers, tofu, and bok choy have become common fare. Cantonese cooking still dominates, but there is a growing appreciation of cuisines from other regions of China, including Beijing, Shanghai, Hunan, and Szechwan. And whereas previously, Americans had frowned on Chinese traditional practices, they now respect and in some cases join Chinese Amer-icans in seeking solace in Buddhism and Taoism; good health in the martial arts, acupuncture, and herbal medicine; and cultural enrichment in study-ing Chinese language and arts.

Second and third generations of American-born Chinese (ABC) have also benefited from the social changes of the civil rights era. They are among the first Chinese Americans to successfully integrate into mainstream society, judging by their middle-class status, suburban residence, social lifestyle, and high rates of outmarriage (54 percent of ABC's were married to non-Chinese in 1990). Even so, many have held on to their strong sense of ethnic pride while negotiating new identities as hapa, gay/lesbian, and generation X. Contrary to the model minority image, ABC's have not been afraid to speak out against racial discrimination and social injustices, to advocate for work-ers' rights, and to challenge racist and sexist stereotypes in the mass media. They have also led the way in creating more realistic images of Chinese Amer-icans in literature, film, and television, and by breaking into new areas pre-viously closed to Chinese Americans—broadcast media, law and law enforce-ment, high finance, art and music, sports, and politics.

According to 2000 U.S. census data, Chinese Americans are doing quite well compared to other racial/ethnic groups in this country: 48.1 percent are college graduates, 52.3 percent hold managerial or professional jobs, and 58.4 percent own their homes. Overall conditions have improved for Chinese Americans since the 1960s, but class and racial conflicts have bro-ken out anew in the last two decades because of downturns in the American economy due to the restructuring of global capitalism and competition from abroad. In the face of plant closures, rising unemployment, and urban de-cay, the country once again blamed the Chinese for its economic problems, especially in light of U.S. trade deficits with Japan and China. Two cases in particular, the murder of Vincent Chin by two white autoworkers in 1982 and the wrongful imprisonment of nuclear scientist Wen Ho Lee for espionage in 1999, serve as strong indicators of the resurgence of anti-Asian violence and stereotyping of Chinese Americans as perpetual foreigners in this country. According to a 2001 national survey sponsored by the Committee of 100 (an organization of prominent Chinese Americans), while a majority of the American public admires Chinese Americans for their devotion to family and emphasis on education and achievements, a disturbing one-third believe that Chinese Americans are more loyal to China than to the United States, and nearly a quarter disapprove of intermarriage with a Chinese American. Other evidence of growing anti-Chinese sentiment includes incidents of ethnic slurs in the mass media, anti-immigrant legislation, setbacks in affirmative action and bilingual education programs, and racial scapegoating of Chinese Americans in a number of high-profile political scandals. There is obviously still much more to be done before Chinese Americans are accepted as an integral part of America.

The voices in Part III mirror the linguistic, cultural, political, and socioeconomic diversity of the Chinese American community in contemporary times. Included in this section are the stories of war brides, refugees, and new immigrants struggling for a foothold in America as well as those who have achieved the American dream of socioeconomic success. There are poems, essays, and interviews with ABC's about their assimilation experience and the identity issues they confronted growing up in communities outside of Chinatown and during a time of great social ferment. Finally, the broad range of perspectives endemic to a period of intense political change is well represented in the editorials of various Chinese-language newspapers, the testimonies by victims of McCarthyism, China bashing, and hate crimes, and the speeches and writings of community activists fighting for workers' rights, civil rights, and political empowerment. Quite appropriately, we end the section with the story and final words of David Ho, who was named *Time* magazine's Man of the Year in 1996 for his research on AIDS: "We all know we are Americans; we're just of a different heritage."

San Francisco
Chinese Papers Blame
Immigration Practices in
Suicide of Chinese Woman (1948)

Chinese News Service

Although World War II ushered in better times for Chinese Americans, the removal of anti-Chinese discriminatory laws and practices occurred slowly. The Chinese exclusion laws were repealed, but only 105 Chinese immigrants worldwide were allowed into the country annually. In 1947 the War Brides Act of 1945 was amended to include wives of Chinese American veterans on a nonquota basis. But Chinese war brides, upon arrival, were treated no differently than during the exclusion period at Angel Island. Locked up and detained at the immigration building on Sansome Street for weeks and sometimes months, they too were subjected to interrogations about their family background in order to prove their identities and marital relationships. When one war bride, upset at the long delays, committed suicide, over one hundred inmates went on a hunger strike, and the Chinese community responded with concern and anger—as reflected in the following newspaper editorials gathered by the Chinese News Service (CNS).[1]

There existed five dailies and one weekly newspaper in San Francisco Chinatown at the time. Despite their different political slants, all of the newspapers blamed the suicide on racial discrimination and the unreasonable immigration procedures that put undue stress on Chinese immigrants. They also pointed to the irony of the situation in which "the most democratic country in the world," while espousing liberty and justice in the postwar era, would so mistreat the wives of Chinese American veterans. Six years later, the detention quarters at 630 Sansome Street were closed, and U.S. officials began determining an applicant's admissibility at the port of departure rather than the port of entry. Although the Chinese American sex ratio narrowed as a result of the in-

1. The Chinese News Service, located in downtown San Francisco and with offices in New York, Chicago, and Washington, D.C., was the official Chinese government news agency and information bureau in the United States. It operated under the control of the Kuomintang (Chiang Kai-shek's Nationalist Party) and the Chinese consul general in San Francisco.

creased immigration of women during the postwar era, it did not reach parity until well after the passage of the Immigration Act of 1965.

[CNS] Editor's Note: On September 21, a Chinese woman, Leong Bick Ha, wife of a former U.S. Army sergeant, Ng Bak Teung of New York, hanged herself in the immigration detention quarters at 630 Sansome Street, San Francisco. Mrs. Ng (nee Leong) had been detained since her arrival on June 30 pending immigration investigation to confirm her marital status. Her 15-year-old son, Ng Lung Tuck, was held in another part of the building.[2] The incident occasioned widespread editorial comment in San Francisco's Chinese-language newspapers, which unanimously condemned existing immigration practices against the Chinese. The following is a roundup in translation of some of the Chinese editorial opinion.

RACIAL PREJUDICE SEEN AT WORK

Chung Sai Yat Po,[3] in a two-part editorial published on September 22 and 23, said: "From press reports we frequently learn that even European refugees, coming to America in small boats, have been granted permission to enter by the U.S. Government. Mr. Ng served in the U.S. Army for several years before securing the right to bring his wife to America. But despite his sacrifices, Mrs. Ng suffered prolonged detention because she lacked proof of marriage. This is in sharp contrast to the ease with which the white races from Europe can enter the United States. So who could believe that the Immigration Office does not have any racial prejudice?

"The United States is at present the most democratic country in the world, and its government and administration are most efficient, yet on one small immigration case it has strangely spent several months, even years. Moreover, in recent years, the families of overseas Chinese, applying for entry permit into the United States, are all examined and approved by the American consuls in Hong Kong, Canton, and Shanghai. The examination is conducted so thoroughly that it is usually several months before permission is granted. Then, upon arrival in the U.S., the immigrant is held for months while a perfectionist, hair-splitting investigation is made. If these Federal agencies operate independently of each other, it only serves to make the world wonder how much to credit the word of the United States Government.

"We know there is a small number of obstinate and myopic Americans

2. According to an article in the *San Francisco Chronicle* on September 22, 1948, Leong Bik Ha had been separated from her husband for fifteen years. This situation was not uncommon, due to the Chinese exclusion laws, which had kept Chinese families apart for decades.

3. Literally meaning "China-West Daily," *Chung Sai Yat Po* was founded by Rev. Ng Poon Chew in 1900. Influenced by American republicanism and Western middle-class values, the newspaper favored reform in China and advocated equal rights for Chinese Americans.

who, whenever they read of the cases of one or two Chinese being smuggled across the border or who falsify passports to enter the country, would come to the conclusion that this is being done by the majority of the Chinese immigrants, and that the examination of immigrants should be harshly conducted. Actually, among the white people as among the yellow races, there are good and bad. The newspapers have reported quite frequently of white people sneaking into the United States from the Atlantic, or illegally entering the country by air from Mexico. Would it be fair to place the crime of these few violators on the whole white race? And yet there is no denying the far greater ease with which members of the white race can enter the country and be assimilated, as compared to the Chinese. This inflexibility and prejudice of the American immigration policy is apparent to all.

"Racial discrimination and unfair treatment can lead to social and even international conflict. So to maintain and enhance international goodwill, the far-seeing American authorities should not overlook the discriminatory practices in immigration."

IMMIGRATION AUTHORITIES CRITICIZED

The *Young China* (morning paper)[4] published an editorial on September 25, in which the writer said: "The bureaucratic and ruthless behavior of the Immigration Office here is both illegal and inhuman, for it is rooted in racial discrimination. Because of racial discrimination, the U.S. immigration laws cannot be equitable. At present, the American Government is devising ways to bring in a large number of displaced Europeans,[5] yet it has no legal protection for the wife of a Chinese-American veteran. But what is more exasperating is the Immigration Office here, which acts in excess of the unfair laws: (1) It presumes that Chinese who enter the country mostly attempt to circumvent the law, and on this basis devises rules and regulations for their detention. (2) It does not recognize the verification of American consuls, and makes Chinese arriving here undergo further examinations. (3) Seeing everything in the light only of American domestic law, rather than the spirit of private international law, it will not recognize

4. The *Young China Morning Post* was founded in 1910 as the official party organ of the Tongmenghui, Sun Yat-sen's Revolutionary Party. The newspaper supported the Western Hills Faction that opposed Sun's alliance with the Soviet Union and acceptance of Chinese Communist Party members into the Kuomintang. This led to a left-right split in the party in the Chinese American community that resulted in the founding of the *Kuo Min Yat Po (Chinese Nationalist Daily of America)* by the left in 1927, while the *Young China* became the voice of the right.

5. Congress had just passed the Displaced Persons Act to admit primarily European refugees escaping Communism into the United States. However, after China became a Communist country in 1949, some five thousand Chinese students and scholars already in the United States were allowed to adjust their status and remain in the country.

reasonable explanations concerning marriage and birth certifications. (4) It will not give speedy examinations to the detained immigrants, so that they have to spend lengthy periods in prisonlike surroundings, which is in contravention of explicit rules of American legal proceedings, and the fundamental spirit of English and American law. (5) The detained Chinese are not criminals, yet their place of detention is not even as well equipped as a common jail. Even the chief commissioner of immigration said it was deplorable and regrettable.

"At just about the time the case of Leong Bick Ha came up, Secretary of State Marshall was giving a speech at the General Assembly of the United Nations at Paris defending human rights. We heard him urge respect for the 'freedom from arbitrary arrest and detention' and 'preservation of the dignity and worth of the individual.' And ironically we have confronting us the action of the Immigration Office.

"However, the Americans are a progressive people and their racial prejudice is bound to be eliminated eventually. The action of a few men in the Immigration Office is a black spot on American society, which may not have the sympathy of the large majority of the American people. When we see the self-criticism of higher immigration authorities and the protests and appeals of American civic bodies and the press, we know that justice is in the hearts of the people and that there is hope of improvement of the immigration question."

PAPER ADVANCES THREE SUGGESTIONS

The *Chinese World*[6] on September 22 published the first of three editorials on the death of Leong Bick Ha, which said: "It is a tragedy we cannot bear to hear. Coming from afar to seek her husband, she had already borne much suffering, and upon arrival to be detained for two months, awaiting examination, the torment in her mind was inconceivable.

"According to reports, the Immigration Office, being shorthanded, cannot speedily get through the large number of accumulated cases. This may be true, but improvement is not impossible. It is to be recalled that when the case of Mrs. Wong Loy took place, a number of questions were brought up by this paper: ([CNS] Editor's note: On June 1, Wong Loy, a Chinese woman held in the immigration detention quarters, was narrowly saved from jumping off the 14th floor of a Sansome St. building.)[7]

---

6. The *Chinese World (Sai Gai Yat Po)* newspaper was founded as the weekly *Mon Hing Bo* in 1891. It fell under the control of the Baohuanghui (Chinese Reform Party) in 1899 and began publishing daily in 1901.

7. Wong Loy, wife of a Chinese American GI in Aberdeen, Washington, had failed to prove her marital relationship and been detained for six months pending an appeal. Distraught over

"(1) Why were not the examinations of immigrants completed when applications were first made for entry permission; why must the examination be conducted after arrival and under detention?

"(2) After the arrival of the immigrants, why could they not be examined immediately? And if the immigration office is shorthanded, why were the immigrants not permitted to post bond and be released while awaiting examination?

"(3) If the immigration office decided to send the immigrants to their place of origin, why were they not sent immediately? And if the immigrants appealed the deportation order, why could they not be allowed to post bond while awaiting review?

"We are fortunate that the immigration authorities have heeded the third question we brought up, and that all who are ordered deported may now be released upon posting of bonds. But our first two questions have not had their attention, so that the tragedy of Leong Bick Ha has to take place. But this is not only the misfortune of Ms. Leong; it is a very unfortunate thing in the friendly relations between China and the United States."

LEONG BICK HA AND MRS. KASENKINA

The *Chinese Pacific Weekly*,[8] in an editorial entitled "Minor International Incidents," wrote on September 25: "In the past two months, two minor international incidents have taken place. They are minor only in comparison with the present civil war in China and the tense international picture." The first, said the paper, was the case of Mrs. Kasenkina, who jumped from the third floor of the Russian consulate in New York because of her desire to stay in the United States. The second was the suicide of Leong Bick Ha because of her desire to enter the United States to rejoin her husband. Like Mrs. Kasenkina, she was detained and held incommunicado, and like Mrs. Kasenkina, she preferred death to imprisonment.

"We are not being jealous when we say that the United States treated the Russian woman better than the Chinese woman, but beyond this, there are a lot of things which seem incomprehensible to us.

"One thing which is worthy of our interest is that the Russian woman, although not protected by the Soviet Government, received protection from

---

the long delay and possibility of deportation, she made newspaper headlines on June 1, 1948, when she perched on the fourteenth-floor parapet of the immigration building for three and a half hours, threatening to jump whenever rescuers approached her. After her rescue, she was released and allowed to stay in the country by remarrying her husband in a civil ceremony.

8. Founded by liberal-minded Gilbert Woo in 1946, the *Chinese Pacific Weekly* focused primarily on news and issues of concern to the Chinese American community.

the American Government, while the Chinese woman, coming to the United States, was devoid of any protection. . . .

"We do not expect that there will be any liberal immigration policy within the next few years. This is of course a misfortune to us Chinese, but it will not be of benefit to the United States. Now, at a time when the American authorities are highly proclaiming liberty and justice in the hope of leading the peoples of the world against aggression, there is not one manifestation of humanity and justice. This does not portend well for the future of the nation of Lincoln, Wilson, and Roosevelt!

"If the Chinese Communists were seeking for material to make their anti-American attacks, the cases of Leong Bick Ha and Wong Loy would furnish them with their best propaganda material."

In another article the *Chinese Pacific Weekly* commented on the suggestion of the American Civil Liberties Union to move the detained Chinese either to Angel Island[9] or to the Tanforan Race Track,[10] in order to ease the congestion at the Immigration Office detention house. The paper declared: "Local Chinese are not interested in this solution, and many regarded the change as boding more ill than good. They pointed out that the suicide of Leong Bick Ha was not because of her dislike of the Sansome Street building. There is no connection between her place of detention and her suicide. Being detained too long and under emotional stress, she could have committed suicide at the race-track camp as in the Sansome Street building.

"Under the present conditions, the husband and friends of the detained women can come from Chinatown to the detention house in less than five minutes to visit them. This would be inconvenient if they were moved to places ten or twenty miles from the city. . . .

"The Chinese in Chinatown also pointed out that Americans do not understand the psychology of Chinese women. The Americans are interested in material things—in sunshine, in fresh air, and in living among sanitary conveniences. But Chinese women coming to the United States are not interested in these things. Their suffering is mental and not due to the lack of material things. And no matter where their place of detention is moved, whether to Angel Island or to Tanforan Race Track, it will not lessen their mental anguish."

September 28, 1948

SOURCE: Chinese News Service, "San Francisco Chinese Papers Blame Immigration Practices in Suicide of Chinese Women," Special Release, September 28, 1948, American Civil Liberties Union file, California Historical Society, San Francisco.

9. After a mysterious fire closed down the Angel Island Immigration Station in 1940, the detention quarters were moved to the Appraiser's Building at 630 Sansome Street.

10. Located south of San Francisco, the Tanforan Race Track was converted into an assembly center to temporarily house Japanese Americans until they could be moved to concentration camps in desolate areas of the United States during World War II.

OTHER REFERENCES

Judy Yung, *Chinese Women of America: A Pictorial History* (Seattle: University of Washington Press, 1986).

Xiaojian Zhao, *Remaking Chinese America: Immigration, Family, and Community, 1940–1965* (New Brunswick, N.J.: Rutgers University Press, 2002).

I Want to Marry
an American Girl (1955)

Eddie Gong

Mainstream images of Chinese Americans began to improve in the 1950s. Though still portrayed as a minority group with a distinct background, they were no longer perceived as a threat to the American way of life. Some articles, anticipating the "model minority" image that would be widely promoted in the 1980s, even suggested that Chinese Americans, with their strong family values and work ethic, could be welcome additions to the national family. Chinese Americans themselves sometimes helped to popularize the idea that they were eager and ready to assimilate into white, middle-class life.

In September 1955, the American Magazine published the following provocative article, "I Want to Marry an American Girl." In contrast to fears about miscegenation expressed in earlier times, this article seemed to endorse interracial marriage. The state of California had repealed its antimiscegenation law in 1948, but twelve states still prohibited intermarriage between Chinese and whites. The article's main intent, however, was to show that Eddie Gong, representative of a new generation of Chinese Americans, was quickly discarding the old ways of his traditional parents and fully embracing American individualism and culture, including its standards of love and beauty.

According to the magazine's introduction to the article, Eddie Gong was "Boy President of the U.S.A." in 1947, when he was a high school junior in Miami, Florida, and met President Harry Truman at an American Legion ceremony in Washington, D.C. Gong went on to Harvard and graduated cum laude in 1952. He was attending Harvard Law School when he wrote this article, describing his dilemma in fulfilling the wishes of his parents to find a Chinese wife in Hong Kong. As it turned out, Gong did go to Hong Kong in 1955 and worked there briefly as a journalist. But he did not find a Chinese wife. He returned to the United States and became a highly successful attorney and political figure in Florida, serving in the Florida state legislature from 1963 to 1972 and as the Florida manager of Republican John Lindsay's presidential primary effort in 1972. He married twice, neither time to a woman of Chinese ancestry. Ironically, one of Gong's sons wrote a senior essay as a Harvard un-

"My ideal of grace and beauty runs more to pretty girls like this," says Eddie Gong. (*American Magazine*, September 1955)

dergraduate in 1987 honoring his grandfather's "courage and spirit" and the hard-ships that the Chinese had endured in America, since "sometimes the later generations of Chinese-Americans tend to forget this dark side of their past."[1]

I am leaving today for Hong Kong, China, the home of my ancestors. At the request of my parents, and in accordance with ancient Chinese tradition and custom, I am looking for a wife—to be chosen by me from a group of Chinese girls carefully selected by my 80-year-old grandmother, Hoo See, whom I have never met. But, in my own heart, I hope I do not find a wife in Hong Kong. I was born in America, of Chinese parents, and consider myself an American. Therefore, I want to marry an American girl and to choose my wife myself, in American fashion, rather than have her chosen for me, in the Chinese way.

This will be the first time that I have ever left the United States, where I was born 25 years ago. But as a dutiful son—the only son in our family—I believe I owe my parents at least one attempt to find a Chinese girl I could fall in love with.

Back of this conflict between my wish to be obedient to my mother and

1. Edmond Joseph Gong, Jr., "The Base on Which I Stand," thesis, Harvard University, 1987.

father, and my desire to marry in the American way, is a clash, not only between two different generations, but between two cultures, the East and the West. To understand my dilemma, you must know something about my family background, and my own upbringing. . . .

I guess you could describe me as a typical American boy, except that my last name is Gong and my parents are from China. I speak Cantonese and English with a Southern accent and am equally proficient with chopsticks and jukeboxes. My background is a blend of the wisdom and teachings of the East and the new spirit of America. For centuries my ancestors tilled the soil of China and although I belong to this long line, I am the first generation born in the New World. Through my parents I have strong ties to my ancestral people, but my heart lies in America, a country which has given to me and my family a way of life which the old country could never have dreamed of.

Picture, if you can, a young man who is carefree and sentimental, who loves to talk to all kinds of people; a guy who has an average frame of about 5 feet 10 and who weighs 160 pounds. He would rather dance than eat, but his favorite dish is real Italian spaghetti. He prefers the genuine and sincere type of person for a friend, and has a fancy for any natural kind of gal who has long hair, a nice figure, and coquettish femininity. Although he achieved fairly good marks at Harvard, studies are definitely not his forte. To him there is nothing greater than the feel of a well-hit tennis ball or a close, wide-open football game, or the "cool" music of Dave Brubeck. He's extroverted, likes crowds, and loves parties. Add a Joe College crew cut, tweed sport coat, a pair of dirty white bucks, throw in a line of Air Force jet chatter, and we have met.

As you see, there's nothing particularly unusual about me as a person. I'm just an average guy, like most of my school and college friends. Many of these kids have parents who came from "the old country," and have been brought up in a combination of Old and New World backgrounds. I know many youngsters of Greek and Polish backgrounds, and they do not feel that for that reason they must seek their mates in Greece and Poland, or that they can marry only persons of similar ancestry. But since my parents come from Asia, where customs are strikingly different from those in America and Europe, and where parents exercise greater control over their offspring all during their lives, my problem in finding a wife is more complex.

My grandfather's name was Joe Lin Gong, and he came to the United States in 1885, when he was 23. Although he spoke no English, he made his way in America by starting a laundry, first in Boston, Mass., then in Fall River. But he found these cities crowded and noisy, and so made his way South, to Albany, Ga., and then to Tifton. He was so sold on the American way of life and form of government that he named his enterprise the "Republic Laundry"!

Operating the laundry was practically a round-the-clock backbreaking job seven days a week, and Grandfather never felt that he could bring Grandmother to America and ask her to share in his toil. In fact, his heart always was in China rather than America. He saved his pennies, and managed to get back to China once or twice before he returned there for good in 1917, and died in the land of his ancestors in 1925.

Like countless thousands of Americans, my own parents had the courage to emigrate from a secure life to a new but uncertain existence in a land of boundless opportunity. One reason I respect them so highly is that they showed vision and courage like that of the Founding Fathers who made America great.

My father, Joseph Fred Gong, was born in a little village near Canton in 1900, and Grandfather sent for him when Father was 15. In 1924, Dad returned to China for the same reason that I am going today—to find a wife. But there was then no conflict in his heart as there is in mine today. Chinese in this country were not so Americanized then as they are now, and it never occurred to my father to question his parents' wisdom, or their right to decide whom he should marry.

My mother, Wong Shee, was 17 when my father married her, in a quaint and colorful Chinese marriage ceremony, with paper lanterns decorating the cottage and paper dragons for good luck, and firecrackers popping gaily afterward. Then father left his bride and returned to America, where he sent for her two years later. He tried the laundry business, in Tifton and then in Miami, and finally decided to open a small grocery store, which is our family business today.

In my judgment, Mom and Dad have reared a pretty fine family. To give us the opportunities they never had, they worked seven days a week in the store. I know that I owe them a debt, which I can never repay, and my four sisters feel as I do. . . .

In school and in our daily lives we have always tried to follow our parents' teachings. They taught us respect for elders, especially our parents and our teachers, gave us a desire for education, and demonstrated, by their practice and example, the true meaning of the Golden Rule. . . .

My relationship with my parents has been a little different than that of my sisters. When I was born in Miami on October 7, 1930, it was a joyous occasion, for I was the first son. And by the Chinese custom, the news was conveyed to friends of my parents by the presentation of red-dyed eggs. This custom takes place only when a son is born. Shortly thereafter, gifts began coming to Mom and Dad. They were in the form of silver and paper money wrapped in Chinese red paper. When the news reached my grandparents in China, they dug deep into their precious money and sent a soft gold bracelet to honor the happy event.

To Chinese parents the birth of the first son is a time of happiness because they have, in large part, fulfilled their ancestral obligation. The remainder of their duty is to see their son marry and, in turn, have his own son. It is so important because the family name must be carried on with an unceasing effort to uphold the family tradition. My parents took great care to choose a name for me. They decided to name me "It Main," or Edmond. The Chinese characters which make up my name mean, "One who will do great deeds which will bring respect and honor to the family name." They are the only Chinese characters I can write.

Ever since I was old enough to understand, my parents have tried to make me realize the great responsibility I carry as the only Gong son. Being the only son in any family means duties and obligations that do not run to the daughters. I know today that my parents wanted very dearly to have another son and, in the characteristic Chinese way, June's name in Chinese means literally, "Turn the next one into a boy!" But as it turned out, I am the number one and only son. That is why the question of my marriage is so important to the entire family. . . .

I believe the first time that I was really aware of the responsibility of being the only son was shortly before I left for Harvard University in 1948. Dad called me in for a man-to-man talk. He told me that I was the first man of the Gong family to have the opportunity of attending college, and that I must always keep that in mind through thick and thin.

My first year of college was a trying one and my grades were below average. I did not maintain honor grades and therefore lost my scholarship. I was ashamed and could not face my parents, but I had no alternative. When I told Dad about it he was not angry. I felt that maybe I was immature and I wanted to enlist in the Army. He looked me straight in the eye, smiled, and said that he was confident that I would make the grade, and that Gongs did not give up so easily. With his understanding and confidence in me, I was inspired. It was one of the happiest moments of my life when I wrote to him and Mom in my senior year to tell them I was to graduate with honors in political science.

Shortly after I graduated from Harvard I was commissioned in the Air Force. After graduating from radar school, I was assigned to the All-Weather Fighter Interceptor School at Moody Air Force Base, Valdosta, Georgia. It was quite a coincidence that I was stationed 30 miles from Tifton, Georgia, where Dad settled when he came to this country, and where his father had operated a small Chinese hand laundry in the village square.

I think that the first time the wires got crossed in my relationship with my parents came one year shortly after I got home for the summer. Mom and Dad and I were talking after dinner, like we always do at home. My sisters were all out at a movie. Mom, in a slightly scolding tone, asked me why I wasn't interested in girls of Chinese ancestry. She said that it was important I should think of girls in terms of marriage, and should prepare myself for the day I would go to China to seek a bride, as Father had done.

I laughed quietly, and jokingly said that I was too young. Anyway, I said, there weren't any Chinese girls and it would be against my nature to make a special trip to find one. But Dad said that in Hong Kong the girls were beautiful, and that I must not think otherwise. He said he was sure that Grandmother could pick out a beautiful girl for me to marry.

Teasingly, and not too seriously, I said, "Dad, I bet the girls in Hong Kong can't jitterbug." This was just enough to cause him to raise his voice and to say that the girls in China were just as modern, as well educated, and as sophisticated as American girls. . . .

How can you explain to the parents whom you love and respect so deeply, and whom you want to please and obey, that you cannot go along with their advice when it comes to marriage? Up to this time I had always been an obedient son, but this was something different. What do you tell them to make them understand that America is your country and not China? . . .

My parents' main argument for my marrying a native Chinese girl is that, in China, girls are brought up to wait on the man they marry, and to devote themselves entirely to their husbands. In America, they said, most American girls, even those of Chinese ancestry, expect their husbands to wait on *them!*

But this to me is a problem that can and should be settled by the marriage partners, rather than by the parents. In my heart, I have my own dreams of the girl I will some day marry. While a girl of Chinese ancestry might be the best choice for me, I have never met or seen such a girl who really attracted me. I have tried to admire them, but I cannot fool myself. My ideal of grace and beauty runs more to someone like Grace Kelly or Ava Gardner. While I haven't yet met such a girl, I want to be free to make my own choice.

I do not think my way of thinking is wrong, or that I am trying to be something I am not. But how can I explain to my parents just why I think and act and feel like an American? What *is* an American? I am not sure I can answer such questions, but I do know what I believe, and no one, not even my parents, can make me think otherwise.

NEVER in my life have I been a victim of prejudice because my name was not Jones or Smith or because I happen to be of Chinese ancestry. I am sure people to whom I tell this do not believe it possible, but it does not matter, for it is the truth and it makes me realize what America means to me.

I do not think it at all strange that my closest friends are Americans and not Chinese. I choose my friends by what they are themselves, and not on the basis of ancestral backgrounds that happen to be identical. It does not seem unusual to me when my friends tell me that after they got to know me they never thought of me as Chinese, but only as an American. To me, it is just one of those things which my country stands for.

The increasing pressure that my parents put on me to consider marriage as they understood it, caused me to rebel. The wires completely fell down between us. They did not realize or comprehend how Americanized I was, and I still cannot entirely appreciate why they want me to marry a girl from China. . . .

And so I finally decided that I would go to Hong Kong as they ask and make an attempt to meet a Chinese girl whom I would want to marry. If I do not meet such a girl, I will always be able to say, to my own conscience, and to my parents, that I tried to carry out their wishes.

Nothing in the world would make my mother happier than to go to Hong Kong with me, but Dad cannot afford the transportation. And so, very soon, I shall be seeing my grandmother, whom I have never met, and who has never been outside China. She will play my mother's role in seeking girls of suitable ancestry and background. Since the Communists overran her native village, she has lived in Hong Kong. Active and vigorous, she has a wide acquaintance, and will make all the necessary arrangements for me to be presented to Chinese girls and their families. Just as she did for my father.

I should be gay and carefree as I leave for the home of my ancestors to find a wife. But I am neither gay nor carefree. In my heart, I cherish a hope that I may meet American girls in Hong Kong, but I realize that it is unlikely. As I said in the beginning, what I really hope is that I do not find a wife in China at all—so that I can come back to America, and start the search over again, here in the country of my choice, and look for an American girl, as an American should.

SOURCE: Eddie Gong, "I Want to Marry an American Girl," *American Magazine* 160, no. 3 (September 1955): 15–17, 82–85.

OTHER REFERENCES

Colleen Fong and Judy Yung, "In Search of the Right Spouse: Interracial Marriage among Chinese and Japanese Americans," *Amerasia Journal* 21 (winter 1995/1996): 77–97.

Betty Lee Sung, *Chinese American Intermarriage* (New York: Center for Migration Studies, 1990).

Betty Lee Sung, *Mountain of Gold* (New York: Macmillan, 1967).

My Bitter Experience
in the United States (1956)

Hsue-shen Tsien

In the late 1930s and 1940s, Hsue-shen Tsien (Qian Xueshen) was one of the most accomplished and distinguished Chinese scientists in the United States. He had arrived in 1935 as one of a small number of Chinese students with a Boxer Indemnity scholarship. The United States began the scholarships in 1909 with indemnity funds obtained from China as a result of America's participation in the suppression of the Boxer Rebellion at the turn of the century.

After a brilliant graduate career in engineering at the Massachusetts Institute of Technology (MIT) and at the California Institute of Technology (Cal Tech), Tsien remained in the United States and quickly established himself as one of the world's leading authorities in the still-infant field of rocketry. During World War II, he received high-level security clearance to work on classified military research. In the spring of 1945 he traveled with the U.S. Army to help interrogate German scientists and study military research installations. Following the war he joined the faculty at MIT and in 1947 was promoted to full professor of engineering at the age of thirty-five.

By all indications, it appeared that Tsien planned to stay in the United States permanently. In 1949, after he moved back to Cal Tech to direct the Jet Propulsion Laboratory, he applied for U.S. citizenship. He and his wife, whom he had met during a return trip to China, began to raise their two American-born children in a house near the campus. But during the Cold War hysteria in the 1950s, federal authorities began an intensive investigation of Tsien, accusing him of joining the American Communist Party while a graduate student at Cal Tech. Tsien vehemently denied the charges and began making plans to return to China. Soon, he faced both federal deportation and restraining orders. The humiliating treatment left him permanently embittered toward the United States.

In 1955, Washington allowed Tsien and 120 other scholars and scientists to return to China. Its decision was part of an outgrowth of U.S.-China negotiations on issues arising from the Korean War that permitted the repatriation of nationals in each

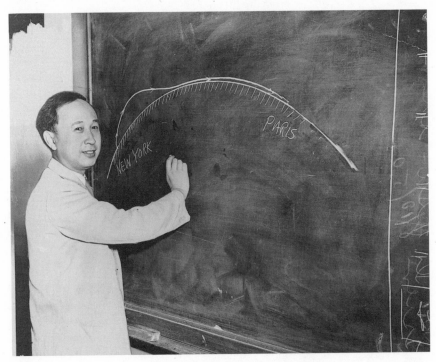

Hsue-shen Tsien demonstrating the flight of a theoretical jet in class at Cal Tech, 1949. (Courtesy of University of Southern California Library)

other's territory. In late 1955, Tsien, with his family, left the United States, never to return. In China, he became director of China's first aerospace and missile institute and known as the "father" of China's rocket program.

The following essay was first published in Chinese in a Hong Kong journal in early 1956. Tsien's sentiments toward the United States have changed little since then. In 1989, after the Tiananmen Square incident, when a protest by students advocating political reform in China was suppressed by armed troops, Tsien published a commentary supporting the Chinese government's position and reminded his readers of the humiliating treatment he had suffered at the hands of the U.S. government in 1950.

On December 16, 1955, a spokesman of the State Department declared that the charges made on the same day by the Chinese Foreign Ministry spokesman relating to alien residents of both China and the United States were groundless. Moreover, he said that the American government had faithfully carried out the agreement reached during the ambassador-level meetings in Geneva. What the American government is doing is putting on a false face of respectability before the peace-loving people of the world to trick them into believing that it is a good and moral government. All this reminds me of an old Chinese saying: "Speak words of justice and moral integrity; harbor the intents of thieves and whores." Let me annotate this with my own experience.

In 1935 I left China to study in the United States. Because China had been under the control of the Chiang Kai-shek clique, I remained in America even after I graduated, and became involved in scientific research and teaching. When mainland China was liberated in 1949, I wanted very much to go home. In the summer of 1950, I made plans to leave the United States. I was going to enter China via Hong Kong after flying there from Canada. All the books and journals that I had accumulated over the years were crated by a freight company for shipment to Hong Kong. But the American Secret Service got wind of my plans. First, I received an official notice from Immigration for-bidding me to leave the States. If I were caught trying to leave the country I would be fined and/or imprisoned. That was in August 1950. Of course I could not leave the States then. Yet even as I was busy returning my airline ticket and trying to recover my books and luggage, U.S. Customs impounded all my possessions, claiming that they contained top-secret documents, tele-graph codes, diagrams of weapons, and photographs of jet engines. And still the American government was not satisfied. A few days later, at the begin-ning of September, another official directive arrived from the Immigration and Naturalization Service (INS), this time telling me that I was a member of the American Communist Party and thus, by law, must be deported. In preparation for such an action, they locked me up in what looked like a jail cell in an INS detention facility. Well, they had certainly tried every dirty trick in the book. One minute they forbade me to leave, and another minute they wanted to deport me. In truth, all they wanted to do was to lock me up.

Fair-minded Americans would never approve of such arbitrary violation of human rights. A few of my colleagues at Cal Tech, where I worked, could not stand such injustice, and through their efforts I was finally released on bail. Considering that the usual kidnap ransom cost only $1,000 to $2,000, I should have been very proud that my bail was set at U.S. $15,000. Natu-rally I could not come up with such an amount of money. It was my friends who paid it for me. I was locked up for a total of fifteen days. During that period, I was not allowed to talk to anyone. In the night someone would open the door and turn on the lights every ten minutes to make sure I had not escaped. This was no normal life; this was persecution and cruel treatment. As a result, I lost thirty pounds in those fifteen days.

I was released, but things were far from being over. I was "questioned" over and over again, mostly about my relationships with other people in an effort to prove that I was a member of the Communist Party. But to fabri-cate something out of nothing is not easy. Since I was never a member of the American Communist Party, their accusation was simply bluster. My Ameri-can friends sitting in as observers and an American newspaper reporter all said that during the proceedings it was the interrogated who was confident and forthright, not the interrogator. What I remember clearly is that when asked by the INS officer as to what country I owed allegiance, I answered that my allegiance was to the Chinese people, and that I would be loyal to any government who would do good to the Chinese people and would oppose any government who would do harm. Then he asked, "So your choice of allegiance is not dependent on a government?" My answer was, "To whom I give my loyalty is decided by myself." At this point, a smug smile of victory appeared on his face, as if he had finally proven that I was an incorrigible "renegade" and, as such, had to be a Communist. I was sorely tempted to ask him, "Did not your Lincoln once say that your government must be a government who carries out the will of its people? Have you forgotten?"

In addition to the interrogations, FBI agents kept me under surveillance, checking on who came to visit me, whom I went to visit, and what kind of letters I received. Consequently, I seldom went out and lived a lonely life. Actually, even if I had gone out, I had nowhere to go. The INS confined me within the perimeters of the Los Angeles area, where I lived. That was how I spent those couple of years, with one order forbidding me to leave the U.S. and another ordering my deportation. They kept my books from me for two years. Finally, in 1953, after searching for over two years, they had to admit that they could not find any secret documents. The charges of hidden telegraph codes, diagrams of weapons, and photos of jet engines were wild concoctions, so they had to return my books, thus proving that what the American government had done two years before was a kind of persecution by false accusation.

Of course, the American government has always maintained in the American and international newspapers that it has never detained any overseas Chinese nationals. The fact is I did not receive any notice from the INS until August 4, 1955, informing me that the ban against my leaving the U.S. was lifted and that I was free to go. There was no mention in the notice of my deportation. So why had they forbidden me to leave in the first place, and why had they now lifted the injunction? There was no explanation. Actually, the riddle was not that hard to solve. August 4 was the fourth day of the ambassadorial talks in Geneva between China and the United States, and for the American government to accomplish something in three days is impossible, unless it is a "red hot" emergency. We can imagine the fear and panic the American government experienced, like "a fox spirit forced to reveal its true features," when Ambassador Wang Bingnan brought up, with concrete evidence, the issue of Chinese nationals residing in the U.S.

Of course, I will never forget the many Americans who would not let justice slide and supported me during the five years I was detained in the United States. Those Americans and the peace-loving people of America are different from the American government. The actions of the American government are not the actions of these people. The Chinese people feel no animosity toward the American people. On the contrary, the Chinese people want to be friends and coexist with the American people in peace.

SOURCE: Hsue-shen Tien, "Wo zai Meiguo de zaoyu [My bitter experience in the United States]," in *Bazhishe xiangei zhuguo* [Intellectual contributions for the homeland] (Hong Kong: Zhoumo Bao, 1956), pp. 47–51. Translator: Ellen Yeung.

OTHER REFERENCES

Iris Chang, *Thread of the Silkworm* (New York: Basic Books, 1995).

Him Mark Lai, "The Chinese Marxist Left, Chinese Students and Scholars in America, and the New China, Mid-1940s to Mid-1950s," *Chinese America: History and Perspectives*, 2004, pp. 7–25.

Father and Son (1995)

Maurice Chuck

In 1955 Everett Drumwright, U.S. consul general in Hong Kong, helped fan the fires of anti-Communist hysteria by charging that many Chinese were immigrating to the United States illegally, raising the specter of Communist infiltration. The Justice Department had been investigating Chinese immigration fraud since the late 1940s, but after China went Communist, and especially now with the release of the Drumwright report, they stepped up their efforts, which in turn caused a panic in the Chinese community. To avoid mass prosecutions and deportations, various community leaders helped to establish the Chinese Confession Program, a procedure by which a Chinese illegal immigrant could disclose his or her false status and become eligible for a suspension of deportation and permanent resident status. On the positive side, the Confession Program legalized the status of over eleven thousand Chinese Americans who confessed to having entered the United States fraudulently, allowing them to reclaim their real names, become naturalized citizens, and send for their relatives from China. On the negative side, the political right took advantage of the situation to persecute and purge the community of left-wing activists. The program also created bitter feelings among family members and relatives, and close to twenty thousand persons implicated by the confessions were subjected to undue stress and agony.

The following excerpt from a short story by Maurice Chuck, editor and publisher of two progressive newspapers, San Francisco Journal *and* Chinese Voice, *is based on the true experiences of the author in the Chinese Confession Program. Chuck had immigrated to the United States in 1948 at the age of fifteen to join his father, who was himself a paper son. Against his father's wishes, he had become active in a left-wing organization, Min Qing (Chinese American Democratic Youth League), and often written articles for the* China Daily News, *a pro-Communist China newspaper. Both Min Qing and the* China Daily News *were targeted by federal investigators and eventually destroyed. According to "Father and Son," Chuck's radical views while serving in the U.S. Army also contributed to his indictment in 1962 for fraudulent en-*

Maurice Chuck (holding banner honoring "labor heroes") at a Min Qing function in San Francisco, 1951. (Courtesy of Laura Lai)

try into the United States. After his father confessed to coming in as a paper son, he was subpoenaed to testify against his own son. The emotional stress this situation created in the father-son relationship was repeated many times over among other Chinese American families that found themselves caught in a similar predicament during the Cold War era.

The Greyhound bus sped along Highway 101 toward Seattle, Washington. However, the destination of Yu Rongzu and son Nianzu was not Seattle, but a town not far away, called Tacoma. Ten years ago, when Nianzu was serving in the Army, he was stationed nearby in Fort Lewis. Almost every weekend he would go to a Chinese restaurant in Tacoma for a Chinese meal. He also applied for his citizenship at the Immigration office there. Who would have thought that ten years later today he would revisit this town because he had to appear in court to defend his rights as a citizen? And his father, who was accompanying him on the trip, was actually going there as a witness for the Immigration and Naturalization Service (INS). . . .

In the summer of 1955, Nianzu had gotten into trouble with the Army. His speeches and his writings had gotten him into hot water. After he was indicted, all his books, papers, and diary while he was in the service were confiscated. At the military hearing, he was interrogated for over a week. To

Rongzu, his son's trial was the most stunning incident to occur during his decades of stay in the United States. He was frightened and worried sick. His friends and relatives distanced themselves from him, chiding him behind his back for having such an unworthy son.

As for Nianzu, he was completely taken by surprise. He never expected that the little dissent he had expressed against the government and the views he had held toward U.S.-China relations would bring such serious consequences.

The verdict from the hearing was guilty, and Nianzu was dishonorably discharged from the Army.

The Nianzu who returned home after being discharged fought often with his father over the incident. His father was constantly scolding him. "A man cannot survive on principles. You now hold a shameful and undesirable discharge. Who would dare or be willing to hire you? How are you going to live from now on?" What the father said was true, and for a long time, Nianzu remained unemployed. Except for enrolling in a couple of evening classes, he passed his days idly and in boredom. Finally, his unemployment problem was solved when his father dragged him to work as a kitchen helper. But after a few months, someone ratted on him to the owner and he was fired. Fortunately, the American Civil Liberties Union (ACLU) went to bat for him and countersued the Army. In convicting him for his thoughts, they had stripped him of his human rights and his right to freedom of belief. The case dragged on for a long time, but finally his conviction was overturned, and Nianzu was reissued an honorable discharge.

Close on the heels of this reprieve, however, came the so-called Confession Program engineered by the INS, requiring the Chinese to come forth voluntarily to confess to illegal entry into the United States. The entire Chinatown was in turmoil; everyone was alarmed. Rongzu was admitted into the country and eventually became naturalized under the family name of Zhou. Whether he confessed or not would implicate a whole group of kinfolk. Rongzu had always been a timid man, afraid of trouble. He discussed the matter with some of the clan elders, who agreed that this was a chance for him to tell all to the INS and clear the records so he could get his status adjusted, reclaim his original name, and be naturalized again.

Nianzu objected to this, calling it a conspiracy. This Confession Program in effect made the involved party incriminate himself by admitting to illegal entry. After the confession, there was no guarantee that the individual would have his status adjusted. Besides, this problem, which had dogged most Chinese for several generations, was the result of the exclusion movement in the past against the Chinese in the United States, and was a product of history. The Confession Program was targeted at certain people and was a way for the INS to convict these unwelcome elements. Rongzu was half convinced by his son's explanation, which seemed to make sense, but he was berated by his clansmen, who said if he did not participate in the Confession Program, he would jeopardize not only himself, but a whole bunch of clansmen as well. Finally, with pressure coming from all sides, he reluctantly headed for the INS to make a clean breast of everything.

Nianzu refused to confess. Not long after, he received an official letter from the INS ordering him to surrender his citizenship certificate; otherwise, he would have to suffer the consequences. He sought advice from the ACLU attorney, Besig, who told him, "You don't have to pay attention to them."

.   .   .

A mild, sunny afternoon. Grant Avenue in Chinatown, as usual, was hopping with activity, with thronging pedestrians and heavy traffic clogging the streets. Suddenly two burly Westerners appeared in the childcare center in Chinatown, where Nianzu was working, telling him in harsh tones, "We have orders to arrest you."

It was so unexpected that Nianzu was momentarily paralyzed with shock. The children and the teachers in the center were scared and confused, not understanding what was happening. Nianzu tried to remain calm. "What crime have I committed?" he asked. "How can you just come here and arrest me? Please show me your warrant."

"You are an illegal immigrant!" one of the officers said coldly. "Here's the warrant." He produced a document from his pocket, showed it to Nianzu, and quickly took it back. Then he handcuffed Nianzu.

"That's ridiculous! Not only did I enter the country legally, but I also hold an official U.S. Naturalization certificate," Nianzu countered angrily.

"Your father has already confessed to the INS that his real family name is Yu, not Zhou." The officers pushed Nianzu out the door, leaving the teachers to look at each other in dismay.

A police car was waiting at the curb. The officers shoved him inside, where he found his best friend, Chen Xuming, already sitting.

"They've arrested you, too?" Nianzu said in surprise.

"When they drove this way, I knew they were coming for you," said Xuming.

At the city jail, they were booked, fingerprinted, ushered into the showers, and finally photographed in prisoner uniforms. According to the law, they had the right to make one outside phone call. Nianzu called Besig at the ACLU, and told the attorney of the arrest of Xuming and himself. In less than two hours, Attorney Besig was at the jail and bailed the two of them out.

.   .   .

An hour before the trial, Nianzu went to see Attorney Wilson to discuss his case. Because Rongzu was a witness for the government, he did not accompany Nianzu, but arranged to meet him at the courthouse.

At the beginning of the trial, the judge said, "This is a case of illegal entry into the United States. Attorney Wilson, how does your client plead?"

"Your Honor, my client pleads not guilty," answered Attorney Wilson.

Nianzu was called by the prosecution to the box. After he had been sworn in, the chief prosecuting attorney said, "Please state your name."

"My last name is Zhou, and my first name is Yunian."

"Is that your true name?"

"That is my legal name in the United States."

"When did you come to the U.S.?"

"In 1948."

"Did you come together with your father?"

"Yes."

"When did you apply for naturalization?"

"In 1954."

"What name did you use to apply for citizenship?"

"Zhou Yunian."

"What is your father's name?"

"Zhou Yurong."

At this point, the prosecuting attorney turned to the judge. "Your Honor, I would like to end my questioning here, but reserve the right to recall the defendant to the box."

"Do you have any questions for your client?" asked the judge of the defense attorney.

"Yes," said Attorney Wilson. Standing, he said, "Who gave you the name Zhou Yunian?"

"My father."

"Is your father in court? Please point him out."

"That is my father," said Nianzu, pointing to Rongzu.

"Is your father here to testify for you?" asked the attorney.

"No," answered Nianzu. "He has been summoned to testify on behalf of the prosecution."

Feigning surprise, the attorney said, "To testify against his own son for the prosecution!"

"I don't think he has any choice," said Nianzu.

"Your Honor, I have no more questions," said Attorney Wilson.

Then the prosecution summoned Yu Ronzu. After he had been sworn in, the attorney asked, "Please state your name."

"I am called Zhou Yurong."

"Is that your true name?"

"No," said Rongzu with discomfort. "But I have used that name."

"Then what is your true name?"

"Yu Rongzu."

"Is your family name Zhou or Yu?"

"It's Yu."

"Are you saying that you used a false family name to enter the U.S.?"

"Yes."

"So at the time you knew full well that you were using false papers to enter the U.S.?"

"I used the name Zhou . . ."

When it was time for Attorney Wilson to cross examine him, he kept pursuing two questions.

"Your son's name, Zhou Yunian, was a name given him by you. Right?"

"Right," answered Rongzu.

"Your son knew this name to be legal or illegal?"

"Legal, of course," said Rongzu. "Because I also used the family name Zhou to apply for naturalization."

The prosecuting attorney also questioned Rongzu. "Is it true you have already confessed to the INS that your true family name is really Yu instead of Zhou, that Zhou is a false name? And now you have reverted to your true name, and have adjusted your status under the name Yu Rongzu, and have been naturalized again."

"Yes."

After the two attorneys argued their cases, the judge ruled in favor of the prosecution. He thought the prosecution presented clear evidence that since the father had admitted to using a false family name to enter the country illegally, then the son, who had used the same false family name for immigration, also entered the country illegally.

The defense attorney's closing statement insisted that the son was innocent. Regardless of whether the name is true or false, what else can a son do but take his father's name? If a crime had been committed, then the crime was the father's, since he was the first to use the bogus family name.

However, the judge did not agree with the defense attorney's deductive reasoning. He thought that if the defendant had done what his father did, that is, accepted the advice of the INS and cooperated with the government by confessing and adjusting his status, subsequently reverting to his true family name and reapplying for naturalization, would not the problem have been solved? Yet the defendant gave up the chance and therefore must accept the consequences.

At the end, the judge asked Nianzu, "Do you have anything to say?"

"I do!" said Nianzu with firm conviction. "I believe what is really on trial here is not me, but the American judicial system."

"What do you mean by that?" The judge was not happy.

"Because today's problem is a result of past exclusionary acts against the Chinese by the U.S.," said Nianzu indignantly.

"Well, you do have the right to express yourself," said the judge. "America is a free and democratic country."

"Let me remind you, Your Honor," Nianzu continued. "The minute my grandfather and father entered as legal immigrants into this so-called democratic and free country, they immediately lost their freedom. Like the tens of thousands of Chinese in those days, they were confined to the detention center on Angel Island in San Francisco Bay. Similarly I also lost my freedom the moment I entered this country when I was locked up by the INS."

Nianzu was found guilty and sentenced to three months in jail, and five years of probation after release. As he was being led away by a prison guard, Rongzu rushed up to him and, grasping his hands, cried out in anguish, "I am so sorry. It's I who have done this to you." And watching his son being taken away, Rongzu wept.

SOURCE: *The Literati*, October 1, 1995. Translator: Ellen Yeung

OTHER REFERENCES

Amy Chen, *The Chinatown Files* (New York: Filmmakers Library, 2001), VHS.

Him Mark Lai, "Unfinished Business: The Chinese Confession Program," in *The Repeal and Its Legacy: Proceedings of the Conference on the 50th Anniversary of the Repeal of the Exclusion Acts, Nov. 12–14, 1993* (San Francisco: Chinese Historical Society of America and Asian American Studies, San Francisco State University, 1994), pp. 47–57.

Mae Ngai, "Legacies of Exclusion: Illegal Chinese Immigration during the Cold War Years," *Journal of American Ethnic History* 18, no. 1 (fall 1998): 3–35.

Xiaojian Zhao, *Remaking Chinese America: Immigration, Family, and Community, 1940–1965* (New Brunswick, N.J.: Rutgers University Press, 2002).

"We gave workers a sense of dignity"

The Story of a Union Social Worker (1982)

Ah Quon McElrath

While conducting research on Chinese women in Hawaii in 1982, Judy Yung was told by a number of people to be sure to interview Ah Quon McElrath, a retired labor organizer who still maintained a passionate interest in the plight of the working class and the poor. During their ninety-minute interview, Yung could hear that passion in her voice, in her choice of words, and in the stories McElrath told nonstop, with an occasional outbreak of laughter as she reflected on her past.

Compared to other Chinese women in Hawaii, McElrath struck Yung as unusual, from her given name to her choice of profession and her radical politics. Born in Honolulu in 1915 of immigrant parents from Zhongshan District in Guangdong Province, McElrath explained that her given name was a diminutive of her Chinese name, Leong Yuk Quon, and that she was too embarrassed to tell anyone what Christian name actually appears on her birth certificate. (She took the surname McElrath after her marriage to union official Bob McElrath in 1941.) The sixth child in a family of seven children, McElrath grew up in poverty and had to work multiple jobs to support herself through college. She graduated from the University of Hawaii with a B.A. in anthropology and sociology in 1938. While her peers chose respectable professions such as teaching, law, and medicine, she chose to go into labor organizing, becoming the first social worker and the only woman on the staff of Local 142 of the International Longshoremen's and Warehousemen's Union (ILWU).

Much of her interview with Yung delved into her childhood growing up in Hawaii, her political views on race, class, and gender discrimination, and how she became involved in labor organizing and the civil rights movement in the South. Yung found her to be straightforward and highly analytical in her responses. A born storyteller and a woman of strong political convictions, McElrath apparently enjoyed reminiscing about the past and providing anecdotes to make her points. Parts of her interview have been rearranged for a smoother read, but the words, manner of speech, and ideas remain very much hers.

Ah Quon McElrath teaching a class on union benefits and services to members of Local 142. (Courtesy of Ah Quon McElrath)

"WE ALL WORKED AT A VERY TENDER AGE"

I was born in 1915, in Honolulu, in a little spot called Iwilei, which was the official red-light district. And we had a house in an area that was very near the beach, filled with *kiawe* trees, and it was very convenient. My father was a part-time carpenter, hack driver, egg producer, gambler, alcohol maker— call it what you will, he was all those things. And, I suspect because it was cheap, we lived there for quite a number of years. See, my father died when I was about five, and so we had to make it on our own after he died.[1] My mother never really worked at any job at all. She had bound feet and barely spoke English. So we were a truly bilingual family as we were growing up.

Typical of all the immigrant women, she cooked, washed clothes, tended the chickens, did a bit of sewing for us. She'd make Chinese clothes for the girls. I remember going to school in pantaloons and the jackets that had the frog [buttons] on the sides. And one of the really charming stories I remember

---

1. In another interview that was published in Brigid O'Farrell and Joyce Kornbluh's *Rocking the Boat,* Ah Quon McElrath said her father was put in jail for smoking opium and later died of a ruptured appendix because the family was too poor to afford a doctor. After he died, the children were scattered among relatives and friends until the family moved into a company camp, where they lived among many other ethnic and poor families.

is that she used to make underclothes of sugar and rice bags, so that one side of your buttock would read "Honolulu," and the other one would read "Plantation." *(laughter)* You could never wash off that ink. *(laughter)*

There were seven [children]. I think two died at birth. And the story I like to tell about the place in the family as concerned my brother and me is that we were the sixth and the seventh child. Mother had me when she was forty-two and forty-four when she had my brother. So we said that, for all intents and purposes, we should have been idiots. *(laughter)* Well, it's interesting that we, who should have been idiots, were the only two in the family who went on to higher education—finished university. My brother got his master's in social work, and I did some graduate work at the School of Social Work at Michigan.

We all started working when we were quite young. We went out and picked *kiawe* beans and dried bones and sold them to the fertilizer company, because we lived very near the fertilizer company. At that time they used dray horses and they used the *kiawe* beans to feed the horses. And we'd also go out and pick brass that was discarded—that was on the beach or wherever we could find it and sell it. And then, of course, my older brother left school when he was sixteen so that he could go to work and support us. But we all worked at a very tender age. We worked in the pineapple canneries when we were twelve, thirteen. You know, there was no child labor law then. So what we would do was to rouge our faces, wear high heels, and stand outside the gate of a pineapple cannery and try to make ourselves tall so that the superintendent who was picking workers could see us. We could go five, six days at a time and never get picked. But then, the fruit kept coming in, and they needed more workers, so we had the opportunity to be picked. You know, my sister worked for five cents an hour. When I started, I was lucky: I think I made thirteen and a half cents an hour in the pineapple cannery. *(laughter)* And she [the oldest sister] went to Normal School, which was a teacher's training school, and at the age of eighteen, I believe, she got a teaching position. And that was how we were supported.

When I finished college in 1938, I really wanted to go on to graduate school, except that when I talked to my sociology professor about it, he said, "Well, Ah Quon, you've got two things which make it difficult. One, you're a woman. Two, you're Oriental." And I suppose I probably would have spat in his face maybe *(laughter)*, if, one, I had more gumption, or two, if I didn't feel such a strong obligation to contribute to family support. See, at that time, the family had bought a piece of property near the university and then built a house. And everything that I earned, all the savings that I had from working in the cannery and doing five jobs when I was a senior in college, was taken out to pay for the house. So I didn't strike out and go on for graduate work, although I was very interested in further research and I felt that I wanted to go into the academic area. But it never happened.

"WE GAVE WORKERS A SENSE OF DIGNITY"

At the time, the legislature had established the Board of Public Welfare following the enactment of various titles of the Social Security Act. So I figured, gee, I'd move in there. When I went to work for the department, I helped to organize a union [for social workers and clerical staff], and it was on an industrial basis. We did a lot of things. We raised questions about housing, adequacy of welfare payment, adequacy of wages paid to social workers. Then I got married.[2] World War II came on, I worked for a couple of years. But all during this time I was still volunteering for the union, the ILWU, and I'd make speeches to longshoremen and tell them why I felt they should join the union, and worked with the wives of longshoremen to get them to get their husbands to join the union. Won a couple of elections, but didn't do very much good because it was just during the war and everything kind of stagnated. You know, there was that "no strike" pledge on the part of the AFL and CIO, and so we didn't get very far in longshore organizing. And I had a couple of children[3] in the interim and I resigned from the department. And in 1946, when I was on leave, there was this big sugar strike. What I did was organize all of the welfare activities—trained people how to fill out applications, told them what they were entitled to, told them what the requirements were for sanitation, informed the people what they had to do—because we had units on four islands. There were 28,000 workers who went out on strike on twenty-six plantations. And that's a huge group to take care of.

Other than improving their working conditions through better wages, better fringe benefits, I think I am most proud of the fact that for the first time we gave a sense of dignity to immigrant workers who had been so put down by their bosses all of these years. We gave them a sense that they were worthwhile human beings. Let me tell you one anecdote that really highlights this kind of newfound feeling about themselves. In 1946, just before the sugar strike, I had gone out to volunteer my services as a social worker because of the tidal wave that had occurred on April First in the town of Hilo, on that island which had suffered the most damage from the tidal wave. We were sitting in the union hall waiting for me to get a ride to go out and do the investigations. A telephone call comes through, and someone answers the phone and he says, "No, I don't know what you got to do, but did you do this? Well, look, I tell you what, I'm going to put Frank Thompson on the phone."

2. In another interview, Ah Quon McElrath described her family's reaction to her marriage to Bob McElrath: "When I told my family I was going to get married to this 'haole,' a white, and a seaman to boot, 'My God! Don't you ever come home. You are not welcome.' I mean, here was a Chinese woman marrying a white man and a white who at the time had no job. This was unheard of. Shame on the family" (O'Farrell and Kornbluh, *Rocking the Boat*, p. 143).

3. Their daughter, Gail, was born in 1943, and their son, Brett, in 1945.

Frank Thompson was a man who came over here from Sacramento, an old IWW—you know, a Wobbly,[4] a person who really sparked up the organizing of sugar workers on all of the islands. And seated in the room were Chinese, Japanese, Koreans, Filipinos, Hawaiians, Portuguese, Spanish, all officers of the various units at that time of the ILWU. So Frank Thompson picks up the phone and he says, "Yeah, you tell that son-of-a-bitch to call me up and I'll be waiting right here." And the "son-of-a-bitch" was the manager, who had apparently forbade the workers to do a certain kind of thing. And so he hung up the phone. Few minutes later he gets a telephone call. Frank says, "This is Frank Thompson, ILWU organizer." And apparently the manager said, "Well, this is Joe Doe, the manager of so-and-so company." So Frank says, "Look, you no good son-of-a-bitch, you better just let those workers go to a meeting or we'll shut down your goddamn place."

And as he was talking this way, everybody's mouth dropped [open]. They just could not understand how anyone could talk that way to a plantation manager, who was a literal king of everything he surveyed. And in a way, this summarizes the kind of dignity that rank-and-file workers of all ethnic groups got. It had never happened before. That story, you see, has never been written. How do you write a story of how people gained a feeling of themselves as human beings with some degree of control over their jobs? And this is what the union gave them.

I am most proud of the fact that I helped to extend the level of understanding of people so that they could understand medical plans, they could understand pension plans, they could understand why these things are so important and feel that, by golly, they have a contribution to make, that they are the backbone of the union and that, in fact, it's only in building a sense of community through the union, helping one another, that we can really get ahead. It's an extremely fascinating thing when you have cane hauler operators, irrigators, rat catchers, packers, trimmers, or whatever it is, being officers of the particular union, running for business agents. Because all of our officers are elected officers; nobody is appointed to the job except the international office representatives here who are appointed by the international office in San Francisco. They're able to sit down with their bosses on an equal basis and say, "Look, we think that the houses are in a bad state of repair. Why don't you do this?" The whole provision for grievance procedure is extremely important in terms of investing in rank-and-file members the ability to sit down with a boss and say, "We think you are doing a wrong thing in not paying this man ten cents an hour on a temporary transfer," or, "We think you discriminated against him." That kind of thing.

4. Founded in 1905 in Chicago, the Industrial Workers of the World (IWW) was established in opposition to the craft unionism of the American Federation of Labor (AFL) and had as its objective the overthrow of capitalism by socialism.

I think one of the other kinds of things is that in our agreements, although it did take some time, we have eliminated the sex bias on wages. And while the ILWU may not be entirely responsible for it, at least we were the catalyst. Because we came at a time, right after World War II, when the returning AJAs [Americans of Japanese Ancestry], through the G.I. Bill of Rights and because of their experience overseas, had a new sense of themselves, even though 110,000 of them had been put into concentration camps. Through the G.I. Bill of Rights, they were able to go to school, become lawyers, become doctors—not that they hadn't become such before, but this was at least the impetus for them to move forward in the professions. And a number of things have been said about the ILWU. For example, Andrew Lind, who was for many years professor of sociology at the university, has said that more than any other organization in Hawaii, the ILWU was responsible for racial equality. John A. Burns, the late governor of this state, has said that it was the ILWU which brought true economic, political, and social democracy to the islands. He was pilloried for making that statement. But it is true. All these things might have come, but we brought them to the islands sooner. And that's why one has to feel a great deal of pride, joy, and happiness that one was in that particular fight and struggle, even though many of us personally suffered because of our identity with the labor movement.

During the Smith Act trial,[5] I lost almost all of my friends. I used to walk down the street and when they'd see me, they'd cross the street. They wouldn't say hello to me. You know, the Cold War and all the anti-Communist feelings came to the front. I remember my kids suffering a great deal of disapprobation in school. And they'd come home and ask us why we worked for the union and why they were called "Communist." And it was tough on them and tough on us, because how do you tell your children, look, you believe sincerely in working people and their right to join unions of their own choosing and to feel, politically, however they wanted to feel? You know, we're supposed to be a democracy, capable, presumably, of embracing any kind of dissidence. And this wasn't true. It wasn't happening. So that made it difficult. And everybody seemed to think, "Well, my God, we fed on steaks every day of the week." That isn't true. You know, my husband who was an international representative,[6] he was making $75 a week. That ain't a hell of a lot of money. Kids had to go to school, you had to clothe them. I sewed all of the kids'

5. The Cold War period unleashed a vicious attack against militant unions like the ILWU, and union leaders in Hawaii who were accused of being Communist conspirators were put on trial for violating the provisions of the Smith Act. Ah Quon McElrath worked as a legal secretary for the law firm that was retained by the ILWU and helped to research the background of all potential witnesses in the trial.

6. Her husband, Bob McElrath, worked for the ILWU for over thirty years as a publicist and representative, and became the regional director in 1969.

clothes. I never bought anything. You know, I learned the lessons well from my mother. *(laughter)* God, I can remember the days when we were kids, eating lard and rice and *siyau* [soy sauce] because we were so poor.

"OURS IS A HIGHLY RACIST SOCIETY"

[During the civil rights days] I worked in an OEO program out of Tuskegee Institute.[7] It merely solidified my feelings, which I had formed very early in the game, that ours is a highly racist society. Of course, it's highly sexist as well. But I got to know a lot of people, and I think I gave them some feeling [about] how important it was to join a union. I remember one of the early things that happened with the janitors at Auburn University. They were trying to form a union, and apparently the dean of students had heard about the organizing attempts. So he called all of the janitors and janitresses into the room, took his key, locked the door, threw the keys on the table in a very contemptuous fashion, and said, "Any one of you with guts enough, you'll pick up that key and open the door and you can walk out." That was literally threatening them. Of course, they caved in. They were making 50 cents an hour then, and I think they wanted to get 75 cents an hour. And so none of them continued in their attempts to form the union because it was so hard for them to get jobs. And that's understandable.

Although the AFL-CIO at the time supported the organizing efforts down south, there wasn't a lot of money put into the organizing of workers. They just didn't have it. They concentrated on basic industries. The South was always a very conservative bastion—always turned aside organizing. And I remember going to a Dan River textile factory to talk with one of the indigenous leaders in that particular county of Alabama, and asking him whether he felt there was a need for a tutorial center there to beef up the language skills of the black children. And he didn't know whether or not he could devote very much time because he was working as a mechanic there in the Dan River plant. And I said, "Gee, how much are you making?" He says, "$2.50 an hour." I said, "My God, mechanics make a hell of a lot more than that in even unorganized plants up north." And he says, "Well, it sure beats chopping cotton for a dollar a day." (This was in 1966.)

I lived with a black family there in Lowndes County, where Viola Liuzzo and the two priests were shot.[8] I lived a half a mile away from the jail where

---

7. In 1965 Ah Quon McElrath took a leave of absence from her ILWU job to do advanced study at the University of Michigan. She was assigned to work in the Office of Economic Opportunity (OEO) program of Tuskegee Institute, an accredited coeducational institution for African Americans in Alabama that emphasized industrial and vocational training.

8. Viola Liuzzo was a medical laboratory assistant who was married to Teamster Anthony Liuzzo. She was in Alabama to participate in the civil rights march to Selma when she was killed

the priests were shot and killed. And it was so obvious that there was discrimination—just rank discrimination. For example, I remember going to an outside toilet in a black high school, and the seat was made of steel. And I sat on it. Oh my God, I jumped to the ceiling. It was so hot because this was in the summer, when it was 110 in the shade. Then you'd go to a white school, and there would be flush toilets and all that kind of stuff. And no paper in the black outhouses.

I remember living with Mrs. McCall for over a month, and I'd have to carry the water in from the well, pour it in a number three tub, and take a bath in the number three tub; then take out the water and throw it on the plants because there was really no water around. You couldn't just use it flagrantly. And in the morning when I brushed my teeth, fill up a glass about that high with water, brush your teeth, spit the water on the plants—that kind of thing. And then go out to the outhouse. So I made it a point never to drink anything that was diuretic in nature because it would mean that I'd have to get out at night, get the flashlight or light the lantern. And there was no running water in the house, so we did our dishwashing and everything by carrying water in from the well. And then, of course, what Mrs. McCall did was to buy a truckload of coal, and it was dumped right on the side of her house, and she used that for fuel, and we cooked on a pot-bellied stove sitting right in the middle of her kitchen.

I remember walking in to a garage in Fort Deposit and being just absolutely flabbergasted because I was very thirsty and I went to the water fountain—[one marked] "For Colored Only," and then the other, "For Whites." And I asked the shop foreman, "Oh, I thought you didn't do this kind of thing anymore, that the law eliminated that kind of stuff." And he says, "Well, these here people, they don't all mind doing this." And talking with patients who went to the doctors, for example, who still maintained the For Whites and For Coloreds separate entrances. And it was a fascinating eye-opener, simply because you got, at first hand, what race relations were down south. And because I was working on a health project, I could get a really good idea of what the power politics were—getting licenses for the doctors, trying to get the health department to give us chlorine tablets to put in the wells, and going through some of the very gross findings of the health examinations that we did.

We did over two thousand of them—men, women, and children. Some of these people had never had a physical examination before. So I had trained a lot of so-called paraprofessionals so that each one of us did this or that— the hemoglobin, the urine analysis, the vaginals, the pelvic examinations,

---

by three Ku Klux Klansmen on Highway 80 while transporting marchers between Montgomery and Selma.

and the family planning questionnaire. The gross findings showed that 90 percent of the people whom we examined had anemia of one degree or another, and we knew that a heck of a lot of it was because of tapeworms, which the people got because they couldn't afford buying shoes, and the lack of sanitation. You also got the very obese black women, simply because they ate a lot of starches. It was the cheapest thing.

My experience down south merely reinforced what I had known intellectually and what I had learned during World War II in some of my contacts with black servicemen. They'd come to the house and they would tell us these awful stories. And you get some feeling of how the whites treated the blacks. There was nothing benign about it, despite some of the histories on slavery and the "We treated our people very well" kind of business. I remember walking across the street to go to a Piggly-Wiggly store in this town, Fort Deposit, to get some food for lunch. I was with one black woman and two black men, and everybody stopped smack in the middle of the street and turned around and looked at us. And the reason for it is that they just didn't know what I was. See, one of the tactics we used was whenever you go to a new county, you go see the sheriff, the newspaper editor, and the mayor. Just let them know that you are in town and what you are doing. This was one way of ingratiating yourself into the power structure, the white power structure. And I remember going to see the sheriff in Green County, and there are two black women, three black men with me, and we told them what we were about. He just couldn't make out what I was. He looked at me. I'm not white, I'm not black, so what the hell am I? *(laughter)* And so when I said I was from Hawaii, oh, that broke the ice. "You're a hula-hula girl," he said. He was so gracious. "Yes, we all are here to help you in whatever way we can."

But we had some fairly harrowing experiences, too. I remember driving from Tuskegee, and we went through Alabama, on our way to Lowndes County, and there was this pimply young man who followed us in his car [and then passed us]. Well, on the divided highway there was just enough room for two cars, and he would never let us pass. He would look out of the car, and we knew something was amiss. And so when we had a chance, we very quickly moved out past him and we stopped at a place and called the chief of police and said that there seemed to be a car following us. And you see, at that time there were two white students and a black woman and myself. And we never made a white sit in the front with a black driver. So I would always ride in the front with a black driver and put the two white students [in the back]. We called the chief of police and told him that we thought we were being followed. We gave our car number, the description of the other car, the person in the other car, and as we were driving out we saw this young man turn right into a service station. And we were on our way. But it was a pretty harrowing ten minutes. Those kinds of things—I can just imagine how they would have shot a person like Viola Liuzzo and killed those three civil rights workers.[9]

"A GOOD DEAL OF IT IS TIED UP WITH ECONOMICS"

As a member of a minority group, certainly my family and my friends and I suffered discrimination. Certainly [I was familiar with] the plantation system [in Hawaii], where representatives of all ethnic and cultural groups were imported as plantation laborers and were subject to racism. And while it may not seem to have been as oppressive as that in the South, you know, it was bad enough. For example, the official view of immigrant laborers can be found in the statement that Richard A. Cooke, who was president of the Hawaiian Sugar Planters Association, once made, which was, "I view the importation of laborers no different from the importation of jute bags from India."

And then, of course, there was the segregation of ethnic groups into various segregated plantation camps: there's Codfish Camp, Pake Camp, Korean Camp, Japanese Camp, Spanish Camp, all of those kinds of names. And while it may have been done not for the overt purpose of segregating people but supposedly for the purpose of keeping each ethnic group within a homogeneous situation, nonetheless, a lot of the writings of sugar planters, especially following labor disputes, [showed] that they didn't want workers fraternizing with each other and talking with each other. The success of this kind of thing, in terms of Hawaiian labor history, is the fact that the Chinese, the Hawaiians, the Portuguese, the Filipinos, and the Japanese were able to break each other's strikes and not present a united front in their demands.

A good deal of it, you see, is tied up with economics, the burgeoning capitalist system, which was started here as a result of the Great Mahele, when the merchants and the representatives of missionary families could buy land, which was extremely important to the growth of the sugar industry.[10] So that started the capitalist development here, and the accumulation of capital and all of these kinds of things that made it possible for them for over a century to wield economic, political, and social hegemony over the rest of the people. The Republican Party became the political arm of the rising industrialists in Hawaii, and for many, many years, for example, there was hardly a Democratic Party here, for the simple reason that people were afraid to join the Democratic Party. There's no doubt there was a financial oligarchy here, which completely controlled the lives of the people. It's a fascinating kind

9. In 1964, during the Freedom Summer campaign to register black voters in Mississippi, James Chaney, Michael Schwerner, and Andrew Goodman were kidnapped, beaten, and shot to death by Klansmen.

10. The Great Mahele (division) of 1848 was a new land ownership system that divided the lands into three parts—for the king, chiefs, and tenants. It paved the way for foreigners to own land in Hawaii by purchasing it from chiefs who were eager to get rich quickly.

of even brush-over economic analysis of the islands when you look at the interlocking directorates. I remember our union did a chart once that showed they controlled all of the auxiliary industries and the banks. One thing about education is that it can be, if used correctly, corrosive of the kinds of things that a dominant society wants to hang on to. Because the more you read, the more you find out what's going on elsewhere. And that's the way I found out a lot of things, not just in Hawaii, but in the United States and in the rest of the world as well.

[How I came to this analysis of the situation], it's a combination of things. I remember, when I was in intermediate school, reading at that stage about what was happening in the Soviet Union. I think the second five-year plan or ten-year plan was being promulgated, and I was fascinated that here was this society that was organized in a completely different way, that apparently they were putting people to work, that there was a respect for all of the people, and that it was not based on making profit. The difference between a socialist and a capitalist economy—I was fascinated by that kind of thing. It was [also] a time that was very vibrant, you know, with the Spanish Civil War, the heavy organizing of the CIO, and the name of John L. Lewis right up there in front.[11] And the longshoremen here had already been organized in the ILA [International Longshoremen's Association], and then, after the General Strike in San Francisco, they became the ILWU. And they became involved in the Inland Boatmen's Union strike in 1938.[12]

I remember they used to have huge rallies in Aala Park. I used to go to those rallies and listen because the professors in economics who were Marxists talked about these things and I wanted to know what it was all about. And interestingly enough, there was a kind of sundry store there called the Dew Drop Inn [that] sold a left-wing periodical called *The New Masses*. And I used to buy that every week and read it. It was strictly a Marxist magazine. And it put a completely different complexion on events that up to then were interpreted in the strict, traditional way. Here was a kind of theory that seemed to make so much sense. That—plus the professors, plus going to those rallies— really interested me in the strike and what was going on. And so I read everything that there was to read. I made the acquaintance of Jack Hall, one of the early leaders of the strike, who subsequently was instrumental in the organizing of workers into the ILWU. I got to know him, and pretty soon I found myself helping them with the mailing of *The Voice of Labor*, which was a labor

11. John L. Lewis was president of the United Mine Workers of America and in 1935 helped establish the Committee for Industrial Organization, later called the Congress of Industrial Organizations (CIO), which advocated organizing the labor movement by industry rather than by craft.

12. In 1938 longshoremen in Hawaii went on strike for 171 days for wage parity comparable to their West Coast counterparts, and won.

newspaper. And I remember going to the office and mixing flour and water. You know, that was the cheapest way of getting paste for your labels. And that was how it all started.

Then, of course, these professors and I used to go to forums. And then I remember I invited some person from the International Typographical Union to speak to a women's campus organization, and the administration put the kibosh on it and said he couldn't speak on campus. "This was too radical." But we managed to hold a lot of those meetings, and what we did in this particular case was to move him off campus. And I went to a number of benefits to raise money for Spain. Those kinds of things occurred during that period.

"IT IS EXTREMELY DIFFICULT TO ACHIEVE TOTAL EQUALITY"

I think that it's not possible to achieve complete racial, social equality for a number of reasons. One, the capitalist economy doesn't encompass that kind of philosophy. Two, I think that human behavior is such that one never really achieves full understanding of human beings, because of the uneven quality of education. And there will always be some people who will need, for either group or individual reasons, to scapegoat another group that appears different. In a dominant culture, such as the one we live in, which is white Western, any dissidence from that kind of culture will make it extremely difficult to achieve total equality.

I also think that, until we evolve or until there is a revolutionary change in the way men and women are put together, there will be inherent differences between men and women. I think you can erase a heck of a lot of the differences in terms of attitudes, in terms of education, but there are some basic anatomical and physiological differences. Short of a revolutionary change in the way we're put together, that will never make it possible for us to achieve total equality.

And equality can mean many different things. Some people argue equality in terms of becoming a combat soldier, that kind of stuff. Like the fight over whether the draft should have included women. Well, to me, that kind of argument is useless. I think we should spend our energy on finding alternative ways of settling our disputes instead of having war—although obviously, from a Marxian point of view, as long as you have a capitalist system competing against a socialist system, and the earth getting smaller and smaller in terms of access to raw materials, you ain't going to be able to, you see. But I feel that our energy should be spent on those kinds of things, rather than on whether or not women should be combat soldiers. That's like working for the nuclear freeze, or working for détente. It's like working for a reduction of our arms budget, rather than saying, "We need security." Security against what, when you're going to be pulverized anyway?

And I think that more women need to have that kind of understanding, although apparently, instinctively, they understand this about [U.S. president Ronald] Reagan. Because there is less approval of Reagan's policies among women than there is among men, you see? And I think that [we need to concentrate on] affording women the opportunity for all kinds of ways in which to learn about themselves and others—through education, through forums, or whatever it might be—so that they will begin to see that some of the kinds of things that television and radio and magazines tell us are important are really unimportant. And that we spend our energies on things that make us truly human, truly compassionate, honest, caring human beings. That's the important thing about what we can do. And maybe out of that can arise the true equality that we're thinking about.

Following her retirement from the ILWU, Ah Quon McElrath worked for two years with the Villers Foundation (which became the well-known Families USA, Inc.) in Washington, D.C., making substantive changes in the Supplemental Security Income (SSI) program. She also cofounded Hawaii's Committee on Welfare Concerns, a coalition of organizations in Hawaii responsible for legislative changes in public assistance payments, death with dignity, and universal health coverage. In 1988 McElrath was awarded an honorary doctorate from the University of Hawaii, where she presently serves as a member of the Board of Regents.

SOURCE: Ah Quon McElrath, interview with Judy Yung, Chinese Women of America Research Project, January 18, 1983, Honolulu, Hawaii. A version of this interview was published in *Chinese America: History and Perspectives,* 2003, pp. 15–22.

OTHER REFERENCES

Clarence E. Glick, *Sojourners and Settlers: Chinese Migrants in Hawaii* (Honolulu: Hawaii Chinese History Center and the University Press of Hawaii, 1980).

Robert H. Mast and Anne B. Mast, *Autobiography of Protest in Hawaii* (Honolulu: University of Hawaii Press, 1996), pp. 305–17.

Brigid O'Farrell and Joyce L. Kornbluh, *Rocking the Boat: Union Women's Voices, 1915–1975* (New Brunswick, N.J.: Rutgers University Press, 1996), pp. 135–58.

"All the daddies were Chinese and all the mommies were white"

Growing Up Biracial in Minnesota (2002)

Sheila Chin Morris

Sheila Chin Morris was born in St. Paul, Minnesota, in 1946. Her father, Harry Chin, was an immigrant from Guangdong Province; her mother was raised in Winnebago, Minnesota, and of German descent. Their second child, Roger, was born in 1948. The Chinese population in Minnesota at the time totaled 720, and the Chins were one of approximately one hundred Chinese American families residing in the Twin Cities area. As Morris recalls, there were many other interracial families in their social group. Many of the Chinese men had moved to the Midwest to escape Chinese persecution on the West Coast and to look for business and job opportunities. Most ended up doing laundry and restaurant work. And unlike many other states, there was no law against interracial marriage in Minnesota.

In the following interview conducted by Sherri Gebert-Fuller for the Minnesota Historical Society in 2002, Morris provides a personal account of her childhood while paying tribute to her father's courage as an immigrant and hardworking life as a cook. She painfully recalls the times that she was called names and made to feel ashamed of her racial background. Compounding matters were the many skeletons in her father's closet—that he had entered the country fraudulently as a "paper son" and that he had left behind in China a wife and daughter. Given the historical context of the Chinese Exclusion Act of 1882, the Confession Program instigated by the American government during the Cold War period, and the break in diplomatic relations between China and the United States after 1949, it should come as no surprise that these same issues existed for other Chinese American families as well. But as Morris reveals in her interview, these secrets would have damaging consequences on every member of her family. Part of the healing process for her has been to share the story with others.

A graphic designer for over thirty years, Sheila Chin Morris resides in Waseca, Minnesota, with her husband, Rick, a florist and county commissioner. They have three grown children. She currently works as a photo archivist for the Waseca County Historical Society, and continues to freelance in graphic design.

272

Sheila Chin Morris with her parents, Harry and Laura Chin, in 1947. (Courtesy of Sheila Chin Morris)

"WAS THERE SOMETHING WRONG WITH ME?"

I remember when I was little, all of our good friends got together for dinners on Sunday afternoons and some holidays. All the daddies were Chinese and all the mommies were white. My mom was of German descent. She was from a small town in Minnesota—Winnebago, Minnesota—and my father left China when he was seventeen. They met in a Chinese restaurant in downtown St. Paul, where she was working as a waitress [and he, a cook]. I remember on Christmas Eve, my dad would always make beef, green pepper, and tomato chop suey because it was red and green and it looked Christmas-y.

I didn't think that we were very different than anybody else. But I remember—maybe I was six or seven—going over to my friend Sharon's house for supper and other people's cooking was very different. *(chuckles)* I had my first cauliflower with only butter on it and thought, "Gee, what the heck is this? Where's the gravy?" I thought everybody cooked their broccoli, cauliflower, and vegetables stir fry and had a little gravy and rice with it. And, I thought it was normal that my dad cooked when he was home for the evening, and certainly on Sunday, he always cooked, even the pot roast. My mom was sort of the second fiddle.

When I was about ten years old, my dad tried running his own restaurant. He bought Twin Towns Take-Out on Lake Street. We moved from the east side of St. Paul, where I was very comfortable, where I knew everybody on the block, to South Minneapolis, in Richfield. My mother [said we] moved from a place where you had coffee in your housedress over the back fence to a place where you put on nylons and a hat just to go have coffee.

We went to the Sister Kenny School, where we made a few friends. I had a very good teacher, but I did have one or two negative experiences that year. Nobody had ever called me names or put me down for any reason. But, there was a little boy named Lyle in that class and when I think back, it was only ten years after World War II but people were still sensitive about the Japanese. I remember him really hurting me one day when I was in line with him. He moved so that he didn't have to be right next to me. Then, when he did, he quietly said to the other boy, "Oh, you have to stand next to *her*." You know, it made me feel very hurt and I started to think that there was something wrong with me. I started to look at myself in the mirror and wonder why he didn't like me.

Then, we moved from South Minneapolis to Roseville and I had just the opposite experience. Nobody ever treated me like that little Lyle did. I went to Fairview Junior High School. The first day of school, I remember two little boys getting up and letting me have their seat, so I was really confused at that point. *(laughter)* But then I also remember when I was in high school, I had a girlfriend who invited me to her house. When I met her mother for the first time, she looked at me and her first reaction was, "Oh, you're a pretty one," as if to say that intermarriage was okay if the kids came out like me.

MY CHINESE SIDE OF THE FAMILY

My father spoke Cantonese, but I never tried to learn Chinese formally until I was an adult. I found out later that my mother didn't want my dad to teach us Chinese. She loved Chinese art and the Chinese things that my dad gave her. She had a Kuan Yin statue, the Goddess of Mercy that held significance for her. In every other way, she embraced Chinese culture, but she didn't want to be left out of the conversation between my dad and us kids. She felt left out enough when his friends would come over and they would speak Chinese.

Chinese New Year was my immersion in the Chinese side of the family. When we were at home, we would have pot roast on Sundays or roast chicken or something Chinese, barbeque ribs. But, when we went to the On Leong[1]

---

1. The On Leong Merchant's Association, counterpart to the Chinese Six Companies in

Chinese New Year's dinner, it was a lot of Chinese talking, a lot of, "What did he say, Dad?" There were huge round tables, banquet tables with ten people each. My dad was always so happy when he'd go there because he would see old friends and he could talk Chinese, and they would catch up on news. I'm sure there was some exchange about what was happening in China and if everybody's relatives were okay, and if there were new ways of helping each other out because it was kind of a support group for them.

The On Leong Association club was rented and upstairs over a Chinese restaurant. You'd go up the steps and you'd come into the main room, which had a lot of Chinese teakwood furniture and an altar with a Buddha. On New Year's, there would be incense burning and oranges and the boiled chicken before the statue of Buddha. You'd go down a hallway and one side was a big kitchen and there were always several members who would volunteer to cook. Then, on the other side, there were various rooms that you could go into. I think there was some gambling afterward in one of these rooms. From what I understand, this was also a place for new immigrant Chinese men. If they had absolutely no place to go on their first night, they could always get a bed there before they would find another place for them to stay.

MY FATHER, THE COOK

My first memory of visiting my dad at work was when he worked at the Snelling Cafe on Snelling [Avenue] and Selby [Avenue in St. Paul]. We'd always go to the backdoor of the restaurant, which was a screen door. And my dad was always dressed in white and he had his long apron on and his cook's hat, which I just loved, the puffy chef's hat. He'd be glad to see us and he'd say, "Well, what's going on, here? Who are these little kids?" We'd come in the kitchen and it was so hot and greasy! He'd show us how to get through the kitchen to the dining room, and then he'd have us on the stools at the counter and ask us what we wanted. He'd generally get us a dish of ice cream or maybe a Coke or something. He and my mom would talk, and then we'd be on our way. It was always a big deal. I always loved it, because the other cooks were always glad to see Harry's kids. So, they would maybe slip us a quarter or tell me how pretty I looked. *(laughter)*

I was always curious about what they were doing. When my dad was cooking chow mein—the wok was about thirty inches in diameter, it was huge. So, he'd bring out a big bin-full of ground pork and put that in with the oil and he'd stir fry that, and then he'd add a big bin-full of celery, and to stir it, you've got to use both arms going one clockwise, the other one counter

San Francisco, was established to serve the social, economic, and legal needs of Chinese immigrants in the Midwest.

clockwise at the same time, stirring all of this stuff. Then, you'd have to get it up to a boil and you'd add all the soy sauce, salt, sugar, and in those days MSG [monosodium glutamate]. Then, you have to make a big bowl full of cornstarch, and when it [the wok] was bubbling, you'd put in the cornstarch. You'd have to stir it really fast so it didn't get clumpy. So, my dad had very strong shoulders. He'd come home from work and, for years, I would, at the age of ten, eleven, or twelve, rub his feet with alcohol because his feet would be burning when he got home.

When he worked at the Snelling, he'd go to work at five-thirty or six in the morning to get all the American food, the roasts and chicken, whatever, going early in the morning. Then he'd come home at three. He would nap for an hour, go to Kee's Chow Mein at four and work till eight. He did that six days a week, and every other Sunday he worked an afternoon at Kee's. Occasionally, he'd ask me to rub his back and he'd stretch out on the floor in front of the TV and I'd sit up on top of him and just give him a really good backrub with some alcohol. He appreciated that.

Then, he got this job at the Nankin. I thought that was pretty cool because I knew about the reputation of the Nankin. By then I was all grown up and I had my own business in the IDS Center (Investors Diversified Services was the tallest building in Minneapolis then)—Sheila Chin Design, graphic design. I was designing cookbooks for Pillsbury and corporate logos for new businesses, posters. During those years, I loved to go see my dad at the Nankin. If I were working late, I'd go over for dinner, and if I could get in there and let him know I was there, then he'd treat me. (*laughter*)

My father was very proud of me. That's actually a great Chinese characteristic, I think: pride in your children and then, racking up your grandchildren and showing them off. Their children's success meant that they were successful, no matter what they were doing at the time. It goes back further, too. Getting to this country meant that they seized that opportunity, and the family is successively successful, so that is a point of real pride. When I went to college, it was hard and I had to decide whether I was really going to finish or not. Getting the degree meant, for me, being the first one on both sides of the family to get a college degree. So, I wanted to do that for both my parents, because neither one of them went past the eighth grade. I especially wanted to do it for my dad.

MY REAL CHINESE NAME

I was about thirteen or fourteen when my mother told me that Daddy might get deported. It was just frightening. We learned that President [John F.] Kennedy or Congress had said that if you just go through naturalization again, you'll be automatically forgiven [for being a paper son] and allowed to stay. I know that was because they found out how many families, American fam-

Business logo with the Chinese character "Liang" designed
by Sheila Chin Morris in honor of her father's true surname.
(Courtesy of Sheila Chin Morris)

ilies, were going to be absolutely uprooted and destroyed if they actually tried
to deport all these fathers. I'm sure most of the Chinese men were in business, so that would have made a large dent in many local businesses.

Then I find out that his name is really Liang Cheung You, so that was a
real bolt from left field. Then, my dad had the choice of going with his real
name, Liang, or staying with Harry Chin. My dad doesn't like to make waves.
I guess it was more important for him to just keep the order that we had had
in our lives. The mortgage was in that name. Their marriage certificate was
in that name. Our birth certificates were all in that name. Why go through
all that change? And so he let our name be Chin.

That would be a second regret that I would have—first, he didn't teach
me Chinese—second, that he didn't let me have my real Chinese name
when he had the opportunity. I grew in reverence knowing that I have that
name, but the only way I got to use it was when I was creating a new logo
for myself. I always wanted a blind embossed letterhead. So, I took the Chi-

nese character for Liang and fit it into a nice little square box and blind embossed it on the letterhead that said, "Sheila Chin Design." Many people would ask me, "What does that character mean?" Then, I would say, "Well, it's our real Chinese family name." And I would quickly tell them about the "paper sons."

MY DAD'S OTHER FAMILY

I'm not sure which came first, the announcement about his name or the knowledge that my dad had another family. What happened was that one summer when I was fourteen, my mother said that a cousin was going to come to visit from China, that she had just gotten married, and that she was Uncle Johnny's daughter—Uncle Johnny was my "paper uncle," the pretend brother, from Milwaukee. Eventually, I was told that she was my sister and not my cousin. She had grown up in Hong Kong with her mother, who had been married to my dad before he left China. She was only two months old when my father left, and her mother had matched her with Ben, her husband, because he had American citizenship and a business in Philadelphia. He could bring her to the United States so she could see her father and live here.

I don't know what went on between my mom and dad over that issue. I never saw or heard fighting, and I don't remember actually seeing any tears either. I remember my mom trying to embrace the situation and make the best of it. I think it was very difficult for Susan [the Chinese sister] because her mother was still alive and living in Hong Kong at this time. I think my mother was assured that that wasn't going to be a problem. But of course, it did become a problem.

I was in college when Susan's mother came to the United States. Her name was Yuet, Y-u-e-t (meaning "moon"). She came to Philadelphia and visited with Susan. When she came to Minneapolis, she wanted to see my dad. He saw her a few times and tried to send her away. "Go live with Susan or go back to Hong Kong or whatever, but I can't be with you." I don't know if he gave her money or what. But, I try to understand everybody's part in this and I have compassion for everybody, probably most of all for my dad, because I think he was really trying to take care of everybody. He tried to tell both my mother and Yuet what they wanted to hear, and I don't think he could follow through.

Our lives changed forever on September 19, 1970, when my mother took her own life. For whatever other reasons—poor health, depression, menopause, grown children—the situation between my parents had really worsened more than I realized. I was completely devastated with the death of my mother. I believe my brother still suffers from depression because of it. (I got counseling some years later and feel resolved now.)

When they finally did get together after my mom died, I was really curious about whether he was going to be happy, and that's part of how I came to accept her because she did make my dad happy. They only had six years together [she passed away in 1976 of lung cancer], but he was much more animated and sociable. They went out to dinner, and would go visit Chinese friends. I think he introduced her as his number one wife. She loved mahjongg, so they'd sometimes stay up late playing mahjongg with friends, or they would go to Las Vegas to gamble. She brought the old ways with her when she came. She brought stuff that he hadn't thought of making for years. There would be these funny little steamed cakes or dumplings and he would show it to me like it was a new artifact. He'd say, "Sheila, I haven't seen it since I was a boy in China. Look at this. This is called 'bun ga min' in Chinese."

I learned as I got to know her that she really did love Rog and me, and I knew she really loved my dad. It wasn't that she had to cultivate us as a second wife might have to do in other blended families. But she claimed us, that was that. She'd just revel in cooking for us. In fact, we became *extremely* close over the years, so all was forgiven, because she had her situation, too.

When I first heard about another family, I didn't think it had happened to anybody else, but of course, it's happened hundreds, maybe thousands of times to a lot of these Chinese men who were stranded in America, and they couldn't be reunited with their families during the whole Communist era. Many of them started new families. So I know I'm not the only one.

.   .   .

I feel that being the daughter of Harry Chin has given me an incredible depth that not everybody gets to experience. When I was a little girl, there were some times when I just hated being Chinese. I didn't want to be different. I just wanted to have blue eyes and light hair. I just wanted to blend in, to be one of the kids on the block. In some cases I was, but then in some cases, I definitely was not.

I grew up being afraid of people, not knowing whether they were going to love me or if they were going to, like when I was a little girl, call me a name. Even when I moved to this small town, Waseca, in 1980, I was thinking about the stereotypes. I'm a Chinese person, are they going to like me? None of that materialized. I've learned to celebrate my uniqueness, I've learned about communication, and I've learned about getting involved in communities. I think I've done a good job with my kids and I know I have a great marriage. I don't have a lot of money, but I *know* I feel like I'm a very successful person. If I die tomorrow, I'd die happy.

SOURCE: Sheila Chin Morris, interview with Sherri Gebert-Fuller, Minnesota Historical Society, October 2, 2002, Waseca, Minnesota. A version of this interview was published in Sherri Gebert-Fuller, *Chinese in Minnesota* (Minneapolis: Minnesota Historical Society Press, 2004), pp. 83–87.

OTHER REFERENCES

Peggy Spitzer Christoff, *Tracking the "Yellow Peril": The INS and Chinese Immigrants in the Midwest* (Rockport, Me.: Picton Press, 2001).

Erika Lee, *At America's Gates: Chinese Immigration during the Exclusion Era, 1882–1943* (Chapel Hill: University of North Carolina Press, 2003).

Huping Ling, *Chinese St. Louis: From Enclave to Cultural Community* (Philadelphia: Temple University Press, 2004).

Sarah R. Mason, "The Chinese," in *They Chose Minnesota: A Survey of the State's Ethnic Groups,* ed. June D. Holmquist (St. Paul: Minnesota Historical Society, 1981), pp. 531–45.

Eleanor Wong Telemaque, *It's Crazy to Be Chinese in Minnesota* (New York: Thomas Nelson, 1978).

"I always felt out of place there"
Growing Up Chinese in Mississippi (1982)

Bonnie C. Lew

By the time Bonnie Lew moved with her family from San Francisco Chinatown to the Mississippi Delta in 1954, Chinese had been settled in that area for over one hundred years. Recruited initially to replace freed African slaves after the Civil War, many Chinese found plantation work undesirable and moved on to running grocery stores that catered to black farmhands. Once established, they sent for family and helped other relatives to start grocery stores. The business required little English but long hours, the labor of all family members, and the ability of the Chinese to maintain good relations with both the black and white communities.

In this interview conducted by Judy Yung for the Chinese Women of America Research Project in 1982, Bonnie Lew candidly recalls what it was like growing up Chinese in Mississippi, "squished between the whites on top and the blacks on the bottom," and why she always felt so out of place there. She was eight years old when her family moved to Cleveland, Mississippi, to open a grocery store, and twenty-four years old when she finally moved back to California, where she founded the Chinese Folkdance Troupe in Stockton and today works as supervising librarian for the Stockton–San Joaquin Delta County Public Library.

MOVING FROM SAN FRANCISCO

My mom was born in San Francisco Chinatown and lived there all her life until she married my father. My father came over from China when he was ten or twelve. They met in a music club in Chinatown. I was the second born and middle child. I have an older brother who now lives in Concord [California] and a younger sister still in Mississippi. I guess I had a happy childhood in San Francisco, except that I remember staying with my grandmother a lot because both my parents worked. My mother worked during the day at Deb's Department Store and my father worked nights as a cook. Oftentimes they left my brother and myself at home alone. I was six or seven then, and I remember just sitting and looking out the window and watching the cable cars go up Washington Street for days and days on end. And it always had to be quiet during the day because my father was asleep. He had Sundays off and that's the only time I ever saw my father. On Sundays we would go to Golden Gate Park. In a way, life was really lonely in San Francisco for me because my parents never let us out. When we got home from school, we stayed inside the apartment. We never went anywhere unless my grandmother took us to the park on Clay Street. That was it.

Then my great-aunt, my grandfather's sister, came out to California one summer to visit. She had married a gentleman who had settled in Mississippi and opened a grocery store in Boyle, Mississippi. And my father's sister, Kim Gwoo, had also settled in Mississippi with a man who opened a grocery store there. They told my father that there was no life in San Francisco, that this was no place to raise three children. "Your wife work during the day, you work during the night, nobody ever saw each other, that wasn't a good family life." They encouraged him to move to Mississippi, said they would help him open a business.[1] And because it was such a rat race for them in California, they decided to move to Mississippi in '54. It was a real traumatic experience for my mother because she was very close to her four brothers and sisters and to my grandmother who had raised them. And she was already thirty-four, thirty-five then. I was eight years old at the time.

LIFE IN MISSISSIPPI

When we first moved to Mississippi, we lived in Cleveland for two years. Frank Wong was the one who told my father that his place of business in Cleveland was no good.[2] Kim Gwoo was the one who said, "Come to Clarksdale, I'll give you a little money and help you set up. There's too many Chinese in Cleveland for you to try and compete with them." So we moved to Clarksdale and they made a good business because those were the years when the blacks didn't drive. We moved into a black neighborhood, right next to a government housing area. We seldom went out in the streets to play because the streets weren't paved. They were gravel and there were pit holes and mud holes in the street. And our parents didn't want us associating with the blacks. You either associated with the Chinese down the street or your family. If you

---

1. According to Lucy Cheung (Bonnie's mother), the aunt was building a new grocery store in Cleveland and wanted the Cheungs to move there to run it (Lucy Cheung interview with Judy Yung, Chinese Women of America Research Project, June 4, 1982, Clarksdale, Mississippi).

2. Also according to Lucy Cheung, business was poor at this location because the store was isolated, set back from the street, and on the wrong side of the freeway.

really had any white friends, your parents didn't have time to cart you across town to visit them.

As a result, my brother and I played a lot together. We played a lot of war games and checkers, swept a lot of floors, filled a lot of Coke cases, stocked a lot of shelves, and played with our dogs. Then when my sister was old enough, my mother taught the three of us how to play MJ [mah-jongg]. She had waited until all three of us were grown up enough so she could find three legs to play MJ with her. *(laughs)* I also ironed a lot, read a lot, and we worked in the grocery store a lot . . . *a lot.*[3] There were days when the cotton pickers would go out at 5:30 in the morning. We would get up and open the door for the cotton pickers to come in and steal you blind. *(laughs)* No, they won't, that's what we were there for. We would be strategically placed in front of the Twinkies or in front of the milk box, my brother and I, then my mother and father behind the counter, and we would watch the people as they came through and bought their things for lunch. Then they went out and got in their bus. It took about forty-five minutes. Then we would close the store, climb back into bed and sleep until eight or nine o'clock (this was all summer long during cotton season). But if we wanted spaghetti or something else exciting for lunch, we had to get out of bed and watch the store so my mom could come back in and cook because we lived in the back of the store like *so* many of the Chinese did.

My mom and dad had one bedroom, and my brother, sister, and I had the other. Our bedroom was essentially the bedroom, the dining room, and the living room. I remember lying in bed and watching Friday night wrestling, and I can remember eating on the Wonder Bread trays. That was our dining room table for I don't remember how many years, and we children would sit on either crates or boxes around our bedroom to eat. It probably wasn't very sanitary because we lived with a lot of roaches and a lot of mice, but it was an inevitable thing because we were living in a grocery store and roaches just grow naturally in a hot and damp climate. In fact, it was worse than living in San Francisco, where we at least had a nice apartment. But my parents were being frugal and trying to scrimp and save every penny to pay back the relatives and friends who had subsidized them, so we had to live meagerly the first few years. I don't begrudge any of that; it was just all a part of my growing up.

I think my mom always kept a really healthy attitude. She always said, "In California it won't be like this," or "We're going to go home, we're going to go to California." It wasn't like we were living in Mississippi for the rest of our lives. That's how come I always knew I was going to end up here [in California]. It was something that she had instilled in me. It was like we were so-

3. Lucy Cheung said in her interview that store hours were usually 7 A.M. to 12 midnight, seven days a week.

journers in Mississippi. My father always kept a really positive attitude too, even though things got really bad, because he could up and go off. He was the only one in the family who could drive, and he could just take off when he wanted and go hunting and fishing with his friends. So he had an outlet, whereas our outlet was my mother. She was really the strong person who kept all of us up all the time, just kind of kept us going . . . silently supportive, not necessarily verbally or with any show of affection, just the fact that you felt that she knew there was a better life out there than what we were living here in Mississippi.

MY SCHOOLING

I was in the third grade when I started school in Mississippi, and I flunked math. My brother and I both flunked math. We went to summer school for two solid summers because neither of us could add or subtract or multiply . . . other than five, ten, fifteen, twenty and make change. We didn't know fractions. I don't know if it was something that we didn't pick up when we were in school out in California or what, but the teachers in Mississippi thought we were really lacking. I wasn't that conscientious of a student and my parents didn't pressure us. They never said, "You better study really hard or you'll never get out of this place." They just sent us to school and if I got S's (Superior) and G's (Good), my mother would say, "That's good." I never got any flak for the grades I made.

Apparently it was only two years prior to our move that the Chinese could go to school with the whites. So I attended a school that was strictly white with a few Chinese. I was treated fine when I was in grammar school. In fact, when I was in the sixth grade, I was invited to a couple of birthday parties. These parties were given by a lot of the rich, white Southern families in town whose children were in school with me. But as soon as I got into junior high school, all social activities stopped and I was ignored, period. Maybe it was because I was Chinese, or maybe I was unattractive, or maybe I didn't have the brightest personality in the world. And I had asthma, that's the other thing, so my mom never let me do anything . . . like join the band. That was something that a lot of Chinese in Clarksdale did, and they got into school activities that way. They got to go to the football games, the basketball games, and to the Lions Club parades all over the state. And because I wasn't in band, or I wasn't in anything, I was really pretty much a loner until I graduated from high school and I went on to college. It didn't hit me that it was really discrimination until I went back to the same high school to teach after college. The mothers of the students that I had been shunned by the whole time that I was in the seventh through the twelfth grade, were coming up to me and saying, "Oh, you're Miss Cheung, weren't you in Troy's class?" and calling me "Ma'am" and this whole bit. And they had been the same ones that had not even looked my way. It was really difficult to handle because I knew inside what they really felt. But because my status had changed and because I was now a teacher of their children, they were treating me with respect.

Growing up, I wanted to become a schoolteacher because I guess I didn't have anybody else to look up to . . . except teachers and librarians. That's what I worked toward, and college wasn't a choice that I had to really make either. After high school, you either go out to work or you go on to college. Ever since I can remember, we spent our summers rolling nickels, dimes, and pennies from the bubble gum machines in the store to take us to college. Every time my mom emptied the little candy machines, she would dump that money in a box and that's what she sent her children to school on. There was no other alternative. You just went from high school into college . . . it was just an extension. And we came home every weekend from college and worked at the grocery store.

My mom had always told me, "You're going to go back to California," so I had always planned on going to college there, but financially my parents were not able to send me . . . plus I think in a way my mother didn't think I was ready. So I went to Delta State College, and one of my big things then was to go to church on Thursday evenings, because I was living in the dormitories and I could only go out one night a week. But church didn't count, so I could go to church one night and still go out another night a week. Church was an outlet for us, especially after Rev. Wu and their kids came to Mississippi. Johnny and Terry were like a breath of fresh air because they were from California. And they talked about being in California, doing this with the kids and doing that with the Chinese, and all the fun things that you always read about but never did. And Madie used to tell us about going to Sacramento and all the dates she had, and we would sit there and just suck it all in. *(laughs)* They were like people from outer space. We did so many different things, like talent shows, because they were really big into singing and stuff like that. We sat around and talked, talked, talked to the wee hours of the morning. Then we would sneak Johnny and Terry out the back window because they had a curfew *(laughs),* and we would go ride around. Those were fun days.

OUR SOCIAL LIFE

For a long time my mom kept herself apart from the Chinese people in Mississippi because she felt that they were too close-knit, that if they got to know you, they'll talk about you . . . plus she wasn't Chinese-born, she was American-born, although she spoke Chinese like a pro. She worked in the store and never had a social life. The closest person she ever got to was my father's sister, Kim Gwoo. And on occasional Wednesdays in the summertime, we would close up in the afternoon after lunch. That was like the normal day for Chinese stores to be closed because it was the slowest. We would go down to Cleve-

Chinese grocers and their families at a social function in the Mississippi Delta, 1950s. (Courtesy of Nancy Bing Chew)

land to see my aunt and play with the kids, or they would all come up to see us. Then if there was a wedding or a *daai saang yat* [big birthday] or *moon yuet* [baby party] or something like that on a Sunday, then stores closed on that Sunday and people would go to that. But if you ask about our social life, it was nil.[4] We worked in the store. That was our family and our social life. We did our homework in the grocery store and we took our meals there.

The one thing my mother felt strongly about was that everybody sit at the table and eat together. So for a long time we would wait until we closed the store up and then eat. Sometimes there would be people in there sitting around and drinking beer until eleven o'clock, and she would hold dinner until those people left because she felt that as a family we had to sit and eat together. During the school year sometimes we would eat in shifts, but in the summertime, some nights we didn't find ourselves eating dinner until 11:30. That was a big thing with her, and that was a big thing with us. So eating became a big part of our lives. For a while we were eating two meals of rice a day, which is a lot. That's why I was really fat. By the time I

4. According to Lucy Cheung, the family made occasional trips to Memphis, and her husband sometimes took the kids fishing.

graduated from high school, I was 178 pounds. *(laughs)* My father had been a chef in San Francisco, and my mom, having lived near North Beach, cooks Italian food better than any Italian I've ever met. So, you know, it was good eating at my house.

It was really hard for her to keep up the Chinese traditions in Mississippi. There were things that she kept doing only because her mother had always done them, like making *tay* [pastries] at certain times of the year or making *joong* [tamales] at certain times of the year. My parents never said, "You are Chinese and this is what you have to do." It was more subtle than that. For example, when I was sixteen or seventeen, my grandmother asked me what I wanted for my birthday, and I told her I wanted a hair dryer. She didn't send it to me until after Chinese New Year because my birthday that year was so close to Chinese New Year. She was afraid I was going to wash my hair on Chinese New Year's eve. And to this day, I don't wash my hair on Chinese New Year's eve because it's considered bad luck. Another example, one of the reasons I enjoy Chinese folkdance now is because we heard so much Chinese music in my home. My mom *loves* her Chinese opera. She had her Chinese records and she would play them all the time. Or my sister and I would play them over and over again, and we got used to hearing it. Then I think the fact that she always felt that Chinatown was home, that when we visited San Francisco, it was not just the feeling that you were in Chinatown with all these other Chinese people, but you were home with your family and the people that always made you happy. And that's the kind of thing that she always instilled in us, that happiness was with your family, and your family was in Chinatown. So it just kind of drew you back there, because her ties were so close to Chinatown that being Chinese was real natural and normal.

But my father grew to love it in Mississippi. He learned to speak English very fast, and he assimilated. He became a big hunter and a big fisherman, and he planted Chinese vegetables on one acre of land and farmed. Ninety-nine percent of the store's customers were black. The one percent that was white were the garbage men and the city workers. They came after work because Tom [her father] was a regular guy and you could always get a cold beer there, and you could sit there as long as you wanted to and talk to him about hunting, fishing, and the things that men like to talk about. The wives never found them there and they weren't at a bar, so it was quite a social place. It was pleasant because my father got to know quite a few people in the city offices, and the tax assessor became one of my father's best friends. They would go hunting, and Mr. Leslie did a lot of things for my father. My father did a lot of things for him. But the main thing that Mr. Leslie did was to buy the house that my father wanted and turn it over to him. In 1964, when people heard that we were looking for a house, a lot of realtors in town said, "There's a Chinese looking for a house, don't sell." My father came up against a lot of barriers, so Mr. Leslie said, "I can't have this. Tom wants to buy a house. Give me the money and I'll go out and buy your house." So my father gave him $11,000. He went out and bought the house my father wanted and it was in a white neighborhood.

RACE RELATIONS IN THE SOUTH

If you lived in the South and saw the blacks the time we were growing up . . . of course, a lot of it is different now, a lot of them are more educated . . . many of them were illiterate. You know, my mother signed more welfare checks—it was her handwriting on the back of one million and ten of them. And once, one of the women had her daughter sign the back of the check, and the check came back to her and they said, "Hey, this is not the same person. Did you get your money?" She said, "Oh, no, no. Miss Tom used to sign my checks for me, but I got my daughter to sign it because she can write now." They would come in just to cash their checks and buy two dollars' worth of groceries, and we would charge them a dime to sign and cash their check. That was a lot of dimes. My mom use to say, "Geez, they must think my name is Hattie Lou Smith." *(laughs)* But it was strictly business—that was all. Although I had one black friend that I used to run around with, and her name was Baby Lou. My parents didn't mind because I would run over to Louise's house and run back. I didn't stay gone very long, maybe an hour or so. It was very seldom that we would play with the black kids. A lot of them were very dirty. Even as a child I knew that I didn't want to associate with a lot of them. They lived in poverty and it was not something that they could really help, you know, when you have just one faucet in the house. I was growing up in a black neighborhood that was really poor. We had ditches and gravel on the street, the whole bit, it was like living out in the country. It wasn't until 1963 that they paved the street in front of our house, and it was a city street. It's just hard to tell you how it's like. The mud comes rushing in with the water after the rain and stuff like that.

You know, everyone has to have someone to be better than, I mean, no matter whether you're a poor black living in a rat-infested hole, you're better than somebody out there. The blacks were the only people that the Chinese could be better than. The whites were on top, and we were squished in the middle. I came home from school one time all fired up about something political. It must have been from American government or civics class; I don't even remember what it was. I just remember the comment my father made: "You don't talk about them (the whites) like that. You're Chinese and you have nowhere to go." He knew his place, and essentially he was right. You can't go down, you definitely couldn't go up at that time. I can't remember whether I was in the ninth grade or twelfth grade at the time, but I remember the comment more than anything else. Later when I returned to California, I noticed that prejudice was more blatant here. They do it to your face, whereas in Mississippi you knew your place or you knew where everybody belonged. A funny thing, my father used to fish so much in the summertime that he would get really dark. He was refused service at a couple of restaurants when he walked in with his white friends because they thought he was black. Chinese were not stopped from going anywhere the whites were as long as you looked lighter. That's just how it was and you lived with it. It was just all part of growing up.

LEAVING MISSISSIPPI

I wasn't that happy at home, and I always felt that I was missing out on something. I was an avid reader and I read everything I could at the library—Carolyn Haywood, Du Jardin, and I must have read *Fifteen* by Beverly Cleary 110 times. You know, I went to the senior prom and my date asked me half way through the Grand March why I wasn't having any fun. *(laughs)* It was a riot, I always felt out of place. I didn't have the boyfriends in the convertible cars or anything else. There was so much out there that I was reading and so much that I was missing that I always felt that I didn't want to be where I was, that Mississippi was the last place in the world to be. Maybe if I came to California, I thought, then I would look like everyone else and feel a little more at ease with myself.

I taught school for two years and the second year I taught school, they semi-integrated the school. What sold me on the idea to finally leave Mississippi was the fact that some male black students came through the hall one day, and I was walking from the library to the principal's office, and they go, "Hi, baby," or they made some derogatory remark to me about being cute or whatever. And I decided at that point I didn't think I could go back to school and teach that next year, because I didn't think I was mature enough to handle that kind of a situation. That was one of the major boosts for me to leave Mississippi, to pick myself up and get going.

When I got back to Chinatown after I moved back to California, it was like I was home. It was almost like I had never left, I mean I could walk to where I wanted to go. I could remember the streets in order—Sacramento, Clay, Washington, Jackson, Pacific—and it was a place that I could drive through and feel comfortable, not like I was lost. And I knew which streets went one way and which streets went the other way, I didn't have to be told. It was like I was home . . . it was just a good feeling.

There were few adjustments for me to make, although Bobby [her husband] used to tell me that I was so un-Chinese. He used to say, "You're so white." I said, "Gee, I'm the most Chinese person I know." *(laughs)* So few of my girl friends spoke Chinese as well as I did, I thought. He's changed his thoughts about it since, but it was something I had to reevaluate and think about. And at that time in the early seventies, all the Chinese and Asians

were into Third World and Yellow Power and stuff like that, and I wasn't thinking about that, so maybe that's what they were talking about.

One major adjustment I had to make was losing my Southern accent. I lost
it the day someone called me Mississippi Bonnie. This black woman was following me around in the stacks at the library. She couldn't figure out what I
was, I guess because I had this Southern accent. So I worked at losing it, although I didn't have that much of a Southern accent, because my mother was
from San Francisco and we came out every second and third year to visit. My
sister or their children . . . gosh, you couldn't tell them from black children.
They sound so Southern, you know, they're terrible. *(laughs)* I don't mean
that. It is really cute when you see a little Chinese with almond eyes and they're
speaking, "Y'all come back, now, Uncle Bobby and Auntie Bonnie."

Having been exposed to liberal thinking and being freer with my mind
and with my mouth, I don't think I could ever go back to live in Mississippi,
which is essentially a closed society, even though it's come a long way. Even
as a teacher, a cut above a student or a person who worked in the grocery
store, I was still a Chinese and unable to speak my mind. Another reason I
won't go back to live is I don't like the way white people look at you. Growing up, you knew you were going to get stared at because you're Chinese
when you went anywhere, so it didn't faze you, whereas now when I go back
and people look at me, I want to say, "What's wrong with you? Your eyes itchy?
Why are you staring at me?"

As for my parents . . . I guess the Chinese had been having problems with
the blacks for a while, especially with the civil rights movement coming on
and the people getting a little more militant. During the mid-sixties, there
were a number of boycotts of the Chinese grocery stores[5] because the blacks
from the North said, "The whites are exploiting you and the Chinese are exploiting you. All the Chinese are is an extension of the whites. If they wanted
to be like us, they would have come to our schools, they would have moved
into our neighborhoods, and they would be helping us and working with us
rather than being apart from us." Then they started throwing Molotov cock-
tails through the windows and that kind of thing. At that time my parents
didn't live in the back of the store anymore, and that was a good thing. Someone threw a Molotov cocktail into the back storeroom and it started a fire
and it burnt the store down. So that's why my parents retired five years ago.
They were burned down and there was no reason to open the store back,
because the business had gotten so slow. And there was another Chinese grocery store a block away. They said that with the insurance and everything,
they'd just take the money and retire, even though they were both still young.

But my father didn't want to leave Mississippi. I think it is because he has

5. According to Lucy Cheung, one boycott in 1968 lasted over three months and business
declined so drastically that many Chinese grocers had to borrow money from the banks.

made a life in Mississippi for himself. He's been able to reach his aspirations in Mississippi as a man and he's raised his children. He never would have done it in California, making the meager wages he was making. Living in that large of a city, he never would have achieved personal satisfaction and become the big hunter and big fisherman he is. If my father were to say, "Okay, let's pack up and leave," my mother would do it in a minute. Well, maybe she'll do it in two minutes, because my sister is there, and she has her three children. And that's one reason my mother is still there, because she gets the grandchildren occasionally and that helps my sister.[6]

SOURCE: Bonnie C. Lew, interview with Judy Yung, Chinese Women of America Research Project, March 26, 1982, Stockton, California.

OTHER REFERENCES

Christine Choy, *Mississippi Triangle* (New York: Third World Newsreel, 1987), VHS.

James Loewen, *The Mississippi Chinese: Between Black and White* (Cambridge, Mass.: Harvard University Press, 1971).

Robert Seto Quan, *Lotus among the Magnolias: The Mississippi Chinese* (Jackson: University Press of Mississippi, 1982).

6. According to Lucy Cheung, after thirty years she had adjusted to living in rural Mississippi, and she actually preferred staying there than returning to the more hectic pace of life in San Francisco. Penny Cheung (Bonnie's sister) said that she too preferred living in Mississippi over California because, unlike her brother and sister, she had no memories of life in California, and when she had visited San Francisco, she had found the pace of life there too fast. Moreover, her husband was a local Chinese boy who had taken over his father's farm (Penny Cheung, interview with Judy Yung, Chinese Women of America Research Project, June 5, 1982, Clarksdale, Mississippi).

"It was not a winnable war"

Remembering Vietnam (1998)

Johnny Wong

The legacy of the Vietnam War, which continues to haunt America today, holds special meaning in the memories of the Chinese American baby boomer generation—those born after World War II. The Tet Offensive in 1968 marked a turning point in America's effort to stop the spread of communism in Indochina and the beginning of their involvement in the war. On the homefront, those who joined the antiwar movement questioned the racial and moral implications of the war in relation to their newfound identities as Asian Americans. At the warfront, those who served in Vietnam suffered not only combat trauma but also the race-related stress of being treated as "gooks" by fellow Americans. Moreover, when they returned from the war that the United States lost, they were spat on rather than saluted, adding to the severity of their post–traumatic stress disorders.

Jason Chang, an undergraduate working on an oral history paper, explores these issues in the following interview with Vietnam War veteran Johnny Wong. Specifically, he wanted to know: What were Wong's experiences as a Chinese American in the Vietnam War? Was racism in the military more pronounced for him because he looked like the enemy? Did he suffer post–traumatic stress disorder upon his return, and if so, how did he deal with it? Wong had never openly talked about his memories of the Vietnam War, and as the interview progressed, it became apparent that he had his own story to tell, beginning with his troubled childhood in San Francisco, his first experience with racial prejudice, and the events that led to his tour of duty in Vietnam. In the last analysis, Johnny Wong's story is about one soldier's survival of mind, body, and soul in a senseless and unwinnable war.

GROWING UP

I was born on November 22, 1945, in Canton City, China. I immigrated to this country when I was about two and a half; I can vaguely remember living close to Chinatown in a hotel, and then we moved down by the Embarcadero Center in San Francisco. My father ran a laundry, so we were living on top of the laundry. My brother and I stayed in a small room. So I kind of grew up down there until about ten or eleven. Then we moved out here by the tunnel on Geary Boulevard. That was the home that I was in for a long time, until after high school. I attended Washington Irving Elementary School, went to Francisco Junior High School, and from Francisco I went to George Washington High School. Then I got kicked out and finished up at John Adams Adult School. After that I attended City College of San Francisco, and then I was drafted.

As far as the places I hung around while growing up, I would say that it was in Chinatown and North Beach. I hung out at Cameron House.[1] My parents wanted to give us some religious or some sense of group activity involvement. It was a place to meet friends. On Fridays we had club meetings, played some sports. Once they started talking about religious things, most of us just turned a deaf ear because that wasn't what we were interested in. I started going in the seventh grade and lasted until about the tenth grade. Going there, it did give me a sense of belonging because my family life when I was young wasn't kosher. My parents were very strict. They adhered to Chinese customs and upbringing. My mother was very demanding and always had negative things to say, like I was bad and always looking for trouble—this constant barrage of nagging, nagging, and nagging. I remember many times being physically abused, of going to junior high and having welts on my back and being ashamed to take off my shirt because it would have been obvious that I had gotten hit. If that happened today, they would probably throw my mom in jail and throw the key away.

In elementary school there were some Caucasians and blacks, but it was predominantly Chinese. When you are young and growing up, the first thing you learn is people swearing and talking bad. When somebody calls you a "Chink" or a "slant-eye," you wonder why they would say things like that. But it's more like bullying—picking on somebody. I think I learned to distinguish being bullied versus having somebody be racist, which was having somebody demonstrate a certain prejudice toward me. That happened later in my life and while I was in the service.

I remember back in the sixties, probably '63 or '64 when I was getting out of high school, the Free Speech Movement was going on at Berkeley, the civil rights movement, and it was the beginning of a lot of demonstrations. What that brought in terms of awareness for me was that a whole mass of people was demonstrating on behalf of something they believed was right.

1. The Donaldina Cameron House, located in San Francisco Chinatown, was established as the Presbyterian Mission Home in 1874 to rescue and help Chinese prostitutes and abused slave girls. Beginning in the 1940s, it turned its attention to youth work in the Chinese community.

I was no longer living at home but with the family of a Puerto Rican friend from high school. Right after high school, he invited me to go down to Puerto Rico. In order for me to get to Puerto Rico I had to take a Greyhound bus. So I went across the United States and I planned to stop off in the Detroit area because my older brother was attending medical school at Wayne State University. I remember going downtown to a Woolworth's and wanting to be served. This was my first time being on my own; I was only about eighteen. The person that was serving behind the counter was black and I just waited and waited and she wouldn't come. As a last resort, I asked her why I wasn't being served and she said *(pauses)*, I can't remember exactly what she said, but I just got the feeling that something was being taken out on me, and I just picked up and walked out of there.

Just before I made the decision to sign up for the military my father admitted that he came to this country illegally.[2] I wasn't born here, I was naturalized here, so for years I had to carry a green card. When he made that statement it put my older brother and me in a very precarious situation. Because my father admitted to having come to this country illegally, my brother and I would have to go through the process of naturalization again. At that time I had to make a decision about going into the service even though I was against the war. I could voluntarily enlist or my other option was to not go at all. My Puerto Rican friend's mother, who was a teacher, told me one of my options was to leave the country, go to Canada. Looking back at it now, if I had made that decision I would probably have never come back because I wasn't a citizen. I felt that by enlisting I would be giving myself a choice as to some kind of training versus none if I were drafted. Although I would be obligated to serve one extra year, I didn't want to take a chance ending up in the infantry. These were some of the circumstances that pushed me to enlist.

The situation back then was that if you continued schooling, it would give you a deferment from the draft, but you had to carry a full course load. Under those circumstances, it was a lot of pressure just to think that there was a war going on, so that staying in school and taking a full course load was very hard. What was I trying to accomplish while I was in school? Was I in school to not get drafted, or what if something happened and my grades were to slip? My grades slipped and I knew that most likely I was going to be drafted. I tried to sign up for the navy, but it was too late. I never really considered signing up for the air force because it was a four-year commitment. The other alternative was the marines, and I definitely didn't want to go into the marines. Back then, they had the reputation as being those who were really gung-ho. So my only option was the army. To give you an example, the

2. Johnny Wong's father had entered the United States as a "paper son" in 1930 in order to circumvent the Chinese Exclusion Act. In 1966 he took advantage of the Chinese Confession Program that allowed paper sons to disclose their false status and claim their true identities.

month that I was drafted—October 1966—48,000 guys got drafted in that one month. Of course I contemplated dodging the draft. I had a friend, I remember going to the physical right after we got the draft papers, he took a load of soy sauce and drank it to try and mess up his body. From what I remember, he got away with it.

LIFE IN THE ARMY

When I was at Fort Lewis, Washington (boot camp), the drill sergeant picked me and some others to be squad leaders. Whether he did that intentionally or not I can't be sure, but that was not the right environment for me to be assertive or aggressive because I was not there by choice. I just wanted to be done with it and get on to the next step in terms of what we had to do. I happened to be in command of a group of rednecks, and that didn't work out for me at all. They called me "slant-eye," "Chink," and things like that. Being bombarded with all this verbal garbage was something that I really wasn't accustomed to. When I grew up I learned to take care of myself. I could handle somebody trying to bully me, but all these racist comments coming from more than one individual was something different. I just tolerated it as much as I could, I didn't go out and explode or anything like that. I had enough problems as it was, trying to be their type of soldier when it was totally uncomfortable.

I remember this incident where I was learning to handle a rifle, M14, and I remember we were sitting down and they were demonstrating how to load the magazine. So we were loading the cartridge and I was putting a round into the chamber but I accidentally pulled the trigger. *(laughs a little)* So fire, you hear a shot. I said, "Holy shit." *(laughs)* I mean, I knew it was a blank, but I really didn't know what a blank can do and not do. It came really close to this person that was sitting next to me, and when that round went off, it totally silenced everybody. The drill sergeant immediately says, "Who fired that round?" I felt like digging myself all the way to China, but I'm raising my hand and going through this uncomfortable situation. How they'd address you is like, "Come here and stand at attention." And then the officer says, "What do you do when you're in front of an officer?" You're supposed to salute, you know, but shit, I was uncomfortable enough going through all this. In essence, they pulled me from being a squad leader. I felt pretty bad and my self-esteem just went down twenty levels. Not only had I been reprimanded, but they took my squad away and I ended up doing k.p. duty because of this mishap.

I had enlisted for supply training, so after basic training at Fort Lewis, I had orders to go to Fort Dix in New Jersey. I remember feeling relief because I was getting further away from Vietnam. Then after spending six or eight weeks in New Jersey, I got orders to go to Hanau, Germany. I thought how lucky because I was getting even further and further away. I still had two more years to do and I was hoping that this was where I would stay for the remainder of my service. I was put in a motor pool with a section called PLL (Prescribe Load Lists), which supplied the artillery units with trucks, parts, etc. We were to ensure the unit's combat and mission readiness by keeping accurate records of parts and parts supplied. After about three months I was sent to another supply school, where I graduated sixth out of a class of thirty. Then it was back to Hanau. By then, all I was doing was going to work every day, getting everything ready, and at night listening to my friends bitch and drink. I remember that I wanted to go back on the West Coast, to be closer to home. I remember discussing that with some of my superiors and they said that I could try. Then out of the blue came orders saying that I was going to Nam. What was mind-blowing was that there were 400 guys in the battalion and I was the only one who got the order. I was just in shock at the time. I went down to personnel and asked, "Why me?" This is the answer he gave me— there's nothing I can say to disprove it or say that it's not fair—he said that a computer in Washington, D.C., kicked my name out. I was saying, "Jesus Christ!!" There were a lot of guys with my M.O. [military occupation] and more time left in the service, and he was telling me that the computer picked my name. How can I believe that, but at the same time who am I going to question? I tried to come up with gimmicks about why I couldn't go. I'm not a citizen and other stuff, but it didn't make a difference because they could send noncitizens to Vietnam.

THE VIETNAM WAR

I got into Vietnam on April 1, 1968. The reason they sent so many soldiers in that year was because of Tet.[3] What the American people had been told up to that point by General Westmoreland was that South Vietnam was more or less under control. What had happened was that all the major cities had gone under attack, including Saigon. Everything had totally broken down, and that is part of the reason I was going to Vietnam. President Johnson had made a commitment that he was going to commit up to 500,000 more troops. Prior to my going there, there were probably already over 300,000 troops. And he was committing 500,000 more?

I remember arriving in Vietnam at about two in the afternoon and the air-conditioning was turned off and the door of the plane was opened. As the humidity filled the plane, I kept thinking that this was the biggest joke of my life. My original orders were to go to another artillery unit. But for

---

3. The Tet Offensive, which began in 1968 during the Vietnamese New Year, was a decisive turning point in the Vietnam War as the Viet Cong overwhelmed cities and towns across South Vietnam, shattering U.S. confidence about winning the war.

some reason, during the three days that I spent in processing, the orders were changed and they told me that I was going to the 25th Infantry Division in Cu Chi (20 miles northwest of Saigon). I'm freaking out and saying to myself, "Jesus Christ, why them [the infantry]?"

When I arrived in Cu Chi, I was assigned to a mechanized battalion as a PLL clerk in the motor pool. The first person that greeted me in Nam was this Asian guy, very dark, and he was wearing fatigues with no insignia. I couldn't tell if he was a Vietnamese or someone else. He introduced himself as Jimmy *(chuckles to himself)* and talked kind of funny because he was Chinese and from New York. He was in the infantry. Going through supply school and being in Germany was nothing compared to what he had gone through already. We talked about why he didn't show his insignia. He thought it was safer to not wear the insignia so that the Vietnamese might mistake him for one of their own and not fire on him. But at the same time, wouldn't the American soldiers maybe mistake him for being a Vietnamese? The difference is, when you're out in the field you know who your buddies are so you rely on them to watch your back. Jimmy took me aside and taught me not to panic should we come under attack. Try to calm yourself before reacting. He said that the Viet Cong knew our routine and that I should always be careful before coming out in the morning for reveille. Learning these things made me feel like someone was there to help me. As we got to know each other in a short period of time, I couldn't help but feel more compassion for him. Later, I was happy to hear he made it home.

Sure enough, the first day that I got into my base camp, I was walking to report in and I heard these sounds. It was like "ptooo, ptooo, ptooo," like something coming out of a tube. As I am walking toward the door, about to open the screen door, I see two guys—one guy going this way and one guy going the other way *(gestures in opposite directions with his hands)*, so I'm going like this *(gets down on his hands and knees)*. I'm not lying down flat because I don't know what it is. Well, those are mortars and when it hits the ground it makes an explosion. The other guys are running out, I don't know where they're running because I'm not familiar with the base camp and it was semi-dark. But I go in the front door and out the back door and they've gone into a bunker, so I *jump* right into the bunker! Instead of running down into the bunker I jumped, I mean we're talking about ten feet! That's how scared I was. That was the mentality in terms of learning—you had to learn as quickly as possible what was really going on. Yeah, we were in a big base camp. Did I feel safe? No.

After I was there for two weeks, we went under a rocket attack. I mean Jesus Christ! It was worse than a mortar round. It was like you could just hear it going, "schwooo!!" That's how it sounds, and then there is a ripple effect. You hear that and you're petrified. That one particular evening we were under that constant barrage. We were inside the hooch—that's where we lived—

Johnny Wong *(left)* with his buddy Jimmy in Vietnam.
(Courtesy of Johnny Wong)

not one of us took a chance and said, "Let's get the hell out of here." Each
hooch has a bunker in front or on the side, so when you're under attack,
the first thing you do is hit the ground, and then during the period when
you don't hear anything, you get up and run to the bunker as quickly as you
can. The bunkers are about twelve feet deep and filled with sandbags so I
felt a hell of a lot safer in them. I will never forget that night. I was so petrified
I was under the mattress. Of course if the roof caved in we'd all be gone. But
all of a sudden I remembered hearing a second lieutenant come running in
there and yelling, "What the fuck are you guys doing in here? Get the fuck
out of here!" And I was thinking, this guy's got balls. Then one guy said, "You
think we should go for it?" I said, "Hell yeah, go for it!" And then, "vooom!"
from both ends, because there was an entrance on both sides of the hooch.
We stayed in the bunker all night. In the morning I saw the damage. Right
next to the bunker was a hole about six feet deep by twelve feet wide where
a rocket had hit. I was thinking, shit, I have to go through this! I had just
been there a couple of weeks.

You asked earlier if I had seen any fighting because I was in the rear—there was no such thing as the rear, it was all Vietnam. It wasn't like you could take point A, clear it out completely, and be safe. No. How it was set up was that the United States and other countries—you even had Korean soldiers there and maybe Australians—would disperse soldiers out on patrol to contact with "Charlie" or V.C.'s. Once contact was made with "Charlie," all available fire power would be used in these operations (artillery, helicopter gunship, fighter jet napalm, and B-52 bombing). That was called a "search and destroy" mission and how the war was fought. That's what a lot of people don't understand, there was no safe place.

After spending three months with the mechanized unit, I was transferred to the 25th Infantry Division's Command Maintenance Management Inspection (CMMI) team. In my new assignment I was responsible for inspecting all of the division's PLLs. The 25th Division had three main base camps: Cu Chi, Tay Ninh, and Dau Tieng. Our inspection team would fly by helicopter to these base camps and return to Cu Chi after our inspection. Because we were constantly flying, this became the hazardous part of my job. Fortunately, we were never shot down.

Overall, there was a lack of autonomy in the army. All orders had to be followed. I remember one time I disobeyed orders because I felt they were unfair. Usually in the morning because we go from one base camp to another base camp, they would tell us if we were to pull any duty, like sentry duties or k.p., before we flew out. On this one morning, nothing was said to me in terms of duties, so I flew out to another base camp, did my inspection with the team, came back, and then I was told I had to do duties. I didn't think that was right, so I talked to my sergeant, and he said he would try to do something for me. Well, the next day, nothing was done on my behalf and I was called in to see the commanding officer for disobeying a direct order. Prior to seeing him, I spoke to my major, who was in charge of our inspection team. He assured me everything would be all right. Apparently, he had discussed my situation with the colonel who was in charge of all the units under his command. Because of the severity of my action, it was still necessary for me to see my commanding officer. He chewed me out for over twenty minutes and threatened me with an Article 15 (reprimand and penalty). I knew his actions were only a show and for him to save face. I left without being punished and knew I had dodged a bullet.

Not long after this incident, I approached my major for advice. I found out the 25th Infantry Division Artillery wanted me. My major gave his approval for the transfer. I knew he was leaving Vietnam shortly and that once gone I would no longer have his protection or support. On the day of my transfer, after a brief conversation with my major, he saluted me. I was totally taken aback by this and felt very honored and proud. To this day, I will always cherish that moment. Deep in my heart, I know my major had genuine respect and understanding for who I was and what I had accomplished while a member of his inspection team.[4]

The two most frightening experiences occurred in the latter part of my tour. After transferring to the Division Artillery, I worked as a PLL clerk and continued to assist other artillery PLLs in preparation for their CMMI inspection. I was in Tay Ninh for a week. When I came back, right where my bed was, a mortar had hit and the roof was all shredded. There was metal and shrapnel all over the place. That really blew my mind! After seeing this, I was hoping the rest of my tour would be less dangerous. Well, all hell broke out about forty days before I came home. What happened in this artillery unit was that the whole base camp exploded under attack one night. The V.C. hit where I was and they hit another portion where the tanks were and they hit the helicopter pad. What they were trying to do was destabilize our forces. The first initial report that we got was that "Charlie" had hit the perimeter, come through about fifty yards, and was shooting r.p.g. rounds at some of our armors (r.p.g. rounds are used to take out heavy artillery). This soldier came back in serious condition because they were throwing grenades and the closeness of the blasts had given him shell shock. By this time all of us had to go out, and I was a specialist E-5, which was equivalent to a sergeant, so there was a certain perimeter that I had to be in command of. We were there all night waiting to see if we were going to be probed or come under heavy attack. All night we fired at any movement or flashes aimed at the base camp. The next morning you could see a lot of dead bodies out there and some Viet Cong were decapitated. That was probably the most terrifying experience for me. I made a promise to myself that if I had an opportunity to come back [safe], then everything and everyday I would appreciate my life more. If you have had anything traumatic happen to you, getting into a bad auto accident or somebody close to you gets injured, it can be a cold feeling. But this thing in Nam, of being stressed out or fearful for a long duration of time, was difficult for a lot of people, including me.

COMING HOME

The best way to describe how I felt at the end of my tour was, by the time I got into the airplane and I knew that I was up, even though I was still in Vietnam air space, I said to myself, I don't really give a shit what happens now. I don't really care if this plane blows up, I'm out of Vietnam. It was a great

4. Johnny Wong received numerous written commendations for his outstanding performance as a PLL inspector in Germany and Vietnam as well as the Army Commendation Medal and the Bronze Star Medal for his meritorious service while with the 25th Infantry Division in Vietnam.

sense of relief from feeling scared like hell every day of my life. Flying back home, all I did was sleep. I mean, after that whole year of sleeping with one eye open and your rifle by your bed, I really slept.

The reality of how I got processed out was that I went to Oakland and spent about 24 or 36 hours there. One of the requirements was that we had to put on the uniforms when we stepped out. I remember I wanted to just walk out and take a cab home and that's it. A lot of Vietnam veterans came back and were not able to adjust because one of the things that I felt, and I'm pretty sure a lot of guys felt this way, was a sense of not having any respect or having any feeling that we had done a good job. I remember this chaplain saying to everyone, "Would you like to re-up [sign up] again?" And all of us were saying, "Fuck you!" It was just a really bad joke. It was a lonely feeling coming back and knowing what the country was going through, and we were just let go like that. They didn't situate us in a group and say, this is what we expect. It was just like that's it, it's over, but for a lot of people it wasn't over.

I can't remember if I took a cab home or if they had a bus. All I remember is approaching my parents' house and seeing a lot of Asian families. There wasn't any joy one way or the other. It was just like, you're home. All I can remember was what I wanted to do was rest, to release my feelings without being bombarded by any distractions. For about four or five months, I didn't really do anything. It was like I was in a daze. Is this real? Am I safe? For a long time I didn't think about anything more than two or three hours in front of me, and now that I was back home, I had no real game plan for what I was gonna do. Eventually I thought, maybe I'll finish up school, maybe I'll get a job, things like that. But it just came gradually.[5]

A high school friend that I bumped into in Vietnam, he came back. We became friends and subsequently, we began playing mah-jongg together. I still remember this one time we were playing and he was sitting there *(points across from him)* and I was sitting here. It was close to the Fourth of July and we heard this "whoosh!!" That same sound I told you about for the rockets. Well, he went this way and I went that way *(waves his hands in opposite directions)* and the other two guys we were with were like, what the fuck are you guys doing? It was just a gut reaction. We freaked out and they laughed at it and we laughed at it afterward, but it was just our normal reflexes. And this was two years after I came back! I will never forget that sound. Like every April 1, April Fool's Day, it's really traumatizing because I always think back to Vietnam. May 22, when I got out. You know, those things that I won't forget . . . *(starts to cry).*

5. Wong eventually earned his B.A. degree in recreation from San Francisco State University and worked for the San Francisco Parks and Recreation Department for a few years before returning to work for the U.S. Postal Service.

It took me more than two years to be able to express any of my feelings. I knew that I had changed a hundred percent. And I knew that friends and people in general were relatively sane. I mean, they weren't impacted by something traumatizing like Vietnam, so how could they relate to me if they never experienced that? Once you have felt that constant pressure of being fearful, like it's each minute of each day, you couldn't go beyond that. The only reason I kept my sanity in Vietnam was by concentrating on what I had to do. As much as I thought we should not be there, I felt what I was doing was important and possibly might save some lives. Even though I wasn't out there on a daily basis fighting, you had these young kids out there fighting. If they didn't get the support from people responsible for that, then they would have more to worry about. That's why I felt a genuine regard toward my responsibilities. On one hand, I was worrying about myself every day. Then on the other hand, I tried to do what I could to help others. I think the combination helped me get through it all.

I had come back from Vietnam more or less in one piece, other than a few psychological problems. I wasn't going to go overboard and feel obsessed with anything. I wouldn't let myself be bothered by trivial things. One of the things I had problems with while I was growing up was my patience. If I didn't like hearing something, I would just totally explode, I would just go bonkers. I have since learned tolerance. It's like waiting in line, sometimes you get a lot of static from people saying things like, what's going on and why is this taking so long? Well, I just say, hey, I'll put up with it. And if I don't want to put up with it, I just walk away because I don't want to waste my time. What I went through in Vietnam just changed everything. It changed the way I thought, and it changed the way I felt, and it changed the way that I wanted to be in relation to my life. Whatever I do in my life I have to enjoy, and if I don't enjoy it, there's no sense in going through the process. I might as well dig the hole now and go under.

I thought a lot about why the U.S. was involved in Vietnam. Putting it in proper context, there was some sincerity in helping South Vietnam out. I knew that, but to what extent do you help out when it's a civil war? The big difference was that in World War II, you had guys like Hitler. The mentality [in the sixties] was the domino effect. If you don't stop communism here, it will act like a row of dominos, but that proved to be wrong. My feelings were, hey, enough is enough. I felt that the U.S. should get out of there because it was not a winnable war. They didn't have a plan or an objective. They just went in and fought and bombed and destroyed things at random. Like the last line in the film *Platoon:* "It doesn't mean a thing." That's how I felt. That's how a lot of soldiers felt because the majority didn't want to be there. I know that for a fact. I feel sad for those people who didn't come back home. Back then and still now I feel sorry for the whole country of Vietnam and for the people because they shouldn't have to go through so much war.

The [memorial] wall in Washington, D.C., did a lot of healing. Just knowing the fact that they, the government, went out of their way to engrave the names of all the people that died. That was the start of the healing. I think it would take more than courage for me to go there, I don't think I have the heart. I think I would be overwhelmed. At one time they had a replica of the wall out here and a friend of mine told me about it and I just didn't have the courage to go.

. . .

There was this guy that went to the same high school as me and we were in the same boot camp. It was during my last week and a half in boot camp, and I was really sick, and the last thing we all had to do was go through this fifteen-mile run and hike. It was tough because I had a backpack and I had to carry my rifle, and this guy—he was black and his name was Niles—saw me struggling and he helped me carry my rifle. Prior to that, the drill sergeant had said if you fell out you'd have to go through another six weeks of boot camp. I didn't want to go through another period like this, so without this guy helping me, I wouldn't have made it. When I got out of the service I found out he got killed in Vietnam, and you know, that really bothered me. It really comes down to a lot of wasted life, because you or I don't know what any of these people could have done in terms of accomplishments and living a full life. That's how I look back at it. Close to 60,000 servicemen died in this war, for what? Really, for what?

SOURCE: Johnny Wong, interview with Jason Chang, February 8 and 25, 1998, San Francisco, California, Special Collections, McHenry Library, University of California, Santa Cruz.

OTHER REFERENCES

C. A. del Rosario, *A Different Battle: Stories of Asian Pacific American Veterans* (Seattle: Wing Luke Museum and University of Washington Press, 1999).

Peter Kiang, "About Face: Recognizing Asian and Pacific American Vietnam Veterans in Asian American Studies," *Amerasia Journal* 17, no. 3 (1991): 22–40.

Chalsa Loo and Peter Kiang, "Race-related Stressors and Psychological Trauma: Contributions of Asian American Vietnam Veterans," in *Asian Americans: Vulnerable Populations, Model Interventions, and Clarifying Agendas,* ed. Lin Zhan (Boston: Jones & Bartlett Publishers, 2003), pp. 19–42.

Alethea Yip, "Enemies All Around: Asian American Vietnam Vets Paid a Special Price for Service to Their Country," *Asian Week,* November 3, 1995, p. 17.

"I'm a Chinaman"

An Interview with Frank Chin (1970)

Jeffery Paul Chan

The era of the antiwar, black power, and Asian American movements motivated many second-generation Chinese Americans to challenge white racism and assert their ethnic identity as neither Oriental nor white American, but uniquely and integrally as Chinese American. One of the most outspoken and influential writers of this period was Frank Chin. Born in 1940 in Berkeley, California, he did his undergraduate studies at the University of California at Berkeley, and also attended the University of Iowa Writers' Workshop and the University of California at Santa Barbara. Upon graduation, Chin purposefully got a job as a brakeman with the Southern Pacific Railroad before moving to Seattle to write scripts for the King Broadcasting Company. In 1969 he moved back to California, where he lectured in Asian American studies at the University of California, Davis, and San Francisco State College while helping to found the Combined Asian Resources Project (CARP)[1] and the Asian American Theater Workshop.

At the time of this interview with his colleague Jeffery Paul Chan, a short story writer and chair of Asian American studies at San Francisco State College, Chin had just been physically knocked down by Alex Hing, leader of the Red Guard, a revolutionary organization in San Francisco Chinatown, for calling the organization "a yellow minstrel show." More important, the interview is one of the earliest records of Chin's views on white racism, the emasculation of Chinese men in mainstream media, and the need for Chinese American writers to reclaim an authentic cultural identity — themes that would reoccur in his later writings. The interview was published in East / West, *a bilingual weekly founded in 1967 to cover events and concerns of interest to Chinese Americans throughout the country. The paper folded in 1985.*

1. CARP consisted of a group of teachers, scholars, and writers who were interested in promoting a deeper understanding of Chinese American sensibilities through conducting oral histories and creating curriculum materials for schools. The group also helped to get literary classics such as John Okada's *No No Boy* and Louis Chu's *Eat a Bowl of Tea* republished.

Frank Chin. (Photo
by Connie Hwang)

Regarded as the "Godfather of Asian American literature," Chin first won acclaim when his plays The Chickencoop Chinaman *(1972) and* The Year of the Dragon *(1974) became the first Chinese American plays to be produced on the New York stage and on national television. Chin is also known for the groundbreaking* Aiiieeeee! An Anthology of Asian-American Writers *(1974) and* The Big Aiiieeeee! An Anthology of Chinese American and Japanese American Literature *(1991), both of which he coedited with Lawson Inada, Shawn Wong, and Jeffery Paul Chan. His other published works include* The Chinaman Pacific and Frisco R.R. Co., *a collection of short stories; two novels,* Donald Duk *and* Gunga Din Highway; *and* Bulletproof Buddhists and Other Essays.

Why did you come back from Seattle to Chinatown?
I didn't come back just to be beaten up . . . I came back because . . . well, there was you [the interviewer, Jeffery Paul Chan] and a few others, and I felt that the Chinese were beginning to speak out more on their own. It seemed that Chinatown was becoming more aware of itself and its own terms. It was also very obvious to me, outside working in an admittedly white world, that the stereotypes were very confining. That even though I was out, a free

individual, an agent, that I was very confined by the stereotypes. I was always being measured against the stereotypes and having to say I was or I wasn't what someone else thought I was before he'd ever met me.

What stereotype/types?
The Chinese American, native born, has attributed to him all of Chinese culture. Well, not all of Chinese culture, but the good image—the high aesthetic Chinese culture. This is the China of the literary . . . the China of the watercolor painting, the China of the civil service administration, and it's the China I don't relate to because I don't relate to China at all. I was born here. The other side of the coin, well, besides having all this great Chinese culture—we're very Americanized. And the proof of this is . . . well, we're engineers, we enter the professions . . . but these are all . . . as a mass . . . the apex of our achievement . . . places us in the role of being nothing but servants . . . servants to a larger machine, servants of Boeing, of Lockheed, of TRW [Thompson-Remo-Woolridge Corporation]. That we have not among us any who are known for pushing just something Chinese American, achieving on just Chinese American terms, the way the blacks have, Chicanos, the Indians. That we never really contributed to the culture.

What's wrong with a benign stereotype . . . we seem to live comfortably within it, under it?
Yes, it's benign, yet it becomes very frustrating to individual Chinese Americans, I think. The most insidious part of the stereotype is . . . not in so many words—they don't say this—but under analysis, looking for masculine characteristics, you find none. That the stereotype of the Chinese is utterly without masculine prerogatives. The only images of Chinese Americans—Chinese here under Western eyes—are waiters, laundrymen—okay, that's the old. And the new ones, you know, the good engineers, the nice doctors, all very nice, all very conservative . . . all passive. This makes them the ideal subject race, the ideal employees, the ideal servants.

Have you modified your thinking about "masculine prerogatives" when you were met with a street faction within Chinatown that displayed a hostile, aggressive posture toward you?
(laughter) Well, no. I've been beaten up, and I've been beaten up. *(laughter)* Ahh . . . I don't consider the American Legion more masculine or more manly because they beat me up. I think I was beaten up kind of Western style. Maybe I was lucky in that . . . that I didn't have one of these legendary forms of Oriental self-defense used on me. But what style of masculinity were they asserting? Styles of masculinity are important. If we consider ourselves to have no style of our own and are compelled, therefore, to imitate others—and this is something I think we've been taught from birth. We have to imitate English, or we have to imitate Chinese, though we're neither. Then, when

we hit puberty, to become men, we have to imitate the Chicanos or the blacks or the whites or somebody else. And this serves to keep us in Chinatown . . . because in imitation—you know there is something contemptible about imitation—and when that's the only option open to us . . . when we adopt a role, when we imitate, we are also taking on a certain amount of self-contempt. And this is something the culture itself has taught us to do here.

Make a distinction between imitation and assimilation.
Assimilation is a very general term. To my mind it's not just adapting or adjusting to the culture, it's being able to take certain traits, certain values of the culture and turn them into your own. And then, turn them into something else. Just what the blacks have done. Let's say they assimilated the English language. But they turned the language into something of their own. It's not just strictly American English. So that the language they speak is an act of assimilation in that it's based in English, but it is not the English that is generally spoken or acceptable in schools. It's simply Black English. The language communicates the unique black experience. And in turn it has affected the general culture. So it demands that the general culture assimilate some of the black experience.

How can you compare the black experience to the Chinese experience in America? I mean, haven't the unique Chinese institutions, language, etc., done a lot to keep the two cultures distinct?
Well, I think the continuity of Chinese culture from China to America is largely mythical. One of the institutions . . . the family . . . we're told the strong Chinese family—this is why the low crime rate and this is why Chinese are more obedient and passive. Well, you know, women were barred from entry, Chinese women were barred from entering California into this country. Until the turn of the century, when a few of them began to appear in noticeable numbers, then . . . at the turn of the century, there were twenty-eight men for every woman. This means that for the larger part of our history here, our population has been male. And I ask you, what kind of Chinese family do you maintain with just a transient male population? The other part of the mythical Chinese culture is that . . . well we are culturally passive. This is not so, and it isn't even so of Chinese American history: that between 1850 and 1905, there were Chinese in the Supreme Court of the United States or California protesting against city ordinances, state laws, union activities that they felt were unconstitutional. Going to the Supreme Court is far from passive resistance. The stereotypes, historically, of Chinese having no manhood, were false. The stereotypes of the continuity of Chinese culture between China and here were false. And this myth of Chinese culture has been used to confine us, to oppress intellectually, culturally, and to certainly suppress and restrain our individual development. I don't know that this was a calculated plot, but it's working out that way.

What has all this got to do with this play you've written? Does the play take the above into account?
Well, now, with this play, we dredge up a lot of these old stereotypes that are still operating here, now.

What's it called?
Dear lo fan, fan gwai, whitey, honey babe.[2] It's addressed to the whites, because I see that the stereotypes were not manufactured by the Chinese at all, but by the whites. The white point of view is—well, "You Chinese, you take care of yourselves. If you have any problems in Chinatown, why, that's your hang-up." I don't think that's so. If we have problems in Chinatown, it's largely the fault of the whites. They don't want to take responsibility, they don't admit to holding these stereotypes, and yet when you talk to them long enough, you see that they do. I think they have to be convinced that Chinese can speak for themselves. Remember that Mary Ellen Leary article in the *Atlantic Monthly*, in March, she says the most aggrieved minority in San Francisco cannot speak for themselves, and that's supposed to be us.[3]

Now in the play, we hit Mary Ellen Leary by name. I mean, we're obviously speaking English, or a kind of English, and at least enough so we can understand her. And we dress up in the play in grotesque imitation of her, just as whites have dressed up in grotesque images of us and we read what she has to say: That the Chinese can't speak English. If this doesn't make her nervous, well . . . there's nothing we can do but blow up everything. I think it will make her nervous.

Do you attack other writers who have written similarly about the Chinese in the play?
Yeah. A Christian writer, a Rev. John L. Nevius who pushes very hard . . . in the positive sense . . . the stereotype of the Chinese who has no masculinity.[4] He justifies this by saying that we are characteristically timid and docile and he rationalizes that this is good. Remember this is from the white point of view about a subject race, and he reasons that while the Chinese are deficient in active courage and daring, they are not in passive resistance. Now this attitude comes out more clearly in another writer we attack in the play, Jack London, great American author. If you're deficient in active courage and daring, this means that when you get whipped, you're not going to jump up and do anything about it. But in passive resistance, if you have a lot of passive resistance, you'll just sit there and endure it. Some things we'll endure and some things we won't, as a people, as an individual. I am not personally up to enduring

2. The play consisted of a series of skits written by students, staff, and faculty at San Francisco State College that attempted to skew racial stereotypes of Chinese Americans.
3. Mary Ellen Leary, "San Francisco Chinatown," *Atlantic Monthly*, March 1970, pp. 32–42.
4. John L. Nevius (1829–93) served as a Presbyterian missionary in China for over forty years and wrote *China and the Chinese* (New York: Harper & Bros., 1869).

much more white trash written about us. Over the past year, about eight articles have been written about us, in national magazines. Only two were written by Chinese—one by you, and they boxed that, they put a black border around it, as if to say gee whiz, Jeffery Chan's a real Chinaman.[5] So again, you were put in the role of a servant, to a white man at that. And that's a crime.

Look at the other one by Min Yee in *Newsweek,* February 23rd.[6] It was an article on Chinatown written by a Chinese American, it ran down old information about Chinatown but information that has not received national attention from a major news magazine. But what he did wrong was close his article with the admission that he was whitewashed. This is not just an individual confession, it was for us. You can see this if you were to pick up an article by a black writer on the ills of the black ghetto in Oakland, California. No black writer in his right mind would end such an article saying, I never had such problems, but then, I'm an Uncle Tom. Min Yee does just that by ending his article saying "but then I never had such problems because I was whitewashed." Here he is, our only national journalist in how many years, admitting that the only way to success is to become white. And he's not talking to Chinese, nor is he talking for them, but he's talking for whites and the Chinese are again eavesdroppers.

This play doesn't do that. Here we are, speaking as Chinese Americans. We hold our audience in contempt, the white audiences, and we are talking to the whites not about the problems in Chinatown as isolated incidents, but as problems that they were and are largely responsible for. Chinese America is larger than any one community, even larger than San Francisco's Chinatown. The identity problem that faces many Chinese Americans is centered around the myth that the only real Chinatown, the real Chinese America, is San Francisco's Chinatown. If they were all to act on that, the density rate would be a lot worse than it is now. As we travel with this play, I hope we'll give the Chinese themselves a larger view of Chinese America. That they should think of Chinese America not just in terms of Chinatown, San Francisco, but in terms of the whole country.

The opening passage of the play introduces what you would call a Chinese American folk song: Chink, Chink Chinaman, etc. I find that objectionable. Nobody calls me a Chink or Chinaman.
This is a white folk song that came out of the gold rush . . . and if we forget it, we've lost proof, documentary proof of white racism against the Chinese.

5. Jeffery Paul Chan's "Let 100 Problems Bloom" appeared in the *Los Angeles Times's West* magazine on January 4, 1970, p. 15, following a longer article by Kenneth Lamott, "The Awakening of Chinatown," pp. 6–14.
6. Min Yee, "Chinatown in Crisis," *Newsweek,* February 23, 1970, pp. 57–58.

This is a grotesque but not unfair analogy: ask the Jews, why talk about Auschwitz and the concentration camps? Just forget the names. But . . . they remember the names. Not for their own humiliation, but to remind Germany of their guilt. If we lose Chink, Chink Chinaman, then we've effectively buried white guilt.

Now dramatically, in the play, the puppet narrator is the character who represents the Chinese American controlled, being puppeted by the white culture. He sings Chink, Chink Chinaman. In the play, he encourages the audience to sing along with him. And once they get involved singing, we tell them to shut up. That this is a terrible song, that they've been singing it to us for a long time, for over a hundred years, and that tonight we're going to sing them this song . . . we don't want it anymore . . . it's their song . . . not ours. And the gesture is to insult the audience, to make them aware that the song is offensive. That it has offended us. The way to respond to that—the insults—was to say, that kid's stupid, don't pay any attention. Well, I don't think our kids have to put up with that anymore. I think we should try to encourage people who sing these songs to not sing them anymore. We are the right people to sing this song, to remind the whites, to document their white racism.

Do you think of yourself as a Chinese, Chinese American, Chinaman?
I do think of myself as a Chinaman. I'm fifth generation here. My great-grandfather, great-great-grandfather came over here to work on the railroad. He was called a Chinaman. He worked honorably as a Chinaman. He probably lost his life as a Chinaman. The whites, they laughed at that name. But, it's the only name I know my ancestors by and it's not my ancestors who made it a bad name. Great-grandfather was an honorable guy, as a Chinaman . . . that's what the whites called him. So . . . I'm a Chinaman. But, I do demand respect for the name. Not as a term of derision . . . in the same way that *black* used to be a term of humiliation . . . and they fight over it. But they've turned this word into an act of pride. And I think the term *Chinaman*, because it is our only connection with our ancestors, is something to be proud of. I think we should all be Chinamen.

SOURCE: *East/West*, April 22, 1970, pp. 5, 8.

OTHER REFERENCES

Frank Chin, "Confessions of the Chinatown Cowboy," *Bulletin of Concerned Asian Scholars* 4, no. 3 (fall 1972): 58–70.

Frank Chin and Jeffery Paul Chan, "Racist Love," in *Seeing through Shuck,* ed. Richard Kostelanetz (New York: Ballantine, 1972), pp. 65–79.

Gloria Heyung Chun, *Of Orphans and Warriors: Inventing Chinese American Culture and Identity* (New Brunswick, N.J.: Rutgers University Press, 2000).

David L. Eng, *Racial Castration: Managing Masculinity in Asian America* (Durham: Duke University Press, 2001).

Elaine Kim, "Chinatown Cowboys and Warrior Women: Searching for a New Self-Image," in *Asian American Literature: An Introduction to the Writings and Their Social Context* (Philadelphia: Temple University Press, 1982), pp. 173–213.

Major Education Problems Facing the Chinese Community (1972)

L. Ling-chi Wang

Following on the heels of the civil rights movement, Chinese Americans began to agitate for equal rights and social change in the areas of education, employment, housing, health, immigration, and services to youths and the elderly. In 1970 Chinese parents filed a class action suit (Lau v. Nichols) *against the San Francisco Unified School District for denying their non-English-speaking children equal education according to the Civil Rights Act of 1964. The lawsuit went through two appeals before the U.S. Supreme Court ruled in its landmark decision of January 21, 1974, that the school district, in failing to provide special assistance to Chinese-speaking students, had denied them "a meaningful opportunity to participate in the public education program." Thus, in the midst of heated discussions in the nation over desegregation and busing, bilingual education programs were formally launched in the public schools.*

One of the chief strategists behind Lau v. Nichols *and a strong proponent of bilingual education was Ling-chi Wang, a doctoral student at the University of California, Berkeley, and the director of the Youth Service Center in San Francisco Chinatown at the time. Born in Xiamen, Fujian Province, Wang had emigrated as a student from Hong Kong in 1957 to study Semitic languages and literature at Princeton University. But after relocating to the San Francisco Bay Area, he found his true calling in political activism. Prior to making the following speech before the U.S. Senate Committee on Equal Educational Opportunity, he had been instrumental in organizing a protest march in Chinatown to call attention to growing social problems in the community and in founding Chinese for Affirmative Action to deal with these problems. A social reformist at heart, Wang believed institutional and systemic change was key to improving the life chances of all Chinese Americans. Tackling the public schools was a necessary first step. Wang would go on to spearhead many other civil rights battles and head the Ethnic Studies Department at UC Berkeley.*

Headed by Senator Walter F. Mondale, the Committee on Equal Educational Opportunity was formed to ensure the uniform application of school desegregation stan-

Ling-chi Wang *(right)* and Larry Lew *(left)* accepting the 1971 Emmy Award for the Sut Yung Ying Yee English-learning series produced by KPIX-TV and Chinese for Affirmative Action. (Photo by Connie Hwang)

dards and funding throughout the nation. Public hearings were held from the end of 1970 to early 1973 on all aspects of equal educational opportunity. Wang joined other educators and community activists in the San Francisco Bay Area on March 5, 1971, to apprise the Senate committee of desegregation efforts and the overall quality of education in their local public schools. Statistical tables and the Q & A discussion that followed his speech have been omitted.

Mr. Chairman, my name is L. Ling-chi Wang; I am the director of the Youth Service Center in Chinatown, an organization that works with delinquent and pre-delinquent school youth in the Chinese community in San Francisco. I welcome this opportunity to address this committee on what I consider major educational problems facing the Chinese community—problems facing the community which are deeply embedded in a traditional school system that has been denying equal and quality education to our youth.

In academic year 1969–70, there were 115,457 students attending the public schools in San Francisco. Of these, 16,574 or 14.4 percent were Chinese. . . .

These figures reflect a unique situation in San Francisco. The San Francisco Bay Area has the distinction of being the only area in the U.S. with a high concentration of Chinese population. This, of course, is not the result of historical accident; rather, it is the result of the perpetuation of a policy designed to exploit and discriminate against the Chinese. It is not my intention here to recount that history nor is it my purpose to seek your sympathy. My intention, rather, is to present facts, historical and contemporary, as far as they are related to equal educational opportunity for the Chinese students. My hope is that your committee, and later, the Congress of the U.S., will act appropriately and promptly to correct the injustice of the past and restore our rights.

An understanding of the problems I am about to enumerate is inseparable from the past. I, therefore, will begin with some remarks on some historical efforts established to prevent the Chinese from attaining equal educational opportunity.

In 1860, the California State Legislature declared that "Negroes, Mongolians and Indians shall not be admitted into the public schools," but that separate schools might be established for their education. No segregated school, however, was established until 1887, when present-day Commodore Stockton School was founded. Thus, from the very beginning, the Chinese were denied access to education. The Legislature liberalized this policy in 1866 by providing that the restriction only applied to Negroes, Mongolians, or Indian children "not living under the care of white persons," and that children not so cared for "whose education can be provided in no other way," such as [a] segregated school, could attend a school for white children if the school board approved and if a majority of the white parents did not object. The separate school policy was upheld by the California Supreme Court in 1874 and remained in the law until 1947. In 1880 the Legislature amended its Political Code to provide local school boards with the power to exclude "children of filthy or vicious habits, or children suffering from contagious or infectious diseases." The San Francisco schools used this amendment to exclude the Chinese students. However, in 1885, the California Supreme Court held that Mamie Tape, a Chinese girl, was entitled to enter the San Francisco schools, pointing out also that "it is not alleged that she is vicious, or filthy, or that she has a contagious or infectious disease *[Tape v. Hurley]*." Nine days after the decision, the Code was amended to read, "When separate schools are established, Chinese or Mongolian children must not be admitted into any other school." This amendment was upheld by the Federal Court in 1902 *[Him v. Callahan]*. As I mentioned above, the segregated school law was not repealed until 1947, although admittance of Chinese students into white school gained wide acceptance during and after World War II.

I. THE LANGUAGE PROBLEM

Gaining admission into white schools, however, in no way guaranteed equal and quality education, nor did it improve significantly the opportunity of

Chinese students to compete with white students in higher education and in achieving equal employment opportunity in the society. I will now address myself to four areas of great concern to the Chinese community: (1) the language problems, (2) the disciplinary problems, (3) curriculum and the Chinese, and (4) discrimination against Chinese teachers and administrators.

No reliable figures are available for the number of non-English-speaking Chinese students in San Francisco because there has never been any standardized test designed to test Chinese students for their English language proficiency. Surveys, to date, on students' English language proficiency have been conducted crudely and unscientifically through information supplied by classroom teachers and on-site principals. Not only were the teachers not trained in the method of assessing students' language ability, [but] not all schools participated in these surveys and not all teachers took these surveys for their schools. Immigrant students, in most cases, are placed in classes commensurate with their ages, rather than their language ability and intellectual development. . . . It is important to note that 42 percent of the Chinese-speaking students in the elementary level are not receiving special instruction, 54.5 percent at junior high and 21.8 percent at senior high. It is also significant to note that among those registered as receiving special instruction in English, most are receiving at most 50 minutes of special instruction a day.

What do these figures mean? They mean quite simply that thousands of Chinese students at all levels are being placed in classes by their ages, sent through the school system and graduated sometimes not knowing the language; they mean that many of the non-English-speaking students are falling hopelessly behind their classmates; they mean that these students are spending anxious and frustrated hours in schools daily; they mean considerable numbers of them are truant and becoming potential drop-outs, a phenomenon least likely to occur among the Chinese.

The San Francisco Unified School District has tried to overcome this serious problem with 29 full-time and 15 part-time teachers over and above the regular school staffing. They hardly meet the needs of all non-English-speaking students. Besides, many of these teachers are untrained and unprepared to face this problem. They have been given little or no special curriculum designed to teach the Chinese.

In this connection, I would like to point out that the approach used by the Unified School District in teaching these Chinese-speaking students has been almost exclusively audio-lingual method, commonly known as the ESL method. This method is quite different from the bilingual approach spelt out under Title VII of the ESEA.[1] I have no objection to the use of ESL as a

1. Passed by Congress in 1967, Title VII of the Elementary and Secondary Education Act recommended bilingual education programs as a way to improve the education of non-English-speaking schoolchildren.

means of instructing English to non-English-speakers, but I strongly object to the use of ESL as an end in itself. I am referring specifically to the exclusive use of ESL in such a way that the native language, culture and knowledge of these children are systematically suppressed and downgraded. The desire on the part of many well-meaning ESL teachers to help students in acquiring English as quickly as possible may be perfectly sincere and innocent. Yet in their innocence they are causing serious permanent damage to the overall growth of these same students. Exclusive use of the ESL method entertains no consideration of the children's native intelligence, provides no respect for their native language and culture and ignores and negates everything they know in their native language. Inadvertently, students are humiliated and abused. I am fearful that we are doing injustice to our Chinese- and Spanish-speaking children and I regret that, by ignoring and suppressing the Chinese language and culture, we are depriving American students of one of the richest cultural heritages brought to this country by immigrant children. I believe the best method of overcoming the language problem is the use of bilingual education as conceived by the Congress of the United States under Title VII of the ESEA.

In conjunction with the problem of teaching a new language, I would like to further point out another highly destructive and racist attitude current among many white teachers. I am referring to teachers who delight in publicly ridiculing and humiliating students speaking English with a slight Chinese accent. To them, no one speaks more accurate English than they do. They delight themselves in picking on the speech behavior of the Chinese students and finding fault in every student from the Chinese community. This attitude easily causes severe psychological damage to the students and greatly inhibits students from active participation in classroom activities. Little wonder Chinese students have gained the reputation of being docile, quiet and hardworking! I am further distressed by the prevailing attitude that persons speaking English with a Continental accent are generally looked up to as being sophisticated and upper class. I guess for these teachers, a Chinese accent destroys the English language while a Continental accent enhances its beauty.

These teachers, to me, are ignoring the simple fact that a language—any language—is merely a means of communication and that communication is by no means impeded by a slight accent. Besides, there is no such thing as a "standard" English.

II. THE DISCIPLINARY PROBLEM

As I mentioned above, the Chinese students hold a reputation of being docile, quiet and hardworking among white teachers in San Francisco. To them, Chinese students do not question or challenge the teachers. Unfortunately, this stereotype often encourages teachers to do anything that they wish to foist upon their students. As a result, schools with predominantly Chinese students become the most sought after schools for experienced and often aging teachers with seniority. This peculiar personnel pattern soon led in Chinatown to the formation of all-white faculties, entrenched and rigid. A combination of the stereotype image of the Chinese students and the inflexible white faculty results frequently in severe disciplinary problems.

A case in point is Galileo High School. During academic year 1969–70, the 2,802 student body was made up of 1,535 Chinese (64.8 percent), 578 whites (20.6 percent), 444 blacks (15.8 percent), 145 Spanish-surnamed (5.2 percent) and a small number of other minorities. In spite of such a high percentage of Chinese students, Galileo had over 95 percent white and about 3 percent Chinese on its teaching and administrative staffs. Normally, this kind of condition at Galileo is described as a teacher's paradise because students are supposed to have no serious disciplinary problems, and teachers are not confronted with questions and challenges by students. Yet, what used to be unthinkable or rare among the "docile" Chinese students, such as absenteeism, suspensions, disciplinary problems, disciplinary transfers, dropouts, and delinquent behavior, have become normal routine at Galileo. For example, during the academic year 1968–69, Galileo ranked second in the city with 433 suspensions. Between September 10, 1969, and January 23, 1970, Galileo actually achieved the distinction of being Number One in the number of suspensions among all high schools. (Galileo registered 566 suspensions; the second highest, Wilson, showed 322.) In the same period, Galileo also ranked among the highest in the number of disciplinary transfers. As for the delinquency problem, police figures on arrests and citations of Chinese juveniles indicated that the problem increased by 600 percent during the period 1964–69. Significantly, the Chinatown–North Beach Area Youth Council's study of police records reveals that delinquency rates among Chinese youths are lowest during the summer months, indicating a close correlation between school attendance and delinquency.

What has happened to the good old days in schools with predominantly Chinese students? Are the Chinese students behaving worse today than yesterday? The clue to these and other related questions rests on the fact that the Chinese community has changed considerably in recent years,[2] yet the white teachers and administrators in Chinatown schools remain largely unchanged. To begin, the personnel pattern at Galileo is not in tune with the times. The need to recruit Chinese teachers on the faculty was never taken

2. Later, during the Q & A discussion, Wang elaborated on the causes of juvenile delinquency—dislocated Chinese families and parental neglect due to the long hours of harsh working conditions, and frustrated youths who felt trapped by their lack of English-language ability, cultural differences, and inability to get out of Chinatown and find jobs.

seriously. Secondly, the stereotype image of the Chinese students became obsolete as Chinese students became more conscious of their ethnic origin and more aware of their rights. Furthermore, recent increases of non-English-speaking students brought new problems to the teachers who were not prepared to deal with them. Instead of accepting these changes and seeking new solutions, the school chose to ignore or suppress these problems. Result: frustration and anger among students and parents. More and more students became alienated from their white teachers, counselors and administrators. Failure to recognize these problems and to cope with them creatively and open-mindedly led the schoolteachers and administrators to resort to traditional tactics, that is, the use of disciplinary measures. Unfortunately, these repressive means could never resolve the educational problems at school. In fact, they merely aggravated the problems. And in the meantime, students are being denied an opportunity to receive equal and quality education.

III. CURRICULUM AND THE CHINESE

Another area of inequality in education is the curriculum. As one of the minority groups in the U.S., the Chinese have been given no fair treatment in school textbooks and in curriculum in general.

In textbooks, almost without exception, the Chinese are depicted variously as vicious, cruel, stupid, sneaky, untrustworthy, inscrutable, filthy, etc. These depictions came directly from historical attitude and treatment of the Chinese in California. Unfortunately, little or nothing is being done to remove these obviously racist portrayals of the Chinese. The effects of these misconceptions of the Chinese are tremendous and quite detrimental to the welfare of the Chinese people in the U.S. For example, many of our youngsters are brought up to be ashamed of their own people and to look down upon anything Chinese. They are taught exclusively white, Anglo-Saxon, middle-class values in schools. Daily their Chinese value system is shot down or ridiculed by a value system presented to them as being superior. As a result, many have lost their self-respect and have developed a strong sense of inferiority complex.

Others try to lose their Chinese identity and tongue by rebelling against their parents and refusing to have anything to do with their parents. On account of this, many homes in our community are broken.

Equally destructive are the effects of these racist depictions on fellow students and the general public. Often times, Chinese become victims of public hostility and mistrust. We are denied equal employment and educational opportunity; we are prevented access to certain schools, recreational facilities and neighborhoods.

Looking now at the school curriculum, it is ironic to note that it has so little to do with one of the most important races and cultures of the world.

In terms of language and culture, the Chinese people have as much, if not more, to offer to the world. Yet our school curriculum continues to ignore the Chinese and their contribution to world civilization, denying, therefore, the American students the right to know more about China and her people and culture.

It is in this connection that I wish to plead for better and fairer treatment and coverage of the Chinese people, language and culture. It is high time that the Chinese heritage be rightfully restored to our students.

IV. DISCRIMINATION AGAINST CHINESE TEACHERS, ADMINISTRATORS

We come now to an area of discrimination which has considerable influence over the quality of education for the Chinese students. I am referring to the lack of Chinese teachers, counselors and administrators in the Unified School District.

It is common knowledge that urban public schools are in the midst of serious and seemingly unsolvable problems. Aside from perennial financial difficulties, public schools now face insurmountable problems dealing with school-community relations, counseling services, etc. All these problems, which we dealt with earlier, could be traced back to the problem of school administration and the quality of teaching staff. Unfortunately, students and communities, especially minority communities, are quite alienated from the schools at the moment. Certainly, one of the major causes of alienation is the failure of schoolteachers, counselors and administrators to relate with the needs of minority students and communities. This failure, I submit, is caused largely by the lack of minority school personnel. I will now comment on this subject from the Chinese perspective.

According to statistics compiled by the S.F. Unified School District, there were 115,457 students in the elementary, secondary and adult schools in academic year 1969–1970. Of these, 43,980 or 38.1 percent were white, 29,275 or 25.4 percent black, 17,026 or 14.7 percent Spanish surname, and 16,574 or 14.4 percent were Chinese. However, figures on teaching and administrative staff of the SFUSD for the same academic year show that 3,980 or 83 percent are white, 355 or 7 percent black, 121 or 3 percent Spanish surname and 204 or 4 percent Chinese.[3]

The most important cause for the present lack of Chinese teachers, counselors and administrators in the SFUSD is discrimination. It was only in the last ten years that Chinese faces first appeared on the staff of the SFUSD in small numbers. Discrimination takes many forms. Potential Chinese teachers are excluded basically for the following reasons: (1) qualified Chinese

---

3. According to Wang in the Q & A discussion following his speech, the San Francisco school district had a policy that the faculty ethnic composition should reflect the student population.

teachers are outrightly turned away, (2) potential teachers are discouraged from entering teacher's training programs, (3) unfavorable stereotypes such as "all Chinese speak English with a Chinese accent," "Chinese are mostly not qualified to teach," "Chinese possess no public speaking skill," "Chinese bilingual teachers are all bad teachers," "immigrant teachers don't know teaching methods," etc., and (4) qualified bilingual teachers are excluded as a potential threat to monolingual teachers. In addition, (5) absence of sound and objective criteria for hiring teachers, (6) cumbersome bureaucracy, (7) elaborate patronage system and (8) tradition-bound personnel management continue to block efforts to recruit and hire more Chinese teachers, counselors and administrators. . . .

Other things being equal, in an age when the quality and effectiveness of education depend heavily on the teacher's ability to understand and relate to students, parents and communities, various ethnic and linguistic backgrounds, it is imperative that the composition of teaching staffs be reflective of the student body. The crying need for bilingual teachers and counselors is yet another reason for hiring more Chinese teachers.

It is time for the SFUSD to evaluate its recruiting, hiring and promoting policies, to reset its priorities on personnel matters and to pursue a policy that will bring justice both to qualified unemployed Chinese teachers in San Francisco numbering perhaps up to 300, and to the quality of education.

Mr. Chairman, I thank you for the opportunity to address the committee. I hope something constructive will generate from these hearings. Thank you.

SOURCE: "Prepared Statement of L. Ling-chi Wang," Equal Educational Opportunity: Hearings before Select Committee on Equal Education Opportunity of the U.S. Senate, Part 9A, 92nd Congress, 1st Session, 1972, pp. 4229–35.

OTHER REFERENCES

Victor Low, The Unimpressible Race: A Century of Educational Struggle by the Chinese in San Francisco (San Francisco: East/West Publishing Company, 1982).

L. Ling-chi Wang, "Lau v. Nichols: History of a Struggle for Equal and Quality Education," in Counterpoint: Perspectives on Asian America, ed. Emma Gee (Los Angeles: UCLA Asian American Studies Center, 1976), pp. 240–63.

On the Normalization of Relations between China and the U.S.

Prior to World War II, Chinese immigrants, subjected to white racism and political disenfranchisement in America, remained closely involved in China politics. Their involvement was also encouraged by the different political factions fighting for control of China and vying for their financial support. However, as their social and economic status improved after World War II and the United States severed diplomatic relations with "Communist China" in 1949, the Chinese began to stake their political future in America. At the same time, the Kuomintang regime in Taiwan, capitalizing on the anti-Communist atmosphere in the United States in the 1950s, seized the opportunity to dominate Chinatown politics. For the next two decades, the Chinese community would remain divided on the two-China issue.

In 1971, when the General Assembly of the United Nations (UN) voted to admit the People's Republic of China to the UN, thus displacing the Nationalist Chinese government in Taiwan, Chinese Americans were at first cautious about expressing any jubilation. But the Chinese Six Companies, as seen below, was quick to condemn the vote and proclaim unwavering support for Chiang Kai-shek and "Free China" on behalf of the entire overseas Chinese community.

Soon after, President Richard Nixon made his historic visit to Beijing to begin normalization of diplomatic relations with the People's Republic of China. As trade and traveling restrictions were lifted and full diplomatic relations with China resumed in 1979, Chinese Americans became less wary about expressing their opinions on the two-China issue. Gilbert Woo, whose anti-Kuomintang voice had been muzzled during the McCarthy period, was among the first to speak out for normalization. His editorial, which appeared in the Chinese Pacific Weekly, *espoused a new perspective, one that paid no allegiance to the Nationalists or Communists but instead urged Chinese Americans to focus their attention on community issues closer to home—"home" meaning not China, but America.*

PROCLAMATION BY THE CHINESE
SIX COMPANIES OF SAN FRANCISCO (1971)

On September 18, 1931, Japanese warlords invaded Shenyang in Manchuria. For fourteen long and arduous years, the Republic of China, as constituted by Dr. Sun Yat-sen, resisted the transgressions and massacres committed by Japanese troops and unstintingly gave up millions of human lives and innumerable material possessions to defend national territory and to struggle for the freedom of mankind. Finally, fascism was defeated and victory was achieved. In 1944, in order to "save succeeding generations from the scourge of war, which twice in our lifetime has brought untold sorrow to mankind,"[1] China participated in the Dumbarton Oaks Conference to create the United Nations and, on April 25, 1945, in the founding conference of all nations in San Francisco to draft the UN charter. Chapter 1, Article 1, states outright the purpose of the organization:

> 1. To maintain international peace and security, and to that end: to take effective collective measures for the prevention and removal of threats to the peace, and for the suppression of acts of aggression or other breaches of the peace . . .

And Article 2 says: "4. All members shall refrain in their international relations from the threat or use of force . . ."

To affirm equal rights for people, Chapter 9, Article 55, Section C of the UN Charter further states: "[The UN shall promote] universal respect for, and observance of, human rights and fundamental freedoms for all without distinction as to race, sex, language, or religion."

Chapter 5, Article 23, clearly stipulates that the Republic of China is one of the five permanent members of the Security Council. With the outside world, each member nation must maintain peace and stop aggression. With its own people, it must respect human rights; protect fundamental civil liberties and racial equality, equality of the sexes, and the freedoms of speech and religion. These high ideals and noble goals are indeed worthy of our respect and esteem. From the beginning until now, the Republic of China, as a permanent member of the Security Council, has in all sincerity discharged its obligations and with unfailing diligence remained true to its promise. Yet the current session (the 26th) of the General Assembly actually approved a motion by Albania and other pro-Communist countries to admit into the United Nations Communist China, a renegade government, which, on June 25, 1950, dispatched armed troops into South Korea, thus starting the Korean War, and, in fighting with the United Nations, killed over 200,000 American young men.[2] This is the government which was roundly condemned as

---

1. Taken from the text of the United Nations charter.
2. According to an official source, 36,913 Americans died in the Korean War (Richard Kolb, "Killed in Korea: The Untold Story," *VFW*, June/July 2000, p. 23).

an invader by the General Assembly, and is currently still in Vietnam, destroying peace and continuing to kill Americans and Vietnamese. And on the Chinese mainland, this government has been responsible for the willful slaughter of 60 million innocent lives, the trampling of civil rights, the stripping away of the fundamental liberties and rights of 700 million people, and the persecution of Christians, Catholics, Muslims and Tibetan Buddhists by arrests and imprisonment, and by the wanton destruction of their churches and temples. This renegade government is in fact the public enemy of the entire Chinese race, and, in no way, does it represent our 700 million compatriots within and without China.

In allowing Communist China to replace the Republic of China in the organization and in the Security Council, the UN is in effect violating the goals and principles of its own Charter, ignoring morals and justice, kneeling to gangsters, and bowing to the devil. Such action is shameful as well as pitiful. A once noble and respectable organization, which our Republic, through the shedding of blood and the sacrifice of countless lives, had helped to create at a great price to defend world peace, the UN is now reduced to a nesting place for rats and snakes, a den of iniquity. This organization has lost its moral compass, its noble ideals, and its reason for existing. That is why our entire overseas Chinese community unanimously approves of the withdrawal of the Republic of China from the United Nations, supports the declaration in President Chiang's message that, "With respect to the passage by the current session of the General Assembly of the illegal resolution which violates the stipulations of the Charter, the government and the people of the Republic of China absolutely refuse to recognize its validity," and is prepared to struggle. We earnestly hope that every member of our community will remain loyal and steadfast to our cause, cultivate self-reliance and remain calm in the face of misfortune, and continue to support and defend international justice and world peace. With such firm conviction and unwavering resolve, we will surely be successful in our sacred mission to recover Mainland China and to rebuild our homes. Such is the intent of this proclamation.

October 28, 1971

SOURCE: *Young China Morning Post*, October 29, 1971, pp. 2, 8. Translator: Ellen Yeung.

A TURNING POINT IN CHINATOWN (1979)

Gilbert Woo

Today's Chinese American community has reached another turning point. Based on past experience, a transition period is not necessarily a peaceful and harmonious time. During the 1911 Revolution, the Revolutionaries and the Reformists went through a period of strife. During the Northern Expedition days [1926–27], the Kuomintang and the Constitutionalists had their share of skirmishes. Both times the *Young China Morning Post* took the sides of the Revolutionaries and the Kuomintang, respectively.[1] The first time, someone charged into the pressroom to cause trouble; the second time, the newspaper was boycotted by the Ning Yung District Association.[2] Then during 1949 when the Chinese mainland turned Communist, there was a bloody battle in the Chinese-American Citizens' Alliance auditorium.[3] These were all unusual occurrences during transition periods.

This time, on the second day after the normalization of relations between China and the United States, a joint edition of the two newspapers in the city used the headline "A Peaceful Chinatown" when it reported the reaction of Chinatown.[4] This of course referred to the situation on the surface, but the fact that the newspapers treated "A Peaceful Chinatown" as newsworthy showed that they had anticipated a certain degree of confusion, or at least had believed in the possibility of conflict.

There were reasons why Chinatown was completely peaceful during the first week. First, most people knew this event was going to happen, sooner or later. Granted, the news broke quite suddenly (which showed the incompetence of Kuomintang intelligence), but people who have been reading this newspaper were definitely not taken by surprise. Second, since the breakup of the Gang of Four, the negative feelings of the community toward

1. Both the Tongmenghui (Revolutionary Party), which called for overthrowing Manchu rule and establishing a republic in China, and the Baohuanghui (Chinese Empire Reform Association), which wanted to reform the imperial system from within, vied for the financial support of overseas Chinese communities. In 1911, the Tongmenghui succeeded in its goal and under the leadership of Sun Yat-sen, the Kuomintang (Chinese Nationalist Party) emerged as a major political force in China in the early 1920s, accepting Communists as members. But after Sun's death in 1925, the Kuomintang split into left and right factions, with the right Kuomintang falling under the control of Chiang Kai-shek. During the Northern Expedition to rid the country of warlords, Chiang took the opportunity to kill off as many Communist members as he could, while in the United States, the Kuomintang competed against the Chinese Constitutionist Party (previously Baohuanghui) for control of the Chinese community. The *Young China Morning Post*, which was the official party organ of the Tongmenghui in 1910, became the voice of the Kuomintang right after the political split.

2. At the instigation of the Constitutionist Party, the Ning Yung Benevolent Association, which had the largest membership of Chinese immigrants, organized and sustained a boycott of the *Young China Morning Post* for eight years in retaliation for the newspaper's criticism of Ning Yung and the Chinese Six Companies.

3. During a celebration of the founding of the People's Republic of China at the Chinese-American Citizens' Alliance auditorium on the evening of October 9, 1949, the local Kuomintang leadership sent hoodlums to break up the meeting. The next day, Kuomintang elements passed out leaflets marking fifteen progressive Chinese men for death.

4. The two newspapers were the *San Francisco Chronicle* and *San Francisco Examiner*.

the Communist government have begun to abate.[5] Not a few community leaders have gone to the mainland to visit and to spend their vacation. Third, everybody realizes that it is local community affairs that have a direct bearing on us, and there is no point getting too serious about foreign politics. Consequently, the number of Chinese registering as voters is on the rise. Then there is the triumph of the residents of the Ping Yuen Housing Project over the Housing Authority.[6] These are the best possible examples. In addition, many of the overseas Chinese are from Hong Kong, who read the newspaper purely for enjoyment and are rarely moved by inflammatory rhetoric to take action.

As a result, the first protest march against the normalization of relations was not sponsored by the Chinese community, but rather by Taiwanese students from the University of California, Berkeley. Those spreading propaganda at the corner of Jackson and Kearny Streets in Chinatown spoke Mandarin, not Cantonese—a rare sight. They may have said, "We have not come to Chinatown to demonstrate. We are here to protest to the Americans." But there were more television shots about the protest march by supporters of the Independent Taiwan Movement the next day than of the demonstration by Kuomintang students. One group was criticizing the United States for recognizing China, while the other was expressing support for the recognition of China (but calling for Taiwan independence), thus canceling each other out. Television news loves conflicting stories, and was particularly interested in the action of the Taiwan independence supporters, as if it was some kind of breakthrough that deserved special coverage. Such a development has never occurred before during past political struggles in Chinatown.

The biggest difference lies in the role played by the United States this time. Formerly, Chinatown political strife pitched Chinese against Chinese. The normalization this time is due to the intervention of the American government. The instruction to the Taiwan embassy and consulate to lower their flags came not from the "leftist" elements in Chinatown, but from the U.S. government. If the loyalists want to vent their anger, they should direct it toward President Carter. Actually, they did that, which was why almost every slogan posted in Chinatown by the loyalists accused Carter, thus helping to neutralize the tension in Chinatown, creating the "peaceful Chinatown" as described in the *Examiner*.

In reality, whatever changes there are following the normalization, except for the fact that the community leaders cannot have their photographs taken

---

5. The Gang of Four, consisting of Jiang Qing, Zhang Chunqiao, Wang Hongwen, and Yao Wenyuan, were arrested and blamed for the excesses of the Cultural Revolution in 1976. Their sentences ranged from death (later commuted to life in prison) to twenty years in prison.

6. The San Francisco Housing Authority Commission had just agreed to provide security guards at the Ping Yuen housing projects in Chinatown after a three-month-long rent strike triggered by the rape and murder of a nineteen-year-old female tenant.

any more with the Kuomintang consul-general, there is very little impact on everybody's daily life. Even if they cannot stop thinking about Taiwan, they can still eat Taiwanese food and travel to Taiwan to appreciate the one and only authentic Chinese culture. Moreover, they also have the chance to visit their relatives and go sightseeing in mainland China. Therefore, at this time when the sun is setting for the loyalists, neither urging the overseas Chinese to participate in their political activities nor resorting to trickery to win their sympathies is a practical plan.

In our local city elections, the political strength of the Chinese cannot be discounted. Every vote cast wields some power. But when it comes to international political changes, we can only express our opinion; we cannot influence the outcome. The Taiwan lobbyists in America were quite successful, and almost convinced the whole country to regard Communist China as a kind of malignance. Yet it took just one trip by [President] Nixon to turn the situation around. Chiang Ching-kuo [president of the Republic of China] was feeling free and easy when 70 percent of Americans opposed giving up Taiwan. Yet it took just one broadcast by Carter and all that remained of those 70 percent Americans was one small group of three or four individuals led by Goldwater.[7] (They kept insisting that Taiwan should not be given up. But is Taiwan an American territory? And what is all this talk of "giving up" and "not giving up"? This kind of thinking is no more than a throwback to nineteenth-century colonialism.) One can see that these events are in no way influenced by us.

"There are circumstances beyond man's control." This may seem like a hackneyed saying, but it still holds true to a certain extent. By accepting this, Chinatown will weather this transition period without any difficulty.

SOURCE: *Chinese Pacific Weekly,* January 4, 1979. Translator: Ellen Yeung.

OTHER REFERENCES

Brett de Bary and Victor Nee, "The Kuomintang in Chinatown," in *Counterpoint: Perspectives on Asian America,* ed. Emma Gee (Los Angeles: UCLA Asian American Studies Center, 1976), pp. 146–51.

Him Mark Lai, "China and the Chinese American Community: The Political Dimension," *Chinese America: History and Perspectives,* 1999, pp. 1–32.

L. Ling-chi Wang, "The Structure of Dual Domination: Toward a Paradigm for the Study of the Chinese Diaspora in the United States," *Amerasia Journal* 21, nos. 1–2 (1995): 149–69.

7. Barry Goldwater, U.S. senator from Arizona and Republican presidential candidate in 1964, was known to be a conservative Republican and extreme anti-Communist.

Asian American Women and Revolution: A Personal View (1983)

Sadie Lum

The political ideologies of the antiwar, Asian American, and women's liberation move-
ments in the 1970s heightened Chinese American women's awareness of racial, gender,
and class oppression in their lives, inspiring many to become political activists. Some
chose to participate in community service programs, others in mainstream politics, and
still others, like Sadie Lum, chose the revolutionary route. As a member of the League of
Revolutionary Struggle, she firmly believed that society's problems were caused by the
capitalist system and that the solution was to organize the oppressed classes—workers
and racial minorities—to bring socialism to the United States. As a woman, she also
believed in the Chinese slogan "Women hold up half the sky"—in other words, that women
should be allowed full and equal participation in the revolutionary movement.

In the following essay, originally published in a special Asian American women's
issue of East Wind *magazine,[1] Lum recalls an exciting period of political involve-*
ment and personal growth, when anything and everything seemed possible. At the same
time, she remembers the difficulties she had juggling the multiple responsibilities of wife,
mother, worker, and activist while at the same time struggling against male chauvin-
ism at home and in the movement. How she was able to contribute to the revolution-
ary cause, deal with the personal conflicts, and come out of the process a stronger per-
son is the underlying message of this retrospective essay.

The position and role that we, Asian women, occupy—our potential and how
to tap and unleash our resources and full capabilities—is an important question to understand and address. Failure to do so will cripple the Asian
peoples' struggle for full equality as well as harm the struggle for revolutionary change in the U.S.

---

1. *East Wind,* a progressive Asian American politics and culture magazine, was published
from 1982 to 1989.

I was asked to share some of my experiences as an Asian woman active in the revolutionary movement with *East Wind* readers. I am looking forward to reading *East Wind*'s Focus section on Asian women, as it is by sharing and learning from each other's life experiences that we become stronger, collectively and individually. Collectively we have a common oppression—oppressed just because we are yellow-skinned and oppressed because we are women. Asian working women also bear the added weight of being exploited and oppressed as workers. We have many different, as well as similar, experiences in dealing with our oppression. In sharing them we become stronger as our understanding is broadened and deepened with experiences and lessons going beyond our own personal lives.

I am and have been a member of the League of Revolutionary Struggle (Marxist-Leninist), and organizations that came before it,[2] for over the past ten years. Our organization was born and grew up as an integral part of the new, contemporary revolutionary movement in the U.S. dating back to the 1960s. In our early history we embraced the view capsulized in the slogan we learned from the Chinese Revolution: "Women Hold Up Half the Sky!" This has guided our work to promote and develop the full participation of women in the peoples' struggles and in the revolutionary movement.

Like many Asian women of our generation, I was deeply affected by the times and circumstances in the late 1960s and early 1970s. My political history dating back to that time is also the history of my life growing up and maturing as a woman, a mother and a communist.

It was an explosive time—the rage of the peoples' militant struggles here inside the U.S. and around the world exploded with such a force that you could not be untouched by it. It was a time when our emotions ran a full spectrum—we cried at the military viciousness of the U.S. imperialists in Viet Nam; and we screamed our anger at many anti-war demonstrations in support of our brothers and sisters in Southeast Asia. We were inspired as we saw Vietnamese and Cambodian women take up arms to liberate their people. We marched, picketed and chanted against racist injustice and for our rights. We talked to everyone we could talk to—we learned a lot, we educated ourselves about ourselves and the world around us. We organized, organized, organized to fight. And throughout this entire process, in every aspect of this process, Asian women were right there—leading, contributing, working hard and inspiring others!

Most of us Asian women were brought together because of the times, and there was great diversity in who we were. Many of us had had very different

2. A Communist organization that sought to mobilize the working class and oppressed people of color to overthrow the U.S. capitalist state and replace it with a socialist one, the League of Revolutionary Struggle incorporated the Red Guard, I Wor Kuen, and other political groups before disbanding in the early 1990s.

life experiences. Our ages ranged from over 50 years old to 18 years old. Some of us were working women from the community and some of us were students from universities and campuses from all over the U.S. One of our greatest strengths was our ability to come together and to learn and share the lessons from our lives.

Among the most active of us, we were convinced and motivated by the understanding that in order to deal with the particular issues facing Asian peoples, we had to bring this whole capitalist system down! We could not just change one piece here and there. We had to change the whole thing!

We committed ourselves to the goal of revolutionary struggle to establish socialism right here in the U.S. It was with this outlook, this consciousness, that we carried out day-to-day organizing in the community. We set up programs and took up issues affecting the majority of our people, the working and poor people in the community—the people who have no choice but to fight if they want a decent and better life.

For Asian working women, this reality hits to the heart of their daily existence, i.e., to even try to improve something in their basic, day-to-day situation and position at home, they have to fight. *(Equality between husbands and wives? Equal distribution of the work at home? Where did that come from?)* So, to deal with this, in any real way, women must fight to change their immediate situation and must do this as part of fighting to change the society that puts us in this position in the first place and then keeps us there.

This time in my life was very important. Doing community work in Chinatown and being involved in the anti–Viet Nam war movement gave me new eyes—a new outlook—to look at myself and at life. It was through my political activism that I came to believe in socialist revolution and communism and came to see how Asian women like myself would really win liberation. The developing revolutionary movement turned my life around. It gave me an understanding of myself which enabled me to bring my life under my control and give it direction. It gave me belief that my life was of value and that I was worth something and had something to contribute to society for the betterment of mankind. This may seem very simple, but it was not an easy or simple realization.

I was raised in San Francisco Chinatown in the Ping Yuen housing projects. My mother, a single parent, working mother (a wonderful and strong woman), raised me and my two sisters on her own. I went to Francisco Junior High and Galileo High School and "hung out" at the Chinese Recreation Center and Commodore Gym and in the streets of Chinatown. I grew up conditioned to feel that human life is not worth much generally. *(You read and hear so much about people being killed and dying every day.)* I now understand that to cover their crimes against the people and the decadence of this capitalist society, the ruling class must promote an atmosphere of indifference and numbness towards the value of human life. Also, as a Third World woman from a working-class family, I felt I had very little to hold my head up about, since everything promoted in this society as things to be proud of and to strive for were not relevant to me. This includes almost everything, from all kinds of material possessions, to what you looked like and how you acted, to what school you went to, to where you lived, to what job you were going to get, to almost anything you can think of—was someone we were not and never would be; and were things we did not have nor would we ever have in our lifetime. *(What were we doing here, then?)*

This kind of thinking led me to strive hard for what I thought I could have, and to draw sharp limitations on myself. To avoid experiencing repeated disappointments in my life, I made up all kinds of justifications to not want more. It was also this kind of thinking that nurtured my greatest insecurities about who I was and my self worth.

I grew up judging a woman's value and goals in life with: who you were *(lucky enough)* to marry; then to be a good wife and mother, period. *(Is this all our life is?)* Who you married determined your economic status in life and your new circle of friends—his friends. That's why there was always so much emphasis on going out with the "right guy," a guy with a "future." It got to be so that I thought there was something wrong with me because all the guys I went out with either couldn't even get a job or their "futures" were in the post office or the phone company (or something like that). Later I realized that it wasn't just my luck to end up with the "wrong" guy, but that the majority of Asian guys at my school were working-class guys whose futures were to be workers.

I had my first daughter when I was still in high school. I went to work right after she was born and struggled to deal with being a young mother and a wife. Life was hard. It was hard to make enough money. *(My husband was unemployed most of the time.)* I really wanted to move out of the apartment, into our own place, without his mother. *(Who wanted to live their entire life there, or even most of it?)* I was tired when I got home, but I had to pick up my daughter, do all the cleaning, all the cooking—everything. *(Why can't he do some of it, especially since he isn't even working?)* And I took care of and had the main responsibility for raising my daughter. *(Of course, I'm the mother!)* Fights and frustrations. Frustrations and more fights.

About three years later, I began to become more aware of the importance of the rebellions taking place all across America, and saw that the war in Viet Nam was a plunderous war being waged by the U.S.—people here and overseas were really fighting against the *same* enemy. By this time I had left my husband and was in a really oppressive relationship with this possessive man who thought and acted as though he owned me and all my emotions and my thoughts—everything that's me. I really felt I would suffocate and die (or be beat to death) in this relationship. I never had the nerve or strength to just break it off. The extreme insecurity I had about myself kept me tied to him.

At this same time, some of my friends were beginning to become politically active in the San Francisco State Strike (a massive Third World student strike in 1969 at the San Francisco State University),[3] and in doing youth work, draft counseling, etc., in the community. They had formed an organization—the Red Guard Party, a revolutionary organization. I was really interested and began to go around to see what was happening. This did not sit well with the guy I was going with. According to him, I could only be interested in the Red Guard and community work because I was interested in some guy there! Doesn't that sound terribly, typically awful? Women can't have any other independent reason for interests in her life separate from liking a guy or doing things because of a guy.

It was this realization that actually made me more determined to get involved in political work. I was going to stake out my own claim in life, and do what I wanted to do. Amazingly, this was the first time in this completely oppressive relationship that I felt I had the strength to break up with this guy. I must have told him and myself, at least 20 times in the year we were together, that I was going to break this off. But this time I actually did it! It was like a hundred pounds lifted off my shoulders.

I joined the Red Guard Party and later, I Wor Kuen (IWK), a revolutionary Marxist-Leninist organization. It was the community organizing work that led us to become Marxist-Leninists, as this was the only scientific, only real way to bring socialism to the U.S.

We got completely involved in doing community organizing work—to build a strong base and ties among the masses in the community. We paid special attention to developing our work among women. The women I met and worked with taught me a lot, reinforced my feelings of independence and pride and inspired me deeply. Some of us became like sisters, and with the older women, we became their daughters and they, our mothers.

It was at this time (1971) that I had my second daughter and settled into a stable relationship with my present husband. (We just celebrated our tenth wedding anniversary.)

Some of the work IWK did among women included the Hsin Hua School (New China School), which was a full daytime childcare and after-school program; the Asian Women's Health Team that provided free community health services such as TB testing; and we started a Women's Group in the Chinese Progressive Association[4] to promote support and discussion among the women. In addition to these programs, the women were also very active

3. In 1968 students of color at San Francisco State College sustained a strike for five months, winning concessions from the university administration to establish an ethnic studies program.

4. Founded in 1972, the Chinese Progressive Association advocated for normalization of relations between the People's Republic of China and the United States, and continues to serve as a grassroots organization offering social services in Chinatown communities.

Sadie Lum speaking
at the May First International
Workers' Day celebration in San
Francisco Chinatown, 1975.
(Courtesy of Sadie Lum)

in the different community issues that we took up around housing, police brutality, education in the schools, and immigration cases.

One big area of our work was in supporting People's China as the real representative of the Chinese people, not the Taiwan regime. We actively fought for the normalization of state-to-state relations between the U.S. and China and conducted mass educational work about People's China, including the role of women in New China.

In August 1974, a significant struggle broke out in San Francisco Chinatown involving 135 Chinese women garment workers—the Jung Sai garment strike. These women, against numerous odds, organized themselves and went out on strike for the right to unionize and for decent wages, benefits and working conditions. The Jung Sai garment sweatshop was a typical Chinatown sweatshop with the exploitative conditions: low-pay piecework, long hours, bad lighting, fire hazards, etc. The women even had to bring their own toilet paper to work! The strength and power of the strike rested in the fact that the women saw their fight as an important part of the struggle for all Chinese people to be treated justly. The workers' demand for the basic right of unionization has been historically denied to Chinese workers in this country, as have many of their basic rights.

IWK was actively involved in the direct support work for the strike. The

Jung Sai workers were determined to get their demands. Even when the boss closed down the shop and the union dragged its feet, the workers were not disheartened. They kept up the picket lines and their optimism. The majority of the women were married and mothers. For them to have sustained the strike for over eight months was no easy thing. This determination and strength of Chinese working women has been documented many times before and since then, such as the 1938 strike by Chinese women garment workers at the San Francisco National Dollar Department Store for unionization to the recent walkout of over 10,000 Chinese women garment workers who demanded and won a union contract in New York Chinatown in July 1982.

Doing the political work was much more difficult for the women than for the men. There were both very practical problems limiting the participation of women as well as mental and emotional pressures on us. For the women who were working full-time and raising a family, doing community and political work was very difficult. Whether we had children or not, we paid a lot of attention to trying, where possible, to collectivize home responsibilities. For instance, we would do food shopping for each other, help pick up the different children and watch them, help cook dinner, and help wash the clothes. We offered each other a lot of practical support and help.

A common problem that kept coming up was the bad attitudes of husbands/boyfriends towards the women doing political work. Some husbands would absolutely prohibit it and would demand that the woman stay home. In some of these cases, we would organize the meetings and discussions at the woman's house and organize the work for the weekends when it was easier for her to get out of the house. Sadly, in some cases the pressure of the men forced the women to drop out of political work, and they, while interested and wanting to be active, would give it up to keep peace in the home. In one case, a woman in her late forties decided that she wanted to continue her political work even after her husband threatened a divorce if she didn't stop. She kept up her work and tried to talk him out of it, but he filed for divorce anyway. At the divorce hearing, he sat on the stand and went on and on about how he was leaving her because she was a communist. She got custody of all seven children, and he got most of the money and property. But she never regretted the decision. She taught me a lot about the importance and value of your own life and that we all had the right and the duty, to ourselves, to make our lives what we want them to be and to be happy. Especially when we know that to be a revolutionary is right and important. Her strength helped all of us to deal with the pressures, guilt feelings and conflicts that we all went through at some time or another.

Some other common things were: the more active political women were labeled as not being "feminine" and guys would make jokes about us and not want to go out with us; and that to be bold in taking up the work and to have strong opinions and state them, we were seen as "nags" and "bitches."

These were just ploys by some of the men to try to undermine the validity of our political ideas, to discredit us and limit our political impact. What they didn't even realize was that their backward attitudes hurt all of us in our common struggle. Thus, in order to ensure the women's contributions to the work, we had to develop a clear perspective on how we were going to handle the question of fighting male chauvinism. We had to develop a situation where the women could fully participate with ease of mind.

From our experiences we knew that a daily struggle against women's oppression in its most concrete forms had to take place. For women to stand up and be politically active was an integral part of the actual struggle against our oppression—it was a step toward our own liberation. We established the principle and firm belief that women can and should strive to do anything a man can do. That, as women, we should struggle to be active in the political movements and to take up political leadership, even when in leadership over men. We should not define limitations for ourselves just because we are women.

It was this outlook that guided us in handling, very successfully, the questions and situations facing women in our daily lives as political and revolutionary women. With this perspective, we were able to maintain and develop a high level of participation by women at all levels of the work, including many of the main leadership roles.

That tradition has carried forth with us over the years. In all the political and revolutionary work that the League is involved in, there is a high level of women's participation in all different kinds of political work and at all levels of work, including the most demanding and difficult work.

For myself, my life is grounded in the fact that I am a communist. I believe that an important responsibility as a woman and a mother is to be a communist—for the good of my children and for mankind. I do believe communism is our future. I also believe that as a communist I am a better mother. The understanding I have of life, of society, enables me to raise my children in a far-sighted, objective way. It gives me a way to understand them—the social influences and pressures on them; it gives me the understanding that I alone cannot determine all their views and attitudes; and it enables me to build friendships with them because I can understand and respect them as independent people, seeing all sides of them. I want to continue to build a good marriage and raise my daughters to be good people and prepare them for their futures. I also want to have the ability to continue to carry out my political work, make the contributions and take up the responsibilities that I feel are very important to do, and that I want to do. My family and political work are part of the fabric of my life, and in turn my family takes pride in my political work and beliefs.

Many of us came into the peoples' struggles and into the revolutionary movement because of our oppression as Asians, as women, and for many of us, as workers. For me to be able to live my life in the way I do has only been

possible through a lot of conscious work to promote and pay special attention to the participation and contributions of women. This is an important
tradition and precedent to promote and continue in all our lives and in our
work. And without us women, where would our movement be?

*As of 2004, Sadie Lum has worked as a legal secretary with the same San Francisco
law firm for fourteen years, and has been married to Irwin "B. M." Lum for thirty-
three years. They are the proud parents of two college-educated daughters and have
one sixteen-year-old grandson, and they remain active in political issues such as the
antiwar movement, women's rights, and labor.*

SOURCE: *East Wind* 2, no. 1 (spring/summer 1983): 46–50.

OTHER REFERENCES

Asian Women (Asian American Studies, University of California, Berkeley, 1971).
Steve Louie and Glenn Omatsu, eds., *Asian Americans: The Movement and the Moment*
(Los Angeles: UCLA Asian American Studies Center Press, 2001).
William Wei, *The Asian American Movement* (Philadelphia: Temple University Press,
1993).

"In unity there is strength"

Garment Worker Speaks Out at Union Rally (1982)

Shui Mak Ka

Chinese women garment workers made history on July 15, 1982, when more than twenty thousand people turned out at a strike rally called by the International Ladies Garment Workers Union (ILGWU) to fight for a three-year union contract that would give workers increased wages and benefits. It was the largest labor strike in New York Chinatown to date, and it had come about at the insistence of the workers after the owners of five hundred factories in Chinatown voted down the contract for a second time.

One of the key organizers and speakers at this historic event was Shui Mak Ka, a fifty-year-old garment worker who was once a medical doctor in China. After coming to the United States in 1973, she had resorted to supporting her family of three children by working in a Chinatown garment shop during the day and a Chinese restaurant in Brooklyn at night. When her husband, Sun Fook Ka, chief physician of a major hospital in China, arrived a year later, he too ended up working in a Chinatown garment shop. Underemployment was a common situation for many well-educated but non-English-speaking Chinese immigrants like the Kas, who poured into the United States after the passage of the Immigration Act of 1965. Arriving in New York Chinatown when the garment industry was prospering and union organizing going strong, it was not surprising that Shui Mak Ka would end up working as a seamstress and, given her forceful personality and firm belief in social justice, that she would end up being chosen shop representative by her fellow workers.

At the time of the strike, six out of every ten families in New York Chinatown had someone working in the garment industry, and 430 out of the 500 Chinatown shops were union shops, which meant that there were twenty thousand Chinese members in ILGWU's Local 23–25 (85 percent of them women). Employers in five eastern states had approved the new contract; only the owners of New York Chinatown's 500 shops refused. Disgruntled over the contract they had signed three years ago and smarting from losses in their margin of profit caused by global competition and changes in the city's garment industry, Chinese contractors voted to reject the contract on June 10.

"The grasshopper cannot stop the car in its tracks!" says Shui Mak Ka at the union rally in New York Chinatown, 1982. (Courtesy of Shui Mak Ka)

More than 20,000 people attend the rally in support of Local 23–25's strike for a union contract, 1982. (Courtesy of Shui Mak Ka)

They obviously underestimated the power and militancy of their women workers, who in no time mobilized fifteen thousand people to attend a union rally at Columbus Park in the heart of New York Chinatown to pressure their employers to sign the contract. The following speech, sprinkled with analogies from Mao Zedong's poetry, was given by Shui Mak Ka at this first rally on June 24, 1982.

Dear brothers and sisters of Local 23–25, greetings to all of you!

On behalf of all sewing factory workers, first please allow me to convey our thanks to our union representatives. The union has been fighting hard for our rights as expressed in the three-year contract. Many of them have been busy working day and night, putting aside their own need to eat and sleep; please give them a big round of applause to express our highest sense of gratitude and respect.

The three-year contract is something we absolutely must have. We work very hard, and deserve every bit of the wages and benefits contained in the contract. The bosses depend on our sweat and labor, and have profited quite a bit of money to buy their houses and cars. But capitalists are never short on desire and wants. They oppose the three-year contract. We must clear our eyes, and not allow them to substitute a fish eye for a pearl or let them fish in muddy waters.[1] We must unite around the union's banner, because in unity, there is strength. The grasshopper cannot stop the car in its tracks!

It is not spring when one flower blossoms; only when a hundred thousand flowers bloom is it spring. If we close up ranks, work in unity, and move forward with one heart, no matter how tumultuous the coming waves, no matter what kind of difficulties stand before us, we will remain steadfast and strong. In unity there is strength. In unity there will be victory. Our struggle for the three-year contract will be victorious.

That's all I have to say. Thank you!

SOURCE: © 1982 Shui Mak Ka. All rights reserved. Translator: Shiree Teng

The rally succeeded in getting over twenty organizations to sign petitions supporting the workers, but failed at getting the employers to approve the contract when they took another vote on June 29. Some of the contractors went as far as to shut down their shops for two days, in effect locking out their employees, in retaliation. The union had no choice but to call a strike on July 15. In front of 20,000 supporters at Columbus Park that day and broadcast on radio, Shui Mak Ka gave the following speech, which was translated by Shiree Teng at the rally:

We are very angry about the actions of a small handful of employers in the

1. Meaning that the employers are trying to get away with substituting a "fish eye" for a "pearl," which is what employees deserve, and that they are also trying to stir up the dirt in the pond to stop people from seeing clearly.

recent days. Enough is enough! They have faced their desire to negotiate, and in the end they rejected the contract for the second time. The action is totally irresponsible. The worst thing is that this small bunch of employers also has been using all kinds of threats and intimidations to force other employers to close shop. The way that these people are behaving is like a blind bat trying to knock down the tree. It's like a grasshopper's attempt to stop the car in its tracks. They are daydreaming and we tell them, you are nuts. They are trying to substitute a fish eye for a pearl, and they're trying to fish in muddy waters. And we tell them, you are wrong.

According to Xiaolin Bao's account of the rally and the outcome,[2] the rally had started at 11 A.M. that morning. By 1 P.M. all of the Chinatown shop owners but one had approved the contract. Shui Mak Ka made it her job to track down the last holdout and succeeded in getting him to sign the contract. The strike was declared a victory for Local 23–25 at 1:15 P.M. that same day, thus ending a six-week labor dispute in the shortest strike in New York Chinatown's history. Ka would go on to work full-time for the ILGWU as its liaison to the Chinese community until her retirement in 1999.

SOURCE: Gail Pellett, *We Are One* (New York: Local 23–25, ILGWU, 1982). VHS.

OTHER REFERENCES:

Xiaolan Bao, *Holding Up More Than Half the Sky: Chinese Women Garment Workers in New York City, 1948–92* (Urbana: University of Illinois Press, 2001).

Peter Kwong, *The New Chinatown* (New York: Hill & Wang, 1996).

Miriam Ching Louie, *Sweatshop Warriors: Immigrant Women Workers Take On the Global Factory* (Cambridge, Mass.: South End Press, 2001).

Shiree Teng, "Women, Community and Equality: Three Garment Workers Speak Out," *East Wind* 2, no. 1 (spring/summer 1983): 20–23.

2. Xiaolan Bao, *Holding Up More Than Half the Sky: Chinese Women Garment Workers in New York City, 1948–92* (Urbana: University of Illinois Press, 2001), pp. 211–12.

The Words of a Woman
Who Breathes Fire (1983)

Kitty Tsui

Community activist and poet Kitty Tsui became the first Chinese American lesbian to come out publicly when her collection of poetry and prose, The Words of a Woman Who Breathes Fire, *was published by Spinsters, Ink, in 1983. Born in Hong Kong in 1952, Tsui grew up in Liverpool, England, and immigrated to the United States in 1968. She graduated from San Francisco State University with a B.A. in creative writing in 1975. Inspired by the independent life style of her grandmother Kwan Ying Lin, a Chinese opera star, as well as the gay liberation movement, Tsui chose to come out to her family when she was twenty-one. "It was one of the hardest periods of my life," she said, "but I had my tools for survival: a typewriter, a voice that was screaming to be heard, and my best friend, alcohol."[1] With the support of feminist writers and gay sisters, Tsui overcame alcoholism and marginalization by taking up bodybuilding, writing poetry, and becoming an activist in the Third World and gay communities.*

As the following two poems from her anthology attest, Asian American lesbians must not only grapple with discrimination and homophobia from within their families and ethnic communities, but they must also contend with racism, sexism, and homophobia in the larger society. Determined to overcome invisibility, break silence, and assert her multiple identities as a Chinese American lesbian, Tsui has continued to make waves with her writing. Her poetry, short stories, and essays have been included in over seventy anthologies, and she is the author of two other books: Breathless, *a collection of erotic short stories, and* Sparks Fly, *a novel about the adventures of a gay man in San Francisco.*

---

1. Kitty Tsui, "Breaking Silence, Making Waves and Loving Ourselves: The Politics of Coming Out and Coming Home," in *Lesbian Philosophies and Cultures,* ed. Jeffner Allen (New York: State University of New York Press, 1990), p. 55.

Cover of the first book by a Chinese American lesbian, published by Spinsters, Ink, in 1983. (Book design and calligraphy by Kitty Tsui, cover photograph by Cathy Cade)

A CHINESE BANQUET

for the one who was not invited

it was not a very formal affair but
all the women over twelve
wore long gowns and a corsage,
except for me.

it was not a very formal affair, just
the family getting together,
poa poa, kuw fu without *kuw mow*[2]
(her excuse this year is a headache).

---

2. *Poa poa* means grandmother; *kuw fu* means uncle; and *kuw mow* means aunt.

aunts and uncles and cousins,
the grandson who is a dentist,
the one who drives a mercedes benz,
sitting down for shark's fin soup.

they talk about buying a house and
taking a two week vacation in beijing.
i suck on shrimp and squab,
dreaming of the cloudscape in your eyes.

my mother, her voice beaded with sarcasm:
you're twenty six and not getting younger.
it's about time you got a decent job.
she no longer asks when i'm getting married.

you're twenty six and not getting younger.
what are you doing with your life?
you've got to make a living.
why don't you study computer programming?

she no longer asks when i'm getting married.
one day, wanting desperately to
bridge the boundaries that separate us,
wanting desperately to touch her,

tell her: mother, i'm gay,
mother i'm gay and so happy with her.
but she will not listen,
she shakes her head.

she sits across from me,
emotions invading her face.
her eyes are wet but
she will not let tears fall.

mother, i say,
you love a man.
i love a woman.
it is not what she wants to hear.

aunts and uncles and cousins,
very much a family affair.
but you are not invited,
being neither my husband nor my wife.

aunts and uncles and cousins
eating longevity noodles

fragrant with ham inquire:
sold that old car of yours yet?

i want to tell them: my back is healing,
i dream of dragons and water.
my home is in her arms,
our bedroom ceiling the wide open sky.

THE WORDS OF A WOMAN
WHO BREATHES FIRE

a woman was asked to conduct
a workshop of a conference
to talk about the kinds of oppression
she had experienced
as a gay asian woman in america.

the woman was asked to do
her presentation as part of
the female sexuality workshop.
as if being a lesbian
is merely a sexual personality.

a week later the woman was informed
by the coordinator that
she was to do her presentation
as part of another workshop
because it was feared that

the family counselor who was to lead
the female sexuality workshop,
might feel uncomfortable
sitting next to a woman
talking about her lesbianism.

the woman shouted,
the woman screamed:
what does it mean to be a lesbian?
i am a woman, they call me a bitch, a cunt.
i am asian, they call me a slant-eyed whore.

the woman shouted,
the woman screamed:
i am not a professional homosexual.
i am my grandmother's youngest daughter,
a warrior, a worker, a writer.

I am a visionary who creates
blood and courage soaked stories
of countless *ah goongs* and *ah poas.*[3]
i link arms with women, with men to fight
the diseases of a patriarchal past.

i am a warrior who grapples with three
many-headed demons: racism, sexism, homophobia;
a twenty-four hour worker;
a writer with the will to change
the age-old inheritance of inequality.

i am a warrior, a worker, a writer,
my grandmother's youngest daughter,
a feminist who does not believe in silence.
i am a woman who loves women,
i am a woman who loves myself.

Source: Kitty Tsui, *The Words of a Woman Who Breathes Fire* (Argyle, N.Y.: Spinsters, Ink, 1983), pp. 12–13, 51–52. Reprinted by permission of the author.

OTHER REFERENCES

David L. Eng and Alice Y. Hom, *Q & A: Queer in Asian America* (Philadelphia: Temple University Press, 1996).

Sharon Lim-Hing, ed., *The Very Inside: An Anthology of Writing by Asian and Pacific Islander Lesbian and Bisexual Women* (Toronto: Sister Vision Press, 1994).

Barbara Noda, Kitty Tsui, and Z. Wong, "Coming Out: We Are Here in the Asian Community," *Bridge* 7, no. 1 (spring 1979): 22–24.

Trinity A. Ordona, "Asian Lesbians in San Francisco: Struggle to Create a Safe Space, 1970s–1980s," in *Asian/Pacific Islander American Women: A Historical Anthology,* ed. Shirley Hune and Gail M. Nomura (New York: New York University Press, 2003), pp. 319–34.

Kitty Tsui, "Breaking Silence, Making Waves and Loving Ourselves: The Politics of Coming Out and Coming Home," in *Lesbian Philosophies and Cultures,* ed. Jeffner Allen (New York: State University of New York Press, 1990), pp. 49–61.

3. *Ah goongs* means grandfathers, and *ah poas* mean grandmothers.

Anti-Asian Violence
and the Vincent Chin Case

*In the 1980s, as the United States deindustrialized and sank into a recession in re-
sponse to rapid changes in the global economy, hate crimes against Asian Americans
erupted. It was not a coincidence that the first outbreak occurred in Detroit, Michigan,
where the auto industry, unable to compete with foreign imports, had all but collapsed.
In 1982 unemployed workers and the mass media were blaming Japanese imports for
the depressed economy when Vincent Chin, a twenty-seven-year-old Chinese American,
was brutally killed in a barroom brawl by two white auto workers. During the fistfight
that preceded the murder, one of the men was heard saying, "It's because of you motherfuckers that we're out of work." They had obviously mistaken Chin for a Japanese as
well as unfairly blamed all Asian people for the economic problems of the country.*

THE NEW VIOLENCE (1984)

Helen Y. Zia

Helen Zia was working as a journalist for the Detroit Metro Times *and* Metropolitan Detroit *when she heard the shocking news about Vincent Chin. Inspired by
the antiwar and Asian American movements while an undergraduate at Princeton
University, she had moved to Detroit in 1976 to do grassroots organizing. For two
years she had worked as a large-press operator at a Chrysler plant before being laid
off. Although she could understand the underlying causes behind the Vincent Chin
murder, she could not believe or accept the lenient sentences that the judge meted out
to the two killers; nor could the Asian American community. Helen Zia ended up leading a national campaign to seek justice for Vincent Chin. The following article, one
of many that she wrote on behalf of American Citizens for Justice (ACJ), was published
in* Bridge, *a leading national Asian American magazine, in 1984.*

345

In 1982, in America, a Chinese American named Vincent Chin was beaten to death with a baseball bat by two men—after being accused by them of causing the unemployment of U.S. autoworkers. His killers were each fined $3,000 and given three years' probation.

When news spread of the lenient sentences given for the crime of brutally taking a life, there were storms of protest.

The Vincent Chin case has come to mean far more to Asian Americans than a failure of the criminal justice system, though this aspect of the case serves as a lesson to all. This case has come to represent the racial hatred, scapegoating and very real discrimination that Asian Americans of all our diverse nationalities have been forced to endure since our forebears set foot on this land. To the extent that what happened to Vincent Chin could happen to any one of us, all Asian Americans are in jeopardy.

The Chin case is also a mandate to those of us who are fortunate enough not to have suffered Vincent's fate. The nationwide response to it symbolizes what can—and must—be achieved by Asian Americans acting together on behalf of our common need to live in our nation free from the threat of racial violence and innuendo. This case has proven that Americans from China, Japan, Korea, the Philippines, Southeast Asia, India and other Asian heritages can make a powerful impact by working together for our mutual interests.

On the night of his slaying, Vincent Chin was 27 years old and his future was promising. He was doing well at work in computer graphics, was well liked, and was looking to buy a new home for his wife and his widowed mother. In fact, Vincent's story typified the experiences of many Asian American immigrants: his father, Chin Wing Hing, came from Guangdong Province to America in search of a new life, which he found in the laundries and restaurants of Detroit. When World War II began, he enlisted, and after serving honorably in the U.S. Army, became eligible for citizenship. As a reward of citizenship, Mr. Chin was permitted to bring his wife, Lily, to this country. There were no children, and a few years later, the couple adopted a five-year-old boy from Guangdong, whom they named Vincent.

Friends and teachers say Vincent was a fun-loving, happy kid. His mother says he could have studied harder, but that he was a good boy, the kind who would help others. When he was nine, he began working in local Chinese restaurants, bussing tables. He had two passions: fishing and reading. "Whenever he had a chance, Vince would try to get to a lake and drop a line—it was his way of relaxing," remembers boyhood friend Gary Koivu, who was with Vincent the night he died.

And Vincent had a sensitive side to his personality—he often wrote poetry to his fiancée, Vikki Wong. She is trying to renew her life and is reluctant to talk publicly about Vincent, but some memories stand out, such as a Valentine's Day poem that Vincent placed in a classified section of a local paper:

There is no life without you
There is no joy or laughter
There is no brightness, no warmth
All the mornings after.

So stay with me
And we'll face the tomorrows
To find if our love
Can overcome the sorrows.

Though Vincent began college studying architecture, he later changed his mind, thinking that it might not be a secure profession. "Vince said he did not want to work his whole life in laundries and restaurants like his father did," Vikki recalls. So he later studied computer operations at a local trade school, and graduated with honors. He found a job at an engineering firm, combining his drafting and computing skills in computer-aided design work. To help save money for a house, Vincent also worked on weekends as a waiter.

Like many a "red-blooded American male," Vincent enjoyed going out on the town with his buddies. But unlike those other Americans, Vincent had an Asian face. On that warm Saturday night, Vincent and three friends decided to celebrate his upcoming wedding by going to a nude go-go joint that Vincent frequented during his carefree bachelorhood. Though his mother told him he shouldn't go out so close to the wedding date, he laughed and reassured her that "it would be his last night out with the guys." That night, Vincent was the target of a racial attack, and he died four days later as a result of that assault.

The bar that Vincent and his friends—two white and one Asian—went to was a seedy strip joint where women dance by the dollar: one dollar buys a few gyrations right in front of the customer—the more dollars, the more gyrations. Vincent and his friends had gone to have a good time, bringing plenty of dollar bills. But the more time the dancers spent with the free-spending Asian American, the more provoked two other patrons became.

Ronald Ebens, a tall, heavy-set white man, then 43 years old, and his step-son Michael Nitz, a tall, slim 22-year-old, were seated across from Vincent. Dancers from the bar say that Ebens, perhaps resentful that an Asian man should be receiving so much attention while he was not, began calling Vincent racially offensive names, needling Vincent, suggesting that he wasn't a man, talking about what he could do with his mother. One dancer heard Ebens say explicitly, "It's because of you motherfuckers that we're out of work."

A good-natured Vincent uncharacteristically stood up to them as the epithets continued, and a scuffle ensued. Vincent and his friends left the club, followed closely behind by Ebens and Nitz. Outside, in the parking lot, Ebens went straight to the trunk of his car and pulled out a baseball bat. Vincent ran, chased by Ebens and Nitz. When the two larger men were outdistanced by Vincent, they returned to the lot, where Vincent's two white friends and Jimmy Choi were standing—and they homed in on Jimmy, who had been uninvolved in their assaults against Vincent. But Jimmy also had an Asian face, and the two began chasing Jimmy, Ebens still wielding his bat. "I ran for my dear life," shudders Jimmy.

Intent on their purpose, Ebens and Nitz embarked on a search-and-destroy mission. For the next 20 minutes, they drove through streets and alleys searching for Vincent and Jimmy. They hired a third man to "help them get the chinks," as that man, Jimmy Perry, freely admits today. And they found the two Asian Americans waiting outside of a fast-food restaurant for a bus or a car or anything to get them away from their assailants. Ebens, Nitz and Perry crept up behind the two unsuspecting Asians, who noticed their attackers too late. Nitz grabbed Vincent in a bear hug, and his stepfather pummeled Vincent's legs, arms, body—and finally, sent four grand-slam swings into the back of Vincent's skull.

Two off-duty police officers stopped the carnage at gunpoint. "I ordered halt twice; if I hadn't stopped him, he would have gone for another 20 blows," recounts one officer. But for Vincent, it was over. Doctors operated on his battered head all night; surgeons said it looked like someone had beaten an animal. Vincent was placed on life support systems—his brain was already dead. Four days later, on June 23, 1982, his grieving fiancée and his stricken mother consented to turning off the life supports. Instead of attending Vincent's wedding, his friends went to his funeral.

What might have been just another senseless tragedy then turned into a carnival of bungling and sheer incompetence—the product of an insensitive, overburdened system where there is often no justice—just another case. And Vincent Chin was treated as just another case. No one went to the bar to find out what had initiated the murderous hunt. No one even thought to ask if race might have been a factor. A dough-faced detective (from what is reported to be one of the state's most inadequate police departments) says the killing was no big deal and that he is sure there was nothing racial about it—even though he acknowledges he made no effort to find out. Two defense lawyers managed to get the case moved from courtroom to courtroom within Wayne County, and found one judge to set the charges at second-degree murder, prompting another judge to comment on the record, "I am of the opinion that the defendants were undercharged. The elements of first-degree murder are here."

Finally the case went before Judge Charles Kaufman, who overlooked a probation officer's recommendations of incarceration and a psychiatric report warning that Ebens was an "extremely hostile and explosive individual . . . with a potential for uncontrollable hostility and explosive acting out." While the prosecutors didn't even bother to show up at the plea-bargained manslaughter sentencing, Kaufman ignored the previous courtroom testimony and listened to the killers' lawyers say that Vincent provoked his own death while Ebens and Nitz were innocent bystanders. Judge Kaufman took ten minutes to consider the charges, and sentenced Ronald Ebens and Michael Nitz each to $3,000 in fines and $780 in court costs, payable at $125 per month with no interest, and three years' probation.

That was the total value placed on the life of 27-year-old Vincent Chin, whose only crime was having an Asian face at a time when anti-Japanese and anti-Asian sentiments were rampant.

In rendering his now-infamous sentence, Kaufman offered several rationalizations: "These aren't the kind of men you send to jail . . . We're talking here about a man who's held down a responsible job for 17 or 18 years, and his son is employed and is a part-time student. You don't make the punishment fit the crime, you make the punishment fit the criminal."

News of the killers' sentences and the judge's opinion drew an immediate response from a shocked and disbelieving Chinese community. A grief-stricken Mrs. Chin, friends and members of the community struggled to understand what had happened and to discover what might be done about the clearly flawed judicial decision. There were emotional meetings of hundreds of Asians and others who had never before come together, suddenly talking about the pain, humiliation and suffering that we had endured silently for generations. We knew that what happened to Vincent Chin endangered all of us, and we knew that we could no longer stand in silence.

March 31, 1983, stands out in the history of Asians in America, for it was the night that individuals and representatives of local and national Asian organizations came together in Michigan and recognized that our fate and indeed our lives depended on our willingness to work in cooperation and in coalition with one another. In the drafty hall of the Detroit Chinese Welfare Council,[1] there was a joining of liberals and conservatives, youths and seniors, scientists, businessmen, Chinese, Japanese, Filipinos and Koreans, Christians and Buddhists, Cantonese- and Mandarin-speakers, American-born and immigrants—all of us put aside the differences that kept us apart and agreed that night to form a new organization to protect our rights as Americans of Asian ancestry, and we named it "American Citizens for Justice."

In the ensuing days, weeks and months, the many volunteers of ACJ donated money, time, effort, and whatever else was needed to discover what caused this miscarriage of justice. We engaged an attorney to look into legal recourse. (Our small force of Asian American attorneys in the Detroit area could not support a sustained *pro bono* effort, unlike some larger com-

---

1. Affiliated with the long established Chinese Consolidated Benevolent Association and On Leong Merchants Association, the Detroit Chinese Welfare Council represented the interests of Chinatown to the city and at political functions. Vincent Chin was one of its younger members.

munities.) Obtaining court records and reconstructing the events of that tragic evening took much hard work and persistence in a system that seemed all too eager to cover up the mistakes made. The more established civil rights organizations of Detroit recognized our concerns and helped us open doors in an unwieldy bureaucracy. Bit by bit, we were able to reconstruct what happened to Vincent and what happened in the courts.

The more we learned about the case, the more evident it became that a grievous wrong had occurred. ACJ deliberately avoided making accusations of racism against the judge and did not call the killing a racial attack—until statements of additional eyewitnesses, who had never been questioned by police, prosecutors or anyone else from the criminal justice system, forced an inescapable conclusion: that the crime of violating Vincent Chin's civil rights on the basis of his race had taken place, and that it was time for a governmental body to review the evidence that this fledgling civil rights organization had uncovered. In May 1983, an FBI investigation was initiated by the Justice Department; in September, a grand jury probe was announced, and in November, 23 grand jurors returned indictments against Ebens and Nitz for the violation of Vincent Chin's civil rights.

During that long summer of 1983, as the news of what happened in Detroit spread throughout the U.S. and across the globe, Asians began to respond to what many had recognized long ago: the knowledge that the welfare and livelihood of each of us, regardless of national origin, depends on our ability to work together. Even our personal safety is at risk, subject to bigotry and scapegoating for economic or foreign policy problems since we "all look alike." Demonstrations and support activities took place in San Francisco, Oakland, Los Angeles, Denver, Chicago, Toronto, New York, and a huge demonstration was held in Detroit. Mrs. Chin and ACJ were invited to address groups all over the country as new organizations formed in San Francisco, Los Angeles and Chicago. We were able to bring our concerns about anti-Asian sentiments to the nation for the first time, whereas previously Asians were usually featured as the "national threat" or the "national superminority." Mrs. Chin and ACJ representatives appeared on national television—all three news networks, *The Donahue Show*, NBC's *First Camera*, and local TV documentaries in Detroit—and Sacramento ACJ addressed the founding meeting of the Democratic Party's Asian Pacific American Caucus. In Japan, coverage by newspapers and TV prompted Japanese to question visiting American businessmen and government officials who were soliciting Asian business whether Asians are safe in the U.S. and whether Asians can get equal treatment here. The example of cooperative effort set by the Detroit groups was taken up nationally by the Japanese American Citizens League, the Organization of Chinese Americans, and the National Chinese Welfare Association, among others.

While many minority and civil rights groups greeted the Asian American

presence in the civil rights arena as a long overdue event, others instead questioned the right of Asians to join the civil rights coalition. ACJ representatives were at times treated to tedious and absurd arguments that Asians are
not truly a minority in America, and to the equally absurd question of whether
racial slurs make a racial incident. Indeed ACJ was advised by some constitutional lawyers that Asians are not protected under the federal civil rights
statutes and that it would be ill advised to consider a civil rights violation. Some
legal organizations wrote tortuous essays on the dangers of double jeopardy
for the killers—often a specter in civil rights crimes—while other liberal legal groups were either strangely and unusually silent or eager to jump to fellow liberal Kaufman's defense. Conservatives, meanwhile, were quick to jump
on the case as a law-and-order issue, but completely ignored its racial aspects.
Mostly, though, the response of legal professionals was one of alarming indifference to injustice, which, they say, happens all the time. Partly, it seems,
because of their total unwillingness to do anything about it.

There were the usual difficulties encountered when organizations learn
to work with one another. Still, support for the efforts of the ACJ and the
growing Asian American civil rights network continues. We are living in a
depressed economic period that makes it all too easy and convenient to direct frustrations and anger at us. What happened to Vincent Chin was not
an aberration or an isolated quirk of fate. The list of assaults and killings of
Asians since the Chin case, maintained through an informal network, continues to grow:[2]

- A 17-year-old Vietnamese student was stabbed to death in his Davis,
  Calif., high school after weeks of racial harassment by a group calling
  itself the "White Student Union."
- A gun was pulled on a Chinese American telecommunications market-
  ing professional working in Texas.
- A Vietnamese man was stabbed to death in Dorchester, Mass., report-
  edly in a racial incident.
- A Buddhist temple in Greenview, Mass., was blown up by Vietnam
  War veterans who said they wanted to get even for what happened
  to them in Vietnam, even though the temple has no Asian members.
- A Vietnamese family was forced from its farm in West Virginia after
  several cross-burnings.
- The words "Nips Go Home" were spray painted on the store of a
  Korean family in Davis, Calif.

2. The National Asian Pacific American Legal Consortium, an organization of legal and
civil rights organizations formed in 1993 as a result of the Vincent Chin case, is committed to
documenting, monitoring, and educating the public about hate violence. Its *Audit of Violence
against Asian Pacific Americans* in 2001, the year of the 9/11 terrorist attack, reported 507 incidents of anti-Asian violence.

- The word "Chink" appeared on the cover of *National Review* magazine, a conservative publication. Its editors say they didn't think it would be offensive.
- A 19-year-old pregnant Chinese woman was decapitated by a train when she was pushed in front of it at a New York subway stop by a man whose lawyer says the murderer was "overcome by a fear of Asians."
- A Chinese graduate student, also in Davis, was stabbed to death and police have not ruled out a racial motivation in his killing.
- Every day of the week, countless Asian Americans are insulted, intimidated, threatened, cursed at and told to "go back home" by total strangers, for no reason other than because we look Asian. How many of these insults will turn into senseless racist murders?

The flurry of Asian American activism throughout the country that followed the shocking sentence by Kaufman may seem strange to some observers, but it is a natural result of two centuries of oppression and the final straw for many who've suffered a lifetime of indignities. For many of us, the killing of Vincent Chin and the sentences of probation for his murderers shattered the illusion that Asians are being treated as equals of other Americans. Instead we learned that little has changed: in 1873 a rancher could kill his Chinese servant and be fined $20; in 1982 two men could beat a Chinese American to death and be fined $3,000. No matter how long we stay in this country, and no matter how "accent-free" our children learn to speak English, we are still regarded as foreigners, and as "foreigners" we are suspect as an enemy from overseas.

For us, the price of personal safety in the U.S. is eternal vigilance and involvement. While we, like other Americans, cherish our heritages, we cannot afford the luxury of being silent or isolated from other groups. Our ability to demand the protection of our constitutional rights depends on our willingness to work together and maintain the fragile network that has been woven as a result of the Vincent Chin tragedy. It is to the credit of thousands of Asian Americans who sacrificed their time, money and effort to make sure we did not turn our backs on this life-threatening issue. In doing so, we have written another page in our history. But until the day groups like ACJ can disband because their work is done, we all still have much to do, to try to ensure there will be no more Vincent Chin cases.

SOURCE: *Bridge* 9, no. 2 (1984): 18–23.

A LETTER FROM LILY CHIN (1983)

Lily Chin was the moral backbone behind ACJ's national crusade for justice. A Chinese immigrant woman of great courage and fortitude, she never gave up in her quest

Lily Chin speaking at a rally for Vincent Chin, with Jesse Jackson *(left of podium)* and Helen Zia *(right of podium)* in attendance. (Courtesy of Renee Tajima-Pena)

for justice and the hope that no other mother would ever have to lose a child to hate and prejudice again. Her presence and active participation in the national campaign helped to galvanize broad-base support for the first Asian American civil rights case against hate crime. In 1983, after Judge Charles Kaufman sentenced Ebens and Nitz each to $3,000 in fines and three years' probation for the killing of Vincent Chin, Lily Chin wrote the following letter in Chinese to the Detroit Chinese Welfare Council:

I, King Fong Yu (wife of Bing Heng Chin), grieve my son, Vincent Chin, who was brutally beaten to death by two assailants with a baseball bat. The two killers were apprehended by police and prosecuted in court. During the court proceedings, I, because I am widowed and poor, with no money in my bed, could not retain legal counsel to press the case for my deceased son. As a result, the murderers' attorney had the say. Yesterday, I read in the newspaper, the sentence was only a fine and probation; and the killers were set free. There was also no compensation for the victim's family. This is injustice to the gross extreme. My son's blood had been shed, how unjust can it be? I grieve in my heart and shed tears in blood. Yes, my son cannot be brought back; and I can only wait to die. It is just that my deceased son, Vincent Chin, was a member of your council. I, therefore, plead to you. Please help me. Please let the Chinese American community know, so they can help me raise funds and hire legal counsel to appeal. You must put the killers in prison so my son can rest his soul; and my grief vindicated. This old woman will be forever grateful.

I, King Fong Yu, respectfully submit this letter of appeal.

March 18, 1983

SOURCE: Courtesy of Helen Zia.

In 1984, the U.S. District Court sentenced Ebens to twenty-five years in jail for violating Chin's civil rights and acquitted Nitz. But the victory was short-lived. Ebens's attorney succeeded in appealing the decision on a technicality and getting a retrial in the conservative city of Cincinnati, Ohio, where the jury returned a verdict of not guilty on May 1, 1987. Ebens was acquitted of all charges. Although Vincent Chin's mother, Lily Chin, later won a $1.5 million civil suit against Ebens and Nitz for the loss of Vincent's life, no money was ever paid; nor did Ebens or Nitz ever serve a day in jail for the murder of Vincent Chin. Grief-torn and bitter over her son's murder and the miscarriage of justice, Lily Chin moved back to China to live out the remainder of her days. She returned to Detroit after a long illness and died on June 9, 2002, at the age of eighty-two.

OTHER REFERENCES

Christine Choy and Renee Tajima, *Who Killed Vincent Chin?* (New York: Filmakers Library, 1989), VHS.

Patricia Wong Hall and Victor M. Hwang, *Anti-Asian Violence in North America: Asian American and Asian Canadian Reflections on Hate, Healing, and Resistance* (Walnut Creek, Calif.: Alta Mira Press, 2001).

Helen Zia, *Asian American Dreams: The Emergence of an American People* (New York: Farrar, Straus & Giroux, 2000).

A Journey of Bitterness (1999)

Lily Wang

In 1989, Lily Wang (pseudonym) was one of 50,000 Chinese that year to be smuggled into the United States from the Fuzhou area in southeast China. In the next decade, approximately 150,000 others would follow her, almost all seeking better economic opportunities in New York City. Lacking a legitimate way to immigrate to the United States as sponsored relatives or skilled and technical workers, many Fuzhounese fell prey to a human smuggling syndicate that profited handsomely in arranging for their clandestine passage into the United States. More often than not, the journey proved difficult and dangerous, forcing immigrants to risk their lives, endure physical discomforts and abuse, and incur enormous debts before ever reaching their destination. Then began the difficult task of toiling for years as undocumented workers in the underground economy—at construction sites, restaurants, garment shops, and factories—in order to pay off their smuggling fees, estimated to be $30,000 in the early 1990s.

The following story by Lily Wang came out of a survey of three hundred Chinese illegals in New York City conducted by criminologist Ko-lin Chin for his book Smuggled Chinese: Clandestine Immigration to the United States. *The majority of his subjects were men, and although many of them had harrowing stories to tell about their hazardous journey and harsh lives in America, in some ways, as shown by Wang's story, it was worse for the women.*

I left China mainly for non-financial reasons. When I was in China, I met an overseas man in a barbershop where I was working, and we developed a very close relationship. Later, he went back to America. When he was about to leave, he promised he would return in a year to marry me and bring me to America. However, I did not hear from him again. I believed he looked down on me. Later, through a flashy guy who came frequently to my hair salon to get his hair done, I made contact with a snakehead [human smuggler] from Tingjiang. I heard say that he was really cool and very good at what he was doing.

When I first made contact, the agreement was for US$30,000, US$1,000 up front as deposit and the balance payable on arrival in America. All expenses during the trip were to be included. The first part of the trip would be by air. Then we would enter the U.S. by land, via auto. At first the snakehead supplied me with tourist documents for Hong Kong so I could enter Hong Kong from Shenzhen on a tourist bus. Supposedly it was for a ten-day tour, but in reality all the passengers were destined for other countries. After I arrived in Hong Kong, I was picked up and delivered to a guesthouse by a Cantonese-speaking Fuzhou man. The food and accommodations were quite good. We were also allowed to go out and have fun. Then the snakehead in Hong Kong gave me a passport to Bolivia, supposedly to visit relatives.

With that document we first went to Thailand. There were only five of us going from Hong Kong to Thailand: two women, three men. After we disembarked at the airport, we were picked up by a Fuzhou man, who brought the five of us to a guesthouse. The snakehead in Thailand then collected our passports and gave us Taiwan passports. We flew to Bolivia and waited for him there. The person who met us there was Chinese. We had absolutely no problems passing through customs. The man could speak the Fuzhou dialect. He was big and tall and treated us quite well. He picked us up and set us up in a private residence. Our food and accommodations were all provided by him.

A week passed and there was still no word about the next lap of our journey. Then one day he took me and the other woman out, saying he needed our help to buy food. So we accompanied him and we enjoyed ourselves on the outing. When it got dark, he said we were going to a nightclub. We felt absolutely no threat from him so we followed him. We had a good time. Then suddenly someone else showed up and greeted us. He was Chinese too. It appeared that he knew our snakehead. When it got very late we wanted to go back and rest, but the two of them refused and said that we were going to stay at a good hotel. We became scared and said no. They said if we wanted to go back we could go by ourselves. We were afraid. Using threats and coercion by turns, they "invited" us to a guesthouse. We knew everything was over, that we were completely at their mercy. Afterward they said if we didn't cooperate they would not help us, and furthermore, they would send us to some remote rural area far away. So that day the two of us fell prey to them. During the next fortnight, they took us out practically every night, and we had to go with them. Sometimes I was the only one "invited" out. I was young then, and in a foreign country far from home. I was scared they would abandon me in some far-off place, and in order to continue my journey, I had no choice but to submit.

Finally the snakehead in Hong Kong made contact with him, telling him to send me to Hong Kong as soon as possible. I wept with joy when I heard the news because it meant I would soon leave this country and leave him as well. Even as we boarded our boat in Bolivia, it seemed as if he could not bear to let me go. On the outside I was all smiles to him, but inside I was seething with anger. I don't know how long the voyage was, but all the time I was foolishly going through my mind as to what had happened to me during those ten-odd days in Bolivia. As I faced the ocean, I felt no sense of fear. On the boat they gave us fruit and candy. We disembarked in the night, and only then did we find out that we had arrived in Mexico.

Once we set foot on land, we were met by a Mexican. We continued by car, making rest stops on the way to stretch our legs. Sometimes we traveled on mountain roads. During the trip our Mexican guide opened our luggage and confiscated at will the good things. At that time we were all secretly carrying American dollars on our persons. When he couldn't find any cash in our luggage, he gestured at us and said something. Though we didn't understand the language we knew full well he wanted money and shook our heads. He didn't do anything to us and we continued on our way.

On the mountain I just couldn't walk a step further and sat down. He screamed at me. It was terrifying. He had a cane in his hand and could have hit me with it at any time. When we arrived at the U.S.-Mexican border, he told us to wade across the river. We women couldn't swim and we were afraid to go into the water. He spoke to us in English, but still we didn't dare do it. When the men in the group saw that we wouldn't go into the water, they also stopped. The Mexican finally gestured to show us that the water only came up to our chest. I wasn't sure if I should believe him, but I was half pushed and half dragged into the water. Actually the water was not deep, but I was still scared. The guide waved at me to cross the river quickly. When we arrived on the other side, we were all wet and shivering with fear. After walking some distance we reached the highway, scaled a fence, and entered U.S. territory.

Some henchman hired by the snakehead came to meet us. He treated us quite well in the beginning. First, he picked us up in a car and took us to a private residence. After one night in Los Angeles, they sent us on a plane to New York early the next morning. In New York they kept us in a private villa. The food and the accommodations were fine. A few days later the snakehead showed up. Afterward he and his snakehead cronies asked me to go out to dinner with them and bought me some clothes. He was still quite nice to me. The next few nights he had me accompany some of his friends to dinner and karaoke and then took me home. Later I was frequently asked to accompany them when they went out, and then they asked me to spend the night, telling me that it would help retire my debt. If I didn't agree I would have to pay back the sum in full within a week, or I would be sold to a massage parlor. Since the snakehead was decent to me, the collector also showed me some consideration. Eventually I moved in with the snakehead.

I worked in a garment factory for a while, but later started working as a call girl, doing things I could not explain to you. I am making $4,000 a month now. I know I have become a very low-class person, but I cannot get out of this predicament. I had relatives here, but I rarely got in touch with them. Later, the friends of the snakehead sexually harassed me, but I didn't think I could report it to the police because of who I am.

I endured a lot during the journey. The price I had to pay to come to the U.S. was incalculable. My journey was a chronicle of bitterness. It's too late for regrets now, and there is not enough money to buy back the life I lost. All this talk about love and affection in America is a big lie. The same is true in China. America is not a paradise; it's a hell.

SOURCE: Ko-lin Chin, *Smuggled Chinese: Clandestine Immigration to the United States* (Philadelphia: Temple University Press, 1999). Translator: Ellen Yeung.

OTHER REFERENCES

Kenneth Guest, *God in Chinatown: Religion and Survival in New York's Evolving Immigrant Community* (New York: New York University Press, 2003).

Peter Kwong, *Forbidden Workers: Illegal Chinese Immigrants and American Labor* (New York: Free Press, 1997).

Paul Smith, ed., *Human Smuggling: Chinese Migrant Trafficking and the Challenge to America's Immigration Tradition* (Washington, D.C.: Center for Strategic and International Studies, 1997).

Snakeheads: The Chinese Mafia and the New Slave Trade (New York: Downtown Community TV Center, 1994), VHS.

Immigrant Women Speak Out on Garment Industry Abuse (1993)

Fu Lee

On a sunny May morning in 1993, two hundred workers, community supporters, and elected officials gathered at the Oakland Museum to hear Chinese immigrant women speak out against the deplorable working conditions in the garment industry. In addition, Chinese immigrant subcontractors came forth and blamed the manufacturers for controlling the contract prices, wages, and working conditions; scholars and experts linked the local problems with "free trade" and the global economy; and specific recommendations for industry reform were made to local elected officials.

The hearing was initiated by Asian Immigrant Women Advocates (AIWA), a grassroots organization in Oakland, California, committed to working with immigrant women to improve working conditions in the garment, hotel, and electronics industries, and was spurred by a recent labor dispute in which twelve Chinese women at Lucky Sewing Company were laid off with $15,000 back wages owed them. Because the sewing company had gone bankrupt after manufacturer Jessica McClintock, Inc., terminated their contract, the workers, with the support of AIWA, decided to go after the manufacturer for their back wages. When Jessica McClintock refused to accept corporate responsibility for the loss of the workers' wages and jobs, the workers decided to take their case to the public. Fu Lee, one of the twelve garment workers laid off by Lucky Sewing Company, was among the speakers that day. Her testimony was given in Chinese and translated into English as follows.

Hello, my name is Fu Lee. I am forty-one years old, married, and I have a nine-year old daughter. I have been living in Oakland Chinatown since I left Hong Kong twelve years ago.

I want to tell you about the kind of exploitative working conditions I have had to endure in the sweatshops. I also want to tell you why me and my co-workers felt we had to stand up against the manufacturers to take responsibility for our loss of jobs and pay.

When you see Jessica McClintock's holiday windows this year, think about the reality behind them: Sweatshop women facing a cold, grim Christmas.

FANTASY vs. REALITY

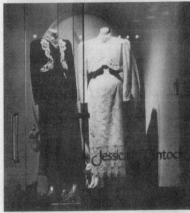

A few weeks ago, we bought a page in this newspaper to appeal to S.F. clothing magnate Jessica McClintock's better nature.

The ad was paid for by donations from concerned people in the Bay Area.

It was our plea on behalf of seamstresses cheated out of months of pay when a sweatshop with long-time ties to Jessica McClintock took shelter in Chapter 11 bankruptcy.

We went public only after Ms. McClintock refused to meet with us or discuss ways to help these women.

Rather than show compassion, Ms. McClintock's answer was her own ad — quite different from the highly romantic ads her $145 million fashion empire usually runs — accusing the unpaid seamstresses of "intimidation and a blatant shakedown."

Her ad was so odd in tone, and so disappointing to many who think of Jessica McClintock as an ethical designer, that we can only assume that she was poorly advised to issue such an angry and distorted response to our reasonable, humanitarian appeal.

FANTASY: That these low-income, non-English speaking women are any kind of threat to Jessica McClintock's $145 million operation.

REALITY: Bay Area sweatshop workers are so fearful of reprisals if they show support for the women seeking back pay, some attend rallies wearing masks. One sweatshop woman was fired after being spotted

at a rally outside Jessica McClintock's headquarters.

Can you imagine the courage it takes for these women to stand up to threats of blacklisting from sweatshops captive to companies like McClintock?

"Intimidation," Ms. McClintock? "Shakedown"? Tell us all about it.

FANTASY: Ms. McClintock's ad claimed that she had contracted with

> ## THE WOMEN WHO SEW IN THE SWEATSHOPS HAVE STILL NOT BEEN PAID. WITH HOLIDAYS COMING UP, WE ALL HAVE A CHOICE TO MAKE.

the bankrupt sweatshop "only for a period of six months," and "we paid them for the work they did for us."

REALITY: Despite a fictitious name change, evidence suggests the family who owned the bankrupt sweatshop had relied on McClintock business for years. When expected production quotas from McClintock did not materialize, the company headed into bankruptcy.

FANTASY: Jessica McClintock says she finds the working conditions we described "abhorrent" and claims that her company will only work with a contractor who "abides by all

federal and state hour, safety, and other laws" — as if written agreements actually reflect reality.

REALITY: The women in this sweatshop were required to work ten hours a day, six to seven days a week. They were never paid overtime as required by state law. They were forbidden to use the bathroom. There was poor lighting. Inadequate ventilation. No health benefits. And they worked for far less than minimum wage on Ms. McClintock's dresses — in fact, in the end, they were paid nothing at all.

FANTASY: The ad over McClintock's signature included a "pledge" to work to improve the lot of garment workers.

REALITY: Jessica McClintock, Inc., belongs to a trade association which lobbied hard to kill California legislation that would have extended protection to contract workers in the

garment industry, protection already enjoyed by contracted farm and construction labor. It is hypocrisy for Jessica McClintock to say she favors better treatment of garment workers while Jessica McClintock, Inc., opposes it.

Jessica McClintock's fantasy is of the lace and frills of yesteryear. But her contract workers face a starker reality.

We again appeal to Jessica McClintock to show her good faith...and her compassion.

With the holidays approaching, many of these women are without any means to celebrate.

The plight of these unpaid seamstresses is a matter of conscience. It is a terrible social injustice for such hardworking women to be exploited in the name of "romanticism."

We thank you for your understanding and your support. Please, let Ms. McClintock know how you feel.

> "The price of a garment is determined...
> by what the department stores are
> willing to pay for it. Then the person
> doing the pricing works backward to
> determine how much can be spent for
> materials and labor. Usually the cost of
> labor [cutting, sewing, pressing, etc.]
> and the materials combined must be
> kept under 1/8 the retail price: labor
> and materials split this amount 50-50.
> Thus a garment that will sell in the
> stores for $168 can only be produced if
> the labor costs $10. I am thrilled that
> someone is taking a stand about this. I
> hope your efforts will be the wedge that
> starts people re-evaluating their basic
> assumptions, like Rosa Parks refusing
> to move to the back of the bus."
>
> — letter from a former production
> supervisor for Jessica McClintock

Jessica McClintock & Ben Gollober
1400 16th Street, San Francisco, California 94103

I appeal to you as the thoughtful people you are reputed to be. I know what your lawyers and PR consultants are telling you. But I also know it's time to change a system that sweats non-English speaking women for profit — the way the system changed for California's farmworkers. You know what the right thing to do is in this case. Pay these women for the work they've done. And contract with them directly for high-quality party dresses, sportswear and children's wear worthy of my family's consideration this holiday season.

NAME

ADDRESS

Asian Immigrant Women Advocates
Room 302, 310 Eighth Street, Oakland, California 94607 / PHONE (510) 268-0192

The two pages you have been compelled to buy in this newspaper add up to several thousand dollars, paid for by donations from courageous seamstresses who have decided to stand up for themselves and from people like me who applaud their courage. □ I wrote Ms. McClintock and her business partner Ben Gollober. □ I'm enclosing my tax-deductible support for your non-profit educational and advocacy efforts □ $25 □ $50 □ $100 or $_____

NAME

ADDRESS

Full-page ad placed in the *New York Times* on December 2, 1992, by Asian Immigrant Women Advocates to appeal to clothing magnate Jessica McClintock's "better nature." (Courtesy of Asian Immigrant Women Advocates)

I worked as a seamstress at Lucky Sewing Company for two years. Before that, I worked as a seamstress at other similar sweatshops. All of the workers worked long hours, ten to twelve hours a day and six to seven days a week. We were paid by the piece, which sometimes was below the minimum wage. Overtime pay was unheard of. You may think sewing is an easy job. But it requires a lot of skill. For fancy dresses with laces, tiny buttons, and tricky fabric patterns, you really have to concentrate so you do not make any mistakes. My wage was never enough money for our family to live on. We always worried about our daughter getting sick because we had no health insurance.

My eyes hurt from straining under poor lighting; my throat hurt because of the chemical fumes from the fabric dye. Sometimes, I wore surgical masks so I would not have to breathe in all the dust from the fabric. My back never stopped hurting from bending over the sewing machine all day. Our boss was like a dictator. He was always pushing us to work faster. There was a sign in the shop that said, "No loud talking. You cannot go to the bathroom." When we did talk loudly or laugh during work, he would throw empty boxes at us and tell us to go back to work. When there was a rush order, we had to eat lunch at our work station.

Last year, my employer closed his shop and left us holding bad paychecks. We found out that he had filed for bankruptcy and had no intention of paying us our meager wages. The twelve Chinese seamstresses including myself were so mad. After working so hard under such horrendous working conditions, we should at least get our pay.

With the help of Asian Immigrant Women Advocates, we began searching for ways to get our pay. We were shocked to find out that the dresses we sewed were selling for $175 at an exclusive Jessica McClintock boutique in San Francisco. Our boss would receive only $10 for these dresses from Jessica McClintock, the manufacturer, and we seamstresses would be paid less than $5 for each of these dresses. And in our case, we got nothing! We also discovered that the main reason why our employer went out of business was because Jessica McClintock Inc. had terminated its contract with my employer, after ten years of exclusive dealings. We felt that since Jessica McClintock made the most profit from the dresses we sewed, she should pay us for our work when our boss cannot. So we asked Jessica McClintock Inc. to pay us our back wages.

When Jessica McClintock said no, we held public rallies in front of her stores. We had gone out to rallies wearing masks because we were still afraid of being blacklisted in our community. We would be called troublemakers and have a difficult time finding a job. You see, because we do not speak English and the American society does not recognize our skills, we have no choice but to go back to these dead-end jobs. But instead of listening to our demands, Jessica McClintock called our public rallies "a blatant shakedown" and "intimidation."

Our story is not unique. The San Francisco Bay Area's garment industry is the third largest in this country. There are over twenty-five thousand garment workers in the Bay Area. Eighty percent are women, most of whom are immigrant women like myself. For over a century, immigrant women have been the backbone of America's garment industry. Manufacturers use immigrant women's labor because it is cheap and no one speaks against the awful working conditions. To me this is terrible discrimination against immigrant women like me and my friends. Why else do you think the working conditions of sweatshops have been tolerated over a century? I also heard that attempts to pass reform legislation have been killed by powerful corporate lobbyists and unsympathetic politicians.

These are some realities, violations of immigrant women, which exist in the garment industry that sells fantasy to the public.[1] I never dreamed I would be living this kind of life when I came to America. I hope you can help women like me so the next generation of immigrant women do not have to experience the things that me and my friends do now. Thank you.

With courage, determination, and the support of labor, community, and student activists, the women waged a four-year battle involving a consumer boycott, pickets, public actions, national mobilization of support, media coverage, and appeals to elected and government officials. In 1994, Jessica McClintock finally gave in. The settlement included payment of back wages, educational and scholarship funds for the workers and their children, and a bilingual hotline for workers to report violations in sewing factories contracted by McClintock. The victory holding manufacturers accountable to their workers was unprecedented and paved the way for a broader antisweatshop movement.

SOURCE: *Immigrant Women Speak Out on Garment Industry Abuse: A Community Hearing Initiated by Asian Immigrant Women Advocates*, Oakland, California, May 1, 1993, p. 5.

OTHER REFERENCES

Miriam Ching Louie, "Immigrant Asian Women in Bay Area Garment Sweatshops: 'After sewing, laundry, cleaning and cooking, I have no breath left to sing,'" *Amerasia Journal* 18, no. 1 (winter 1992): 1–27.

Miriam Ching Louie, *Sweatshop Warriors: Immigrant Women Workers Take On the Global Factory* (Cambridge, Mass.: South End Press, 2001).

Xiaolan Bao, *Holding Up More Than Half the Sky: Chinese Women Garment Workers in New York City, 1948–92* (Urbana: University of Illinois Press, 2001).

1. "Fantasy" is in reference to the text of an advertisement placed in the *New York Times* (see p. 360) by AIWA, which in part read: "Jessica McClintock's fantasy is of the lace and frills of yesterday. But her contract workers face a starker reality."

Chinese and Proud of It (1996)

Jubilee Lau

In 1996 Jubilee Lau was a nineteen-year-old student attending the College of San Mateo in northern California when she won second place in the "Growing Up Asian in America" competition with the following essay about adjusting to life in Idaho as a six-year-old immigrant from Hong Kong. Started by the Asian Pacific Fund in 1995 to celebrate national Asian Pacific American Heritage Month, the contest seeks to encourage Asian American youths in the San Francisco Bay Area to share their ideas and experiences through creative writing and art.

For the 1996 contest, students were asked to address the topics of parents and family, coming to America, career choices, or growing up in a bicultural environment. Out of close to 1,500 entries in all age categories, Lau placed second in the 18–22 age group. Her essay, "Chinese and Proud of It," gives us hope that racial prejudices, language barriers, and cultural differences can be overcome even in places like Nampa, Idaho. Lau graduated from the University of California, Berkeley, with a B.A. in mass communications in 1999, and currently works as a wedding consultant in Santa Clara, California.

It was 11:00 A.M. on January 23, 1983. I lifted the panel to the window on the airplane and timidly peered outside. I glanced back at my parents and my eight-year-old sister sitting beside me and felt reassured by the grins on their faces. My parents began talking excitedly in Cantonese and hugged each other in happiness. We had finally made it to America. Hand in hand, the four of us stepped onto the carpeted floor of the San Francisco International Airport and stared in awe at the people around us. They all spoke English. We, the non-English speakers, were guided to our luggage by a friendly bilingual stewardess, and we were soon greeted by my aunt and uncle at the crowded greeting area. I had never seen such happy laughter from my parents as they kept repeating in disbelief, "Finally, we've come to America!"

My family immigrated to the United States when I was six years old. I was too young to realize that the plane ride that I had been so excited about was actually going to transform my whole life. My parents left Hong Kong, our longtime home, with high hopes to "make something of their lives." They dreamed of coming to America, the land of opportunities, to recreate our lives for the better. They were convinced that America could offer my sister and me the best education and future. To them, America promised success and a steady life. Therefore, with high hopes and determination, we left our families, friends, and home country behind to pursue a new and better life.

When we first arrived as new immigrants, we rented a small apartment near Chinatown. Although my uncle, who has adapted to the lifestyle in America, frequently tried to take us to "American" shopping malls and tourist areas, we would still end up going to Chinatown at least once a day. There, we felt more at ease because we could buy Chinese groceries and hear people speaking the same language as us. Whenever we were in the "white areas" of San Francisco, I would hold on to my father's hand tightly for security and shyly ask in Cantonese, "Daddy, what are those English people saying?" During my six years of life in Hong Kong, I had never been acquainted with the strange language, which everyone was speaking so rapidly on the streets of San Francisco. Both my mom and dad spoke limited English, and they found it hard to translate for me.

After a week, my sister and I began attending the Chinese Educational Center, an elementary school for new immigrants who didn't know English at all. My parents sent us to school with sparkles of hope in their eyes. "This is a new beginning," my mom would remind us. "Study hard in school, and don't worry about anything else." My parents would often fantasize how proud they would be when they will be able to brag about their two college-graduate children from the United States to their friends and families in Hong Kong. It didn't matter that they couldn't find a high-paying job with their poor English skills, or the fact that people snickered silently at their terrible pronunciation. The hope that they put on my sister and me was enough to keep them going.

Learning English proved to be much harder than I imagined. I still remember the first day of school when I wanted to know where the bathroom was. I shyly walked up to a teacher and whispered, "Do you know the toilet?" The teacher didn't even try to cover up her laughter as she pointed to the other direction. "The *bathroom*," she emphasized, "is right down the hallway." I was so embarrassed that I refused to try to speak English again. I was so afraid that other people were going to laugh in my face again, and I wasn't going to let that happen. After a while, my parents noticed that my English was not improving a bit. Everyday after school, they would ask me to speak in English, but I would always refuse and went in the living room to watch Chinese television programs. Frustrated, my parents decided that this couldn't go on.

Jubilee Lau *(left)* with her parents and older sister Mimi at Lucky Peak Park in Idaho, 1987. (Courtesy of Jubilee Lau)

I thought the worst day of my life was when my parents announced that we were moving to Idaho. After getting loans from the bank and relatives, my parents collected enough money to buy a restaurant in Idaho, where we would start our lives all over again. I had overheard my parents talking in their bedroom one night, and I knew that Idaho was a place where I would have to speak English, whether I chose to or not. My parents thought that this would be the only way for my sister and I to adapt to the American way of life and really start learning English. Within a month, we packed our bags and were on our way.

Idaho was everything that I had feared. There was no Chinatown for us to "hide," no Asians, and nothing but farms, cows, and the "English people." I cried every day during the first week of our arrival. I was so afraid of living there that I refused to step out of the house. I felt so unsafe and so scared that I often had nightmares about speaking in English. However, I was too young to have a say in any decision. My parents quickly found a school for my sister and me, and we were to start school in three days. I dreaded starting school, and seeing the difficulties my parents were having in getting people to understand how they wanted the restaurant to be renovated made me feel worse.

Everything did not go the way that I expected. On the first day of school, I was caught by surprise when I stepped inside the carpeted floors and air-conditioned hallways of Centennial Elementary School. My eyes widened as students trampled past me without their shoes. Friendly smiles greeted me as I continued walking down the hall, holding on to my dad's hand. When the principal, an extremely nice lady, took me to my new classroom, my heart skipped a few beats as other classmates eyed me curiously. My fear didn't stay very long though, because I could sense the friendliness all around me. My teacher, a pleasant-looking young lady, gently steered me to the front of the class and introduced me. Then, she turned to me and said very slowly, "We are very happy to have you here. You are the only Asian we've ever had in this school, and we hope you'll feel right at home." She pronounced each word carefully and accurately, and I was amazed that I actually understood her words. When recess came, all the other kids surrounded me and began shooting questions at me excitedly. "Are you from China? Hey, then you must know Kung Fu!" "What do you eat for dinner? Snakes?" "Say something in Chinese!" "How come your eyes aren't slanted like they should be?" I was startled by their bundles of questions, but I also felt pleased that they were so interested in me. Taking a deep breath, I tried to answer their questions the best I could. To my surprise, none of them seemed to mind that my English wasn't fluent, or the fact that my pronunciation was poor. That day, I went home feeling confident and great.

The next few years in Idaho were the most memorable ones in my life. I learned English much quicker than anyone expected, and I realized that I was smarter than most of the people in my class. Pretty soon, I spoke English fluently, read the Sweet Valley Book Series that everyone else read, sang Christmas songs as loudly as anyone else, and played Double Dutch at recess. When class officer elections came around, I didn't even hesitate. With help from my dad, I created a great campaign and won with a majority of votes. My parents were so proud of my improvements in school, and smiled modestly when my teachers praised me continuously. I remember when one of my classmates lost to me in a Spelling Bee, he asked, "Are all Asians that smart?" My classmates and teachers never stopped taking an interest in my Chinese culture. They continued to fire questions at me once in a while, and sometimes begged me to teach them some Chinese. I enjoyed the attention very much, and felt prouder about my cultural background than ever. At home, I would ask my parents to tell me more about my cultural background so I can transfer the new information to my fellow classmates. I had never felt so good about myself.

My family really benefited from our decision to move to Idaho. My parents not only had a steady business, but they also learned to speak English a lot better by constant practice with customers at the restaurant. I realized that not all Americans look down on the new immigrants who can't even pronounce the simplest English. Idaho made me see a completely different side to the American culture. It also made me aware of my own culture and how interesting it really is. Although I am now an American citizen who can speak English fluently, I still don't consider myself an all American. I will always be a hyphenated American because I am from Hong Kong, my ancestors are from China, and I will always be Chinese.

SOURCE: *Growing Up Asian in America: Prize Winning Essays and Artwork, 1996* (San Francisco: Asian Pacific Fund, 1996), pp. 43–44.

OTHER REFERENCES

Arar Han and John Hsu, *Asian American X: An Intersection of 21st-Century Asian American Voices* (Ann Arbor: University of Michigan Press, 2004).

Maria Hong, ed., *Growing Up Asian American: An Anthology* (New York: W. Morrow, 1993).

Vickie Nam, ed., *Yell-Oh Girls! Emerging Voices Explore Culture, Identity, and Growing Up Asian American* (New York: Harper Collins, 2001).

Learning to See
the Man Himself (1997)

Marilee Chang Lin

Interracial marriage has been a controversial topic and practice for Chinese Americans historically and to this day. In most states, antimiscegenation laws prohibited marriages between Chinese and whites until the U.S. Supreme Court ruled these laws unconstitutional in 1967. Even today, most Chinese immigrant parents would prefer that their children marry within their own ethnic or racial group. Yet statistics show that interracial marriages between Chinese and white Americans have been steadily increasing since the 1970s, with American-born Chinese women out-marrying at higher rates than American-born Chinese men. Journalists and scholars alike have been wondering: Is this trend a sign of Chinese American assimilation and social acceptance, the internalization of racial and gender stereotypes, or hypergamy—people intermarrying to improve their social status?

While Asian American intermarriage, especially the pairing of Asian women and white men, attracts much attention from those interested in analyzing its underlying racial meaning and social causes, we often forget that statistics show that in-group Chinese marriage still predominates, accounting for about three of every four Chinese marriages in the United States. The out-marriage rate among American-born Chinese, however, was as high as 46 percent in 1990. Thus, the following story of "Chinese girl meets and marries Chinese boy," despite the demographic odds in white suburbia, is an unusual one. It is told with humor by Marilee Chang Lin from Needham, Massachusetts, in A. Magazine: Inside Asian America, *a popular journal intended for Asian American co-eds.*

As the daughter of parents of Chinese ancestry who was raised in Honolulu, educated on the East Coast, and three and four generations removed from China, I grew up daydreaming about the "all-American boy-next-door." In our suburban Boston home, that meant a haole [white].

At the time, Needham, Massachusetts, was hardly a model of ethnic di-

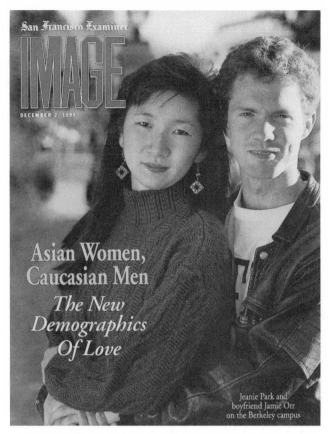

Magazine cover showing popular interest in the controversial topic of interracial dating and marriage among Asian Americans. (*San Francisco Examiner,* December 2, 1990, photo by Elizabeth Mangelsdorf)

versity, and through all my years of public school I encountered only a handful of other Asian kids. The prospects for dating a "nice Chinese boy" were slim indeed, and though my maternal grandfather, Goong-goong Thom, occasionally asked me if I had met any of these nice Chinese boys at school, I was practiced at saying "No" as if to say, "Not recently" rather than "It'll never happen." Otherwise, there was little pressure to date within racial boundaries, and through high school and college I was free to go out with whomever I liked as long as they were careful drivers, polite conversationalists, and hard workers—the usual parental dictates.

John, just like me, was thoroughly assimilated, though he was a first-generation American. An avid outdoorsman and athlete, a scholar and teacher, a photographer and gourmet cook, he was the antithesis to any of the number of warped stereotypes of Asian males that were firmly rooted in my Americanized Chinese brain. For years I'd been thinking, Goong-goong can inquire and cajole all he wants; there's no way I'm going to date, much less marry, some serious, bespectacled computer geek who cares more about standard deviations and MCAT scores than the hues of a sunset or a good fall line on a snowy mountainside. I was well convinced of my destiny to marry a "nice haole boy" and raise hapa-haole kids who would look like my mixed-race Hawaii cousins.

Months before I was to start a new teaching job (my first real job) at a big Eastern boarding school north of Boston, however, I had begun hearing reports of John, one of a handful of other new hires. He, too, was Chinese, an English teacher, and a former rower. I couldn't help feeling slightly offended when people openly speculated about our getting together, a virtual eventuality in some minds that rated high in the "cute factor": two single, Chinese American, English-teaching, crew-coaching new faculty were surely meant for one another. Before long, I began to feel as if we were everyone's Chinese version of Barbie and Ken. Although the matchmakers meant well, I already resented John before we'd exchanged a single syllable. At my most charitable, I supposed we could be friends, amiable colleagues, once all the intrigue had diffused into the everyday routine of school life.

Needless to say, I overcame my own preconceptions, my grudge against this stranger whose only apparent fault was the shared slant of an eye, cast of complexion, and straight, black hair. And despite my resolve to prove that race wasn't everything, I found that race, along with a confluence of interests and values and goals, was something. The coincidence of culture that defined race, the body of tradition and habit and language that transcended the physical play of features and pigments, suddenly mattered. To speak even of food from our childhoods (*jook* [rice gruel], almond junket, *char siu bao* [barbecued pork bun]) was to communicate in some kind of delicious secret code. Our friendship was surprising and comfortable, both despite and because of our common heritage. Moreover, letting myself get to know John as a human being and not some representative of race pulled me out of that worn groove of thinking that I was bound for a certain kind of relationship whose parameters, I was convinced, had been drawn from the moment of my birth in Yankee Connecticut.

Of course, John and I are like any other couple, whether mixed or "matched" in an onlooker's eye; being of the same ethnic background doesn't magically erase differences in temperament and style. And it's hardly something I'm conscious of as I go through the motions of daily life. But when I reflect on the small flashes of understanding I've had as I've grown older, I breathe a sigh of gratitude knowing that in at least this one instance, I managed to shake off a kind of blindness, my own seemingly benign presumptions that I harbored to defend myself against the presumptions of others.

In the end, skin color matters and it doesn't matter. It is indeed the cover of the proverbial book, which gives us clues about the text within, but it's strangely incidental when you get in deep, reading because you can't help being interested, glad that you took it off the shelf at all. My Goong-goong in his great wisdom said it best when I called him, seven years ago now, with the news of our engagement, smug in my expectation that John's background would render him ecstatic. His response, following the few-second delay between Boston and Honolulu, came across loud and clear: "As long as he is a good man," he said in his gentle, serious way. And that was it.

What more needed to be said? Goodness, after all, is the only true standard of measurement when making choices in this life. I did marry a "nice Chinese boy," but the emphasis, I realized, was and always had been on nice, the quality of character, and not the race, that defined the man.

SOURCE: *A. Magazine: Inside Asian America,* July 1997, p. 30.

OTHER REFERENCES

Colleen Fong and Judy Yung, "In Search of the Right Spouse: Interracial Marriage among Chinese and Japanese Americans," *Amerasia Journal* 21, no. 3 (winter 1995/1996): 77–98.

Nazli Kibria, *Becoming Asian American: Second-Generation Chinese and Korean American Identities* (Baltimore: Johns Hopkins University Press, 1982).

Larry Hajime Shinagawa and Gin Yong Pang, "Asian American Panethnicity and Intermarriage," *Amerasia Journal* 22, no. 2 (1996): 127–52.

Betty Lee Sung, *Chinese American Intermarriage* (Staten Island, N.Y.: Center for Migration Studies, 1990).

The Best Tofu in the World
Comes from . . . Indiana? (1998)

Ellen D. Wu

What is a Chinese immigrant family to do about finding comfort foods like fresh tofu in a place like Indianapolis, Indiana, in the early 1970s? Caught in this dilemma, Paul and Anita Wu resorted to making their own tofu — a long and arduous process as described in this heartwarming essay written by their daughter while a student at UCLA. The essay was subsequently published in Yolk, an Asian American magazine that covered entertainment, lifestyles, and popular culture for the "generasian next" from 1994 until it ceased publication in 2003.

Little has been written about the Chinese in the Midwest, although their history in the region dates back to the 1870s, when Chinese immigrants on the West Coast moved east to escape the anti-Chinese movement and in search of work. Almost all of them ended up operating restaurants, laundries, and grocery stores spread out across the midwestern states. Except in Chicago, their population would remain small until the arrival of Chinese students and professionals from Hong Kong, Taiwan, and China in pursuit of higher education and job opportunities in the 1960s. In the state of Indiana, where the Wus settled and raised their two children, Ellen and Simon, the Chinese population increased sevenfold, from 2,115 in 1970, to 14,703 in 2000, according to the U.S. census. Unlike the earlier Chinese settlers, these new immigrants tended to be Mandarin speaking, highly educated, and lived in white suburban communities. Even so, as Wu's story bears out, they still had to deal with cultural adjustments, especially in areas with relatively small Chinese populations.

Born and raised in Indianapolis, Ellen Wu received her B.A. in biology and history from Indiana University and her master's degree in Asian American studies from UCLA. She is currently a Ph.D. student in history at the University of Chicago, where she is completing her dissertation on Chinese and Japanese Americans during the post–World War II period.

My parents moved to Indianapolis, Indiana, in 1973. At the time there were only a handful of Chinese families in the area—hardly surprising for a mid-

Family portrait of Ellen; brother, Simon; and parents, Anita and Paul Wu.
(Courtesy of Ellen D. Wu)

size, midwestern metropolis situated in the "Hoosier Heartland," just eight
years after Congress revamped the country's policy toward Asian immigration. The city's small number of Asians was only enough to sustain one Asian
food market, AB Oriental, which was located on the other side of town from
my parents' home. The nearest Chinatown, in Chicago, required a three-
and-a-half-hour road trip. Thus, the familiar foods of my dad's native Taiwan
and my mom's native Hong Kong were difficult to obtain, while the items
that were more readily available were often of dubious quality.

To satisfy their cravings for Chinese dishes of the non–sweet 'n' sour chop
suey nature, my parents began experimenting in order to re-create the comfort foods that they missed. As a child, I taste-tested their versions of *shao-
bing youtiao* (Shanghainese style sesame seed pastries and fried dough sticks),
chashao and *doushabao* (barbecued pork and sweet red bean steamed buns),
huajuan (flower rolls), *jook* (Cantonese style rice porridge), *dan tat* (egg cus-
tard tarts), and *luobogao* (shredded turnip cakes with Chinese sausage). Sometimes they followed recipes out of *Pei Mei's Cookbook* or friends' suggestions;
other times they used trial and error until they hit upon the right combination of ingredients and cooking methods.

One of the most successful concoctions was my parents' homemade tofu and its myriad of variations. Although it is found in almost all mainstream markets today, tofu, a staple of the Chinese diet, was something of a rarity in Indianapolis grocery stores circa 1973. The supply available frequently lacked the freshness my parents desired. One solution, therefore, was to turn our kitchen into a part-time tofu factory. My parents, however, were recipe-less (hardly anyone makes tofu at home) and had to *xiang banfa*—a Chinese term which translates roughly into thinking of ways, means, and methods—in order to produce it from scratch. They knew that tofu was made from pressing soybean milk. The first step, they concluded, was to make the milk. The process was long and arduous.

My mom or dad would first purchase soybeans in bulk from a local farmer. After hauling the sacks of beans back home, they would hand soak the beans in water overnight to soften them. The next morning I would awaken to the loud sounds of the beans grinding in the blender, reverberating throughout the house. After they pulverized the beans, they poured the watery mash into filtering bags improvised from muslin or cheesecloth. At this point, they would close the bags and twist them to extract the milk, leaving the solid bean parts behind.

I can still picture my mom on tiptoes at the kitchen sink, grunting and squeezing the beans as hard as she could.

Finally, they would boil the raw milk in large pots on the stove. The second part of tofu making, they deduced, was to press the milk into squares. A liquid, however, will not metamorphose into a solid without some sort of physical or chemical alteration. Luckily my father, a research pharmacist, had training in the sciences. He reasoned correctly that a coagulant needed to be added to the soybean milk. My parents tried a number of different substances until they found calcium sulfate to be a satisfactory additive.

After mixing this magic substance into the soybean milk, my parents would then pour the mixture into square wooden frames that they had constructed. A considerable amount of weight was necessary to press the tofu to the correct firmness, so my mom would gather heavy objects from around the house to stack on top of the frame—our old manual typewriter and selected volumes from our *World Book Encyclopedia* collection usually sufficed. This makeshift tower of assorted items would sit in our kitchen sink overnight until the next day, when the tofu—creamy, silken, and of the utmost freshness—would finally emerge ready to be cooked and consumed.

My mom would remove the finished product from the wooden frames and place each block carefully in a Tupperware container full of water to keep the tofu moist while it sat in the refrigerator. For a couple of weeks thereafter we would enjoy tofu in different soup and main dishes, such as hot and sour soup, fried tofu stuffed with ground meat, and *mapuo doufu*, at the dinner table. Due in part to my parents' tofu-making escapades, my mom gradually gained a reputation among the local Chinese American community for being a talented Chinese cook.

My parents, always adventurous, continued to experiment not only with tofu dishes but also with modifications of tofu itself. Soybean milk was the most basic of the variants. Chinese people like to drink it sweet or salty, hot or cold. My father tried to coax me into drinking the milk, chilled and sweetened, by adding chocolate syrup to it, probably thinking the cocoa flavor would appeal to my "American" taste buds. The syrup and the milk did not mix together well, however—I recall the drink looking rather spotty. It tasted even worse than it looked—I held my nose while downing my glass as quickly as possible—and to this day, I still avoid sweet soybean milk, with or without chocolate syrup. I do like the salty kind, however. My dad would serve it steaming hot in bowls with a bit of vinegar and dried shrimp and green onions sprinkled on top.

Doufuhua was a dish that is "in between" soybean milk and tofu. It is extremely soft and slippery and served hot and sweetened. Again, to entice his second-generation daughter, my dad would serve it to me with an American sweetener, maple syrup. I thought it to be delicious. *Doufugan,* tofu pressed longer and flatter than "regular" tofu, was at the opposite end of the consistency spectrum. After pressing it, my mother would flavor the outside of the tofu blocks with Chinese five-spice powder, then slice it thinly and cook it in soups or stir-fries. Brown on the edges and white in the middle, *doufugan* was, and still is, one of my favorites. I love it with all types of soups and dishes and even as an appetizer.

As the years progressed, however, the tofu making became less and less frequent for a number of reasons. Fresh tofu became more readily available as increasing numbers of Asian immigrants settled in Indianapolis, spawning a small wave of Asian market openings. When my dad passed away in 1987, my mom lost some of her drive to re-create the foods that he dearly loved and missed. Most significant, however, were the practical considerations of *liqi* (strength), *gongfu* (energy), and *shijian* (time). My mom, a petite woman who stands barely five feet, found it more and more difficult to handle large amounts of soybeans, squeeze the raw milk out of the cheesecloth bags, and manipulate the heavy objects necessary to press the tofu.

Furthermore, as a single mother working full-time as a nurse, she had much less energy and time to spend in the kitchen. Nevertheless, we still enjoy homemade tofu every once in awhile. My mother proudly feeds her tofu to my brother and me when we go home on weekends and breaks. She always reminds us that it is not only tasty, but also nutritious. She occasionally prepares tofu dishes for holiday potluck dinners with family friends. Her tofu is the highlight of our *huoguo* winter meals (Chinese-style *shabu-shabu,* which involves cooking raw foods in a pot of boiling water in the middle of the dinner table).

Growing up on my mom's homemade tofu has spoiled me and turned me into a quasi–tofu snob. I refused to touch what passed for tofu in my college dorm cafeteria. I was horrified by the vegans at school who drank soybean milk, not in the Chinese fashion, but with their breakfast cereal. I never buy tofu at mainstream supermarkets. And even though I now live in Los Angeles, where I can find soybean milk, tofu, *doufuhua, doufugan,* the infamous stinky tofu, and tofu "salad" (cold tofu topped with shaved bonito flakes, seaweed, and soy sauce, a dish I recently tried at my Japanese American boyfriend's house) almost anywhere, I hardly eat the stuff anymore.

I long for my mother's tasty and nutritious tofu, the symbol of both her love and my parents' ingenuity, a gastronomic link to their homeland and a culinary link to my childhood. I eagerly anticipate my next trip home to Indianapolis when I will finally have the opportunity to eat some of the best tofu in the world.

SOURCE: *Yolk* 5, no. 2 (summer 1998): 20.

OTHER REFERENCES

Ling-li Chang and R. Bruce Sanders, eds., *Mid-America Chinese Resource Guide,* Chinese American Librarians Association–Midwest Chapter, 1995; available at http://lark.cc.ukans.edu/~eastasia/calamwrg/midwest951.html. Accessed September 23, 2004.

Ken Hom, *Easy Family Recipes from a Chinese-American Childhood* (New York: Alfred A. Knopf, 1997).

R. Keith Schoppe, "Chinese," in *Peopling Indiana: The Ethnic Experience,* ed. Robert M. Taylor and Connie A. McBirney (Indianapolis: Indiana Historical Society, 1961), pp. 86–104.

Reflections on Becoming American
(1999)

Binh Ha Hong

Take no one's word for anything, including mine—but trust your experience.
Know whence you came.
If you know whence you came, there really is no limit to where you can go.
JAMES BALDWIN

Binh Ha Hong and her family were among the 270,000 Vietnamese to flee their home-
land by boat after relations between China and Vietnam deteriorated following the end
of the Vietnam War. About one-half of the "boat people" were ethnic Chinese like the
Hongs, forced out by the new Communist regime. They were also among the lucky sur-
vivors, as an estimated 80 percent of the boats were attacked by pirates and over
100,000 died at sea. Along with one million other Southeast Asian refugees, the Hong
family finally resettled in the United States, making Portland, Oregon, their home.

Binh Ha Hong was only three years old at the time, but the memories of war, escape,
and resettlement would continue to haunt her. After graduating from Northwestern
University with degrees in journalism, she worked at various local newspapers in south-
ern California and is currently pursuing a Ph.D. degree in history at the University
of California, Irvine. In the following essay, which was first published in the Ontario
[Calif.] Daily Bulletin *on Independence Day, 1999, Hong pays tribute to her par-*
ents' courage and sacrifices on the twentieth anniversary of their escape from Vietnam
and reflects on what it means to be Chinese, Vietnamese, and American.

My father's hands are tanned from years in the sun. The blunt edges of his
fingernails are closely clipped. Permanent calluses have created a stiff, leath-
ery texture on his palms. Black residue from motor oil lines the cracks and
crevices of his nails and fingers. His hands are capable of any task—from dis-
mantling a car's transmission to rocking a baby back to sleep.

My mother's hands are soft and pale from working with fabrics for 16 years.
The skin is a bit more elastic, but still as graceful as they were in her youth.
They are warm and reassuringly maternal with the knowledge of having pre-
pared countless meals and nursing me through fitful colds.

Binh Ha Hong *(left)* with her mother, Hoa Thi Dang Hong; brother, Vu The Hong; and father, Ho Phu Hong, in Tuy Hoa, Vietnam, two days before her father was sent to a reeducation camp for the second time, 1978. (Courtesy of Binh Ha Hong)

Neither of my parents wears a wedding ring. They were pawned long ago to buy our passage to freedom. Ho Phu Hong and Hoa Thi Dang Hong teach by example. My parents rarely speak of their childhoods, the Vietnam War, or adjusting to the United States. There is no point dwelling on things that cannot be changed.

My father emphasizes education because his was disrupted when he was drafted into the army at 21. My happiness is their American dream. For this reason, they started life over—learning a new language and new skills so they could give me the basics.

Yet, it is what they do not say that has given me so much more. I learned the value of a dollar by watching my parents struggle for each penny. I learned to endure hardships because there was no other choice. But most important, I learned that through the roughest times family is what really matters.

In July 1979, my family fled Vietnam. The events that so drastically changed my life and those of two million Vietnamese expatriates have been replaced in the world's consciousness by other wars and other refugees.

The experiences—deprivations after the Vietnam War ended, the uncertainty of the future, and learning how to do without—can never be erased. Those years shaped who I am today. My extended family now is scattered across five continents. Family members built new lives—learning English, Spanish, or Norwegian, getting married, switching careers, and having babies. My generation and my younger cousins are more versed in pop culture than Vietnamese culture. The only time I speak Vietnamese is when I address my elders. I think, write, and even dream in English.

And yet the surest way of passing on history and heritage is through exposure. Because of that, the expatriate elders from my village created the Chinese Compatriot Association of Tuy Hoa (my birthplace in central Vietnam). They celebrate the Lunar New Year, the Mid-Autumn Festival, and, on Independence Day in 1999, a banquet to commemorate the twentieth anniversary of when we all fled Vietnam. An estimated 600 people gathered to eat, to watch their children and grandchildren show off their talents, and to catch up on gossip.

I cannot separate where my Vietnamese side ends and my Chinese side begins. I grew up with an amalgam of both. My birthplace was Vietnam, but the Chinese association's existence proves my Chineseness. Only my grandmother and my oldest uncle spoke Chinese. And yet, I grew up addressing some of my cousin's relatives by the Chinese version of aunt or uncle. As the oldest grandchild, my cousins on my father's side called me "chi," a title of respect for older females. I didn't realize that was a Chinese custom until I returned to Vietnam for the first time in 1994. My mother was the second youngest child in her family. My maternal cousins, who were half of my nineteen years of age but whose parent was older in the family hierarchy, followed Vietnamese custom and simply called me by name, without that title of "chi." One of my mom's most mouthwatering dishes was actually a recipe she learned from my father's family, who hailed from Hainan Island (off the southeast coast of China), where the chicken rice is famous.

The distinctions between my two halves come out in subtle ways. Around purely Chinese people, I am reminded of my "Vietnameseness" because I cannot speak Chinese. Around Vietnamese people, customs that I assumed were Vietnamese actually turned out to be Chinese. All I know is that each time I help my grandmother in the kitchen, wiping banana leaves to wrap around dumplings or plucking herbs for dinner, I am introduced to another segment of my history.

My parents were married on January 1, 1975, a scant four months before

Saigon fell, and along with it, our world. Because my father had served in the Army of the Republic of South Vietnam (ARVN), he was detained in a reeducation camp after the war. He was there when I was born. My father refers to it as prison. He was sent to a remote outpost to do hard labor in the jungle. "Reeducation" for an estimated 1 million South Vietnamese military officers and soldiers, government employees, and political dissidents meant communist ideology indoctrination classes, starvation, torture, and even death. My father was released after eighteen months. He rarely speaks about what he went through.

Former prisoners were blackballed by the communists and not allowed to work or receive food rations. Homes and businesses were confiscated and redistributed. Because my father and uncles had served on the losing side, I and my cousins would never be allowed to get an education. We would always be discriminated against because my family had Chinese blood and fought for South Vietnam. The future seemed bleak.

In December 1978, Vietnam invaded China-backed Cambodia. In retaliation in February 1979, China invaded Lang Son province in North Vietnam, and 26,000 people were massacred. The new government of Vietnam panicked, uncertain whether China intended to start another war. So they intensified their campaign against the Chinese in Vietnam, encouraging them to emigrate.

In the ensuing months, my family sold everything we owned for gold. The pawned wedding rings and other valuables were enough to bribe my father out of the reeducation camp and to gain passage on a tiny fishing boat for my grandmother, my parents, 13 aunts and uncles, and 11 grandchildren. Though the Vietnamese government tried to expel the ethnic Chinese, passage on the boats and bribing officials cost money.

Children cost four ounces of gold, or $1,800. For adults the price jumped up to nearly $3,000.

We snuck out in the middle of the night in July 1979, aiming for Hong Kong. The fishing boat was packed with several hundred people. We drifted at sea for four nights and three days. We were one of the lucky ones. The route to Hong Kong was popular because it avoided the Thai pirates that preyed on boats headed toward camps in Malaysia, the Philippines, and Indonesia. They raped, tortured, and killed countless victims.

I was 3 years old. I vaguely recall throwing up on my youngest aunt and demanding ice cubes to cool myself from the broiling South China Sea sun.

We docked in Hong Kong harbor and were placed in Shanshuipo Transit Centre, a refugee camp operated by the United Nations High Commissioner for Refugees. My family was given one bunk bed. Later refugees slept on wooden slats. I shared the top bunk with my grandmother and youngest aunt. My father, mother, and brother had the bottom. I remember playing hide-and-seek among the bunk beds. My mother remembers asking for discarded chicken wingtips from nearby restaurants to supplement our food rations.

On June 16, 1980, my family came to the United States. We were sponsored by the nuns at Marylhurst University in Oregon City, a suburb of Portland, Oregon. In many ways, I think we were fortunate there was not a large Vietnamese or Chinese ethnic community around. It forced us to learn English quickly in order to understand and communicate with others. My parents only have a mild accent. I don't have one at all.

Even with language barriers, those early years were filled with scattered memories of the kindness of strangers. Our landlady baked a pineapple upside-down cake to introduce us to American cuisine. Ladies from a local church taught my mom and aunts how to make Christmas stockings. A pick-your-own fruit farmer swallowed his losses after my family, confused by the sign, picked a truckload of peaches, thinking he would pay them by the pound instead of the other way around.

My parents worked for minimum wage as janitors in the education building at the college. My mother, who had once been a bank executive in Vietnam, became a seamstress at Pendleton Woolen Mills to get us off welfare. My father, who once dreamed of becoming a doctor or a lawyer, chose to get an associate's degree in auto mechanics because it required little knowledge of English and could be completed in 18 months.

They desperately took any odd job they could find to bring in extra money. These years taught me not to ask for anything, knowing we could not afford it. I remember my parents waking up at the crack of dawn to pick strawberries, blackberries, blueberries, and raspberries. Oregon farmers paid in cash—two dollars for a flat of berries and thirty-three cents for a pound of cucumbers. My parents learned to knit intricate woolen reindeer and snowflake patterned sweaters. They were paid $15 for each handknit creation. Their janitorial job required them to dump office trash cans each night, but they took home the contents. For years my brother and I sorted and boxed piles of white, color, and computer paper so my father could take it to the recycling plant for a little bit of cash.

After six years of scrimping, my parents had saved enough to buy a house and moved us to Portland to be closer to my dad's auto shop.

Decades later, those hardships become memories. A thousand miles away from home, and thousands more away from my birthplace, I want to tell my parents that their sacrifices have not been in vain. But my parents have never asked for that.

Their accomplishments aren't summed up in the house they bought or the business they started. Their pride hangs in the family room where gigantic picture frames hold my Northwestern University degree and my brother's University of Pennsylvania diploma.

The reflections on my past come rarely. I made a living writing about other people's lives, other people's thoughts, other people's histories. For once I'm writing about mine.

So mom and dad, this one's for you.

SOURCE: A version of this article was published in the *Ontario [Calif.] Daily Bulletin,* July 4, 1999, p. D9.

OTHER REFERENCES

Nathan Caplan, *The Boat People and Achievement in America: A Study of Family Life, Hard Work, and Cultural Values* (Ann Arbor: University of Michigan Press, 1989).

Mary Terrell Cargill and Jade Quang Huynh, eds., *Voices of Vietnamese Boat People: Nineteen Narratives of Escape and Survival* (Jefferson, N.C.: McFarland & Company, 2000).

Tricia Knoll, *Becoming Americans: Asian Sojourners, Immigrants, and Refugees in the Western United States* (Portland, Ore.: Coast to Coast Books, 1982).

Affirming
Affirmative Action (1995)

Chang-Lin Tien

The national debate over affirmative action as a remedy for addressing racial discrimination reached a new crossroad in the 1990s. Focusing on affirmative action policies in higher education, neoconservatives argued that affirmative action was in fact "reverse discrimination" against whites and Asian Americans. Under pressure and in support of this view, the University of California (UC) Board of Regents voted in 1995 to eliminate the consideration of race, ethnicity, and gender in admissions, hiring, and contracting. That same year, Chinese American parents sued the San Francisco Unified School District for requiring higher scores of their children to get into the prestigious Lowell High School, and the Asian American community was divided over Proposition 209, the California Civil Rights Initiative that would end affirmative action in the state by prohibiting "preferential treatment" on the basis of race.

It was within this context that Chang-Lin Tien,[1] then chancellor of UC Berkeley, wrote the following commentary in defense of affirmative action for A. Magazine: Inside Asian America, later reprinted in the New York Times. As the first Asian American to head a major U.S. university, Chancellor Tien was internationally known as an expert on heat transfer and thermal science, a formidable fundraiser for the university, and a staunch advocate of "excellence through diversity."

I never rode the city buses when I attended the University of Louisville in Kentucky. I had no car, so sometimes I had to walk seemingly endless miles

---

1. Chang-Lin Tien was born in Wuhan, China, in 1935. He fled with his family to Taiwan after China turned Communist in 1949. In 1956 he came to the United States to attend graduate school at the University of Louisville in Kentucky. Upon receiving his Ph.D. in mechanical engineering from Princeton University in 1959, he joined the faculty at UC Berkeley. In 1962, at age twenty-six, Tien became the youngest professor to win Berkeley's Distinguished Teaching Award, and in 1990 he became the first Asian American to head a major U.S. university.

Chancellor Chang-Lin
Tien at the University
of California, Berkeley.
(Courtesy of University
of California, Berkeley)

back and forth from the campus to downtown. It was not simply the lack of money that forced me to walk, although I was a poor immigrant when I was accepted as a graduate student there in 1956. Rather, I refused to ride the buses because I found it humiliating.

Today, I can still recall my shock when I first boarded a city bus and found that whites rode in the front and "coloreds" rode in the rear. Just where exactly did an Asian fit in? I too have a skin color, but I am not black. And if I chose the front section, what kind of statement was I making about the black men, women, and children relegated to the rear?

This great country has made phenomenal progress since those days of Jim Crow segregation. The Civil Rights Act of 1964 paved the way for the desegregation of our society.[2] Yet this country's leaders realized that de facto segregation would remain, so long as blacks and other minorities were not afforded equal opportunities in hiring, contracting, and admission to institutions of higher education. Their concerns led to the establishment of affirmative action policies.

---

2. The Civil Rights Act of 1964 guaranteed people of all racial backgrounds equal access to public accommodations and protection from employment discrimination.

These historic social changes did not come easily. The debates were heated. Pitched battles frequently erupted. Yet most would agree that our country is a better place as a consequence.

The Asian American community reaped substantial benefits from these efforts to integrate American society. Affirmative action opened doors previously closed to immigrants and natives alike, offering broader opportunities for housing and employment. It is now acceptable in America for an Asian to be CEO of a major corporation. Some Asians, like myself, have even become chancellors of prominent universities. This would have been unthinkable in the America of the 1950s.

Now, the debate over affirmative action has surfaced once again. There are serious proposals to do away with these policies altogether. I do not agree with these proposals. I am particularly concerned about the impact these policies would have on institutions like the University of California at Berkeley. I worry that we may be turning back the clock, with harsh consequences for all minorities, including Asian Americans.

I remain firmly convinced that diversity is the key to the continued academic excellence that is Berkeley's hallmark. I base this belief on the many successes my campus has recorded over the last decade, as it has grown increasingly diverse.

Berkeley is a public university that is charged with educating the diverse population of the state of California. In the 1990 census, ethnic minorities represented 43 percent of California's population. Any policy that does not enhance access for these minorities to our university is shunning our most basic charge.

Achieving this diversity while maintaining excellent academic standards is not a simple task. It requires an admissions process that takes into account traditional academic standards such as grade point average and SAT scores. Yet the process must go further. It also must assess the relative potential of applicants as measured by that person's special talents, the hardships he or she had to overcome, and the contributions he or she may make to society if afforded a quality education. It must take into account the obstacles to academic success posed by an applicant's race or ethnicity.

When we embarked on our journey to diversify our student body while preserving our excellence, there were no model admissions programs for us to follow. In many senses Berkeley has been charting new territory. And whenever you travel in unfamiliar terrain, you expect to stumble at times and strike off in the wrong direction at others. This has been our experience and we have learned along the way.

The Asian community is painfully familiar with some of our missteps. In the 1980s, a controversy brewed over the fairness of our freshmen admission standards. Some critics—including campus administrators such as myself— argued that proposed standards were weighted heavily against Asian Americans. The public outcry triggered investigations that ultimately resulted in a refining of our standards to insure fairness.[3]

At the same time, we reformed the process of setting standards. As a result, the details of our freshmen admissions process are very much open to public scrutiny. Our admissions standards are a model copied across the country.

The new standards also define diversity more broadly. We want to make sure our doors are open to low-income students, immigrant students, older students, disabled students, and students from rural and urban regions alike.

Today, Berkeley has one of the most diverse populations of any major American university. No racial or ethnic group is in the majority. In the fall of 1994 undergraduate student population, Asians represented 39.4 percent, whites 32.4 percent, Chicano/Latinos 13.8 percent, African Americans 5.5 percent, and American Indian/Native Americans 1.1 percent.

Critics of affirmative action say that opening the door to minorities does not guarantee their success, and yet our graduation rates have improved as the campus has become more diverse. Other critics predict that academic standards will decline as the numbers of minority students increase.

At Berkeley, that simply is not true. The fall 1994 freshman class is stronger academically from top to bottom than the freshman class of 10 years ago. Measured by almost any academic criteria one chooses, the excellence of our students is evident. The mean high school grade point average is 3.84, for example, and the mean SAT score is 1,225—high by any standard. The overall academic quality of our student body has been improving consistently over the past 10 years.

And the pool of highly qualified students applying for admission continues to grow. For the fall 1995 semester, we received 22,700 freshmen applications—an increase of 9 percent over last year. These highly talented applicants included about 9,500 students with a 4.0 high school grade point average. The fact is, our 1995 fall freshmen class will consist of 3,470 students.

Furthermore, our graduation rates have climbed steadily over the past 10 years for all students. Currently, 74 percent of our students graduate within five years. In the mid-1950s, just 48 percent of our students graduated within five years. The numbers dispel the notion that diversity has somehow sacrificed the quality of our institution. In fact, the diversity has been coupled with rising standards.

I know there are Asian community leaders who argue that traditional academic criteria—grade point averages and SAT scores—should be the sole

---

3. In 1985 the Asian American Task Force on University Admissions found evidence that a series of policy changes had discriminated against Asian American applicants at UC Berkeley. This was later confirmed in a subcommittee hearing of the State Assembly. Chancellor Michael Heyman publicly apologized to the Asian American community in 1988, and a more inclusive and fairer admissions policy was instituted after Tien became chancellor in 1990.

determinants for admission. I would point out that no major university admits students solely on this basis because such an approach ignores other factors that differentiate an excellent student from a good one. Elite private institutions routinely give special preferences to the children of alumni and of major donors. Yet no one argues that these practices have caused the academic quality of the Ivy League schools to decline.

The fact remains that diversifying our student body is sound educational policy in a country undergoing profound demographic changes. Today's education student must be able to effectively teach in a multicultural classroom. The medical student who cannot comfortably interact with African American, Latino, or Asian patients will fail to address modern society's medical needs. The business student who can't work in concert with colleagues from Hong Kong, Korea, or Mexico will have a hard time climbing the corporate ladder.

Our country has come a long way since the days of segregated buses. But if we fail to provide access to higher education for all minorities, major sectors of our population will not succeed in a society that increasingly mandates advanced academic skills. I fear that the net result will be a two-tiered society, divided like those old buses along racial and ethnic lines.

The Asian community has always been united by a strong sense of justice. I am confident that that sense will prevail as the current debate on affirmative action unfolds.

To counter the impact of the UC Regents' ban on affirmative action and the passage of Proposition 209 the following year, Chancellor Tien initiated broader and more inclusive admissions standards, and launched the Berkeley Pledge, a program designed to maintain campus diversity by preparing underprivileged high school students for the University of California. He retired in 1997, after a successful thirty-eight-year teaching career and seven-year term as chancellor. Five years later, he died of a brain tumor and stroke at the age of sixty-seven.

SOURCE: *A. Magazine: Inside Asian America,* June/July 1995, pp. 87–88.

OTHER REFERENCES

Sucheng Chan, "Asian American Struggles for Civil, Political, Economic, and Social Rights," *Chinese America: History and Perspectives,* 2002, pp. 56–70.

Gena A. Lew, ed., *Common Ground: Perspectives on Affirmative Action and Its Impact on Asian Pacific Americans* (Los Angeles: LEAP Asian Pacific American Public Policy Institute, 1995).

Paul M. Ong, "The Affirmative Action Divide," in *Asian American Politics: Law, Participation, and Policy,* ed. Don T. Nakanishi and James S. Lai (Lanham, Md.: Rowman & Littlefield, 2003), pp. 377–405.

Dana Y. Takagi, *The Retreat from Race: Asian-American Admissions and Racial Politics* (New Brunswick, N.J.: Rutgers University Press, 1992).

Countering Complacency

An Interview with OCA Director
Daphne Kwok (1996)

Alethea Yip

Daphne Kwok remembers growing up in a Virginia suburb where she and her brother were among the few minorities in school. "I thought it was time to start an Asian American organization, but there weren't enough Asian Americans at the school. So then I said, 'Okay, we'll start an international club.'" It wasn't until college, at Wesleyan University in Connecticut, that she became aware of the Asian American movement and what it meant to be an Asian American. Since then, she has tried to build that awareness among as many Asian Americans as she can reach. As executive director of the Organization of Chinese Americans (OCA) from 1990 until 2001, Kwok oversaw one of Asian America's leading civil rights groups.

Founded in 1973, OCA has forty-five chapters in twenty-five states and maintains a national office in Washington, D.C. In 1996, when this interview was conducted, Kwok was thirty-four and had already spearheaded several important victories; nevertheless, she believed that the biggest challenges for the organization still lay ahead, particularly in the areas of immigration reform and affirmative action. Here, Kwok reflects on where OCA has been, where it is going, and what her hopes are for the future of Asian America.

OCA was founded in 1973 when the Asian American population was half of what it is now and where there was little political organization among Asian Americans, especially on the national level. How has the agenda of the organization changed over the years?
Unfortunately, the agenda remains the same. We need to continue to improve the image of Asian Americans and Chinese Americans here in the United States, to seek equal opportunity and equal treatment as Chinese Americans and Asian Americans. I think our mission and role is even more important now with this whole anti-immigrant sentiment that is pervading this country at the local level as well as the national level.

Daphne Kwok
in Washington, D.C.
(Courtesy of Daphne Kwok)

Over the last two decades, what do you think has been the most difficult time for Asian Americans?
I think it is now. Unfortunately, too many Asian Americans in our community have bought into the whole model minority myth—that we're OK as we are, that life is OK as it is. Unfortunately, it's not for most Asian Americans, and until this country becomes a colorblind society, we really are going to be seen as Asian, still perceived as foreign, and still not really accepted as true Americans.

I think that all of this is now starting to show in the pieces of legislation in Congress that are really starting to question and differentiate between citizens—whether you are born here or naturalized citizens—it's a very scary thought.

A lot of it is aimed particularly at the Latino community and the Asian American community. Because we are so physically distinct from the European immigration, people, when they see us, they assume, first of all, that we are from Asia directly even though we may be fourth-generation American. They have the concept and perception that we are not Americans and so, therefore, we are treated differently as such.

What has changed then in the way of progress? What do you think have been OCA's most significant accomplishments?
I think that so far what we've been able to do is really in the immigration field. We worked hard on the 1990 Immigration Act to ensure that the Asian American community still retained the family preference category, specifically the fifth preference—the brothers and sisters category—which most Asians come in under. We were also able to have Hong Kong be recognized as a sovereign nation and to be able to receive the same number of immigration slots as other countries. Prior to that, it was only receiving about 500 slots a year. So, by being able to elevate Hong Kong as a regular country and receiving the same kind of immigration visas, that was one of the major accomplishments. Also, I think our efforts in coordinating a national voter registration drive and really having full support from the community have been very successful as well.

What do you see as the main issues facing Chinese Americans as well as the Asian American community?
Right now, the main issues are affirmative action, the importance of Asian Americans to still continue to support affirmative action because we have been impacted by it. We have benefited from affirmative action and it's not just a beneficial piece of legislation for the African American community or women, but Asians have very much been involved. I think that people unfortunately don't see the link between affirmative action and the glass ceiling. Too many people in our community are advocating that they have been affected by the glass ceiling and yet, on the other hand, they are also saying that we should abolish affirmative action. There is a direct link. If we can't get into the door in the first place, how are we ever going to be able to hit the glass ceiling?

This is an important election year for Asian Americans. Some say it is the first time national politicians will make a serious effort to win the Asian American vote. What role will OCA play in the '96 election?
We do not endorse candidates; we educate and we endorse issues. We want to educate our community about how these various pieces of legislation would impact our community.

We really see OCA as an educational organization, educating not only the Chinese American community or the Asian American community, but the broader community about the issues that impact the Asian American community.

How do you decide which issues to go after?
The board decides, but many of the issues are part of OCA's history. We've always been involved with fair immigration practices. We've always been involved with employment issues, making sure that Asian Americans have

equal access to employment opportunities. All these issues really are following all the same goals and issues that we've had for the last 20 some years, but if new issues come about, yes, we take it up before the board to decide upon.

OCA asserts that it is one of the preeminent national civil rights organizations. How does it relate to other civil rights organizations like the NAACP?
We work very closely with the other civil rights groups. We are one of 180 organizations that are part of the leadership conference on civil rights here in Washington, D.C., and that is made up of minority groups like the NAACP, the National Council of La Raza, the Mexican American Legal Defense and Education Fund, the church groups, the AFL-CIO, the disabled community, the women's community. As one of the members of that coalition, we work on all these civil rights issues in a broader civil rights coalition.

OCA or any other Asian American organization would not be able [to exist] and is not effective by itself. We are, unfortunately, still too small, we're still not really able to pull our political weight and we rely heavily on coalition partners in order to be able to advance our agenda. We are very thankful to the Jewish community, the Latino community, and the African American community for helping us along on issues that impact us as well.

Some say the OCA needs to do more, to become a more visible player on the community scene. How do you respond to that?
I think it's very true, too. At the community level, we really rely on our chapters to be able to have an impact and to be able to have some presence on the local level. OCA being a national organization, we really couldn't be national without our chapters. Yet, we also need to realize that everybody is a volunteer outside of the national staff—and right now we only have a staff of four—and, unfortunately, because of financial resources, we really aren't able to have more of a presence. As we all know, everything takes money. One thing that is unfortunate, not just for OCA, but for other Asian American advocacy organizations, is that we are not supported by the community when it comes to financial resources. What we are working for and fighting for is a very long-term goal, and we're not going to clean up or eliminate discrimination in just a year or two years. It's a long-term investment and I think most Asian Americans don't realize that importance, and so, financially, the [need for more] financial resources is what holds us back from doing what we really need to be doing.

How do you respond when a Chinese American comes up to you and asks, "What has the OCA done for me?"
What I would say to that person is that what we've been trying to do is to ensure that when laws get passed, that lawmakers are not passing laws that dis-

criminate against Asian Americans, that would adversely impact Asian Americans. And basically, what we're trying to do is to protect the civil rights of Asian Americans and all Americans. What we're doing is really at the policy level, and that's not tangible. And unless you are discriminated against, maybe what we're doing will never impact you. And we hope that would be the case for people, but unfortunately our history has shown that if you're a person of color, you're bound to be affected at some point in your life, just because of the color of your skin.

You've been heading OCA for six years now. How did you first get involved in OCA?
I've been involved with the Asian American community since I was in high school. And in college, I was very much involved with the Asian American organization on campus. When I got out of school I was looking for an Asian American group to get hooked up with, and that turned out to be OCA.

Why OCA?
I think it was because it was a national Chinese American organization that was working on issues, not just a social organization, because that was not my interest; and that they were working on some really tough issues and ones that I felt really strongly about: discrimination. So that's what drove me to OCA initially.

And your personal motivation?
I've just always been involved. My parents have always been involved in community volunteer and nonprofit organizations. So, it was instilled in us the need to be involved. So, by just seeing their example and helping them with their nonprofit work it has always been a part of us and very enjoyable and fulfilling. And so I always knew that it was something I wanted to do with my career, hopefully helping others. Hopefully what I'm doing is impacting people throughout the country. One of the most fulfilling parts of my job now is working with students. OCA does have an internship program where we give them a Washington, D.C., experience, a nonprofit experience, and they go back to their campuses with a better knowledge of how D.C. works and what really happens here at the national level. But I think seeing their interest in coming out of college and working with the community really is very inspiring to me, and that really keeps me going.

What have been your goals as executive director?
One of my main goals has been to solidify and stabilize the organization, and I hope that during my tenure with OCA for six years now I've been able to do some of that. Prior to that, we were having presidents coming in and out every one to two years, executive directors every two years, and so there was tremendous [turnover]. It seemed like we were always starting all over again from the beginning. Hopefully, by putting into place stan-

dard and regular events and meetings we've been able to move ahead in our agenda on the issues as well as raise the organization to a higher level of professionalism, and continue to gain more visibility for the organization as well.

So, you're saying that Asian Americans are not yet as politically mobilized as other groups of color. Then, what would it take for Asian Americans to reach political maturity?
I think it's going to take some unfortunate incident to occur to the Asian American community. With the Japanese American community, unfortunately, there was the internment process that really got that community mobilized. I think right now what's anti-immigrant sentiment is to a certain extent the main issue that is kicking the Asian American community in its behind and finally getting us going. I think until issues directly hurt and impact the Asian American community, we're still going to remain complacent. In a way, a lot of us want to thank the immigration restrictionists because their adverse policies and viewpoints finally awakened the Asian American community.

What is your vision for OCA?
Ideally, my vision for OCA would be that there would be no more need for OCA, that our mission and goals will have ended—that there is no more discrimination here in the United States, that there is no more need for organizations like OCA advocating for civil rights. That's ideally what we're trying to work toward. But in reality, I don't think that is going to come anytime soon, unfortunately.

What are the next steps for OCA?
I think just the continued presence and the need to get more of our members to take on more speaking engagements at the local level, to really be involved in the mainstream community by serving on local boards, whether it's the Red Cross or the homeless boards or literacy boards—just to become active participants of American society. I think that's extremely critical and that's what OCA's been working toward—to get people involved, whether it's on the political level or the volunteer level, just for us to be active Americans and involved Americans. We're here in the U.S. and we need to improve our lot here in the United States and we need to be involved. We just can't stay home and be sheltered and hope that someone else takes care of our problems for us.

After eleven years as the executive director of OCA, Daphne Kwok left the organization in 2001 to head the Asian Pacific American Institute for Congressional Studies in Washington, D.C.

SOURCE: *Asian Week,* June 27, 1996, p. 12.

OTHER REFERENCES

Gordon H. Chang, ed., *Asian Americans and Politics: Perspectives, Experiences, Prospects* (Stanford: Stanford University Press, 2001).

Benson Tong, "Political Mobilization and Empowerment," in *The Chinese Americans* (Boulder: University Press of Colorado, 2003), pp. 165–200.

Helen Zia, *Asian American Dreams: The Emergence of an American People* (New York: Farrar, Straus & Giroux, 2000).

"One mile, one hundred years"

Governor Gary Locke's Inaugural Address (1997)

Gary Locke made history on January 15, 1997, when he gave the following inaugural address as Washington's twenty-first governor and the first Chinese American governor in U.S. history. Born into an immigrant family in 1950, Locke grew up in a public housing project and worked in his father's grocery store while attending public school. He received his B.A. in political science from Yale University in 1972 and his law degree from Boston University in 1975. Prior to becoming governor, he served as a deputy prosecutor, a legislator in Washington's House of Representatives and chair of its powerful Appropriations Committee, and chief executive of King County. Locke was known as a hard worker, a budget wizard, and a strong advocate for education, affirmative action, welfare reform, and environmental protection. At the time of this speech, he and his wife, news reporter Mona Lee, were expecting their first child.

The personal story he told that day would be repeated in other speeches, including his "Democratic Response to President Bush's State of the Union Address" in 2003 on national television: "My grandfather came to this country from China nearly a century ago, and worked as a servant. Now, I serve as governor just one mile from where my grandfather worked. It took our family a hundred years to travel that mile— it was a voyage we could only make in America." Locke firmly believed that the ideals and values that had served him and his family—education, hard work, and family solidarity—could help many others to realize the American dream. It was his intention to apply these same principles to the difficult tasks ahead of him as governor of the state of Washington.

Mr. President, Mr. Speaker, Madam Chief Justice, distinguished justices of the Supreme Court, statewide elected officials, members of the Washington State Legislature, other elected officials, members of the Consular Corps, fellow citizens, and friends of Washington State across America and around the world:

Governor Gary Locke.
(Photo by S. Vento)

I am humbled by the honor of serving as your governor. And I am deeply grateful to all those who have made our American tradition of freedom and democracy possible.

I also want to express my gratitude to members of my family, and to introduce them to you. First I'd like you to meet my father, Jimmy Locke, who fought in World War II and participated in the Normandy invasion. I'd like you to meet my mother, Julie, who raised five children, learned English along with me when I started kindergarten, and who returned to school at Seattle Community College when she was nearly sixty. And I'd like to introduce my brother and sisters, Marian Monwai, Jannie Chow, Jeffrey Locke, and Rita Yoshihara. And finally, it is my greatest pleasure to introduce Washington's new First Lady, Mona Lee Locke. This truly is a wonderful day for the Locke family.

One of my ancestors—a distant cousin, actually—was a merchant who immigrated to Olympia in 1874 and became a leader of the Chinese-American community just a few blocks from this state Capitol. He acted as a bridge between the Chinese and white communities, and became friends with the other downtown merchants, and with the sheriff, William Billings.

In 1886, an anti-immigrant, anti-Chinese mob threatened to burn down the Chinese settlement here. But what happened next is a story that every Washington resident ought to know: Sheriff Billings deputized scores of Olympia's merchants and civic leaders. And those citizen deputies stood between the angry mob and the Chinese neighborhood at Fifth and Water Streets. Faced by the sheriff and the leading citizens of Olympia, the mob gradually dispersed. Not a single shot was fired, nor a single Chinese house burned.

For the Locke family, that incident helped establish a deep faith in the essential goodness of mainstream American values: the values that reject extremism and division, and embrace fairness and moral progress; the value of working together as a community; and the values of hard work, hope, enterprise, and opportunity.

Just a few years after that Olympia show of courage, my grandfather came to America to work as a "house boy" for the Yeager family, who lived in a house that's still standing, less than a mile from here.

His purpose was to get an education, and so the Yeager family agreed to teach him English in return for his work. Like everyone else in our family, my grandfather studied and worked hard, and he eventually became the head chef at Virginia Mason Hospital in Seattle.

So although I may be standing less than a mile from where our family started its life in America, we've come a long way. Our journey was possible because of the courage of Sheriff Billings and the heroes of Olympia history. And our journey was successful because the Locke family embraces three values: Get a good education, work hard, and take care of each other.

Our family history is more the norm than the exception. There is Governor [Albert] Rosellini, this state's first Italian-American governor, whose parents migrated to America at the beginning of this century. There is Representative Paul Zellinsky, whose grandfather was a Russian sea captain. There is Senator Dan McDonald, whose ancestors were among the pioneer families of this state. And there is Senator Rosa Franklin, whose family rose from slavery in South Carolina to civic leadership in Tacoma.

There are millions of families like mine, and millions of people like me— people whose ancestors dreamed the American Dream and worked hard to make it come true. And today, on Martin Luther King's birthday, we are taking another step toward that dream.

In the 108 years since Washington became a state, we have gone from riding horses to flying in jets; from sending telegrams to sending e-mail; and from woodstoves to microwave ovens.

Can anyone even guess what the next hundred years will bring? We already know that computers will think, that telephones and television will merge, and that biotechnology will reveal the secrets of our genetic code. Many of our children will produce goods and services that haven't even been invented yet.

For us, the challenge is to embrace change rather than to fear it. We have no time to waste.

To keep the American Dream alive in a high-tech and unpredictable future, we have to raise our sights, and our standards. We must raise our sights above the partisanship, the prejudice, and the arrogance that keep us from acknowledging our common humanity and our common future. And we must raise our standards of academic achievement, of government productivity and customer service, of the careful preservation of the natural environment we cherish, and of our determination to protect the well-being of Washington's working families.

The principles that will guide me in this quest for higher standards—and the principles that will guide my response to legislative proposals—are clear and simple. My first principle is that education is the great equalizer that makes hope and opportunity possible. That's why I am passionately committed to developing a world-class system of education. In the last century, the drafters of our Constitution made the education of children the "paramount duty" of the state. But learning is not just for kids anymore. For the next century, the paramount duty of this state will be to create an education system for lifelong learning—a system that every person regardless of age can plug into for basic skills, professional advancement, or personal enrichment.

My second principle is to promote civility, mutual respect, and unity, and to oppose measures that divide, disrespect, or diminish our humanity. I want our state to build on the mainstream values of equal protection and equal opportunity, and to reject hate, violence, and bigotry. And I want our state to be known as a place where elected officials lead by example.

My third principle is to judge every public policy by whether it helps or hurts Washington's working families. Everyone who works hard and lives responsibly ought to be rewarded with economic security, the opportunity to learn and to advance in their chosen field of work, and the peace of mind that comes from knowing that the essential services their families need—like health care insurance and child care—will be affordable and accessible. And every senior citizen who has spent a lifetime contributing to the freedom and prosperity we enjoy deserves dignity and security.

My fourth principle is to protect our environment, so that future generations enjoy the same natural beauty and abundance we cherish today.

These principles require self-discipline, and a commitment not to settle for quick fixes, Band-Aids, or political expediency. To help us live up to these principles, I intend to set clear, challenging goals, and to measure our progress toward achieving those goals. Everyone in state government will be held accountable for achieving results—not for convening meetings, creating commissions, or following reams of clumsy regulations.

I want to liberate the creativity and expertise of every state employee, and to make working for government as prestigious as building airplanes, designing software, or inventing new medical technologies.

I call on every state employee to search for new and better ways of doing our work, to strive toward a higher level of customer service to citizens, and to show greater respect for every hard-earned tax dollar that we collect.

In fact, let's take a moment to thank both state and local government employees for the truly heroic work they've done during the storms of the past few weeks.

They made visible something too many of us often don't see: that we truly can't live without basic government services, and that these services are provided by people—our dedicated public employees. In the storm and its aftermath, those public employees focused on helping citizens and solving problems and they achieved results.

Now it's time to harness that same energy and sense of urgency to solve problems and achieve results in our education system. We have to do a better job of making our schools safe, and ensuring that students respect their teachers, and each other.

We must hold both schools and students accountable for learning, not just for following all the rules or sitting through the required number of classes. We will not break our promise to raise academic standards. Every third grader must read at the third-grade level, and every high school graduate must master basic academic skills and knowledge.

To meet these ambitious goals, our schools need a stable base of funding, including the ability to pass school levies with the same simple majority that it takes to pass bond measures to build other public facilities.

But money alone is not the whole solution. Greater accountability, coupled with more local control and more flexibility, is also essential to school improvement. To meet the growing demand for education in our colleges and universities, my administration will present a proposal to increase enrollments, to improve quality, and to provide more management flexibility while insisting on greater productivity and accountability.

To do all this, we will make education the first priority in every budget we write. That will not be easy. Developing a quality education system depends on the soundness of our fiscal and tax policies.

That's why it's so important to write budgets that are sustainable beyond the current biennium. And that's why we ought to maintain a prudent reserve, so we'll have funds to see us through a recession without cutting schools or vital services.

This year, a balanced approach to budgeting will also include tax relief. In the last biennium, we gave almost a billion dollars in tax breaks to business. Isn't it time to help working families? To me, that means property tax relief for middle-class homeowners.

Of course, I also support rolling back the business and occupation tax to pre-1993 levels. We raised that tax in a time of fiscal emergency. That emergency has passed, and it's important that we keep faith with the business community by repealing the increase.

We also have a host of other problems that urgently need our attention. We need to agree on a bipartisan, comprehensive plan to invest in our transportation system, on which all our jobs and our economic growth depend.

Our farmers need good highways and rail systems to get their crops to market. Our commuters must have transit and carpool lanes, so they can spend more time with their children and less time stuck in traffic. Our ports need a transportation system that supports the growth of our international trade, which generates so many of our new jobs. There is a great deal the state can and must do to secure our competitive position in the world economy. We have an opportunity to improve Washington's international trade climate. I'm committed to establishing strong personal relationships with overseas government and business leaders to help Washington companies expand existing export markets and establish new ones.

It's also time to stop procrastinating and make some tough decisions about how to use and protect our water resources, which have been tangled in a web of conflicts and controversies year after year. And it's time to fine-tune our commitments to manage growth, to protect fish and wildlife, and to preserve the vitality of our farms and our forest products industry.

As a result of last year's federal welfare reform legislation, we have a once-in-a-lifetime chance to redesign our social safety net, so that it reflects our mainstream values of hard work, hope, and opportunity. If we do this right, we can reduce poverty and protect children—and that ought to be our purpose.

So I will propose a system that puts work first—a system designed to help people in need build on their strengths rather than be paralyzed by their problems. To make welfare reform succeed, we need to become partners with the business community to find jobs and to improve training programs, so that every entry-level job in Washington is the first step on a career ladder rather than a treadmill that keeps the poor stuck in place. And to make work the solution to poverty, we will make sure that work pays better than public assistance.

At the same time, we have a duty to ensure that the ill, elderly, and disabled live with dignity, and that legal immigrants are accorded equal treatment and equal protection.

And finally, we have already waited too long to fix our juvenile justice system—a system that lets kids get away with too much; that misses too many opportunities to turn kids around; and a system that leaves too many of us vulnerable to violent and dangerous young criminals.

To procrastinate on any one of these issues—from education to water to juvenile justice—is to court disaster. The clock is ticking. A new century is coming at us like a bullet train. And it's up to us to either rise to these challenges, or to watch as that train passes by.

If we cultivate the habit of genuine partnership—partnership entered with a commitment to solving problems and achieving results—we can accomplish all our goals.

Students, parents, and teachers can create the best schools in the world. Community leaders, local and state governments can shape a transportation system second to none. And farmers, city-dwellers, tribal governments, and developers can, if they work as real partners, untangle the web of water disputes and find ways to protect this precious resource.

We must all come together, work together, and stay together until our work is complete. Let's work as hard as our parents and grandparents did. Let's match their record of accomplishment, and their level of responsibility to the next generation.

As most of you already know, Mona and I are expecting our first child in March. So in very rapid succession, I will be blessed with two titles that carry immense responsibility and immense honor: Governor and Dad.

As the advent of fatherhood gets closer, I am more and more conscious that everything I do as governor—and everything we do together—we do for our children.

Our child will be a child of the 21st century. He or she will come of age in a world that we can scarcely imagine. But it is his or her world that we must now work together to create. For our children and yours, I want to foster a new century of personal responsibility, of community, and of hope and optimism.

Please help me carry on the Locke family tradition of focusing on those three crucial values: get a good education, work hard, and take care of each other.

With your hand in partnership, and with an abiding faith in the essential goodness of the people of our great state, I want to devote the next four years to making the American Dream come true for children whose faces we have yet to see.

Thank you.

Locke was reelected to a second term as governor in 2000, and after his high-profile speech in response to President George W. Bush's State of the Union Address in 2003, there was talk that he might become the first Chinese American president of the United States. In 2004, however, he announced that he would leave politics and not run for a third term as governor, citing family considerations as his reason. By then, he was the father of two young children—Emily, 7, and Dylan, 5—with a third child on the way. In a message to citizens, he said, "As profoundly important as it is to be your governor, it is just as important to me to be a good husband and father."

SOURCE: "Governor Gary Locke's Inaugural Address, January 15, 1997." Available at www.governor.wa.gov/speeches/speech-view.asp?SpeechSeq = 107. Accessed June 1, 2004. Reprinted by permission of Governor Gary Locke.

OTHER REFERENCES

Gordon H. Chang, *Asian Americans and Politics: Perspectives, Experiences, Prospects* (Stanford: Stanford University Press, 2001).

Don T. Nakanishi and James S. Lai, *Asian American Politics: Law, Participation, and Policy* (Lanham, Md.: Rowman & Littlefield, 2003).

Donald Young, *Searching for Asian America* (San Francisco: National Asian American Telecommunications Association, 2003), VHS.

Helen Zia, *Asian American Dreams: The Emergence of an American People* (New York: Farrar, Straus & Giroux, 2000).

A Second-Generation
Call to Action (1999)

Kristie Wang

Immigration from Taiwan to the United States began with the arrival of over 18,000 students in pursuit of higher education in the 1950s and 1960s. Upon finishing their degrees, the vast majority chose to remain in the United States to take advantage of greater freedoms and opportunities here. Many more came after 1965 in response to America's call for highly skilled and technical labor, so that by 2000, the Taiwanese population in America had grown to some 145,000, according to the U.S. census. Although the number is small compared to the 2.7 million Chinese now living in the United States, Taiwanese Americans stand out because they are generally well educated and well off, and many insist on a Taiwanese identity in keeping with their political views that Taiwan is not a part of China but an independent country. To this end, they succeeded in lobbying the U.S. government for a separate immigration quota in 1982 and to begin listing Taiwanese as a separate ethnic group in the 1990 census.

The importance of claiming a Taiwanese identity is the focus of Kristie Wang's keynote address at the first annual West Coast Intercollegiate Taiwanese American Student Association (ITASA) Conference at UC Berkeley. Organized by the Taiwanese Student Association and Berkeley Students for a Sovereign Taiwan, the conference was intended to educate second-generation Taiwanese Americans about their identity, history, and culture and to arouse their support and participation in the Taiwanese sovereignty movement, which had picked up once martial law was lifted in 1987.

A veteran activist in the democracy movement and a passionate speaker, Kristie Wang immigrated to the United States from Taiwan with her family when she was seven years old. She credits her mother's side of the family for her strong interest in politics and sense of Taiwanese identity. After receiving a master's degree from Harvard's Kennedy School of Government, she worked for three years as program director at the Center for Taiwan International Relations in Washington, D.C. She is currently communications director at Children Now in Oakland, California, and has two young children to whom she speaks Taiwanese.

Kristie Wang speaking at a Cornell University rally in support of Taiwanese president Lee Teng-hui's visit to the United States in 1995. (Courtesy of Kristie Wang)

INTRODUCTION

Most of us who grew up in the United States are quite familiar with the stories of the American civil rights movement. We all are familiar with the courageous tales of Harriet Tubman and the underground railroad, Rosa Parks's refusal to move to the back of the bus, and Martin Luther King's march on Selma. We know how individuals like them have brought about dramatic changes in American society.

Every successful political and social change movement has its own stories of people who stood up in the face of injustice and demanded their rights to dignity and freedom. These stories also are filled with the numerous unsung heroes who participated in the protests, joined the marches, and supported the causes. The story of Taiwan and of Taiwanese in America is no different.

DRAMATIC DEMOCRATIZATION

Many of you probably know of Taiwan's dramatic ten-year transformation to democracy. Of course, the transformation actually was more than ten years in the making, but the concrete political gains began in 1986 with the formal establishment of the first opposition party, the Democratic Progressive Party, or DPP. It seemed that each year after that, Taiwan took another dramatic step toward democracy.

To recap the highlights, in 1987 the almost forty years of the longest period of martial law in world history was lifted in Taiwan. In 1988 freedom of the press began to be recognized, as restrictions on the print media were lifted. In 1989 the DPP was allowed to field candidates for elections. In 1990 the octogenarian parliamentarians elected in China in the 1940s were given generous pensions to retire—though in fact, many of them had slept and drooled their way through sessions for many years. In 1991 wartime emergency laws were lifted.

Sedition Law 100 and the blacklist were abolished in 1992, thus freeing many political dissidents from long prison sentences and overseas Taiwanese from their exile. Middle-age, formerly exiled overseas Taiwanese, many of whom were Taiwanese Americans, raced back to the homeland they had been barred from and reunited with aged parents and siblings they last saw when they were only college students.

Perhaps most exciting of all, in 1996 Taiwan's democratization was declared complete when, for the first time in its 400-plus-year history, the island held a direct, democratic election for president. The historical significance of this election was not lost on the 21 million residents of Taiwan, nor on news media from around the world, which flocked to the island. Every major and minor media outlet was in Taiwan for weeks leading up to the big event.

The election was all anyone in Taiwan talked about, and campaign paraphernalia covered every available public space. There was an electrified air of excitement all over the island. On Election Day, 76 percent of the population turned out to vote. This high voter turnout was particularly unbelievable for those of us from the United States, where presidential elections in recent years have typically drawn 30 to 33 percent of eligible voters.

NEED TO RECALL TAIWAN'S PAST

This has been a very exciting and historical time for Taiwan. Yet it's important to remember where Taiwan came from and where it was, just a very uncomfortably short time ago. I would like to recall a little bit of Taiwan's political past, because it's integral to every aspect of Taiwanese life yesterday and today, and any effort to avoid these issues would be disingenuous.

But before we do that, let's talk about why it seems Taiwanese people constantly need to retell Taiwan's history. Among second-generation Taiwanese Americans, there are those who are highly aware and hardcore supporters of Taiwan's democracy movement. You all probably know some of these people—many of them planned this conference. They're the ones people sometimes point to and whisper, "she's political" or "he's political."

What we need to realize is that the person who identifies herself as Taiwanese and knows her history is no more political than the person who identifies herself as Chinese because she doesn't think it's important to make the distinction. The reason is, given Taiwan's history and current political climate, those who don't think it matters to differentiate between Taiwanese and Chinese are, in fact, buying into and legitimizing China's claim to Taiwan. They are, in fact, supporting Chinese efforts to wipe out a distinct Taiwanese identity, language, and culture. If you indeed agree with that, then recognize and acknowledge that you are making a political statement when you don't distinguish between Taiwanese and Chinese, and don't mislead yourself into thinking that you're being politically neutral because you don't insist on a separate Taiwanese identity.

There also are many of us who fall into one or more of these categories: there are people who think that those who pushed for human rights and democracy in Taiwan are troublemakers or are unfairly heaping blame on the KMT [Kuomintang, or Nationalist Party under Chiang Kai-shek's leadership]. There are those who feel they've heard enough from their parents and friends about Taiwan's history and think it's a tired topic. They may think that retelling these stories is divisive, that it's time to get over it. And then there are those who don't know much about what happened in Taiwan's past and, frankly, don't care to.

It's important that we examine and challenge these feelings in ourselves and in each other. For those who believe in ignorance being bliss, we'll talk later about why it's important for us to know and care [about] what happened in Taiwan's past. First, let's address the issue of putting blame on the KMT. Reports of the brutal oppression of Taiwanese people are fact, not fiction. For a long time, these stories have not been told and legitimized because of tight, authoritarian controls on their retelling.

For many years, the stories were shared and passed on in secret from person to person, thus lending them the aura of legend or even unproven or exaggerated storytelling. Since Taiwan has opened up politically in recent years, these stories are beginning to be told and documented. Even the KMT government finally has admitted to its role in the "2–28 massacres."[1] We have to remember the words of American writer and feminist Meridel Le Sueur, who said, "The history of an oppressed people is hidden in the lies and the agreed-upon myth of its conquerors."

For those who think the Taiwanese political dissidents were troublemakers, this is a label they wore proudly. Rosa Parks was a troublemaker. Martin Luther King was a troublemaker. Like them, Taiwanese dissidents were fighting for very basic human rights, and it was imperative for their survival and the survival of the Taiwanese people that they rock the boat. If they had not overcome their fear, apathy, and oppressed minds and [acted], I have no

---

1. Resentment by native Taiwanese against KMT rule erupted in a riot on February 28, 1947, after the police beat a woman vendor and killed a protesting bystander. Military forces called in to quell the rebellion killed several thousand Taiwanese.

doubt that Taiwanese people at home and abroad still would be denied their very basic freedoms.

For those of you who've heard the litany of KMT atrocities and think no good comes from dwelling on it, consider this. It's easy when we sit here and recount Taiwan's recent glory and when we visit Taiwan and see the relatively free political society, to think that its oppressive history is far behind us. But remember that Taiwan was fully democratized only three years ago, and until 1992, Sedition Law 100 still prevented political dissidents from airing their views.

Besides, consider this range of very plausible scenarios. The politically hardline New Party in Taiwan, which split off from the KMT because they didn't like the political liberalization of recent years, could win a major election and begin to turn back the democratic progress that has been made. China, which has been gaining greater economic and military strength, could attempt to take Taiwan by force. U.S. policy toward Taiwan, which has flipped and flopped to the political winds, can withdraw its already vague assurances of security for Taiwan. Taiwan's democratization is far from being a done deal.

If there's one thing we can learn from other movements for political and social change, it's that we can never be reticent. You all know the saying: those who forget history are doomed to repeat it. No matter how many times we've heard it before, we all still need to be reminded of Taiwan's very recent past.

MARTIAL LAW AND WHITE TERROR

So let's remind ourselves a little. Some of you may know that in Taiwan's 400-plus-year history, the island has been occupied and colonized by people like the Dutch, the Chinese, and the Japanese. Taiwan's most recent experience with the Nationalist Chinese, or KMT, who escaped to Taiwan after losing the civil war in China in 1949, has been particularly brutal. After all, it was during this period of authoritarian rule that began in 1945 and continued into the 1990s that some 20,000 Taiwanese leaders were systematically murdered during what is known as the "2–28 Incident." It was during this almost half-century, known as "white terror," that Taiwanese were prohibited from speaking their native language, from criticizing the government, from electing their own representatives, from freedoms of speech, assembly, and the press. This was the time of campus spying on overseas Taiwanese students and of the blacklist, which barred many from returning to Taiwan, even to see their parents before they died. It was during these almost forty years of martial law that political dissidents and even their family members were imprisoned and sometimes killed.

This truly was a very dark period in Taiwan's recent history, when brutal examples were made of anyone who dared indicate displeasure with the authoritarian rule of the Nationalist Chinese. These measures were largely successful because they frightened subsequent generations of Taiwanese into fear and inaction. Yet in the face of all this, there were those who dared to speak out and organize. It took many decades and far too many deaths and sacrifices, but in the last 13 years, Taiwan finally began to walk out of the shadows of this brutal repression.

ROLE OF STUDENTS

Many of the people who played critical roles in Taiwan's democratization were students and many were Taiwanese Americans. By some estimates, there were only 50 Taiwanese in the U.S. in 1950, and all of them were students. The first waves of Taiwanese to come to the U.S. and reside here were all students who had come to pursue graduate studies. So it makes sense that the first Taiwanese American organizations were student groups and were campus-based. In fact, students have always played an important role in Taiwan's political development.

I'd like to tell you about a few of them. Kang-lu Wang came to the U.S. from Taiwan in late 1964 to pursue graduate studies. He incurred the wrath of the KMT when he helped organize the first Taiwanese student organization in the U.S. in 1967. The mere existence of an organization that called itself the "Taiwanese Students Association" (TSA) was political, in the sense that it is a statement of a unique Taiwanese identity, separate from "Chinese." Remember, this was 1967, deep in the period of "white terror" when the KMT was systematically suppressing Taiwanese identity by harassing, imprisoning, and even murdering dissidents.

This also was during the time when KMT student spies were rampant on American college campuses. In 1985 Michael Glennon, who had been on the staff of the U.S. Senate Foreign Relations Committee, testified in Congress that KMT intelligence agents had harassed, intimidated, and spied on U.S. residents, in order to identify critics of the KMT government. He testified, "Once the critics are identified, several things may occur. They may be threatened or assaulted. Relatives in their homeland may be harmed. Upon returning home, the critic may be imprisoned, possibly tortured. On rare occasions, he or she may be murdered here in this country."

Mr. Glennon had worked on the Senate Committee's investigative report on this matter, which found that the CIA estimated the KMT had placed 45 intelligence officers in the U.S., with nine on university campuses. An FBI report cited 25 KMT officers on American college campuses. Whatever the precise number, even one campus spy was enough to send a clear message to the students that they were not safe from the oppressive eyes of the KMT regime, even though they were halfway across the globe from Taiwan.

This is the political climate under which Taiwanese students in America formed these student organizations. For daring to help organize the first such student group, Kang-lu Wang was harassed by the KMT government. Students who dared to join these campus organizations, though they primarily were social in nature, also were harassed and eventually all ended up on the blacklist and were barred from returning to Taiwan, even for short visits.

On December 10, 1979, a peaceful rally of 60,000 people in Kaohsiung, Taiwan, to honor International Human Rights Day turned into a riot when KMT police tried to put an end to the demonstration. The government subsequently arrested four to five hundred participants and imprisoned the leaders. On the campus of the University of Washington, Taiwanese graduate student Mei-chin Chen and her Dutch friend Gerrit van der Wees learned of this event, known as the "Kaohsiung Incident," and the related injustices and began to write and distribute a newsletter in English about what was going on in Taiwan, because the KMT had tight controls over the press. Mei-chin and Gerrit felt it was important that Americans and the rest of the world know what was going on inside Taiwan.

I could stand here all day recounting the number of first-generation Taiwanese Americans who, under the dark cloud of threats and tragic losses of their compatriots in the struggle for freedom, continued to speak up about the KMT's human rights abuses and injustices. They organized letter-writing campaigns, planned marches and demonstrations, and talked to any U.S. policy maker who would listen—and there weren't many back then. They did all this, despite fear of KMT reprisals, language difficulties, initial lack of knowledge about the American political system and culture, completing their educations and raising families, little available funding for these activities, and ignorance and apathy from the general public. This is why it's such an insult and disservice when the KMT regime or any other group tries to take credit for Taiwan's political development. Why would the KMT voluntarily give up the sweet deal they had in Taiwan? Remember the words of Frederick Douglass: "Power concedes nothing without demand; it never has and it never will."

Make no mistake. Taiwan's political achievements were bought and paid for by the blood of the murdered dissidents and their families, by the courage of those who dared speak up for justice, and by the spouses and children of political leaders and activists who had to devote much of their time and energy to the movement.

In our own second generation of Taiwanese Americans, there are inspirational people who as students took action to do their part for the future of Taiwan. Many of you know Tim Chuang, who back in 1991, along with several other Taiwanese American students on various college campuses, took [the] initiative in organizing the first-ever conference of the Inter-collegiate Taiwanese American Students Association, or ITASA. They wanted to use the conference as a vehicle for building a network and community of second-generation Taiwanese Americans, as well as an opportunity to educate themselves and others about Taiwan's history and current developments.

Today the annual ITASA conference has become an institution on the East Coast, attended by 400-plus students each year. In the last few years, colleges in the Midwest also have been holding annual ITASA conferences. This year, thanks to more trailblazers, ITASA has come to the West Coast.

You truly are at the start of something very exciting and important. It's so thrilling to think of the number of Taiwanese American students who— no matter where in the U.S. they go to school—now have the opportunity to take a couple of days out of their four years of college education and learn something about their heritage. If you think about the number of students who—since the first ITASA conference in 1991—have been impacted because of the initiative of Tim and his friends, it is so inspiring.

But it's important to remember that none of these people could have made any difference without the people who went to the conferences they planned, marched in their demonstrations, signed their petitions, and donated money to their causes. Each of us has a role to play.

WHY WE SHOULD CARE

Before we talk about what that role is, let's take a moment and talk about why we should care about Taiwan. After all, we live halfway across the globe, and most of us don't ever plan to live there. Let me give you a few very good reasons why we should care.

First, Taiwan is at a historical crossroads. We've reviewed the low points of Taiwan's recent history and its glorious successes. We also talked about the threats from hard-liners in Taiwan, an insecure China, and unpredictable international politics. Taiwan's future is far from determined. It is so critical that each and every one of us learn about Taiwan's past and keep updated on its current situation so we can educate others and speak up for our brothers and sisters in Taiwan if necessary.

Second, as a Taiwanese American, what happens in Taiwan and to Taiwan always will reflect on you. Even if you want to stay blissfully ignorant of what is going on there and even if you don't really know your relatives there, what happens in Taiwan still will affect you.

The third reason why we should care is that we are in a unique position as second-generation immigrants to play a critical role in the future of our native country. We have a direct link to the first generation, from whom we can learn about Taiwan's history and political struggles, but we have better language capabilities, cultural understanding, and societal connections in the United States to educate Americans about Taiwan's struggles and to affect public policy.

Fourth, young people often talk of the desire to make a difference and leave a mark on the world. Well, here is the perfect opportunity. Taiwan's history is being made right now, and we can and are needed to get involved.

Things are happening and changing very quickly there, and we are in a position to influence events.

Fifth, first-generation Taiwanese Americans have paved the way for us. They have helped to bring about a vibrant, multi-party democracy in Taiwan, bring an end to the blacklist and campus spying, and bring home the freedoms that we enjoy in this country. The first generation was able to take the legacy of oppression and injustice they inherited and pass on to us a legacy of activism, passion, and courage. We cannot pass on to third-generation Taiwanese Americans a legacy of apathy and ignorance.

A sixth reason why we should care [about] what happens to Taiwan is: because it's easy to. Previous generations of Taiwanese didn't have the political, economic, and educational opportunities that we do. What we don't have is any reason to fear getting involved. We don't have to worry about campus spies, blacklists, or imprisonment for speaking our minds, but we may have to if we don't work actively to make sure progress continues.

Finally, we need to care about Taiwan because first-generation Taiwanese Americans are ready to retire from the movement for Taiwanese sovereignty. Believe me, nothing would excite these old revolutionaries more than to be able to "pass the torch" to our generation and feel that they are leaving it in good hands. The good news is, we can do this. A lot of groundwork already has been done. We just need to kick up our level of commitment and training to the next stage.

These are seven good, solid reasons why second-generation Taiwanese Americans need to care about Taiwan and need to carry on the struggle of previous generations. Now let's talk about exactly how we can do that.

HOW TO CONTRIBUTE GENERALLY

The first and most important way we can contribute to and support the political struggle of Taiwan is to identify ourselves individually and as a community as Taiwanese or Taiwanese Americans. Normally, I wouldn't tell anyone how to identify themselves, and frankly, if you weren't of Taiwanese descent I wouldn't really care. But I do care in this case because Taiwan's identity has been co-opted many times throughout its history. Today Taiwanese people finally have the freedom to identify themselves solely and uniquely with the island of Taiwan. But as I said before, this freedom still is being threatened. If you know something of the political developments in Taiwan today, you know that Taiwan's national identity is being determined right now. Our brothers and sisters in Taiwan are a mere one hundred miles from a China that is constantly threatening with words and missiles to force its identity on the people of Taiwan. It is imperative that Taiwanese around the world promote this identity and stand up for it.

And if you are ever in a situation where you have made a name for yourself, please insist on your identity as a Taiwanese American. As our community has continued to grow and diversify, our members have achieved distinction in many varied professions and endeavors, including academics, business, science and technology, the arts, sports, and government service. You might not know that Miss USA 1984 [Mai Shanley] was a Taiwanese American and that a Taiwanese American scientist [Yuan-tse Lee] won a Nobel prize in 1986. Unfortunately, many of them do not insist on their identification as Taiwanese Americans. So please, if you make a mark and a name for yourself, make one for the community, too, and insist on your identity as a Taiwanese American.

The second way we can contribute to the community is by learning the history of Taiwan and learning from the first generation about their struggles—both so we can gain from this experience and so we can pass it on to future generations. Once we educate ourselves, we need to educate others—Taiwanese and non-Taiwanese. We need to speak up, speak out, and speak often about Taiwan's struggles and build a strong international movement to support Taiwan's fragile democracy. This is our historical responsibility, and it is critical that we fulfill it.

A third way to make a contribution is by strengthening the network of Taiwanese Americans. Each year conferences like this one, holiday celebrations, and summer camps for Taiwanese Americans take place all across the country. Unfortunately, the number of second-generation participants is usually quite small at these events. We need to strengthen these networks and build up our community.

There's something in it for you if you do. I can give you many examples of people who have been helped by complete strangers, simply because they both were of Taiwanese descent. When you graduate and go out to look for a job, you'll appreciate having a network of people to turn to for job advice or job leads. It's immensely comforting to know that when you need it, you have a community of people who will lend a helping hand.

A fourth way that you can contribute to the community is by becoming a good U.S. citizen. That means learning about our system of government, knowing who your elected representatives are, registering and voting in elections, and being an active participant in our civic affairs. I'm sure you've all heard the phrase "Think globally and act locally." Your ability to effect change in Taiwan can only be strengthened by your political roots here in this country.

HOW TO CONTRIBUTE SPECIFICALLY

Those are some general ways we can contribute to the Taiwanese American community. If you are inclined to contribute to the political struggle of the Taiwanese specifically, then here are some ways you can do that.

There are many, many ways we can support Taiwan's political struggle.

The best way to do it is by sharing our talents and skills. If you're a good organizer, plan a conference or other activities on campus and in your community. If you have computer skills, offer to set up and maintain a Web site for a Taiwanese American organization. If you are a performer or artist, explore ways to express these ideas through your craft. Follow the lead of people like Philip Wu and Mynor King and try to revive and keep alive traditional Taiwanese art and music and find opportunities to educate people about Taiwanese culture and its ties to Taiwan's political past.

If you're not the type to get out there and organize people, then contribute your time and support. Participate in the events that others organize. Go to their conferences. Pick up a sign and march in their protests. Join their organizations. Lend a helping hand when they need it.

Each of you in this room has played an important part in making possible this first West Coast ITASA Conference. This conference could not have happened without the people who took the initiative to organize it, the many people who put in their time and energy to put it all together, and the presenters who came to share their experiences and expertise. But it also couldn't have happened without all of you who came to participate. A movement cannot be sustained by a small group of people. We all must get involved. Once you complete your educations and get out into the professional world, if you find that what you do best is make money, then contribute that.

Contribute your hands and your dollars, where possible. But make sure you contribute in a productive way. Unity is important to every cause and every community, and it is even more so for a community as small in number as ours. Support people's efforts; don't stand on the sidelines and criticize. Find ways to bring people together, not new ways to divide.

As Taiwanese American college students, there are some specific ways you can get involved in the movement. Spend a summer interning with a Taiwanese American organization. If your campus doesn't have a Taiwanese American students organization, form one. If there is one, but it's not active or political, challenge yourselves to make it so. Politics is not a scary word; it really isn't. We no longer have anything to fear in getting involved. This is a gift the first generation gave us.

We no longer have to fear campus spies, blacklists, or other repercussions for our activism, but I can't guarantee that this will always be the case if we don't work actively to prevent a turning back of the progress that's been made. Unfortunately, we don't have the luxury to sit back and watch. So be overtly political and fight the ignorance and apathy of those who don't want to get involved, by educating them.

Those of you who are here now are a self-selected group. You made the effort and time to come to this Taiwanese American conference. After these two days, you now have been trained and can go back to your campuses and spread the word among Taiwanese and non-Taiwanese alike. Think about all the Taiwanese American students you know who didn't come to this conference and make sure you bring them with you to next year's conference.

Opportunities to contribute to the Taiwanese cause are everywhere around us. We can educate people at school, at work, and at home. This is a historical opportunity for Taiwan to finally step out permanently from the shadows of its oppressive past, and we all need to get involved now.

Our community also is beginning to expand into a third generation. We need to make sure that they know their heritage. In the face of the worst injustices and obstacles, the first generation has made amazing strides. If they have been deficient in anything, it is that in their modesty, their engagement in the struggle, and fear of exposing their families to reprisal, the first generation has not done such a great job in educating their children about the movement. We need to take the initiative to fill that gap and pass on this knowledge to future generations.

Finally, if you never go to another Taiwanese American conference or event and you never actively participate in the community again, but you do insist on your Taiwanese American identity, then that is enough. This is the minimum that you have to do to contribute to our community, and it is perhaps the most important thing you can do. There are very few other causes that you can make such a significant contribution to by doing so little.

Many people throughout Taiwan's history have tried to co-opt or wipe out the Taiwanese identity, and many Taiwanese have died or been punished merely for insisting on it. Those days are over—for now—and this identity is ours to claim and perpetuate. If you are of Taiwanese descent or identify your country of origin primarily with the island of Taiwan, then insist on this label. It is the most important thing you can do right now, while the 21 million people of Taiwan are engaged in a struggle over their identity as a nation and as a people.

CALL TO ACTION

As we approach a new century, the most important thing we can do is ensure that Taiwan continues to move forward and that its progress is not turned back. We must not waste this great opportunity to make it our finest hour. This is a call to action for our generation. Be an activist. Carry on the revolution. Change never happened when people were afraid to push the envelope. Challenge yourself and others to make a difference for Taiwan. Take the baton. The race has yet to be won.

SOURCE: 1999 West Coast ITASA Conference, University of California at Berkeley, April 11, 1999. Berkeley Students for a Sovereign Taiwan, University of California, Berkeley. Available at <http://www.ocf.berkeley.edu/~bst/itasa/rclosing.html>. Accessed June 1, 2004. Reprinted by permission of Kristie Wang.

OTHER REFERENCES

Iris Chang, "The Taiwanese Americans," in *The Chinese in America: A Narrative History* (New York: Viking, 2003), pp. 283–311.

Hsiang-Shui Chen, *Chinatown No More: Taiwan Immigrants in Contemporary New York* (Ithaca, N.Y.: Cornell University Press, 1992).

Sibyl Chen, *Our Treasury: The Shaping of First-Generation Taiwanese Americans* (Boston: Intercollegiate Taiwanese American Student Association, 2002).

brenda Lin, *Wealth Ribbon: Taiwan Bound, America Bound* (Indianapolis: University of Indianapolis Press, 2004).

Franklin Ng, *The Taiwanese Americans* (Westport, Conn.: Greenwood Press, 1998).

The Los Alamos Incident and Its Effects on Chinese American Scientists (2000)

Cheuk-Yin Wong

One of the most disturbing and damaging cases of racial profiling against Chinese Americans in recent times centers on nuclear scientist Wen Ho Lee. Born in Taiwan in 1935, Lee came to the United States for graduate studies in 1965. He became a naturalized U.S. citizen, and in 1978 began working as a physicist in the weapons section of the Los Alamos National Laboratory. In 1999 Lee was falsely accused of spying for China, fired from his job at Los Alamos, arrested and denied bail, and placed in solitary confinement for nine months pending trial. After he pleaded guilty to one out of fifty-nine counts of mishandling classified government data, he was freed on September 13, 2000, with an unprecedented apology from U.S. District Court judge James Parker for the "unfair manner" in which the executive branch had treated him.

According to the following speech delivered by scientist Cheuk-Yin Wong[1] at the American Physical Society meeting at Long Beach, California, on April 29, 2000, the science community was deeply shaken by the case. Chinese American scientists were particularly disturbed that Lee had been singled out for investigation because of his ethnicity and that his constitutional rights had been violated in the process. In turn, they were adversely affected by the high-profile case, the perception of Chinese Americans as "perpetual foreigners," and the resulting climate of distrust and suspicion in the defense industry. Along with many other scientific groups, civil rights organizations, and American citizens across the country, they were not going to stand by quietly and allow one of their peers to fall victim to racism and political scapegoating.

On March 6, 1999, the *New York Times* broke the news about an alleged "Chinese spy." The attention of the media and the government was soon focused

---

1. At the time of this speech, Cheuk-Yin Wong was chairman of the Overseas Chinese Physics Association (OCPA), a professional organization consisting of 400 members, and a fellow of the American Physical Society (APS). He earned his Ph.D. from Princeton in 1966 and has

Wen Ho Lee as he
appears on the cover
of his book, *My Country
versus Me,* published
by Hyperion in 2001.
(Photograph by Deborah
Feingold)

on Dr. Wen Ho Lee of the Los Alamos National Laboratory as the suspect.
On March 8, 1999, Dr. Wen Ho Lee was fired from his Los Alamos position.
After many months of investigation, Dr. Lee was charged, not for spying, but
for mishandling classified information. He has been detained without bail
in a New Mexico jail since December 10, 1999.[2]

The Los Alamos incident has affected the Chinese American science community adversely in many ways. Chinese American scientists wish to state at
the outset that they strongly support rigorous measures to safeguard America's national and military secrets. They recognize the importance of the
proper handling of classified information. They make no judgment about
the guilt or innocence of Dr. Wen Ho Lee, which will be decided by a court
of law. However, they are painfully aware of the tragic Chinese Exclusion

---

been working at Oak Ridge National Laboratory for the past thirty-four years. In addition to
speaking out against the deteriorating work environment and media stereotypes in connection
with the Wen Ho Lee case, OCPA got two of the largest science organizations in the country,
APS and the American Association for the Advancement of Science, to issue statements protesting the harsh treatment of Dr. Lee and denouncing wrongful portrayals of immigrant scientists.

2. Treated worse than a common criminal, Wen Ho Lee was put in solitary confinement
and was shackled and chained whenever he left his cell.

Act of 1882 and the internment of Japanese Americans in 1942. They are therefore deeply concerned and disturbed that Dr. Lee might have been singled out for investigation because of his ethnicity, as stated recently by Robert Vrooman, the chief counterintelligence officer at Los Alamos from 1987 to 1998.[3]

The Chinese American community is also concerned that the statutes under which Dr. Lee was charged for mishandling classified data were used to prosecute Dr. Lee selectively while a well-known non-Chinese American government official, John Deutch of the CIA, who mishandled classified data, did not face similar prosecution.[4]

Chinese American scientists are troubled by the extended pretrial detention. The Bill of Rights guarantees fundamental due process to all criminal defendants, and the Eighth Amendment explicitly forbids excessive bail in criminal cases. Yet Dr. Lee has been in detention since his arrest on December 10, 1999, without bail despite the willingness of Dr. Lee and his supporters to post reasonable bail. The isolation of Dr. Lee from his family and lawyers is thus an abrogation of his constitutional right of posting bail.

The justification for the abrogation of Dr. Wen Ho Lee's constitutional right is based on the contention that, if released, Dr. Lee is likely to pose a grave threat to our national security. Such an abrogation of a defendant's constitutional right in the name of national security is a very serious matter because we will be judged by history. Our abrogation of the constitutional rights of the Japanese Americans during WWII in the name of national security led to an apology from our Government to the Japanese Americans many years later, in addition to painful human sufferings and a dark chapter in our history.

Recent news reports indicate that the alleged downloaded data were originally classified as "Protect as Restricted Data." Only after Dr. Lee was fired and investigated was the classification of these data elevated to become "Secret Restricted Data" or "Confidential Restricted Data" with much stricter rules of handling.[5] Therefore, in considering the merits of Dr. Wen Ho Lee's constitutional right, we urge the government to seek ways to confine Dr. Lee in his home that will also protect the security of the United States against possible actions by Dr. Lee.

3. Robert Vrooman would later testify at Wen Ho Lee's trial that Dr. Lee was singled out for investigation by the FBI because he is ethnic Chinese.

4. John Deutch, former director of the CIA, was found to have downloaded thirty-one top-secret CIA files to his unsecured home computer. He was pardoned by President Clinton during his last hours in office. However, Clinton declined to do the same for Wen Ho Lee.

5. Reclassification of the data provided grounds for denying Wen Ho Lee bail. Wen Ho Lee was charged with fifty-nine counts of violating the Atomic Energy Act and the Federal Espionage Act in his mishandling of classified nuclear data, with the maximum penalty of life in prison for thirty-nine of the counts. Later testimony at the trial would prove that the data were not the "crown jewels" of America's nuclear arsenal but readily available in open literature.

The perception that Dr. Lee is not being treated justly has caused great consternation in the Chinese American community. It has shaken their faith in the fairness of the justice system. Chinese Americans will follow the proceedings of the legal case and will speak out for justice, equality, and due process of law.

Before we discuss how the Los Alamos incident has affected the Chinese American science community, we would like to briefly describe this community. Most Chinese American scientists came to study in this country as foreign students. After they finished their education they became permanent U.S. residents and were later naturalized to become American citizens. However, a good number were born in this country.

By recent accounts, Chinese American scientists make up about 8 percent of the American workforce in science and technology. Among recent Ph.D. recipients in science and engineering, about 25 percent are ethnic Chinese. Chinese CEOs started about 20 percent of all Silicon Valley companies. They are leading 2,000 Silicon Valley companies, employing more than 58,000 workers.

Chinese American scientists are therefore an important component of the workforce in American science and technology, both in unclassified research and classified works. They have contributed their shares to the advancement of American science and technology, and to the development of American national defense. In their ranks are six Nobel Laureates and numerous recipients of science and technology awards. Chinese American pioneering AIDS researcher David Ho was *Time* magazine's 1996 Man of the Year. Chinese American entrepreneurs Jerry Yang of Yahoo and Charles Wang of Computer Associates have made important contributions to the Internet and computer industry. Chinese Americans, along with other American scientists, have been working hard to advance American science, technology, and national defense.

How has the Los Alamos incident affected the Chinese American science community? Past espionage allegations were centered on the individuals without implicating the ethnic group of a suspect. This was, however, not the case with Dr. Wen Ho Lee. Without taking time to check the evidence, certain members of the media stated uncritically that the hundred thousand Chinese students and scientists working in this country provided ready targets for PRC intelligence gathering. The source of these categorical statements was the Cox Report, which was published on May 26, 1999.[6]

Although these categorical statements were subsequently refuted by an

6. Chaired by Christopher Cox, the House of Representatives Select Committee on U.S. National Security and Military/Commercial Concerns with the People's Republic of China reported that China had been systematically stealing military secrets from the United States and that Chinese spies had penetrated the U.S. national weapons laboratories.

independent report from Stanford University,[7] they had already incited irrational public fears and misconceptions in the general public about the ethnic Chinese American science community. The good reputation of Chinese American scientists, which took many generations of hard work to build, has been tarnished and damaged. Their loyalty and their contribution to the progress of this country have been challenged and questioned. These wrongful categorical statements reinforce further the prejudices existing already in American society.

One immediate consequence is that many Chinese American scientists performing classified work in weapons labs, defense subcontractors, and space subcontractors find their loyalty severely questioned. In such a climate of distrust and suspicion, some Chinese Americans in classified work have requested transfers to unclassified projects. Some have opted for early retirement. Others stay on knowing very well that their upward mobility would be limited. They worry that in this atmosphere, project managers in weapons labs, defense subcontractors, and space subcontractors may have reservations about employing Chinese American scientists, about promoting Chinese Americans to leadership roles, and about putting them to head a major project. They also worry that in the case of a downsizing, they will be first to be laid off. The working environment of these Chinese American scientists has deteriorated as a result. Their contribution to American science, technology, and national defense may also suffer as a consequence.

For those Chinese American scientists doing unclassified research in national laboratories and universities, the immediate impact is not as severe. They are, however, concerned whether the negative image propagated by news media might affect the perception of science programming officers and proposal reviewers when they apply for research grants.

For those Chinese nationals working in unclassified research in national laboratories, there are now greater restrictions on security matters and on funding of some areas of unclassified research. These restrictions apply to foreign nationals from sensitive countries, which include Chinese nationals. For example, in one of the unclassified areas of a laboratory, nationals from sensitive countries performing unclassified work must be escorted by Americans when they walk outside their own building to go to the cafeteria or the library. In another national laboratory, postdoctoral fellows have not been renewed based on newly applied criteria, foreign nationals have been denied the opportunity to apply for laboratory positions for which they are qualified, and foreign national staff members are sometimes unsure about their sources of funding. A number of laboratory staff members who tradi-

7. This is in reference to Alastair Johnston, *Cox Committee Report: An Assessment* (Stanford: Center for International Security and Cooperation, Stanford University, 1999).

tionally mentor postdoctoral fellows have decided not to recruit foreign nationals because of their uncertain future.

As a result of the Los Alamos incident many Chinese American scientists and Chinese nationals consciously steer away from defense- and space-related work and from weapons laboratories, because they fear that their ethnicity alone would make them suspect. Five prominent scientists left Los Alamos to go to academia or industry, citing a harsh and uncertain working environment. The number of Asian postdoctoral fellows at Los Alamos decreased from 70 to 55. The number of Chinese graduate students applying for Los Alamos' Director's Postdoctoral Fellowships has also decreased. A resolution calling upon all Asian American scientists and engineers not to apply for jobs at the national labs was recently passed by the Asian Pacific Americans in Higher Education.[8]

The fact that the alleged action of an individual can bring with it a wrongful characterization of an entire ethnic group shows that racial prejudices come in many different ways and appear in many forms. Some of the prejudices are so well entrenched that people holding these prejudices may not be aware of them. It is necessary to alert the public to the existence of these tendencies so that they may be avoided in the future.

The elimination of these prejudices calls for a full acceptance and inclusion of Chinese Americans as a vital and vibrant part of America. Admittedly, Chinese Americans are in a much better time than that of their forefathers in terms of equality. But the road to equality and full acceptance is long indeed. America should not be content with herself looking back at the distance she has traveled since the Chinese Exclusion Act of 1882.

It has been known for a long time that Chinese Americans as well as Asian Americans are often considered as "outsiders" or "perpetual foreigners." For example, employment statistics show that there exists a disparity between the Asian American population and their ranks as senior managers and administrators. This occurs in national laboratories, in industries, and in universities.

In a typical science subcontractor or a four-year public university, about 14 percent of the white-male scientists or faculty members are in official and senior manager positions, but only 4 to 6 percent of the Asian American scientists or faculty members are. Chinese Americans are greatly underrepresented in senior management and leadership positions. In another example, studies by groups of Asian American employees at the Lawrence Livermore National Laboratory indicate that their average salaries are consistently lower than those of their white counterparts. In some departments, the difference

---

8. Soon after, a similar resolution was passed by the Association for Asian American Studies. The boycott ended two years later and succeeded in getting three weapons laboratories to change their hiring and promotion practices for Asian Americans, other minorities, and women employed by the laboratories.

is as large as $1,000 per month. While part of these disparities may be due to the characters of Chinese Americans themselves, a very significant part arises from prejudices that view Chinese Americans as "outsiders" in the matter of upward mobility and leadership positions. The end result is the existence of a glass ceiling through which Chinese Americans (and other Asian Americans) have great difficulty breaking. The additional distrust brought on by the Los Alamos incident will only further reinforce existing prejudices.

Looking ahead, we can expect that the legal proceedings involving Dr. Wen Ho Lee's case will take one or more years. The high-profile trial will split the American public and will lead to unnecessary animosity between ethnic groups. The trial could lead to anti-ethnic Chinese sentiments. The energy of the society will be spent on resolving social discords rather than on the full utilization of America's valuable human resources.

It is important to rectify this situation by first recognizing the presence of prejudicial tendencies in America and then carrying out a change within America, in order that America can use fully her greatest asset—her people, including Chinese Americans. The change must be a change of sentiment and attitude, leading to the full acceptance and inclusion of Chinese Americans as a vital and vibrant part of American society, and not as "outsiders" or "perpetual foreigners." The acceptance of Chinese Americans into all roles of the society, including top leadership roles, will enable America to utilize the talents of all her people to the fullest degree, for the benefits of the nation and the whole world.

Such a change will take time, but it is the right thing to do, in accordance with the honorable American tradition of fairness, justice, and equality.

To conclude my talk, I wish to quote my son, Albert Wong, who wrote in a national essay contest when he was sixteen, "People come and settle in America from all areas of the globe, each bringing his own special skill, his own special instrument. America is a land where all of these instruments are made into one symphony. Each of us is important to the symphony of America. Together America can produce the most beautiful sounds in the world, but separated it produces a discord of noises. Let us try to make the symphony of America play the beautiful music that we know it can."

SOURCE: Cheuk-Yin Wong, "The Los Alamos Incident and Its Effects on Chinese American Scientists," April 29, 2000. Available at www.wenholee.org/cgi-local/viewnews.cgi?newsid 956981796.1144. Accessed July 8, 2003. Reprinted by permission of Cheuk-Yin Wong.

OTHER REFERENCES

Wen Ho Lee with Helen Zia, *My Country versus Me: The First-Hand Account by the Los Alamos Scientist Who Was Falsely Accused of Being a Spy* (New York: Hyperion, 2001).
Dan Stober and Ian Hoffman, *A Convenient Spy: Wen Ho Lee and the Politics of Nuclear Espionage* (New York: Simon & Schuster, 2001).

"We are Americans"

The Story behind Time Magazine's Man of the Year (2003)

David Ho

In 1996 David Ho was named Time magazine's Man of the Year for his pioneering research on the causes and treatment of acquired immune deficiency syndrome (AIDS). Born in Taichung, Taiwan, in 1952, Ho immigrated to the United States with his family when he was twelve. By focusing on his schoolwork and achievements, he overcame language and cultural barriers and went on to graduate from the California Institute of Technology and Harvard Medical School in the 1970s. He subsequently did his clinical training in internal medicine and infectious diseases at the UCLA School of Medicine and Massachusetts General Hospital, respectively.

The director of the Aaron Diamond AIDS Research Center in New York since its inception in 1990, Ho is internationally known as the foremost authority on the human immunodeficiency virus (HIV), which causes AIDS. In the following excerpts from an interview with Bill Moyers for the PBS television series Becoming American: The Chinese Experience, *Ho speaks candidly about his family's experience as immigrants from Taiwan, why he chose to pursue a career in the sciences, and how he came to discover a treatment that would help to reduce the death rate from AIDS.*

My father left the mainland to teach in Taiwan, actually prior to the Communist takeover of the mainland. And my mother was born in central Taiwan in a town called Taichung. They met because he was the teacher and she was the student—an old story. I was born in Taichung, then a sleepy little town in central Taiwan. Today it's a pretty busy place with a few million people, and the third largest city in Taiwan.

The educational system in Taiwan is highly competitive, and even at the elementary level we were told that you had to excel, because if you didn't, you wouldn't get into middle school. And of course everyone wanted to get into the best, or the better ones. And so starting about third or fourth grade you have school and then you have additional school or course work at night

David Ho on the cover of *Time* magazine, December 30, 1996/January 6, 1997. (Photo by Gregory Heisler)

where tutors would be brought in. And we were doing algebra in the fifth and sixth grade. I'm not sure that's necessarily healthy, but we were told to focus on education.

As a young boy, I saw my father leave Taiwan to pursue higher education in the U.S. and, ultimately, become an engineer. Similarly I had, on my mother's side, an uncle who did the same. The fact that they left Taiwan to pursue higher education was valued a great deal by friends and relatives, and that already told me that doing something like that—scholarly—was a good thing. And then interestingly in the late '50s, so I would have been just eight or nine years old, two physicists from China, Yang (Chen Ning) and Lee (Tsung-Dao), won the Nobel Prize. That was such a big development that they were glorified; they were deified. All the kids were told this is what you ought to follow. Science became a big part of what I was thinking about from then on.

When he [my father] left in 1957 he left behind my mother, a younger brother, and myself. We did not see him until 1965, when the three of us came over. He did it that way because he wanted to finish school, establish himself, and become stable before moving us over. I've heard him over the years talk about his initial years in America trying to study and work at the same time while sending some money back home to support the family, and there was a great deal of hardship. Just as an example, he tells us, frequently, about one job. While he was going to school he had to put eggs in cartons. The white workers were bigger; they had hands that were substantially bigger. My father is a small man with very small hands and he could not keep up because he could only put two eggs in his hands at a time. He has told us about doing that job for hours and falling behind other workers because he was not as well equipped to do the job. And to hold that kind of job and have to study at the same time, worrying about family and being so far away and not being able to see your sons and your wife, that's hardship enough.

Looking back, I think he's really very happy that he made that move to come over there because it really broadened the opportunities for the entire family. We were finally able to join him in 1965 because the climate for immigrations became much more favorable by then. To this day my father worships JFK and LBJ for what they did to have the laws changed so that his family could come. Certainly for a lot of Chinese Americans I know it's crucial, myself included. As I have gotten older, I truly appreciate the personal sacrifices he made. I've tried to tell his story to my own kids. They always think that I'm exaggerating. But comparatively speaking, they have it pretty nice compared to me, who in turn had it pretty nice compared to my father.

I was twelve when I came and I remember thinking it's truly a different world. You know, you go from bicycles to cars, from shopping in the village market to supermarkets, and from Chinese to English. I was a sixth grader and my brother was a fourth grader, and in Taiwan one does not learn English until you get to middle school, so we had absolutely no exposure to the language. We did not know the alphabet. So we started from step one, and it was a culture shock on top of a language barrier. It was a tough time for me in the sense that, in Taiwan, I had been a pretty good student and then all of a sudden, I couldn't communicate. Therefore, I was generally viewed by others as the dummy in the class—you know, kids can be cruel at times.

For me, during the early years, there was always some emphasis on the quantitative sciences, probably because I had a father who is an electrical engineer and also because science and math are great equalizers in that if you have a handicap in communication those are much more objective fields. There's a right answer and there's a wrong answer and if you get it right you're right, whereas in English or social sciences, it's more of a subjective field.

That's why many of the immigrants in my father's generation, and to some extent my generation, go into areas like science and engineering, where the language handicap would not be as significant a factor. With the next generation, our kids go on to tackle other things—in law, in media, and so on. I have kids—16, 21, and 24. The oldest is in the process of applying to business school. Our son who is 21 is a senior at MIT but his major is in economics. Perhaps there's a chance for the youngest one to go into science.

So I went through middle school and high school with a great deal of interest in the sciences. I went to Cal Tech, which is a science school, but my interests within science shifted a great deal over the years. Initially I was interested in the physical sciences, physics and so on. Then I saw that a new biology was emerging in the early '70s and the impact that might have on the medical profession. That's why, rather late in the college years, I decided that I would pursue medical research.

I became involved in the HIV epidemic as a young physician. I had finished my medical school and was in the process of finishing up my training in internal medicine in Los Angeles in 1980–81, and I had taken on an extra year to be the chief medical resident. It was during that period when a few gay men were coming in to the hospital with a multitude of infections, and these were not usual infections. These are infections that are only seen in immune-compromised individuals—cancer patients who had been on chemotherapy, transplant patients who had been on rejection medications. The immune systems were wiped out and therefore they were susceptible to these infections by an organism that would normally not cause trouble. Yet these previously healthy young men were coming down with these diseases, which suggested that their immune system had been destroyed by something.

I got interested because it was a scientific curiosity. I never realized that this would turn into the plague of the millennium. HIV has already infected, cumulatively, over 60 million individuals worldwide. Right now, it is killing approximately 20-plus million, and about 42 million people are living with viral infection. We know that each day this epidemic continues to grow at a rate of about 14,000 new cases per day. Of the 42 million people living with HIV, at least three-quarters of them are in sub-Saharan Africa. In those African countries, the patients do not have access to the kind of therapies we have in the U.S. and Europe, and therefore they're condemned to die a slow and miserable death. The second wave of the epidemic is now spreading into Asia, where half of the population resides, so there's no doubt that the problem will get worse. Projections suggest that over the coming decade in India and China, we could have perhaps 40 million infections by 2010. This epidemic gained importance when we realized we were not only tackling a fascinating scientific issue but we were also addressing a major public health concern. That's doubly gratifying.

I think our biggest contribution to the field—the one I feel most proud of—is the fact that we showed the world what HIV is doing in the body of an infected person. Through our study of patients, we realized that the virus infects and replicates continuously, relentlessly, at extremely high levels. It's constantly churning away, producing more progeny virus, which in turn infect more of these important cells in the immune system. This just goes on remorselessly for years and years. In that process, it wears down the immune system so that the person infected becomes susceptible to a multitude of ordinary bugs in our environment. The ramification of this discovery is that we could actually quantify how fast the virus replicates and to what level. We also learned that every time HIV replicates, it makes mistakes, it makes mutations. You could say that's pretty stupid of the virus to make mistakes while trying to copy itself because many of the progeny virus would be defective or dead, but in fact it's a very clever strategy because some of the viruses will survive and those are more fit. The consequence is that when you try to treat HIV, because it's so capable of making these mutations, it will evade the drugs very quickly. It will evolve forms that become drug resistant. And therefore the drugs will fail after a short period of time.

We found that by doing the numbers and doing the proper calculations we could actually figure out a new strategy. You corner the virus and force it to make multiple mutations to evade multiple drugs at a given time. When you crunch the numbers you realize it becomes increasingly difficult for HIV to do this if you put three or four drugs in at the same time. We then took this implication and tested it in patients. By mid-1996 we had a bunch of patients whose virus loads were controlled to an undetectable level using such a strategy. So we now have therapies that can control the virus, but we still have a long way to go. There's absolutely no cure and there's no effective vaccine yet, so there's a lot to be done.

. . .

When my parents found out I had made the cover of *Time* magazine, they were of course really excited and proud. My father couldn't have been prouder. And in his own way, he told every one of his friends and relatives. He's not the kind who would hug you and kiss you—you know, the typical stern Chinese father figure. But you could tell there was a great deal of joy in his heart at that crucial moment. And seeing them so happy and proud, I couldn't help but enjoy it with them.

. . .

I actually became a naturalized citizen in 1970, about five years after coming, but I always thought of myself as an immigrant, a foreigner to some extent, and it is really through the fact that our kids are clearly American that we are American. And you know, I have this ambivalence. I've been here so long that I sometimes forget I'm an immigrant, but there are times when I am reminded that I'm an immigrant—by our society. People will come up and say, "Where are you from?" "I'm from New York." And then they say, "Well, where were you born? Where are you really from?" And then I would go into my history because I am an immigrant, and then I tell them that I was born in Taiwan, came over to California when I was twelve. But then, for my children it's really tough. They say, "I was born in California and then raised in New York," but then people say, "Well, where are you really from?" And they don't really have much of an answer for that. There's a certain attitude that an Asian face is automatically non-American. And yet we all know we are Americans; we're just of a different heritage.

SOURCE: David Ho, interview with Bill Moyers, Public Affairs Television, 2003. Available at www.pbs.org/becomingamerican/ap_pjourneys_transcript3.html. Accessed June 1, 2004. Reprinted by permission of David Ho.

OTHER REFERENCES

Howard Chua-Eoan, "The Tao of Ho," *Time*, December 30, 1996/January 6, 1997, pp. 69–70.

Christine Gorman, "The Disease Detective," *Time*, December 30, 1996/January 6, 1997, pp. 56–64.

1368–1644	Ming dynasty rules China.
1600s	Chinese reach Mexico on the ships of the Manila galleon.
1644–1911	Qing dynasty (Manchu) rules China.
1683	Manchus take over Taiwan from Ming loyalists, who had ousted the Dutch in 1681.
1784	U.S.-China trade begins with the voyage of the *Empress of China* from New York to Canton.
1785	Three stranded crewmen, Ashing, Achun, and Accun, are first Chinese to land in the U.S. at Baltimore.
1818	Five Chinese students arrive to study at the Foreign Missions School in Cornwall, Connecticut.
1830s	Chinese start sugar industry in Hawaii; Chinese sailors and peddlers seen in New York; Chang and Eng Bunker, the original Siamese twins, appear with P. T. Barnum in New York.
1839–42	China defeated in Opium War against Britain; Treaty of Nanking opens five ports, cedes Hong Kong to Britain, grants extraterritorial rights to foreigners, and imposes indemnity of 21 million silver dollars.
1844	U.S. and China sign first treaty giving U.S. consular jurisdiction over American nationals in China.
1848	James Marshall discovers gold in California; Chinese begin to arrive.
1850	California imposes first Foreign Miners' Tax of $20 a month.
1851–64	Taiping Rebellion against the Qing dynasty sweeps through South and Central China.
1852	Chinese contract laborers land in Hawaii; over 20,000 Chinese

	enter California; Foreign Miners' Tax of $3 a month imposed on the Chinese.
1854	Yung Wing is first Chinese to graduate from an American college (Yale); *People v. Hall* rules that Chinese, Negroes, and Indians cannot testify against whites in court (repealed 1872).
1856–60	Britain and France defeat China in Second Opium War; Treaty of Tientsin opens more ports, legalizes opium, imposes further indemnity, and cedes Kowloon to Britain.
1858	California passes law to bar entry of Chinese or Mongolians.
1862	Chinese Six Companies is loosely formed to protect the interest of the Chinese community in San Francisco (formalized as Chinese Consolidated Benevolent Association in 1882).
1865	Central Pacific Railroad Company recruits Chinese workers.
1866	Chinese laborers work in the cane fields of Louisiana, some brought over from Cuba.
1867	Two thousand Chinese railroad workers strike for same pay and hours as white workers.
1868	U.S. and China sign Burlingame Treaty recognizing the right of their citizens to immigrate without restrictions but not be granted naturalization rights.
1869	First transcontinental railroad is completed; Chinese work on Alabama and Texas railroad lines; plantation owners hold conference in Memphis, Tennessee, and propose replacing black slaves with Chinese laborers.
1870	California passes law against importation of Chinese, Japanese, and Mongolian women for prostitution; 75 Chinese laborers are recruited to Sampson's shoe factory in North Adams, Massachusetts, as strikebreakers.
1871	Anti-Chinese violence in Los Angeles; Chinese are employed by planters in Mississippi, Georgia, and Arkansas.
1872	Chinese Educational Mission, headed by Yung Wing, sends first of 120 students from China to the U.S. to study science and technology.
1874	Presbyterian Mission Home for Girls is established to rescue Chinese prostitutes and abused slave girls.
1875	Congress passes Page Law to bar entry of Chinese prostitutes, felons, and contract laborers into the U.S.
1877	Workingman's Party of California, founded under the leadership of Denis Kearney, instigates riot against the Chinese in San Francisco.
1878	The Zhigongtang (Triads), a secret society, is formed to help overthrow the Manchus and restore the Ming emperor to the throne.
1879	California constitution prohibits further immigration of Chinese laborers and their employment on public works; U.S. Circuit Court rules that Chinese can be denied naturalization rights on the basis of race *(In re Ah Yup)*.

1880	California prohibits marriage between whites and "Mongolians, Negroes, mulattos and persons of mixed blood" (repealed 1948).
1882	Chinese Exclusion Act suspends immigration of Chinese laborers for ten years and denies naturalization rights to Chinese.
1885	Chinese miners are massacred in Rock Springs, Wyoming; California Supreme Court rules in *Tape v. Hurley* that Chinese children should be admitted into the public schools; U.S. Supreme Court prohibits discrimination against Chinese laundrymen in *Yick Wo v. Hopkins.*
1887	Brutal massacre of Chinese miners occurs in Snake River, Oregon.
1888	Scott Act renders 20,000 Chinese reentry certificates null and void.
1892	Geary Law renews exclusion of Chinese laborers for another ten years and requires Chinese to register; the next year, *Fong Yue Ting v. U.S.* upholds constitutionality of Geary Law.
1894	Sun Yat-sen establishes the Xingzhonghui (Revive China Society) in Honolulu to overthrow the Qing dynasty and establish a republic.
1895	Japan defeats China in Sino-Japanese War and Taiwan is ceded to Japan; Native Sons of the Golden State (later Chinese-American Citizens' Alliance) is founded in San Francisco.
1898	*Wong Kim Ark v. U.S.* decides that Chinese born in the U.S. cannot be stripped of their citizenship; Hundred Days Reform to modernize China fails and Empress Dowager imprisons the Emperor Kuang-hsu; U.S. annexes Hawaii and the Philippines after the Spanish-American War.
1899	Chinese reformer Kang Youwei establishes the Baohuanghui (Protect the Emperor Society) in Victoria, B.C., which favors a constitutional monarchy under the Manchu emperor, and later tours the U.S. to recruit members.
1900	Boxer Rebellion against foreigners in China fails; U.S. establishes a scholarship fund for Chinese students to study in America.
1902	Chinese Exclusion Act is extended another ten years; immigration raid in Boston's Chinatown.
1904	Chinese Exclusion Act is made indefinite and applicable to U.S. insular possessions.
1905	Chinese in U.S. and Hawaii support boycott of American products in China to protest mistreatment of Chinese immigrants in the U.S.; Sun Yat-sen organizes Tongmenghui (Chinese United League) in Tokyo to overthrow the Manchus.
1906	Earthquake and fire in San Francisco destroy municipal records, facilitating the entry of Chinese immigrants as "paper sons."
1910–40	Immigrants from Asian countries are processed at the Angel Island Immigration Station, but only the Chinese are singled out for long detentions and harsh interrogations because of the Chinese Exclusion Act.
1911	Sun Yat-sen's followers succeed in overthrowing the Qing dynasty and establishing the Republic of China.
1913	Second revolution to overthrow Yuan Shih-kai, president of the

republic, fails and Sun Yat-sen flees overseas; California passes alien land law prohibiting "aliens ineligible to citizenship" from buying land or leasing it for longer than three years.

1916–28   Yuan Shih-kai dies (1916) and warlords rule China with the support of foreign powers.

1919   May Fourth Movement breaks out in China in response to the Treaty of Versailles, which awarded German concessions in China to Japan.

1921   Chinese Communist Party is formally organized under the leadership of Mao Zedong.

1922   Cable Act stipulates that any American female citizen who marries an alien ineligible for citizenship will lose her citizenship (repealed 1931).

1924   Immigration Act excludes all aliens ineligible for citizenship, including Chinese wives of U.S. citizens; Sun Yat-sen accepts Soviet aid and forms First United Front with Chinese Communist Party.

1925   Warring tongs in U.S. declare truce; Sun Yat-sen dies and Chiang Kai-shek becomes commander in chief; Chiang leads the Northern Expedition and succeeds in ridding China of warlords.

1927   Chiang leads anti-Communist coup and reduces their forces by four-fifths; Kuomintang splits into Nationalist camp in Nanjing and left camp in Wuhan.

1931   Japan occupies Manchuria.

1933   Chinese Hand Laundry Alliance is formed in New York and successfully opposes a discriminatory ordinance against Chinese laundries.

1934–35   Communist Long March to Northwest China is completed.

1936   Chiang Kai-shek is kidnapped in the Xian Incident and forced into the Second United Front with the Chinese Communist Party.

1937   War breaks out between China and Japan after the Marco Polo Bridge Incident; Chinese Workers' Mutual Aid Association joins the American labor movement.

1938   Chinese garment workers strike for thirteen weeks against the National Dollar Stores chain and form the first Chinese chapter of the International Ladies Garment Workers Union.

1941   Japan attacks Pearl Harbor and U.S. enters World War II as China's ally.

1943   Congress repeals the Chinese Exclusion Acts, establishes an annual quota of 105 Chinese immigrants, and grants naturalization rights to the Chinese.

1945   Japan is defeated, World War II ends, and Taiwan is returned to China.

1946   Act of August 9, 1946, exempts Chinese wives of U.S. citizens from quota restrictions.

1947   Amendment to the War Brides Act of 1945 allows Chinese wives of U.S. veterans to immigrate; civil war breaks out in China between the Kuomintang under Chiang Kai-shek and the Communist Party under Mao Zedong; in "2–28 Massacre" military forces are called in to quell a rebellion by Taiwanese civilians against Kuomintang control of the island, resulting in the deaths of several thousand Taiwanese.

1948   Displaced Persons Act allows Chinese scholars already in the U.S. to change their status to residents after China falls under Communist control; California repeals anti-miscegenation law.

1949   Communist Party under Mao Zedong establishes the People's Republic of China; Kuomintang under Chiang Kai-shek flees to Taiwan, making Taipei the capital of the Republic of China.

1950–53   People's Republic of China opposes U.S. military forces in the Korean conflict; Kuomintang consolidates control in Chinatown communities.

1952   McCarran-Walter Act retains Chinese quota of 105 per year but exempts Chinese aliens married to U.S. citizens from quota.

1953–65   Refugee Relief Acts admit close to 50,000 Chinese refugees into the U.S.

1956   California repeals alien land laws.

1957   In response to the Drumwright Report, which called attention to fraudulent entry practices among the Chinese, the National Chinese Welfare Council is formed to lobby against mass deportation of Chinese, resulting in the Confession Program and FBI persecution of progressive elements in the Chinese American community.

1959   Hiram Fong becomes the first Chinese American to be elected to Congress as a U.S. senator after Hawaii becomes the 50th state to join the union.

1965   Congress passes Immigration and Naturalization Act of 1965, putting China on an equal footing with other countries at 20,000 immigrants per year, with preference given to family reunification and skilled and professional personnel; U.S. involvement in the Vietnam War escalates.

1966   *U.S. News and World Report* touts Chinese Americans as model minorities; start of the Cultural Revolution in China.

1967   U.S. Supreme Court rules that states cannot outlaw intermarriages by race.

1968–69   Student strikes at San Francisco State College and UC Berkeley succeed in establishing ethnic studies programs.

1969   Chinese for Affirmative Action is founded as a civil rights organization in San Francisco.

1970   Asian Americans organize separate contingent in the anti–Vietnam War movement.

1971   United Nations votes to admit the People's Republic of China, thereby ousting Chiang Kai-shek's Republic of China.

1972   President Richard Nixon visits Beijing in support of normalization of relations between China and the U.S.

1973   Organization of Chinese Americans is founded in Washington,

	D.C.; Chinese scholars in America protest U.S. turnover of Diaoyutai Islands to Japan.
1974	March Fong Eu is elected California's secretary of state; *Lau v. Nichols* rules that failure to provide some form of bilingual education to non-English-speaking students violates their constitutional rights; Chinese agitate for construction jobs in Confucius Plaza site in New York Chinatown.
1975	20,000 Chinese protest police brutality in New York City; Vietnam War ends and refugees from Vietnam, Cambodia, and Laos begin arriving in the U.S.
1976	*Hampton v. Wong Mow Sun* rules that lawful aliens may not be denied federal employment on the basis of race or national origin.
1979	U.S. recognizes and resumes diplomatic relations with the People's Republic of China.
1981	U.S. creates a separate quota of 20,000 for Taiwan.
1982	Vincent Chin, a Chinese American draftsman, is clubbed to death with a baseball bat by two white autoworkers in a racially motivated hate crime in Detroit, Michigan; more than 20,000 Chinese garment workers strike in New York Chinatown and succeed in winning a new union contract.
1984	Henry Liu is assassinated in his home in Daly City, California, for writing an unfavorable biography of Chiang Ching-kuo, president of the Republic of China.
1986	Immigration Reform and Control Act grants amnesty to illegal immigrants and penalizes employers who knowingly employ illegals; U.S. increases Hong Kong's immigration quota from 600 to 5,000 per year.
1987	Thirty-five years of martial law end in Taiwan.
1989	Ming Hai "Jim" Loo is murdered by two white brothers avenging the deaths of American soldiers in the Vietnam War outside a pool hall in Raleigh, North Carolina; in the Tiananmen Square Incident in Beijing, armed troops suppress protest by thousands of college students advocating political reform.
1990	Immigration Act raises annual immigration from all countries of the world to 700,000 and revises system of preference to encourage immigration of professionals and business investors.
1992	In response to the Tiananmen Square Incident, President George Bush issues an Executive Order granting over 60,000 students and scholars permanent residence status in the U.S.; Americans adopt 200 orphans from China, mostly baby girls (numbers grow to 33,000 by the year 2000).
1993	*Golden Venture,* a cargo steamer carrying 286 illegal immigrants from Fujian Province, runs aground in New York harbor, calling attention to the clandestine smuggling of Chinese into the United States.
1994	California voters pass Proposition 187 to deny undocumented immigrants education, health, and social services (ruled unconstitutional in 1998).
1995	U.S. increases Hong Kong's immigration quota to 20,000.

1996   California voters pass Proposition 209 (Civil Rights Initiative) to
        bar "preferential treatment" in public employment, education, and
        contracting on the basis of race; Immigration Reform and Immigrant
        Responsibility Act tightens legal recourses for political asylum; Taiwan
        holds first direct presidential election.

1997   U.S. Senate investigates charges of illegal campaign contributions,
        targeting foreign donors in Asia but implicating Asian Americans as
        a whole; Hong Kong is returned to the People's Republic of China.

1998   Number of H1B visas is doubled to encourage immigration of highly
        skilled guest workers from India and China; California voters approve
        Proposition 227 to end bilingual education in public schools; Washing-
        ton voters pass Initiative 200 to eliminate "preferential treatment" in
        public employment, education, and contracting on the basis of race;
        Angel Island Immigration Station is granted National Historic Land-
        mark status.

1999   Wen Ho Lee, a Taiwan-born U.S. citizen working as a physicist at the
        Los Alamos National Laboratory, is falsely arrested and jailed on
        charges of spying for China; Macao is returned to the People's Repub-
        lic of China; Gary Locke becomes the first Chinese American to be
        elected governor of a state (Washington); U.S. bomb accidentally hits
        the Chinese embassy in Yugoslavia during the war in Kosovo.

2000   According to the U.S. census, Chinese Americans are the largest Asian
        ethnic group, numbering 2.8 million, an increase of 1.2 million from
        1990; President Bill Clinton signs the China Trade Bill, scrapping the
        practice of annual review of China's trade privileges and promoting
        trade between the two countries.

2001   Elaine Chao, appointed secretary of labor by President Bush, becomes
        the first Chinese American to serve in a president's cabinet; American
        spy plane collides with a Chinese fighter jet, causing the death of a Chi-
        nese pilot and strained Sino-American relations; China is admitted into
        the World Trade Organization; national survey by the Committee of
        100 finds that one-fourth of the American population still hold nega-
        tive attitudes toward Chinese Americans; terrorist attack on the World
        Trade Center causes 3,000 deaths and injuries, economic damage to
        New York Chinatown, and racial backlash against Arab Americans,
        Muslims, Sikhs, and other immigrants.

2002   An outbreak of Severe Acute Respiratory Syndrome (SARS) in south-
        ern China and Hong Kong revives xenophobic fears and dampens
        travel and trade between the U.S. and Asian countries; protesters
        convince Abercrombie & Fitch to pull T-shirts that negatively stereo-
        type Chinese Americans.

2003   Captain James Yee, Muslim chaplain at the U.S. detention facility
        in Guantanamo Bay, is arrested on suspicion of espionage and put
        in solitary confinement for 76 days (all charges dropped in 2005).

CHINESE GLOSSARY

Ashing, Achun, Accun	亞成, 亞全, 亞宮
Asing, Norman	袁生
Bahtuhlu	巴圖魯
Baishi	白石
Baohuanghui	保皇會
Bok-fat-lik	博弗叻
Bow On Guk	保安局
Canton City	廣州市
Chaap Kuen	椺權
Chan Dak Gwong	陳德廣
Chan Kiu Sing	陳九盛
Chan Woon Sui	陳垣瑞
Chang Foyin	張康仁
Chaozhou	潮州
chashaobao	叉燒飽
Chee Lai	起來
Chen Lanbin	陳蘭彬
Chen, Mei-chin	陳美津
Chen She	陳涉
Chen Xuming	陳烱明
Cheung Hau Association	昌後堂

Chew Mon Sing	趙萬勝
chi	姼
Chiang Ching-kuo	蔣經國
Chiang Kai-shek	蔣介石
Chin Gee Hee	陳宜禧
Ching dynasty	清朝
Ching Ming	清明
Choi Gei Gwong	蔡基廣
Chui Jau	徐州
Chui Waan	徐環
Chun Doshim, Mrs.	伍資深夫人
Chung Mun-yao	鐘文耀
Chung Sai Yat Po	中西日報
daai saang yat	大生日
dan tat	蛋撻
Diaoyutai	釣愚台
Dawang City	大王市
doufugan	豆腐乾
doufuhua	豆腐花
doushabao	豆沙飽
Doushan	斗山
Duanwu Festival	端午節
faat choi	髮蔡
Fenshuijiang	汾水江
Fong, B. S.	鄺发炳舜
Fu Lee	傅李
Fucha	夫差
Fujian Province	福建省
Fung Biu	馮標
Fuzhou	福州
gamsaanhaak	金山客
gamsaanpoh	金山婆
Go Hap Yuen	高洽源
Gong Moon	江門
Gong Yan	江恩
Gong Yuen Tim	江潤甜
gongfu	工夫

Gongyi	公益
goong-goong	公公
Goujian	句踐
Guangdong Province	廣東省
Guangxu	光緒
Guangzhou	廣州
gum jum	金斜
Ha-si-jin-ji	蟀士甄治
Haamfung	咸豐
Haikuan Taotai	海關道臺
Hainan Island	海南島
Hakka	客家
Han dynasty	漢朝
Han Xin	韓信
Hankow	漢口
Hanlin	翰林
Heungshan District	香山縣
Hezuo	合作
Ho Man Gwong	何文光
Hom Ah Wing	譚亞榮
Hom Gong Village	潭岡鄉
Hong, Dang Thi Hoa	洪鄧氏花
Hong, Ha Binh	洪夏萍
Hong, Phu Ho	洪輔瑚
Hong, The Vu	洪世武
Hop Lee Laundry	合利洗衣館
Hop Wo Company	合和會館
Hsiang Shan District	香山縣
huajuan	花卷
Huang Sih Chuen	黃錫銓
Huang Zunxian	黃遵憲
Huangliang Du	黃梁都
Huaxian	花縣
Huie Kin	許芹
Huie Kin-kwong	許芹光
huoguo	火鍋
It Main	一鳴

Jau Dung Sing	周東成
Jau Fung Gui	周逢舉
Jau Hing	周興
Jau Taan	周檀
Jee Gam	朱金
Jew Baak Ming	趙弼明
Jew Cheuk Faan	趙卓凡
Jew Ji Faan	趙子蕃
Jian Fu	堅夫
Jiang Qing	江青
Jiangmen	江門
Jim Tien Yu	詹天佑
jin	斤
jo poh	祖婆
jook	粥
joong	粽
Jui Ying Building	聚英樓
Jung Sai Garment Factory	中西車衣廠
Ka, Shui Mak	賈麥穗
Ka, Sun Fook	賈山福
Kaiping District	開平縣
Kam Wah Chung	錦華昌
Kang Youwei	康有為
Kaohsiung	高雄
Kin-Chang Railroad	京張鐵路
Kong Chow Company	岡州會館
Kuan Yin	觀音
Kuang-hsu	光緒
Kuo Min Yat Po	國民日報
Kuomintang	國民黨
kuw fu	舅父
kuw mow	舅母
Kwan Ying Lin	關影憐
Kwangtung Province	廣東省
Lam Yam Yin	林任賢
Langmei Village	朗美村
Lee, K. P.	李桂攀

Lee, Lim P.	李泮霖
Lee Ming How	李銘侯
Lee Tsung-Dao	李政道
Lee, Wen Ho	李文和
Lee, Yan Phou	李恩富
Lee, Yuan-tse	李遠哲
leisi	利是
Leong Yuk Quon	梁玉群
Leung Ju	梁住
Leung Naam	梁楠
Leung Tai Kee	梁泰記
li	里
Li Hung Chang	李鴻章
Li Ling	李陵
Li Shimin	李世民
Liang Cheung You	梁長有
Liang Kiang	兩廣
Liang Tung-yen	梁敦彥
Liangshanpo	梁山泊
Lik Bui Village	瀝貝村
Lin Chien Fu	林堅夫
liqi	力氣
Liu Liangmo	劉良模
Lok Cheung Village	洛場村
Lok Gau	駱九
Low Hop Lee	劉合意
Lu Zhishen	魯智深
luobogao	蘿蔔糕
Ma Din	馬典
Ma-che-haang-mei	馬車坑尾
Ma-sun-dong	孖慎當
Man Dak	文德
Manchu	滿族
Mao Zedong	毛澤東
mapo doufu	麻婆豆腐
maqua	馬褂
Mark, C. S.	麥英俊

Min-Cheh	閩浙
Min, King	愍王
Min Qing	民青
Min Ziqian	閔子騫
Ming dynasty	明朝
Ming Leung	明亮
Ming Seung	明尚
Minnan	閩南
Mok Fai Bak	莫輝北
Mon Hing Bo	文興報
moon yuet	滿月
mou	畝
mui nui	妹女
mui tsai	妹仔
Mukden	瀋陽
muk-uk	木屋
Nam How	南頭
Nanking	南京
Ng Poon Chew	伍盤照
Ng Yiu Ming, Mrs.	吳耀明夫人
Ngui Hoi	外海
Nianzu	念祖
Nie Er	聶耳
Ning Yung Company	寧陽會館
Niuwan	牛灣
On Leong Association	安良堂
Ou Lei Sewing Shop	區利車衣廠
Panyu District	番禺縣
Peng, Le Shan	彭樂善
poa poa	婆婆
pu-erh tea	普弭茶
Punti	本地
Qin, Prince	秦王
Qin, state of	秦國
Qing dynasty	清朝
Qizhi	啓者
Qu Yuan	屈原

Quong Tuck Company	廣德號
Sai Gai Yat Po	世界日報
Sam Yup Company	三邑會館
Sang Yuen	生原
Sanzi Jing	三字經
Seeto	司徒
shantang	善堂
shaobing youtiao	燒餅油條
Shenyang	瀋陽
Shenzhen	深圳
shijian	時間
Shui Wu Chu	稅務處
Sin Siu	冼韶
Siyau	豉油
Siyi	四邑
So Mo	蘇戊
Su Wu	蘇武
Sun Yat-sen	孫逸仙
Sunning District	新寧縣
Sunwui District	新縣
Suzhou	蘇州
Taichung	台中
Taishan City	台城
Taishan District	台山縣
Tanka	蛋家
tay	米茲
Tian Han	田漢
Tian Heng	田橫
Tien Chang-lin	田長霖
Tientsin	天津
Tin Fook Jewelry Shop	天福金鋪
Ting Yi-chang	丁日昌
tofu	豆腐
Tom Kai Shau	譚啓秀
Tong Shao-yi	唐紹儀
Tong menghui	同盟會
Tongzhi	同治

Tsai Ting-kai	蔡廷鍇
Tsai Ting-kang	蔡廷幹
Tseng Kuo-fan	曾國藩
Tsien, Hsue-shen	錢學森
Tung Meng Hui	同盟會
Wah Fong	華芳
Wang Bingnam	王炳南
Wang, C. T.	王正延
Wang Chung-hui	王寵惠
Wang Chung-yao	王寵佑
Wang Hongwen	王洪文
Wang, Kang-lu	王康陸
Wang, Ling-chi	王靈智
Wang Yu Cho	王煜初
Wen Bing Chung	溫秉忠
Wen, King	文王
Wong, Cheuk-Yin	黃卓然
Wong Chin Foo	王清福
Wong Kai	黃啓
Wong Liu Tsong	黃柳霜
Wong Sei	黃泗
Woo Sung	吳淞
Woo Tze-teng	吳子登
Woo Ying-foo	吳應科
Wu, King	武王
Wu Song	武松
Wu, state of	吳國
Wu Yong	吳用
Wuchang	武昌
Wuhan	武漢
wujiapi	五加皮
Xiamen	廈門
Xian	西安
Xianfeng	咸豐
xiang banfa	想辦法
Xiangshan District	香山縣
Xingzhonghui	興中會

Xinhui City	新會城
Xinhui District	新會縣
Xinning Magazine	新寧雜誌
Xiongnu	匈奴
Yalu River	鴨綠江
Yan Hui	顏回
Yan Wo Company	人和會館
Yang Chen Ning	楊振寧
Yao Wenyuan	姚文元
Yat Ging Lau	一景樓
Yee Kai Man	余桂鳴
Yeong Wo District Association	陽和會館
Yik Hau	益厚
Yik Jook Yee Jook	一囑二囑
Yim Geng	嚴根
Youli	羑里
Yu Cheuk	余灼
Yu Gau San	余苟新
Yu King Fong	余瓊芳
Yu Rongzu	余榮祖
Yu Sun	禹慎
Yuan Shih-kai	袁世凱
Yue, king of	越王
Yuet Chung Paak	越松柏
Yung Wing	容閎
Yung Wo Company	陽和會館
Zhang Chunqiao	張春橋
Zheng Zaoru	鄭藻如
Zhiduoxing	智多星
Zhigongtang	致公堂
Zhongnan Mountain	終南山
Zhongshan District	中山縣
Zhou Yunian	周宇年
Zhou Yurong	周宇榮

Aarim-Heriot, Najia. *Chinese Americans, African Americans, and Racial Anxiety in the United States, 1848–1882.* Urbana: University of Illinois Press, 2003.

Arkush, R. David, and Leo O. Lee, eds. *Land without Ghosts: Chinese Impressions of America from the Mid–Nineteenth Century to the Present.* Berkeley: University of California Press, 1989.

Asian Women. Asian American Studies, University of California, Berkeley, 1971.

Bao, Xiaolan. *Holding Up More Than Half the Sky: Chinese Women Garment Workers in New York City, 1948–92.* Urbana: University of Illinois Press, 2001.

Barlow, Jeffrey, and Christine Richardson. *China Doctor of John Day.* Portland, Ore.: Binford & Mort, 1979.

Barth, Gunther. *Bitter Strength: A History of the Chinese in the United States, 1850–1870.* Cambridge, Mass.: Harvard University Press, 1964.

Bieler, Stacey. *"Patriots" or "Traitors"? A History of American-Educated Chinese Students.* Armonk, N.Y.: M. E. Sharpe, 2004.

Bonner, Arthur. *Alas! What Brought Thee Hither? The Chinese in New York, 1800–1950.* London: Associated University Presses, 1997.

Bridging the Centuries: History of Chinese Americans in Southern California. Los Angeles: Chinese Historical Society of Southern California, 2001.

Caplan, Nathan. *The Boat People and Achievement in America: A Study of Family Life, Hard Work, and Cultural Values.* Ann Arbor: University of Michigan Press, 1989.

Cargill, Mary Terrell, and Jade Quang Huynh, eds. *Voices of Vietnamese Boat People: Nineteen Narratives of Escape and Survival.* Jefferson, N.C.: McFarland & Company, 2000.

Chan, Anthony B. *Perpetually Cool: The Many Lives of Anna May Wong.* Lanham, Md.: Scarecrow Press, 2003.

Chan, Sucheng. "Asian American Struggles for Civil, Political, Economic, and Social Rights." *Chinese America: History and Perspectives,* 2002, pp. 56–70.

———. *Asian Americans: An Interpretive History.* Boston: Twayne, 1991.

————, ed. *Entry Denied: Exclusion and the Chinese Community in America, 1882–1943.* Philadelphia: Temple University Press, 1991.

————. *This Bitter-sweet Soil: The Chinese in California Agriculture, 1860–1910.* Berkeley: University of California Press, 1986.

Chang, Gordon H., ed. *Asian Americans and Politics: Perspectives, Experiences, Prospects.* Stanford: Stanford University Press, 2001.

Chang, Iris. *The Chinese in America: A Narrative History.* New York: Viking, 2003.

————. *Thread of the Silkworm.* New York: Basic Books, 1995.

Char, Tin-Yuke. *The Sandalwood Mountains: Readings and Stories of the Early Chinese in Hawaii.* Honolulu: University Press of Hawaii, 1975.

Chen, Amy. *The Chinatown Files.* New York: Filmmakers Library, 2001. VHS.

Chen, Hsiang-Shui. *Chinatown No More: Taiwan Immigrants in Contemporary New York.* Ithaca: Cornell University Press, 1992.

Chen, Jack. *The Chinese of America.* New York: Harper & Row, 1980.

Chen, Shehong. *Being Chinese, Becoming Chinese American.* Urbana: University of Illinois Press, 2003.

Chen, Sibyl. *Our Treasury: The Shaping of First-Generation Taiwanese Americans.* Boston: Intercollegiate Taiwanese American Student Association, 2002.

Chen, Yong. *Chinese San Francisco, 1850–1943: A Trans-Pacific Community.* Stanford: Stanford University Press, 2000.

Cheng, Lucie, and Edna Bonacich, eds. *Labor Immigration under Capitalism: Asian Workers in the United States before World War II.* Berkeley: University of California Press, 1984.

Cheng, Lucie, Yuzun Liu, and Dehua Zheng. "Chinese Emigration: The Sunning Railroad and the Development of Toisan." *Amerasia Journal* 9, no. 1 (1982): 59–74.

Chew, Ron, ed. *Reflections of Seattle's Chinese Americans: The First 100 Years.* Seattle: University of Washington Press, 1994.

Chin, Frank. "Confessions of the Chinatown Cowboy." *Bulletin of Concerned Asian Scholars* 4, no. 3 (fall 1972): 58–70.

Chin, Frank, and Jeffery Paul Chan. "Racist Love." In *Seeing through Shuck*, edited by Richard Kostelanetz, pp. 65–79. New York: Ballantine, 1972.

Chinn, Thomas W. *Bridging the Pacific: San Francisco Chinatown and Its People.* San Francisco: Chinese Historical Society of America, 1989.

————, ed. *A History of the Chinese in California: A Syllabus.* San Francisco: Chinese Historical Society of America, 1969.

Chiu, Ping. *Chinese Labor in California, 1850–1880: An Economic Study.* Madison: State Historical Society of Wisconsin, 1967.

Choy, Christine. *Mississippi Triangle.* New York: Third World Newsreel, 1987. VHS.

Choy, Christine, and Renee Tajima. *Who Killed Vincent Chin?* New York: Filmmakers Library, 1989. VHS.

Choy, Philip P., Lorraine Dong, and Marlon K. Hom. *The Coming Man: 19th-Century American Perceptions of the Chinese.* Hong Kong: Joint Publishing Co., 1994.

Christoff, Peggy Spitzer. *Tracking the "Yellow Peril": The INS and Chinese Immigrants in the Midwest.* Rockport, Me.: Picton Press, 2001.

Chu, Doris C. J. *Chinese in Massachusetts: Their Experiences and Contributions.* Boston: Chinese Culture Institute, 1987.

Chu, Judy. "Anna May Wong." In *Counterpoint: Perspectives on Asian America*, edited by Emma Gee, pp. 284–89. Los Angeles: Asian American Studies Center, UCLA, 1976.

Chua-Eoan, Howard. "The Tao of Ho." *Time,* December 30, 1996/January 6, 1997, pp. 69–70.

Chun, Gloria Heyung. *Of Orphans and Warriors: Inventing Chinese American Culture and Identity.* New Brunswick, N.J.: Rutgers University Press, 2000.

Chung, Sue Fawn. "The Chinese American Citizens Alliance: An Effort in Assimilation, 1895–1965." *Chinese America: History and Perspectives,* 1988, pp. 30–57.

Cohen, Lucy M. *Chinese in the Post–Civil War South: A People without a History.* Baton Rouge: Louisiana State University Press, 1984.

Coolidge, Mary Roberts. *Chinese Immigration.* New York: Henry Holt, 1909.

Crowder, Linda Sun. "Mortuary Practices in San Francisco Chinatown." *Chinese America: History and Perspectives,* 1999, pp. 33–46.

Daniels, Roger. *Asian America: Chinese and Japanese in the United States since 1850.* Seattle: University of Washington Press, 1988.

Daws, Gavan. *Prisoners of the Japanese: POWs of World War II in the Pacific.* New York: William Morrow, 1994.

Del Rosario, C. A. *A Different Battle: Stories of Asian Pacific American Veterans.* Seattle: Wing Luke Museum and University of Washington Press, 1999.

Dicker, Laverne Mau. *The Chinese in San Francisco: A Pictorial History.* New York: Dover, 1979.

Dirlik, Arif, ed. *Chinese in the American Frontier.* Lanham, Md.: Rowman & Littlefield, 2001.

Djao, Wei. *Being Chinese: Voices from the Diaspora.* Tucson: University of Arizona Press, 2003.

Duberman, Martin. *Paul Robeson.* New York: Alfred A. Knopf, 1988.

Eng, David L. *Racial Castration: Managing Masculinity in Asian America.* Durham, N.C.: Duke University Press, 2001.

Eng, David L., and Alice Y. Hom, eds. *Q & A: Queer in Asian America.* Philadelphia: Temple University Press, 1996.

Fong, Colleen, and Judy Yung. "In Search of the Right Spouse: Interracial Marriage among Chinese and Japanese Americans." *Amerasia Journal* 21 (winter 1995/1996): 77–97.

Fong, Lawrence Michael. "Sojourners and Settlers: The Chinese Experience in Arizona." In *The Chinese Experience in Arizona and Northern Mexico.* Tucson: Arizona Historical Society, 1980.

Fong, Timothy P. *The First Suburban Chinatown: The Remaking of Monterey Park, California.* Philadelphia: Temple University Press, 1994.

Fuller, Sherri Gebert. *Chinese in Minnesota.* St. Paul: Minnesota Historical Society Press, 2004.

Gibson, Otis. *The Chinese in America.* Cincinnati: Hitchcock & Walden, 1877.

Gillenkirk, Jeff, and James Motlow. *Bitter Melon: Stories from the Last Rural Chinese Town in America.* Seattle: University of Washington Press, 1987.

Glick, Clarence. *Sojourners and Settlers: Chinese Migrants in Hawaii.* Honolulu: Hawaii Chinese History Center and the University Press of Hawaii, 1980.

Gorman, Christine. "The Disease Detective." *Time,* December 30,1996/January 6, 1997, pp. 56–64.

Guest, Kenneth. *God in Chinatown: Religion and Survival in New York's Evolving Immigrant Community.* New York: New York University Press, 2003.

Gyory, Andrew. *Closing the Gate: Race, Politics, and the Chinese Exclusion Act.* Chapel Hill: University of North Carolina Press, 1998.

Hall, Patricia Wong, and Victor M. Hwang. *Anti-Asian Violence in North America: Asian American and Asian Canadian Reflections on Hate, Healing, and Resistance.* Walnut Creek, Calif.: Alta Mira Press, 2001.

Han, Arar, and John Hsu. *Asian American X: An Intersection of 21st-Century Asian American Voices.* Ann Arbor: University of Michigan Press, 2004.

Hildebrand, Lorraine Barker. *Straw Halls, Sandals and Steel.* Tacoma: Washington State American Revolution Bicentennial Commission, 1977.

Hing, Bill Ong. *Making and Remaking Asian America through Immigration Policy, 1850–1990.* Stanford: Stanford University Press, 1993.

Hirata, Lucie Cheng. "Free, Indentured, Enslaved: Chinese Prostitutes in Nineteenth-Century America." *Signs: Journal of Women in Culture and Society* 5, no. 1 (autumn 1979): 3–29.

Hodges, Graham Russell Gao. *Anna May Wong: From Laundryman's Daughter to Hollywood Legend.* New York: Palgrave Macmillan, 2004.

Hoexter, Corinne K. *From Canton to California: The Epic of Chinese Immigration.* New York: Four Winds Press, 1976.

Hom, Ken. *Easy Family Recipes from a Chinese-American Childhood.* New York: Alfred A. Knopf, 1997.

Hom, Marlon K. "Fallen Leaves' Homecoming: Notes on the 1893 Gold Mountain Charity Cemetery in Xinhui." *Chinese America: History and Perspectives,* 2002, pp. 36–50.

———. "Gold Mountain Wives: Rhapsodies in Blue." *Chinese America: History and Perspectives,* 2002, pp. 32–35.

———. *Songs of Gold Mountain: Cantonese Rhymes from San Francisco Chinatown.* Berkeley: University of California Press, 1987.

Hong, Maria, ed. *Growing Up Asian American: An Anthology.* New York: W. Morrow, 1993.

Hsu, Madeline. *Dreaming of Gold, Dreaming of Home: Transnationalism and Migration between the United States and South China, 1882–1943.* Stanford: Stanford University Press, 2000.

Hu-DeHart, Evelyn, ed. *Across the Pacific: Asian Americans and Globalization.* Philadelphia: Temple University Press, 1999.

Huie Kin, *Reminiscences.* Peiping: San Yu Press, 1932.

Jacobs, Paul, and Saul Landau, with Eve Pell. *To Serve the Devil.* Volume 2: *Colonials and Sojourners: A Documentary Analysis of America's Racial History and Why It Has Been Kept Hidden.* New York: Vintage Books, 1971.

Jue, Willard. "Chin Gee Hee, Chinese Pioneer Entrepreneur in Seattle and Toishan." *Annals of the Chinese Historical Society of the Pacific Northwest,* 1983, pp. 31–38.

Kiang, Peter. "About Face: Recognizing Asian and Pacific American Vietnam Veterans in Asian American Studies." *Amerasia Journal* 17, no. 3 (1991): 22–40.

Kibria, Nazli. *Becoming Asian American: Second-Generation Chinese and Korean American Identities.* Baltimore: John Hopkins University Press, 2002.

Kim, Elaine. *Asian American Literature: An Introduction to the Writings and Their Social Context.* Philadelphia: Temple University Press, 1982.

Kim, Hyung-chan, ed. *Distinguished Asian Americans: A Biographical Dictionary.* Westport, Conn.: Greenwood Press, 1999.

Knoll, Tricia. *Becoming Americans: Asian Sojourners, Immigrants, and Refugees in the Western United States.* Portland, Ore.: Coast to Coast Books, 1982.

Koehn, Peter H., and Xiao-huang Yin, eds. *The Expanding Roles of Chinese Americans in U.S.-China Relations.* Armonk, N.Y.: M. E. Sharpe, 2002.

Kumashiro, Kevin K., ed. *Restoried Selves: Autobiographies of Queer Asian/Pacific American Activists.* New York: Harrington Park Press, 2004.

Kung, S. W. *Chinese in American Life: Some Aspects of Their History, Status, Problems, and Contributions.* Seattle: University of Washington Press, 1962.

Kwong, Peter. *Chinatown, N.Y.: Labor and Politics, 1930–1950.* New York: Monthly Review Press, 1979.

———. *Forbidden Workers: Illegal Chinese Immigrants and American Labor.* New York: Free Press, 1997.

———. *The New Chinatown.* New York: Hill & Wang, 1996.

La Fargue, Thomas. *China's First Hundred.* Pullman: State College of Washington, 1942.

Lai, Eric, and Dennis Arguelles. *The New Face of Asian Pacific America: Numbers, Diversity and Change in the 21st Century.* San Francisco: Asian Week, 2003.

Lai, Him Mark. *Becoming Chinese America: A History of Communities and Institutions.* Walnut Creek, Calif.: Alta Mira Press, 2004.

———. "China and the Chinese American Community: The Political Dimension." *Chinese America: History and Perspectives,* 1999, pp. 1–32.

———. "The Chinese-American Press." In *The Ethnic Press in the United States: A Historical Analysis and Handbook,* edited by Sally M. Miller, pp. 27–43. New York: Greenwood Press, 1987.

———. "The Chinese Marxist Left, Chinese Students and Scholars in America, and the New China, Mid-1940s to Mid-1950s." *Chinese America: History and Perspectives,* 2004, pp. 7–25.

———. *Cong huaqiao dao huaren—ershi shiji Meiguo Huaren shehui fazhan shi* [From overseas Chinese to Chinese American—History of the development of Chinese American society in the twentieth century]. Hong Kong: Joint Publishing Co., 1992.

———. "Historical Development of the Chinese Consolidated Benevolent Association/Huiguan System." *Chinese America: History and Perspectives,* 1987, pp. 3–51.

———. "Roles Played by the Chinese in America during China's Resistance to Japanese Aggression and during World War II." *Chinese America: History and Perspectives,* 1997, pp. 75–128.

———. "To Bring Forth a New China, to Build a Better America: The Chinese Marxist Left in America to the 1960s." *Chinese America: History and Perspectives,* 1992, pp. 3–82.

———. "Unfinished Business: The Chinese Confession Program." In *The Repeal and Its Legacy: Proceedings of the Conference on the 50th Anniversary of the Repeal of the Exclusion Acts, 1993,* pp. 47–57. San Francisco: Chinese Historical Society of America and Asian American Studies, San Francisco State University, 1994.

———. "A Voice of Reason: Life and Times of Gilbert Woo, Chinese American Journalist." *Chinese America: History and Perspectives,* 1992, pp. 83–123.

Lai, Him Mark, Joe Huang, and Don Wong. *The Chinese of America, 1785–1980.* San Francisco: Chinese Culture Foundation, 1980.

Lai, Him Mark, Genny Lim, and Judy Yung. *Island: Poetry and History of Chinese Immigrants on Angel Island, 1910–1940.* San Francisco: HOC-DOI, 1980.

Lee, Erika. *At America's Gate: Chinese Immigration during the Exclusion Era, 1882–1943.* Chapel Hill: University of North Carolina Press, 2002.

Lee, Marjorie, ed. *Duty and Honor: A Tribute to Chinese American World War II Veterans of Southern California.* Los Angeles: Chinese Historical Society of Southern California, 1998.

Lee, Rose Hum. *The Chinese in the United States of America.* Hong Kong: Hong Kong University Press, 1960.

———. *The Growth and Decline of Chinese Communities in the Rocky Mountain Region.* New York: Arno Press, 1978.

Lee, Wen Ho, with Helen Zia. *My Country versus Me: The First-Hand Account by the Los Alamos Scientist Who Was Falsely Accused of Being a Spy.* New York: Hyperion, 2001.

Lee, Yan Phou. *When I Was a Boy in China.* Boston: D. Lothrop, 1887.

Leong Gor Yun. *Chinatown Inside Out.* New York: Barrows Mussey, 1936.

Leong, Karen. *The China Mystique: Pearl S. Buck, Anna May Wong, Mayling Soong, and the Transformation of American Orientalism.* Berkeley: University of California Press, 2005.

Leong, Russell, ed. *Asian American Sexualities: Dimensions of the Gay and Lesbian Experience.* New York: Routledge, 1996.

———, ed. *Moving the Image: Independent Asian American Media Arts.* Los Angeles: UCLA Asian American Studies Center and Visual Communications, 1991.

Lew, Gena A., ed. *Common Ground: Perspectives on Affirmative Action and Its Impact on Asian Pacific Americans.* Los Angeles: LEAP Asian Pacific American Public Policy Institute, 1995.

Liang, Hua. "Fighting for a New Life: Social and Patriotic Activism of Chinese American Women in New York City, 1900 to 1945." *Journal of American Ethnic History* 17, no. 2 (winter 1998): 22–38.

Lim-Hing, Sharon, ed. *The Very Inside: An Anthology of Writing by Asian and Pacific Islander Lesbians and Bisexual Women.* Toronto: Sister Vision Press, 1994.

Lin, brenda. *Wealth Ribbon: Taiwan Bound, America Bound.* Indianapolis: University of Indianapolis Press, 2004.

Ling, Amy. "Yan Phou Lee or the Asian American Frontier." In *Re/collecting Early Asian America: Essays in Cultural History,* edited by Josephine Lee, Imogene L. Lim, and Yuko Matsukawa, pp. 273–87. Philadelphia: Temple University Press, 2002.

Ling, Huping. *Chinese St. Louis: From Enclave to Cultural Community.* Philadelphia: Temple University Press, 2004.

———. *Surviving on the Gold Mountain: A History of Chinese American Women and Their Lives.* Albany: State University of New York Press, 1998.

Linking Our Lives: Chinese American Women of Los Angeles. Los Angeles: Chinese Historical Society of Southern California, 1984.

Liu, Eric. *The Accidental Asian: Notes of a Native Speaker.* New York: Vintage Books, 1998.

Liu Pei Chi. *Meiguo Huaqiao shi, 1848–1911* [A history of the Chinese in the United States of America, 1848–1911]. Taipei: Liming Wenhua Shiye Gufen Youxian Gongsi, 1976.

———. *Meiguo Huaqiao shi, xu bian* [A history of the Chinese in the United States of America, vol. 2]. Taipei: Liming Wenhua Shiye Gufen Youxian Gongsi, 1984.

Lo, Karl, and Him Mark Lai. *Chinese Newspapers Published in North America, 1854–1975.*

Washington, D.C.: Center for Chinese Research Materials, Association of Research Libraries, 1977.

Loewen, James. *The Mississippi Chinese: Between Black and White.* Cambridge, Mass.: Harvard University Press, 1971.

Loo, Chalsa. *Chinatown: Most Time, Hard Time.* New York: Praeger, 1991.

Loo, Chalsa, and Peter Kiang. "Race Related Stressors and Psychological Trauma: Contributions of Asian American Vietnam Veterans." In *Asian Americans: Vulnerable Populations, Model Interventions, and Clarifying Agendas,* edited by Lin Zhan, pp. 19–42. Boston: Jones & Bartlett, 2003.

Lost Battalion Association, 2nd Battalion, 131st Field Artillery, USS Houston Survivors, 2002 Roster.

Louie, Miriam Ching. "Immigrant Asian Women in Bay Area Garment Sweatshops: 'After sewing, laundry, cleaning and cooking, I have no breath left to sing.'" *Amerasia Journal* 18, no. 1 (winter 1992): 1–27.

———. *Sweatshop Warriors: Immigrant Women Workers Take On the Global Factory.* Cambridge, Mass.: South End Press, 2001.

Louie, Steve, and Glenn Omatsu, eds. *Asian Americans: The Movement and the Moment.* Los Angeles: UCLA Asian American Studies Center Press, 2001.

Low, Victor. *The Unimpressible Race: A Century of Educational Struggle by the Chinese in San Francisco.* San Francisco: East/West, 1982.

Lowe, Pardee. *Father and Glorious Descendant.* Boston: Little, Brown, 1943.

Lum, Arlene, ed. *Sailing for the Sun: The Chinese in Hawaii, 1789–1989.* Honolulu: University of Hawaii Center for Chinese Studies, 1988.

Lydon, Sandy. *Chinese Gold: The Chinese in the Monterey Bay Region.* Capitola, Calif.: Capitola Book Company, 1985.

Lyman, Stanford M. *Chinese Americans.* New York: Random House, 1974.

Ma, L. Eve Armentrout. *Revolutionaries, Monarchists, and Chinatowns: Chinese Politics in the Americas and the 1911 Revolution.* Honolulu: University of Hawaii Press, 1990.

Mark, Diane Mei Lin, and Ginger Chih. *A Place Called Chinese America.* Dubuque, Iowa: Kendall/Hunt, 1982.

Mason, Sarah R. "The Chinese." In *They Chose Minnesota: A Survey of the State's Ethnic Groups,* edited by June D. Holmquist, pp. 531–45. St. Paul: Minnesota Historical Society, 1981.

Mast, Robert H., and Anne B. Mast. *Autobiography of Protest in Hawaii.* Honolulu: University of Hawaii Press, 1996.

McClain, Charles. *In Search of Equality: The Chinese Struggle against Discrimination in Nineteenth-Century America.* Berkeley: University of California Press, 1994.

McCunn, Ruthanne Lum. *Chinese American Portraits: Personal Histories, 1828–1988.* San Francisco: Chronicle Books, 1988.

———. *An Illustrated History of the Chinese in America.* San Francisco: Design Enterprises, 1979.

McKee, Delber L. *Chinese Exclusion versus the Open Door Policy, 1900–1906.* Detroit: Wayne State University Press, 1977.

McKeown, Adam. *Chinese Migrant Networks and Cultural Change: Peru, Chicago, Hawaii, 1900–1936.* Chicago: University of Chicago Press, 2001.

Mears, Eliot Grinnell. *Resident Orientals on the American Pacific Coast.* New York: Arno Press, 1978.

Miller, Stuart. *The Unwelcome Immigrant: The American Image of the Chinese, 1785–1882.* Berkeley: University of California Press, 1969.

Minnick, Sylvia Sun. *Samfow: The San Joaquin Chinese Legacy.* Fresno, Calif.: Panorama West, 1988.

Morton, James. *In the Sea of Sterile Mountains: The Chinese in British Columbia.* Vancouver: J. J. Douglas, 1974.

Moyers, Bill. *Becoming Americans: The Chinese Experience.* Princeton, N.J.: Films for the Humanities and Sciences, 2003. VHS.

Nakanishi, Don T., and James S. Lai. *Asian American Politics: Law, Participation, and Policy.* Lanham, Md.: Rowman & Littlefield, 2003.

Nam, Vickie, ed. *Yell-Oh Girls! Emerging Voices Explore Culture, Identity, and Growing Up Asian American.* New York: Harper Collins, 2001.

Nee, Brett De Bary, and Victor Nee. "The Kuomintang in Chinatown." In *Counterpoint: Perspectives on Asian America,* edited by Emma Gee, pp. 146–51. Los Angeles: Asian American Studies Center, University of California, 1976.

Nee, Victor G., and Brett de Bary Nee. *Longtime Californ': A Documentary Study of an American Chinatown.* New York: Pantheon Books, 1972.

Ng, Franklin, ed. *The Asian American Encyclopedia.* New York: Marshall Cavendish, 1995.

———. *The Taiwanese Americans.* Westport, Conn.: Greenwood Press, 1998.

Ngai, Mae. "The Architecture of Race in American Immigration Law: A Reexamination of the Immigration Act of 1924." *Journal of American History* 86, no. 1 (June 1999): 80–88.

———. *Impossible Subjects: Illegal Aliens and the Making of Modern America.* Princeton: Princeton University Press, 2004.

———. "Legacies of Exclusion: Illegal Chinese Immigration during the Cold War Years." *Journal of American Ethnic History* 18, no. 1 (fall 1998): 3–35.

Noda, Barbara, and Kitty Tsui and Z. Wong. "Coming Out: We Are Here in the Asian Community." *Bridge* 7, no. 1 (spring 1979): 22–24.

Odo, Franklin, ed. *The Columbia Documentary History of the Asian American Experience.* New York: Columbia University Press, 2002.

O'Farrell, Brigid, and Joyce L. Kornbluh. *Rocking the Boat: Union Women's Voices, 1915–1975.* New Brunswick, N.J.: Rutgers University Press, 1996.

Ong, Paul M. "The Affirmative Action Divide." In *Asian American Politics: Law, Participation, and Policy,* edited by Don T. Nakanishi and James S. Lai, pp. 377–405. Lanham, Md.: Rowman & Littlefield, 2003.

Ong, Paul, Edna Bonacich, and Lucie Cheng. *The New Asian Immigration in Los Angeles and Global Restructuring.* Philadelphia: Temple University Press, 1994.

Ordona, Trinity A. "Asian Lesbians in San Francisco: Struggle to Create a Safe Space, 1970s–1980s." In *Asian/Pacific Islander American Women: A Historical Anthology,* edited by Shirley Hune and Gail M. Nomura, pp. 319–34. New York: New York University Press, 2003.

Pan, Lynn. *Sons of the Yellow Emperor: A History of the Chinese Diaspora.* New York: Kodansha America, 1994.

Pascoe, Peggy. *Relations of Rescue: The Search for Female Moral Authority in the American West, 1874–1939.* New York: Oxford University Press, 1990.

Peffer, Anthony. *If They Don't Bring Their Women Here: Chinese Female Immigration before Exclusion.* Urbana: University of Illinois Press, 1999.

Quan, Robert. *Lotus among the Magnolias: The Mississippi Chinese.* Jackson: University Press of Mississippi, 1982.

Riggs, Fred. *Pressure on Congress: A Study of the Repeal of Chinese Exclusion.* New York: Columbia University Press, 1950.

Salyer, Lucy E. *Laws Harsh as Tigers: Chinese Immigrants and the Shaping of Modern Immigration Law.* Chapel Hill: University of North Carolina Press, 1995.

Sandmeyer, Elmer Clarence. *The Anti-Chinese Movement in California.* Urbana: University of Illinois Press, 1973.

Saxton, Alexander. "The Army of Canton in the High Sierra." *Pacific Historical Review* 35, no. 2 (May 1966): 141–52.

———. *The Indispensable Enemy: Labor and the Anti-Chinese Movement in California.* Berkeley: University of California Press, 1971.

Schoppe, R. Keith. "Chinese." In *Peopling Indiana: The Ethnic Experience,* edited by Robert M. Taylor and Connie A. McBirney, pp. 86–104. Indianapolis: Indiana Historical Society, 1961.

Seward, George F. *Chinese Immigration in Its Social and Economical Aspects.* New York: Charles Scribner's Sons, 1881.

Shah, Nayan. *Contagious Divide: Epidemics and Race in San Francisco's Chinatown.* Berkeley: University of California Press, 2001.

Shinagawa, Larry, and Gin Yong Pang. "Asian American Panethnicity and Intermarriage." *Amerasia Journal* 22, no. 2 (1996): 127–52.

Siu, Paul. *The Chinese Laundryman: A Study of Social Isolation.* New York: New York University Press, 1987.

Smith, Icy, ed. *Voices of Healing: Spirit and Unity after 9/11 in the Asian American and Pacific Islander Community.* Gardena, Calif.: East West Discovery Press, 2004.

Smith, Paul, ed. *Human Smuggling: Chinese Migrant Trafficking and the Challenge to America's Immigration Tradition.* Washington, D.C.: Center for Strategic and International Studies, 1997.

Smith, William Carlson. *Americans in Process: A Study of Our Citizens of Oriental Ancestry.* Ann Arbor, Mich.: Edwards Brothers, 1937.

Snakeheads: The Chinese Mafia and the New Slave Trade. New York: Downtown Community TV Center, 1994. VHS.

Stewart, Jeffrey, ed. *Paul Robeson: Artist and Citizen.* New Brunswick, N.J.: Rutgers University Press, 1998.

Stober, Dan, and Ian Hoffman. *A Convenient Spy: Wen Ho Lee and the Politics of Nuclear Espionage.* New York: Simon & Schuster, 2001.

Storti, Craig. *Incident at Bitter Creek: The Story of the Rock Springs Chinese Massacre.* Ames: Iowa State University Press, 1991.

Sung, Betty Lee. *Chinese American Intermarriage.* Staten Island, N.Y.: Center for Migration Studies, 1990.

———. *Mountain of Gold.* New York: Macmillan, 1967.

Tachiki, Amy, ed. *Roots: An Asian-American Reader.* Los Angeles: Continental Graphics, 1971.

Takagi, Dana Y. *The Retreat from Race: Asian-American Admissions and Racial Politics.* New Brunswick, N.J.: Rutgers University Press, 1992.

Takaki, Ronald. *Pau Hana: Plantation Life and Labor in Hawaii, 1835–1920.* Honolulu: University of Hawaii Press, 1983.

————. *Strangers from a Different Shore: A History of Asian Americans*. Boston: Little, Brown, 1989.

Tchen, John Kuo Wei. *New York before Chinatown: Orientalism and the Shaping of American Culture, 1776–1882*. Baltimore: Johns Hopkins University Press, 1999.

Telemaque, Eleanor Wong. *It's Crazy to be Chinese in Minnesota*. New York: Thomas Nelson, 1978.

Teng, Shiree. "Women, Community, and Equality: Three Garment Workers Speak Out." *East Wind* 2, no. 1 (spring/summer 1983): 20–23.

Tong, Benson, ed. *Asian American Children: A Historical Handbook and Guide*. Westport, Conn.: Greenwood Press, 2004.

————. *The Chinese Americans*. Boulder: University Press of Colorado, 2003.

————. *Unsubmissive Women: Chinese Prostitutes in Nineteenth-Century San Francisco*. Norman: University of Oklahoma Press, 1994.

Tsai, Shih-shan Henry. *China and the Overseas Chinese in the United States, 1868–1911*. Fayetteville: University of Arkansas Press, 1983.

————. *The Chinese Experience in America*. Bloomington: Indiana University Press, 1986.

————." The Chinese in Arkansas." *Amerasia Journal* 8, no. 1 (1981): 1–18.

Tseng, Timothy. "Chinese Protestant Nationalism in the United States, 1880–1927." In *New Spiritual Homes: Religion and Asian Americans*, edited by Daivid K. Yoo, pp. 19–51. Honolulu: University of Hawaii Press, 1998.

Tsui, Kitty. "Breaking Silence, Making Waves, and Loving Ourselves: The Politics of Coming Out and Coming Home." In *Lesbian Philosophies and Cultures*, edited by Jeffner Allen, pp. 49–61. New York: State University of New York Press, 1990.

Tung, William L. *The Chinese in America, 1820–1973: A Chronology and Fact Book*. Dobbs Ferry, N.Y.: Oceana Publications, 1974.

Wang, An, with Eugene Linden. *Lessons: An Autobiography*. Boston: Addison-Wesley, 1986.

Wang, L. Ling-chi. "*Lau v. Nichols:* History of a Struggle for Equal and Quality Education." In *Counterpoint: Perspectives on Asian America*, edited by Emma Gee, pp. 240–63. Los Angeles: [UCLA Asian American Studies Center,] 1976.

————. "Politics of the Repeal of the Chinese Exclusion Laws." In *The Repeal and Its Legacy: Proceedings of the Conference on the 50th Anniversary of the Repeal of the Exclusion Acts*, pp. 66–80. San Francisco: Chinese Historical Society of America and Asian American Studies, San Francisco State University, 1994.

————. "Race, Class, Citizenship, and Extraterritoriality: Asian Americans and the 1996 Campaign Finance Scandal." *Amerasia Journal* 24, no. 1 (1998): 1–21.

————. "The Structure of Dual Domination: Toward a Paradigm for the Study of the Chinese Diaspora in the United States." *Amerasia Journal* 21, nos. 1–2 (1995): 149–69.

Wang, Xinyang. *Surviving the City: The Chinese Immigrant Experience in New York City, 1890–1970*. Lanham, Md.: Rowman & Littlefield, 2001.

Wei, William. *The Asian American Movement*. Philadelphia: Temple University Press, 1993.

Wickberg, Edgar, ed. *From China to Canada: A History of the Chinese Communities in Canada*. Toronto: McClelland & Stewart, 1982.

Wong, Anna May. "The True Life Story of a Chinese Girl." *Pictures*, August 1926, pp. 28–29, 106–8; September 1926, pp. 34–35, 72, 74–75.

Wong, Jade Snow. *Fifth Chinese Daughter.* New York: Harper & Brothers, 1950.

Wong, K. Scott. *Americans First: Chinese Americans and the Second World War.* Cambridge, Mass.: Harvard University Press, 2005.

Wong, K. Scott, and Sucheng Chan, eds. *Claiming America: Constructing Chinese American Identities during the Exclusion Era.* Philadelphia: Temple University Press, 1998.

Wong, Marie Rose. *Sweet Cakes, Long Journey: The Chinatowns of Portland, Oregon.* Seattle: University of Washington Press, 2004.

Wong, William. *Yellow Journalist: Dispatches from Asian America.* Philadelphia: Temple University Press, 2001.

Woo, Wesley. "Chinese Protestants in the San Francisco Bay Area." In *Entry Denied: Exclusion and the Chinese Community in America, 1882–1943,* edited by Sucheng Chan, pp. 213–45. Philadelphia: Temple University Press, 1991.

Wu, Cheng-Tsu. *"Chink!" A Documentary History of Anti-Chinese Prejudice in America.* New York: World Publishing, 1972.

Wu, Frank H. *Yellow: Race in America beyond Black and White.* New York: Basic Books, 2002.

Yang, Fenggang. *Chinese Christians in America: Conversion, Assimilation, and Adhesive Identities.* University Park: Pennsylvania State University Press, 1999.

Ye, Weili. *Seeking Modernity in China's Name: Chinese Students in the United States, 1900–1927.* Stanford: Stanford University Press, 2001.

Yee, Alfred. *Shopping at Giant Foods: Chinese American Supermarkets in Northern California.* Seattle: University of Washington Press, 2003.

Yin, Xiao-huang. *Chinese American Literature since the 1850s.* Urbana: University of Illinois Press, 2000.

Yip, Alethea. "Enemies All Around: Asian American Vietnam Vets Paid a Special Price for Service to Their Country." *Asian Week,* November 3, 1995, p. 17.

Young, Donald. *Searching for Asian America.* San Francisco: National Asian American Telecommunications Association, 2003. VHS.

Yu, Renqiu. *To Save China, to Save Ourselves: The Chinese Hand Laundry Alliance of New York.* Philadelphia: Temple University Press, 1992.

Yung, Judy. *Chinese Women of America: A Pictorial History.* Seattle: University of Washington Press, 1986.

———. *Unbound Feet: A Social History of Chinese Women in San Francisco.* Berkeley: University of California Press, 1995.

———. *Unbound Voices: A Documentary History of Chinese Women in San Francisco.* Berkeley: University of California Press, 1999.

Yung Wing. *My Life in China and America.* New York: Henry Holt, 1909.

Zhang, Qingsong. "The Origins of the Chinese Americanization Movement: Wong Chin Foo and the Chinese Equal Rights League." In *Claiming America: Constructing Chinese American Identities during the Exclusion Era,* edited by K. Scott Wong and Sucheng Chan, pp. 41–63. Philadelphia: Temple University Press, 1998.

Zhao, Jianli. *Strangers in the City: The Atlanta Chinese, Their Community, and Stories of Their Lives.* New York: Routledge, 2002.

Zhao, Xiaojian. *Remaking Chinese America: Immigration, Family, and Community, 1940–1965.* New Brunswick, N.J.: Rutgers University Press, 2002.

Zhou, Min. *Chinatown: The Socioeconomic Potential of an Urban Enclave.* Philadelphia: Temple University Press, 1992.

Zhu, Liping. *A Chinaman's Chance: The Chinese on the Rocky Mountain Mining Frontier.* Niwot: University Press of Colorado, 1997.

Zia, Helen. *Asian American Dreams: The Emergence of an American People.* New York: Farrar, Straus & Giroux, 2000.

INDEX